ExamSim

Experience realistic, simulated exams on your own computer with Osborne's interactive ExamSim software. This computer-based test engine offers both standard and adaptive test modes, knowledge-based and Case Study–based questions like those found on the real exams, and review tools that show you where you went wrong and why. ExamSim features also include automatic benchmarking of your progress, and a score report that shows your overall performance on the exam.

Knowledge-based questions present challenging material in a multiple-choice format. Answer treatments not only explain why the correct options are right, they also tell you why the incorrect answers are wrong.

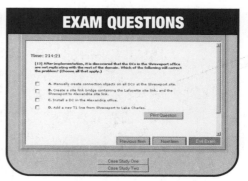

Realistic designing Windows 2000 **Case Study–based** questions challenge your ability to analyze and synthesize complex information in realistic scenarios similar to those on the actual exams.

Additional CD-ROM Features

- Complete hyperlinked **e-book** for easy information access and self-paced study

- **DriveTime** audio tracks offer concise review of key exam topics for in the car or on the go!

System Requirements:

A PC running Internet Explorer version 5 or higher

The **Score Report** provides an overall assessment of your exam performance as well as performance history.

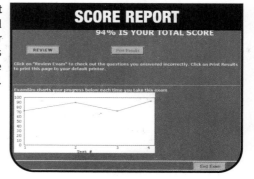

STEPHEN OSSOWSKI

MICROSOFT CERTIFIED SYSTEMS ENGINEER

MCSE Designing a Windows® 2000 Network Study Guide

(Exam 70-221)

Syngress Media, Inc.

Osborne/McGraw-Hill
Berkeley New York St. Louis San Francisco Auckland Bogotá Hamburg London Madrid Mexico City
Milan Montreal New Delhi Panama City Paris São Paulo Singapore Sydney Tokyo Toronto

Osborne/**McGraw-Hill**
2600 Tenth Street
Berkeley, California 94710
U.S.A.

For information on translations or book distributors outside the U.S.A., or to arrange bulk
purchase discounts for sales promotions, premiums, or fund-raisers, please contact
Osborne/**McGraw-Hill** at the above address.

MCSE Designing a Windows® 2000 Network Study Guide (Exam 70-221)

1234567890 PCP PCP 019876543210

Book P/N 0-07-212492-X   and   CD P/N 0-07-212493-8
parts of ISBN 0-07-212494-6

Publisher Brandon A. Nordin	**VP, Worldwide Business Development Global Knowledge** Richard Kristof	**Indexer** Carol Burbo
Vice President and Associate Publisher Scott Rogers	**Series Editors** Dr. Thomas W. Shinder Debra Littlejohn Shinder	**Computer Designers** Gary Corrigan Dick Schwartz
Editorial Director Gareth Hancock	**Technical Editors** Dr. Thomas W. Shinder Henry Maine	**Illustrator** Micheal Mueller
Associate Acquisitions Editor Timothy Green		**Series Design** Peter F. Hancik
Editorial Management Syngress Media, Inc.	**Copy Editor** Nancy Faughnan	
Acquisitions Coordinators Tara Davis Jessica Wilson	**Proofreader** Susan Elkind	

This book was composed with Corel VENTURA™ Publisher.

From Global Knowledge

At Global Knowledge we strive to support the multiplicity of learning styles required by our students to achieve success as technical professionals. In this series of books, it is our intention to offer the reader a valuable tool for successful completion of the MCSE Windows 2000 Certification exams.

As the world's largest IT training company, Global Knowledge is uniquely positioned to offer these books. The expertise gained each year from providing instructor-led training to hundreds of thousands of students worldwide has been captured in book form to enhance your learning experience. We hope that the quality of these books demonstrates our commitment to your lifelong learning success. Whether you choose to learn through the written word, computer-based training, Web delivery, or instructor-led training, Global Knowledge is committed to providing you the very best in each of those categories. For those of you who know Global Knowledge, or those of you who have just found us for the first time, our goal is to be your lifelong competency partner.

Thank you for the opportunity to serve you. We look forward to serving your needs again in the future.

Warmest regards,

Duncan Anderson
President and Chief Operating Officer, Global Knowledge

The Global Knowledge Advantage

Global Knowledge has a global delivery system for its products and services. The company has 28 subsidiaries, and offers its programs through a total of 60+ locations. No other vendor can provide consistent services across a geographic area this large. Global Knowledge is the largest independent information technology education provider, offering programs on a variety of platforms. This enables our multi-platform and multi-national customers to obtain all of their programs from a single vendor. The company has developed the unique Competus™ Framework software tool and methodology which can quickly reconfigure courseware to the proficiency level of a student on an interactive basis. Combined with self-paced and on-line programs, this technology can reduce the time required for training by prescribing content in only the deficient skills areas. The company has fully automated every aspect of the education process, from registration and follow-up, to "just-in-time" production of courseware. Global Knowledge Network through its Enterprise Services Consultancy, can customize programs and products to suit the needs of an individual customer.

Global Knowledge Classroom Education Programs

The backbone of our delivery options is classroom-based education. Our modern, well-equipped facilities staffed with the finest instructors offer programs in a wide variety of information technology topics, many of which lead to professional certifications.

Custom Learning Solutions

This delivery option has been created for companies and governments that value customized learning solutions. For them, our consultancy-based approach of developing targeted education solutions is most effective at helping them meet specific objectives.

Self-Paced and Multimedia Products

This delivery option offers self-paced program titles in interactive CD-ROM, videotape and audio tape programs. In addition, we offer custom development of interactive multimedia courseware to customers and partners. Call us at 1-888-427-4228.

Electronic Delivery of Training

Our network-based training service delivers efficient competency-based, interactive training via the World Wide Web and organizational intranets. This leading-edge delivery option provides a custom learning path and "just-in-time" training for maximum convenience to students.

ARG

American Research Group (ARG), a wholly-owned subsidiary of Global Knowledge, one of the largest worldwide training partners of Cisco Systems, offers a wide range of internetworking, LAN/WAN, Bay Networks, FORE Systems, IBM, and UNIX courses. ARG offers hands on network training in both instructor-led classes and self-paced PC-based training.

Global Knowledge Courses Available

Network Fundamentals

- Understanding Computer Networks
- Telecommunications Fundamentals I
- Telecommunications Fundamentals II
- Understanding Networking Fundamentals
- Implementing Computer Telephony Integration
- Introduction to Voice Over IP
- Introduction to Wide Area Networking
- Cabling Voice and Data Networks
- Introduction to LAN/WAN protocols
- Virtual Private Networks
- ATM Essentials

Network Security & Management

- Troubleshooting TCP/IP Networks
- Network Management
- Network Troubleshooting
- IP Address Management
- Network Security Administration
- Web Security
- Implementing UNIX Security
- Managing Cisco Network Security
- Windows NT 4.0 Security

IT Professional Skills

- Project Management for IT Professionals
- Advanced Project Management for IT Professionals
- Survival Skills for the New IT Manager
- Making IT Teams Work

LAN/WAN Internetworking

- Frame Relay Internetworking
- Implementing T1/T3 Services
- Understanding Digital Subscriber Line (xDSL)
- Internetworking with Routers and Switches
- Advanced Routing and Switching
- Multi-Layer Switching and Wire-Speed Routing
- Internetworking with TCP/IP
- ATM Internetworking
- OSPF Design and Configuration
- Border Gateway Protocol (BGP) Configuration

Authorized Vendor Training

Cisco Systems

- Introduction to Cisco Router Configuration
- Advanced Cisco Router Configuration
- Installation and Maintenance of Cisco Routers
- Cisco Internetwork Troubleshooting
- Cisco Internetwork Design
- Cisco Routers and LAN Switches
- Catalyst 5000 Series Configuration
- Cisco LAN Switch Configuration
- Managing Cisco Switched Internetworks
- Configuring, Monitoring, and Troubleshooting Dial-Up Services
- Cisco AS5200 Installation and Configuration
- Cisco Campus ATM Solutions

Bay Networks

- Bay Networks Accelerated Router Configuration
- Bay Networks Advanced IP Routing
- Bay Networks Hub Connectivity
- Bay Networks Accelar 1xxx Installation and Basic Configuration
- Bay Networks Centillion Switching

FORE Systems

- FORE ATM Enterprise Core Products
- FORE ATM Enterprise Edge Products
- FORE ATM Theory
- FORE LAN Certification

Operating Systems & Programming

Microsoft

- Introduction to Windows NT
- Microsoft Networking Essentials
- Windows NT 4.0 Workstation
- Windows NT 4.0 Server
- Advanced Windows NT 4.0 Server
- Windows NT Networking with TCP/IP
- Introduction to Microsoft Web Tools
- Windows NT Troubleshooting
- Windows Registry Configuration

UNIX

- UNIX Level I
- UNIX Level II
- Essentials of UNIX and NT Integration

Programming

- Introduction to JavaScript
- Java Programming
- PERL Programming
- Advanced PERL with CGI for the Web

Web Site Management & Development

- Building a Web Site
- Web Site Management and Performance
- Web Development Fundamentals

High Speed Networking

- Essentials of Wide Area Networking
- Integrating ISDN
- Fiber Optic Network Design
- Fiber Optic Network Installation
- Migrating to High Performance Ethernet

DIGITAL UNIX

- UNIX Utilities and Commands
- DIGITAL UNIX v4.0 System Administration
- DIGITAL UNIX v4.0 (TCP/IP) Network Management
- AdvFS, LSM, and RAID Configuration and Management
- DIGITAL UNIX TruCluster Software Configuration and Management
- UNIX Shell Programming Featuring Kornshell
- DIGITAL UNIX v4.0 Security Management
- DIGITAL UNIX v4.0 Performance Management
- DIGITAL UNIX v4.0 Intervals Overview

DIGITAL OpenVMS

- OpenVMS Skills for Users
- OpenVMS System and Network Node Management I
- OpenVMS System and Network Node Management II
- OpenVMS System and Network Node Management III
- OpenVMS System and Network Node Operations
- OpenVMS for Programmers
- OpenVMS System Troubleshooting for Systems Managers
- Configuring and Managing Complex VMScluster Systems
- Utilizing OpenVMS Features from C
- OpenVMS Performance Management
- Managing DEC TCP/IP Services for OpenVMS
- Programming in C

Hardware Courses

- AlphaServer 1000/1000A Installation, Configuration and Maintenance
- AlphaServer 2100 Server Maintenance
- AlphaServer 4100, Troubleshooting Techniques and Problem Solving

About Syngress Media

Syngress Media creates books and software for Information Technology professionals seeking skill enhancement and career advancement. Its products are designed to comply with vendor and industry standard course curricula, and are optimized for certification exam preparation. You can contact Syngress via the Web at www.syngress.com.

Contributors

Carol Bailey (MCSE+I). Based in London, the UK, Carol has over ten years of experience in networking, and currently has more than a dozen Microsoft exams to her name. She is a Senior Technical Consultant working for Metascybe Systems Ltd., a company that specializes in PC software communications, offering their own connectivity products in addition to project work and consultancy for a diverse customer base. Working for a Microsoft Solutions Provider has provided Carol with a wide range of technical opportunities. Her work includes supporting the in-house networking services as well as all aspects of external customer support and consultancy.

David Blue (MCP+I, Seicor Fiber Certified, Compaq Certified) has, for the past year, been the Vice President and Director of Operations for Review Technology Group. David has also worked for the last 8 years at Meijers Inc., where he is the Network Administrator and Tech Specialist over WAN/LAN for ITS. David obtained his education at Central State University, Edison State Community College, Sinclair Community College and at ICB, where he received a Bachelor's Degree in MIS and Computer Science and an Associates Degree in Communications. David would like to dedicate this book to his family.

Jerrod Brokaw Couser (MCSE+I, MCP+I, CCA, A+) is currently a technical author at Review Technology Group. Jerrod has previously worked as a Technology Coordinator at Newton Local School District in Ohio, where he got his training in the education field. Jerrod's love of writing and technology has made him a valuable asset to Review Technology Group. Jerrod would like to dedicate his work to his fiancé, without whose support nothing in his life would be possible.

Michael Cross (MCSE, MCPS, MCP+I, CNA) is the Network Administrator, Internet Specialist, and a Programmer for the Niagara Regional Police Service. In addition to administering its network, programming, and providing support to a user base of over 800 civilian and uniform users, he is also Webmaster of the service's Web site at www.nrps.com. Michael also owns KnightWare, a company that provides consulting, programming, networking, Web page design, computer training, and various other services. He has served as an instructor for private colleges and technical schools in London, Ontario, Canada. He has been a freelance writer for several years, and has been published over two dozen times in numerous books and anthologies. He currently resides in St. Catharines, Ontario, Canada.

Brian Frederick (MCSE, MCNE, Network+) is a Systems Engineer with over seven years of technical background. Brian started working with computers with an Apple II+. He attended the University of Northern Iowa and is married with two adorable children. Brian is a Senior Systems Engineer for Stockpoint Inc., a leading business-to-business provider of global online investment tools and market information. His hobbies include his kids, family, and golf. Brian owes his success to his parents and brother for their support and backing during his Apple days and his college days, and to his wife and children for their support and understanding when dad spends many hours in front of their computer.

Feridun Kadir (MCP, MCP+I, MCSE, MCT) is a freelance IT Consultant and Trainer who has worked in the field of IT since 1988. He remembers selling a TRS-80 home PC with 4Kilobytes RAM (yes kilobytes!) in the early 1980s for over $1000. His early IT experience was with UNIX systems and local area networks. In more recent years he has worked with Microsoft products. Having discovered that he liked giving presentation, he became an MCT and regularly teaches Microsoft technical courses including Windows NT4.0, Windows 2000, TCP/IP, and SQL Server 7.0 Administration. Feridun also provides IT consulting services to all types of businesses. Feridun lives with his wife, Liz, and newly born son, Jake, in Stansted, Essex in England. He can be contacted by e-mail at feridun@sfax.co.uk.

Joseph M. Lamb has over ten years of experience with systems and services related to networking, managing, and directing Information Systems groups within organizations such as Automatic Data Processing, BellSouth, The CIT Group, Witness Systems, and TechGeorgia Nexus. Mr. Lamb now serves as the President and Chief Executive Officer of Thello Consulting Services, a consulting firm located in Atlanta, Georgia, specializing in Microsoft Networking. Mr. Lamb has a broad range of technical skills, specializing in LAN/WAN Design utilizing Microsoft

Network Operating Systems and Services. Mr. Lamb has taught several training classes on Microsoft Networking, including Microsoft Exchange Enterprise Implementation, Administering Windows NT 4.0 networks, TCP/IP Networking, and Internet Architecture and Design.

Neil MacMurchy (MCP, MCP+I, MCSE, MCSE+I, MCT, CCNA, A+, Networking+). Neil has worked in the IT industry for 14 years and has done everything from repairs, to network consulting, to technical training. In addition to the certifications listed above, he also holds designations from Apple (Apple Technical Specialist/System Engineer) and Compaq (Accredited System Engineer). Neil currently divides his time between network consulting, training Microsoft Official Curriculum at Microage Niagara in the Niagara Falls, Canada area, and spending time with his wife Ellen and two daughters, Ashley and Heather. He has been working with Windows 2000 since beta one of Windows NT 5.0 and with NT since the 3.1 beta.

Jeffery A. Martin (MCSE, MCT, MCP+I, CCI, CCA, CNA, A+, Network+, I-Net+, CIW) has been working with computers and computer networks for over 15 years. Jeffery spends most of his time working with Internet-related startup companies and consulting for large international media companies. When not consulting or spending time managing his numerous business interests, he works as a technical instructor and enjoys training others in the use of technology.

Michael F. Martone (MCSD, MCSE, MCP+I) is a consultant and author based in Lakewood, Ohio. Mike was one of the first thousand MCSDs in 1995, and in addition to his Microsoft certifications, he has also obtained the Lotus LCNAD. Mike has six years of consulting experience (Big 5 and independent), has contributed to three previous Syngress/Osborne books, and has co-authored the April 2000 cover article for InfoPro magazine. Mike is currently pursuing his Masters in MIS from Case Western Reserve University, and can be reached at mfm11@po.cwru.edu.

Debra Littlejohn Shinder (MCSE, MCP+I, MCT) is an instructor in the AATP program at Eastfield College, Dallas County Community College District, where she has taught since 1992. She is Webmaster for the cities of Seagoville and Sunnyvale, Texas, as well as the family Web site at www.shinder.net. She and her husband, Dr. Thomas W. Shinder, provide consulting and technical support services to Dallas-area organizations. She is also the proud mom of a daughter, Kristen, who is currently serving in the U.S. Navy in Italy, and a son, Kris, who is a high school chess champion. Deb has been a writer for most her life, and has published numerous articles in both technical and nontechnical fields. She can be contacted at deb@shinder.net.

Thomas W. Shinder, M.D. (MCSE, MCP+I, MCT) is a technology trainer and consultant in the Dallas–Ft. Worth metroplex. Dr. Shinder has consulted with major firms, including Xerox, Lucent Technologies, and FINA Oil, assisting in the development and implementation of IP-based communications strategies. Dr. Shinder attended medical school at the University of Illinois in Chicago, and trained in neurology at the Oregon Health Sciences Center in Portland, Oregon. His fascination with interneuronal communication ultimately melded with his interest in internetworking and led him to focus on systems engineering. Tom works passionately with his beloved wife, Deb Shinder, to design elegant and cost-efficient solutions for small and medium-sized businesses based on Windows NT/2000 platforms.

Russell Thomas (A+, MCSE, MCP+I, MCT) is currently the President and CEO of Review Technology Group. RTG specializes in bringing the value of technology to businesses and individuals. Through the use of various types of media, Review Technology Group has set a new standard as leaders in Training, Consultation, and Service. Russell has had many years of experience as a Certified Trainer with on-line training companies such as Ziff-Davis University and SmartPlanet, as well as on-site with New Horizons and numerous universities. A member of the International Who's Who in Information Technology, Russell works daily to share with others the tremendous opportunities that technology makes available to everyone. The staff of RTG would like to dedicate their work to their families, without whose support nothing in their lives would be possible.

Technical Editors

Thomas W. Shinder, M.D. (MCSE, MCP+I, MCT) is a technology trainer and consultant in the Dallas–Ft. Worth metroplex. Dr. Shinder has consulted with major firms, including Xerox, Lucent Technologies, and FINA Oil, assisting in the development and implementation of IP-based communications strategies. Dr. Shinder attended medical school at the University of Illinois in Chicago, and trained in neurology at the Oregon Health Sciences Center in Portland, Oregon. His fascination with interneuronal communication ultimately melded with his interest in internetworking and led him to focus on systems engineering. Tom works passionately with his beloved wife, Deb Shinder, to design elegant and cost-efficient solutions for small and medium-sized businesses based on Windows NT/2000 platforms.

Henry Maine (RHCE, MCSE+I, MCT, MCP) is a principle consultant with Maine Consulting Inc. He has a B.S. in Computer Science from Tennessee

Technological University and has over 12 years of experience as a network administrator in both UNIX and Microsoft environments. He currently specializes in providing system administration consultation services as well as training for system and network administration and programming.

Series Editors

Thomas W. Shinder, M.D. (MCSE, MCP+I, MCT) is a technology trainer and consultant in the Dallas–Ft. Worth metroplex. Dr. Shinder has consulted with major firms, including Xerox, Lucent Technologies, and FINA Oil, assisting in the development and implementation of IP-based communications strategies. Dr. Shinder attended medical school at the University of Illinois in Chicago, and trained in neurology at the Oregon Health Sciences Center in Portland, Oregon. His fascination with interneuronal communication ultimately melded with his interest in internetworking and led him to focus on systems engineering. Tom works passionately with his beloved wife, Deb Shinder, to design elegant and cost-efficient solutions for small and medium-sized businesses based on Windows NT/2000 platforms.

Debra Littlejohn Shinder (MCSE, MCP+I, MCT) is an instructor in the AATP program at Eastfield College, Dallas County Community College District, where she has taught since 1992. She is Webmaster for the cities of Seagoville and Sunnyvale, Texas, as well as the family Web site at www.shinder.net. She and her husband, Dr. Thomas W. Shinder, provide consulting and technical support services to Dallas-area organizations. She is also the proud mom of a daughter, Kristen, who is currently serving in the U.S. Navy in Italy, and a son, Kris, who is a high school chess champion. Deb has been a writer for most her life, and has published numerous articles in both technical and nontechnical fields. She can be contacted at deb@shinder.net.

ACKNOWLEDGMENTS

W e would like to thank the following people:

- Richard Kristof of Global Knowledge for championing the series and providing access to some great people and information.

- All the incredibly hard-working folks at Osborne/McGraw-Hill: Brandon Nordin, Scott Rogers, Gareth Hancock, and Tim Green for their help in launching a great series and being solid team players. In addition, Tara Davis and Jessica Wilson for their help in fine-tuning the book.

- Monica Kilwine at Microsoft Corp., for being patient and diligent in answering all our questions.

CONTENTS AT A GLANCE

CONTENTS

This book's primary objective is to help you prepare for the MCSE Designing a Windows 2000 Network Infrastructure exam under the new Windows 2000 certification track. As the Microsoft program transitions from Windows NT 4.0, it will become increasingly important that current and aspiring IT professionals have multiple resources available to assist them in increasing their knowledge and building their skills.

At the time of publication, all the exam objectives have been posted on the Microsoft Web site and the beta exam process has been completed. Microsoft has announced its commitment to measuring real-world skills. This book is designed with that premise in mind; its authors have practical experience in the field, using the Windows 2000 operating systems in hands-on situations and have followed the development of the product since early beta versions.

Because the focus of the exams is on application and understanding, as opposed to memorization of facts, no book by itself can fully prepare you to obtain a passing score. It is essential that you work with the software to enhance your proficiency. Toward that end, this book includes many practical step-by-step exercises in each chapter that are designed to give you hands-on practice as well as guide you in truly learning how to design a Microsoft Windows 2000 Network Infrastructure, not just learning *about* it.

In This Book

This book is organized in such a way as to serve as an in-depth review for the MCSE Designing a Windows 2000 Network Infrastructure exam for both experienced Windows NT professionals and newcomers to Microsoft networking technologies. Each chapter covers a major aspect of the exam, with an emphasis on the "why" as well as the "how to" of working with and supporting Windows 2000 as a network administrator or engineer.

On the CD

The CD-ROM contains the CertTrainer software. CertTrainer comes complete with ExamSim, Skill Assessment tests, CertCam movie clips, the e-book (electronic version of the book), and Drive Time. CertTrainer is easy to install on any Windows 98/NT/2000 computer and must be installed to access these features. You may, however, browse the e-book direct from the CD without installation. For more information on the CD-ROM, please see Appendix A.

In Every Chapter

We've created a set of chapter components that call your attention to important items, reinforce important points, and provide helpful exam-taking hints. Take a look at what you'll find in every chapter:

- Every chapter begins with the **Certification Objectives**—what you need to know in order to pass the section on the exam dealing with the chapter topic. The Objective headings identify the objectives within the chapter, so you'll always know an objective when you see it!

- **Exam Watch** notes call attention to information about, and potential pitfalls in, the exam. These helpful hints are written by authors who have taken the exams and received their certification—who better to tell you what to worry about? They know what you're about to go through!

- **Practice Exercises** are interspersed throughout the chapters. These are step-by-step and conceptual exercises that allow you to get the hands-on experience you need in order to pass the exams. They help you master skills that are likely to be an area of focus on the exam. Don't just read through the exercises; they are hands-on practice that you should be comfortable completing. Learning by doing is an effective way to increase your competency with a product. The practical exercises will be very helpful for any simulation exercises you may encounter on the MCSE Designing a Windows 2000 Network Infrastructure exam.

- The **CertCam** icon that appears in many of the exercises indicates that the exercise is presented in .avi format on the accompanying CD-ROM. These .avi clips walk you through various system configurations and are narrated by Thomas W. Shinder, M.D., MCSE.

- **On The Job** notes describe the issues that come up most often in real-world settings. They provide a valuable perspective on certification- and product-related topics. They point out common mistakes and address questions that have arisen from on the job discussions and experience.

■ **From The Classroom** sidebars describe the issues that come up most often in the training classroom setting. These sidebars highlight some of the most common and confusing problems that students encounter when taking a live Windows 2000 training course. You can get a leg up on those difficult to understand subjects by focusing extra attention on these sidebars.

■ **Scenario & Solution** sections lay out potential problems and solutions in a quick-to-read format:

SCENARIO & SOLUTION

Is Active Directory scalable?	Yes! Unlike the Windows NT security database, which is limited to approximately 40,000 objects, Active Directory supports literally millions of objects.
Is Active Directory compatible with other LDAP directory services?	Yes! Active Directory can share information with other directory services that support LDAP versions 2 and 3, such as Novell's NDS.

■ The **Certification Summary** is a succinct review of the chapter and a restatement of salient points regarding the exam.

✓ ■ The **Two-Minute Drill** at the end of every chapter is a checklist of the main points of the chapter. It can be used for last-minute review.

Q&A ■ The **Self Test** offers questions similar to those found on the certification exams. The answers to these questions, as well as explanations of the answers, can be found at the end of each chapter. By taking the Self Test after completing each chapter, you'll reinforce what you've learned from that chapter while becoming familiar with the structure of the exam questions.

■ The **Lab Question** at the end of the Self Test section offers a unique and challenging question format that requires the reader to understand multiple chapter concepts to answer correctly. These questions are more complex, and more comprehensive than the other questions, as they test your ability to take all the knowledge you have gained from reading the chapter and apply it to complicated, real-world situations. These questions are aimed to be more difficult than what you will find on the exam. If you can answer these questions, you have proven that you know the subject!

The Global Knowledge Web Site

Check out the Web site. Global Knowledge invites you to become an active member of the Access Global Web site. This site is an online mall and an information repository that you'll find invaluable. You can access many types of products to assist you in your preparation for the exams, and you'll be able to participate in forums, online discussions, and threaded discussions. No other book brings you unlimited access to such a resource. You'll find more information about this site in Appendix B.

Some Pointers

Once you've finished reading this book, set aside some time to do a thorough review. You might want to return to the book several times and make use of all the methods it offers for reviewing the material:

1. *Re-read all the Two-Minute Drills,* or have someone quiz you. You also can use the drills as a way to do a quick cram before the exam. You might want to make some flash cards out of 3 x 5 index cards that have the Two-Minute Drill material on them.

2. *Re-read all the Exam Watch notes.* Remember that these notes are written by authors who have taken the exam and passed. They know what you should expect—and what you should be on the lookout for.

3. *Review all the S&S sections* for quick problem solving.

4. *Re-take the Self Tests.* Taking the tests right after you've read the chapter is a good idea, because the questions help reinforce what you've just learned. However, it's an even better idea to go back later and do all the questions in the book in one sitting. Pretend that you're taking the live exam. (When you go through the questions the first time, you should mark your answers on a separate piece of paper. That way, you can run through the questions as many times as you need to until you feel comfortable with the material.)

5. *Complete the Exercises.* Did you do the exercises when you read through each chapter? If not, do them! These exercises are designed to cover exam topics, and there's no better way to get to know this material than by practicing. Be sure you understand why you are performing each step in each exercise. If there is something you are not clear on, re-read that section in the chapter.

MCSE Certification

This book is designed to help you pass the MCSE Designing a Windows 2000 Network Infrastructure exam. At the time this book was written, the exam objectives for the exam were posted on the Microsoft Web site, and the beta exams had been completed. We wrote this book to give you a complete and incisive review of all the important topics that are targeted for the exam. The information contained in Table 1-1 will provide you with the required foundation of knowledge that will not only allow you to succeed in passing the MCSE Designing a Windows 2000 Network Infrastructure exam, but will also make you a better Microsoft Certified Systems Engineer.

The nature of the Information Technology industry is changing rapidly, and the requirements and specifications for certification can change just as quickly without notice. Microsoft expects you to regularly visit their Website at http://www.microsoft.com/mcp/certstep/mcse.htm to get the most up to date information on the entire MCSE program.

TABLE 1-1	Windows 2000 Certification Track

Core Exams		
Candidates Who Have <u>Not</u> Already Passed Windows NT 4.0 Exams All 4 of the Following Core Exams Required:	OR	Candidates Who Have Passed 3 Windows NT 4.0 Exams (Exams 70-067, 70-068, and 70-073) Instead of the 4 Core Exams on Left, You May Take:
Exam 70-210: Installing, Configuring and Administering Microsoft® Windows® 2000 Professional		**Exam 70-240**: Microsoft® Windows® 2000 Accelerated Exam for MCPs Certified on Microsoft® Windows NT® 4.0. The accelerated exam will be available until December 31, 2001. It covers the core competencies of exams **70-210, 70-215, 70-216, and 70-217.**
Exam 70-215: Installing, Configuring and Administering Microsoft® Windows® 2000 Server		
Exam 70-216: Implementing and Administering a Microsoft® Windows® 2000 Network Infrastructure		
Exam 70-217: Implementing and Administering a Microsoft® Windows® 2000 Directory Services Infrastructure		
PLUS – All Candidates – *1 of the Following Core Exams Required:*		
*****Exam 70-219**: Designing a Microsoft® Windows® 2000 Directory Services Infrastructure		
*****Exam 70-220**: Designing Security for a Microsoft® Windows® 2000 Network		
*****Exam 70-221**: Designing a Microsoft® Windows® 2000 Network Infrastructure		
PLUS – All Candidates – *2 Elective Exams Required:*		
Any current MCSE electives when the Windows 2000 exams listed above are released in their live versions. **Electives scheduled for retirement will not be considered current.** Selected third-party certifications that focus on interoperability will be accepted as an alternative to one elective exam.		
*****Exam 70-219**: Designing a Microsoft® Windows® 2000 Directory Services Infrastructure		
*****Exam 70-220**: Designing Security for a Microsoft® Windows® 2000 Network		
*****Exam 70-221**: Designing a Microsoft® Windows® 2000 Network Infrastructure		
Exam 70-222: Upgrading from Microsoft® Windows® NT 4.0 to Microsoft® Windows® 2000		
*Note that some of the Windows 2000 core exams can be used as elective exams as well. An exam that is used to meet the design requirement cannot also count as an elective. Each exam can only be counted once in the Windows 2000 Certification.		

Let's look at two scenarios. The first applies to the person who has already taken the Windows NT 4.0 Server (70-067), Windows NT 4.0 Workstation (70-073), and Windows NT 4.0 Server in the Enterprise (70-068) exams. The second scenario covers the situation of the person who has not completed those Windows NT 4.0 exams and would like to concentrate ONLY on Windows 2000.

In the first scenario, you have the option of taking all four Windows 2000 core exams, or you can take the Windows 2000 Accelerated Exam for MCPs if you have already passed exams 70-067, 70-068, and 70-073. (Note that you must have passed those specific exams to qualify for the Accelerated Exam; if you have fulfilled your NT 4.0 MCSE requirements by passing the Windows 95 or Windows 98 exam as your client operating system option, and did not take the NT Workstation Exam, you don't qualify.)

After completing the core requirements, either by passing the four core exams or the one Accelerated exam, you must pass a "design" exam. The design exams include Designing a Microsoft Windows 2000 Directory Services Infrastructure (70-219), Designing Security for Microsoft Windows 2000 Network (70-220), and Designing a Microsoft Windows 2000 Network Infrastructure (70-221). One design exam is REQUIRED.

You also must pass two exams from the list of electives. However, you cannot use the design exam that you took as an elective. Each exam can only count once toward certification. This includes any of the MCSE electives that are current when the Windows 2000 exams are released. In summary, you would take a total of at least two more exams, the upgrade exam and the design exam. Any additional exams would be dependent on which electives the candidate may have already completed.

In the second scenario, if you have not completed, and do not plan to complete the Core Windows NT 4.0 exams, you must pass the four core Windows 2000 exams, one design exam, and two elective exams. Again, no exam can be counted twice. In this case, you must pass a total of seven exams to obtain the Windows 2000 MCSE certification.

How to Take a Microsoft Certification Exam

If you have taken a Microsoft Certification exam before, we have some good news and some bad news. The good news is that the new testing formats will be a true measure of your ability and knowledge. Microsoft has "raised the bar" for its Windows 2000 certification exams. If you are an expert in the Windows 2000 operating system, and can troubleshoot and engineer efficient, cost effective solutions using Windows 2000, you will have no difficulty with the new exams.

The bad news is that if you have used resources such as "brain-dumps," boot-camps, or exam specific practice tests as your only method of test preparation, you will undoubtedly fail your Windows 2000 exams. The new Windows 2000 MCSE exams will test your knowledge, and your ability to apply that knowledge in more sophisticated and accurate ways than was expected for the MCSE exams for Windows NT 4.0.

In the Windows 2000 exams, Microsoft will use a variety of testing formats which include product simulations, adaptive testing, drag-and-drop matching, and possibly even "fill in the blank" questions (also called "free response" questions). The test-taking process will measure the examinee's fundamental knowledge of the Windows 2000 operating system rather than the ability to memorize a few facts and then answer a few simple multiple-choice questions.

In addition, the "pool" of questions for each exam will significantly increase. The greater number of questions combined with the adaptive testing techniques will enhance the validity and security of the certification process.

We will begin by looking at the purpose, focus, and structure of Microsoft certification tests, and examine the effect that these factors have on the kinds of questions you will face on your certification exams. We will define the structure of exam questions and investigate some common formats. Next, we will present a strategy for answering these questions. Finally, we will give some specific guidelines on what you should do on the day of your test.

Why Vendor Certification?

The Microsoft Certified Professional program, like the certification programs from Cisco, Novell, Oracle, and other software vendors, is maintained for the ultimate purpose of increasing the corporation's profits. A successful vendor certification program accomplishes this goal by helping to create a pool of experts in a company's software and by "branding" these experts so companies using the software can identify them.

We know that vendor certification has become increasingly popular in the last few years because it helps employers find qualified workers and because it helps software vendors like Microsoft sell their products. But why vendor certification rather than a more traditional approach like a college degree in computer science? A college education is a broadening and enriching experience, but a degree in computer science does not prepare students for most jobs in the IT industry.

A common truism in our business states, "If you are out of the IT industry for three years and want to return, you have to start over." The problem, of course, is *timeliness*; if a first-year student learns about a specific computer program, it probably will no longer be in wide use when he or she graduates. Although some colleges are trying to integrate Microsoft certification into their curriculum, the problem is not really a flaw in higher education, but a characteristic of the IT industry. Computer software is changing so rapidly that a four-year college just can't keep up.

A marked characteristic of the Microsoft certification program is an emphasis on performing specific job tasks rather than merely gathering knowledge. It may come as a shock, but most potential employers do not care how much you know about the theory of operating systems, networking, or database design. As one IT manager put it, "I don't really care what my employees know about the theory of our network. We don't need someone to sit at a desk and think about it. We need people who can actually do something to make it work better."

You should not think that this attitude is some kind of anti-intellectual revolt against "book learning." Knowledge is a necessary prerequisite, but it is not enough. More than one company has hired a computer science graduate as a network administrator, only to learn that the new employee has no idea how to add users, assign permissions, or perform the other day-to-day tasks necessary to maintain a network. This brings us to the second major characteristic of Microsoft certification that affects the questions you must be prepared to answer. In addition to timeliness, Microsoft certification is also job-task oriented.

The timeliness of Microsoft's certification program is obvious and is inherent in the fact that you will be tested on current versions of software in wide use today. The job task orientation of Microsoft certification is almost as obvious, but testing real-world job skills using a computer-based test is not easy.

Computerized Testing

Considering the popularity of Microsoft certification, and the fact that certification candidates are spread around the world, the only practical way to administer tests for the certification program is through Sylvan Prometric or Vue testing centers, which operate internationally. Sylvan Prometric and Vue provide proctor testing services for Microsoft, Oracle, Novell, Lotus, and the A+ computer technician certification. Although the IT industry accounts for much of Sylvan's revenue, the company provides services for a number of other businesses and organizations, such as FAA pre-flight pilot tests. Historically, several hundred questions were developed for a new Microsoft certification exam. The Windows 2000 MCSE exam pool is expected to contain hundreds of new questions. Microsoft is aware that many new MCSE candidates have been able to access information on test questions via the Internet or other resources. The company is very concerned about maintaining the MCSE as a "premium" certification. The significant increase in the number of test questions, together with stronger enforcement of the NDA (Non-disclosure agreement) will ensure that a higher standard for certification is attained.

Microsoft treats the test-building process very seriously. Test questions are first reviewed by a number of subject matter experts for technical accuracy and then are presented in a beta test. Taking the beta test may require several hours, due to the large number of questions. After a few weeks, Microsoft Certification uses the statistical feedback from Sylvan to check the performance of the beta questions. The beta test group for the Windows 2000 certification series included MCTs, MCSEs, and members of Microsoft's rapid deployment partners groups. Because the exams will be normalized based on this population, you can be sure that the passing scores will be difficult to achieve without detailed product knowledge.

Questions are discarded if most test takers get them right (too easy) or wrong (too difficult), and a number of other statistical measures are taken of each question. Although the scope of our discussion precludes a rigorous treatment of question analysis, you should be aware that Microsoft and other vendors spend a great deal of time and effort making sure their exam questions are valid.

The questions that survive statistical analysis form the pool of questions for the final certification exam.

Test Structure

The questions in a Microsoft form test will not be equally weighted. From what we can tell at the present time, different questions are given a value based on the level of difficulty. You will get more credit for getting a difficult question correct, than if you got an easy one correct. Because the questions are weighted differently, and because the exams will likely use the adapter method of testing, your score will not bear any relationship to how many questions you answered correctly.

Microsoft has implemented *adaptive* testing. When an adaptive test begins, the candidate is first given a level three question. If it is answered correctly, a question from the next higher level is presented, and an incorrect response results in a question from the next lower level. When 15 to 20 questions have been answered in this manner, the scoring algorithm is able to predict, with a high degree of statistical certainty, whether the candidate would pass or fail if all the questions in the form were answered. When the required degree of certainty is attained, the test ends and the candidate receives a pass/fail grade.

Adaptive testing has some definite advantages for everyone involved in the certification process. Adaptive tests allow Sylvan Prometric or Vue to deliver more tests with the same resources, as certification candidates often are in and out in 30 minutes or less. For candidates, the "fatigue factor" is reduced due to the shortened testing time. For Microsoft, adaptive testing means that fewer test questions are exposed to each candidate, and this can enhance the security, and therefore the overall validity, of certification tests.

One possible problem you may have with adaptive testing is that you are not allowed to mark and revisit questions. Since the adaptive algorithm is interactive, and all questions but the first are selected on the basis of your response to the previous question, it is not possible to skip a particular question or change an answer.

Question Types

Computerized test questions can be presented in a number of ways. Some of the possible formats are used on Microsoft certification exam and some are not.

True/False

We are all familiar with True/False questions, but because of the inherent 50 percent chance of guessing the correct answer, you will not see questions of this type on Microsoft certification exams.

Multiple Choice

The majority of Microsoft certification questions are in the multiple-choice format, with either a single correct answer or multiple correct answers. One interesting variation on multiple-choice questions with multiple correct answers is whether or not the candidate is told how many answers are correct.

EXAMPLE:

Which two files can be altered to configure the MS-DOS environment? (Choose two.)

Or

Which files can be altered to configure the MS-DOS environment? (Choose all that apply.)

You may see both variations on Microsoft certification exams, but the trend seems to be toward the first type, where candidates are told explicitly how many answers are correct. Questions of the "choose all that apply" variety are more difficult and can be merely confusing.

Graphical Questions

One or more graphical elements are sometimes used as exhibits to help present or clarify an exam question. These elements may take the form of a network diagram, pictures of networking components, or screen shots from the software on which you are being tested. It is often easier to present the concepts required for a complex performance-based scenario with a graphic than with words.

Test questions known as *hotspots* actually incorporate graphics as part of the answer. These questions ask the certification candidate to click on a location or graphical element to answer the question. For example, you might be shown the diagram of a network and asked to click on an appropriate location for a router. The answer is correct if the candidate clicks within the *hotspot* that defines the correct location.

Free Response Questions

Another kind of question you sometimes see on Microsoft certification exams requires a *free response* or type-in answer. An example of this type of question might present a TCP/IP network scenario and ask the candidate to calculate and enter the correct subnet mask in dotted decimal notation.

Simulation Questions

Simulation questions provide a method for Microsoft to test how familiar the test taker is with the actual product interface and the candidate's ability to quickly implement a task using the interface. These questions will present an actual Windows 2000 interface that you must work with to solve a problem or implement a solution. If you are familiar with the product, you will be able to answer these questions quickly, and they will be the easiest questions on the exam. However, if you are not accustomed to working with Windows 2000, these questions will be difficult for you to answer. This is why actual hands-on practice with Windows 2000 is so important!

Knowledge-Based and Performance-Based Questions

Microsoft Certification develops a blueprint for each Microsoft certification exam with input from subject matter experts. This blueprint defines the content areas and objectives for each test, and each test question is created to test a specific objective. The basic information from the examination blueprint can be found on Microsoft's Web site in the Exam Prep Guide for each test.

Psychometricians (psychologists who specialize in designing and analyzing tests) categorize test questions as knowledge-based or performance-based. As the names imply, knowledge-based questions are designed to test knowledge, while performance-based questions are designed to test performance.

Some objectives demand a knowledge-based question. For example, objectives that use verbs like *list* and *identify* tend to test only what you know, not what you can do.

EXAMPLE:

Objective: Identify the MS-DOS configuration files.

Which two files can be altered to configure the MS-DOS environment? (Choose two.)

    A. COMMAND.COM

    B. AUTOEXEC.BAT

    C. IO.SYS

    D. CONFIG.SYS

    Correct answers: B, D

Other objectives use action verbs like *install, configure,* and *troubleshoot* to define job tasks. These objectives can often be tested with either a knowledge-based question or a performance-based question.

EXAMPLE:

Objective: Configure an MS-DOS installation appropriately using the PATH statement in AUTOEXEC.BAT.

Knowledge-based question:

What is the correct syntax to set a path to the D: directory in AUTOEXEC.BAT?

    A. SET PATH EQUAL TO D:

    B. PATH D:

    C. SETPATH D:

    D. D:EQUALS PATH

    Correct answer: B

Performance-based question:

Your company uses several DOS accounting applications that access a group of common utility programs. What is the best strategy for configuring the computers in the accounting department so that the accounting applications will always be able to access the utility programs?

A. Store all the utilities on a single floppy disk and make a copy of the disk for each computer in the accounting department.

B. Copy all the utilities to a directory on the C: drive of each computer in the accounting department and add a PATH statement pointing to this directory in the AUTOEXEC.BAT files.

C. Copy all the utilities to all application directories on each computer in the accounting department.

D. Place all the utilities in the C: directory on each computer, because the C: directory is automatically included in the PATH statement when AUTOEXEC.BAT is executed.

Correct answer: B

Even in this simple example, the superiority of the performance-based question is obvious. Whereas the knowledge-based question asks for a single fact, the performance-based question presents a real-life situation and requires that you make a decision based on this scenario. Thus, performance-based questions give more bang (validity) for the test author's buck (individual question).

Testing Job Performance

We have said that Microsoft certification focuses on timeliness and the ability to perform job tasks. We have also introduced the concept of performance-based questions, but even performance-based multiple-choice questions do not really measure performance. Another strategy is needed to test job skills.

Given unlimited resources, it is not difficult to test job skills. In an ideal world, Microsoft would fly MCP candidates to Redmond, place them in a controlled environment with a team of experts, and ask them to plan, install, maintain, and troubleshoot a Windows network. In a few days at most, the experts could reach a valid decision as to whether each candidate should or should not be granted MCDBA or MCSE status. Needless to say, this is not likely to happen.

Closer to reality, another way to test performance is by using the actual software and creating a testing program to present tasks and automatically grade a candidate's performance when the tasks are completed. This *cooperative* approach would be practical in some testing situations, but the same test that is presented to MCP candidates in Boston must also be available in Bahrain and Botswana. The most workable solution for measuring performance in today's testing environment is a *simulation* program. When the program is launched during a test, the candidate sees a simulation of the actual software that looks, and behaves, just like the real thing. When the testing software presents a task, the simulation program is launched and the candidate performs the required task. The testing software then grades the candidate's performance on the required task and moves to the next question. Microsoft has introduced simulation questions on the certification exam for Internet Information Server 4.0. Simulation questions provide many advantages over other testing methodologies, and simulations are expected to become increasingly important in the Microsoft certification program. For example, studies have shown that there is a very high correlation between the ability to perform simulated tasks on a computer-based test and the ability to perform the actual job tasks. Thus, simulations enhance the validity of the certification process.

Another truly wonderful benefit of simulations is in the area of test security. It is just not possible to cheat on a simulation question. In fact, you will be told exactly what tasks you are expected to perform on the test. How can a certification candidate cheat? By learning to perform the tasks? What a concept!

Study Strategies

There are appropriate ways to study for the different types of questions you will see on a Microsoft certification exam.

Knowledge-Based Questions

Knowledge-based questions require that you memorize facts. There are hundreds of facts inherent in every content area of every Microsoft certification exam. There are several keys to memorizing facts:

- **Repetition** The more times your brain is exposed to a fact, the more likely you are to remember it.

- **Association**   Connecting facts within a logical framework makes them easier to remember.

- **Motor Association**   It is often easier to remember something if you write it down or perform some other physical act, like clicking on a practice test answer.

We have said that the emphasis of Microsoft certification is job performance, and that there are very few knowledge-based questions on Microsoft certification exams. Why should you waste a lot of time learning filenames, IP address formulas, and other minutiae? Read on.

Performance-Based Questions

Most of the questions you will face on a Microsoft certification exam are performance-based scenario questions. We have discussed the superiority of these questions over simple knowledge-based questions, but you should remember that the job task orientation of Microsoft certification extends the knowledge you need to pass the exams; it does not replace this knowledge. Therefore, the first step in preparing for scenario questions is to absorb as many facts relating to the exam content areas as you can. In other words, go back to the previous section and follow the steps to prepare for an exam composed of knowledge-based questions.

The second step is to familiarize yourself with the format of the questions you are likely to see on the exam. You can do this by answering the questions in this study guide, by using Microsoft assessment tests, or by using practice tests on the included CD-ROM. The day of your test is not the time to be surprised by the construction of Microsoft exam questions.

At best, performance-based scenario questions really do test certification candidates at a higher cognitive level than knowledge-based questions. At worst, these questions can test your reading comprehension and test-taking ability rather than your ability to use Microsoft products. Be sure to get in the habit of reading the question carefully to determine what is being asked.

The third step in preparing for Microsoft scenario questions is to adopt the following attitude: multiple-choice questions aren't really performance-based. It is all a cruel lie. These scenario questions are just knowledge-based questions with a story wrapped around them.

To answer a scenario question, you have to sift through the story to the underlying facts of the situation and apply your knowledge to determine the correct answer.

This may sound silly at first, but the process we go through in solving real-life problems is quite similar. The key concept is that every scenario question (and every real-life problem) has a fact at its center, and if we can identify that fact, we can answer the question.

Simulations

Simulation questions really do measure your ability to perform job tasks. You must be able to perform the specified tasks. There are two ways to prepare for simulation questions:

1. Get experience with the actual software. If you have the resources, this is a great way to prepare for simulation questions.

2. Use the practice test on this book's accompanying CD-ROM, as it contains simulation questions similar to those you will find on the Microsoft exam. This approach has the added advantage of grading your efforts. You can find additional practice tests at www.syngress.com and www.osborne.com.

Signing Up

Signing up to take a Microsoft certification exam is easy. Sylvan Prometric or Vue operators in each country can schedule tests at any testing center. There are, however, a few things you should know:

1. If you call Sylvan Prometric or Vue during a busy time, get a cup of coffee first, because you may be in for a long wait. The exam providers do an excellent job, but everyone in the world seems to want to sign up for a test on Monday morning.

2. You will need your social security number or some other unique identifier to sign up for a test, so have it at hand.

3. Pay for your test by credit card if at all possible. This makes things easier, and you can even schedule tests for the same day you call, if space is available at your local testing center.

4. Know the number and title of the test you want to take before you call. This is not essential, and the Sylvan operators will help you if they can. Having this information in advance, however, speeds up and improves the accuracy of the registration process.

Taking the Test

Teachers have always told you not to try to cram for exams because it does no good. If you are faced with a knowledge-based test requiring only that you regurgitate facts, cramming can mean the difference between passing and failing. This is not the case, however, with Microsoft certification exams. If you don't know it the night before, don't bother to stay up and cram.

Instead, create a schedule and stick to it. Plan your study time carefully, and do not schedule your test until you think you are ready to succeed. Follow these guidelines on the day of your exam:

1. Get a good night's sleep. The scenario questions you will face on a Microsoft certification exam require a clear head.

2. Remember to take two forms of identification—at least one with a picture. A driver's license with your picture and social security or credit card is acceptable.

3. Leave home in time to arrive at your testing center a few minutes early. It is not a good idea to feel rushed as you begin your exam.

4. Do not spend too much time on any one question. You cannot mark and revisit questions on an adaptive test, so you must do your best on each question as you go.

5. If you do not know the answer to a question, try to eliminate the obviously wrong answers and guess from the rest. If you can eliminate two out of four options, you have a 50 percent chance of guessing the correct answer.

6. For scenario questions, follow the steps we outlined earlier. Read the question carefully and try to identify the facts at the center of the story.

Finally, we would advise anyone attempting to earn Microsoft MCDBA and MCSE certification to adopt a philosophical attitude. The Windows 2000 MCSE will be the most difficult MCSE ever to be offered. The questions will be at a higher cognitive level than seen on all previous MCSE exams. Therefore, even if you are the kind of person who never fails a test, you are likely to fail at least one Windows 2000 certification test somewhere along the way. Do not get discouraged. Microsoft wants to ensure the value of your certification. Moreover, it will attempt to so by keeping the standard as high as possible. If Microsoft certification were easy to obtain, more people would have it, and it would not be so respected and so valuable to your future in the IT industry.

1
Introduction to Designing a Microsoft Windows 2000 Network Infrastructure

CERTIFICATION OBJECTIVES

W elcome to one of Microsoft's most important new elective/core topics for the Windows 2000 Microsoft Certified Systems Engineer (MCSE) certification track. Networking is what Microsoft's new operating system—and computing in general—is all about today. Understanding how to build, use, maintain, and troubleshoot the network infrastructure is essential to performing the duties of an administrator and must be mastered in order to obtain certification as a systems engineer.

CERTIFICATION OBJECTIVE 1.01

Introduction

Exam 70-216 covers the implementation and administration of the Windows 2000 networking infrastructure, while the exam addressed by this book, 70-221, focuses on design aspects. In this chapter, we will discuss how the two subjects differ and how they tie together.

It is recommended that you first study and test on the core topic, Implementation and Administration, prior to tackling the Design exam. At first glance, this might seem to be a backward approach; after all, you must design a network *before* you implement and administer it. However, Microsoft sees the Design exams as topics requiring a higher level of knowledge and expertise, with the ability to gather the appropriate data, analyze and evaluate requirements and specifications, and conceptualize the "big picture." This is the task of a true enterprise architect, a step beyond the duties of the engineer in the field who carries out those plans after they've been formulated.

Although networking fundamentals remain the same at the physical level, designing a network from the ground up requires many skills that were not required to obtain the Windows NT 4.0 MCSE. With new features such as Active Directory, and a new emphasis on topics that were only touched on lightly, such as DNS, Windows 2000 is changing the world of networking and the way administrators perform common tasks.

To design a network based on the new operating system, you *must* first have a thorough understanding of basic TCP/IP concepts such as Domain Name Services (DNS), the Dynamic Host Configuration Protocol (DHCP), Routing and Remote Access Services (RRAS) including Network Address Translation (NAT), the Windows Internet Name Service (WINS), Certificate Services, and the TCP/IP and

NWLink protocol suites upon which modern networks are based. These are topics covered by the Implementation and Administration exam (70-216).

Then you must go a step further. To pass the Design exam, you will need to know about more than computer networks. You will need to understand business models and company processes. You will need to understand how organizations are structured and what effect organizational structure has on network design. You will need to be able to analyze factors that influence company strategies as well as be able to conduct an analysis of the structure of the company's IT management.

Part of designing a network is knowing the technical requirements of the organization. You should not only be able to analyze the technical environment in which the company is presently operating, but also have a good grasp of the company's goals in terms of technology and growth.

Specifically, you will be expected to demonstrate the ability to design a TCP/IP networking strategy. This is why a thorough understanding of the TCP/IP protocol suite and how it is implemented is vitally important. Within that objective, you should be capable of designing a DHCP strategy and planning the design of name resolution services for the network.

As important as TCP/IP is, there are still many enterprise environments in which it coexists with other network protocols. Thus you must also be able to design a multi-protocol strategy which incorporates IPX/SPX (still popular in networking environments that run Novell NetWare servers) and Systems Network Architecture (SNA), used to connect PC LANs to mainframe networks.

Many of these requirements are issues commonly faced by those who design NT 4.0 networks. However, the Windows 2000 Design exams will introduce other concepts that may not be addressed by the NT 4.0 professional. For instance, you will need to know the specifics of designing a Distributed File System (DFS) strategy, and you will be required to design connectivity solutions (Internet and intranet) that are supported as new features in Windows 2000. This includes Internet Connection Sharing (ICS) and Network Address Translation (NAT), as well as load balancing, proxy and firewall solutions, and remote access strategies.

Planning for wide area networking (WAN) implementation, including RRAS, RADIUS, demand-dial routing, and virtual private networking (VPN) will be likely exam topics as well.

Finally, you must be prepared to design strategies for monitoring and managing the Windows 2000 network services. Many of these, such as LDAP services and global catalog services, are new to Windows 2000. Others, such as DHCP, DNS, WINS, routing and remote access, and certificate services, have been modified and improved in the new operating system. It will be essential that you understand why and how to plan for the management of network resources, creating a strategy that allows for the growth of the network in the future.

Correlation Between Windows 2000 and NT 4.0 Exams

Although it is possible to draw some sort of correlation between the Windows 2000 core exams and their NT 4.0 counterparts (for instance, the Windows 2000 Professional and NT Workstation exams, or the two Server exams, or even the combination of Networking Essentials and TCP/IP compared to the Implementing and Administering a Network Infrastructure exam), it is impossible to map the Windows 2000 design exams to anything in the NT MCSE certification track.

It has been rumored that the design exams are part of a long-range plan by Microsoft to create an "upper tier" MCSE certification, perhaps conferring the title "enterprise architect." Whether or not this occurs, it is obvious that the company desires to raise the bar for the Microsoft Certified Systems Engineer certification itself, making it more difficult for the so-called "dumpers and crammers" (those who memorize test questions and answers from "brain dumps" distributed on the Internet or who cram "quick review" books as their primary source of study for the exams) to pass the exams.

Target Audience

Microsoft's stated "target audience" for this exam specifies those who have supported networks in which the number of users ranges from 200–26,000 and up, and the number of physical locations ranges from 5–150 or more. According to those specifications, typical network services and applications you have supported should include file and print, database, messaging, proxy server or firewall, dial-in server, desktop management, and Web hosting. You also should have experience in connectivity issues, including connecting individual offices and users at remote locations to the corporate network and connecting corporate networks to the Internet.

Those criteria may seem steep, especially when compared to the NT 4.0 exams. There are good reasons for this. There has been a lot of talk, with the advent of the Windows 2000 certification track, about Microsoft's desire to "raise the bar" and restore the MCSE to the status of a "premium" certification. This is reflected in the suggested prerequisites.

Also keep in mind that the Design exams will logically be taken after passing the following four Windows 2000 mandatory core exams:

- Installing, Configuring, and Administering Windows 2000 Professional (70-210)

- Installing, Configuring, and Administering Windows 2000 Server (70-215)

- Implementing and Administering a Windows 2000 Network Infrastructure (70-216)

- Implementing and Administering a Windows 2000 Directory Services Infrastructure (70-217)

Or, they can be taken after successful completion of the Microsoft Windows 2000 Accelerated Exam for MCPs (70-240), which encompasses the topics covered by the four core exams previously listed.

Although you must take *one* of the three Design exams as a required "core" to obtain the Windows 2000 MCSE certification, Microsoft has made it obvious that the Design exams are the more advanced in topic and scope. Unless you have specific experience as a network architect in the areas covered by the Design exam objectives, it would not be wise to tackle any of them prior to demonstrating that you have mastered the "foundation" knowledge and skills measured by the mandatory core exams.

The Microsoft "target audience" specifications are recommendations, not enforced prerequisites. Realistically, those taking Exam 70-221 can be expected to fall into one of two categories: experienced networking professionals and network "newbies."

Experienced Networking Professionals

According to the Microsoft Web site and documentation, exam candidates are presumed to be networking personnel operating in medium-to-very-large computing environments with a minimum of one year's experience in administering and implementing Windows networking components and supporting 200 or more users in five or more physical locations. It is also presumed that the exam taker is familiar with typical network services and applications, such as file and print sharing, databases, messaging services, proxy and/or firewalls, dial-in remote access servers, Web hosting, and desktop management and control.

What if you've been working as a network administrator for 20 years in a small company with a small network that has only 50 users instead of the "minimum" 200? Or, what if your network has a relatively large number of users all contained in one physical location?

Does this mean you can't take the exam, or that you have no hope of passing it? Of course not. What it does mean to you, however, is that you need to carefully assess the skills set you've developed in that networking situation and evaluate how it differs from Microsoft's "ideal" experiential environment. Some small networks are on the "cutting edge" and have implemented, on a smaller scale, all or most of the same enterprise technologies ordinarily used in large networks. In that case, you might already meet the "target audience" specifications in spirit if not in fact. Even if your network has only two physical locations instead of "5 or more," if you have worked extensively with remote access solutions, proxies and firewalls, IP routing, messaging and database administration, Web hosting, etc., you will be in good shape to prepare for the Design exam.

On the other hand, if your small network has been limited to LAN communications only, primarily using the network for only file and print sharing, and you have no dial-in users and have never connected the local network to the Internet, you may have a bit more study and practice ahead of you. What you will need to do in order to get the background skills you need for this exam, is attempt to emulate the large network environment to the extent possible. If this can't be done on your production network, consider investing in the equipment to set up a home network on which you can test and learn Windows 2000's enterprise-oriented features. Alternately, you might volunteer to work with, or ask to observe, the administrator of a large network as he/she goes about daily tasks. The important thing is not *how* you get first-hand exposure to a network running traditionally large-network services such as RAS servers, Web servers, terminal services, and database servers; the important thing is that you *do* find a way to get hands-on experience in such an environment.

What if You're New to Networking?

Despite Microsoft's recommendations, there will be some who come to this exam as "network newbies." Career-changers and new graduates studying for certification in order to *get* their first networking job will be preparing for these exams as well. The statements from Microsoft regarding target audience do not mean that if you don't have on-the-job experience as a network administrator you won't be able to pass the Windows 2000 exams. They do mean that if you don't meet the description of the exam's "target audience," you will need to study harder, and in particular you will need to get more hands-on practice in working with the products.

This book contains a large number of practical exercises that walk you through the steps of procedures common to working network professionals. In order to really understand the concepts and skills covered by the exam, it is essential that you do more than read through the exercises—you must work through them on a Windows 2000 computer. This can be done on a relatively simple home network, and we highly recommend that you consider setting up a two- or three-system lab if you don't have access to a network on the job or in a classroom situation. The cost of doing so is an investment that can quickly pay for itself in terms of time saved in obtaining the certification.

CERTIFICATION OBJECTIVE 1.02

What Is Network Infrastructure Design?

If you have already taken the mandatory core Exam 70-216, Implementing and Administering a Windows 2000 Network Infrastructure, you are already familiar with the term *network infrastructure,* but let's review what it means.

Infrastructure is a big word that can be used to describe many things. It is often used to refer to the basic facilities, services, and installations necessary for a community or a society to function (such as roads, communications systems, water and sewer services, electrical power lines, etc.). The dictionary gives the following broad definition:

An underlying base or foundation of an organization or system.

From this, we can extrapolate that the infrastructure of a computer network consists of the basic components upon which it is built. We could further divide these into two subcategories:

- Those making up the *physical* infrastructure (the machines themselves, the cables and network interface cards and hubs and routers).

- Those making up the *logical* infrastructure (the networking protocols, the DNS namespace and services, the IP addressing scheme and DHCP strategy, the remote access services, and security protocols).

The first category is hardware-related while the second is dependent on software components and their configuration.

Now, where does the "design" part of this exam title fit in?

New Focus on Design Issues

The Windows 2000 core networking exam (70-216), Implementing and Administering a Windows 2000 Network Infrastructure, is focused almost entirely on the logical infrastructure and how to install, configure, administer, and troubleshoot the services associated with it, such as DNS, WINS, DHCP, RAS, and the TCP/IP protocol suite. Exam 70-216 does not test on the physical infrastructure (as the Windows NT 4.0 Networking Essentials exam did). This is because Microsoft seems to presume that the Windows 2000 exam candidate has prior networking experience and is already familiar with physical issues. It may also reflect the fact that the typical Windows 2000 exam candidate will be working in a company that has a medium-to-very-large network, and in this environment there is more likely to be a division between the personnel who do actual administrative tasks and the technicians who care for the hardware.

At first glance, you may wonder if Exam 70-221 is a recap of the same topics covered by Exam 70-216. The objectives for the latter begin with some familiar issues: routing and IP addressing, DNS, WINS, and RAS. You'll also notice one of those "physical" issues that was part of the NT Networking Essentials exam but left out of the Windows 2000 Implementing and Administering a Network Infrastructure exam: network topologies. Virtual private networking and telephony solutions are mentioned, as well, but we're still talking about network infrastructure issues, so exactly how does the "Design" exam differ from the "Implementing and Administering" exam?

Components of Physical and Logical Infrastructure Design

The physical infrastructure of the network consists of the following:

- Network Topology (layout)
- Cabling/media Types
- Networking Hardware (interface cards, hubs, repeaters, bridges, routers, and switches)

The logical infrastructure includes:

- Network Protocols
- IP Addressing Schemes
- Name Resolution Services
- Remote Access
- Routing and Network Address Translation
- The Security Infrastructure

In order to design a network that will perform most effectively and efficiently, and will be easy to administer and to expand in the future, you will need a good grasp of each of these components.

LAN Topology

The network topology refers to the layout of the cable or the path taken by the signals as they travel along the network. The *physical* topology is based on the shape of the network, what it looks like. The following grid addresses popular physical topologies.

The *logical* topology may be the same, or different from the physical topology. It describes the actual path of data transmission. For example, a network can appear to be a star, with all computers connecting to a central hub. However, if inside the hub the wiring connects each port to the next in a circle, the *logical topology* is a ring. See Figure 1-1.

SCENARIO & SOLUTION

What is a linear bus topology?	The computers are connected in a line, one to the next. The network cabling has a beginning and an end.
What is a star bus topology?	Computers all connect to a central hub or switch.
What is a ring topology?	Similarly to a linear bus, computers are connected one to the next, but the last computer is then connected to the first, forming a circle.
What is a mesh topology?	Computers have redundant connections so that there are multiple pathways between some or all of the computers.

FIGURE 1-1

A physical star can be a logical ring if the wiring inside the hub is connected in a circle

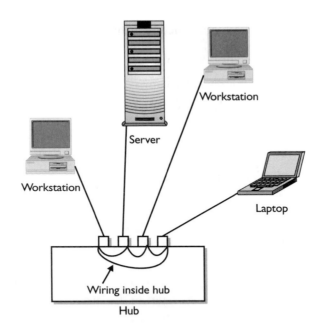

Network topology affects the overall operation of the network in many ways. Certain cable or media types are associated with certain topologies, and media access methods differ according to topology as well.

WAN Topology

It is very important that you understand both LAN topology, as described above, and WAN topology, which has to do with the connections between separate geographic sites. In a Windows 2000 network, this impacts such things as replication of the Active Directory database between domain controllers.

Windows 2000 allows you to configure Active Directory *sites*, which consist of one or more well-connected IP subnets, and specify scheduled times and intervals for replication traffic. This allows you to avoid congesting a slow WAN link during peak business hours.

Configuration of sites is covered in much more detail in Exam 70-217, Implementing and Administering a Windows 2000 Directory Services Infrastructure, but it is important that you have an understanding of how sites work in order to design a network infrastructure.

Cabling/Media Types and Network Hardware

Because an important part of designing a network infrastructure is assessing and evaluating the existing systems and determining whether and what upgrades are needed, you should be familiar with network cabling and media issues, as well as network hardware—especially connectivity devices such as routers and switches.

The following Scenario & Solution reference outlines the advantages and limitations of some of the common network media types.

Networking Protocols

An important component of the logical foundation of a group of networked computers is the protocol(s) those computers use to communicate.

SCENARIO & SOLUTION

What are the characteristics of coaxial cable?	Thin coax is often used for small networks or for small segments or subnets on a larger network. It is inexpensive and relatively easy to work with. It is limited to 185 meters per segment and 10 Mbps transmission. Thick coax can span longer distances per segment (500 meters) but still transmits at 10 Mbps. It is used for backbone connections (connecting hubs to one another). It is more expensive and more difficult to work with. Coax is generally used in a linear bus configuration.
What are the characteristics of twisted pair?	Unshielded twisted pair (UTP) is popular for Ethernet networks and is used in a star configuration. It comes in different grades designated by *category*. Category 5 is standard and can support transmission at 10 or 100 Mbps. It is relatively inexpensive and easy to work with. Segment length is limited to 100 meters.
What are the characteristics of fiber optic?	Fiber is expensive and working with it requires special training and skills. It is capable of very high speeds (up in the Gbps range) and is not subject to the signal loss over distance that plagues copper cable (coax and UTP). Thus segments can be 2000 meters in length. It is often used for backbones to connect two LANs in different buildings, for example.
What are wireless media?	Wireless technologies are developing and improving all the time. These include laser, infrared, radio, and satellite/microwave technologies. Some of these are limited to line-of-sight transmission and some are very slow compared to cable, but wireless is a viable solution in situations where cabling is inconvenient or impossible to implement.

The default LAN protocol for Windows 2000 is TCP/IP, and Exam 70-221 focuses on designing a TCP/IP networking strategy as one of its main objectives, so understanding protocols, especially the TCP/IP protocols, is essential to passing this exam.

A protocol is a set of rules, or a standardized order of procedures, that the networking components of the systems follow when they transmit data over the network. There are physical layer protocols, which consist of specifications or standards governing the hardware components, and there are numerous other protocols that operate at higher layers of the networking model. But the term "network protocol" is usually used to refer to the network and transport layer protocols (often part of a protocol "stack" or "suite") used for communication over a local area network (LAN).

Although Windows 2000, like Windows NT and the Windows 9x operating systems, supports other LAN protocols such as NWLink (a Microsoft implementation of Novell's IPX/SPX protocol stack) and NetBEUI (a simple, fast, low-overhead protocol used primarily in small, nonrouted networks), the "protocol stack of choice" for Windows 2000 networks is, not coincidentally, the set of protocols upon which the global Internet is based: the Transmission Control Protocol/Internet Protocol, or TCP/IP suite of protocols.

Networking Models   In order to fully understand how networking protocols function, you should be familiar with some of the popular networking models that describe the networking architecture and serve as the framework for standardization of the steps involved in network communications. The Open Systems Interconnection, or OSI model, has become a common reference point for discussion of network protocols and connection devices.

The OSI model uses seven layers or levels to represent the communications process. This layered approach provides a logical division of responsibility, where each layer handles prescribed functions. The Open Systems Interconnection model is used as a broad guideline for describing the network communications process. Not all protocol implementations map directly to the OSI model, but it serves as a good starting point for gaining a general understanding of how data is transferred across a network.

Figure 1-2 shows a graphical representation of the OSI networking model, from the "top down."

The seven layers
of the Open
Systems
Interconnection
(OSI) model

Communication takes place between corresponding layers on the Sending and Receiving computers. The data that is created by a user application (such as an e-mail message) enters the network communication process at the Application layer, and travels down the levels, with each layer adding header information that will be processed by its corresponding layer on the other side. At the Physical layer, the data is turned into electrical impulses, pulses of light, or radio signals (depending on the physical media being used) and sent out over the cable or over the air to the destination computer. When it arrives there, the networking components on that system process the data in the opposite order, finally delivering it (with the intervening headers stripped off) to the user application program (such as the recipient's e-mail program) at that end.

Note that the Data Link layer as represented in the original implementation of the OSI model was later divided into two sublayers:

- Logical Link Control (LLC)
- Media Access Control (MAC)

Figure 1-3 shows how this process works.

Communication occurs between corresponding layers of the OSI model

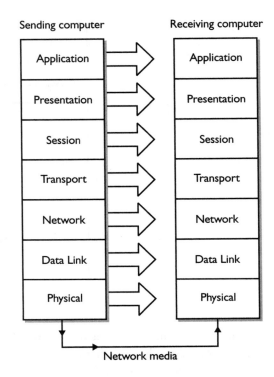

The model is important to understanding protocols because in a protocol stack such as TCP/IP, different protocols work at different layers in conjunction with one another. We will discuss the separate functions of TCP, UDP, and IP a little later in this chapter.

The OSI model is not the only networking model in use. If you do much study of TCP/IP, you will encounter the DoD (Department of Defense) model. Microsoft has also developed its own Windows networking model that intersperses layers called "boundary layers" representing open standards with vendor-specific components of its networking software.

OSI is an international standard, however, and Microsoft exams have traditionally required some knowledge of its structure and which protocols operate at which levels.

Why TCP/IP?   The TCP/IP protocol suite is the current standard for large networks, up to and including the Internet itself. Although it is slower and requires more resource overhead than other common network/transport protocol stacks, it has the advantages of being easily routable and compatible with most platforms and operating systems. Using the TCP/IP protocols to connect to the Internet, a computer user in Los Angeles using a Windows system can communicate with someone in London using a MacIntosh or someone in Tokyo using a Sun Solaris workstation. TCP/IP is the common "language" that makes it possible.

It would be difficult for an administrator to find a network environment today in which knowledge of TCP/IP is not required. Even Novell's NetWare server operating system, which relied on the IPX/SPX protocol stack for communications for a long time, has included support for "pure IP" with the debut of NetWare 5.0.

TCP/IP was originally designed for use on the ARPAnet, the predecessor of the Internet. The U.S. Department of Defense, in conjunction with major universities, developed the nationwide system (which then was extended throughout the world) to provide highly reliable, redundant communications links that could withstand even a nuclear war. TCP/IP has also survived efforts to replace it with other protocols, most notably the Open Systems Interconnect (OSI) suite.

Because of its continuing popularity and its role as a foundation of communications on large (and more and more small) networks today, TCP/IP is an essential topic of study for an aspiring MCSE. The Windows NT 3.51 and 4.0 certification tracks included an elective exam devoted to TCP/IP. The Windows 2000 track does not. This is not because a mastery of TCP/IP is less important in the new certification track; rather, it is because it has become so much more important that the fundamentals of TCP/IP are now incorporated into the required core exams. A thorough understanding of TCP/IP and those topics formerly included in the TCP/IP exam material (DNS, WINS, DHCP) is required to pass the Networking Infrastructure exams (both the core Implementing and Administering a Windows 2000 Network Infrastructure Exam 70-216 and the elective Designing a Windows 2000 Network Infrastructure, Exam 70-221).

exam
ⓦatch

Because Exam 70-221 focuses on skills needed to design a large TCP/IP network, it is imperative that you be intimately familiar with the more "advanced" aspects of TCP/IP, such as dynamic routing, and how to integrate TCP/IP with existing WAN requirements.

While you will need to know specifics of how to use the Windows 2000 interface to configure TCP/IP for Exam 70-216, this exam (70-221) presumes that knowledge, and expects you to go beyond mere administrative tasks to concentrate on conceptual issues. However, some design questions may be difficult to understand

and answer if you don't have the basic "how to" knowledge. If you have not already taken Exam 70-217, we recommend that you at least review a study guide, such as the Osborne/Syngress study guide for Implementing and Administering a Windows 2000 Network Infrastructure, before you attempt to master design issues covered in this book.

on the

Job

One of the most difficult tasks for many in designing a large, multi-location TCP/IP network from the ground up is determining a strategy for dividing the network into IP subnets. Subnetting is necessary on a large network to cut down on broadcast traffic and enhance security, but networks are sometimes divided into subnets somewhat haphazardly, thus the administrator's shrug and grinning comment that "it just grew that way." Planning your subnetting scheme carefully can make your job easier down the road, so make this a priority item when you design your new network.

IP Addressing Schemes

In addition to the protocols themselves, another important component of the infrastructure of a TCP/IP-based network is the addressing scheme used by IP to ensure that data transmissions reach the proper destination. This is the basis of network/subnet design.

Version 4 of the Internet Protocol (IPv4), the current implementation, uses 32 bit binary addresses, which are expressed in most cases as their equivalent in "dotted decimal," the familiar four-octet format (example: 192.168.1.45). This is also sometimes referred to as "dotted quad" because there are four groups of digits separated by dots.

IP Address Assignment   Address assignment—both manual assignment in which an administrator individually configures the TCP/IP properties of each computer on the network and automatic addressing methods such as DHCP and NAT—must be understood and mastered in order to work with TCP/IP. An administrator also needs to understand the "internals" of IP, how the logical addresses assigned at this level are mapped to the physical (Media Access Control) addresses that are ultimately used to get the data to its intended destination.

This means you need to know about protocols such as ARP (the Address Resolution Protocol) and RARP (Reverse ARP) and how they work.

Windows 2000 includes some new features that pertain to IP addressing. Automatic Private IP Addressing (APIPA), which allows a DHCP client computer that is unable to find a DHCP server to assign itself a temporary address and the auto addressing used by Internet Connection Sharing (ICS) are likely to be subjects of exam questions as well.

You should also be aware of the differences between "classful" and "classless" IP addressing, and know the default subnet masks for the common network classes, as shown in the following Scenario & Solution.

IP Subnetting   An important (and, both for network newbies and many experienced administrators, difficult) part of IP addressing is subnetting. This is the art and science of properly dividing a network into smaller connected IP networks (subnets), using a 32 bit number called the subnet mask to indicate the network ID.

exam
ⓦatch

Although some study guides and instructors may tell you that all you need to do to pass the IP subnetting portion of the Microsoft exams is to memorize tables defining subnet masks based on number of network and/or host IDs, there is no way to truly understand subnetting without learning to work with binary. Being able to convert dotted decimal addresses and masks to binary and then calculate and perform common operations such as ANDing on the binary digits will give you a big edge in answering subnetting questions on the exams. Not only will you be able to determine the correct answer, you'll know why it's correct.

The binary (base two) numbering system may seem confusing if you've never worked with anything but our common base ten system. However, you'll find that it's really pretty simple once you know the "tricks." In binary, there are only two digits: 0 and 1. This is particularly appropriate for computer calculations because it's

SCENARIO & SOLUTION

What default mask should I use for a Class A network?	255.0.0.0
What default mask should I use for a Class B network?	255.255.0.0
What default mask should I use for a Class C network?	255.255.255.0

FROM THE CLASSROOM

Classless InterDomain Routing

Classless InterDomain Routing (CIDR, pronounced "cider") is a means of addressing the shrinking number of Class B ("medium sized") network numbers available to be allocated. Using CIDR addressing, the subnet mask becomes a part of the routing table and a route is made up of the IP address and subnet mask. CIDR addresses are defined as "slash X" addresses because they include, appended to the usual four octets, a slash and a number that represents the number of bits used for the network ID. For instance, if the address is notated as 192.204.76.0/14, the "14" indicates that the first 14 bits of the address identify the network and the remaining 18 identify the host.CIDR allows for both dividing networks into subnets and for combining small networks with a common network prefix into supernets. In order to use CIDR, the routing protocols must support it. Dynamic routing protocols that support CIDR include version 2 of RIP and OSPF. Both the Routing Information Protocol v1 and v2 and Open Shortest Path First are included in the Windows 2000 Server.

—Debra Littlejohn Shinder, MCSE, MCP+I, MCT

easy to represent these two digits as electrical impulses or pulses of light—if the current or light is off, that's a 0 and if it's on, that's a 1. This is the basis of digital signaling; it is also called *discrete state* signaling.

Using this system, every possible number in our familiar base ten system can be represented by the 0s and 1s. Converting binary to decimal is not difficult, and is a necessary skill for learning IP subnetting, because the "real" numbers that the computer works with (and that you should work with in order to understand the process) are binary, but the software converts them to the "dotted decimal" format for entry into Properties boxes.

Of course, the easiest way to covert decimal to binary or vice versa is to use the Windows calculator in scientific mode (choose "Scientific" from the View menu). Just check the "dec" radio button and enter the number in decimal, then click on the "bin" radio button and tada! As if by magic, you have the binary equivalent.

Microsoft certification exams generally make the Windows calculator available for your use in performing these calculations; however, it is a good idea to know how to convert binary to decimal without the calculator.

The problem with using the calculator is that if you don't really understand how binary is converted to decimal, you may be confused by the calculator's results. For instance, when you convert the decimal 1 to binary, the result is 1. Let's say you are converting the last (right-most) octet in the IP address 192.168.1.1 to binary.

You know that an octet has eight digits, but the calculator only displays one. Do you put seven zeros before or after the 1? If you know how to do the conversion manually, it's obvious.

We have eight binary digits, and each of them represents a decimal value, beginning with the right-most digit and working our way back to the left-most. Note that the right-most digits are sometimes referred to as the low order bits and the left-most as the high order bits.

Each bit that is "turned on" (that is, shows a 1 instead of a 0), represents the value of that bit as shown in Figure 1-4. As you can see, the value increases by a power of 2 as you move from right to left. A bit that is "turned off" (represented by a 0) counts as 0. All we have to do then is add up the values of the bits that are "on."

You can use this simple formula to convert an octet in binary form, such as 10111001, to decimal. To do so, start at the right and look at which digits are turned on. We see that the bits represented by 1s have decimal values of 1, 8, 16, 32, and 128. If we add up those values, we get a total of 185 for the octet, which matches up with the value we get when we use the scientific calculator to convert 10111001 to decimal.

FIGURE 1-4

The value of each bit in an octet

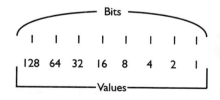

Another way of seeing how this is done when you're first learning how to convert to binary is to "line" up the numbers in three columns like this:

128×1=128
64×0=0
32×1=32
16×1=16
8×1=8
4×0=0
2×0=0
1×1=1

Then add up the number in the last column, which in this case is 185.

If all bits in an octet are "off," the decimal value is 0 and if all are "on," the value (total of 1, 2, 4, 8, 16, 32, 64, and 128) is 255.

The intricacies of subnet masking are covered in the study guide for Exam 70-216, Implementing and Administering a Windows 2000 Network Infrastructure.

DHCP   Designing a DHCP strategy is another important element in overall network design, and as such is an objective in Exam 70-221.

The Dynamic Host Configuration Protocol (DHCP), derived from BOOTP, allows a server computer configured to be a DHCP server to automatically assign IP addresses from a specified pool to client machines that are configured to be DHCP clients.

The Windows 2000 implementation of DHCP includes new functionality, such as integration with DNS, better logging, the ability to create multicast scopes, detection of "rogue" (unauthorized) Windows 2000 DHCP servers, and support for automatic client configuration via APIPA. For this, you'll need to know how to integrate DHCP with Windows 2000, and how to design a DHCP implementation for remote locations, as well as having a good understanding of monitoring and optimizing the performance of DHCP.

Designing Name Resolution Strategies

Another very important component of a networking infrastructure is name resolution. Another objective of Design exam 70-221 is the ability to design a strategy for deploying name resolution services for the network. For this reason, you need to have a good understanding of both the Domain Name System (DNS) and Microsoft's Windows Internet Naming Service (WINS).

Why is name resolution important? Because computers and humans are inherently different. The machines can only recognize and work with numbers (and only binary numbers, at that). To your computer, another system on the network with which it communicates is identified by numbers. As human beings, we are more comfortable if we can use "friendly names" to identify computers, Web sites, and other network resources that we wish to access.

A good example of this occurs when you browse the World Wide Web. If you want to access Microsoft's Web site, you type **www.microsoft.com** into your browser's URL box. Imagine having to remember, instead, the IP address 207.46.130.14—or worse yet, the binary form of that: 11001111 00101110 10000010 00001110—and having to type that in each time you wanted to go to the Microsoft site.

Well, without some form of name resolution, we would be stuck with keeping track of at least the dotted decimal version of all those Web sites. Incidences of Web addiction might decrease, but it would certainly make for a more frustrating user experience. Name resolution services, such as the Domain Name System service (DNS) and the Windows Internet Name Service (WINS) allow you to use friendlier names while they take over the task of getting those names converted into an IP address that the computer can use.

on the job

In designing a new network, you will be faced with providing the most efficient means of resolving both host names and—unless your Windows 2000 network is running with no "downlevel" (pre-Windows 2000) computers and NetBT has been decommissioned—NetBIOS names as well. This means you will need to design deployment strategies for both DNS and WINS, taking into account such factors as security and the impact on network bandwidth of replication between name servers.

DNS and WINS servers are machines that maintain databases matching up names to IP addresses and accept queries from other machines on the network that need this information. Think of them as similar to the directory assistance service provided by your phone company; if you know the person's name but not his phone number, you call up, query directory assistance, and then you can connect directly (by calling) to the person with whom you want to communicate.

DNS and WINS work similarly, but deal with different types of names. DNS resolves *fully qualified domain names* (also referred to as FQDNs) to IP addresses. These are the "dotted" or hierarchically structured names such as those used for Web sites. WINS resolves NetBIOS names, used by Windows operating systems prior to Windows 2000 and by many applications, to IP addresses. These are "flat" names, such as COMPUTER12 (the same computer's DNS name might be computer12.mydomain.com).

DNS   The mandatory core exam will expect you to know how to install and configure a DNS server and how to set up DNS clients, as well as how to troubleshoot problems that occur in the DNS name resolution process. For this exam, the emphasis is on how to design a troublefree DNS environment.

exam
ⓦatch

The DNS in Windows 2000 is dynamic (thus the term Dynamic DNS or DDNS). Unlike the DNS service in Windows NT 4.0, which had to be manually updated, the Windows 2000 DDNS database supports a new specification to the DNS standard for dynamic update. This permits hosts that store name information in DNS to dynamically register and update their records in zones maintained by DNS servers that can accept and process dynamic update messages.

In Windows 2000, DNS can be integrated with the Active Directory, making for more efficient replication of the DNS records. The Design exam is likely to focus heavily on planning the DNS namespace for a Windows 2000 network, and you will be expected to know how to create a DNS environment that is optimized for security, availability, and performance.

You will also need to understand how a DNS server deployment is planned and implemented, and the different types of DNS servers. The following Scenario & Solution reference is a handy summarization of the server types and how you would use each in real-world networking situations.

WINS   Windows 2000 provides for the eventual decommissioning of WINS and disabling of NetBIOS, but this will not become a reality for most production networks for some time to come. Microsoft recognizes this and many improvements have been made to the service in Windows 2000. The Networking Infrastructure Design exam will expect you to know how to plan the deployment of WINS servers and clients, how WINS replication works, and how to optimize and secure the WINS service.

SCENARIO & SOLUTION

What is the function of the primary DNS server?	The primary read/write copy of the DNS zone file is located on the primary DNS server. This server is known as "authoritative" for the domain or domains contained in the zone file it hosts.
What role does the secondary DNS server play?	The secondary DNS server contains a copy of the zone database file that is stored on the primary. You should have a secondary DNS server for fault tolerance. It also provides load balancing functionality so the query load can be distributed among multiple DNS servers.
What is a caching-only server and why would I need one?	The caching-only DNS server doesn't contain any zone information; it only stores (caches) the results of previous queries it has issued. You might want to place a caching-only server on the other side of a slow WAN link, since they don't generate zone transfer traffic.
What are forwarder and slave servers for?	A DNS forwarder accepts requests to resolve host names from another DNS server. A forwarder can be used to protect your internal DNS server from access by Internet users.

Enhancements to WINS in Windows 2000 include:

- **Persistent connections**   Now you can configure each WINS server to maintain a persistent connection with one or more of its replication partners. This will increase the speed of replication and do away with the overhead involved in opening and terminating connections.

- **Manual tombstoning**   Windows 2000 allows you to manually mark a record to eventually be deleted (this is called *tombstoning*). The tombstone state of the record replicates to other WINS servers, and this prevents any replicated copies of the deleted records from re-appearing at the same server where they were originally deleted.

- **Better management utility**   WINS is now managed through the MMC. This provides you with a powerful and more user-friendly environment that can be customized for better efficiency. The new MMC-based utilities are easier to use and operate more predictably, as they follow a common design.

- **Easier configuration of features**   Several of the WINS features from earlier versions of Windows NT Server that required editing of the Registry to configure can now be configured more easily and directly. These include the ability to block records by a specific owner or WINS replication partner (formerly known as Persona Non Grata), or allow override of static mappings (formerly known as Migrate On/Off).

■ **Better filtering and search of records**   Improved filtering features and new search functions allow you to locate records more easily, by displaying only those that fit the criteria you specify.

■ **Dynamic record deletion and multi-select**   The WINS MMC snap-in allows you to point, click, and delete one or more WINS static or dynamic entries. (In NT, you had to use command-based utilities, such as Winscl.exe, to accomplish this). Windows 2000 also makes it possible to delete records that use names based on nonalphanumeric characters.

■ **Record verification and version number validation**   You can now check the consistency of names stored and replicated on your WINS servers quickly and easily. Record verification compares the IP addresses returned by a NetBIOS name query of different WINS servers. Version number validation examines the owner address-to-version number mapping tables.

■ **Export**   Using the Export feature, you can place WINS data in a comma-delimited text file and then export this file to Microsoft Excel or similar programs for analysis and reporting purposes.

■ **More and better fault tolerance for clients**   WINS clients running Windows 2000 or Windows 98 can now specify more than two WINS servers (up to a maximum of 12 addresses) per interface. This provides fault tolerance, as the extra WINS server addresses are used only if the primary and secondary WINS servers fail to respond.

■ **Dynamic re-insertion of client names**   WINS clients in Windows 2000 don't have to be restarted after they use WINS to force re-insertion and update of local NetBIOS names. There is a new option available in the Nbstat command, –RR, which provides the means of doing this. The –RR option can also be used with WINS clients that are running Windows NT 4.0, updated to Service Pack 4 or later.

■ **Read-only feature on the WINS console**   You can add members to a special group, the WINS Users group, which is automatically added when WINS is installed, and provide read-only access in the WINS console to WINS-related information on the server for members of the group. This way you can allow nonadministrators to view WINS related information, but they cannot make changes.

- **Command-line WINS administration tools**   Although Windows 2000 Server includes a full graphical user interface for managing WINS servers, there is also a fully equivalent WINS command-line based tool for those who prefer to work at the command line.

- **Better WINS database engine**   WINS in Windows 2000 uses the same performance-enhanced database engine technology that is used in Active Directory.

Connectivity Issues

Internet connectivity (and using the remote access service to accomplish it) is another very important component of Windows 2000 networking infrastructure design. Remote access is becoming a more and more common way of connecting to the enterprise network, as well as being used by home users and small businesses to connect to an Internet Service Provider (ISP) to gain access to Internet resources.

Remote Access Connections   A remote access connection most typically uses common telephone lines and modems to establish a temporary, dial-in connection to a server. Windows 2000 also supports a second type of RAS connection, via virtual private networking (VPN). A remote access *node* (a node is a computer or device on the network) is able to function in the same way as a computer that is physically cabled to the network onsite, except that the connection will generally be slower. Windows 2000's RRAS (Routing and Remote Access Services) provides for a robust and easy-to-use remote access server service, as well as the ability to function as a RAS client.

For the exam, you will need to understand the basic concepts of remote access and be familiar with the WAN protocols used to establish a remote link so that you can plan the best implementation for your network's unique needs. The same network/transport protocols used on your LAN (TCP/IP, IPX/SPX, NetBEUI) can be used with RAS, but another protocol, which operates at the Data Link layer, is required for the wide area part of the connection. Windows 2000 supports the same two WAN link protocols (also sometimes referred to as "line protocols") as Windows NT 4.0:

- **PPP**   The Point-to-Point Protocol (PPP) can be used by a Windows 2000 machine acting as a RAS client or by a Windows 2000 remote access server. PPP is the most popular of the wide area link protocols and supports encryption, compression, and dynamic IP address assignment.

■ **SLIP** The Serial Line Interface Protocol (SLIP) is an older WAN link protocol that does not support encryption or compression and requires a manually configured static IP address. It can be used only on the Windows 2000 RAS client and is used now primarily to connect to remote servers running the UNIX operating system.

exam
ⓦatch

Network Address Translation (NAT) and Internet Connection Sharing (ICS) are the subject of important objectives in Exam 70-221. ICS is available in both Windows 2000 Professional and Server, while the full-fledged NAT service is included only on the Server operating systems. ICS can be thought of as "NAT lite," providing the basic functionality of address translation but without the flexibility and configuration options available in the more full-featured version.

Virtual Private Networking

The exam also requires that you know how to design a virtual private networking (VPN) strategy for allowing clients to connect to a Windows 2000 VPN server. This would include planning for security, choosing the appropriate tunneling protocol, PPTP or L2TP, and developing VPN access policies.

The following Scenario & Solution reference will answer some of your questions about the differences between the two tunneling protocols included in Windows 2000.

SCENARIO & SOLUTION

What are some of the characteristics of PPTP?	The Point-to-Point Tunneling Protocol is used to establish VPN connections. It is an extension to the Point-to-Point Protocol (PPP) and supports the authentication, compression, and encryption mechanisms of PPP.
How does L2TP differ from PPTP?	The Layer Two Tunneling Protocol (L2TP) supports multi-protocol VPNs that allow remote users to access corporate networks securely across the Internet. It is similar to PPTP in that it can be used for tunneled end-to-end Internet connections through the Internet or other remote access media. However, unlike PPTP, L2TP doesn't depend on vendor-specific encryption technologies to establish a fully secured and successful implementation. L2TP utilizes the benefits of IPSec for better end-to-end security.

IP Routing

Exam 70-221 requires knowledge of IP routing and how to integrate software routing into existing network environments. Routing refers to the process of forwarding computer communications traffic along the pathways of an internetwork (a network of networks). A computer set up to support routing receives transmitted messages and forwards them to their correct destinations over the most efficient available route, even if many routes are possible. The distance traveled from one router to the next is called a hop, and at each router, the destination IP address on the packet is compared to the routing table, and the best route is used to decide the endpoint of the next hop.

Fast, efficient, reliable routing of data is at the heart of all large networks, up to and including the global Internet.

IP routing can be done by specialized dedicated devices called routers, or by a computer whose operating system supports IP forwarding. Windows 2000 is designed to function as an IP (or IPX) router.

exam
🐶atch

A router is also often referred to as a gateway. When an exam question mentions the "default gateway," it means the router (or computer functioning as a router) that serves as the "way out" of the network or subnet for sending of data to other networks. A network interface can have only one active default gateway at a time, although multiple gateways can be configured in Windows 2000 for fault tolerance purposes.

Be aware for exam purposes that there are two basic types of routing: static and dynamic.

Static Routing   *Static routing* requires that an administrator manually construct a routing table, which contains the pathways to outside networks.

Dynamic Routing   *Dynamic routing* uses routing protocols, such as the Routing Information Protocol (RIP) or Open Shortest Path First (OSPF), to allow routers to communicate with one another to automatically and dynamically update their routing tables without human intervention.

You should know that Windows 2000 supports the following routing protocols:

- RIPv1
- RIPv2
- OSPF

RIP is known as a *distance vector protocol.* This means that it has a maximum path length of 15 hops. If a packet must pass through more than 15 routers (gateways) to reach its destination, RIP considers the destination "unreachable." Another drawback of these protocols is that they are vulnerable to routing loops. RIP and the other distance vector protocols were designed for use in moderately sized networks, not for huge internetworks. However, RIP is a well-established standard and offers many advantages over static routing. Link state protocols are more efficient and scale better than distance vector protocols, but they are also more complex.

OSPF belongs to a different group, the *link state protocols.* This type of protocol maps the network and updates the mapping database (called the link state database) whenever any changes are made to the network. Link state protocols are more efficient but more complex than distance vector protocols.

The Microsoft exams will expect you to know the differences between these protocol types, and how to plan and implement an effective routing strategy for your network using dynamic routing protocols. You will need to know how to design demand-dial routing solutions, as well as how to plan connectivity of remote locations through IP routing.

CERTIFICATION OBJECTIVE 1.03

Overview of Exam 70-221

For a list of the learning objectives for Exam 70-221, see the Microsoft Web site at http://www.microsoft.com/mcp/exam/stat/SP70-221.htm. The objectives are somewhat broad, and you'll note that they are both conceptual in nature and performance-based. The objectives are divided into two broad areas, Analysis and Design, which can be further broken down into logical categories:

Analysis

■ **Analysis of business requirements** For this objective, you'll need to know how to analyze the existing and planned business models and how to analyze the company model and the geographical scope of the organization.

exam **Watch** *Models include regional, national, international, subsidiary, and branch offices.*

- **Analysis of company processes**   The processes in question include information flow, communication flow, service and product life cycles, and decision making. You will also need to understand how to analyze the existing and planned organizational structures. This includes such considerations as the management model; company organization; vendor, partner, and customer relationships; and acquisition plans.

- **Analysis of factors that influence company strategies**   Toward that end, you should be able to identify company priorities, plan for projected growth, and develop a growth strategy. You will need to be able to identify relevant laws and regulations, as well as recognize what the company's tolerance for risk entails. A new focus in the Windows 2000 exams is TCO—total cost of ownership or operations. Be sure you can analyze the structure of IT management in the company, taking into consideration the type of administration (centralized or decentralized), the funding model, the role of outsourcing, the decision-making process, and the change-management process within the company.

- **Analysis of the company's existing and planned technical environment and goals**   Mastering this objective will require that you be able to analyze company size and user and resource distribution, and assess the available connectivity between the geographic location of worksites and remote sites. You'll need to be capable of assessing net available bandwidth and latency issues within the network. You should also know how to analyze performance, availability, and scalability requirements of services that are running on the network, and analyze data and system access patterns in order to optimize performance. You should also be comfortable with analyzing network roles and responsibilities and be able to analyze security considerations, given the needs of the network.

- **Analyze the impact of infrastructure design on the existing and planned technical environment**   This means being able to assess current applications and determine how they fit into the organization's function and whether they need to be retained, upgraded, or replaced. You should also be able to analyze the network infrastructure, protocols, and host computers on the network. It is very important that you be able to analyze the TCP/IP infrastructure, including the subnetting scheme. You should be able to assess current hardware and make decisions regarding deployment, and be aware of any existing and planned upgrades and rollouts. You must analyze the technical support structure and assess its effectiveness, and then evaluate and analyze both extant and planned network/systems management policies and practice.

■ **End-user (client) analysis**   You will need to be able to analyze the needs of end-users, and monitor and assess their usage patterns so as to optimize the design of the network to better serve their purposes.

■ **Analysis of disaster recovery plan**   It is very important that you be able to analyze the existing strategy for disaster recovery, in regard to servers, clients, and the network infrastructure, and identify areas that require improvement.

Design

■ **Designing the network topology**   This objective requires knowledge of physical network layout (LAN topologies) and implementation of WAN links to connect distant geographic locations.

■ **Designing the TCP/IP strategy**   Expect TCP/IP to be an important part of this exam, now that there is no separate exam on the topic. You will need to know how to analyze IP subnet requirements and design a TCP/IP addressing and implementation plan. You'll also be expected to demonstrate your ability to measure and optimize a TCP/IP infrastructure design, and to be able to integrate software routing into an existing network. Finally, be familiar with strategies for integration of TCP/IP with existing WAN requirements.

■ **Designing a multi-protocol network**   Also in relation to networking protocols, familiarize yourself with NWLink (IPX/SPX) and Systems Network Architecture (SNA) and know how to design a network in which multiple protocols must coexist.

■ **Designing name resolution strategies**   For the DNS exam objective, you will need to be familiar with planning deployment of DNS servers in a large network, best practices for managing DNS/DDNS in a Windows 2000 network, how to monitor DNS performance, and basic troubleshooting of common DNS problems. Specifically, you'll need to know how to create a secure, yet highly available DNS design which is integrated fully with Windows 2000 Active Directory. Even though WINS may be "on the way out," it is still very much alive and well in the first release of Windows 2000 and likely to be the subject of at least a few exam questions. So be sure you pay particular attention to WINS replication, management, and monitoring.

- **Designing a Dfs strategy**   The exam will expect you to understand the components of the Distributed File System (Dfs) and be able to design a Dfs deployment strategy that includes proper placement of the Dfs root and development of a root replica strategy.

- **Designing a DHCP strategy**   In relation to DHCP, you must be familiar with how DHCP is integrated with DNS and Active Directory, and know how to integrate DHCP into a routed network environment. Monitoring, measuring, and optimizing the DHCP infrastructure design will also be necessary skills to pass the exam.

- **Designing an Internet Connectivity strategy**   To meet this objective, you will need to know how to design both Internet and extranet access solutions that include such enterprise-level components as proxy servers, firewalls, routing and remote access, NAT and ICS, Web hosting, and implementation of a mail server. You should also be able to design a load-balancing strategy to reduce the burden on specific servers.

- **Designing a WAN infrastructure**   You must be able to design a wide area networking infrastructure using remote access and implement a dial-in strategy. You also should be able to design RRAS-based remote access solutions and be able to integrate authentication with RADIUS. It is necessary that you understand the deployment of Remote Authentication Dial-in User Service (RADIUS) and demand-dial routing.

- **Designing ICS and NAT solutions**   Internet Connection Sharing and Network Address Translation are new features in Windows 2000 that are sure to come up in exam questions. You should know the difference between ICS (built into both Windows 2000 Professional and Server) and NAT (available only with the Server products), and how to develop strategies for deploying both.

- **Designing a management and implementation strategy**   The exam will expect that you are able to design strategic plans for monitoring and managing such Windows 2000 network services as global catalog servers, LDAP (the Lightweight Directory Access Protocol), certificate services, and proxy servers. You should be able to plan for the placement and management of network resources, understand the difference between centralized and decentralized administration and be able to design solutions for both situations, and ensure that your plans take future growth into account.

Although much of the knowledge and some of the network design concepts you may have gained from working with NT in the past are transferable to Windows 2000, it is imperative that you not make assumptions that the solutions which were applicable to NT-based networks will be the most effective—or even work at all—in a Windows 2000 network.

CERTIFICATION OBJECTIVE 1.04

What We'll Cover in this Book

Each of the topics covered in the Exam 70-221 list of objectives will be addressed in this book. However, we will go beyond the basic "how to" aspect even though the certification objectives are written almost exclusively as performance-based statements. We know that in order to really understand what you're doing, you need to know the theory behind it. If you have many long years of on-the-job experience working with NT *and* have been involved in the design and deployment strategies of networks in the past, you may already be familiar with the concepts behind these design-oriented objectives. Otherwise, it will benefit you to read the explanatory text carefully as well as performing the exercises in each chapter.

Knowledge

In the beginning of each chapter, we will try to provide you with a foundation of knowledge upon which conceptual comprehension and practical design skills can be built. This includes definitions of new terms, explanations of processes, and discussion of relationships between components.

Topic Tie-ins

We will cross-reference subjects that appear elsewhere in the book that tie in to the topic of the chapter and/or that will aid you in understanding the material to be presented in the chapter.

Concepts

In addition to basic knowledge-based information such as definitions and relationships, we will provide an overview of the concepts behind the skills-based exercises. For example, designing a WINS deployment strategy involves a skill set. An understanding of the *concept* of WINS—resolution of NetBIOS names to IP addresses and why this needs to be done—is necessary in order to perform the task correctly.

The authors will attempt to make all abstract concepts as easy to understand as possible, using analogies and graphical illustrations.

Practical Skills

The heart of Windows 2000 exam preparation is development of practical skills—the ability not just to know about the operating system, but also to use it to perform common network administration tasks. Although the Design exams cover topics that are more conceptual in nature than the core exams, they are still performance based, as is obvious from the wording of the exam objectives, almost all of which use action verbs such as "design, analyze, assess, evaluate, plan" and the like. These are action verbs, indicating that you should be able to *perform* the designated tasks.

The exercises in this and other Design exam preparation books will often involve problem-solving, determining which deployment solution is appropriate for a given situation, and defending your decision. This differs from the more task-oriented exercises for using the operating system interface that you will find in the books that address the mandatory core exams.

More so than with the NT exams, it is imperative that you do the practical exercises in each chapter, experiment with various settings and options, and get hands-on experience in performing the tasks you read about.

Many of the exam questions will be relatively simple for those who have worked with Windows 2000 and designed networks based on the operating system, and almost impossible to answer for someone who hasn't gone through the processes themselves. In this book, we attempt to simulate the Windows 2000 working environment as much as possible by liberal use of graphic illustrations and detailed descriptions of every aspect of the environment in which you are working; however, there is no substitute for *doing it yourself.*

CERTIFICATION OBJECTIVE 1.05

Networking Terminology

For those who are beginning their study of Windows 2000 with little exposure to real-life networking, one of the most important (and perhaps most tedious) tasks is to "learn the language" of computer networking. At times, as you read through the study material, you may feel as if you're floating in a sea of acronyms and unfamiliar words.

In this book, our policy is to spell out all acronyms in full the first time they appear and to define new terms within the text whenever possible. However, what's a well-known term to a networking professional may be "new" to you, and in a book this size, trying to flip back through the pages to find the first occurrence of a word could be a time-consuming process.

We suggest that you make liberal use of the glossary. If you run across a word or term whose meaning you're not sure of, and that's not obvious from the context, don't just skim over it and hope it will be clarified later. Taking the time to look it up may seem to slow down your study, but in actuality it's one of the best ways to ensure that you remember the meaning later.

"Double Meanings"

Don't despair if you find that definitions are not always absolutely consistent from one source to the next. Within the computer industry, and even within the more narrowly defined networking world, there are many subspecialty areas that have their own brand of jargon.

For example, you may hear the word "segment" used to describe a length of cable, or the computers that are connected to a length of backbone cable. You will hear the same word used in discussions of TCP/IP to describe the "chunks" into which data is broken down to be transmitted across the network. Likewise, "cell" means one thing in the context of wireless communications and something else when discussing ATM technology.

The following Scenario & Solution reference lists some of these more confusing "double meanings" that you are likely to encounter in your studies of networking infrastructure fundamentals.

SCENARIO & SOLUTION

What is a segment?	In discussions of the physical networking infrastructure, "segment" usually refers to a length of cable, or the portion of the network connected to a length of backbone between repeaters. In TCP/IP terminology, "segment" is the term used to describe the chunk of data sent by TCP over the network (roughly equivalent to the usage of "packet" or "frame").
I see the acronyms DN, DNM, DNS and DDNS. What does it all mean and what, if any, is the relationship between them?	DN, in Active Directory parlance, stands for Distinguished Name, an LDAP way of uniquely identifying an object. A DNM is a Domain Naming Master, one of the operations masters roles played by domain controllers in a Windows 2000 network. DNS is Domain Name System, used to map fully qualified domain names to IP addresses. Dynamic DNS is the enhanced version used in Windows 2000. In the Networking Infrastructure exam, Dynamic DNS is the one you are more likely to encounter. The only relationship is their common status as components of Windows 2000. DNS will be familiar to NT 4.0 administrators; the others may not be.
What does PVC mean?	In discussing the physical networking infrastructure, PVC refers to polyvinyl chloride, the material out of which standard Ethernet cable is made. In discussions of networking concepts, PVC is used to mean Permanent Virtual Circuit, referring to a network pathway in which all packets follow the same route (as opposed to a switched virtual circuit).
Why does the word "gateway" seem to have two different meanings?	"Gateway" is used in networking to refer to a router or a computer functioning as one, the "way out" of the network or subnet, to get to another network. The word "gateway" is also used in regard to software that connects a system using one protocol to a system using a different protocol, such as the Systems Network Architecture (SNA) software that allows a PC LAN to connect to an IBM mainframe, or the Gateway Services for NetWare used to provide a way for Microsoft clients to go through a Windows NT or Windows 2000 server to access files on a Novell file server.
What's the difference between OSI, ISO, and IOS?	OSI stands for Open Systems Interconnection and is used in all standard basic networking texts and classes in regard to the OSI layered networking model. The ISO is the organization that created this and other international standards; its name is the International Organization for Standardization and its short form, ISO, is not really an acronym but a derivative of a Greek word. IOS is the dedicated operating system used by Cisco routers.

CERTIFICATION OBJECTIVE 1.06

For "Newbies" and "Old Pros"

For those who are brand new to the world of networking, this chapter contains a section providing background information that, although not specifically covered by the Windows 2000 exam objectives, is essential to understanding the chapter topic(s). And for experienced administrators, there will be special tips for NT pros, pointing out the areas in which Windows 2000 differs (subtly or drastically) from its predecessor and warning you of common pitfalls that you may encounter in making the transition to Microsoft's new way of doing things.

For Networking Newbies

If you are new to computer networking, we recommend that you take a course or study a good book in basic networking concepts before you even sit for the mandatory core exams. Even if you are following the Windows 2000 MCSE certification track, it would benefit you to study one of the NT 4.0 Networking Essentials study guides and/or take the Windows 2000 Network and Operating Systems Essentials course. Then take—and pass—the core exams before you move on to the Design exams.

Even though it might *seem* as if design issues are simple and "less technical" than implementation and administration issues, you will find that it is difficult or impossible to plan strategies for deployment of services when you don't thoroughly understand how these services work or the basics of installing, configuring, and troubleshooting them.

You will find that familiarizing yourself with basic networking concepts—such as physical topologies, characteristics of different cable and other media types, the popular networking architectures such as Ethernet, AppleTalk, and Token Ring, and often referenced networking standards and models such as the OSI, DoD, and Windows models and the IEEE 802 specifications—will benefit you in many ways. Not only will the knowledge provide a solid foundation for the material you will be studying in the process of obtaining Microsoft certification, but most employers will expect you, as an MCP or MCSE, to recognize these fundamental concepts.

The very best investment a networking neophyte can make, though, is that of building your own network from the ground up. Even a simple two-computer thinnet network will give you a taste of the challenges faced by Enterprise pros in the field, and many of the setup, maintenance, and troubleshooting scenarios associated with large production networks can be simulated on a smaller scale with a small home network.

This will give you a golden opportunity, and one that is invaluable to the aspiring network architect: the chance to design and deploy a Windows 2000 network from scratch. Even on such a small scale, the experience will teach you many valuable lessons about the difference between a plan that "looks good on paper" and one that really works in the field.

There are a number of excellent books, as well as numerous Web resources, available to guide you through the challenging experience of getting those first two computers to "talk" to one another. Once you've accomplished that, there is no limit to your experimentation. In some ways, you have an advantage over the working IT professional who is unable to make significant changes to the production network environment.

For NT Pros

If you are already certified and/or experienced in NT 4.0, you may be able to skip the parts of this book that provide basic information about protocols and services with which you are already familiar. But don't skip too much! Windows 2000 is built on the NT kernel and you will find much in the new operating system that feels like "home"—but you will also discover, as you delve deeper, that there are many fundamental changes, even to "old friends" like DNS and WINS. And remember that there is nothing in the NT certification process that prepares you for the Design exams. Analysis of business and technical requirements and development of strategic deployment plans simply were not covered, at least not in any depth or detail, in the NT exams.

NT professionals will need to guard against the possibility that your experience and mastery of the earlier operating system will be your biggest enemy on the Windows 2000 certification exams. Expect questions that try to "trick" you by providing solutions that *would* have been correct if you were using NT; questions which measure whether you're aware of the differences between the two operating systems (just as there were traditionally questions on the NT certification exams that used a test-taker's experience with Windows 9x against him in the same way).

We cannot emphasize enough that you *must* master the basics of Windows 2000 before you can intelligently analyze and solve design issues. Learn to use and administer the operating system first—then tackle the more subjective areas of strategy and design.

We certainly don't advise NT pros to "forget everything you ever knew" about network operating systems, but we do encourage you not only to study Windows 2000, but to actually use it on a day-to-day basis. If possible, upgrade your primary workstation to Windows 2000 Professional so that the slightly different ways of performing routine tasks, the subtle differences in the interface, become second nature to you. And work with Windows 2000 Server or Advanced Server—on the job if you can, at home, or in the classroom. It's in the server products that the real differences between NT and Windows 2000 show themselves. As you work with the Windows 2000 network, consider how design decisions that were made during the pre-implementation stage affect the ease of administration (or lack thereof) on a day-to-day basis.

Your NT experience can put you a step ahead of the networking newcomers—*if* you remember not to make too many assumptions (generally a good policy to follow in all areas of life).

CERTIFICATION SUMMARY

This chapter has provided a brief introduction to the Windows 2000 certification exam process, in general, and an overview of the objectives of Exam 70-221, Designing a Microsoft Windows 2000 Networking Infrastructure, in particular.

We have discussed some very fundamental concepts of Microsoft networking, such as IP addressing, name resolution, remote access, and security. We have also discussed those specific topics which are the focus of the Design exam, such as DNS/DDNS, WINS, IP routing, TCP/IP, DHCP, NAT/ICS, VPNs, Dfs, and Internet connectivity.

We examined the two-part breakdown of the exam objectives, which represents the two steps involved in preparing a strategy for deployment of a Windows 2000 network infrastructure: analysis and design. We looked at specific areas that must be analyzed and evaluated prior to beginning the actual design stage, including business requirements and technical requirements of the organization.

We briefly touched on the importance of mastering common networking terminology, and provided examples of a few common cases of acronyms or terms that may have unclear or dual meanings.

We also discussed the differences in focus between the mandatory core exams and the design exams on the corresponding topics. We looked at some of the issues involved in assuming the role of network architect, and why it is essential that you first have a thorough understanding of administration practices and Windows 2000 networking services before attempting to design strategies for deploying them.

In closing, we addressed the special needs of the two very different audiences who are likely to use this book: the networking novice who is beginning his or her career with the study of Windows 2000, and the networking professional who has experience working in the field with, and may already be certified in, other network operating systems.

TWO-MINUTE DRILL

❑ The Windows 2000 "Design" exams are more conceptual in nature than the corresponding "Administration and Implementation" mandatory core exams, and exam objectives are divided into two broad parts: analysis and design.

❑ Microsoft's "target audience" for the Windows 2000 exams consists of networking professionals with at least one year's experience; this does not mean that you can't pass the exams without that experience, but it does mean that you will need to do more hands-on practice with the operating system.

❑ Unless you have a great deal of experience in designing networks, you should first study and pass the mandatory core exams before you attempt the Design exams.

❑ A computer network has both a physical and a logical infrastructure. The former consists of hardware components; the latter is software-based and includes protocols and services upon which network communications depend. Exam 70-221 requires knowledge and understanding of the components of both.

❑ The TCP/IP protocol suite, on which most of today's medium-to-large networks (including the Internet) run, is an important component of the logical networking infrastructure, and a good understanding of how it works will be essential to mastering the exam objective of designing a TCP/IP infrastructure.

❑ Name resolution is an important component of the infrastructure because it allows "friendly" host names or NetBIOS names to be mapped to IP addresses (and the latter is used by the networking protocol for one computer to communicate with another). You will need to understand how to design a name resolution strategy in a large network in order to pass Exam 70-221.

❑ The Domain Name Service, DNS, maps fully qualified domain names to IP addresses. The Windows 2000 implementation, Dynamic DNS (DDNS), is an essential component of Windows 2000 networks. How to deploy DNS servers and configure replication between them are likely to be the subjects of one or more questions on Exam 70-221.

❑ The Windows Internet Naming Service (WINS) resolves NetBIOS names to IP addresses. Although WINS plays a lesser role in Windows 2000 networks, Microsoft has made several significant improvements to the service and the exam will require that you know how to design a secure, optimized WINS infrastructure.

❑ The Dynamic Host Configuration Protocol (DHCP) is used for automatic assignment of IP addresses. Windows 2000's implementation of DHCP is integrated with DNS, and Exam 70-221 will require that you understand how to integrate DHCP with Windows 2000 in a routed environment and be able to design a DHCP service for remote locations.

❑ Internet connectivity solutions will be important on the Network Infrastructure Design exam, and you will need to know how to design remote access solutions including both dialup and Virtual Private Networking (VPN).

❑ Network Address Translation (NAT) and Internet Connection Sharing (ICS) are important new features in Windows 2000 that allow you to connect an entire LAN to the Internet via one modem or ISDN/DSL/cable interface and one ISP account. For exam purposes, you will need to understand the differences between the two and how to best design a strategy for deploying one or both in a Windows 2000 network.

❑ IP routing is fundamental to any medium-to-large networking environment, and for Exam 70-221, you will need to know how to design a Routing and Remote Access Services solution to connect locations, as well as how to implement demand-dial routing.

❑ The Distributed File System (Dfs) is another important feature that makes it easier for users to access files in Windows 2000. You will need to know how to design a Dfs strategy, including planning for the best placement of the Dfs root.

❑ It is important that the network design process take into consideration such factors as the administrative model (centralized or decentralized) and future growth of the network. You will need to develop a monitoring and management strategy that addresses these issues.

SELF TEST

The following questions will help measure your understanding of the material presented in this chapter. Read all of the choices carefully, as there may be more than one correct answer. Choose all correct answers for each question.

1. Which of the following describes Microsoft's target audience for Exam 70-221?

    A. Administrators with five years of experience supporting networks of 50 or more users at two or more locations

    B. Administrators with two years of experience supporting networks of 100 or more users at one location

    C. Administrators with one year of experience supporting networks of 200 or more users at five or more locations

    D. None of the above

2. Which of the following is a difference between Exam 70-216, Implementing and Administering a Windows 2000 Network Infrastructure, and Exam 70-221, Designing a Windows 2000 Network Infrastructure (select all that apply)?

    A. Exam 70-216 should generally be taken after Exam 70-221.

    B. Exam 70-221 should generally be taken after Exam 70-216.

    C. They cover the same material and you only need to pass one of the two.

    D. The "Design" exam covers more conceptual material, while the "Implementing and Administering" exam covers more task-oriented material.

3. Which of the following is based on the shape or layout of a local area network?

    A. The logical topology

    B. The physical topology

    C. Both of the above

    D. None of the above

4. Which of the following LAN topologies is one in which computers have redundant connections so that each computer has multiple connections to some or all other computers?

    A. Star

    B. Ring

C. Linear bus

D. Mesh

E. None of the above

5. Which of the following are components of the logical networking infrastructure (select all that apply)?

A. The networking protocols

B. The networking cable or other media

C. The network topology

D. The name resolution services

6. Which of the following describes the actual path of data transmission, which may or may not be the same as the outer shape or appearance of the network cabling?

A. Logical topology

B. Physical topology

C. Media access method

D. Network architecture

7. In Windows 2000 Active Directory, you can configure one or more well connected IP subnets in order to reduce replication traffic across slow WAN links. Which of the following terms is used to describe this concept?

A. Supernets

B. Sites

C. Domains

D. Organizational units

8. Which of the following is also known as the TCP/IP networking model because it was developed in conjunction with the development of the TCP/IP protocols?

A. The OSI networking model

B. The Windows networking model

C. The Transmission Protocol networking model

D. The Department of Defense networking model

9. What version of the Internet Protocol (IP) is the current standard on the Internet?

    A. IP version 3

    B. IP version 4

    C. IP version 5

    D. IP version 6

10. Which of the following is the term used to describe an eight-bit portion of an IP address?

    A. Subnet

    B. Segment

    C. Octet

    D. Field

11. Which of the following is a DNS server that accepts requests to resolve host names from another DNS server and can be used to protect your internal DNS server from access by Internet users?

    A. Zone server

    B. Secondary DNS server

    C. Primary DNS server

    D. Forwarder

12. Which of the following is a new WINS feature in Windows 2000 (select all that apply)?

    A. Manual tombstoning

    B. Dynamic updates

    C. Persistent connections

    D. Replication partners

13. Which of the following is a difference between PPTP and L2TP (select all that apply)?

    A. It can be used for end-to-end tunneled connections through the Internet.

    B. It doesn't depend on vendor-specific encryption technologies.

    C. It can use IPSec to establish secure connections.

    D. It is included in Windows 2000.

14. Which of the following is a distance vector dynamic routing protocol?

   A. OSPF

   B. RIP

   C. Static Routing Protocol

   D. IPSec

15. Which of the following allows you to connect a local area network to the Internet and give all computers on the LAN access using only one public IP address (select all that apply)?

   A. Routed connection

   B. Internet Connection Sharing

   C. Multihoming

   D. NAT

SELF TEST ANSWERS

1. ☑ **C.** Microsoft's stated target audience for this exam is network administrators with one or more years of experience supporting networks of 200-26,000+ users at 5-150+ locations.
   ☒ **A** and **B** are incorrect because they specify more years of experience and fewer users and locations than Microsoft's specifications.

2. ☑ **B, D.** Exam 70-221 should generally be taken after Exam 70-216, and the Design exam covers more conceptual material than the Implementing exam.
   ☒ **A** is incorrect because it is important to understand the basics of how Windows 2000 network services work, covered in Exam 70-216, before you can properly design strategies for deploying the services, as covered in Exam 70-221. **C** is incorrect because the exams cover different aspects of the topics and one cannot be substituted for the other.

3. ☑ **B.** The physical topology refers to the layout or shape of the network.
   ☒ **A** is incorrect because the logical topology refers to the actual path taken by the data signals, which can be the same or different from the physical topology.

4. ☑ **D.** The mesh topology is most reliable (but also most expensive and most complex) because it involves multiple connections between computers.
   ☒ **B** is incorrect because the ring topology has each computer joined one to the other in line, with the last connected back to the first to form a circle. **C** is incorrect because the linear bus has each computer connected to the next in a line, with a beginning and an end. **E** is incorrect because **D** is correct.

5. ☑ **A, D.** Protocols and name resolution services are components of the logical, or software-based, infrastructure.
   ☒ **B** and **C** are incorrect because both the cabling/media and the network topology are elements of the physical infrastructure.

6. ☑ **A.** The physical topology is the outer shape or layout of the cable, and the logical topology may or may not be the same. For example, a physical star can be a logical ring because inside the hub, the wiring connects the computers in a circle.
   ☒ **C** is incorrect because the media access method refers to the way in which network traffic is controlled, and **D** is incorrect because the network architecture is a combination of the cable type, topology, and access method.

7. ☑ **B.** One or more well connected IP subnets, configured to reduce replication traffic across a slow WAN link, is called a site.

   ☒ **A** is incorrect because supernet is a combination of two or more network IDs to create a large network. **C** is incorrect because domains are the basic administrative boundaries in a Windows network. **D** is incorrect because organizational units are container objects in Active Directory, into which other objects may be placed and to which administrative and access privileges may be assigned.

8. ☑ **D.** The DoD networking model is sometimes called the TCP/IP networking model because the two were developed in conjunction with one another and with the implementation of the ARPAnet, the predecessor to the global Internet.

   ☒ **A** is incorrect because the OSI model is a standard used in most networking courses, but is a seven-layer model as opposed to the DoD TCP/IP four-layer model. **B** is incorrect because the Windows networking model is used by Microsoft to describe the network communications process in Windows operating systems. **C** is incorrect because there is no such thing as the Transmission Protocol networking model.

9. ☑ **B.** IPv4 is the current standard. It is expected that within the next several years, networks will transition to IPv6, also known as IPng (for Next Generation).

   ☒ **A, C,** and **D** are incorrect because none of these is the correct version number of the current standard.

10. ☑ **C.** An IP address consists of four octets of eight bits each, with the octets separated by dots.

    ☒ **A** is incorrect because a subnet is a group of computers on a network with the same network ID and subnet mask. **B** is incorrect because a segment is a length of cable, or a "chunk" of data transmitted by TCP. **C** is incorrect because a field is an area of a packet header that contains information. Each field consists of a specified number of bits.

11. ☑ **D.** A DNS Forwarder accepts requests to resolve host names from another DNS server.

    ☒ **A** is incorrect because there is no such designation as "zone server." **B** is incorrect because the secondary DNS server contains a copy of the zone database file that is stored on the primary DNS server, and is used for fault tolerance and load balancing functionality. **C** is incorrect because the primary DNS server contains the primary read/write copy of the DNS zone file.

12. ☑ **A, C.** Windows 2000 allows you to manually mark a record to eventually be deleted (this is called *tombstoning*). Also new to Windows 2000 is the ability to configure each WINS server to maintain a persistent connection with one or more of its replication partners and thus increase the speed of replication and do away with the overhead involved in opening and terminating connections.

    ☒ **B and D** are incorrect because both dynamic updates of the WINS database and configuration of replication partners were also supported in NT 4.0.

13. ☑ **B, C.** The Layer 2 Tunneling Protocol (L2TP), unlike PPTP, is not dependent on vendor-specific encryption technologies. It can use IPSecurity (IPSec), included in Windows 2000, to establish secure connections across the Internet.

    ☒ **A** is incorrect because PPTP can also be used for end-to-end tunneled connections through the Internet. **D** is incorrect because both PPTP and L2TP are included in Windows 2000 (only PPTP is included in NT 4.0).

14. ☑ **B.** The Routing Information Protocol (RIP) is a dynamic routing protocol known as a distance vector protocol.

    ☒ **A** is incorrect because Open Shortest Path First (OSPF) is also a dynamic routing protocol but it is of the link state type. **C** is incorrect because Static Routing does not require an additional protocol; it requires that the administrator manually configure the routing table. **D** is incorrect because IPSec is a security feature in Windows 2000, not a routing protocol.

15. ☑ **B, D.** Both ICS, included in Windows 2000 Professional and Server, and the Network Address Translation protocol (NAT), included only in Windows 2000, allow you to connect a small LAN to the Internet and give all computers Internet access using only one public IP address. ICS is a "light" version of NAT.

    ☒ **A** is incorrect because although the computers on a LAN can be given Internet access through a routed connection, each computer must have its own public IP address. **C** is incorrect because multihoming refers to putting two network interfaces in one computer, or assigning two IP addresses to one network interface. This does not, in itself, allow you to give the computers on a LAN access to the Internet with one IP address.

2

Analyzing Business Requirements

B usiness requirements are where you begin designing a network infrastructure. The needs of the business are what drive the design of the network, and affect later stages of the project. In this chapter, we'll look at factors involved in analyzing a company's needs, and see how they will as a whole affect the project of designing a network infrastructure.

Overview of Business Requirements Analysis

Business requirements are the foundation on which you build a network infrastructure. Put simply, business requirements are the needs and issues that must be analyzed and addressed when planning a network. Before you plan what operating systems, hardware, applications, data-transmitting media, or other technologies to use, you must first determine what the company is and how it conducts business.

To illustrate the importance of business analysis, let's say you were designing a network for a group of 10 users. These users have been with the company for the last five years, with no one else being hired. Because of this, you decide to install Windows 2000 Professional on all the machines, add a network hub, and create a peer network. A peer network is two-to-ten computers connected together, but doesn't use a central computer as a server. Because of this, there is no centralized administration. The network lacks many of the security features of a network that uses a server, although it is useful for small groups of users who wish to share files and printers, who have a small budget to work with, and who have little to no concern about security. Now that you've created this network, let's say the company goes through a growth period due to a new product they have been working on. Because you didn't investigate the needs and future plans of the company, you had no idea this would occur. Unfortunately, your network is now useless because it failed to meet the business requirements of the company.

While this tiny network could be upgraded, and this is an exercise in make believe, it shows several important points. First, it showed the need to determine what a company does. If you had known a new product was expected to cause growth, you could have taken it into account when planning what kind of network would be used. To meet the requirements of a business, you have to understand the business itself.

Second, it showed the need to account for future growth and changes in the company. As the number of users increase, the network infrastructure should be scalable to those needs. It should also be able to handle increases in users and data transfer as these changes occur.

Finally, it showed that business requirements are transformed into a set of technical specifications. These specifications are influenced by the technical architecture, but they must preserve the intent of the business requirements. In other words, while technology will impact on specifications, the needs of the business must always be first and foremost in the mind of the network's architect.

Business requirements analysis isn't an exact science, but rather a calculation of trade offs. For example, although certain technologies may be available, the business may be unable or unwilling to pay for them. A network medium with lower bandwidth may need to be used, such as coaxial cabling or ISDN, because the company cannot afford one that provides higher speeds, such as fiber optics. As we'll see throughout this chapter, different factors will affect the network infrastructure you create. The way a business is laid out, its ability to change and accept risks, and other variables will each play a part in how a network is planned and implemented.

Business needs change, and the requirements of a business will evolve with those changes. As the number of employees increases or decreases, the number of users on a network will often be affected. As new applications are implemented to serve these users, the speed of your network may be affected. This is often the case when rich media, such as streaming video or video files are used more regularly. Graphic files are larger and consume more bandwidth, causing some networks to slow dramatically. As the business requirements change, these needs will be added to your network's future technical specifications.

Gathering Information and Creating Project Planning Documents

There are a number of techniques that can be used to gather information for business requirements analysis. One of these is using surveys to gather information about a company. Surveys contain a listing of questions that provide information on what people do in the company, what their duties and subsequent needs are, and what they envision the network should be. It allows you to see what their view of the company is, its organizational structure, and how they feel a network will enhance their work. Data collected from such surveys can then be used in interviews with people within the organization.

on the **!** **j** o b   *Documentation is vital to designing a network infrastructure. Previous documentation will show you how the business and its network have changed and current documentation will keep you on schedule and provide information used in future changes.*

Talking with people allows you to get a larger understanding of how different stakeholders envision the network, and how they feel the network will be used. Who should be interviewed can be determined from surveys previously taken. By talking one-on-one or with small groups, you'll be able to fully understand the business's needs. One group may need to use the network for sharing large files, showing a requirement for higher speed transmission. Other users may show a need for downloading information from the Internet, showing a need for firewalls to be implemented in the network's design. By talking to different types of users, you will be able define objectives and business goals, and take the first steps toward planning how the network needs to be deployed.

The information acquired from the people interviewed should be documented in a way that can be understood by everyone involved with the project. In other words, don't convolute your documentation with technical jargon that only you and others in information technology will understand. For example, state that the network needs to support x number of users by a specific time, what concerns (cost, training) are to be addressed, and technical stipulations (such as using existing, older servers as part of the network). This documentation will outline objectives for your project, and detail the business needs that must be addressed. It will also act as a source of reference for what was agreed on by all parties.

There are several types of documentation that will be created during the course of designing your network infrastructure. These include:

- Administrative documents, which identify the scope, goals and objectives of the project.

- Deployment documents, which describe the current network environment (if any), how Windows 2000 will be integrated into this environment, changes that will occur, gaps between the current environment and the one envisioned, issues pertaining to capacity, and an assessment of risks.

- Functional specification, which outlines features to be deployed, and the details of what the network infrastructure will be.

- Communication strategy, which outlines how information about the project will be conveyed and how often.

- Training plan, which outlines issues dealing with how users and support staff will be educated on the new system.

- Capacity plan, which estimates minimum, maximum, and average figures on network usage. This includes such factors as how often users log on to the network, the number of DNS queries, for example.

- Risk assessment, which assesses possible risks that the project may face, and how these risks may affect the project.

While some of these documents may not play a vital role until after business requirements have been established, you should start creating them as early as possible. This will allow you to modify them as needed in the project. Each of these documents, and the topics contained in them, are discussed further in the sections that follow.

FROM THE CLASSROOM

Documenting Business Requirements

In analyzing business requirements, it is important to create documentation. This is used to provide a source of information and reference, and should be written in a way that both laymen and Information Technology (IT) staff can understand.

Documentation acts as a roadmap that outlines the initial needs of a company to how the network infrastructure will be implemented. Issues discussed in this chapter are included in the document, showing how the IT team understands the business and its needs. It allows everyone involved to know what needs are being addressed, and makes owners, stakeholders, and end users part of the process.

Documentation also serves as a contract between owners, stakeholders, end users,

and the Information Technology team on what was agreed on. Requirements are identified in a document so that they can be referred to at a later date. This will avoid possible future conflicts resulting from misunderstanding or miscommunication. All interested parties have the documentation available to them so confusion on what's to be addressed and implemented can't be misconstrued.

Documentation also provides a reference for future changes to the network. As the business changes, so too will its requirements. Existing documentation can be used in determining how the business and its needs have truly changed since previous implementation of the network, its technologies, and resources.

—*Michael Cross, MCSE, MCPS, MCP+I, CNA*

Administrative Documents

Administrative documents are used to identify the scope, goals, and objectives of the project. They provide a clearer vision of what the project hopes to achieve, what business needs must be addressed, and what future phases your project will go through.

In creating administrative documents, you should establish clear phases and milestones. These are points in designing your network infrastructure, which establish where your project team currently is, and where it is going. Each phase of your project culminates in a milestone, showing that a particular phase of the project is complete, and the team is now ready to move on. These phases and milestones keep you from getting away from your project, and keep you on schedule.

A communications strategy should be implemented so that your team and users know the status of the project. A fine example of the need for this was during Y2K upgrades. People were worried that their computers wouldn't be usable after the turn of the century, so it was important that users were updated on how an information technology staff was proceeding. It was also important that the IT staff knew how one another were proceeding with their individual tasks. Scheduling regular meetings, providing progress reports, e-mailing updates to people, and publishing the progress in company newsletters were methods that could be used. Because people were updated and became knowledgeable, this also inspired support and excitement over changes in the current system.

Because knowledge is power, and someone who knows what could happen is better able to deal with it, an assessment of risk should also be performed. Risk assessment looks at possible problems that could affect the project. This may include employees striking, weather conditions (such as winter snow slowing travel with equipment to outlying areas), impending mergers, or the loss of a key personnel or project members of a business.

Administrative documents should also provide basic information that may seem obvious but is vital to the project. One of these basic elements deals with what facilities are available to do the work. Does the business have space to store servers, cabling, and other components used in deploying the network, or will you need to work offsite and deliver computers and cabling to the site as they are installed? Is there sufficient space for your team to work, or will it need additional office space and storage ? Such factors need to be addressed early in the project.

Budgets are another important part of administrative documents. They provide information on how much your network is expected to cost, and how much money has been provided to the project. This is a constraint of the project, keeping you from spending more money than the business has to offer or wants to spend. The budget should also provide some leeway in covering unexpected expenses that may creep into the project.

Finally, you should determine how the project team will be staffed, and what roles each person will play in the team. In assigning roles to members of your team, you should determine who has what skills, and assign a role to each person that matches their individual skills and abilities. These roles include:

- IT management or executive sponsor
- Project management
- Development and design
- Technical and subject matter experts
- Testing
- Documentation
- Training
- Logistics

In the paragraphs that follow, we will look at each of the various roles that make up a project team, the skills required, and what those roles involve.

exam
Watch

While you may not get questions directly involving the team roles, it is important you understand them. This not only helps to understand Microsoft's view of how a network infrastructure is designed and deployed, but will help you understand elements working together in the design of the network infrastructure.

The person acting as IT management or executive sponsor works as an intermediary between the team and the business. As such, this person creates the communication plan. He or she sets priorities for the network infrastructure. They are responsible for setting the vision of what the project entails, establishing a business case, and securing funding for the project. The IT manager or executive sponsor not only needs a knowledge of Windows 2000 features and capabilities, but also needs to know the needs of the business, and how the network will meet those needs.

Project management is responsible for driving critical decisions necessary to deploy the network infrastructure. He or she will look at the business needs and come up with solutions to problems faced by the company. From this, the project manager works with other members of the team to create a functional specification. The person in this role needs a detailed knowledge of Windows 2000 Server and Windows 2000 Professional functionality, and must have the ability to coordinate executive management goals with project team goals.

The person in the development and design role is important in determining what features will actually be used in the infrastructure, and how the network infrastructure will be designed and developed. This person has the responsibility of evaluating solutions, and designing and developing the infrastructure. He or she must have knowledge of Windows 2000 Server and Windows 2000 Professional functionality, experience in developing services, and a firm understanding of technical requirements for the existing and new network infrastructure.

The expert on technical and subject matter is the leader of any subteam created for the project. Subteams are composed of people who are working toward success in one area of the project. Each technical/subject matter expert will be responsible for designing and developing strategies for their particular areas. They need to be experts in the area they supervise, and have management skills to oversee the their subteams.

Testing is, as you might assume, responsible for testing the new system, and determining any issues that other members of the team need to be aware of. The person in this role provides assistance in the initial design, designs and builds test labs to do performance testing and test applications, and determines problems that users may experience. This role requires knowledge of not only Windows 2000, but also of related hardware.

The documentation role has the responsibility of creating planning documents, reports, and white papers. This person creates the documents used by the team throughout the project, and creates the resource material that will be used later when the network is modified or when user documentation is created. While this person needs to know the technologies used in the network infrastructure, and the concepts involved, they do not need technological skills at the level described in previous roles.

Training and user education helps end users attain the skills necessary to use the system. The person in this role works with the user and is responsible for determining the level of training required and the additional skills the user will require, and for developing material and classes necessary for training users. As with the role of documentation, communication skills are a must for this role. The person must have an understanding of the Windows 2000 network infrastructure, and be able to relay that knowledge to users.

Finally, logistics management is responsible for a smooth rollout of the new system, and for ensuring that support groups like training and help desk are in place to assist users. Logistics managers require familiarity with Windows 2000 features.

Deployment Documents

Deployment documents are used to provide insight into where your network is, and what it will develop into. In creating deployment documents, you should start with an overview of your current network. An overview shows you what you're currently dealing with, and answers questions directly related to the design of the network infrastructure. How many users are on the network? What hardware, software, and policies are currently in use? What technologies are currently used? How many servers and computers are on the network, and do they meet the minimum requirements for Windows 2000 or do they need to be upgraded? What is the topology of the network, and how is it geographically spread out? In answering these questions, you'll have a firmer understanding of what work you'll be performing.

Another piece of deployment documentation is the deployment design, which outlines changes in the current system. It details how existing applications and systems will be affected, including how server and client computers will be upgraded and migrated into the new system. It details when, how, and where these upgrades will occur.

A pilot plan is used to detail what goals you want to achieve during the first rollout of the network. The pilot plan includes methods of gathering feedback (such as a feedback page on a local intranet) so that you can determine how users are reacting to the initial rollout, and what problems they're experiencing. You should also include testing and deployment strategies in your documentation. This outlines a plan on how the proposed network infrastructure will be tested, and how it will be deployed.

Other parts of deployment documents are gap analysis, capacity planning, and risk assessment. Gap analysis explains gaps between how your system currently is, and how it will be when the project is completed. A capacity plan is a plan that determines what resources are needed to keep the network from degrading. Risk assessment looks at potential problems that may be associated with the project. We'll discuss each of these in greater detail later in this chapter.

Functional Specification

A functional specification outlines features to be deployed, how they will be configured, and details what the network infrastructure will be. It states each of the features used in your Windows 2000 network, when they will be implemented, and how. For example, if the domain name system (DNS) will be used, you will need to specify which Windows 2000 Server will run DNS, whether other DNS systems (such as BIND) will be used on other servers, and document how the DNS namespace will be set up.

A functional specification is derived from the identification of business requirements. Without knowledge of these requirements, it would be impossible to create a functional specification.

Communication Strategy

A communication strategy is a plan that addresses how a business' management, your project team, and end users will stay connected through the project. It keeps everyone involved in the success of your network in touch with one another. This improves support for your project in several ways.

Communication allows those managing the business to stay aware of problems and successes your team is experiencing. If there is a budget problem, difficulties with certain employees, or other issues, management will be better able to assist you. By staying connected to end users, they will be more willing to accept changes to the current system, and be more excited about changes to come. As you deploy the system, they will have more faith in your abilities because they've seen how far you've already come in the project.

Since communication is such an important factor in meeting business needs, we'll discuss this in greater detail later in the chapter.

Training Plan

It is important to establish a training plan before your network is deployed. By doing this, you can begin creating training material on what users and support staff will need to know before the network is put into place. You can send information technology staff to seminars to provide help desk support on Windows 2000, set training days for users, or establish who will provide training and when. You can decide whether or not key personnel in the business should be trained so that they can provide assistance to their peers. This puts a "resident expert" in offices, providing much of the onsite assistance. You can also determine what level of knowledge users will need, and set out methods (such as scripts, roaming profiles, or folder redirection) to perform tasks or free users from needing to configure their workstations.

When implementing a training plan, it is important to analyze the skills of members of your team. Some may have expertise in training users, while others may have little knowledge of networks. For example, one member of your information technology staff may have knowledge in programming applications or fixing hardware, but no idea what a Windows 2000 Server really does or how network cabling is installed. By looking at the skills of your team, you can determine who should be in charge of particular areas of the project, and what members should be paired up and assist those with greater knowledge.

Capacity Plan

A capacity plan is used to identify what resources are needed to keep the network from degrading. In changing an existing network, you want to ensure that users don't experience sluggishness in using network applications or resources. A capacity plan looks at elements like the type of cabling used in the network, network interface cards, server speed and power, and so on. It ensures that the network design takes into account network and hardware resources needed to support Windows 2000 services and features.

An important part of a capacity plan is creating a baseline that looks at the current available resources and the current workload. This is used to analyze how workload may change, and whether the resources will be able to support these changes. For example, creating a baseline would involve looking at the number of logins on your network, or a particular subnet of that network. You could also look at the number of times users change their passwords, machine account password changes, DNS queries, data transferred over a given time period, and so forth. Once you've gathered such information about your network, you would then calculate the minimum, maximum, and average for each of these elements. This will provide you with information on how many of these events occur, use of processing power, disk space, and bandwidth.

Risk Assessment

Risk assessment isn't a negative thing. By knowing what risks may crop up in a project, you are better able to deal with them. A risk assessment document looks at possible problems that could affect a project, and then offers contingency plans. Risk assessment is an important factor in analyzing business requirements, and a topic to be discussed in greater detail later in this chapter.

Now that we've provided you with an overview of the topics involved in analyzing business requirements and designing a network infrastructure, look at the following Scenario & Solution box for some common questions that students ask.

SCENARIO & SOLUTION

Why should I bother analyzing the requirements of a business? They need a network, so why shouldn't I simply install cabling, servers, and computers to make one?	If you don't understand the requirements of a business, then it's impossible to create an effective network infrastructure. Different businesses have different needs. How the business is organized will affect security issues, topology, and other aspects of a planned network.
I don't have enough people to fill every team role that Microsoft suggests. What should I do?	Multiple team roles can be assigned to each person. For example, a person responsible for creating documentation could also provide user education.

CertCam 2-1

EXERCISE 2-1

Understanding Business Requirements

The president of Positronic Robotics and Housewares contracts to design a network for her company and gives the following information. The company employs 250 people, and has projects that will require hiring another 200 over the next three years. The company uses managers to oversee the work of about 50 employees. Above the managers are a president and vice president. It is important that those in lower positions shouldn't be able to see files of those in higher positions. There is an existing network using older servers that can't support Windows 2000. These servers are experiencing failures more regularly, and users are saying that transferring files is taking an extremely long time. Users are currently working on machines running Windows for Workgroups, and should be able to continue working even if the network is down. As a consultant, you will work with the existing IT Staff, which consists of eight professionals.

1. What business requirements must be met by the network you design?

2. After acquiring this information, who else can provide you with business requirements?

3. Based on the number of IT staff, which team roles can be assigned?

Answers:

1. Three years from now the network must support 450 users. Security will need to be set up in the network so that those in higher levels of the company can see the files of employees below them. This network security should also keep subordinates from viewing the files of their superiors. Current servers will need to be replaced or upgraded to support Windows 2000 Server. The network media, NICs, and other hardware will need to be upgraded to support higher speeds. Client workstations will need to be upgraded or replaced to support Windows 2000 Professional. Terminal services cannot be used, as users will need to continue working if the network is down.

2. Since the president has provided this information, you could gain further insight into the company's requirements by contacting other management (vice president or managers), end users (employees), and the existing IT staff.

3. Team roles include IT management or executive sponsor, project management, development and design, technical and subject matter experts, testing, documentation, training, and logistics.

Analyzing the Existing and Planned Business Models

In determining business requirements, it is important to not only look at what the new system will have, but what the current system already has in place. This is not only limited to technology, but also the business itself. How a company is organized will affect the network, and how the network is designed will affect the company. It is important to understand the specifics of an organization if you are to understand how your network infrastructure works.

If a company is restructuring itself, or changing how it does business, it may affect security and other elements related to your Windows 2000 network. For example, additional offices may be planned in other areas of the city, and new levels of management may be added. As you look at how a business is set up, you may find that certain changes need to be implemented in the organization itself. For example, does the organization have its own information technology staff, or does it need one? If it does, will additional employees be needed to support the new system?

Earlier in this chapter, we discussed the importance of documentation. If the designers of the current network infrastructure have made documentation, you already have a portion of your work done for you. You may need to add additional information to bring the information up-to-date, but it will provide you with insight on how the business and its needs have already changed.

To understand the current and future state of a business, you need to analyze the existing and planned business models. A business model is a comprehensive description of business requirements. A model provides insight into the needs of the business by looking at such factors as what the business does, how information flows, its organizational structure, and how decisions are made. In other words, the business model is a representation of the business as a whole, providing you with an overview of how the business works and what its requirements are.

Business models are comprised of business objects. Business objects are representations of components that make up the business. They include the business name, a definition of the business, attributes, behaviors, relationships, rules, policies, and constraints. For example, a business object can represent people, places, events, concepts or business processes. These include such things as employees, products, or methods in which the company conducts its business.

Conceptual Aids

Conceptual aids provide a visual approach to relaying the information contained in business models. Flowcharts and diagrams can show the structure of a business, how data and communication flows, and other aspects of the business model. Creating these provides an easy-to-use source of reference that is easy to understand by laymen and IT staff alike.

To create flowcharts and diagrams, you must first identify the business objects that will make up the business model. Once you've determined the business objects, you can then organize that information into a structured depiction. The type of flowchart or diagram you create depends on how the information can best be presented.

Entity Relationship Diagrams (ERD) are commonly used when developing applications, but can also be used when diagramming relationships for network design. An ERD shows how different entities, or business objects, relate to one another. Each entity and its relationship to other entities needs to be defined. This allows you to understand how one entity relates to another as the diagram evolves and grows. For example, Figure 2-1 depicts how people in an office are paid. Management makes up payroll sheets that are passed to the finance department.

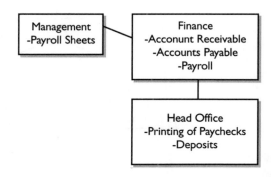

FIGURE 2-1

Entity
Relationship
diagram

Finance has varied responsibilities including payroll. The amount owed to the employee is calculated and passed to Head Office, which prints the paychecks and deposits the money necessary to cover those checks. By diagramming the relationship between these entities, you can see how one area of a business relates to others areas.

You can use hierarchical flowcharts for your business model. As shown in Figure 2-2, a hierarchical structure can be created to show the business objects making up a company. By breaking down the business into these objects and displaying them this way, users are able to understand how the business is structured. This is not only used to show the organizational structure of a business, but also to suggest the workflow.

Such diagrams can be used to display different types of information in a business. You can use functional decomposition to break down tasks in a business process. Each node in the flowchart depicts how a particular task is handled and how a job is performed.

Diagrams are only part of a business model. You can back up nodes in a flowchart with textual information that describes a business object in detail. For example, you could explain how a business process is performed step-by-step, elements or duties in a unit of the organization, or other information describing a business and its requirements.

FIGURE 2-2

Hierarchical
diagram of a
business model

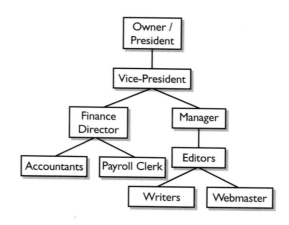

Business Models

1. Create a flowchart showing the organizational structure of a school. Business objects to be used include principal, vice-principal, teachers, and students.

2. Compare your flowchart with the one shown in the answer to this exercise.

This flow chart illustrates the answer to the exercise question:

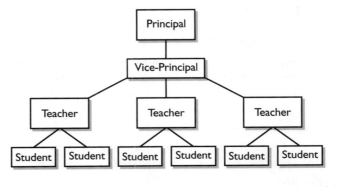

GAP Analysis

By looking at the current system, you can determine what changes will take place between the old system and the new one. A gap analysis involves comparing your current environment to your future environment, which is based on business requirements making up your project's goals. The gap between these two environments will assist you in determining what is needed to close this gap.

exam

watch

A gap analysis is an important part of designing a network infrastructure. It is a documented analysis that looks at the current state of the network and the proposed state (which is based on a business' requirements). A gap analysis then details what will be needed to change the current system into the future system.

A gap analysis often starts by looking at how employees currently work and how the business would like them to work when the new system is complete. This information will help you in deciding what network technologies and Windows 2000 features should be deployed. Remember that a new network infrastructure will affect the performance and methods used to carry out tasks. Once the new system is in place, you can measure the success of your project by how productive workers are when the new system is in place.

Reviewing documents is another important step in gap analysis. Documents on previous upgrades to the network—including server and client upgrades—will provide information on the current system. It will also give you an idea of what succeeded and failed during that project, so you can make similar decisions and avoid previous mistakes. In addition, you should also look at documents from hardware and software vendors so that you can determine what should be replaced, upgraded, or left as is. As you read through documents related to the current system, you should update them as changes are made.

In looking at how users currently perform their jobs, you should identify tasks they commonly perform. You can then determine what resources are required for each task, and determine how they can be performed faster by implementing features found in Windows 2000. You can also decide from this information whether additional resources will need to be provided, and which groups of users can help you in evaluating certain features.

Once you've analyzed this information and created documentation on what needs to be upgraded and added to the current system to make the future network infrastructure a reality, you should provide the gap analysis to decision makers in the company. This will allow those in charge of the business—who will foot the bill for any changes you make—to determine whether your ideas for what's needed are acceptable. If they accept your gap analysis, you'll be ready to go ahead with the proposed changes. If they reject your ideas, you'll need to modify them by revising the contents of your gap analysis.

CERTIFICATION OBJECTIVE 2.03

Analyzing the Company Model and the Geographical Scope

How a company is structured geographically often reflects the type of network it will require. Many of the factors that determine how you design your network are determined by the size of your network. By analyzing the location of units making up the business and how they are located, you will gain significant knowledge of how to design your network infrastructure.

A local area network (LAN) is a group of computers connected in a single location. This may be a single office, floor of a building, or all of the computers in a small company's building. If the computers are spread across a city, this type of network can be referred to as a Metropolitan Area Network (MAN). Often, organizations are larger than this, and have offices or locations that are spread across a region. An example of this would be a police department with precincts or detachments that are spread throughout a city or several cities. Another example would be a bank that may have a central headquarters, but branches across a city, state, or province. If a network is spread across a city, state, nation, or multiple nations, the network is referred to as a Wide Area Network (WAN.)

In analyzing the company model and geographic scope, you determine how units making up the company are separated from one another, and how those units are similar or different. For example, are employees largely grouped together in one area or are they located in widely separated areas? Do these units perform the same tasks or do they have significantly different needs and requirements? Will they need to be under the same domain namespace? These are some of the questions you need to ask yourself, decision makers, and users when determining a business' requirements.

Regional

Outside of creating a LAN in a single building, creating a network for a regional business is the least difficult network infrastructure to design. This is primarily due to staffing issues. When dealing with a network spread across several cities, you can have a single project team working on the entire network. By driving between sites in the region, you will be able to do the business requirements analysis and other work necessary to deploy your Windows 2000 network. When dealing with a network spread across far flung cities (such as those at opposite ends of a state or province), this becomes more problematic. In such cases, you will need to get your team to those sites via shuttle flights, communicate through e-mail or other methods, use multiple teams, or consider outsourcing work (discussed later in this chapter).

With such companies, you also need to determine how much data will be exchanged between the different locations. In many cases, you can get away with putting a server at each location and having routers connected through modems and digital lines. For the most part, these users will only connect to their local server, and only occasionally need to connect to other servers in other locations. If constant connectivity is required, or large amounts of data are transmitted, then you may need to consider faster lines with greater bandwidth, such as T1 or T3 lines. If fast connections such as T-carrier lines are available, then you might even consider using servers at a single location, such as the business' headquarters. This is feasible when a business' facilities are separated across cities or townships that are close to one another.

National

National companies provide a different challenge from ones located within a region. One particular issue deals with staffing. In deploying the network, you will need to decide whether to fly your team members out to other states or provinces to do the work, outsource the work to another company, or have information technology staff in those locations perform necessary tasks. If other teams are used to performing the work, you will need to coordinate these efforts, creating teams in each area and assigning the role of team leader to someone to oversee local work.

When offices making up a national company are connected through a network, they make up a WAN. National companies generally require faster connections, such as T1 or T3 lines connecting their offices. If small offices need only occasional connections, then slower methods of connectivity can be used. So that users can save data to a server, and use resources available through the server, a Windows 2000 Server should be located at each site.

To provide support, you will also need to implement support strategically. It is unfeasible to have members of your IT staff jetting across the country. Imagine doing that every time a tape needs to be changed in tape backup, or repairs need to be performed on a user's Windows 2000 Professional machine or a Windows 2000 Server. As such, you will need to develop a strategy of placing staff at each of the major sites to provide IT support.

International

International companies also have unique problems when implementing a network infrastructure. Like national companies, there is a problem with staffing. You will probably need to delegate responsibilities to information technology staff in those foreign offices, or outsource work to firms in those countries. In doing so, you will need to have additional focus on communicating project status and problems. As is the case with national companies, a coordinated effort is needed between each team in each nation.

Also, as with national companies, international companies have specific hardware needs. They require faster connections, such as T1 or T3 lines connecting their foreign offices. If occasional connections are required, slower methods may be used. This is also the case when considering connectivity between each country's offices. To improve speed, each country's offices will also need servers so that users can save data and use resources available through the server.

Other problems may deal with the country's themselves. You will need to develop a strategy for how information will flow between the countries, when users from different countries speak different languages. Currency, data format, and other issues specific to different locales will need to be decided upon. In other words, when data is exchanged, is it in English, using American dollars, or Japanese, using yen as the currency?

Subsidiary

Subsidiaries are companies that are owned by another company. A subsidiary is run as a separate business, and is generally a business that's been purchased by a larger corporation. Because the subsidiary has already been running as its own business for a while, they usually provide different services or make different products than the headquarters that owns them. They will often have different needs, use different practices, and have their own network infrastructure in place. They may be using UNIX or Macintosh systems, or using network operating systems like Novell NetWare. This means you'll have to determine whether these systems will need to work with the Windows 2000 network at the headquarters, or if their system should be changed to use Windows 2000. You will also need to determine whether the subsidiary and the company that owns it need to be connected. It is possible that decision makers may want the companies separate in every way.

If each subsidiary has its own IT staff, you will have to work with them to make your project a success. The IT staff will have a relationship with those who work for the subsidiary, providing you with greater insight into the subsidiary's needs. They may also have existing documentation on the current network infrastructure and business plans.

Branch Offices

When groups of users are separated and work out of offices in different cities, a question arises over what these users do. Some offices may perform different tasks, such as a finance office or marketing office. Others may supply the same services, but they are duplicated so that they may serve individual cities. You will need to determine what users in these offices do before designing your network.

This is often the case with branch offices. Each office performs the same task and reports to headquarters. In such cases, you are able to analyze one office thoroughly and assume that each of the other offices has the same requirements.

This can be a dangerous assumption to make, however, if you don't verify that all branch offices perform the same tasks. It is important to determine whether all branch offices have the same requirements. You may find that some offices provide additional services to their clientele and so have different needs. To investigate this, you should talk to decision makers in the company and managers of these branch offices.

CertCam 2-3

EXERCISE 2-3

Understanding a Company Model and Geographic Scope

Asimov Robotics Inc. has offices in London, England, Paris, France, and Moosejaw. The headquarters are located in London, while the Paris and Moosejaw offices oversee manufacturing and sales. Recently, it has purchased Positronic Robotics and Housewares, which consists of a single office in New Jersey. This company makes components geared toward home offices, while the company that now owns it manufactures components for corporate use.

1. Into which company model does Asimov Robotics Inc. fall?

2. Into which company model does Positronic Robotics and Housewares fall?

3. You are upgrading Asimov Robotics Inc. to a Windows 2000 network. What issues do the company models and geographic scope of these companies present?

Answers:

1. Asimov Robotics Inc. is an International company. It has two branch offices.

2. It is a subsidiary.

3. Since these companies and the subsidiary are in different countries, date and time issues, currency, and connectivity (they will require faster connections if they are to communicate regularly) are issues that will have to be addressed. Since one country (Paris) may use a different language, language issues should also be considered. Also, since these other countries probably have their own IT staff, you will have to coordinate with them any changes to the network infrastructure. As a subsidiary, you should determine if Positronic Robotics and Housewares already have an existing network infrastructure. If they do, you will need to decide whether to replace their system with a Windows 2000 network, or if the disparate systems need to work together.

CERTIFICATION OBJECTIVE 2.04

Analyzing Company Processes

Every company has its own way of doing business, so it's important that you look at company processes when designing a network infrastructure. A company process is a function within the business that allows it to deliver its products and services. These are the procedures that are followed so that the business can function successfully. This includes workflow, decision making, service and product life cycles, and the flow of communication and information.

When investigating business requirements, it is important to document and diagram key business processes. This is especially the case if you are reengineering business processes. You need to show how business processes will change with the new infrastructure and how this will result in an improvement. If current business processes will be unaffected, you should show how key processes would work within the new infrastructure.

on the
job

Business rules and processes can change dramatically in a business, so you need to consider flexibility in your design. Laws change, policies change, life changes, so your Windows 2000 network must be able to adapt. When someone is promoted into a decision-making role, they want to impress people around them by implementing new policies and procedures. When this happens, your design should be flexible to accommodate these changes.

In diagramming company processes, you can use conceptual modeling to illustrate how a process works. Using terminology that those within the business can understand, the process and subprocesses it contains can be shown through a functional hierarchy diagram. Figure 2-3 shows processes can be grouped into a process family with child processes appearing beneath a core process. The parent

FIGURE 2-3   Functional hierarchy diagram showing a company process, where processes and their sub-processes are grouped into families

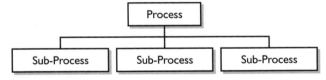

process appears at the top. This shows the major process that takes place, with minor functions that make that process possible appearing beneath it.

You can also take a high-level approach to diagramming company processes, and decompose a functional hierarchy. Figure 2-4 displays how you can show detailed levels that need to be addressed to make key company processes possible. With this approach, you specify a particular process or subprocess at the top, then detail the activities required in that process. Beneath this, you diagram the tasks required for each activity. Using a detailed approach like this, decision makers, users, and other stakeholders will be able to determine implications and potential changes. They are able to look at the diagram and see what specifics need to be performed to make the process to be completed successfully.

Information Flow

Since information technology is the name of the game, it should come as no surprise that detailing the flow of information is part of analyzing business requirements. Decision makers will need information to make critical decisions about business practices. A business process relies on information being available to the people who need it. In diagramming and/or documenting business processes, it is important to show how information flows through the business, and that key data stores are organized and accessible.

To illustrate the flow of information, Data Flow Diagrams (DFDs) can be used. A DFD uses oval shapes to hold business processes. It contains easy to understand terms describing what happens at that stage. Lines are used to connect the various processes, with arrows on the lines showing the direction that information flows. Text above these arrows indicates the name or form of that information.

To make this a little clearer, let's use the example in Figure 2-5. A business sells products over the Internet. When a customer orders a product on a Web page, he or she enters shipping information and a credit card number into fields on the Web

FIGURE 2-4   Detailed conceptual diagram of a company process

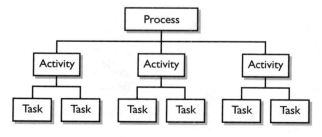

FIGURE 2-5

Data flow
diagram of
information flow

page. This data is passed to a SQL server database. The sales department checks this information, confirming that the credit card number is valid. A shipping order is then sent to the shipping department, which arranges delivery.

EXERCISE 2-4

Diagramming the Flow of Information

You have been hired to create a network infrastructure for a hospital. In analyzing business requirements, you need to document how information flows. When analyzing the hospital kitchen's needs, you interview people to find how the process of determining what food will be served to patients each day. This involves looking at the foods currently in stock, creating a daily menu of what will be served, and then creating a shopping list of items currently out of stock.

Based on the information acquired from the hospital kitchen staff, create a data flow diagram showing the flow of information in determining the food served to patients. This should include analysis of currently stocked food, creation of a daily menu, and creating a shopping list to replenish depleted items.

This diagram displays the answer to the exercise:

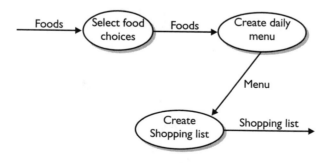

Communication Flow

The flow of communication is another necessary component in documenting company processes. This shows how information is conveyed, and the method and frequency with which it is distributed. By determining this, you will have a firm grasp on communication within an organization, and how your team will provide information about the project.

The details of communication flow can be used in creating a communication strategy for your project. A communication strategy outlines how information about the project will be conveyed. It is a plan designed to transmit information between members of your project, those whom your project team answers to, and those whom the network infrastructure will serve. Your communication strategy should include several different types of audiences, including executive management, information technology, project teams, and endusers. By communicating how the project is going, you will acquire improved support. Those in charge of the business will be able to help with obstacles faced by the team, while users will be better prepared in using the network.

When documenting communication flow, you should first look at how communication is structured. This includes looking at who is involved in the flow, the type of information being distributed, and how it is distributed. Certain people need to be informed of a process so they can authorize its completion. For example, a clerk in purchasing might need a manager to sign off on buying equipment. After this, the information needs to go to accounting so that seller of the equipment can be paid. This shows a clear trail of which company members are involved in the process, and how they are involved. By determining the current communication flow, you can then show how the new infrastructure will enhance communication, making the user's job easier and increasing productivity.

Communication flow involves documenting or diagramming how information will be distributed throughout a company. If a company has an existing intranet or you will be adding one as part of the new infrastructure, you can distribute information quickly and inexpensively. Users, decision makers, and other stakeholders can use browsers to check the intranet for information. Status reports, procedures, or general orders on company policy can easily be referred to in this manner. Also, Web applications and interactive Web pages can be used to allow users to update information themselves or perform key tasks. If no intranet is available, internal or external e-mail can be used to share information. If no electronic methods are used, you can look into printed materials, such as newsletters or memos. However, it is far more cost effective to use electronic methods of communication.

You should include in your documentation of communication flow, how frequently the information needs to be distributed. The frequency rate is usually based on how access to information will impact their job performance or their position in the business. Those in charge of a department or the organization as a whole may require weekly or daily access to certain information. Others, such as stockholders or users not directly involved in a process, will require information less frequently. For these users, they may need updates on a monthly or quarterly basis.

Service and Product Life Cycles

Nothing lasts forever, and some services and products don't last as long as others. Some services and products are geared toward a particular point in time. Good examples of this were services and products that were geared toward Y2K. After January 1, 2000, any clocks that were counting down toward zero hour couldn't be sold. As such, any projects geared toward making these clocks were scrapped. This meant that network security needed to be changed, computers and other resources were relocated, and the business requirements and company processes changed.

From this example, you can see that a company's service and product's life cycles are an important part of analysis. While this was a clear-cut example, many situations may seem clear, but involve questions that must be answered. For example, in a business that prepares tax returns, any income tax software is only good for the current year. When this software becomes obsolete, decisions need to be made as to whether new software should be installed or old software upgraded. Also, you must decide what happens to older data. Is it purged from the system or archived? If archived, for how many years?

Interviewing those closest to a particular business process often provides the information needed to calculate life cycles. In the case of tax preparation, accountants can tell you when an old system becomes obsolete. Other departments can inform you of when laws will be changing.

In determining the life of a product or service, you should include some leeway in your calculations. Internal and external delays will affect replacements or upgrades, as will enhancements to the current product or service. Value adding means adding additional features or qualities, and may possibly lengthen life.

The need for older products or services may also play a part in the life cycle of a product or service. To use the example of Y2K again, many companies will take older computers and put them back into service on a network. A Y2K software company may sell software that will test and fix Y2K problems years into the 21st century. In the case of the automotive industry, parts may need to be stocked or made for cars that were produced several years before.

Decision Making

It is vital that you identify decision makers in an organization early in analysis. While end users may have their own view of what the network infrastructure should be and how company processes work, the head of a department or company will have access to greater amounts of information and may provide a different viewpoint. Identifying decision makers will provide a fuller understanding of company processes, and increase the odds that your project will be successful.

One of the most important reasons for identifying decision makers is that they are the people who sign off on elements of your network infrastructure or on the project as a whole. While interviewing people during requirement analysis, some may present themselves as having more power than they really do. This can waste your time and provide you with false information. In knowing who is in charge of what, you will know who will need to sign off on the project and what responsibility they have in the success of your project.

Understanding decision making in a company is essential to documenting and diagramming work, communication, and information flow. In any process, there is always someone who is responsible for seeing that process achieve successful completion. As such, these people play an important part in how a process runs.

Now that we've discussed so many elements involved in analyzing company processes, look at the following Scenario & Solution box for some common questions students have about this topic.

SCENARIO & SOLUTION

I want to diagram how information flows through a business. In doing so, I want to show company processes and the information passed between each process. What should I use to diagram this?	Data flow diagrams are used to document information flow. A data flow diagram shows business processes in the form of oval shapes, with arrows connecting the various processes. These arrows show the direction information flows, while text above these arrows indicates the name or form of that information.
Why do I need a communication strategy for my project?	A communication strategy outlines how information about a project will be conveyed to decision makers, end users, and other stake holders. It can use current methods for the business' communication flow, or use new technologies implemented as part of the network infrastructure.

Analyzing the Existing and Planned Organizational Structure

The organizational structure of a business shows how the company itself is set up. It shows how it is managed, how the company itself is organized, partner and customer relationships, acquisition plans, and vendor issues. Once you have defined the goals and objectives of a business, it is important to consider what the existing organizational structure is, and how a planned organizational structure will help to achieve those goals.

Management Model

A management model shows how the company is managed, and what the functions of management are. As we saw when we discussed identifying decision makers in an organization, it is important to determine early in business requirements analysis who is really in charge, and of what they are in charge. The management model provides you with an effective view of how the company is administered.

There are many different types of management that can be used in a business. Corporations must ultimately report to stockholders, so a CEO administers the business on their behalf. A board of directors may exist in these and other businesses to oversee the organization as a whole. Other companies may be run by a partnership or sole proprietor. Beneath such lofty levels of the organization there might be vice presidents, and beneath that level of management might be departmental managers. Other organizations, such as the military or police, might use similar models, but include captains, sergeants, chiefs, or other ranks.

A management model can be illustrated using a hierarchical diagram. Such a diagram is similar to an organizational chart. In fact, as we'll discuss in the next subsection, many organizational charts include a management model within them. At the top of the chart is the role of the highest management position. This may be a board of directors or a president. Below this is the next level of management (such as a vice president), which leads to another level that perhaps oversees individual units of the company (such as a departmental manager). Diagramming or documenting the model of management used by a business will tell you who is accountable for a particular level of the business or for the business itself. This is particularly important when a decision needs to be made and the person normally responsible for such decisions is away. In such cases, you need to quickly determine who can sign off on a decision or process.

Company Organization

The organization of a company will have a profound effect on your network infrastructure. Company organization shows the structure of a business and the departments contained within it. Gathering this information gives you a clear view of how the organization is designed as a whole, and what units provide individual services and products within the company.

Company organization can be documented using an organizational chart. An organizational chart starts at the topmost level of the business. If you were looking at a particular component of the organization, such as a subsidiary, you would start with the topmost level of that component. From this point, you show what units of the business fall under each level. In other words, you show what departments are accountable to whom. The organizational chart in Figure 2-6 shows that the Accounts and Payroll departments each fall under the jurisdiction of Finance that in turn reports to the Executive Director.

Many times, organizational charts will include the management structure within them. Functional decomposition is used to break the organizational chart into greater detail. They will show a particular level or an organization, and beneath it, state the role that is responsible. For example, one unit of the structure may be finance, so the finance director is documented as being in charge. Beneath this you could document the name of the person in charge of that particular area.

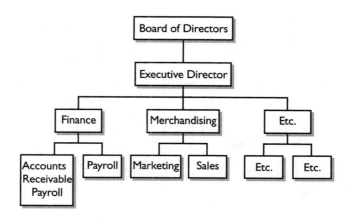

Creating an Organizational Chart

St. Bittysburg Police Department has hired you to design a network infrastructure. During the course of analyzing business requirements, you create an organizational chart. Create an organizational chart with the following business objects:

1. The top level of the organization is the commissioner's office. The police commissioner has responsibility over this office.

2. The chief of police answers to the commissioner's office and has responsibility over the deputy chief.

3. The deputy chief has responsibility over two precincts, run by captains, and the finance department.

4. Each precinct is comprised of a detective office and a uniform unit, made up of sergeants and officers.

5. Finance is made up of a payroll department and an accounts department. The accountants in the accounts department handle either accounts receivable or accounts payable. The accounts department also oversees the purchasing department.

This chart illustrates the structure of the police department organization:

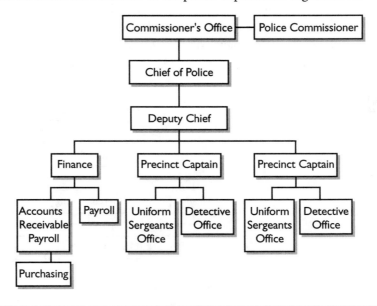

Vendor

Vendors, and their part in the company, should also be considered when analyzing the existing and planned organizational structures. Vendors are individuals or other companies that are autonomous, but sell products or services to your business. Many companies rely on vendors to get their products or services sold and may rely on other vendors to supply products or services that the company needs.

In analyzing the existing and planned structure of an organization, it is important to identify the vendors involved and how they fit into the company. Some companies may require orders to come directly from vendors, so you'll need to take into account any applications and connectivity used in acquiring these orders. Other vendors may receive computer support from the main company and you'll need to consider this when setting up IT staffing.

Partner and Customer Relationships

Not all companies are owned by a single person or rely on a board of directors answering to stockholders. Some companies are partnerships, where two or more people actually own the company. In such cases, you will need to consider the role a partner plays in the existing and planned organizational structure. If a partner is part of the decision making process, you will need to include them in this structure. If they are a silent partner and have no say in how the business is run, you won't need to structure your network security, organizational, and management models to include them.

In addition to partners who have a stake in the company's profitability, many organizations are forming partnerships on individual projects. For example, a company may have a cooperative program set up with a local college or university, where students perform work within the company. In such cases, network security will need to be set up to include necessary levels of security. Other partnerships may involve two or more organizations working together on a project, where information is shared among users of their system, and where users are part of the network infrastructure you're creating. In such cases, you will need to consider dial-up networking, network security, and compatibility issues. The users from the other companies may need to dial into a server, upload or download data, or use folders to which they have access. If information is being shared, you will need to determine the applications they are using, and the file formats being used, so users on your network can access this information.

Customer relationships are always an important factor in analyzing an organizational structure. In terms of ordering products or services, the Internet has opened many doors for increasing sales. It is commonplace to allow customers to order products or services online. It is also not unusual to have kiosks that allow users to access services or order products provided by a business. Such avenues also allow customers access to self-help forms of support. They can access information related to products and services so that the company or customer can cut costs in paying service people, telephone help-desk people, or other methods of support.

If stockholders are part of an organization, the Internet provides a method of relaying information about your own network infrastructure project. Just as the intranet allows you to use Web pages to publish status reports and other relevant data that users can view, you can also publish a version of this to the Internet. This was common during Y2K upgrades, where customers were concerned about organizations being Y2K compliant.

Acquisitions Plans

The design of your network infrastructure needs to be flexible to accommodate company acquisitions, divestitures, and reorganization of companies. While a current design may work for the company as it is now, you need to account for changes that may occur over time.

Over time, aspects of your network may become obsolete or fragmented due to changing standards for computer applications or network technologies. This is especially the case when acquisition plans are involved. One company may merge with another. If another company acquires yours, or your company plans on acquiring another, then different systems will need to work together or be replaced.

It is important that you know of acquisition plans early in designing a network infrastructure, as it is a potential risk to the success of your project. If you have this information, you can take other systems into account during the design and work around such possibilities.

on the
job

Acquisitions, divestitures, and reorganizations can greatly affect your network infrastructure. Other companies will use applications, protocols, topologies, and network technologies that may be different from those you've designed. Merging these infrastructures can be a difficult process, especially when you consider that the other company has its own IT staff, which may be protective about their system and defensive about change.

Analyzing Factors that Influence Company Strategies

There are many factors that can influence a company's strategies, and will have an effect on the success of your project. To deal with these factors, it is important to identify company priorities, projected growth and growth strategies, relevant laws and regulations, risk and total cost of operations. These issues will affect the features going into a project, when these features will be added, and the size of your network infrastructure.

Identify Company Priorities

While you and other members of your project team may have their own ideas of what is a priority of the new network infrastructure, it is important to establish priorities of the company. These are issues that take precedence and must be in place before other features of the project. Because it would be impossible to offer everything at once in a project, tradeoffs must be made.

When tradeoffs are made, it is a matter of adjusting one element of a project for another. Projects have three elements that are interrelated: schedule, features, and resources. A schedule is the timetable that establishes when features of your project will be in place, and sets a due date for completion. Features are requirements part of your network infrastructure, while resources are elements that make the project possible. Examples of resources would include people, facilities, technologies, and available funding. When you adjust your schedule, features, or resources, one of the other two are affected.

Figure 2-7 illustrates these three project elements in a triangulated relationship. Modifying the schedule, features, or resources will alter the project, just as adjusting one of the three lines would alter the shape of a triangle. For example, if the schedule needed to be completed earlier, then certain features might need to be dropped to make that due date. If these features cannot be dropped, then additional people may need to be brought into the project, costing more money. As you can see, an alteration of one element affects the other two.

Triangulated
relationship of
project elements

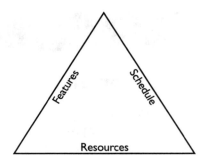

Priorities are set through a process of trading off one element of a project for another. If it is vital that features are in place, then the budget or schedule will adjust to ensure those features are part of the network infrastructure. Also, remember that when one of these three elements is adjusted, it affects the other two.

To establish priorities in a project, and determine what tradeoffs will occur, you can use a tradeoff matrix. A *tradeoff matrix* is a table, like the one shown below, that is used as a reference tool, allowing your team to decide whether it is more important to stay on schedule, on budget, or to pass off certain features until a later date. It is important that you and the business accept one element as a tradeoff. By going over priorities with the business, you can determine which elements should be optimized, constrained, or accepted as a tradeoff. Going over particulars of the project and checking off in the matrix how elements can be traded off, gives you a firm grasp on a business' priorities.

	Optimize	Constrain	Accept
Features			
Schedule			
Resources			

Identify the Projected Growth and Growth Strategy

As a company grows, the network will change. Additional workstations will be added, network traffic will increase, network security will be adjusted to include new groups and user accounts, and new features and technologies will be added. If a new division or unit with great needs is to be added in the future, even a small growth in the company can have a profound impact on your network.

As such, it is important to identify the projected growth and review the growth strategy of a company when you analyze business requirements. Most companies have a business plan that shows what direction it will take over the next few years. Such plans will include information on possible cutbacks or increased hiring, expansion of facilities, and may include new projects the company will undertake. In addition to analyzing the business plan of the company, you should interview key decision makers, asking their views on how many users may be added to the network, new facilities, and other issues related to the network infrastructure.

Identify Relevant Laws and Regulations

Failing to identify relevant laws and regulations related to the business can result in criminal and civil prosecution. You should investigate what is allowed in areas where your network infrastructure will be deployed. Protocols, encryption schemes, and other features used on your network may be prohibited, depending on where the company is located.

Laws and regulations vary from state to state, country to country. What may be legal in one area, may not be in another. A good example of such laws would be the Web browser used on the network. If you decided to use Internet Explorer with 128-bit encryption, you would need to look at what countries allow such encryption schemes. If the business were located in the United States or Canada, this wouldn't be a problem. However, using this encryption scheme in other countries, such as Japan, would cause the company to be in violation of laws.

Issues related to laws and regulations may not apply to the technologies you use, but to the data being transmitted across your network. For example, privacy laws may require extra security measures or encryption. Some people may need to be kept from viewing certain data, unless they have the proper security clearances from the organization. This is particularly relevant when dealing with network infrastructures in military, police, or other government agencies.

Identify the Company's Tolerance for Risk

The only risk that can hurt you is one you haven't planned for. Risk isn't necessarily a bad thing if you take precautions to deal with problems before they actually occur.

Examples of risks include such things as company mergers, economics, changing business needs or user requirements, or natural disasters like storms or floods. A risk management plan is used to identify potential problems before they happen, and prepares your team for a fast response when they actually occur.

The key to risk management is being proactive. In other words, don't wait for a problem to occur and then react to it. Create a management plan that offers contingencies, workaround plans, or solutions. The time to create such a plan is early in designing the network infrastructure, before risk factors raise their ugly heads.

A good risk management plan offers methods of redundancy, which reduces the likelihood that a problem will actually occur. In terms of staffing, no one person on a team should have all the knowledge about a particular aspect of the project. While you want experts on your team, you don't want the project crippled if that person leaves. Documenting procedures and aspects of a person's expertise, and training a person to act as backup for each expert, are valid methods of avoiding such problems.

Redundancy also applies to technology. When setting up your Windows 2000 network, you should plan for the possibility that installation of Windows 2000 servers may not go as expected. To deal with this risk, you should plan installations and rollout to deal with this possibility. For example, in setting up your Windows 2000 network, you could install Windows NT 4 domain controllers, move them to a private network, and upgrade them to install a new domain for the new network. You could also establish trust relationships between Windows 2000 domain controllers and existing Windows NT 4.0 domain controllers. Once these relationships are set up, you could then clone the user accounts. Regardless of the method you choose, you can roll back to the existing Windows NT 4.0 network if problems arise. This keeps users from experiencing loss of service from failure of the upgrade to work as planned.

Earlier in this chapter, we discussed problems with acquisitions and stated that they are risk factors. In mergers or reorganization of a business, you may experience problems with completing your project successfully. You should take this into account, and plan for changes in the organizational structure so that you can deal with them as they arise.

An effective risk management plan involves identifying and analyzing potential risks, quantifying the potential impact of those risks, identifying mission-critical applications, detailing escalation processes, and finding solutions to the risks. You need to assess risk in every area of your project, by asking team members to identify and manage possible risks. When we discussed team roles earlier in this chapter, we saw that each member is responsible for a particular area of the project, so they have the best knowledge of what may jeopardize success.

exam
ⓦatch

It is important to realize that just because one project is more risky than another, it does not mean it's not a viable project. For example, one project may have 10 risk factors, while another has 20. This doesn't mean that the project with more risk factors won't be successful. It means that there are more risk factors that must be addressed in the risk management plan.

Risk management requires communication with senior management and project members so that everyone is kept up to date, and it must be part of everyday project management. If it is not part of your team's normal routine, problems may arise without you realizing it.

on the
Ⓙob

You should make it clear to everyone involved in a project that it is valuable for people to identify risks. Don't allow your team, end users, or management to feel that they are complaining or foretelling doom by pointing out risks.

It is important to prioritize risks so you can identify which ones are most likely to become a problem. Some risks are more likely to occur than others, while others have more severe repercussions. By prioritizing risks, you can address primary risk factors first, then address those that are less likely or severe.

Risk assessment matrices can be a useful resource tool in identifying, assessing, and prioritizing potential risks. Table 2-1 shows a risk assessment matrix. You'll notice that the first column states the risk that poses a potential problem. The second column shows the estimated probability that the risk will become an actual problem. For example, it might be a small chance that an earthquake will occur during the project, so this would be low probability. The Impact column shows the effect this risk would have on the project. For example, if budgetary problems were a risk, then the impact might be high, as there wouldn't be enough money to complete the project. The next column is the Owner column, which states the person who is responsible for this risk. This person will be in charge of keeping this risk from becoming a serious issue, or dealing with the risk when it becomes problematic. The Date Resolved column states when this risk was resolved, while the Mitigation Strategy column states what the proposed strategy is for managing the risk.

TABLE 2-1   Risk Assessment Matrix

Risk	Probability	Impact	Owner	Date Resolved	Mitigation Strategy
What is the risk?	How probable is it the risk will become a problem?	How great an impact will the risk have on the project's success?	What team role is responsible for dealing with this risk?	What date was the risk resolved?	What is the strategy for dealing with this risk?

Creating a Risk Assessment Matrix

Clarke Robotics is located in Tarzana, California. Tarzana hasn't had an earthquake in two years, and they are very proud of this. Despite this, Clarke Robotics occupies an earthquake-resistant building that is designed to experience minimal damage. The only problem they experienced two years ago was losing power for a week, which almost bankrupted them. Recently, Clarke Robotics has been considering a merger with Asimov Robotics, though they are just starting to hash out the details of any merger (if one occurs). Finally, Clarke Robotics has been using desktop operating systems and a network operating system other than Windows. They have no experience with Windows 2000 or previous versions.

1. Draw out the columns and enter the captions included in the Risk Assessment Matrix.

2. Enter the risks, the rate of probability they will occur, what you consider the impact will be, the team role responsible for handling the risk, and any possible strategies you can think of for dealing with the risk.

This table contains the solutions to the exercise:

Risk	Probability	Impact	Owner	Date Resolved	Mitigation Strategy
Acquisition	Medium	High	IT Management		Create strategy for integrating our project team with counterparts in the other organization.
Earthquake	Low	High	Project Management		Install a generator and uninterrupted power supplies to deal with possible power failure.
Users have no experience with Windows	Medium	Medium	Training / Logistics		Develop training and support for users on Windows 2000. Train users before the new infrastructure is in place.

EXERCISE 2-6

Identify the Total Cost of Operations

Total cost of ownership (TCO) is all costs that are involved in information technology. This includes servers, workstations, operating systems, printers, and other elements involved in running a network. It is the amount of expenses and depreciated costs of each asset in a network infrastructure. TCO works on the premise that by optimizing costs, you will have a better return on investment (ROI). In other words, the less that is spent, the more money you have.

The TCO model involves three phases: analyze, improve, and manage. Through these phases you create a baseline of your current costs, identify and take action regarding analysis of this information, and measure progress by comparing change to the baseline. These phases are expounded upon in the paragraphs that follow.

The first step in the TCO model is the analysis phase. During this phase, you create a baseline, which explains the network before any changes occurred. This involves taking an inventory of software and hardware used in the current infrastructure, and cataloging the actual cost of each asset. Current inventories of software and hardware used in the organization and financial records can provide this information.

During this phase, national averages are also collected. These averages are called *metrics*, and they enable you to compare your costs to averages of those of other companies. The metrics should come from the same type of business as the company you are analyzing. In other words, don't compare automotive industry averages to those of a banking institution. By documenting the baseline, these metrics are then compared to average industry costs.

Once these metrics have been collected, you then analyze them. Comparing your costs to national averages may reveal issues that need to be addressed. Areas of your inventory may appear bloated and show overspending, requiring further investigation. Risks revealed by the analysis will need to be analyzed so that you can determine their impact and a strategy to deal with those risks. This comparison of a baseline to national averages creates a baseline report.

The next phase of the TCO model is the improvement phase. During this phase, issues identified by the previous phase become improvement projects. These projects attempt to lower the TCO by making changes to the current environment, and resolve information technology issues.

Once the improvement phase is completed, the management phase begins. This phase occurs after a plan is implemented and change takes place. During this phase, data is then recollected and compared to the metrics so that you can determine whether improvement has occurred. If a positive change has occurred, the costs of the network should decrease. If costs have increased, further analysis may be required. For example, if new technologies were implemented to improve the network and user productivity, then the change will still be positive despite increased costs. If no change or a negative change to the TCO has occurred, then new projects can be implemented to improve the TCO.

SCENARIO & SOLUTION

What is a tradeoff matrix for?	A tradeoff matrix is a tool used to establish priorities in a project, and to determine what tradeoffs will occur. It is a table that is used as a reference tool, allowing your team to decide whether it is more important to stay on schedule, on budget, or to pass off certain features until a later date. It is important that you and the business accept one element as a tradeoff.
I am designing a network infrastructure for an international company. Are there any particular issues I should watch for?	Identify laws and regulations related to the network infrastructure. Determine which laws may affect the network technologies and standards that you plan to put into place.
What is a risk assessment matrix for?	A risk assessment matrix is an important part of a risk management plan used to assess and prioritize risks in a project. It is used to determine what risks are involved in a project, their impact, the rate of probability they will occur, who is responsible for dealing with them, and a strategy to show how they will be dealt with if they become a problem.

CERTIFICATION OBJECTIVE 2.07

Analyzing the Structure of IT Management

Whether you're consulting for a company or working in a company with its own IT staff, there is a need to analyze the structure of IT management. In consulting, you need to determine how IT staff is organized and the functions they currently perform, or should perform with the new system. If you are part of an IT team in a company, you will need to determine if current roles should change with the new system, what team roles each person will play, and how IT Management will be part of implementing the new infrastructure. As we'll see in this section, the type of administration, funding model, decision making, change management, and outsourcing policies are all elements that should be part of this analysis.

Type of Administration

In analyzing the structure of IT management, it is important to look at how the network is administered. There are two types of administration available: centralized and decentralized. In the paragraphs that follow, we will discuss these types of administration.

Decentralized

Decentralized administration requires management to be performed from different locations and possibly through different software. This creates an added burden to administrators when security and a need to centralize tasks are important.

Decentralized administration is good for small networks or groups of users where security is not an issue. It allows such groups to share their resources without having to go through a network administrator. In such an environment, a minimal amount of administration is required because the user performs many common administration tasks. This is particularly true of security. A good example of this is a peer-to-peer network. In such a network, users control access to resources themselves. They can share printers, files and folders, and control what access users will have to these resources (if any). Security can be set using password-protected shares, as seen in

Windows 95 and 98 operating systems, or via localized account databases, as seen with Windows NT or Windows 2000 workgroups.

Centralized

Centralized management is important when administrators need to manage large groups of users and security is an issue. This is particularly important when servers are spread out over a large geographic area and there is a need to manage these servers remotely. In centralized management, servers and user accounts can be administered from a single machine.

Funding Model

Earlier in this chapter, we discussed how IT Management secures funding for the project. Because of this, you need to determine how the project will be funded, and what the budget will be. What sources of revenue are available to the project, and where will the money come from?

Funding is a risk factor, so it is the role of IT management to handle potential funding problems. If the project goes over budget, it is the responsibility of IT management to seek out additional forms of funding. This may include taking money out of another budget, petitioning for additional sources, or other methods. In some cases, the project may need to be delayed so that it is funded from the next year's budget.

When discussing risks, we saw that tradeoffs are part of prioritizing a project. Because cash is a limited resource, and the well eventually will run dry, IT management must ensure there is enough money to fund the new network infrastructure. If there is not enough funding, then tradeoffs must take place. This means that features must be dropped from the project and scheduling will probably be affected.

Outsourcing

Outsourcing is hiring other information technology professionals to perform information technology management functions. Such firms may be brought in to do specialized work, such as programming large applications, analyzing a network, and performing upgrades. In some cases, outsourcing replaces an in-house IT staff so that they perform all functions related to such staff.

In analyzing business requirements, it is important to determine what part (if any) outsourcing plays in an organization. In some organizations, outsourcing is not an acceptable solution. This may be due to security issues, union contracts, or other reasons.

Decision-Making Process

Part of IT management's responsibility is acting as an intermediary between the team and the business. They are responsible for setting the vision of what the project entails, and work closely with both team members and decision makers in the business. While they are higher than other members of the team in the decision-making process, it is important to realize that the requirements dictated by the business are foremost. It is these decision makers in the business who will ultimately sign off on the project.

It is the business that will drive the features and characteristics of the network infrastructure. Each team member working under the business will have his or her own responsibilities for decision making. IT management works with the business and team to set priorities for the network infrastructure. Beneath the IT manager and business decision makers is the project manager, who makes decisions necessary to deploy the network infrastructure. Development and design is a role that makes decisions regarding features included in the design and how the network infrastructure will actually be designed and developed. The technical and subject-matter role makes decisions regarding designing and developing strategies for their particular areas of expertise. The testing role makes decisions regarding testing of the project, and determining any issues that other members of the team need to be aware of. Those in the documentation role make decisions regarding the generation of planning documents, reports, and white papers. Training and user education makes decisions on how users will be trained on the new system. Finally, logistics management makes decisions on how to smoothly roll out of the new system, and determine if support groups like trained and help desk are in place to assist users.

While each of these roles and their responsibilities were discussed at greater length earlier in this chapter, it is important to realize that each role plays his or her part in the decision-making process. At all times, it is the business that makes the ultimate decision on what will become part of the network infrastructure. Decision makers in the organization must sign off on features, functionality, support, and other aspects of the new system.

Change Management Process

Few people appreciate change, and many will treat it with disdain. Initial excitement can quickly lead to frustration and anger when dealing with changes in an environment. Since change is an inevitable part of a project, managing change is critical to the success of the project. In managing change, it is important to recognize that it doesn't merely affect technology, but also people and company processes, and may induce organizational change. Early in a project, you will need to implement processes to assess what can go wrong, determine which changes must be dealt with, and implement strategies for dealing with them.

As we saw with risk management, change management should be proactive. It should identify what will change at the start of a project and assess changes throughout the project. Also like risk management, you will need to prioritize changes and assess their impact on the success of the project. Often, change will result in a drop in productivity for a while, as users adjust to new technologies and methods of performing tasks. Because of this, team members in training and logistics roles will need to use the change management process as part of the functions they provide to the project.

When you incorporate a change management process into your project, it is important that members of your team understand it and follow it. They will need to make it part of their decisions and part of their daily practices. Team members will need to look for changes in elements of the project that they handle so they can identify changes to company processes, technologies, and the way it will affect users.

SCENARIO & SOLUTION

What is the difference between centralized and decentralized administration?	With centralized administration, multiple servers, users, and security is administered from a central computer or computers. With decentralized administration, computers are administered on numerous computers because the user performs many common administration tasks.
Why should I consider outsourcing?	Outsourcing is an excellent option when there are specialized tasks that are beyond the abilities of your IT staff. It is also useful when you don't want to hire additional fulltime staff, but need work performed.

Decision Making

Answer each of the following questions:

1. You are designing a network that has extensive security needs. You are asked whether centralized or decentralized security is better for this network. What type of administration should you use and why?

2. True or false: Change management should be reactive. You should manage problems resulting from change as they occur.

3. When should change management be implemented in a project?

Answers:

1. Centralized management is important when administrators need to manage large groups of users and security is an issue. Decentralized administration is not an option here. Decentralized administration is good for small networks, or groups of users where security is not an issue. It allows such groups to share their resources without having to go through a network administrator.

2. As we saw with risk management, change management should be proactive. It should identify what will change at the start of a project, and assess changes throughout the project.

3. This should be done early in a project. You should assess what can go wrong with a project, determine which changes must be dealt with, and implement strategies for dealing with them

CERTIFICATION SUMMARY

In this chapter, we saw that analyzing business requirements is an important part of planning a network infrastructure. By understanding the needs of the business, we are better able to create a network that enhances the business and allows it to achieve its goals.

We saw that an important part of business analysis is documentation, and that many documents can be created to keep a project on schedule and achieve success. Previous documentation, such as business models, can be used to help understand the business, and newly created models will help current and future work. In addition, you can create a gap analysis to determine what is needed to take a system from its current state to its proposed state.

In designing a network infrastructure, we also saw that there are many elements that determine what shape the network will take. One of the primary elements of how you will design your network is how the company is structured, and how it is spread out geographically. To understand how the company works, you also need to look at company processes, and document or diagram elements involved in a process. This includes workflow, decision making, service and product life cycles, and the flow of communication and information. The structure of an organization, its partnerships and customers, management and other aspects of the existing and planned organizational model also affect your network. Other elements to be considered are those that can influence a company's strategies, and will have an effect on the success of your project. To deal with these factors, it is important to identify company priorities, projected growth and growth strategies, relevant laws and regulations, risk, and total cost of operations. Each of these play a part in a business' requirements and how your network infrastructure will be designed.

Finally, this chapter showed us how IT management fits into the analysis of business requirements and the issues that need to be acknowledged during this analysis. These issues include the type of administration, funding model, decision making, change management, and outsourcing policies that should be part of this analysis.

✓ TWO-MINUTE DRILL

Overview of Business Requirements Analysis

❑ Business requirements are the needs and issues that must be analyzed and addressed when planning a network. Once determined, these are applied to a plan that outlines the technical specifications of a network infrastructure.

❑ Business requirements analysis isn't an exact science, but rather a calculation of trade offs. Different factors affect the network infrastructure you create. The way a business is laid out, its ability to change and accept risks, and other variables will each play a part in how a network is planned and implemented.

❑ There are several types of documentation that will be created during the course of designing your network infrastructure. These include administrative documents, deployment documents, functional specification, communication strategy, training plans, capacity plans, and a risk assessment.

Analyzing the Existing and Planned Business Models

❑ A business model is a comprehensive description of business requirements. It is a representation of the business as a whole, providing you with an overview of how the business works and what its requirements are.

❑ Business models are comprised of business objects. Business objects are representations of components that make up the business.

❑ A gap analysis involves comparing your current environment to your future environment. The gap between these two environments will assist you in determining what is needed to close this gap.

Analyzing the Company Model and the Geographical Scope

❑ Many of the factors that determine how you design your network are determined by the size of your network. As such, analyzing how the company is structured is vital to designing a network infrastructure.

❑ In analyzing the company model and geographic scope, you determine how units of the company are separated from one another. You need to investigate whether these units perform the same tasks for their area, or if they have unique needs.

Analyzing Company Processes

❑ A company process is a function within the business that allows it to deliver its products and services.

❑ When analyzing company processes you need to document or diagram workflow, decisionmaking, service and product life cycles, and the flow of communication and information.

Analyzing the Existing and Planned Organizational Structures

❑ The existing organizational structure shows how it is managed, how the company itself is organized, partner and customer relationships, acquisition plans, and vendor issues.

❑ Organizational charts and management models are used to show how the company is structured and levels of management contained within the business, respectively.

Analyzing Factors that Influence Company Strategies

❑ There are many factors that can influence a company's strategies and have an effect on the success of your project. To deal with these factors, it is important to identify company priorities, projected growth and growth strategies, relevant laws and regulations, risk and total cost of operations.

❑ In setting priorities, you are dealing with three elements of a project: schedule, resources, and features. Altering one of these elements will affect the other two.

Analyzing the Structure of IT Management

❑ Analyzing IT management structure includes scrutiny of the type of administration, funding model, decision making, change management, and outsourcing policies.

❑ In the decision-making process, each team member has responsibilities for making decisions that will affect the project's success. Ultimately, decision makers in the business have the final say, as they sign off on the project.

SELF TEST

The following questions will help you measure your understanding of the material presented in this chapter. Read all of the choices carefully, as there may be more than one correct answer. Choose all correct answers for each question.

Overview of Business Requirements Analysis

1. Which of the following best describes business requirements analysis?

    A. Outlines the needs and issues of a business, but does not affect the technical specifications of a network infrastructure

    B. The needs and issues that must be analyzed and addressed when planning a network. The analyses of these requirements are applied to a plan that outlines the technical specifications of a network infrastructure.

    C. Applies to software development, but does not directly apply to network infrastructure planning

    D. Outlines the needs of a business, but does not outline how a company conducts its business

2. You are designing a Windows 2000 network for a company. You have gathered the initial business requirements and want to document the scope, goals, and objectives of the project. In which of the following types of documents will you document these?

    A. Administrative documents

    B. Functional specification

    C. Risk assessment

    D. Training/user education plan

Analyzing the Existing and Planned Business Models

3. Which of the following best describes a business model?

    A. A definition of the business

    B. A comprehensive description of business requirements

    C. A model made of cardboard or other material that allows you to analyze how cabling should be laid through the environment

    D. An outline of the features and functionality required in the network to show how these features will be implemented

4. You have created documentation that details your current system and outlines what your new system should provide. Which of the following would you create to show what upgrades and/or additions would be needed to change the current system into the proposed system?

   A. Change analysis

   B. Gap analysis

   C. Change management

   D. Functional gap

Analyzing the Company Model and the Geographical Scope

5. A national company has offices connected together with high-speed lines. What kind of network is this?

   A. LAN

   B. MAN

   C. WAN

   D. SPAN

6. You have been hired by the president of Murky Motors to design a network infrastructure. Murky Motors has offices spread across several cities that are located adjacent to one another. Each office occasionally has the need to access a database located on a SQL server at the head office. Which of the following company models does this situation represent, and what issues will you need to address when designing this network? Choose the best answer.

   A. This is a regional company. You will need to upgrade servers at each office, and determine if data transmitted to and from the SQL server requires faster connections.

   B. This is a subsidiary company. Because subsidiary companies usually have their own network infrastructures already in place, you will need to determine whether the new system will work with this existing system, or if you will replace the subsidiaries system.

   C. This is an international company. You will need to address language issues when you design the new system. You will need to upgrade servers at each office and determine if data transmitted to and from the SQL server requires faster connections.

   D. This is a regional company. Because regional companies usually have their own IT staff at each location, you will need to coordinate your efforts with the IT staff at each location.

Analyzing Company Processes

7. You are preparing documentation to show functions required for the business to function properly. You document and diagram workflow, decision making, service and product life cycles, and the flow of communication and information. Which of the following are you analyzing?

   A. Company model and geographic scope

   B. Company processes

   C. Structure of IT management

   D. Laws affecting proposed infrastructure

8. You are designing a network infrastructure for an e-commerce business. During the course of analyzing business requirements, a member of your team creates the diagram shown here:

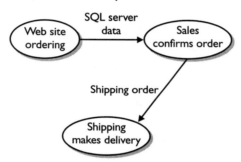

   In reviewing this diagram with the owner of the business, the owner asks which are the business processes. What will you tell him?

   A. Data and shipping order

   B. Web site ordering, data, and sales confirms order

   C. Sales confirms order, shipping order, and shipping makes delivery

   D. Web site ordering, sales confirms order, and shipping makes delivery

Analyzing the Existing and Planned Organizational Structures

9. Refer to this diagram:

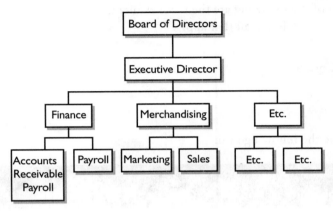

What type of diagram is this, and what does it show?

A. Data flow diagram, showing the management model of the company

B. Data flow diagram, showing company processes

C. Organizational chart, showing the organizational structure of the company

D. Organizational chart, showing company processes

10. You are analyzing the existing and planned organizational structure of a business. Which of the following components of this analysis should be viewed as a potential risk and can instantly fragment your network infrastructure?

A. Organizational structure

B. Management model

C. Acquisition plans

D. Customer relationships

Analyzing Factors that Influence Company Strategies

11. You are setting priorities for your project with decision makers of the business. Using a tradeoff matrix, which of the following are the three elements of a project that can be evaluated as a possible tradeoff? Choose all that apply.

A. Schedule

B. Windows 2000

C. Resources

D. Features

12. Please examine the following grid:

Risk	Probability	Impact	Owner	Date Resolved	Mitigation Strategy
Acquisition	High	High	IT Management		Create strategy for integrating our project team with counterparts in the other organization.

Which of the following tools is this?

A. Data flow diagram

B. Organizational chart

C. Risk assessment matrix

D. Risk assessment plan

13. At which phase of the TCO model do you create a baseline and compare this data to metrics?

A. Analysis

B. Improve

C. Management

D. Resolution

Analyzing the Structure of IT Management

14. You are designing a network infrastructure with a large group of users where security is an issue. What type of administration should be used?

A. Decentralized

B. Centralized

C. Dictatorship

D. None of the above

15. Your network requires network software to perform a number of complicated tasks for users. Creating this software is beyond the abilities of members of your IT staff. Which of the following are options to resolve this problem?

A. Insourcing, so that another IT group can create this software

B. Outsourcing, so that another IT group can create this software

C. Centralized management, so that users do not need to do their jobs

D. Sidesourcing, so that another method of performing these tasks can be found

16. Which of the following team roles is responsible for deciding on features included in the network infrastructure?

A. IT management

B. Technical and subject matter

C. Project manager

D. Development and design

17. You are concerned with how changes to the network infrastructure will affect users and processes. As such, you decide to implement change management as part of your project. When should change management be implemented in the project?

A. At the beginning of the project, before deployment has taken place

B. After training and support mechanisms are in place

C. At the end of the project, when everything has been completed

D. Never

LAB QUESTION

Positronic Robotics and Housewares has contracted you to design a network infrastructure. Currently they have 450 users on their network, and plan on hiring another 50 over the next year. The network will need to be fully operational in one year, to support this increase in users.

In the next two years after this, it is being negotiated that they will hire an additional 75 employees, and the union may strike in the next year to ensure these new employees are hired. They have some older computers that will not support Windows 2000 Professional, but may need to use applications used by Windows 2000.

Perform each of the following tasks:

1. Identify each of the team roles that can be used in this project.

2. Identify each of the types of documentation that will be created during the course of designing your network infrastructure.

3. What initial requirements does the company have?

4. To identify company priorities, what three elements will be involved in a tradeoff?

5. Draw a tradeoff matrix, which will be used in determining company priorities.

6. Determine a risk involved in the project, and create a risk assessment matrix to analyze those risks.

SELF TEST ANSWERS

Overview of Business Requirements Analysis

1. ☑   **B.** Business requirements are the needs and issues that must be analyzed and addressed when planning a network. The analyses of these requirements are applied to a plan that outlines the technical specifications of a network infrastructure.

☒   **A** is wrong because business requirements do affect the technical specifications of a network infrastructure. In fact, business requirements are what help to form these specifications. **C** is also wrong. While business requirements analysis is used in software development, it is also part of planning the infrastructure of a network. **D** is incorrect because business requirements analysis outlines the needs of a business and how a company conducts its business. This helps to form a plan of how the network will play a part in meeting the company's needs as well as helping it conduct its business more efficiently.

2. ☑   **A.** Administrative documents identify the requirements of a business, and identify the scope, goals, and objectives of the project. Administrative documents outline the needs of the business, and include documentation on phases and milestones of the project, communication strategies, facilities, risk assessment, budget, and staffing. They provide a clearer vision of what the project hopes to achieve, what business needs must be addressed, and future phases of your project..

☒   **B** is incorrect because a functional specification outlines features to be deployed, how they will be configured, and details what the network infrastructure will be. It states each of the features used in your Windows 2000 network, when they will be implemented, and how. **C** is wrong because risk assessment identifies potential problems that could occur in the course of the project and offers contingencies to avoid those problems from adversely affecting the project's success. **D** is wrong because a training or user education plan is used to establish training material on what users and support staff will need to know before the network is put into place.

Analyzing the Existing and Planned Business Models

3. ☑   **B.** A business model is a comprehensive description of business requirements. It is a representation of the business as a whole, providing you with an overview of how the business works and what its requirements are. Once created, a model provides insight into the needs of the business by looking at such factors as what the business does, how information flows, its organizational structure, how decisions are made, and so forth.

☒ A is wrong because a definition of a business would be a business object of the business model, not the business model itself. A business model describes the business as a whole, outlining how the business works and what its needs are. C is wrong because a business model isn't a physical model made of cardboard and used to see how cabling should be laid through the environment. D is wrong because this describes a functional specification. A functional specification is derived from the requirements of the business.

4. ☑ **B.** A gap analysis involves comparing your current environment to your future environment, which is based on business requirements making up your project's goals. The gap between these two environments will assist you in determining what is needed to close this gap.

☒ A and C are wrong because change management or change analysis is the process of determining how changes to the infrastructure will impact the applications, technology, and users in the computing environment. D is wrong because there is no such thing as functional gaps.

Analyzing the Company Model and the Geographical Scope

5. ☑ **C.** When offices making up a national company are connected through a network, they make up a Wide Area Network (WAN). A WAN is a network that covers a wide area. The best example of a WAN is the Internet. It is a network spread across a city, state, nation, or multiple nations.

☒ A is wrong because a Local Area Network (LAN) is a group of computers connected together in a single location. This may be a single office, floor of a building, or all of the computers in a small company's building. B is wrong because a Metropolitan Area Network (MAN) is a type of network consisting of interconnected computers spread across a city. D is wrong because there is no type of network called SPAN.

6. ☑ **A.** This is a regional company. You will need to upgrade servers at each office, and determine if data transmitted to and from the SQL server requires faster connections. You need to determine how much data will be exchanged between the different locations. In many cases, you can get away with putting a server at each location, and have repeaters connected through modems and digital lines. This will probably be the case, since there is an occasional need to connect to the SQL server at head office. If large amounts of data are transmitted, you may need to consider faster lines with greater bandwidth, such as T1 or T3 lines.

☒ B is wrong because it is a single company with several offices. C is wrong because the business is spread across several cities that are close to one another. They are not spread across several countries, so this isn't an international company model. D is wrong because when dealing with a network spread across several cities, you can have a single project team working on the entire network. As these cities are located beside one another, this will not likely be an issue.

Analyzing Company Processes

7. ☑ **B.** A company process is a function within the business that allows it to deliver its products and services. These are the procedures that are followed so that the business can function successfully. This includes workflow, decision making, service and product life cycles, and the flow of communication and information.

   ☒ **A** is wrong because analyzing the company model and geographic scope involves looking at how units of a business are organized and separated from one another geographically. **C** is wrong because the elements being documented and diagrammed do not directly affect IT management. **D** is also wrong because none of the elements being documented or diagrammed show information dealing with legislation affecting the proposed infrastructure.

8. ☑ **D.** In a data flow diagram, oval shapes are to hold business processes, while lines are used to connect the various processes, with arrows on the lines showing the direction that information flows. Text above these arrows indicates the name or form of that information. In this diagram, therefore, Web site ordering, sales confirms order, and shipping makes delivery are all business processes.

   ☒ **A** is wrong because this is information passed as a result of a business process. **B** is wrong because Web site ordering and sales confirming the order are business processes, while data is the information passed between these processes. **C** is wrong because sales confirming the order and shipping making the delivery arrangements are business processes. The shipping order is the information passing between these processes.

Analyzing the Existing and Planned Organizational Structures

9. ☑ **C.** Organizational chart, showing the organizational structure of the company. The organizational structure of a company can be shown using an organizational chart. It shows how the company is organized by breaking it into interconnected components.

   ☒ **A** and **B** are wrong because this is not a data flow diagram.
   In a data flow diagram, oval shapes are to hold business processes, while lines are used to connect the various processes, with arrows on the lines showing the direction that information flows. Text above these arrows indicates the name or form of that information. **B** is also wrong for the same reason that **D** is wrong. No company processes are depicted in the illustration.

10. ☑ **C.** Acquisition plans are a potential risk to the success of your project. Due to changing standards dealing for computer applications or network technologies that can occur during an acquisition, your network may become obsolete or fragmented. One company may merge with another. If another company acquires yours, or your company plans on acquiring another, then different systems will need to work together or be replaced.

    ☒ **A, B,** and **D** are wrong because none of these choices can instantly fragment a network infrastructure, or make existing standards obsolete.

Analyzing Factors that Influence Company Strategies

11. ☑ **A, C,** and **D.** Schedule, resources, and features are the three elements of a project that can be evaluated as possible tradeoffs. A schedule is the timetable that establishes when features of your project will be in place, and sets a due date for completion. Features are requirements that are part of your network infrastructure, while resources are elements that make the project possible. Examples of resources would include people, facilities, technologies, and available funding. When you adjust your schedule, features, or resources, one of the other two are affected.

    ☒ **B** is wrong because Windows 2000 isn't an actual element of a project. It is part of the features that will be added to your network infrastructure.

12. ☑ **C.** Risk assessment matrixes can be a useful resource tool in identifying, assessing, and prioritizing potential risks. The columns identify the risk, estimated probability that the risk will become an actual problem, the effect this risk would have on the project, who is responsible for dealing with it, the date it is resolved, and the proposed strategy for managing the risk.

    ☒ **A** is wrong because in a data flow diagram, oval shapes are to hold business processes, while lines are used to connect the various processes, with arrows on the lines showing the direction that information flows. Text above these arrows indicates the name or form of that information. **B** is also incorrect because an organizational chart is used to show the organizational structure of a business. **D** is wrong because a risk assessment matrix is part of a risk assessment plan, but isn't the entire plan itself.

13. ☑ **A.** The analysis phase is where you create a baseline. This involves making an inventory of software and hardware used in the current infrastructure, and cataloging the actual cost of each asset. Current inventories of software and hardware used in the organization and financial records can provide this information. These figures are then compared to national averages called metrics.

☒   **B** is wrong because the improvement phase is where plans are implemented to improve the TCO. This occurs after the baseline has been created. **C** is also wrong because the management phase occurs after the baseline has been created, compared to metrics, and improvement plans have taken place. During this phase it has determined whether the changes made have been positive or not. **D** is wrong because there is no resolution phase in the TCO model.

Analyzing the Structure of IT Management

14. ☑   **B.** Centralized management is important when administrators need to manage large groups of users and security is an issue. This is particularly important when servers are spread out over a large geographic area, and there is a need to manage these servers remotely.
☒   **A** is wrong because security is an issue, and decentralized administration is used on networks where security isn't particularly important. **C** is wrong because there is no network administration called dictatorship, although some users may disagree. **D** is wrong because this network shows a need for centralized administration.

15. ☑   **B.** Outsourcing is hiring other information technology professionals to perform IT management functions. Such firms may be brought in to do specialized work, such as programming large applications, analyzing a network and doing upgrades, or other tasks.
☒   **A** is wrong because insourcing is using members of your IT staff to do a task. **C** is wrong because centralized management is administering a network from a centralized location. **D** is wrong because there is no such thing as sidesourcing.

16. ☑   **D.** Development and design is a role that makes decisions regarding features included in the design, and how the network infrastructure will actually be designed and developed.
☒   **A** is wrong because IT management works with the business and team to set priorities for the network infrastructure. **B** is wrong because the technical and subject matter role makes decisions regarding designing and developing strategies for their particular areas of expertise. **C** is wrong because the project manager makes decisions necessary to deploy the network infrastructure.

17. ☑   **A.** Change management needs to be in place at the beginning of a process and continued throughout. This will allow new changes to be identified.
☒   **B, C,** and **D** are all wrong because change management needs to be implemented early in the design of your network infrastructure.

LAB ANSWER

1. Identify each of the team roles that can be used in this project.
   IT Management or Executive Sponsor, Project Management, Development and Design, Technical and Subject Matter Experts, Testing, Documentation, Training, Logistics

2. Identify each of the types of documentation that will be created during the course of designing your network infrastructure.
   Administrative Documents, Deployment Documents, Functional Specification, Communication Strategy, Training Plan, Capacity Plan, Risk Assessment

3. What initial requirements does the company have?
   The network must support at least 575 users over the next three years. Terminal services will need to be used so that older systems can access data and use applications the same as those running Windows 2000 Professional. There is a one year due date to complete the network.

4. To identify company priorities, what three elements will be involved in a tradeoff ?
   Features, schedule, and resources

5. Draw a tradeoff matrix, which will be used in determining company priorities.

	Optimize	Constrain	Accept
Features			
Schedule			
Resources			

6. Determine a risk involved in the project, and create a risk assessment matrix to analyze those risks.

Risk	Probability	Impact	Owner	Date Resolved	Mitigation Strategy
Employees may strike in the next year.	Medium	High	IT Management		Create a strategy to ensure network work can still be done. Talk to union. Get offsite facilities to do work at.

3

Analyzing Technical Requirements

A fter you have completed the analysis of the business-related requirements that will impact the design of your network infrastructure, you must turn your attention to the technical requirements of your corporate environment. This requires you to evaluate the existing network infrastructure, and that you then determine the company's goals, such as what do users actually *do* with the network? What does the company want the network to be able to do in the future? Is it possible, with the existing infrastructure, to accomplish these goals? If not, what improvements need to be made?

You will need to take a look at the big picture: the overall infrastructure design. Analyze its impact on the network as it is and as you envision it after any planned upgrades or modifications. An important part of this process will be determining the technical requirements that will provide optimum client access. Finally, you must not overlook the possibility that data could be lost, either during the upgrade process or for other reasons. It is imperative that you review your existing disaster recovery plan at this time, analyze its current effectiveness and how effective it will be in the planned environment, and devise and implement a systematic plan for ensuring that all mission-critical data can be recovered in the event of disaster.

This chapter will take a closer look at each of these issues, and provide you with information you need to complete the kind of thorough analysis of your company's technical requirements that will be most useful as you prepare to design a new network infrastructure or adapt your current infrastructure to work effectively in the Windows 2000 environment.

CERTIFICATION OBJECTIVE 3.01

Overview of Analyzing Corporate Technical Requirements

Let's first look at our technical environment as a whole. What do we mean by technical requirements, anyway?

The American Heritage Dictionary defines technical as "used in or peculiar to a specific field or profession." In this case, of course, we refer to that which is used in the information technology area; in other words, what is required in terms of hardware, software, or technical services, such as phone lines and ISP accounts, for the network to serve the necessary company functions?

In the previous chapter, we discussed how to evaluate the company's administrative structure, management model, business philosophies and priorities, and level of tolerance for risk. Building on that knowledge, we will now address the computer network itself and how it fits or doesn't fit the furtherance of those business requirements.

Analyzing your network environment involves far more than an examination of the hardware and protocols in place. You must adopt a broader perspective, and look at the operational environment in which the company conducts its business.

The Analytical Process

Any design project involves several distinct phases or steps. These include:

- Information gathering and identification
- Analysis
- Design
- Implementation
- Evaluation (and revision, if necessary)

This chapter deals with the second step, the analysis phase. However, the steps are not independent of one another; each depends upon the preceding step or steps. So before we can discuss how to analyze the technical requirements pertinent to a particular company's network, we must look at the previous step and ensure that we have gathered all the information necessary to complete an analysis.

Information Needed to Begin the Analytical Process

In order to analyze the technical environment (both current and planned), you need to have certain information recorded and organized in such a way as to make it easily referenced. Before you can begin the analytical process, you should have written documentation of the following:

- An inventory of the current hardware, including computers, connectivity devices, and network media, as well as information on planned upgrades, replacements, and additions
- An inventory of the software applications, utilities, and operating systems being used on the network and any planned to be deployed in the future

■ Diagrams and/or statistical charts showing the number of users, physical locations of users, workstations, servers, and devices

■ A list of the file, print, and Web servers on the network and plans for additional servers

■ Identification of all line-of-business (in effect, mission-critical) applications currently in use, as well as planned upgrades and new software roll outs

■ Security measures in place (and those planned)

Gathering information is easier to do and the information gathered is easier to organize and understand if you use a standardized method of notation. This is particularly true if more than one person has the task of gathering the information. You may find it helpful to construct a fill-in-the-blank form to guide you through the information-gathering process, such as in the following example.

Computer Name and hardware configuration	Computer Placement (physical location, subnet)	Computer Function (DC, File server, DNS or WINS, Work-station)	Software installed (operating system, applications, utilities)	Planned upgrades
ACCTG1 PIII 500 MHZ, 384MB, 30GB	Headquarters Bldg, second floor, Subnet B	Terminal server, accounting dept	Win2000 Server, TS, Office 2000, Norton AV	Upgrade RAM to 512MB, install Visio 2000

Forms can be customized to fit your company's situation. The important point is consistency. This has two purposes:

■ Important information won't be left out

■ The data will be arranged in a standard fashion so that you don't have to hunt for it in different places for different locations

Looking a Step Ahead

As you go through the process of analyzing your network infrastructure and technical requirements, not only must you utilize the documents created in the information gathering stage, but you must also look ahead to the next steps: design and deployment. It's difficult to reach your destination if you don't know where you want to arrive, so keep in mind some of the end products of your analysis, including:

- A comprehensive overview of the networking environment including hardware, software, policies, number/types of users, geographic information, and other relevant data that impact the technical requirements for the network

- A deployment design, detailing how the rollout of Windows 2000 on your network will proceed

- A gap analysis that addresses specific shortfalls between the existing network infrastructure and the planned outcome

- A capacity plan that will address the need for sufficient hardware and bandwidth to meet the goals and support the features that you plan to implement

- A risk assessment that pinpoints any risks inherent in your emerging plan and addresses them

- A problem escalation plan that defines the process to be used in resolving and escalating issues to give them priority and focus

- A pilot plan for limited deployment

- A strategy for testing and deployment

Keep in mind that your analysis should provide a foundation for all of the above.

An Overview of Network Hardware

It goes without saying that your hardware inventory should include all workstations, domain controllers, and member servers, but don't forget to document routers, hubs, printers, modems/modem banks, scanners, and other hardware. A simple list of the existing hardware devices is not enough; a thorough inventory document will also note such things as model numbers, jumper settings, CMOS (BIOS) settings, and hardware configuration information.

You may wish to combine the hardware and software inventory documents into one.

An Overview of Network Software

Software information you should include in your inventory:

- Driver information, such as version numbers, filenames, and sources, such as the URL of the Web site where the driver software can be downloaded

- Operating system information for each computer, including version/build information, service packs applied

■ A list of all software applications on each computer, with versions and special installation options or non-default configurations

exam
ⓦatch

Compiling all the hardware and software information for a large network can be a long, tedious process. There are tools available to assist and expedite the task. For instance, you can use scripts and/or third-party utilities to collect much of this information if Windows Management Instrumentation (WMI) is in use, and Systems Management Server (SMS) can be used to gather detailed information and produce reports.

CertCam 3-1

EXERCISE 3-1

Obtaining Network Settings Information

To obtain protocol configuration information for an NT or Windows 2000 computer network running the TCP/IP protocol, complete the following steps:

1. Open a command prompt (Start | Run | CMD).

2. Type **IPCONFIG /ALL**. You will see a screen similar to the one shown here:

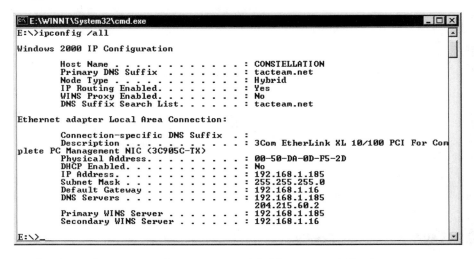

```
E:\WINNT\System32\cmd.exe                                          _ □ ×
E:\>ipconfig /all

Windows 2000 IP Configuration

        Host Name . . . . . . . . . . . . : CONSTELLATION
        Primary DNS Suffix  . . . . . . . : tacteam.net
        Node Type . . . . . . . . . . . . : Hybrid
        IP Routing Enabled. . . . . . . . : Yes
        WINS Proxy Enabled. . . . . . . . : No
        DNS Suffix Search List. . . . . . : tacteam.net

Ethernet adapter Local Area Connection:

        Connection-specific DNS Suffix  . :
        Description . . . . . . . . . . . : 3Com EtherLink XL 10/100 PCI For Com
plete PC Management NIC (3C905C-TX)
        Physical Address. . . . . . . . . : 00-50-DA-0D-F5-2D
        DHCP Enabled. . . . . . . . . . . : No
        IP Address. . . . . . . . . . . . : 192.168.1.185
        Subnet Mask . . . . . . . . . . . : 255.255.255.0
        Default Gateway . . . . . . . . . : 192.168.1.16
        DNS Servers . . . . . . . . . . . : 192.168.1.185
                                            204.215.60.2
        Primary WINS Server . . . . . . . : 192.168.1.185
        Secondary WINS Server . . . . . . : 192.168.1.16

E:\>_
```

Note the IP configuration information provided here, especially the computer name and DNS suffix, the adapter model, hardware (physical) address, IP address, subnet mask, default gateway, and DNS and WINS server IP addresses. All of this information should be recorded for each computer in your inventory documents.

On a Windows 9*x* machine, use the WINIPCFG command. This will display a graphical interface that provides the same IP configuration information.

To obtain network settings for a computer running the NWLink protocols, follow these steps:

1. Open Network and Dialup Connections (Start | Settings | Network and Dialup Connections).

2. Right-click a local area connection, then click Properties.

3. On the General tab, click NWLink IPX/SPX/NetBIOS Compatible Transport Protocol, then click Properties. You will see the dialog box shown here:

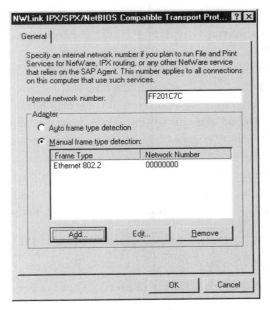

4. Note the value for the Internal Network Number (default value is 00000000).

5. Note the frame-type setting (auto or manual). For manual frame type, note the selected frame type and Network Number.

Note these settings in your inventory document for this computer.

Your hardware and software analyses, when combined with the requirements that will be developed based on needs of the network's users, will help you to set standards for hardware, software, and network configurations as part of the new infrastructure design.

An Overview of the Network Infrastructure

The best way to document your overall network infrastructure is by creating detailed *diagrams* of both the physical and the logical networks. Diagrams can be created manually (by hand) or using one of many excellent diagramming software tools available, such as Microsoft's Visio. The important thing is that the diagram be thorough and understandable.

Diagramming the Physical Network

The diagram of your physical network should include all servers and their roles, workstations, LAN and WAN connection links, and connectivity devices such as hubs, bridges, and routers. Also include any network-connected or shared peripherals, such as printers and modem banks.

A good diagram will contain names of all devices and IP addressing information for each. A sample diagram for a very simple network is shown in Figure 3-1.

For a very large network with multiple geographic locations, you may have separate physical diagrams detailing the infrastructure at each physical location, and then an overall, less detailed diagram showing the links between the geographic sites. The information that should be shown in the physical network diagram includes:

- **Network links**   Cable, analog and ISDN lines, and WAN connections
- **Servers**   Computer name, IP address, role(s), domain membership
- **Workstations and users**   Number per site, including mobile
- **Network devices**   Printers, routers, hubs, bridges, switches, and modems

Diagramming the Logical Network

A diagram of the logical network shows relationships between the network components that make up the domain structure and trust relationships, both implicit and explicit. An example, again vastly simplified, is shown in Figure 3-2.

In Figure 3-2, domain controllers for each domain are shown, with one-way arrows indicating old-style NTLM non-transitive trusts and two-way arrows

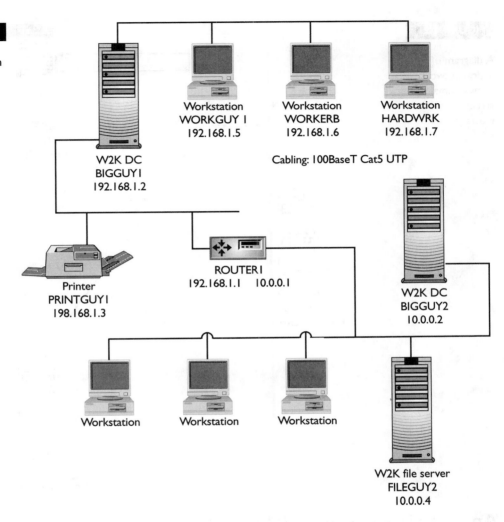

FIGURE 3-1

A simple diagram
of the physical
network
infrastructure

indicating Kerberos transitive trusts within a Windows 2000 domain tree. The
information that should be shown in the logical network diagram includes:

- Domain controllers and their role(s) in the domain structure
- Server roles (DHCP, WINS, DNS)
- Trust relationships, both implicit and explicit

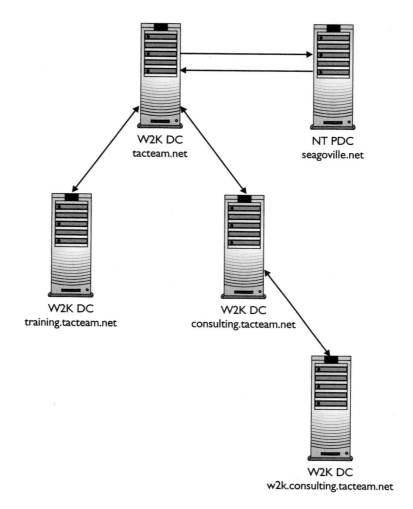

FIGURE 3-2

A diagram of the logical network shows domain structure and trusts

W2K DC
tacteam.net

NT PDC
seagoville.net

W2K DC
training.tacteam.net

W2K DC
consulting.tacteam.net

W2K DC
w2k.consulting.tacteam.net

An Overview of Network Servers

In addition to the very important task of documenting the configuration information for your domain controllers, you should not forget to do as thorough a job of documenting the member servers on your network. Although not involved in authentication, these file, print, Web or other special-purpose servers often provide vital functions.

exam
🅦*atch*

Be especially careful to note the settings for your web and proxy servers, and to consider your security requirements in regard to these servers that are connected to the public Internet.

An Overview of Line-of-Business Applications

Line-of-business applications are those upon which the organization is dependent to perform its necessary operations, that is, mission-critical programs without which the company could not function properly.

Document the function of each core application and ascertain whether each is compatible with Windows 2000. Consult the software vendor for information as to whether the application is certified to run with Windows 2000. Check the Windows 2000 Applications link on the Web Resources page on the Microsoft Web site (http://windows\microsoft.com/windows2000/reskit/webresources) and/or set up a test lab from which you can determine for yourself if and how well your program functions with the new operating system.

on the
🅞*ob*

The rollout of a new operating system like Windows 2000 provides an opportunity to evaluate the suitability and current status of your core application programs, and upgrade or replace those that have become outdated. Windows 2000's Group Policy software deployment feature makes it easy to automate many of the tasks associated with upgrading or installing new software, making the administrator's job easier and offering users the benefits of feature-rich new software versions.

An Overview of Security Analysis

You should consult your company's existing written–and unwritten–security policies, and evaluate how they are implemented within the current infrastructure. Windows 2000 provides many improved security features, which may allow you to discontinue the use of third-party software, for example, to encrypt files or to provide for two-step authentication such as Smartcard logon.

CERTIFICATION OBJECTIVE 3.02

Evaluating the Company's Existing and Planned Technical Environment and Goals

In evaluating the technical environment, as well as the goals dictated by company priorities, philosophies and policies, you will address a variety of issues. A thorough evaluation will include:

- Company size, along with the distribution of company users and resources
- Connectivity that is available between sites that are geographically separated
- Available network bandwidth, latency issues, and how these issues impact the functional operation of the network
- Performance, availability, and scalability requirements of network services
- Data and system access patterns on the network
- Network roles and responsibilities
- Security considerations

Let's take a look at each of these evaluative steps individually.

Analyzing Company Size and User and Resource Distribution

The physical and logical infrastructure that is most efficient and effective for your network will depend in part on the size of the company and number of users, the number and nature of the resources shared across the network, and how those users and resources are distributed geographically if the organization and network encompass multiple physical sites.

It is important that you determine:

- Total number of network users
- Number of users at each geographic location
- Distribution of users in the logical network structure (users per domain)
- Number of users typically accessing the network at one time
- Maximum number of users likely to access the network simultaneously

- Projections of growth in number of network users
- Shared resources
- Physical location of each resource
- Location of each resource in the logical network structure
- Typical amount of network access to each shared resource

This information should then be compared with the information about hardware resources, so that you can determine the requirements for number and placement of domain controllers, name servers, and other infrastructure issues that are impacted by the distribution of users and resources.

Assessing the Available Connectivity Between Geographic Location of Worksites and Remote Sites

It is important that you gather information pertaining to the type and speed of the WAN links that join remote sites to one another. Some possibilities include:

- Analog phone lines and modems
- ISDN, DSL, or other digital lines
- T1 or other dedicated access solutions
- Satellite or other wireless connections
- VPN connections over a public network

The reliability and performance of the wide-area links will help you in determining your Active Directory site structure, planning the creation of IP subnets and determining the placement of domain controllers at each geographic location.

Active Directory sites allow for more efficient use of bandwidth across slow links, by providing control over replication behavior between sites.

Assessing Available Bandwidth and Latency Issues

Network *bandwidth* refers to a measurement of the range of frequencies the signal occupies. Bandwidth is directly proportional to the amount of data transmitted or received per a unit of time. Digital systems express bandwidth as the speed of data transfer in bits per second (bps).

Bandwidth Requirements

Available bandwidth refers to how much of the media's signal path is free for transmitting signals. Here's an analogy: If you have a six-inch diameter pipe that runs from a water storage tank to your home plumbing system, a certain amount of water will be able to flow through the pipe in a given amount of time. If you increase the diameter of the pipe, you will increase the flow capacity (or, if you were sending electrical signals through instead of water, you would have increased its bandwidth). So, the "bigger" the "pipe," the more bandwidth is available.

To analyze your bandwidth requirements, you need to examine what types of applications are being used across the network. If all your users are doing is sending text e-mail, bandwidth is unlikely to be a major issue. If they are doing live videoconferencing, a bandwidth-intensive activity, a high bandwidth connectivity solution will be a priority.

Latency Problems

Latency means delay. In other words, it refers to how much time it takes for a packet of data to get from a designated point to another. Latency can be a problem with applications that are operating in "real time," such as Internet phone programs, "Web cams" that provide a live video feed, and so forth. Low bandwidth and high latency go hand in hand.

In many network applications, latency doesn't present much of a problem. If there is a slight delay involved in the transfer of some of the packets that make up an e-mail message, this has little impact and is not noticeable to the end user. However, if there is a delay in transmission packets containing streaming video data, it will cause the video display to be jerky and perhaps even unwatchable.

It is important to assess whether the applications used on your network will be affected by latency, and if so, whether these are mission-critical applications.

Bandwidth Options

Some LAN and WAN technologies offer higher bandwidth than others, and they do this in different ways. For instance, a T1 line offers 1.544 megabits per second (Mbps) of bandwidth, so large files can be transmitted quickly, or streaming audio and video and other applications that require a large flow capacity can function satisfactorily. Cable television companies now offer data transmission over their cable lines, often at a speed similar to T1. Why, then, would you pay several thousand dollars per month for a T1 connection when cable connections are available in many areas for less than $50 per month?

It is important to understand the differences between connectivity options and to realize that bandwidth is not the only factor to consider in planning your WAN infrastructure. You will have to weigh the costs and disadvantages against the advantages of each connection type in order to determine which option is appropriate for your company's network. Table 3-1 compares the characteristics of various connections.

TABLE 3-1   Characteristics of Different Types of Connection

Type of Connection	Speed, Cost, and Characteristics
T-carrier	T1 (and its "big brothers," T2, T3, and T4) are dedicated digital point-to-point WAN links that provide high speed and high reliability at high cost. T1 delivers 1.544 Mbps, T2, 6.312 Mbps, T3, 44.736 Mbps, and T4, 274.760 Mbps. Unfortunately, this comes at a premium price—depending on the carrier, up to several thousand dollars per month for the line alone.
Cable	Cable TV companies offer a relatively high-speed, shared bandwidth connection to the Internet over their cables at a low cost. In many cases, reliability and service are poor and security is low. The connection is to the Internet only, utilizing the cable company as an ISP. Cable speeds vary from 300 Kbps to over 1.5 Mbps. Monthly fees vary from $25 to $75 per month, depending on location.
Digital Subscriber Line (DSL)	Many phone companies are beginning to offer relatively high-speed digital connections via DSL, a service that is added to your existing copper phone lines. DSL speeds vary from 384 Kbps to over 6 Mbps, at costs from $25 to over $100 per month. Advantages of DSL are the dedicated connection, ability to use an ISP of your choice and ability to use the same line for voice and data transfer simultaneously. Unfortunately, DSL is not yet available in all areas and you must be within set distances of the telephone company central office to obtain DSL service. DSL is an "always-on" technology, like cable.
Integrated Services Digital Network (ISDN)	ISDN service is provided by most telephone companies and is much more widely available than DSL. A typical Basic Rate ISDN line (BRI) costs $50–100 per month and provides a dedicated, reliable, digital connection over two 64-Kbps channels, which can be combined (multi-linked) for a 128-Kbps connection. ISDN service can be dial up or dedicated (always on).
Analog phone lines	Analog lines are almost everywhere, and inexpensive—often as little as $10–20 per month. Unfortunately, analog lines provide a relatively slow and often "noisy" connection; that is, although modems are available that are capable of 56-Kbps transmission, the condition of most analog lines will limit the speed to less than 50 Kbps. Analog connections must be dialed up each time you connect.

Analyzing Performance, Availability, and Scalability Requirements of Servers and Services

It is important to determine, as you did in regard to network bandwidth options, the "need for speed" in your particular environment when you purchase server and workstation hardware. You will also want to analyze requirements for availability of network services, and scalability issues; how much growth is anticipated, and will the servers and the services running on them be able to adapt as the load increases?

You can use two built-in Windows 2000 tools to help monitor and analyze server and network/services performance: Performance Monitor and Network Monitor.

Analyzing Server Performance

To determine the overall usage and performance levels for your network's servers, you need to develop strategies for collection of status data from all servers. You must acquire and analyze many different performance counters in order to be able to assess in detail the operation of a single server running multiple services.

Be aware that the default System Overview log defines data collection on processor usage, current memory page activity, and disk queue length. You can use this data to gain a quick view of a server's resource-usage level.

Network Performance

You don't want network traffic to exceed the LAN capacity. If this happens, performance will deteriorate for all users and services on the network. It is possible to monitor network traffic levels, especially on large routed networks, by using the Network Segment object in the Network Monitor tool.

You can also use the Network Segment Broadcast counter to calculate the bandwidth that is being used by broadcast traffic. Messages sent to the *broadcast address* (typically the network address that contains all 1s as the host ID) are processed by every computer on the network or subnet. Because of this, high broadcast levels can mean lower performance, so this is something you will want to address.

Broadcast traffic can be reduced by subnetting the network, because broadcast messages generally do not cross routers to a different IP subnet.

exam
ⓦatch

Segmenting the network with bridges can reduce overall network traffic, because messages are forwarded across the bridge based on the MAC address of the destination computer, but bridges do not filter broadcast messages and thus do not reduce broadcast-based traffic.

Services Infrastructure Performance

Both Performance Monitor (also called System Monitor) and Network Monitor contain a large number of counters that can be used to collect pertinent information from various parts of the system. For example, Performance Monitor will allow you to track the number of packets sent and received per second by each network interface.

The data can be viewed as it is obtained, or it can be logged to a file for future analysis. You can use the data you collect to derive information about the performance of the overall services infrastructure.

Analyzing Network Services

The status of the network services can be determined based on real-time data, accumulated logs, and calculated result sets. The process of analyzing this data should use the collected status information to create the final result derived from accumulated data.

Using the monitoring tools will allow you to recognize potential bottlenecks; for example, if you find that an NT server which you plan to upgrade to Windows 2000 is already near 100 percent memory utilization, you will know you need to add more RAM prior to the operating-system upgrade.

on the
ⓙob

When charged with the responsibility of designing a new network, it is sometimes difficult to resist the temptation to add the latest and greatest new technologies, whether or not they address the company's needs, and to throw everything but the kitchen sink into your recommendations just because you can. However, you must remember that one objective of your analysis is to remain objective. It is usually prudent to follow the old adage, "if it's not broke, don't fix it." A very real priority for most companies, as they contemplate a major upgrade such as rolling out a new operating system, is staying within a budget. Don't make the mistake of thinking that because your job is on the "technical side," this is not a concern of yours. Assuming you want to continue working for the company— or want a positive recommendation from them when you look for your next job—you must make budgetary constrictions one of your concerns.

Using Network Monitor to Collect Information for Analysis

In the following exercise, you will learn to use the Network Monitor to determine bandwidth use on your network.

1. Open the Network Monitor by selecting Start | Programs | Administrative Tools | Network Monitor

2. In the Capture menu, select Start as shown here:

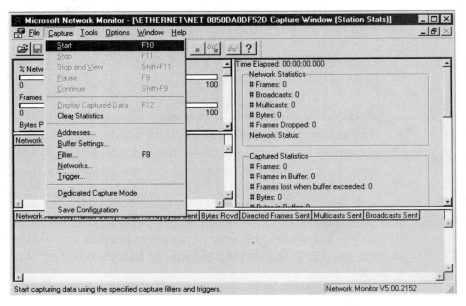

Alternatively, you can click the Start Capture button, which is represented by an arrowhead pointed toward the right.

3. As the monitor begins capturing packets, note the percent of network use shown in the upper left. In this illustration, you see that network use is low, only around eight percent.

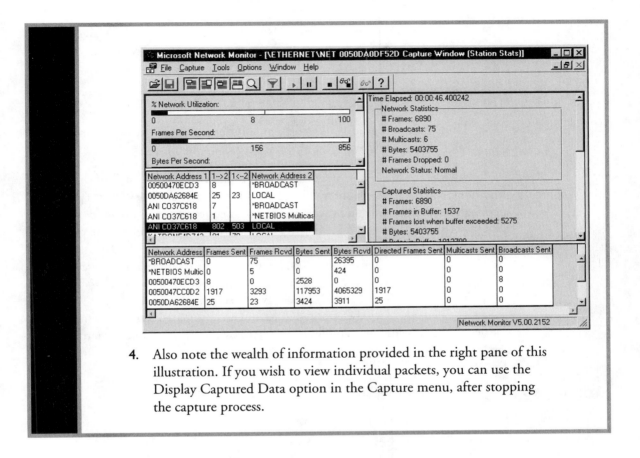

4. Also note the wealth of information provided in the right pane of this illustration. If you wish to view individual packets, you can use the Display Captured Data option in the Capture menu, after stopping the capture process.

Methods of Data Analysis

Use the following techniques and tools to analyze the status information:

- **Manual inspection** Manual processes must specify the source of data and the responses expected from manual interpretation. Manual calculations are, of course, more prone to human error than more automated methods.

- **Excel spreadsheet** An Excel spreadsheet can be used to interpret the status information

- **Microsoft Access or Microsoft SQL Server**   There are several available applications that can be used to analyze status data imported into an Access or SQL Server database

- **Specially written programs**   Applications specially written to perform analysis functions can analyze status information directly

- **Third-party programs**   Third-party solutions exist that incorporate information analysis as part of a management plan

Note that point-in-time analysis can be used to notify operations staff of current conditions, such as service failures or conditions that do not comply with design specifications. Additionally, trend analysis can be used to predict future needs and to notify operations staff when it is necessary to redesign or make configuration changes.

Manual analysis consists of a point-in-time investigation of the current status of a service or a network. This analysis can be used to direct a manual response by the operations staff, if necessary. Manual analysis is often useful in the areas of capacity planning and prediction of required redesign or reconfiguration tasks.

Automated analysis may be required as part of an automated response system that notifies operations staff or reconfigures a system by restarting services or rerouting network paths.

Analyzing Data and System-Access Patterns

The Windows 2000 monitoring tools (and add-on programs, such as Systems Management Server) can help you to gather information and analyze patterns pertaining to when, how often, and how users access the system and the data. In planning for sufficient bandwidth to accommodate user needs, you will need to know what the typical usage of the network looks like. This will also be valuable in determining placement of domain controllers, servers, and other network components.

Analyzing Network Roles and Responsibilities

Determine the role that each server plays on the network. It is likely that in many cases one machine wears many hats, that is, a domain controller could also have the responsibility of functioning as a DHCP server, WINS server and DNS server. A member server might be both a file server and provide shared Internet access as a NAT host. Part of your analysis of the existing network structure requires that you document *all* the roles taken on by each network device.

This does not mean that you will necessarily duplicate that arrangement when you upgrade to Windows 2000. Often a network will be structured in a particular way, not as the result of a well thought out plan, but because the network "just grew that way." In analyzing the current allocation of roles and responsibilities, you must also analyze the effectiveness of that allocation, and the alternatives that might offer better productivity, ease of use, cost savings, or some other benefit.

Analyzing Security Considerations

Windows 2000 makes it easy to connect your LAN to the Internet, which opens up a world of benefits to your network's users. Internet connectivity allows your organization's members to take advantage of the speed and accessibility of e-mail to communicate with people around the world. They will be able to use File Transfer Protocol and Telnet to obtain data from a huge number of sources. Internet connectivity and Windows 2000's Remote Access features can also be used to create virtual networks, to allow customers to obtain information and services from your organization at any time or enable employees to use the company's network resources from home or when on the road.

However (there's usually a "however" to a benefit with such a far-reaching impact), connectivity to the public Internet and access via the public-telephone network can pose security risks, as well.

Part of planning the design of your network involves analyzing the organization's security requirements and implementing technologies that will meet those needs. A security strategy should be an integral part of the planning process from the beginning. Microsoft recommends that even if you have a secure network environment already in place, it is important for you to review your security strategies with Windows 2000 capabilities in mind. Windows 2000 offers many security features and technologies that were not available in Windows NT; therefore, you may find that your security strategy for the Windows 2000-based network will be different. The Windows 2000 Resource Kit suggests that you complete the following tasks as you develop your network security plan:

- Assess your network security risks
- Determine your server size and placement requirements
- Prepare your staff
- Create and publish security policies and procedures

■ Use a formal methodology to create a deployment plan for your security technologies

■ Identify your user groups and their specific needs and security risks

The deployment plan should include security strategies in general, and specific deployment plans for the use of such features as:

■ Group Policy

■ Security groups

■ Public key infrastructure (PKI)

■ Certificate authority deployment

■ Logon authentication methods and strategies

■ Securing Web servers and e-commerce sites

■ E-mail security

■ Delegation of administrative authority

You should identify the categories of users who have access to your network. Each category will have unique security needs and will present particular risks. Microsoft divides users into the following four categories: Everyone, Staff, Users, and Partners. Table 3-2 explains who is included in these categories.

| TABLE 3-2 | User Categories |

Category	Members
Everyone	Everyone who has access to the network from any location. Obviously, this category will overlap with all other categories.
Staff	People who work for the organization, use the company e-mail system, and access the intranet.
Users	People who use network applications to accomplish business objectives. This is a subset of the Staff category.
Partners	People from other organizations who have a special relationship with your company and use facilities similar to staff and users. Partners often are part of an extranet.

Some strategies you should consider for providing network security include:

- Creating boundaries between your network and the outside world and secure those boundaries. One common tactic is to establish a DMZ (de-militarized zone) where servers that are accessed from the Internet are placed.
- Using Microsoft Proxy Server to provide proxy and firewall functions
- Monitoring the security measures using Proxy logging, event logging, auditing, and third-party products to ensure that your security strategies continue to be effective

Planning and Deployment team members who are tasked with analyzing the network's security needs should be familiar with Windows 2000's built-in security technologies designed to protect remote access connections, including Virtual Private Networking (VPN), how L2TP and IPSec can offer better security over a tunneled connection, and Remote Authentication Dial-in User Service (RADIUS).

CERTIFICATION OBJECTIVE 3.03

Analyzing the Impact of Infrastructure Design on the Existing and Planned Technical Environment

This is really a two-part mandate. The impact of the infrastructure design plan must be assessed separately regarding the current technical environment and the planned environment and the two must then be taken together to provide a true picture of how changes to the network infrastructure will affect user access to and use of the network.

Assessing Current Applications

In assessing the current software applications, you should prepare the following documentation at minimum:

- Prioritized list of business applications
- Plan for testing application compatibility

■ Handling of compatibility problems

■ Testing of tracking and reporting system

List of Applications

This should be thorough and should include all applications used on the network to accomplish business purposes, even if only used by one user. When prioritizing, you should take into account the number of users dependent on the application and the nature of the work produced by the application (how mission critical is it?) as well as whether there are available alternatives.

Testing Plan

Before you test the applications for compatibility with Windows 2000, you should develop a *testing plan*. This plan should include the scope of the testing, the priority levels to be addressed, the objectives of the testing, the methodology to be employed (who will perform the test and what the procedures will be), and the hardware, software, personnel, and other requirements to begin the testing.

There should be predetermined criteria for distinguishing between an application that passes and one that fails the test, along with a testing schedule that lays out a realistic time frame under which the tests will be completed prior to the operating system rollout.

Microsoft has provided detailed information in the Windows 2000 Resource Kit that outlines the step-by-step procedure for building and using a test lab. It is highly recommended that you consult this resource as part of the planning process.

Handling Problems with Application Compatibility

It is likely that you will encounter some application compatibility problems. If so, you should assign priorities to them and assign someone to resolve each. The process includes developing a plan for how you will assign these problems. It is very important that you assign the appropriate person(s) to resolve particular problems based on individual experience and expertise.

Resolving the application problems should follow a methodical system. Develop a written procedure, which might encompass some or all of the following:

■ Research Web sites for known problems and solutions and use the experience of those on technical mailing lists and newsgroups. There is no point in reinventing the wheel if others have already encountered and conquered the same problem. TechNet and the Microsoft Knowledge Base provide a wealth of such information.

- Contact the software vendors. Many will have already made available patches, setup programs, or migration DLLs. Check the vendor's Web site and use their tech support lines.

- If all else fails, contact Microsoft Product Support Services. In many cases a solution can be devised within a short time by those who have extensive exposure to the operating system.

- Finally, you may have to debug internally developed applications. In some cases, this will be a simple process. In others, it may be more time- and cost-effective to replace the program with another.

Problems and solutions fall into several categories. Your analysis should help you determine whether to attempt to fix the problem yourself (if you developed the application in-house), request that the software vendor fix the problem if it was purchased commercially, replace the application with a new version or an entirely new application, or just ignore the problem if there is a viable workaround.

Analyzing Network Infrastructure Protocols and Hosts

The next step along the way to developing your thorough analysis of the network infrastructure is to determine what protocols are running on each host machine. You may find that unnecessary protocols have been installed and are negatively impacting network performance (for example, if the binding order places a protocol which is not used by any of the other network computers at the top of a client computer's protocol list).

Determine which protocols are necessary and remove all others. For example, if a client machine needs to access a NetWare 3.11 file server, it will require the NWLink (IPX/SPX) protocol to be installed along with NetWare client software. On the other hand, if all computers on the network are running the TCP/IP protocols, they probably don't need to have NetBEUI installed as well.

In particular, your assessment should include:

- Identification of network protocols installed on each host
- Use of each protocol

■ Plan for removal of unneeded protocols

■ Review of the protocol binding order to optimize multiple protocol use

Windows 2000 networking is designed around the TCP/IP suite, so we will look specifically at the TCP/IP infrastructure in the next section.

Analyzing TCP/IP Infrastructure

An analysis of the TCP/IP infrastructure is a vital step in developing the deployment plan. The TCP/IP suite is the industry standard for large networks and those that connect to the Internet. Windows 2000 offers several new features in its implementation of TCP/IP, such as support for Automatic Private IP Addressing (APIPA), which allows a DHCP client computer that is unable to contact a DHCP server when it comes online to assign itself an IP address. Other new features include under-the-hood improvements like the support for large TCP receive windows, which increases the amount of data that can be buffered on a TCP connection, reducing network traffic and speeding up transfer. Other new features include Selective Acknowledgements and better estimation of Round Trip Time (RTT).

exam
ⓌatcH

Support for large windows is disabled by default; you must specifically enable this feature by editing the Registry in order to benefit from it. However, the default window size in Windows 2000 is larger than that of Windows NT—16 KB as opposed to 8 KB.

TCP/IP Infrastructure Analysis

Assuming your network is already running TCP/IP, now is the time to assess your IP subnetting scheme and determine whether the network is divided in the most effective way to meet the organization's needs and to optimize network performance. Consider such factors as:

■ Network IDs and placement and size of subnets

■ The IP addressing method and placement of DHCP servers (if applicable)

■ Placement of domain controllers and servers running network services

- Placement of routers and assessment of routing protocols
- The network's DNS namespace and structure and placement of DNS servers
- The network's WINS implementation and placement of WINS servers

TCP/IP Planning Considerations

If your network has been running on protocols other than TCP/IP, planning a TCP/IP infrastructure from scratch can be a daunting task. The first step will be to develop a comprehensive IP addressing plan. You will need to consider the following:

- Which address class to use or whether your network will use Classless InterDomain Routing (CIDR)
- How many physical subnets are needed and how many hosts are required in each subnet, both currently and allowing for future expansion
- Whether you will use static routing or dynamic routing and, if the latter, which routing protocols will be deployed
- Whether you will use registered IP addresses on the internal network, which is necessary if you provide a routed connection to the Internet for LAN Internet access
- Whether you will use private addresses internally, which you can do if you use Network Address Translation (NAT) to provide Internet access to LAN machine
- Whether the internal computers will be connected to the public Internet
- Whether you will manually assign IP addresses or use a DHCP server to automatically assign addresses
- Whether you will use the Windows Internet Name Service (WINS) for NetBIOS name resolution and, if so, determine placement of your WINS server(s) on the network
- How to plan your DNS namespace and determine placement of your DNS servers on the network

The Automatic Private Addressing (APIPA) feature in Windows 2000 is one of those features that may prove to be a mixed blessing. In theory it sounds great: if the DHCP server is down when a client comes onto the network, the client machine will not be relegated to the fate it would have faced in NT; that is, unable to initialize the TCP/IP stack because it had no IP address. When an APIPA-enabled machine (Windows 2000 or Windows 98) configured as a DHCP client can't find a DHCP server, not to worry–it simply assigns itself an address. So far, so good. The problem is that the APIPA address range is designated as 169.254.0.1 through 169.254.255.254. Unless this is also the address range of your LAN, the machine with the APIPA-assigned address still may not be able to communicate with the other computers on your network, which will be seen as belonging to a different subnet. APIPA can be useful if all the computers on the network come online after the failure of the DHCP server and all of them are configured to use DHCP to obtain an IP address. Then they will all assign themselves APIPA addresses and can communicate. Unfortunately, it is usually the domain controllers, routers, and other very important interfaces that have manually assigned IP addresses. The APIPA machines won't be able to communicate with them, perhaps resulting in the conclusion that APIPA is more trouble than it's worth. The good news is that if you feel this way, you can turn off the APIPA feature by editing the Registry.

Evaluating Current Hardware

Your assessment of the technical environment must include a plan for upgrading or replacing existing hardware that does not meet the minimum system requirements for installation of Windows 2000. There are several possible approaches to the problem of substandard hardware.

If feasible, upgrade existing hardware. Processors can be upgraded, RAM can be added, and in many cases older machines that do not meet standards can be made to meet the minimum criteria. This may be less expensive than buying new machines, but always do a cost comparison analysis before making that assumption, taking into account the expected lifespan of the equipment.

In some cases, it makes more sense to replace old hardware with newer models that already meet the specifications out of the box. This is particularly true if the old hardware is of a proprietary type and upgrade parts are difficult (or impossible) to find and/or inordinately expensive, or if the vendor is out of business and there is no continued support of the hardware.

If all hardware cannot be upgraded or replaced at once, consider deploying Windows 2000 in phases, rolling out the new operating system on hardware that does meet standards and devising a schedule for the upgrade/replacement/rollout sequence in other areas.

If all hardware cannot be upgraded or replaced and it is important that all users migrate to Windows 2000, consider deployment of Terminal Services as an alternative to installing Windows 2000 Professional on client machines. The Terminal Services client software will run on relatively low-powered machines, under the Windows 95/98 or Windows NT operating systems. There is even a 16-bit client program that runs on Windows for Workgroups 3.11. This means virtually any PC hardware in use can provide the Windows 2000 desktop to users via terminal emulation. Table 3-3 shows the minimum hardware requirements for the Windows 2000 systems.

Let's say you are the network administrator who has been given the task of evaluating your company's network hardware in anticipation of a planned upgrade from Windows NT 4.0 to Windows 2000. You must make recommendations based on two criteria: optimum performance and lowest-cost of implementation. The requirements are to upgrade all domain controllers to Windows 2000 and have all network clients capable of logging on to the servers. The desired result is to have

TABLE 3-3   Minimum Hardware for Windows 2000 Systems

System	Minimum Requirements
Windows 2000 Professional	133MHz processor or higher 64MB RAM 2GB hard disk with 600MB minimum free
Windows 2000 Server	133MHz processor or higher 256MB RAM recommended; 128MB minimum supported 2GB hard disk with 1GB minimum free
Windows 2000 Advanced Server	133MHz processor or higher 256MB RAM recommended; 128MB minimum supported 2GB hard disk with 1GB minimum free

all users familiar with the Windows 2000 interface. Your hardware inventory is as follows:

Six Windows NT servers	– One PDC, a 300MHz Pentium with 256MB RAM and 4GB free disk space; – Three BDCs, all 166MHz Pentiums with 96MB RAM and 2GB free disk space; – One member server (RAS server), a 266MHz AMD K-6 with 128MB RAM and 10GB free disk space; – One member server (new file server), 450MHz Pentium III with 256MB RAM and 5GB free disk space
125 client machines	200MHz Pentiums with 64MB RAM and 2GB free disk space
40 client machines	133MHz Pentiums with 24MB RAM and 800MB free disk space

Here is how you might achieve your objectives. For optimum performance, install Windows 2000 Server on the 450MHz machine and make it the domain controller for the new Windows 2000 domain. Install Windows 2000 Server on the current PDC and make it a domain controller for the new domain as well. Upgrade the 133MHz client machines to at least 64MB RAM and free disk space to 1GB. Install Windows 2000 Professional on all client machines. Additional servers can be used as file servers or an additional domain controller can be added for more fault tolerance and load balancing.

To achieve lowest implementation cost, install Windows 2000 Server on the current PDC and the 266MHz member server and make them domain controllers for the new Windows 2000 domain. Install Windows 2000 Professional on the 125 200MHz client machines. Install Terminal Services on the 450MHz Pentium and install terminal client software on the 40 Pentium 133 machines.

Evaluating Network Services

The next important step in the evaluation/analysis process is to identify the services that are needed on your network and ensure that the infrastructure design will support them. You should also identify services that will be required for future growth and upgrades.

Microsoft recommends that you include the networking services shown in Table 3-4 in your infrastructure design. The function of each service is also noted.

TABLE 3-4	Network Services and Their Functions

Network Service	Function
Dynamic Host Configuration Protocol (DHCP)	Provides automatic assignment of IP addresses and TCP/IP configuration information for DHCP client computers.
Domain Name System (DNS)	Resolves fully qualified domain names (host names) to IP addresses; works with Web-based applications and Windows 2000 Active Directory structure.
Windows Internet Name Service (WINS)	Resolves NetBIOS names to IP addresses on Microsoft networks.
Microsoft Proxy Server	Provides a barrier between the LAN and the Internet and performs address translation and firewall/filtering.
Routing and Remote Access Services (RRAS)	Provides for connectivity between remote locations within a company network, provides for dial-up and VPN connections, provides dynamic routing protocols such as RIP and OSPF; provides Network Address Translation (NAT) for LAN connectivity to the Internet.

Remember to evaluate which of your mission-critical applications depend upon which network services. If important applications fail when network services are off-line, you should consider that service a mission-critical one. Be sure to include support in your network design for redundancy (fault tolerance) for those services upon which your critical applications depend.

Identifying Existing and Planned Upgrades and Rollouts

Planning an effective deployment requires that you identify any software upgrades, including version upgrades or service pack applications, as well as rollouts of new programs that are imminent or anticipated in the future. This is especially important in regard to mission-critical applications and those used by large numbers of users in their everyday work, such as e-mail software.

Although it is likely that the newer version of a program will be compatible with Windows 2000 in contrast to older versions, you cannot make the assumption that because the software upgrade is the latest version, it will automatically work with the new operating system. You should go through the process outlined in the sections on assessing current applications and test the upgrade version in a non-production environment, if possible.

Analyzing Technical Support Structure

Another area you will want to evaluate carefully is the company's current technical support structure. How does the IT department handle user problems? What is the reporting procedure? Is the help desk staff adequately trained and is it available when needed? Is a multilevel tech support program in place to prevent high-level engineers being called to address simple, easily corrected problems?

Some areas you will want to consider in assessing the existing technical support structure and developing the transition plan to Windows 2000 are:

- Training of all technical support personnel to bring them up to speed on the new operating system

- Proactive training of users before the rollout of the new operating system to alleviate some of the workload on the technical staff during the first weeks after deployment

- Consideration of increasing the size of the tech support department temporarily to deal with the anticipated peak period of help desk calls immediately following the transition

- Written documentation to aid in assisting users with common problems

- A system for tracking reported problems and the process through which they are resolved, providing valuable data that will allow for quicker response

The impact on the technical support department of a major rollout such as the upgrade to Windows 2000 can be overwhelming. Be sure to prepare the staff for an increased workload and determine ahead of time how to address such matters as required overtime, performance expectations, and related issues.

CERTIFICATION OBJECTIVE 3.04

Analyzing the Network Requirements for Client Computer Access

Much of your analysis thus far has been concerned with the network components that we think of as the core of the network infrastructure: the servers, routers, network media, and protocols. Now we will turn our attention to the network clients. After all, if there were no clients to access the resources of the network, there would be little need for a network at all.

In this section, we will take a look at what is required for our client computers to access and use the network, paying particular attention to work needs and usage patterns of end users. These factors, taken together, will determine what changes must be made to the infrastructure to allow and optimize client access.

Analyzing End-User Work Needs

In order to deploy Windows 2000 and design your network infrastructure in the most effective way, you must determine the needs, if not the wants, of those who use the network. Some ways to obtain this information are:

- Personal interviews with users to determine what features and functionalities would make their use of the network more productive

- Survey forms to be completed by users, asking directed questions to help you pinpoint potential improvements to the network infrastructure

- Observation of users at work, documenting areas in which the deployment of new features or upgrading of hardware/software could improve performance of workers who rely on the network

Analyzing End-User Patterns of Use

Determining network usage patterns is an important step in collecting the information needed to perform an analysis of the current infrastructure and the basis for planning modifications. Only by gathering detailed information regarding who uses the network when, how much, and for what, will you be able to devise a strategy for optimizing network performance for all users.

You will need to identify trends; for example, there are likely to be periods of peak usage, such as between 8:00 and 8:30 a.m. each day, as users arrive at work and log on the network. This traffic is primarily logon authentication traffic, but if the network is large and has many users, it can slow the network to a crawl. Once you've identified the problem, you can develop solutions. In this instance, there are multiple ways of addressing the bandwidth congestion. It could be done via company policy changes–employee start times could be staggered so fewer employees attempt to log on at one time. Or it could be addressed in the design of the new network infrastructure, by placing more domain controllers on the network to allow for load balancing of the authentication traffic.

Another consideration is to ensure that peak usage times do not coincide with scheduled Active Directory replication, especially replication over a slow WAN link. Windows 2000 offers the capability of creating *sites* for network subnets that are connected by slow links and lets you control the interval and time of day when replication takes place over the slow link.

Designing a Survey Form for Analyzing End-User Patterns

You are the network administrator for a 500-user Windows NT network. You have been tasked with determining the priorities of end users in anticipation of the impending upgrade to Windows 2000. You have decided to conduct interviews of randomly selected users, observe other users at work on a random basis for a period of several weeks, and have all end users complete a survey form to help you analyze their network usage patterns. Here are some questions that would allow you to evaluate usage patterns and identify trends and priorities.

- Which applications do you use at least once per week? How many days per week do you use each one?

- How many times per day do you access the network file server?

- How often do you send or receive large data files (such as graphics, video, audio, or other multimedia files) over the network?

- Where do you store data (documents such as word processing files, graphics created in drawing programs, spreadsheets, and other original data)?

- How much data per week do you store to the local hard disk, a network drive, or removable media?

CERTIFICATION OBJECTIVE 3.05

Analyzing the Existing Disaster Recovery Strategy

Every production network has—or should have—a disaster protection and recovery plan in place. In many cases, however, when you take time to analyze the plan, it turns out to be a hodgepodge of measures, each of which offers some amount of protection in case a disaster such as a server disk crash or physical destruction of important machines occurs. However, there may be no real integrated plan that ensures vital data will be safe regardless of the contingency. That should be the goal of your new and improved disaster recovery strategy, so complete your analysis with a critical eye and that objective in mind.

Disaster recovery plans all consist of two parts:

- Measures to prevent catastrophic data loss from occurring
- Means of recovering data quickly and efficiently if catastrophic loss does occur

A good disaster protection and recovery plan considers cost/benefit ratios and focuses on the most cost-effective prevention and recovery methods. Windows 2000 was designed with fault tolerance in mind.

FROM THE CLASSROOM

Fault Tolerance

There is sometimes confusion among networking students and even among working network administrators as to the exact meaning of the term fault tolerance. Some will tell you that it refers only to RAID, a method for providing redundancy of data by mirroring one disk to another or writing data and parity information across disks so that it can be reconstructed if one of the disks should fail.

The term actually has a far broader meaning. Fault tolerance is the ability of the computer, operating system or software to recover from a catastrophic event without loss of data. RAID is a form of disk fault tolerance, and RAID Level 1 (mirrored volumes) and Level 5 (RAID 5 volumes, which were called stripe sets with parity in Windows NT) are supported by Windows 2000 Server operating systems.

Windows 2000 Professional does not support creation of fault tolerant volumes; however, Professional does use the fault tolerant NTFS file system. The meaning of the term, then, may depend on the context in which it is used.

—*Debra Littlejohn Shinder, MCSE, MCP+I, MCT*

Importance of Disaster Protection

Ask yourself this: How important is it that you are able to log on your system and access resources? The roles the computer and the network play in your company's daily activities and their functionality determine how important it is for you to develop a disaster protection plan. Loss of access to important data may cripple your operation completely, or it may be a mere inconvenience that forces you to spend precious time duplicating previous efforts or taking the long way around to accomplish necessary tasks.

Disaster Protection Features in Windows 2000

Disastrous events most common in today's computer networking environments which should be addressed in your disaster recovery plan include:

- Hard-disk failure due to defect or physical damage
- Damage to operating system or Registry files due to configuration changes
- Complete loss of data and/or operating system and program files, which necessitates reinstallation and restoration from backup tapes or other media

Microsoft includes features in Windows 2000 that make it easier to prevent or recover from these and other disasters and protect the integrity of your data.

Table 3-5 summarizes disaster protection features available in Windows 2000.

Your disaster recovery plan should detail the implementation of fault tolerant volumes, a plan for recovery in the event of fire, flood, sabotage, or equipment failure.

TABLE 3-5   Disaster Protection and Recovery Features in Windows 2000

Feature	Function
Disk fault tolerance	Recovery from failure of a hard drive that is part of a RAID set
Advanced Startup Options	Provides capability to load the operating system when files used in the normal boot process have been damaged or corrupted
Recovery Console	Perform administrative tasks from a command-line utility that can be started from the Windows 2000 setup floppies or installed on your computer
Windows Backup	Provide for manual or scheduled backup to tape or file, and quick-and-easy restoration of backup sets, files, and folders
Emergency Repair Process	Repair problems with the Registry, startup environment, system files, and boot sector that prevent the computer from starting

CertCam 3-3

Using the Windows Backup Program

Don't search in your Start menu programs for the Windows 2000 backup utility—you won't find it. To start and use the backup program, follow these steps:

1. From the Start menu, select Run.

2. Type **ntbackup** in the Run box. This will display the GUI, as shown here:

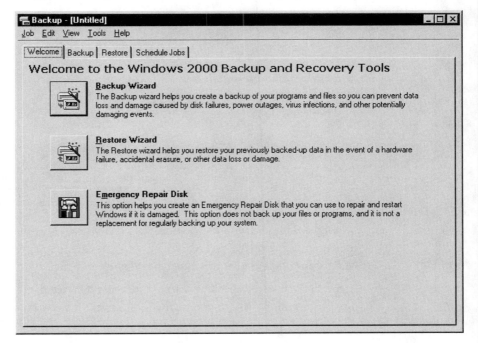

3. Select the Backup Wizard button, and the wizard will guide you through the process to set up the program to perform the desired backup.

4. Click Next at the Backup Wizard splash screen and you will see the dialog box, shown here:

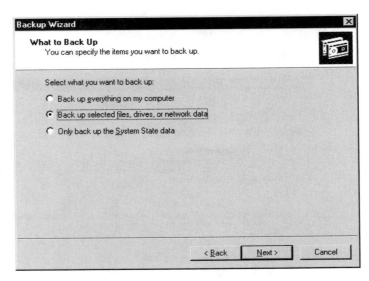

5. Select the data you wish to back up. You have three choices: everything on the computer, selected files, drives or network data, or only system state data. Make your selection (in this case, the second) and click Next.

6. If you have chosen to back up selected files, you will see the dialog box shown next, which allows you to choose the files, drives, or network data to back up.

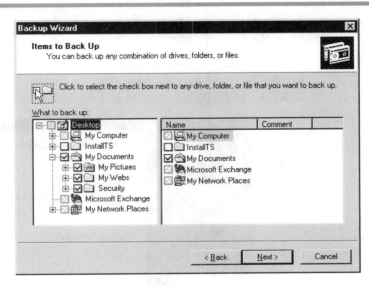

7. Select the data you wish to back up. In this case, select the My Documents folder. Click Next.

8. You will be asked where to store the backup. Select the default, which is to back up to floppy disk. A default file name will be provided, as shown next. You can change the file name if you wish.

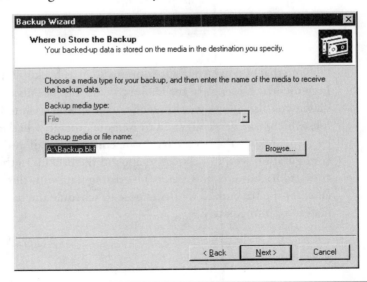

9. Click Next.

10. The next screen, shown here, will summarize the selections you have made. Review the summary and ensure that it is correct. If you wish to make changes, use the Back button to go back and do so.

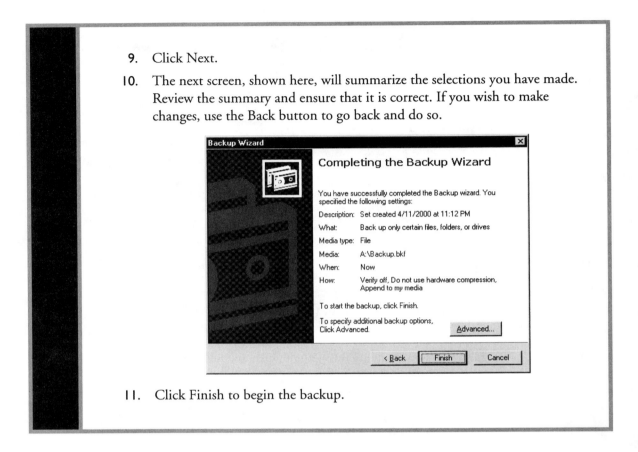

11. Click Finish to begin the backup.

Note that you can configure options such as backup type (Normal, Copy, Incremental, Differential, or Daily) by clicking the Advanced button. The Advanced dialog box also allows you to specify whether you wish to back up the contents of files which have been migrated to Remote Storage, whether to verify the data after backup, and whether to use hardware compression, if available. In the Advanced configuration, you can choose to append the backup to the media if it already contains backups, or to replace the existing data with this backup. You can select a label for the backup, as well as choose to schedule the backup to run at a later time instead of immediately.

Client Computers

Analyze the current measures in place to prevent loss of data in the event of failure of a client computer. Some of these might be:

- Policies that require users to save important data on network drivers, where they can be more easily backed up
- Folder redirection to folders such as My Documents to a network location
- Installation of the Recovery Console on your Windows 2000 client computers

CertCam 3-4

Installing the Recovery Console on a Windows 2000 Professional Computer

With Windows 2000 running, insert your Windows 2000 Professional CD into your CD-ROM drive and follow these steps:

1. Click No when asked if you want to upgrade to Windows 2000.

2. At the command prompt, switch to your CD-ROM drive and type the following:
   \i386\winnt32.exe /cmdcons
   You will see a message box with the following text:
   "You can install the Windows 2000 Recovery Console as a startup option. The Recovery Console helps you gain access to your Windows 2000 installation to replace damaged files and disable or enable services."
   The message also informs you that the Recovery console installation requires 7MB of hard disk space, and asks if you want to install the Recovery Console.

3. Click Yes and Recovery Console will be installed.

4. Use the Recovery Console to enable and disable services, repair a corrupted master boot record, or copy system files from a floppy disk or CD-ROM.

Servers

Servers are most vulnerable to catastrophic data loss, so protective measures will focus on protecting the integrity of server hard disks and the data stored there. This includes:

- Creation of fault tolerant volumes on servers that store mission-critical data so that if one disk fails, the data can be preserved
- Regular backup of data stored on servers, using tape or other backup media and utilizing the Windows 2000 backup utility or a third-party backup program to write the backup to tape, CD, magneto optical disk or other backup media
- Redundant copies of backed-up data that is mission critical
- A plan for storing copies of backed-up data off site, in case of a natural disaster, such as fire or flood, that destroys not only the original disk but any backup tapes or disks that are stored at the same location.

Backup Planning Issues

Before developing and implementing your backup plan, consider the following questions:

Who will have permission to back up data?

By default, all users can back up their own files and folders, and those for which they have Read, Read and Execute, Modify, or Full Control permissions. In addition, Administrators, Backup Operators, and Server Operators can back up all files and folders, including those for which they have no assigned permissions.

Will backups be done manually or unattended?

Unattended backups can be scheduled to take place on a regular basis.

Where will backup data be stored?

Data can be backed up to tape or to file. The latter can be stored on zip or jaz disks or other removable media, or written to compact disks or optical media.

Which files and folders will be backed up?

This will depend on the importance and uniqueness of the data, and how difficult it is to recover or recreate it.

How often will data be backed up?

You must determine whether to back up daily, weekly, or on some other schedule. You may find that some data should be backed up more often than other data.

Once you have answered all these questions, you can begin to develop a strategic backup plan.

CERTIFICATION SUMMARY

In this chapter, we have discussed some of the factors involved in analyzing the technical requirements of your organization and its users in preparation for designing a network infrastructure for your Windows 2000 network. There are a great many considerations, ranging from the size of the network and geographic distribution of its users and resources to the usage patterns observed using the current infrastructure.

The analytical process can be a tedious one, but will proceed more smoothly if conducted in an organized, step-by-step fashion. Forms and surveys can make the job of collecting data for analysis easier, and automated analysis of certain data, such as that captured by Network Monitor and Performance Monitor showing network utilization and other statistical information is more accurate, quicker and easier than performing a manual analysis.

Every aspect of the current infrastructure—hardware configurations, protocols in use, applications (particularly mission-critical ones), bandwidth usage, IP addressing and subnetting schemes, and more—must be factored in as you determine which parts of the infrastructure are sufficient to support the Windows 2000 deployment, which must be improved, and which need to be replaced altogether.

The impact of the changes on users, technical support staff, and network productivity in general should be carefully assessed and made a part of the analytical documents. Contingency plans should be developed, and a good disaster protection and recovery plan should be included and integrated into the overall infrastructure design.

TWO-MINUTE DRILL

Overview of Analyzing Corporate Technical Requirements

❑ A thorough analysis of the technical requirements of the organization, its technical staff, and users should be undertaken before a new infrastructure design is planned and implemented.

❑ The analytical process can be broken down into phases: information gathering and identification, analysis, design, implementation, and evaluation/assessment (including revision, if necessary).

❑ Information needed to begin the analytical process includes hardware and software inventories, network diagrams, documentation of servers, identification of line-of-business applications, and security measures in place or planned.

❑ Forms, customized to fit the needs of your organization, can be useful in collecting needed information.

Evaluating the Company's Existing and Planned Technical Environment and Goals

❑ Network and computer configuration settings for each computer should be documented in the hardware and software inventories.

❑ Both the physical network and the logical network should be diagrammed.

❑ The company's size and geographic distribution of users and network resources are important in determining the best physical and logical infrastructure for the network.

❑ Your analysis should include information about the WAN links connecting remote sites, including analog phone lines, ISDN, DSL, T1, satellite, VPN connections, and other long-distance connectivity solutions.

Analyze the Impact of Infrastructure Design on the Existing and Planned Technical Environment

❑ Bandwidth requirements are dependent on the types of applications in use or planned. High bandwidth applications include live video, streaming audio, CAD and engineering programs, and transfer of very large files.

❑ Network Monitor and Performance (also called System Monitor) are two administrative tools included in Windows 2000 to assist in gathering data to analyze server and network performance.

❑ Windows 2000 includes many enhanced and new security features not included in Windows NT, and security requirements should be assessed in light of the new options available.

❑ Microsoft recommends the security needs of four distinct categories of network users be analyzed—everyone, staff, users, and partners.

❑ You should develop a prioritized list of network applications and test critical applications in a non-production environment prior to the rollout of Windows 2000.

❑ Application compatibility problems can be addressed in many ways. Some can be fixed by in-house programmers, some are addressed by vendors' patches, some by solutions and workarounds on the Web or in mailing lists or newsgroups. Microsoft Product Support can be consulted, or if the problem is minor, you may choose to ignore it or work around it.

❑ Identify all network protocols in use, remove unused protocols, and review the binding order to optimize network performance.

❑ TCP/IP is Microsoft's recommended protocol suite and it is important that you analyze the existing TCP/IP infrastructure and address such issues as subnetting, placement of routers, domain controllers, DNS, WINS, and DHCP servers, and IP addressing.

Analyze the Network Requirements for Client Computer Access

❏ Hardware is carefully evaluated to ensure that it meets minimum requirements for Windows 2000. If it does not, there are several alternatives, including upgrade, replacement, phased deployment, and Terminal Services.

❏ The network services that are critical to the operation of the network and its important applications, including DHCP, DNS, WINS, Proxy services, and RRAS, are identified.

❏ The technical support structure is analyzed, and the impact of changes in the network infrastructure on its personnel is documented. Tech support personnel and users are trained in the new operating system prior to the rollout.

❏ The needs of end users, along with their current usage patterns, are assessed carefully in planning the design of the new infrastructure, with anticipated growth taken into account.

Analyze the Existing Disaster Recovery Strategy

❏ A comprehensive disaster recovery plan should be a part of the infrastructure design, which includes measures to protect both client computers and servers, as well as the integrity of the network itself.

❏ Disaster recovery plans consist of two parts: measures to prevent catastrophic data loss, and a means of recovering data quickly and efficiently if catastrophic loss does occur.

❏ Windows 2000 disaster protection features include those that address hard-disk failure, damage to operating system or Registry files, complete data loss necessitating reinstallation and restoration.

❏ The Windows 2000 Backup utility uses a wizard that guides you through the process of configuring backup options, which is started by the NTBACKUP command.

❏ Servers are most vulnerable to catastrophic data loss, so protective measures should focus on protecting server hard disks and the data stored there.

SELF TEST

The following questions will help you measure your understanding of the material presented in this chapter. Read all of the choices carefully, as there may be more than one correct answer. Choose all correct answers for each question.

Overview of Analyzing Corporate Technical Requirements

1. Your company wishes to upgrade all its computers to Windows 2000 within the next six months. The network consists of two physical locations, with approximately 500 users at the Dallas location and approximately 300 users at the Houston location. There are currently two Windows NT domains, the Dallas domain and the Houston domain. You have a PDC and two BDCs at each location, and several member servers functioning as WINS servers, file and print servers, a Web server, and an FTP server. Each office has a T1 connection to the Internet. As a member of the network design team, you have been tasked with gathering information for analysis of the existing network, including diagramming both the physical and logical networks. Which of the following is information that you should include in the diagram of the physical network? Choose all that apply.

   A. IP addresses of all network devices

   B. Domain membership

   C. Trust relationships between domains

   D. Names of all computers

2. Which of the following addresses the need for sufficient hardware and bandwidth to support and meet the goals of the features that you plan to implement?

   A. The risk assessment

   B. The deployment design

   C. The capacity plan

   D. The gap analysis

3. You are the administrator of a Windows NT network and management has directed you to direct the transition of the network to Windows 2000 by January 2001. There are several proprietary programs in use on the network that were specially written for the company by a staff programmer who no longer works for the company. You are unable to locate the programmer or find any information pertaining to these applications. What should you do regarding these proprietary programs as you prepare for the Windows 2000 deployment?

A. If the programs work on Windows NT, they will work on Windows 2000, so no testing is necessary.

B. Discard all proprietary programs, since they are not certified as compatible and so will not work with Windows 2000.

C. When you have upgraded one machine to Windows 2000, test the proprietary programs on it to determine whether they will work.

D. Set up a test lab environment with Windows 2000 that is not connected to the production network and install and test the proprietary programs.

Evaluating the Company's Existing and Planned Technical Environment and Goals

4. Which of the following are common WAN links to connect two remote sites, such as company branch offices? Choose all that apply.

    A. ISDN

    B. Ethernet

    C. T-carrier lines

    D. Token Ring

5. Your network spans several geographic locations, including branch offices in San Francisco and Boston that are on separate IP subnets. Managers at the two branch offices wish to conduct live video conferences to gain the benefits of face-to-face meetings without the travel costs. Your current network infrastructure includes a 56K modem connection between the two branch offices. Which of the following might present a problem if the videoconferencing software is deployed in the desired manner using the present infrastructure?

    A. Excessive broadcast traffic could cause a shutdown of the network.

    B. Latency could cause jerkiness and other loss of quality in the video.

    C. Routing problems due to the fact that live video cannot be streamed to a different subnet.

    D. The current infrastructure is sufficient to handle the planned deployment.

6. You wish to analyze status information collected with Performance Monitor. It is especially important that the report compiling the results of your monitoring efforts be completely

accurate, that all data be factored in and any calculations be performed without error. What method of data analysis would be preferred to meet these objectives?

A. Manual analysis

B. Trend analysis

C. Automated analysis

D. Redundant analysis

Analyzing the Impact of Infrastructure Design on the Existing and Planned Technical Environment

7. You have tested your mission critical applications in a Windows 2000 test lab, and discovered that one of them does not run properly in the new operating system environment. The program is a proprietary one that was written by an in-house staff member who has since left the company. Which of the following is a viable solution? Choose all that apply.

A. Contact the vendor of a commercial program that performs a similar function and ask for any Windows 2000 patches; these should also work with your proprietary program if the software performs the same task, such as with a database.

B. Contact the person who wrote the program and request assistance in upgrading it to work with Windows 2000.

C. Replace the program with another commercially marketed program that performs the same tasks.

D. Research the Web to find out how others have solved this problem.

8. You are designing an infrastructure for your new Windows 2000 network. The network will include Windows 2000 domain controllers, Windows NT domain controllers, NetWare 3.11 file servers, and a UNIX Web server. The LAN will connect to the Internet through a Microsoft proxy server. Which of the following protocols *must* be installed on the network? Choose all that apply.

A. TCP/IP

B. NWLink

C. NetBEUI

D. PPTP

9. Which of the following is a new feature in Windows 2000 TCP/IP that can help to speed up data transfer and reduce network traffic?

   A. RTT

   B. The Dynamic Host Configuration Protocol

   C. Large TCP window support

   D. APIPA

Analyzing the Network Requirements for Client Computer Access

10. You have been tasked with designing a new network infrastructure based on TCP/IP communications and using Windows 2000 as the only server operating system. Your network will be connected to the Internet through a Network Address Translation (NAT) host computer, which uses an ISDN line and has a registered IP address assigned by your ISP. You must design the IP addressing scheme for the local area network. Management advises that the internal network should fit into the parameters of a Class C network. Which of the following solutions is best in this situation?

    A. Obtain registered IP addresses from your ISP for all computers on the LAN.

    B. Assign IP addresses from the range 10.0.0.1 through 10.255.255.254 to the internal computers.

    C. Assign any IP addresses you wish; they will be shielded from the Internet by NAT, so it doesn't matter what addresses you use.

    D. Assign IP addresses from the range 192.168.0.1 through 192.168.255.254.

11. You have been tasked with analyzing the current hardware on your network and determining what must be done in order to run Windows 2000 on the computers in the Accounting department. The Accounting department's file server is a Pentium 200MHz with 96MB RAM and a 4GB hard disk. There is 800MB of free disk space. The department's client computers are all AMD K-6 166MHz with 64MB RAM and 2GB hard disks, each with more than 1GB of free space. What, if anything, must be done before Windows 2000 can be deployed in this department? Choose all that apply.

    A. The server's processor must be upgraded.

    B. The server's RAM must be increased.

    C. The server's free hard disk space must be increased.

    D. The clients' processor must be upgraded.

    E. The clients' RAM must be increased.

12. You have been assigned the task of analyzing requirements for deployment of network services in a new Windows 2000 network. Your network requires a means of resolving NetBIOS names to IP addresses that can be dynamically updated. You also require the capability of connecting the LAN to the Internet through a single IP address and modem line, and need to be able to filter incoming and outgoing traffic. IP addresses will be manually assigned by the administrator. Which of the following services are required? Choose all that apply.

  A. DNS

  B. WINS

  C. DHCP

  D. Microsoft Proxy Server

Analyzing the Existing Disaster Recovery Strategy

13. Which of the following should be part of a good disaster protection and recovery plan? Choose all that apply.

  A. A program for regularly scheduled backup of all critical data on the servers

  B. A means of providing fault tolerance for server hard disks containing critical data

  C. A strategy for storing copies of critical backups offsite in case of a natural disaster

  D. A policy requiring users to store important files on a network drive that is regularly backed up

14. Your Windows 2000 Professional computer will not start due to an accidental deletion of some system files. The files are on a fault-tolerant mirrored volume. Which of the following is the easiest way to correct this?

  A. Copy the required system files from another Windows 2000 Professional computer to a floppy, boot into DOS, and then copy them to the computer with the missing files.

  B. Use the Windows 2000 Recovery Console to restore the missing files.

  C. Change the ARC path in your boot.ini file and boot to the mirror disk.

  D. Reinstall Windows 2000 Professional.

15. Which of the following is a feature provided in Windows 2000 that is designed to protect the integrity of your data in case of disaster? Choose all that apply.

  A. Windows Backup

  B. Disk fault tolerance

  C. IPSec

  D. APIPA

16. You have been assigned the task of preparing your company's technical support staff for the Windows 2000 rollout. Part of your assignment involves designing the structure of the technical support department after the deployment. Which of the following should you do to ensure as smooth a transition as possible? Choose all that apply.

    A. Immediately deploy Windows 2000 in the tech support department so personnel can learn firsthand how to use it prior to the company-wide deployment.

    B. Prepare written documentation to aid in assisting users when the new operating system is deployed.

    C. Create a one-level support staff, so that all users will have equal access to top-level engineers, regardless of the nature of their problems.

    D. Train technical support personnel on the operating system prior to deployment.

17. Which of the following is the *most* effective way to assess end users' needs when preparing your analysis of technical requirements?

    A. Ask users what they need.

    B. Have users complete survey forms detailing what tasks they perform in using the network, and any problems they have encountered in accomplishing their objectives.

    C. Gather statistical data from national and international sources showing what the typical network user needs in order to perform at peak efficiency.

    D. Base your assessment of user needs on a small prototypical group.

LAB QUESTION

You have been hired on a project basis to design a network infrastructure for a new Windows 2000 network. The network will be for a medium sized law firm that has offices in two locations, Oklahoma City, OK and Little Rock, AR. The Little Rock office has approximately 200 users, and the Oklahoma City office has approximately 150 users. You wish to connect the two offices in the most cost-effective manner at this time. There is a need to share such files as legal documents between the offices, but budgetary considerations are a priority and you do not wish to deploy videoconferencing or other bandwidth intensive applications in the near future. Both offices currently use Windows NT Workstation on client computers, all of which are Pentium 100 MHz machines with 32 MB of RAM and at least 1 GB of free disk space. All users log on to a single NT domain. The PDC, a Pentium 333MHz with 128MB RAM and 3 GB free disk space, is located at the Little Rock office and there is a BDC, a Pentium 200 with 64MB RAM and approximately 600 MB free disk space, at the Oklahoma City office.

Prepare a design plan addressing the technical requirements for redesign of the network infrastructure, keeping in mind the company priorities. Specifically address:

- Number and placement of Windows 2000 domain controllers
- Hardware recommendations
- Site and subnetting recommendations
- WAN link
- Network protocols

SELF TEST ANSWERS

Overview of Analyzing Corporate Technical Requirements

1. ☑ **A, B,** and **D.** Names of computers, IP addresses of all devices connected to the network, and domain membership information are all part of the physical structure. Note that some information will overlap with the logical network diagram.
   ☒ **C** is incorrect because the trust relationship between domains is a part of the logical infrastructure and has nothing to do with the physical layout of the network.

2. ☑ **C.** The capacity plan addresses the need for sufficient hardware and bandwidth.
   ☒ **A** is incorrect because the risk assessment is a document that outlines risks and contingency plans. **B** is incorrect because the deployment design is a guide to how the rollout will proceed. **D** is incorrect because the gap analysis provides documentation of the gap between the existing network infrastructure and that which is planned or required for the Windows 2000 network.

3. ☑ **D.** The best way to determine if a proprietary program will run on Windows 2000 when there is no information available from the vendor is to create a prototype, or test lab, environment that emulates the production environment as closely as possible and test the program there prior to deployment of Windows 2000.
   ☒ **A** is incorrect because you cannot make the assumption that all programs that work with Windows NT will do so with Windows 2000. Although most will, there are significant differences in the operating systems that could cause failure or unstable behavior. **B** is incorrect because it is not cost-effective to assume that the programs won't work without testing them; the certified logo ensures that a program is compatible with Windows 2000, but the lack of one does not ensure that it isn't. **C** is incorrect because it poses an unnecessary risk to the integrity of the network to test the program in the production environment.

Evaluating the Company's Existing and Planned Technical Environment and Goals

4. ☑ **A** and **C.** Both Integrated Services Digital Network phone lines and high-speed dedicated T-carrier lines can be used for remote connectivity.
   ☒ **B** and **D** are incorrect because Ethernet and Token Ring are both LAN links, used to connect local area networks, but unable due to distance limitations that apply to the specified media, to span the geographic scope involved in establishing a WAN link.

5. ☑ **B.** The problem of *latency,* in which some packets are delayed over the slow, unreliable link, may cause loss of quality in the video to the point that it is unusable.

☒   **A** is incorrect because although the high-bandwidth video transmission could impact other network communications, this is not broadcast traffic. Broadcasts would not impact the computers on a separate subnet because broadcasts don't generally cross routers. **C** is incorrect because live video can be streamed across routers to different subnets if bandwidth is sufficient. **D** is incorrect because the current infrastructure will not adequately handle the live video; the WAN link needs to be upgraded to a higher-performance connection such as ISDN, DSL, or a T-1 connection.

6.   ☑   **C.** The best way to ensure that the data is processed accurately, without the chance for human error, is to use automated analysis methods in which the software performs the compilation of the data and outputs the report.

☒   **A** is incorrect because manual analysis is more prone to error. **B** is incorrect because trend analysis can be performed either manually or via software automation, but does not pertain to the accuracy of the analysis. **D** is incorrect because although it's a good practice to repeat the analysis to ascertain that the same results occur, especially when using manual analysis, this does not ensure the accuracy of an automated method.

Analyzing the Impact of Infrastructure Design on the Existing and Planned Technical Environment

7.   ☑   **B** and **C.** If the person who wrote the program is available, he or she may be able to assist you—probably for a fee—in modifying the program to work under Windows 2000. However, your best long-term solution may be to replace the program with a commercially marketed program that is supported by its vendor.

☒   **A** is incorrect because even though two programs perform the same function, it is highly unlikely that a patch written for one would work with another, even without the obvious differences in filenames, for example. **D** is incorrect because although this is an excellent starting point for troubleshooting compatibility problems with commercially marketed programs, if the software was written in-house it is doubtful that you'll find others using it.

8.   ☑   **A** and **B.** The TCP/IP stack is necessary for connecting to the Internet, and will be used to communicate with the UNIX machine. NWLink (Microsoft's implementation of IPX/SPX) is necessary for connecting to the NetWare 3.11 server.

☒   Although **C**, NetBEUI, could be used to connect to the Windows NT machines, it is not required and TCP/IP is preferred. **D**, Point-to-Point Tunneling Protocol (PPTP), is used for establishing a virtual private network (VPN) connection and is not necessary given the situation described.

9. ☑ C. Increasing the size of the TCP receive window can help to decrease network traffic and speed up transfer.

☒ A is incorrect because RTT is the roundtrip time, an estimate of the length of time it takes a packet to travel to a destination and back. B is incorrect because DHCP is used to assign IP addresses and is not new to Windows 2000. D is incorrect because Automatic Private IP Addressing (APIPA) is a means of providing an IP address to a DHCP client when the DHCP server is unavailable.

Analyzing the Network Requirements for Client Computer Access

10. ☑ D. The address range 192.168.0.1 through 192.168.255.254 is designated by the Internet Assigned Numbers Authority (IANA) for private addressing on class C networks.

☒ A is incorrect because, although you could obtain registered addresses for all computers and establish a routed connection to the Internet, NAT translates the private addresses to the one registered public address and the internal addresses are not visible to the Internet. B is incorrect because the address range 10.0.0.1 through 10.255.255.254 is designated for private class A networks. C is incorrect because, although technically you could assign any addresses you want, these would be considered "illegal" addresses; private addresses should be taken from the designated ranges.

11. ☑ B and C. The minimum requirements for Windows 2000 Server are 133MHz processor, 128MB RAM (256MB recommended) and at least 1GB free disk space.

☒ A is incorrect because the 200MHz processor exceeds requirements (although better performance will result from upgrading to a faster processor). D is incorrect because the minimum requirements for Windows 2000 Professional include a 133MHz processor and an AMD (Intel compatible) meets requirements. E is incorrect because the minimum required RAM for Windows 2000 Professional is 64MB and the client machines meet the requirement. Windows 2000 Professional also requires a minimum of 600MB free disk space.

12. ☑ A, B, and D. DNS is an integral part of the Windows 2000 domain structure and is required in order for Active Directory to function. WINS is used to reconcile NetBIOS names to IP addresses. Although this can also be done with an LMHOSTS file, the latter is not dynamically updated. Microsoft Proxy Server can perform address translation, allowing you to connect the LAN to the Internet via a single IP address. It also offers firewall/filtering functions.

☒ C is incorrect because DHCP is not needed, given the statement that IP addresses will be manually assigned by the administrator.

Analyzing the Existing Disaster Recovery Strategy

13. ☑ **A, B, C, and D.** Regularly scheduled backup of critical data is a vital part of any disaster recovery plan. Disk fault tolerance measures (RAID) on the servers will prevent loss of important data in the event of a disk failure. Critical backups should be stored offsite and updated on a regular basis so they will be available even if fire or flood destroys the server and everything in its vicinity. Policies requiring users to store important files in a specified network location ensures that they will be backed up regularly.

14. ☑ **B.** The key to this question is the word "easiest." Although other options might work, the simplest and least time-consuming way to repair the damage is to use the Windows 2000 Recovery Console, which allows you to copy files from a floppy or CD.
    ☒ **A** is incorrect because you will not be able to access a volume on a dynamic disk from DOS. **C** is incorrect because the deletion would have been mirrored to the second disk. **D** is incorrect because, although reinstalling Windows 2000 Professional would fix the problem, it is certainly not the easiest way.

15. ☑ **A and B.** The Windows Backup utility is provided to allow manual or scheduled backups to tape or to file. Disk fault tolerance support, for RAID 5 and mirrored volumes, is included in Windows 2000 Server.
    ☒ **C** is incorrect because IPSec provides data security, but does not offer protection against disaster. **D** is incorrect because APIPA is an automatic addressing feature and does not offer disaster protection.

16. ☑ **B and D.** Thorough written documentation to which the technical staff can refer when assisting users, especially in the early stages of the deployment, will save much time and enhance efficiency. All technical support personnel should receive training in the new operating system prior to deployment.
    ☒ **A** is incorrect because deploying the new operating system in the tech support department without first training personnel in its use would create chaos. **C** is incorrect because a multilevel support structure in which personnel with extensive expertise focus on the most difficult or most mission-critical problems is much more effective than a one-tier system.

17. ☑ **B.** Having your users complete detailed survey forms will give you objective information on which to base your assessment of user needs.
    ☒ **A** is incorrect because asking users what they need is likely to result in their telling you what they *want,* or not being able to come up with anything at all when put on the spot. **C** is incorrect because statistical data based on other networks will not give a true picture of the

unique needs of users in your own network environment. **D** is incorrect because a small prototypical group may not be representative of all users on the network.

LAB ANSWER

Your design plan should address the following points:

- Number and placement of Windows 2000 domain controllers: Best practice is to place a domain controller at each physical location so users will not have to log on over a slow WAN link. If budget permits, a second domain controller at each location will provide fault tolerance.

- Hardware recommendations: The current PDC should be upgraded to 256MB RAM to run Windows 2000 Server with Active Directory at optimal performance, although it will run on 128 MB RAM. The processor does not require upgrading. There is sufficient disk space to install Windows 2000 but it would be preferable to add a hard disk in anticipation of growth. The current BDC must be upgraded to at least 128 MB RAM (256MB preferred) to run Windows 2000 Server with Active Directory. You also need to add at least 1 GB of disk space. Current client computers will run Windows 2000 Professional but meet only the bare minimum requirements. Performance will be slow. Options include upgrading client machines to Windows 2000 Professional if fast performance is not an issue, or continue to use Windows NT 4.0 Workstation as the client to Windows 2000 servers until the budget allows upgrading client hardware, or installing Terminal Services on the servers and running the 32 bit terminal client software on the NT Workstation machines if users need the Windows 2000 desktop and better performance before the client machines' hardware can be upgraded.

- Site and subnetting recommendations: The best practice in this case is to create two IP subnets defined as two separate Active Directory sites, one at each physical location. This will prevent replication traffic over the slow WAN link from clogging bandwidth.

- WAN link: Because budget issues are a priority and there is no need for high performance connectivity at this time, the most cost-effective solution is to use a 56Kbps dialup (modem) connection between the two offices. For better performance at slightly higher cost, 128Kbps ISDN could be used.

■ Network protocols: Although TCP/IP is the default LAN protocol for Windows 2000, in this case because there is no mention of a need for Internet connectivity, you could gain some performance advantage by using NWLink instead, as it is a faster protocol. Although NetBEUI is faster still, it is not routable and thus is not an option if you subnet the network. If you anticipate connectivity to the Internet or other WANs in the future, or compatibility with UNIX machines is an issue, you will want to use TCP/IP.

MICROSOFT CERTIFIED SYSTEMS ENGINEER

4

Designing a TCP/IP Networking Strategy

CERTIFICATION OBJECTIVES

I n previous operating systems, Microsoft included, Transmission Control protocol/Internet protocol was not a given. Proprietary networking protocols were more often in use and the widespread use of Netware file and print servers, with its IPX protocol, was the way most network connectivity was accomplished. Even as late as Windows NT 4.0, IPX was a default protocol along with TCP/IP. However, the market landscape has changed. No business can now survive without access to the Internet or intranets. With this fact in mind, Microsoft has made a shift away from the earlier protocols of NetBEUI and IPX and has made TCP/IP the default protocol on installation of Windows 2000.

But the fact of the matter is that TCP/IP as an access mechanism to the Internet is a small part of what it's capable of doing. It is not merely two protocols slapped together for file and print access. Rather, it is a whole group or suite of protocols and utilities that collectively are known as a stack.

The tools that make up Microsoft's TCP/IP stack have been expanded in Windows 2000 to encompass more than in Windows NT 4.0. The new Requests for Comments (RFCs) published by the Internet Engineering Task Force (IETF) enhance the capabilities of TCP/IP. Such enhancements are most noticeable in the new implementation of DNS where the addition of the SRV record has reduced the reliance on NetBIOS altogether and DNS is no longer a static database requiring administrator input of all DNS records.

There are also some changes that are specific to the core components of TCP/IP. However, even as Microsoft updates the TCP/IP stack, more changes are coming for TCP/IP. It is an evolving platform.

This is in fact one of the many reasons TCP/IP has done so well. Because of its open architecture and the fact that no one company or organization can control the evolution of TCP/IP, it has grown out of an industry need. Other factors that contribute to its widespread use are:

- It is stable and robust, with its core roots going back more than 30 years. We have now had ample time to work out many of the bugs.

- It has been a cross-platform, client-server framework since the beginning. All modern operating systems now support TCP/IP. When Novell released Netware 5, they also signaled a shift as they moved away from IPX and towards TCP/IP by including it as the default protocol. TCP/IP allows you to connect from Unix to Macintosh to PC with relative ease.

- ■ It's routable. You can simply segment off an area of the network and allow routers to pass the traffic based on logically assigned Layer 3 addresses. Some protocols, such as NetBEUI, LAT, and DLC, do not support logical networks (Layer 3 addressing). TCP/IP does.

- ■ Scalable. TCP/IP can accommodate networks from as little as two or three hosts to as many as you might want to imagine. With a class A address under IPv4, you can have as many as 16.77 million hosts per logical subnet. This is an extreme example, but gives you an indication of the range of networks that TCP/IP can support. I can start my new business and watch it grow. My network infrastructure can grow right along with it.

There are many reasons why you would use TCP/IP as your networking protocol of choice. Here we will show you how to design an efficient TCP/IP network.

Overview of Designing TCP/IP Networking Strategies

When designing a TCP/IP network, several things must be taken into consideration. Before you begin the design, you need to understand the main areas of TCP/IP and what components are new to Windows 2000. The underlying theory of the new features is important to a fully functional and optimized network. Let's begin with a few basics as a review of the protocol.

TCP/IP is a suite of protocols. There are various elements of this group that span from Layer 1 to Layer 7 of the OSI model. The TCP/IP model is a four-layer module. Figure 4-1 compares the OSI and TCP/IP models.

The design of Network Interface Layer of the TCP/IP model will not be a consideration here. However, I will quickly go into an overview of the other components listed in Figure 4-1.

FIGURE 4-1   OSI to TCP/IP model comparison

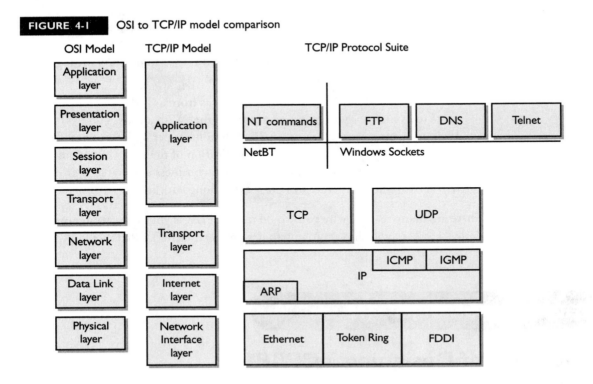

Network Layer

Beginning at the network layer, we see the Address Resolution Protocol (ARP). The actual identification and communication of two hosts on a network is between machines identified at Layer 2 of the OSI model. There is a "burnt-in," or Media Access Control (MAC), address on each Network Interface Card (NIC) that identifies a machine in the data link frame. This is the same information that is in the frame destination and source addresses if you have done a packet analyzer capture.

However, we would like to assign logical addresses that we can manipulate according to our requirements. So, to match up the logical address we assign the physical address that's on the card (TCP/IP uses ARP to figure out who's who). When we request some information from machine 148.51.13.240, TCP/IP sends a hardware broadcast (FF-FF-FF-FF-FF-FF), which is processed by all machines. The machines with the correct IP addresses will respond with their MAC addresses, and a session can be established between the two hosts after the MAC addresses have been resolved.

Internet Layer

The primary purpose of the components at the Internet layer is routing and addressing. Here are the main components of this layer:

Internet Protocol (IP)

The Internet Protocol or IP is the logical addressing mechanism of the group. If you read any books on routing, you will also quickly realize that it is dependent on IP. An IP address not only defines the host on the network, but the network itself. IP decides (with the help of the subnet mask) whether the host is on your network or on another network.

If the host is on the same network as your host, it resolves itself directly for the destination host's MAC address. If the host is on another network, it will first consult an internal table called a *routing table* to assess where the packet should be sent in order to allow it to arrive at its destination.

If there is no route specified to the destination network, the packet will be sent to the default gateway. We will go through a little bit more on IP in a moment and a lot on subnetting.

Internet Group Management Protocol (IGMP)

The Internet Group Management Protocol or IGMP is a grossly underused protocol that assists with multicasting. IGMP informs the routers and hosts on a network that hosts in a group exist. Instead of broadcasting to everyone, or a single host to a single host, IGMP allows us to do the one-to-many communication. More information on IGMP is available in RFC 1112.

Internet Control Message Protocol (ICMP)

The Internet Control Message Protocol or ICMP reports control messages and errors on the IP network. If you have used PING you have used ICMP. Another important component of ICMP is the source-quench message that informs hosts that routers are unable to keep up with the stream of data they are sending them. It is a kind of "shut up for a second" for TCP/IP hosts.

Transport or Host-to-Host Layer

The transport layer, also known as the host-to-host layer, is responsible for either establishing a connection-oriented or connectionless communication session. There are two components of this layer.

Transmission Control Protocol (TCP)

The Transmission Control Protocol or TCP is a connection-oriented, reliable delivery, byte-stream communication service. Early on, communication mediums were weak at best. Errors were as regular as clockwork and *when* an error occurred (not if), you had to have a recovery plan.

TCP uses a three-way handshake to make sure the destination host is available before sending data, and requires an acknowledgment (ACK) for each packet of data that it sends. Each data packet sent via TCP is also assigned a sequence number so that the receiving system can assemble them in the proper order and request that the sending system resend any missing packets. TCP is sometimes referred to as a *streams-oriented* protocol since it ensures that the higher-level protocols depending on it receive information as an unbroken stream of bytes.

User Datagram Protocol (UDP)

The User Datagram Protocol or UDP is TCP's evil twin. It is a connectionless, unreliable communication service. While UDP was designed to operate at the same level as TCP for the same functions, it does not incorporate any of the reliability of TCP. Guaranteed delivery was not part of the design of UDP, speed was.

Each ACK in TCP slows the data transfer process, but does ensure we have received the data. UDP does not use ACKs. Some would have us believe that UDP is only appropriate for small downloads when we can afford to restart the transmission from scratch. Today's networks are not the same as the early 80s and because of this, we are transferring some data types, such as streaming audio, that would be far too choppy if transmission required an ACK for every 8k. But it works very well on UDP.

Application Layer

TCP/IP is an evolving protocol, so not all components of the stack are included in Figure 4-1. Indeed, there are many application layer protocols that are outside the scope of this manual. We will have a look at DNS and a quick peek at RIP in the next few sections. Suffice it to say, we've been building this for 30 years.

One other important point is the little sublayer in between the application and the transport layers. This layer is divided into halves, the NetBIOS over TCP/IP (NetBT) and the Windows Sockets (WinSock) side. These both represent interfaces in what would be considered the session layer in the OSI model. Most of our utilities, and all of the true Unix commands, use the WinSock interface, but the old

NT commands (NET commands) still make use of NetBIOS calls and as such, must pass through the NetBIOS interface or NetBT. Soon we will be able to dispose of NetBIOS altogether, but today is not that day. Most legacy application programs still require the NetBIOS interface, but Windows 2000 is making inroads here.

New TCP/IP Features in Windows 2000

Actually, very few of the components of the stack are listed here. With the latest version of Microsoft's TCP/IP stack for Windows 2000, some new features have been incorporated, such as:

- *Automatic Private IP Addressing (APIPA)*. The first Microsoft product with features was Windows 98. It has now been incorporated into Windows 2000. If a DHCP server is unavailable or the end user has misconfigured the IP addressing settings so that he has chosen to obtain an address from a DHCP server when none exists, a computer can be given a "pretend" address in the range of 169.254.x.x. Although they will now get an IP address from the system, they will only be able to contact other devices who have had their addresses assigned via APIPA. Not really a cure, but for very small networks that will not be connecting to the Internet, the Internet Assigned Number Authority (IANA) has provided a mechanism for easy address configuration without the use of a DHCP server.

- *Bandwidth control*. Two mechanisms that have been added to Windows 2000 are the *BAP* (or *BACP)* and *QoS*. *Bandwidth Allocation Protocol* is described in RFC 2125 and is used for multi-link PPP connections that can be dynamically allocated or de-allocated bandwidth. If you need more bandwidth, BAP gives you more.
  The *Quality of Service* specification (RFC 2212 and 2210) allows you to prioritize the types of traffic on your network. Quite often we may have time-sensitive data such as a desktop conferencing package that is being blocked from functioning by a lower-priority utility, such as e-mail. Although we don't want to abandon the e-mail altogether, we do want more resources allocated to the other types of traffic. Think of it as "smarts" for your network.

- *Security*. For some this is the crown jewel of the new stack. New features in IP filtering and the implementation of *IPSec* (RFC 1825), or for that matter, the addition of *Kerberos* (RFC 1510), *RADIUS* (RFC 2059), and the *Extensible Authentication Protocol EAP* (RFC 2284) have made the insecure nature of TCP/IP much more secure. For those who are security conscious, this means that the Internet is (slowly) becoming a safer place for our data exchanges. *PPTP/MPPE* and *L2TP/IPSec* help as well. Filtering allows you to block all incoming traffic except that which you allow. IPSec provides a mechanism for not only encrypting data (ESP), but also to authenticate (AH and ESP) the system that sent the information.

■ *Improved performance.* The Windows 2000 TCP/IP protocol stack has been tuned for higher performance. First is the TCP Selective Acknowldgement (SACK) defined in RFC 2018. Based on TCP window size in Windows NT 4.0, the receiving host would send an ACK when either the receive window had been filled or two sequenced packets had arrived. If the receiving host only received packets 1, 3, and 5, a NACK or negative ACK is sent to indicate that the sending host should retransmit the information in its entirety, since no two sequenced packets arrived. With SACK, the receiver selectively acknowledges the data it has received and asks the sender to retransmit only packets 2, 4, and 6. Less data needs to be retransmitted, which results in better performance. Second, the TCP extensions for High Performance (RFC 1323) have been added. Microsoft calls this *Large TCP Windows.* It gives us scaled-window sizes and a time stamp that incorporates a Round Trip Time Measurement (RTTM) that improves the performance over WANs by scaling the window size on large data transfers instead of requiring an ACK after a fixed window size.

■ *ICMP router discovery.* This new feature is defined in RFC (1256) and allows a host to send an ICMP packet to find a default gateway when one hasn't been configured. This is very useful in most scenarios; however, this feature is disabled by default. You will have to enable this feature.

■ If you have an RRAS server participating in the discovery process as an "advertiser," you must set up RRAS by selecting IP ROUTING, then GENERAL, then choose the interface you would like to enable. From the GENERAL tab, select ENABLE ROUTER DISCOVERY ADVERTISEMENTS.

■ *DNS Caching.* The DNS caching resolver in Windows 2000 improves the speed of host-name resolution, although with the changes in the caching resolver, the IPCONFIG command has been updated to allow you to view and manipulate the local DNS cache. There are a few other changes to IPCONFIG, so take a look by issuing IPCONFIG /? from the command prompt.

■ *Disabling NetBIOS over TCP/IP (NetBT)*. Windows 2000 has the capability of completely turning off NetBT if you don't need it. Be careful, as this could prompt a few connectivity issues, since many systems will expect it to be turned on. A possible scenario where you might use this capability is on a bastion host between your internal and external networks where you would not want to use NetBT. To disable NetBT, open the adapter Properties, then the TCP/IP Properties. Next, choose Advanced and click on the WINS tab. There you find three choices for NetBT: ENABLE, DISABLE, or USE DHCP SETTINGS. See Figure 4-2.

FIGURE 4-2

Disabling
NetBIOS over
TCP/IP

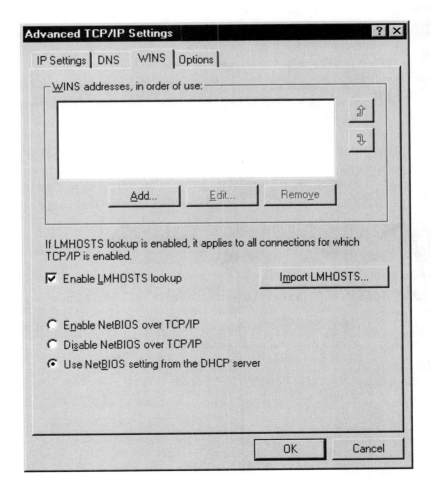

SCENARIO & SOLUTION

I have a network of Windows 2000 Professional, but no servers that supply DHCP addresses. What can I do?	Use APIPA if you do not have a DHCP server. If you require Internet access, you can configure a NAT server to use an IP address from the APIPA network ID on its internal interface.
My network requires improved security. What can I do to create a more secure network?	Use TCP/IP filtering and IPSec to increase your network security.
I have multiple ISDN lines and would like to have another line come up when one is being used at 75 percent. Is there anything that can do this?	Yes. BAP can be configured to automatically bring up another multi-link PPP line if you exceed a pre-set threshold.

There are many new features for TCP/IP in Windows 2000. Do yourself a favor by reviewing the Windows 2000 Help file for another explanation of what has been added to TCP/IP.

There are a few new things that must be taken into consideration for our TCP/IP network. We will look at some of these, such as QoS, IPSec, and filters, in much more detail. For now, let's look at the addressing mechanism and how to subnet.

CERTIFICATION OBJECTIVE 4.02

Analyzing IP Subnet Requirements

IPv4 addresses are 32-bit binary numbers that are converted to dotted decimal notation for our own convenience. IPV4 addresses are divided into a section that identifies networks and individual hosts on each network. As part of the design, you must first decide where to break up your system into networks. Here are some considerations.

Geographic and Business Unit Considerations

In some cases, the boundaries of your network are based on geography or corporate politics. Distance limitations and administrative units will require that physical cable segments be separated by routers. You must have a unique network number for each physical segment of your network. A unique network ID is also required for each wide area connection. With this information in mind, you need to determine how many networks are required for a given organization.

It is also helpful to understand that all hosts on the same network will be doing at least some of their work through broadcasts. As pointed out earlier, ARP must broadcast for a MAC address of units on their own segment. More hosts that exist in a network forces all hosts to process these broadcasts and reduces network performance. Also, in an Ethernet environment we must take into account the concept of collisions and their associated overhead. By reducing the number of hosts in a broadcast domain or a collision domain, we can have increased throughput and decreased collisions. The optimal environment would involve a single machine in a broadcast/collision domain, thereby negating any broadcasts or collisions. However, in a routed environment this is unrealistic. But this is exactly what we do in a switched environment. Using a combination of switches and routers can greatly reduce traffic and improve performance.

Another consideration is the number of routers required using slow WAN links. Expensive WAN links should be minimized if possible. If an organization requires five subnets within a building, but through the use of VLSM and CIDR (explained shortly) we can offer just a single WAN connection to the main office in New York, we've aided that company in two areas. First, we've cut the telephone company charges by a factor of 5 by not having a router connection to New York in all five subnets. Second, we only require a single network ID to go to New York. In this case, we are trying to achieve a flat model for our wide area connections.

Active Directory Replication

If you have delved into Active Directory, you will eventually be presented with the concept of *sites*. A site is one or more well-connected IP subnets. This means they need to be connected together by a fast connection, not a 56K link. While domains are the administrative unit of Windows 2000, sites are the physical units. With the multi-master domain controller environment we need to control how Active Directory replication occurs. However, we can only control it between sites.

All domain controllers within a single site will replicate using RPC based on a change notification. When a change occurs, it is sent immediately (after an interval with a default of five minutes). We also send the information uncompressed. This would not be good over a slow link. Over a slow link it would be much better to send the information at a specified time and compress the traffic. This is, in fact, exactly how replication traffic between sites occurs.

However, all domain controllers are placed in a single site (called Default-First-Site-Name) when you set up Active Directory. It is up to you to create the sites and move the domain controllers to those sites. When replicating within a site, it is important to note that our replication transport will be RPC and only RPC. When replicating between sites, we can choose between RPC and SMTP as our protocols for replication.

exam
ⓌⓐⓉⓒⓗ

Active Directory will be a key component on all Windows 2000 exams. Make sure you understand how replication occurs within a site as well as inter-site replication.

Another piece of the Active Directory design is the placement of domain controllers for efficient access. It is a good design to have at least two domain controllers in each site for redundancy. No sites should be left without a DC, as this will force authentication across WAN connections.

Also consider site link bridges. If you are familiar with exchange replication topology, then you may be familiar with this concept. The standard method of replication is *everyone to everyone*. It may be more efficient to have devices within a site replicate their information to each other in this fashion, since it will produce a "tight consistency" in the Active Directory services data.

When going between sites it would be better to channel the replication data through a single connection to the other side. This is known as a *bridgehead server* and will focus the traffic. It will also allow us to create a path from one site to another. Site A is connected to site B, site B is connected to site C. We can then set up a connector that replicates from site A to C through site B. This is our site link bridge.

The following exercise will show you how to configure Active Directory site links and site link bridges.

EXERCISE 4-1

Designing an Active Directory Site Topology

To complete this exercise will require at least one Windows 2000 server running Active Directory.

ABC Corp. has decided to implement Windows 2000 and you have been hired to configure a server to accommodate this decision. During initial discussions with the IS staff at ABC, you have come up with the following information:

- There are three locations at ABC that will be connected using T1 from Toronto to Detroit and a second T1 from Detroit to Seattle. No location will have more than 200 systems. They have obtained ten class C address ranges for the locations.

- Two distinct business units exist at ABC, an "R&D and Manufacturing" unit and a "Sales and Administration" unit, which will remain autonomous.

- No existing networking infrastructure or Directory Service exists, though they aggressively plan to implement not only an internal network with DNS, but also connectivity to the Internet and a possible Extranet in the future.

You have been authorized to recommend redundant hardware where necessary. You must indicate how many sites, servers, and domains to set up. Your design must also provide an efficient replication mechanism for the Active Directory data.

In this design, you would begin by setting up a TCP/IP design to accommodate the three sites. The Active Directory topology will be more efficient if we can compress the traffic between sites and schedule their delivery. Since they have already obtained the addresses, it is merely an act of implementing them.

Secondly, with two business units we would logically divide these up into two domains, as each wishes to control the users and resources for their own business unit. Since the design allows us to include redundancy, we would likely recommend two domain controllers for each domain per site. Recommending two domain controllers per site increases the availability of logon services in each of the sites and domains. This gives us 12 servers configured as domain controllers.

Please complete the following on your system:

1. To create the sites, we will go into Active Directory sites and services on one of the domain controllers and create our sites. To do this, right-click on the sites node and choose new site. Type in the name of the site you will be creating and, for now, select the "DEFAULTIPSITELINK" object. Create the remaining sites.

2. Next, open the Inter-Site Transport node and right-click on the IP folder and choose new site link. Create a site link for Toronto-Detroit that includes the Toronto site and the Detroit site previously created. Create a second site link called Detroit-Seattle and also create a site link bridge by right-clicking on the IP folder and choosing new site link bridge. Call this Toronto-Seattle and include the site links of Toronto-Detroit and Detroit-Seattle.

3. Lastly, create the three subnets by right-clicking on the subnets folder and choosing new subnet. Enter the IP address and subnet mask for each of the subnets. From the select a site object for this subnet box, select the appropriate site that will be associated with this subnet.

4. One last task left, Under Default-first-site-name, open the servers folder and select a server, right-click it, and choose move. Move the server to the appropriate site and you are now configured for replication. (If you are completing this exercise from a single server, you will only be able to move a single server.)

5. To change the replication schedule, open the Inter-Site Transports and open IP. Right-click the site link for the Toronto-Detroit site link and choose properties. Click the change button at the bottom and choose the hours of 5 a.m. to 9 p.m., Monday to Friday, and click on the replication not available radio button. Complete the same procedure for the second site link. Your replication topology has now been configured.

DNS Zone Replication

DNS has changed significantly in Windows 2000. A great deal of press has been delivered on the SRV record and the Dynamic update features of this implementation. Less noticed is the introduction of IXFR and the ability to include zone replication information in an Active Directory replication.

As part of any normal DNS implementation, the concept is to distribute the information across multiple Name Servers. This is accomplished through a mechanism called zone transfers or zone replication. A primary name server is responsible for maintaining the entries for this or multiple domains or subdomains. This information is kept in a text file (by default) referred to as the *zone* file. A zone is a part of the DNS database for which it is authoritative. Secondary name servers obtain this information from either the primary name server directly or from another secondary name server. In either case, the source of the transfer is known as the *master* server.

In previous generations of DNS, the zone transfer was always initiated by the secondary server and the master would send all of the records in the zone file, not just the updated ones. This transfer of the entire zone file was initiated by an AXFR queries from the Secondary DNS server. RFC 1995 defines a new way of transferring the information using an IXFR or incremental transfer query.

In this method, only the changes to the database are transferred, reducing the amount of data sent. Windows 2000 also allows interoperation with older implementations of DNS through the use of both types of transfer mechanisms.

The Windows 2000 DNS implementation supports a transfer mechanism known as *fast transfers*. The fast transfer allows multiple records to be included in a single DNS message. If the destination DNS server does not support fast transfers, the Windows 2000 DNS server can adjust and use the non-compressed method of transferring zone information.

Also new is DNS NOTIFY (RFC1996) that allows the primary DNS server to inform secondary servers that a change has occurred, as opposed to waiting for the refresh interval on the secondary to expire. The default interval for the refresh interval is 15 minutes, which can lead to communication problems if changes occurring at the primary are not reflected on the secondary. DNS NOTIFY improves this.

Although the zone transfer can occur on any DNS servers that exist in your organization, DNS services on Windows 2000 domain controllers have a distinct advantage over non-domain controllers. DNS can be integrated into the Active Directory service and take advantage of the ADS replication topology. This saves us from setting up masters and Secondary DNS Servers, and allows us to just piggyback off an infrastructure already in place. DNS then becomes an object within the Active Directory and is replicated in a multi-master fashion just like all other ADS replication information. This means that we no longer have a single point of failure at the Primary DNS Server. ADS will also allow for secure, dynamic updates based on ACL entries.

There are two issues to be aware of, though. Only DNS servers implemented on domain controllers can participate in this type of replication. You will still be able to do a standard zone transfer to servers on NT 4 or Unix box. Secondly, only primary DNS zones, not secondary, can be DS integrated.

When you set up your DNS topology, decide if you will be able to go with a Windows 2000 ADS configuration first. If this is possible, then it is much more beneficial to go with the Active Directory integrated DNS. If you must replicate with non-Windows 2000 domain controller installations of DNS, then you should choose to use a secondary at each remote site for redundancy, load balancing, and for the improved performance you will receive by having a local DNS server and not being forced across a slow link to resolve host names. Even choosing to use a caching-only server will improve performance.

Changing between the different configurations is very straightforward and can be changed back and forth at any time. Simply open the DNS manager under administrative tools and select your forward lookup zones property sheet (don't forget to do the same for the reverse lookup zone). Figure 4-3 shows how.

This may, of course, not be possible since corporate politics may become involved. Many large organizations have DNS implemented on Unix servers in place and the thought of passing over control of the name space to the Windows 2000 boxes is not an acceptable option.

If this is the case, you may still be able to integrate Windows 2000 into the existing infrastructure by having a subdomain name space created for the Active Directory services. Planning and consideration must be given as much to what currently exists as to what can be done. If you are receiving pressure from the IS staff to remain with a pure Unix DNS solution, remember that the DNS server must at minimum support SRV records (BIND 4.9.6), or preferably SRV, dynamic updates, and IFXR (BIND 8.2).

FIGURE 4-3

DNS change
zone type

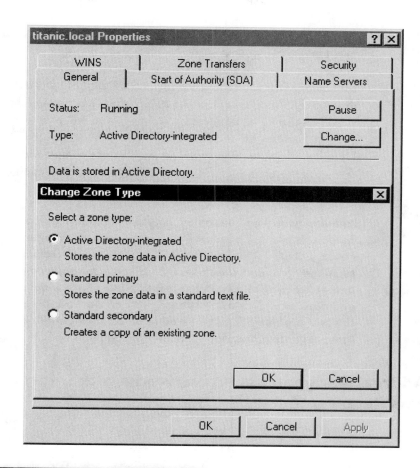

Designing a TCP/IP Addressing and Implementation Plan

Regardless of what you do in the realm of addressing, you will definitely have to choose how you implement your addressing strategy. You may assign IP addresses manually by assigning them at each machine or by configuring a DHCP server. If you choose not to do either, you will be given the previously mentioned automatic private IP address (APIPA).

DHCP is the easiest way to implement the addressing scheme, and it gives you much more centralized control, however you will not be guaranteed a specific address. For servers where an address needs to be static, you will need to use manual IP addressing. This allows you to register the FQDN to IP address mapping in a non-dynamic DNS server such as the BIND 4.3 Name Servers that are in common use.

APIPA should be avoided. Even though you will receive an address, it is not a good mechanism for connectivity if other addressing such as static addresses or DHCP are in place. It also gives you no Internet connectivity unless you are going through a Network Address Translation (NAT) device configured for the 169.254.x.x range.

on the *Job*

APIPA may very well be something you wish to turn off completely on your system. To do this you will need to make some registry changes. Open up regedt32 and HKEY_LOCAL_MACHINE\SYSTEM\CurrentControlSet\Services\Tcpip\Parameters\Interfaces and then open the subtree for your network adapter. Create a new value for IPAutoconfigurationEnabled with a data type of REG_DWORD and data of 0. This will disable APIPA on that adapter. The bad news is that this will probably need to be done on a machine-by-machine basis, since in some organizations, each machine will have a wide variety of NICs.

IP Address Assignments on Networks with Internet Access Requirements

The Internet standard for IP addressing spelled out in RFC 791 (or if you prefer, STD 5) identifies the concept of Classful addresses based on the first four bits of the address, creating five distinct class addresses. (Its predecessor, RFC 760, defines only a single class where the network is the first octet and the hosts are the remaining three octets. It's considered obsolete.) There are five classes of which A through C are given over to individual network/host assignments. Class D is used for multicast groups and Class E is listed as "experimental." Table 4-1 gives a breakdown of the classes and their uses.

When choosing an IP addressing structure, it is important to remember that there are both public addressing and private addressing structures that are defined in RFC 1918. The scheme you choose will in fact be partially decided by your Internet usage.

TABLE 4-1   Class Address Summary

Property	Class A	Class B	Class C	Class D	Class E
W Octet Decimal Value	1-126	128-191	192-223	224-239	240-255
Default Subnet Mask	255.0.0.0	255.255.0.0	255.255.255.0	N/A	N/A
# of available networks	126	16,384	2,098,152	N/A	N/A
# of available host per network	16,777,214	65,534	254	N/A	N/A
Function	Net/Host ID	Net/Host ID	Net/Host ID	Mulitcast Group	Experimental
First four binary bits	0xxx	10xx	110x	1110	1111

All hosts directly connected to the Internet require a unique public address assigned either by American Registry of Internet Numbers (ARIN) or your point of presence provider (likely your ISP). If you have chosen to use a public addressing scheme, there are some serious gotchas. First, there is the security issue. You are directly connected to the Internet. You are left with limited security at best.

The second issue is growth. You will require a unique IP address for each machine directly connected to the Internet and this means there is the potential to run out of assigned addresses as your network grows. If you do run out of addresses, you will have to request additional addresses from your provider. On the plus side, however, you will own the addresses and if you have obtained a large block of addresses directly from ICANN or ARIN (see them at www.icann.org and www.arin.net, respectively), you can sublet the numbers you don't need.

You should only use public addresses if you have a large number of hosts that require direct access to the Internet and you have NO concern whatsoever about the data on your network, as security will be an issue.

The other possibility is to use private addressing for your network.

Intranet Addressing Infrastructure

If the systems you are using are not directly connected to the Internet then you may choose to use a private addressing system. RFC 1918 lists IP address ranges that are reserved for use in private addressing schemes. There are private ranges in classes A through C that allow an organization to assign from 254 to 16.77 million addresses to their network without obtaining an address from ARIN. The class A addresses are in the 10.0.0.1 to 10.255.255.254 range, the class B addresses are from 172.16.0.1 to 172.31.255.254, while the class C addresses are in the 192.168.0.1 to 192.168.255.254 range.

The advantages of a private addressing scheme are visible from the start. Security is improved. Since Internet routers do not forward requests to hosts with private network addresses, you do not need to worry about Internet intruders making direct connections to these computers. We also have an almost unending supply of IP addresses at our disposal. The 16.77 million host addresses should suffice for at least the foreseeable future.

There are always disadvantages that accompany advantages and this is no exception. Yes, security is much better. But you have lost a great deal in functionality. You are not connected to the Internet. Part of RFC 1918 dictates that if we are to agree to these numbers being private, routers should drop packets coming from these networks if they are being forwarded to a public address. If we are to use no other mechanism than private addressing on the network, we will remain unable to connect to the Internet. This is unacceptable.

If we are to have a functional system we are going to need to incorporate functions and features of both public and private addressing systems. To ensure the security of our organization we will use a private addressing system that allows us to use as many addresses as we wish. This will give us a considerable cost saving in the area of IP address leases. (ARIN does provide the price list on their web site. Costs rage from a few hundred to $20,000 per year based on the number of addresses you wish to lease.)

We will, however, buy a few public addresses for an Internet presence. We will gain the security of private addressing and offset the Internet connectivity issue by installing a firewall and Network Address Translation (NAT) device to give us our access to the Public IP address.

If, however, we can use 16.77 million addresses in that class A private address range, we may have bigger issues than connecting to the Internet. If we install all those machines in a single network, our functional design will come crashing to the ground because of an inordinate amount of broadcasts and collisions. We need to break this up into subnets.

Subnetting Based on Number of Subnets or Number of Hosts per Subnet

The only thing you really need to remember about subnetting is $2^n - 2$. After you've finished this section, you'll see why.

First, let's review the reasons for using a subnet mask. Part of the function of IP is to route packets through networks. It does this by using the subnet mask to determine which portion of the address represents the network ID and which represents the host ID. It then compares that to its own address when sending.

For example, if my address is 142.151.107.4 and my subnet mask is the default of 255.255.0.0 and I'm sending to 142.165.32.8, I will compare my first two octets to your first two octets and if they match, I ARP for your address and communication begins. In this case they don't, so I will ARP for the router and pass it on to the other network that way. If, however, I had a subnet mask of 255.0.0.0, these two machines would believe they are on the same network (142), and I would try to ARP directly for the other machine. This would fail, however, if they are on physically separate segments connected by routers.

The problem that I just described is not insurmountable if you know how to play the game. We have been given an enormous group of numbers. Could we not carve this up? In a proper state of mind, I would never put together a network with 16 million PCs, routers, and network attached printers. For one thing, I would be unable to find a building large enough.

RFC 950 says that if I have too many numbers I can subdivide them down into something more manageable. The rules of classful subnetting, however, set up a few rules on how I can divide this large network into smaller ones without purchasing a new network range from ARIN. The only cost to you for implementing this is the cost of the routers, so I can follow the rules to save a couple of bucks.

exam
ⓦatch

Get some practice using the other method of showing subnet masks. Microsoft has adopted the style of using prefixes for the masks instead of using the older standard notation of 10.0.0.0 with a subnet mask of 255.255.0.0. This same mask would be written as 10.0.0.0 /16 in the newer notation, and merely means that the first 16 bits are being used for networks.

What we are planning to do here is to steal some of those 32 bits currently used for host assignment for the use of network IDs. A class B address that uses a prefix of 16 means the same thing as a class B address that uses a subnet mask of 255.255.0.0. A prefix of 16 means that 16 bits are used, or to put it in binary terms,

11111111.11111111.00000000.00000000 equals 255.255.0.0.) We will steal another n amount of bits for the sub network we are going to create.

This brings us to Rule Number One. Steal to the right of the default subnet mask. Going the other way is *supernetting*. We will look at that, too. Next, we have to follow a few other rules that apply to IP addresses.

Rule Number Two is that you may not use all 1s or all 0s in the network or host ID portion of the address. Also, there are no *all 1s* or *all 0s* in the subnet ID. They have a special meaning in IP. *All 1s* is a broadcast. *All 0s* is this network only.

Finally, we have a rule from the "because I said so" department. Rule Number Three is always steal contiguous bits. It's a bad plan to have a subnet mask that is the following form:

11111111.11111111.10101010.00000000

It would make deciding who's on whose network very difficult. Most routers do not support noncontiguous subnet bits.

Now that we understand a few of the rules, it is design time. Using our example from the scenario in the previous section, we have decided to use a private 10.x.x.x number for our addressing convention. We have also decided to break this system up. We have ten offices in various locations; two are major sites that have 1500 machines each. Our business is growing rapidly and we believe that in the next 18 months we will need to possibly double our capacity. We are doing well.

These pieces of information are the kind of thing you need to speak to your customer/organization about to get a good handle on your design parameters.

Ask these questions:

- *Do you have an IP addressing scheme in place?*
  This will tell you if you have to work around some existing infrastructure or can start from scratch. (Sometimes the latter is better.)

- *How many locations do you have?*
  This will give you a clue about the number of networks needed.

- *How many machines are at each location?*
  Look for large collections at a single site as possible candidates for the network segmentation proposal.

- *How much do you plan on growing?*
  Your design must accommodate growth.

Our network will look something like Figure 4-4.

Remember, we will need one network ID for each physical segment and one for each wide area connection. Doing the math, we quickly come up with at least 19 network IDs. There are, however, the 1500 machines in New York and Chicago. We will split this up into three subnets of 500 machines each for this exercise. That now totals nine network IDs for the wide area connections, eight more for the smaller, remote offices side of the routers, and three each in New York and Chicago, for a total of 23 network IDs required. But we also must factor in the doubling in growth over the next 18 months. We will estimate that 46 network IDs will be required eventually.

We also know that the largest number of hosts we will be dealing with is 500 in any one segment. Therefore, our subnetting scheme must accommodate at least 46 networks, each having a minimum of 500 host IDs available on each network. The rest of the subnetting exercise is just math.

Sample network

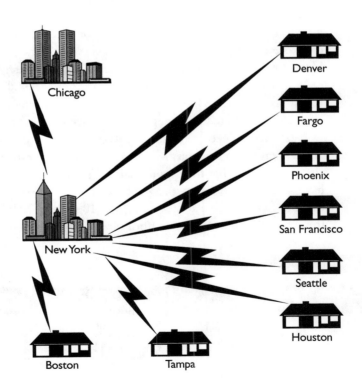

I have a 10.x.x.x network address, which means that my default subnet mask will be 255.0.0.0. Converting this number to binary gives us 11111111.00000000.00000000.00000000. I require 46 subnets, so convert the decimal number 46 to binary. (Do everything in binary and you will learn how IP addressing works. If you choose to use a table someone gave you, you will never really *LEARN* IP addressing.) That equals 101110 (32+0+8+4+2+0 = 46). To make the binary number 46 will require 6 binary digits (bits) locations. This is the number of digits we will require for our subnetting. Therefore, our new custom subnet will be 11111111.11111100.00000000.00000000, which we now must convert back to decimal. Converted back, our subnet mask becomes 255.252.0.0, and we will now use this to determine which machines are on the same network together.

What we've actually done is create 62 subnets. Remember the first paragraph in this section? We will use it now. We've taken 6 bits for our subnet mask $2^6 - 2 = 62$. Rule Number Two says we can't have all 1s or all 0s for the subnet. Therefore, our subnet ID range would start at 000001 and continue on to 111110. We will be unable to use 000000 and 111111 as subnetwork IDs. That's the minus-two part. (Always test your numbers. If we had chosen to use an example needing seven networks, the binary conversion would be 111, leading us to believe we only need three bits for our mask. However, $2^3 - 2 = 6$, not 7. The number we chose, though, is all 1s.)

We have also been left with 18 bits for the hosts. To calculate the number of host IDs available using 18 bits, we can perform the following calculation: $2^{18} - 2 = 262,142$, leaving us with more than enough hosts on each subnet. Table 4-2 shows our breakdown.

Next, we will need to determine which host IDs are valid. We are using the 10.x.x.x range, so let's start by converting the 10 to binary. 00001010 is it. We've also determined that the next available number for the subnetwork is 000001 (can't have all zeros in the subnet). We also can't have all 0s in the host ID, which means that our first available address is 00001010.00000100.00000000.00000001 and this network can continue on until 00001010.00000111.11111111.11111110 (note

TABLE 4-2 Breakdown of Host IDs

Type	Network	Subnetwork	Hosts
IP address	00001010.	000001	00.00000000.00000001
Subnet mask	11111111.	111111	00.00000000.00000000

that the last portion of the host is not all 1s). Each time the subnetwork number increments (from 000001 to 000010 and to 000011), it marks the shift to the next subnetwork and the new physical segment.

This means (if we convert back to decimal) that 10.4.0.1–10.7.255.254 are all on the same network segment, but 10.8.0.1–10.11.255.254 are on the next network up. The next group would be 10.12.0.1–10.15.255.254, then 10.16.0.1–10.19.255.254, and so on up to 10.248.0.1–10.251.255.254. It also means that 10.0.0.1–10.3.254.255 are invalid numbers and so are 10.252.0.1– 10.255.255.254. I'm afraid that's the price you will pay for dividing up the network.

We could also have gone the other way and chosen to decide our mask based on the number of hosts required. I needed at least 500 hosts on a segment to convert that to binary. That's 111110100 or 256+128+64+32+16+0+4+0+0=500. I needed nine bits for the hosts, leaving 15 for the networks. Our subnet mask would then become 11111111.11111111.11111110.00000000, or 255.255.254.0 in decimal notation.

Our mask is different because we based it on required hosts, not networks, and as a consequence, have only 510 hosts (2^9 - 2), but over 32,000 (2^{15} - 2) networks available. Also note that we have subnetted more than one octet. No problem, just make sure that you leave yourself with enough bits for hosts. You also cannot use a single bit for subnetting. After all, that would leave you with a 0 or a 1 in the subnet field. Based on this information, you should design a mask that will accommodate room for growth in both the host and network areas.

CertCam 4-2

EXERCISE 4-2

Designing a Subnet Mask

XYZ Corporation has hired you as a consultant to create their new TCP/IP network-addressing scheme. They have recently moved from a Netware 3.x implementation to Windows 2000 to take advantage of the many new features, but have no existing TCP/IP infrastructure. Since this is a requirement of Windows 2000, they have leased the address range of 158.140.0.0 for their corporation. Your responsibility is to create a subnet mask that will accommodate the entire organization.

XYZ currently has four locations across North America with offices in Denver, Boston, Vancouver, and their head office in New York. All sites are connected via leased lines. The Boston location is a major manufacturing location and currently has over 2000 computers in place, which they would like to break up into smaller groups of not more than 300. New York also has over 900 computers, which could be broken up into smaller groups as well. XYZ has been expanding rapidly over the past few years and is anticipating opening two new smaller locations in the next 18 months.

As part of your design, you must create a subnet mask, determine the number of networks created and the number of hosts created. You may choose to use either the number of hosts or the number of networks as your basis for calculation, as shown in the following table. You must also come up with the addresses of the available hosts.

Design Consideration	Design Solution
Maximum number of hosts per segment	300
Minimum number of networks required	20 based on seven for Boston, four for New York, one each for Denver, Vancouver, and the two new sites, and five for WAN connections, three existing and two new locations
Convert either # of hosts or networks to binary	100101100=300 for hosts, 10100=20 for nets
# of bits you will use for subnet mask	Five bits if based on # of required nets, seven bits if based on number of required hosts
To convert this number back to decimal subnet mask you will use	255.255.248.0 if five bits used, or 255.255.254.0 if seven bits used
# of available Networks	30 if five bits used, or 126 if seven bits used for mask
# of available hosts per network	2046 if five bits used, or 510 if seven bits used for mask
First available host ID	158.140.8.1 (with ranges from 158.140.8.1–158.140.15.254 in the first subnet) if five bits used, 158.140.2.1 (with ranges from 158.140.2.1–158.140.3.254 in the first subnet) if seven bits used

Other design considerations are performance related. Microsoft divides traffic into two major groups: *bandwidth-susceptible* traffic and *latency-susceptible* traffic.

The bandwidth-sensitive traffic has a more one-way flow and is the type of traffic we see in client/server and web applications. Latency traffic is more "bursty" and is usually a packet-by-packet type of traffic. It has the drawback of requiring an acknowledgment of packets before communication to continue. This is more often found in authentication and encryption traffic.

Have you taken into account bandwidth utilization and the size of your broadcast / collision domains? Remember that as we increase the number of hosts on a physical segment, we increase the traffic on that segment.

What about the performance of your routers? Read the router's documentation of the number of hosts that it will support per subnet. What about the impact of your applications on the network? Some of these performance factors can only be measured in a production environment and not as part of a lab or pilot project, so be prepared to reconfigure your network if necessary to improve the performance.

Lastly, have you factored in future growth? Select a mask that will accommodate not only your present requirements, but also will last for the foreseeable future for both the number of hosts and the number of networks.

Also in a LAN, consider the Layer 1 and 2 infrastructure. Are you running a Token Ring or Ethernet network? Ethernet has a Maximum Transmission Unit (MTU) of just 1500 bytes, while Token Ring can use an MTU of over 17,000 bytes. If you must route between Token Ring and Ethernet, your packets will be fragmented to accommodate the smaller size of the Ethernet MTU, which will increase the processor load on the routers and slow traffic.

The MTU includes more than just the TCP encapsulated data portion. The Maximum Segment Size (MSS) is the actual data payload of TCP or UDP, which on an Ethernet network will reduce the amount of data sent in the payload to 1,460 bytes. If the types of network devices you use cause longer delays, such as satellite links might, you may want to place servers closer to the users that need them instead of forcing them across this link. If this is not an option because of a requirement for the server to be available to all users at all times, for example a SQL server that acts as a central repository of data, create multiple servers on either side of this slow link and use software replication to keep the data at both sites consistent. The more data that we can receive from our own side of the link, the better our perceived responsiveness will be.

Optimizing Subnet Designs Using Variable Length Subnet Masks and Supernetting

We are still left with an issue. RFC 950 allows only a single subnet mask to be used beyond the default mask. If I have obtained my address from an ISP, it may already have a subnet mask applied to it. Can I subnet my subnet? What about sending everyone back through to my ISP? Will I need a router for each subnetted subnet? Let's look.

Variable Length Subnet Masks (VLSM)

RFC 1878 provides a mechanism for creating subnet masks of variable lengths. This means that I can have one mask for the outside world and a different subnet mask inside on my network. This is to a certain degree "subnetting the subnet."

Here is how it works. My ISP was assigned the network address of 24.0.0.0 and allowed to lease out subsections of that address to its clients. I was given a block of addresses from 24.144.0.1 to 24.144.255.254 and assigned the subnet mask of 255.255.0.0 This means that the first 16 bits are used for the subnet mask or, to word it a different way, I have a prefix of /16. I still have been left with 16 bits for hosts.

Based on RFC 950, I can't subdivide any further down, but RFC 1878 says you may steal additional bits if I so choose. I would like to create five additional subnets in my office. 101 in binary is 5, so I need an additional three bits. I would increase my prefix to /19, giving me a subnet mask of 255.255.224.0. The first 16 bits are used for the default mask, the next three for the subnet mask assigned by the ISP, and the next three for my internal subnets. My first available host address will be 24.144.32.1 with networks of 24.144.32.0, 24.144.64.0, 24.144.96.0, 24.144.128.0, 24.144.160.0, and 24.144.192.0. The big advantage is the ability to subdivide my network without obtaining another block of addresses from my ISP.

Sounds good, but I will require a routing protocol that supports VLSM. RIP v1 does not support VLSM. RIP v2 and OSPF do, so if you choose to implement VLSM, make sure you have the appropriate protocols in place. You will also have to set up your routers in a hierarchical manner where the top level router will be connected to the ISP and additional routers will be used to connect to your sub subnets.

Finally, you will require routing table entries for each of the internal subnets set up on the top-level router. Parsing the routing table of a large Internetwork can be a very processor-intensive activity. Imagine having hundreds or even thousands of networks.

Classless InterDomain Routing (CIDR) or Supernetting

Routing is a very processor-intensive activity. If we are forced to create large routing tables due to the additional subdividing of our network, we have actually created a performance problem for our network. To improve our network performance and to make our network flatter, we can use Classless InterDomain Routing (CIDR).

CIDR is subnetting turned backward. Instead of stealing host bits to make more networks, we steal network bits to combine more hosts on one network. The specification found in RFC 1519 allows for the combining of IP address ranges into a single range of addresses.

For example, you could take five class B addresses and make them appear as a single IP range. If all five class B ranges are on the same network, they could all pass through the same router, reducing the routing table entries and reducing our cost of routers. To do this, you would again determine how many subnets you wish to combine (five) and convert to binary (101) to determine the number of bits to steal from the network and create your subnet mask in binary (11111111.11111000.00000000.00000000), then convert back to decimal 255.248.0.0.

If you choose to use supernetting, make sure as part of your design that your routers support it. Routers that support RIP v2, OSPF, and Border Gateway Protocol (BGP) routing protocols can all handle CIDR traffic.

Designing Subnetting Solutions for Internetworks Using WAN Connections

A large problem with WAN connections under Windows 2000 is that latency and delays in traffic are amplified. There are some features in the new stack that improve performance, such as the self-tuning nature of the stack, but there are still some changes you can make to improve performance.

Watch for the TCP window size. As with NT 4.0, the receive buffer can be increased if you are experiencing high network delays. But as with NT, it will be a registry hack. As a matter of fact, it's the same hack. Also, keep an eye out for significant packet loss, as this is a sign of errors or congestion on routers you are passing through.

When using point-to-point connections for connecting remote offices, you must use a separate network ID for each internal network and for the transit Internetwork. On the transit Internetwork, you must also supply two IP addresses, one for each end of the transit network for dynamic routing protocols to function.

There are some cases that allow you to use unnumbered connections, but this will force you to use static routes and leaves much more management of the infrastructure in your hands. Multipoint connections, such as X.25 or Frame Relay, will allow you to use a single subnet for all connections. Each virtual circuit on the multipoint network will require an IP address on that subnet. Both of these solutions create essentially a private network. If you have chosen to suballocate addresses from the range in use at the corporation, you must also implement a VLSM/CIDR solution.

As with LANs, you should keep an eye on MTU. If the WAN pipe is unable to accommodate the MTU and is forced to fragment the packets, the data processing requirements will increase. The already smaller MTUs of Ethernet may be a preference of the larger Token Ring MTUs, as fragmentation is less likely with these WAN links. T-1, for example, may be able to transmit the Ethernet packets without any fragmentation, while the 16 MB/s Token Ring would require five or more fragments based on its MTU.

Another method of remote connectivity gaining widespread acceptance is Virtual Private Networks (VPNs). This allows us to use a public, unsecured, but inexpensive network such as the Internet as a backbone to our private networks. It does so by creating a tunnel from one endpoint on our network to another endpoint at the remote network. Each server on this network will require a public address that becomes a tunnel endpoint or terminator. We will also create a pool of VPN addresses that will be assigned to VPN clients so that they will be able to access internal network resources. Be aware that your design will have to accommodate public as well as private addressing in this scheme. The upside is the reduced connectivity costs.

SCENARIO & SOLUTION

I have private addresses now. How can I connect to the Internet?	Use a Network Address Translation (NAT) device such as those found on firewalls or proxy servers.
I have leased an IP address range from my ISP. How can I subdivide this further?	If your routers support it, use VLSM.
I would like to reduce the number of entries in my routing table. How can I do this?	Use CIDR if your routers will support it.

CERTIFICATION OBJECTIVE 4.04

TCP/IP Security Implementations

Windows 2000 contains improved security over TCP/IP in many forms. In this section, we will look at protocol and port filtering as a means of blindly blocking traffic and IPSec and as a more fine-tuned way of selectively restricting access to your servers.

Protocol and Port Filtering

The Internet can be a dangerous place. One means of securing your servers is to hide the ports and protocols from outside access through the use of port filters. These filters block *all* available ports or protocols except those you open up. This is not new to Windows 2000. The advanced IP addressing property page in NT 4.0 had an ENABLE SECURITY check box that would allow you to define which TCP, UDP, or IP ports to block. In Windows 2000 it is very much the same.

Using filters requires a good knowledge of the well-known protocol ports. If you are looking for a copy, it can be found in RCF 1700. It is a very large document (230 pages); however, these numbers are assigned by the IANA and most vendors would like all of their various application layer protocols listed.

Filters should also be used with caution. Although they will secure your system on the network, you may experience a loss in functionality. This is because you are blocking all ports except those you allow to pass through, and with some programs this causes programs that use a dynamic port assignment to fail.

This approach is the complete opposite of a state-full inspection device that will determine whether to allow traffic based on criteria other than just the port number (did traffic originate from our organization or outside our organization, for example). It's a very heavy-handed approach, so it may not be the best option for the client machines, but it will minimize the exposure of ports on servers where these types of applications are not used. On the server, we can just open port 80, for example, for the Web service on that IIS server and know that people will not be accessing other services or causing harm to the system.

The filters in Windows 2000 are a little more advanced. They have an almost wizard-like approach in helping you to configure the filters, but you will still need to know which ports to leave open. See Figure 4-5 for the configuration screen that you will use to configure the filters in the TCP/IP property sheet.

Note also that filters can be enabled through the group policy editor. This is another way of applying the filters on multiple machines at once. If you have an OU that contains only servers, you may want to apply a policy that sets the filters for the entire OU as opposed to going to each server and configuring the filters.

When you are designing a filter solution, be aware of some specific issues with filters. First of all you can create filters based on TCP and UDP port numbers and on IP protocol types, but you cannot block the TCP, UDP, ICMP, IGMP, or IPSec IP protocol types. Also TEST your filters after you have configured them to ensure that you are still able to function. There is no point in being so secure that no one can use the services on your servers. Finally, look out for internal routing (IP forwarding) and filters. Filters will not be applied to traffic that is being forwarded between interfaces.

on the **Job** *If you need a quick reference for the port and protocol numbers, check out the %systemroot%\system32\drivers\etc directory. There you can find a file called services that contains the port numbers and another called protocol that contains a limited list of IP protocol numbers. Whatever you do though, don't delete the ETC directory or TCP/IP will fail to function.*

FIGURE 4-5

TCP/IP Filter configuration

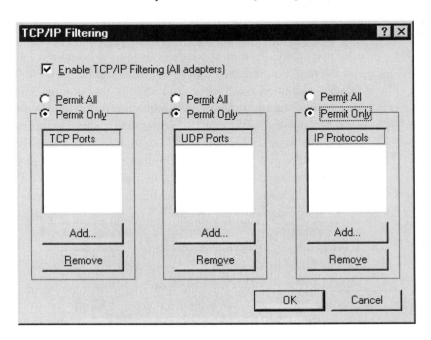

CertCam 4-3

Designing a Security Solution with Port and Protocol Filters

As part of your security design, you have decided to block all Web traffic from your computer using port filters you will also block on another system the FTP ports.

To accomplish this, you must first determine the ports to block for HTTP and for FTP traffic. You will then implement these policies (one at a time) through the IP Security Policy Management MMC.

To complete this exercise you will need an open connection to the Internet to test the filters.

To determine the ports to block, open %systemroot%\system32\drivers\ and open services in Notepad. Find the port numbers for FTP (TCP port 21) and HTTP(TCP port 80).

exam
ⓦatch   *Filters may not always react the way you think they should. For example, blocking TCP and UDP port 7 will not necessarily block ping traffic if you don't block the ICMP protocol. It is a good idea to test a few filters to make sure you fully understand them.*

To block access to http, open the open an empty MMC by opening run box and type MMC. In the Console menu, choose Add/Remove Snap-in and click on the add button.

1. From the list of snap-ins, choose IP Security Policy Management and click Add. Select Local Computer and choose Finish, then Close, then OK to add the snap-in.

2. In the node pane, double-click the IP Security Policy Management icon (you may receive an error message stating that "a policy has been provided by the Domain Controller". Click OK to bypass this message.

3. The Client (Respond only) policy should be assigned. If not, assign it by right-clicking on it and choosing assign. Right-click the Client (Respond Only) policy and choose Properties from the context menu.

4. On the Rules tab, make sure the use add wizard check box is selected, and click the add button. At the welcome screen, click Next and then click Next three more times to select the defaults for the tunnel endpoint, network type, and authentication method.

EXERCISE 4-3

5. In the IP filter list dialog box, click Add and give it a name of "HTTP Filter" (you may call it whatever you wish, but this will help us define what we are filtering), and click Add to start the IP filter wizard. Click Next three times to bypass the welcome screen and to choose the defaults for the IP traffic source and destination (my IP address and all IP addresses). In the Protocol drop down box, choose TCP and select any for the *from* port and 80 for the *to* port. Then click Next and Finish to complete the wizard. Select the HTTP Filter on the IP Filter Lists and click Next. Your screen should look like the one shown here.

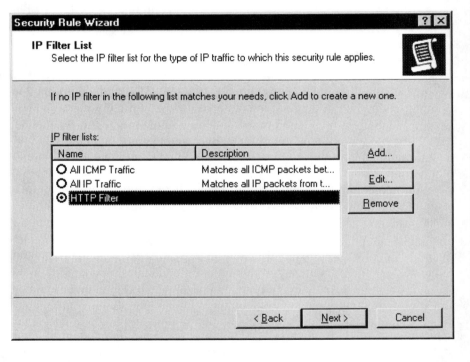

6. In the Filter Action dialog box, clear the Use Add Wizard box and click Add. On the Security Method tab, choose block, and on the General Tab, type **block it** for the filter name. Click OK to close the Add Filter action dialog and choose Block it on the Filter Action page. You should now see the following screen.

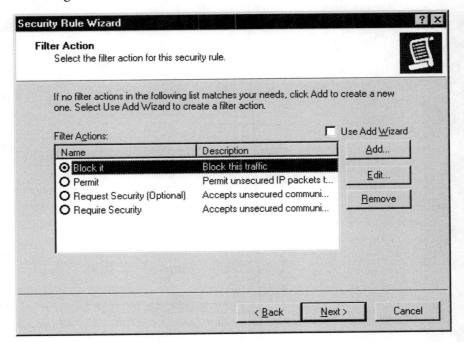

7. Click Next and then Finish, and minimize the MMC. Now we can test our filter by popping up a Web browser, and also from a command prompt try, a ping. The Web browser will time out, but we should be able to FTP to a host such as ftp.microsoft.com.

8. Restore the MMC, double-click Client (Respond only), and repeat steps 3 to 6 to create an FTP filter. Call it FTP filter and you will notice that the "block it" action is still there for you to reuse. Make sure you clear the HTTP Filter box and test the FTP and Web connections again. Your filter should look like the one shown here.

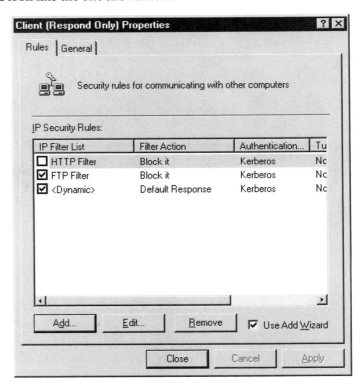

9. To return your system to its previous configuration, right-click the IP Security Policy Management icon in the node pane and choose all tasks and then restore default policy. Say **yes** to the warning and we are back to square one.

exam
ⓦatch
There are different ways to do several tasks in Windows 2000. As this exercise showed, we can apply filters either directly or through security policies. Know different ways to do various tasks for the exam.

You've now created a filter, but we did it a slightly different way. We were in the IP Security Policy management tool. Let's look at that a little deeper.

IPSec

Much of the information that travels across our networks is of a confidential nature. The wide-open nature of TCP/IP is in direct conflict with this. To enhance the security of our network, RFC 2041 says we can add in IPSec to authenticate and encrypt our data.

IPSec has two types of headers that it can add to an IP packet. The AH or Authentication Header provides us with a mechanism for ensuring that the data integrity is valid without encrypting the data itself. This means verifying that I have received that packet without it being changed in transmission and that it was indeed sent by who I think sent it.

The second type of header is the Encapsulating Security Payload or ESP. This not only provides the features of the AH (authentication and integrity), but also encrypts the information during transmission. Furthermore, in "tunnel mode" I can tell the system which two devices will be communicating in the session (the endpoints). The other mode of "transport mode" does not specify endpoints, since it may be received by more than one system. It's not recommended or required to use tunnel mode if you are also using L2TP or PPTP for a VPN.

IPSec Predefined Settings

To set up a IPSec policy, a few conditions must exist. You must first define the policy and the parameters of the policy for IPSec. Next, you must set up an Internet Key Exchange (IKE) to create a Security Association (SA). Finally, the data is exchanged using the SA to encrypt the session. In Windows 2000, there are three IPSec policies already created that you may make use of for your systems. They are the "Client (Respond Only)," "Server (Request Security)," and "Secure Server (Require Security)" settings.

The *Client (Respond Only)* setting will only make use of IPSec if it is requested by another system. If asked, the client will respond to requests for secured communication, but will only secure the requested port and protocol. This would be an appropriate setting for most computers that do not require secured communication on a regular basis.

The *Server (Request Security)* setting will allow traffic to pass that does not use IPSec security, but will always try to use IPSec security first by requesting it from the client. If the client is not IPSec enabled, the server will lower its security to accommodate the client. This would be a good setting for many corporate environments that are using a mix of clients and are not concerned with security issues either because of another security mechanism on the network or because the traffic is not of a sensitive nature.

The *Secure Server (Require Security)* setting will always force the negotiation of IPSec SAs. Any traffic that is not using this security will be immediately rejected. Although this will provide for the highest level of security, it will reject clients who are not IPSec enabled. This may be unacceptable for organizations that have a mix of clients, and some are not capable of this level of security. It's of no use to have a server that is so secure it is not accessible, so this setting should only be used if you know that all clients are capable of securing the traffic using IPSec on your network.

IPSec Custom Settings

If you choose to use a custom security policy, you will need to configure the levels of authentication, encryption, and the Diffie-Hellman groups. These will configure your level of security, but as you increase the security you will adversely affect the performance of your system.

The authentication mechanisms available are the Secure Hash Algorithm (SHA) and Message Digest 5 (MD5) protocols. MD5 provides a 128-bit key authentication, while SHA is the longer 160-bit key. SHA provides a higher level of security, but its longer key length will reduce performance. SHA will be a requirement of U.S. government contracts under the Federal Information Processing Standard (FIPS). If the design is not part of the FIPS requirement, use the shorter key length of MD5 unless the data is of a very confidential nature.

Available encryption algorithms include 40-bit Data Encryption Standard (DES), 56-bit DES, and Triple DES (3DES), which has a 128-bit key length. 40-bit DES will be required for data going into or out of France and will give you better performance, but the lack of security in this method may not be a desirable option. 56-bit DES is a good balance of security and performance for many applications, such as e-mail, where although some lower level security is a benefit, performance is still a driving concern. Using the 3DES encryption should only be used in the highest security environments due to the reduction in processor performance calculating the keys. Use this when performance is of no concern, but security is of utmost importance, such as financial transaction processing systems.

The Diffie-Hellman groups create a kind of *master key* for the communication session. This key is obtained from the Diffie-Hellman key material, which can be either of two groups. Group 1 uses 768 bits of key material and is considered low security, and group 2 uses 1024 bits. Group 2 is still only considered medium security. It is very important that both machines use the same D-H groups or key negotiations will fail. As with the authentication and encryption settings, the higher security you establish, the harder the code is to crack and the slower your system will perform.

Internet Key Exchange

If the two machines that will be communicating are both IPSec enabled, they will need to agree on what level of authentication, encryption, and D-H groups to use. This is accomplished through a process called an Internet Key Exchange (IKE) that uses two protocols created by the IETF to negotiate the security keys. The Internet Security Association and Key Management Protocol (ISAKMP) do the SA management. Oakley, the other protocol used, is for the generation and management of the authenticated keys. The two hosts in the session will also have to set up the authentication method for the SAs. There are three ways this can be done.

First, you may choose to use the Kerberos v5 protocol, which is the default method and is supported for all clients of trusted domains. It's also the simplest to set up. Just click the button and Windows 2000 handles the rest. This is an excellent method if, and only if, all systems will be supporting Kerberos v5. Not all systems will support Kerberos so understand this limitation. It will, however, work very well in a Windows 2000 only environment. Use this method, as part of your design if Active Directory is installed or Kerberos v5 will be supported.

Another method would be through Public Key certificates. These are standard x.509 certificates as supplied by an outside Certificate Authority or through an internal system such as Microsoft's Certificate Server. This method will also be of use if the Internet is a communication method as an External Certificate Authority allows global access to the certificate store.

The final method is by agreement on a "preshared" set of keys. It will require the most amount of configuration since the keys must be manually configured on both machines before any communication over IPSec can take place. Use the Certificate or shared key configuration if your design includes IPSec communication from partner or client organizations where Kerberos v5 will not be used.

These settings and those of the port filters can either be added into a group policy for deployment on all systems in the network or configured under the adapter/IP configuration/advanced/options/IPSec properties (similar to the configuration done with port filters). To apply the IPSec policy in the group policy, open the Administrative Tools/Domain Security MMC snap-in and choose the IP Security Policies. As with any group policy, it may also be applied to OUs as well as Domains and Sites, which may be an effective way to manage your policies.

exam
Watch

Group policies are a new method for applying system configuration changes across all or some of the systems in your domain. Expect Microsoft to test your knowledge of group policies in designing an IPSec network as well as the simpler configuration done through the adapter property sheets.

It is a good idea to plan in advance which policy setting you will use on which machines as you can only have one active policy at a time. If none of the pre-existing policies meets your requirements, you can create a custom policy by editing on of the existing policy settings. Also, plan on opening a few ports on your firewall/proxy/filter to allow the IPSec traffic through. IPSec will require you to open IP protocol 51 for the AH traffic and IP protocol 50 and UDP port 500 for the ESP traffic.

SCENARIO & SOLUTION

I want to use some form of security, but I don't want the processing overhead of the encryption. What should I do?	Use the IPSec AH settings to use just the authentication and not the encryption. Use MD5 Authentication.
I require a secure encrypted transmission with outside partners. How can I make the security keys available to just those partners?	Use a preshared key if the partner is unable to accommodate Kerberos v5.
I would like to secure my communications, but I would like the keys to be available globally. How can I accomplish this?	Use the public key Certificate Configuration and use a Certificate Authority such as Verisign to make the keys globally available.

CERTIFICATION OBJECTIVE 4.05

Measuring and Optimizing a TCP/IP Infrastructure Design

Performance monitoring is much more of an art than a specific science. Although there are some excellent guidelines for what you should and should not monitor, it is just as important to know how to monitor.

As a case in point, remember that any performance monitoring will be a drain on the existing resources of the monitoring system. As such, they will skew the data presented if the monitoring system is also the system being monitored. Whenever possible, keep these systems separate to get a closer interpretation of the data. Also be aware of what I have just mentioned, it will drain resources. It may not be a good idea to have a production server also acting as a monitoring system, as other production applications will be slowed.

Another consideration is when to monitor. Start by creating a *baseline* of activity when the system is functioning normally during normal load. This can then be used as a yardstick for comparing to activity when the system's performance is suspect. Remember, everything is relative and performance is no exception. The end users concept of performance is more from a responsiveness standpoint where perception is the law. As a network matures and additional load is placed on the systems in the network, user responsiveness will decrease. The actual throughput of the system may not have decreased at all, and these are the hard fast numbers that we might not be able to change until the new budget comes in and hardware upgrades are available.

You will find that if you are given an opportunity, you could spend all of your waking hours tinkering with the systems to squeeze that last tiny little drop of speed out of it. Although performance tuning is a good idea, make it functional first. You may have other work to do.

What Events are Worth Monitoring?

This is truly the $64,000 question. If you monitor too little, you will likely miss the resource drain you were looking for. If you monitor too much, you must wade through reams of data that will require spending weeks to filter the information into a usable solution to the problem. For this section we should focus our attention on the issue of design. We will be designing a monitoring approach that will provide us with a usable, but manageable amount of information. It must provide us with the insightful information required to optimize the system, but with a minimum amount of data to sort.

Another aspect to consider is whether this is something that we wish to accomplish on a pilot or production network. As mentioned, the information gathering process of this monitoring is very processor intensive. If at all possible, plan to gather data on a test network rather than a production environment. The details will still give you an idea of what to expect on the production network and will not directly impact the current systems.

Use sampling approaches as well. See how much traffic is generated for a single logon on the network and then multiply that by the number of concurrent logons you anticipate. Other types of data you may wish to sample may be ADS or DNS replication traffic, DHCP traffic, the affects of your IPSec design on processor load, and application specific traffic, such as SQL traffic generated for a typical transaction or traffic generated for sending mail or browsing the Internet. Typical business activity should be monitored. A test lab or pilot lab may not always be available, but it will certainly make life a little easier if you can do it.

on the **Job**

Although test labs are unusual for most organizations, it is something that many VARs would be happy to supply, at a cost, of course. Many resellers that have an onsite training facility will also be able to offer you a mini test lab that consists of their training room, if it's not booked. This will not give you a good idea of what your systems will be like, as hardware will likely differ. However, you will be able to load operating systems and applications and test how they will interoperate and the affect they will have on the network.

Finally, ensure that significant events are sent as administrative alerts to more than one administrator on the network. It's always best to get on top of such errors as quickly as possible. Sending alerts to multiple stations ensures that the issues will be handled as swiftly as possible.

We are, however, looking at the items that are particular to TCP/IP. Therefore, the items most of interest will be in the networking categories. There are some performance counters you should observe.

Designing Redundancy into the Network Infrastructure

A key issue in designing WAN connections is to design for redundancy. If high network availability and top performance is required between sites, add an additional WAN link with routers that support load balancing by setting the metrics for the route to be equal. Routing protocols such as IGRP will even allow load balancing of unequal metrics. This will make the link a larger pipe during regular operation and still provide a path to the other side of the link if one of the routers or links becomes congested or goes down.

If performance is a secondary issue to availability, than use redundant links with differing metrics. For example, we could configure our WAN connection to use a T-1 link with a metric of 1 and also configure a dial-on-demand ISDN connection with a metric of 10. The T-1 link would be used almost all the time, but if the link went down, the router could dial out on the slower ISDN line and still provide the necessary connectivity. This would also be a cost savings vehicle since only one link is required to be up at a time, and the cost of two permanent links would be larger than one permanent backup environment.

Network Monitor

Network monitor is a protocol analyzer that may be used for the recording and analysis of network traffic. It may also be used to capture the information for an in-depth look by Microsoft technical support. It will not, however, allow you to capture the information of other systems on the network. Only data sent to or received from the monitoring machine will be recorded in the Network monitor capture. If you require this additional level, it can be obtained through the version of Network monitor that is supplied with Microsoft's System Management Server (SMS) 2.0. That version will provide functionality as well as allowing you to edit and retransmit the captured frames.

Although the information in Network monitor can be extremely detailed in the amount of information it supplies, it can be used to determine if a system is misconfigured. (Check to see if the system is sending an ARP for an IP address that is not on this network, and you may have an incorrect subnet mask. Or, if you are using a dial-on-demand proxy system that won't shut down, capture some frames and see if a RIP broadcast is keeping the connection to the ISP open.)

If you do use Network monitor, plan to use it when the system is relatively idle. If possible, capture your data at off-peak hours, as the capture will reduce system performance. Secondly, there is a great deal of detail in the data you do capture. Try to keep the amount of data you do gather down to a minimum. Thirty seconds to five minutes of data can often keep you busy looking for a needle in the haystack for a long time. As always, useful, but manageable.

System Monitor

System Monitor is a new name, but a familiar piece in Windows 2000. By opening the Performance MMC snap-in, you will be presented with two nodes—System Monitor and Performance Logs and Alerts.

System Monitor allows you to create the charts and reports found in NT 4.0 performance monitor. Some objects/counters that you may want to add to your chart that pertain to networking would be the Network Interface/Bytes total/sec., Bytes sent/sec., and Bytes received/sec., Network Segment/% Network Utilization and Server/Bytes total/sec., Bytes sent/sec., and Bytes received/sec. A sustained spike in any of these, without a corresponding increase in expected network activity, may be a sign of a network bottleneck that should be investigated further.

Counters that should be observed for TCP/IP, in particular, are the IP Datagrams Outbound Discarded and Datagrams Received Discarded counters, as they will indicate a lack of buffer space. A high number of Datagrams Outbound No Route may also point to a misconfigured system. Check the routing table of the system in question or possibly the default gateway.

Configuration issues are as common as physical network issues. In general, observe all the TCP, UDP, and IP counters during a baseline, and compare them after issues arise to resolve the problems. Don't forget, all counters have an Explain button. Tables 4-3, 4-4, and 4-5 show the counters available for IP, TCP, and UDP, respectively.

TABLE 4-3   Performance Monitor Counters for IP

Counter	Description
Datagrams Forwarded/sec	The rate of input datagrams for which this entity was not their final IP destination, as a result of which an attempt was made to find a route to forward them to that final destination.
Datagrams Outbound Discarded	Number of output IP datagrams for which no problems were encountered to prevent their transmission to their destination, but which were discarded (e.g., for lack of buffer space).

TABLE 4-3   Performance Monitor Counters for IP *(continued)*

Counter	Description
Datagrams Outbound No Route	Number of IP datagrams discarded because no route could be found to transmit them to their destination.
Datagrams Received Address Errors	Number of input datagrams discarded because the IP address in their IP header's destination field was not a valid address to be received at this entity.
Datagrams Received Delivered/sec	Rate at which input datagrams are successfully delivered to IP user protocols (including ICMP).
Datagrams Received Discarded	Number of input IP datagrams for which no problems were encountered to prevent their continued processing, but which were discarded (e.g., for lack of buffer space).
Datagrams Received Header Errors	Number of input datagrams discarded due to errors in their IP headers, including bad check sums, version number mismatch, other format errors, time-to-live exceeded, errors discovered in processing their IP options, etc.
Datagrams Received Unknown Protocol	Number of locally addressed datagrams received successfully, but discarded because of an unknown or unsupported protocol.
Datagrams Received/sec	Rate at which IP datagrams are received from the interfaces, including those in error.
Datagrams Sent/sec	Rate at which IP datagrams are supplied to IP for transmission by local IP user-protocols (including ICMP).
Datagrams/sec	Rate at which IP datagrams are received from or sent to the interfaces, including those in error.
Fragment Reassembly Failures	Number of failures detected by the IP reassembly algorithm (for whatever reason: time out, errors, etc.).
Fragmentation Failures	Number of IP datagrams that have been discarded because they needed to be fragmented at this entity, but could not be (e.g., because their Don't Fragment flag was set).
Fragmented Datagrams/sec	Rate at which datagrams are successfully fragmented at this entity.
Fragments Created/sec	Rate at which IP datagram fragments have been generated as a result of fragmentation at this entity.
Fragments Reassembled/sec	Rate at which IP fragments are successfully reassembled.
Fragments Received/sec	Rate at which IP fragments that need to be reassembled at this entity are received.

TABLE 4-4   Performance Monitor Counters for TCP

Counter	Description
Connection Failures	Number of times TCP connections have made a direct transition to the CLOSED state from the SYN-SENT state or the SYN-RCVD state, plus the number of times TCP connections have made a direct transition to the LISTEN state from the SYN-RCVD state.
Connections Active	Number of times TCP connections have made a direct transition to the SYN-SENT state from the CLOSED state.
Connections Established	Number of TCP connections for which the current state is either ESTABLISHED or CLOSE-WAIT.
Connections Passive	Number of times TCP connections have made a direct transition to the SYN-RCVD state from the LISTEN state.
Connections Reset	Number of times TCP connections have made a direct transition to the CLOSED state from either the ESTABLISHED state or the CLOSE-WAIT state.
Segments Received/sec	Rate at which segments are received, including those received in error.
Segments Retransmitted/sec	Rate at which segments are retransmitted; that is, segments transmitted containing one or more previously transmitted bytes.
Segments Sent/sec	Rate at which segments are sent, including those on current connections, but excluding those containing only retransmitted bytes.
Segments/sec	Rate at which TCP segments are sent or received using the TCP protocol.

TABLE 4-5   Performance Monitor Counters for UDP

Counter	Description
Datagrams No Port/sec	Rate of received UDP datagrams for which there was no application at the destination port.
Datagrams Received Errors	Number of received UDP datagrams that could not be delivered for reasons other than the lack of an application at the destination port.
Datagrams Received/sec	Rate at which UDP datagrams are delivered to UDP users.
Datagrams Sent/sec	Rate at which UDP datagrams are sent from the entity.
Datagrams/sec	Rate at which UDP datagrams are sent or received by the entity.

To build the baseline previously mentioned you will need to use the second item in the Performance MMC—performance logs and alerts. Use this to gather your information over a longer period and then pull that into a chart for further analysis. Unlike creating logs in NT, this tool will automatically schedule when to start gathering the statistics and when to stop, as seen in Figure 4-6.

When designing your System Monitor configuration, remember to keep the monitoring to a single machine where you will monitor all others. From this machine, create a baseline of the other systems by using a log over a period of about a week of normal use. Use a longer sampling interval in the log files to reduce the amount of data in the file. Ten to fifteen-minute samplings will give you about the same amount of information as a five-minute sample if you are gathering the data over a long period, but will consume two-thirds less space in the file size.

FIGURE 4-6

Scheduling log
counters with
Performance logs

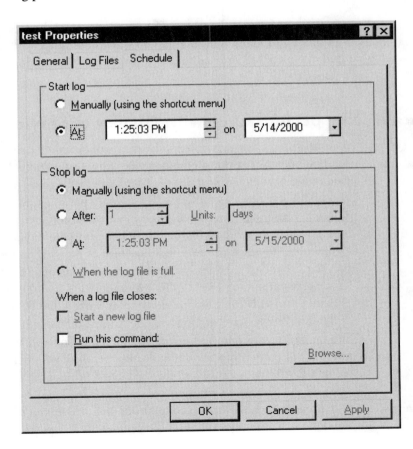

Last, but not least, when you make a change while performance tuning, repeat your monitoring to verify that you have improved the situation. Be careful not to cure one issue only to cause another more drastic issue.

Third-Party Monitoring and Optimization Solutions

Several other organizations provide monitoring and optimization solutions. HP OpenView and IBM Tivoli are excellent products that provide network management capabilities. Network Associates Sniffer has been the standard for packet analyzers for close to ten years. Many other products, such as Microsoft's SMS, provide a suite of management utilities, while others rely on the bare bones approach and simply provide SNMP monitoring only.

When planning to implement any third party solution, you should carefully compare the features that you wish to use and select the product that best meets your needs. In many cases, it's easy to spend too much on a product that you only need one piece of. Shop around and you may find a product that supplies just that one piece.

Guaranteeing performance with Quality of Service (QoS)

As traffic passes through routers, the data will be handled on a first come, first serve basis. While under normal circumstances this is an acceptable approach, in some data traffic it causes important, time-sensitive traffic to be put on hold while potentially second-class traffic, such as e-mail, passes ahead of us through the router. This will cause streaming media such as video teleconferencing or IP telephony to have unacceptable delays. It would be a benefit to these types of applications to have a guaranteed bandwidth or some other form of prioritizing mechanism to ensure that the network itself did not induce additional latency. To do this, Windows 2000 has implemented QoS (RFC 2210-2212 and RFC 2386) to reserve bandwidth and prioritize traffic. It can also prevent protocols like UDP from overusing the network.

The subcomponents of QoS include Admission Control Service (QoS ACS), Subnet Bandwidth management (SBM), Traffic Control, and finally, the RSVP or resource reservation protocol. It is this last protocol where the sender (through the use of a PATH command) and the recipient (through the use of a RESV command) agree on the parameters for their communication. The PATH informs the recipient of the sender and destination addresses as well as the type of traffic that will be sent. The RESV informs the sender of the traffic type it expects to receive.

As part of your design, you should consider QoS if you wish to ensure bandwidth between client and server for time-sensitive applications. However, be aware that this should only be installed if it is supported by the applications and all devices in the path from sender to destination. This will mean that all routers within the communication group must support the RSVP protocols.

CERTIFICATION OBJECTIVE 4.06

Integrating Software Routing into Existing Networks

Routing and Remote access was a download for Windows NT 4.0 that allowed you to increase the capabilities of NT by adding in OSPF routing protocols and Dial-on-Demand routing via RAS. While these capabilities are now built into Windows 2000, they are also enhanced to cover other features such as Network Address Translation (NAT) and Layer 2 Tunneling Protocol (L2TP). When designing your network, consider the software routing possibilities in Windows 2000 as an alternative for higher priced hardware routers. The requirements are very small—a Windows 2000 system with either multiple network adapters or network adapters and dial-out devices.

Windows 2000 Routing and Remote Access Solutions

As you may know, hardware-based routers can be extremely expensive, ranging in price from a few thousand to hundreds of thousands, depending on the configuration and options required. Many organizations cannot afford this type of budget for routing and would like to be offered some other less expensive solution. Bear in mind that software routers will not be comparable to hardware routers in either performance or feature set. But that aside, the expense of software routing in Windows 2000 is the price of additional network cards or dial-out devices. The difficult chore will be configuring the software to do what you want.

There are several ways in which you may do software routing with RRAS. You could choose to use static routes, in which case you will configure all the information as to how to get from one network to another manually, or you might want to use a routing protocol that is capable of *learning* how to get from network to network. Even if you choose to use a routing protocol, Microsoft has given you more than one to choose from.

First, let's look at static routes. In this method we do all the work by specifying which network we want to go to and the subnet mask of that network and the interface that we send it to so that it gets there. When configuring static routing, we don't need to inform the routing table of networks that we are connected to, just the ones we aren't. Let's say I have the network shown below in Figure 4-7.

The system that is acting as a router is connected to both the 131.107 network and the 148.220 network. The only piece of information I need to add into my static routing table is that to get from network 131.107 to 156.110. I should go through interface 148.220.0.2. Once properly configured, I can add static routes in the IP routing, static routes section of RRAS. All I need to provide is the interface, destination network, netmask, gateway address, and metric parameters.

While all of this is wonderful, I have no intention of creating 40 or 50 static routes if I have a large number of subnets. I would much prefer that the router build that information on its own. To do this, we must use a routing protocol.

Routing protocols fall into two categories: Distance Vector and Link State. Distance Vector determines how to get to a network based on how many routers it must pass through. If I have the example shown below in Figure 4-8, I would choose to use the path of A to B even though it is across a 56k line because I only have to go through two routers. Link State's routing decision is a little more intelligent. What kind of line we have is just as important as how many hops we must make. In this case, I would go A-C-B, as there are quicker T-1 lines here.

Microsoft provides OSPF and two versions of RIP in RRAS. There are advantages and disadvantages to both that you should be aware of when you design

FIGURE 4-7   Simple routed LAN

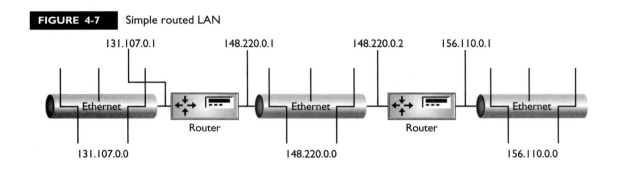

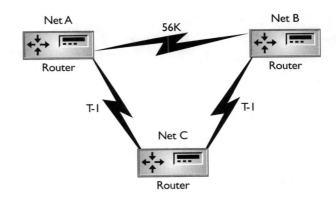

FIGURE 4-8

Routed WAN

your routing infrastructure. Both protocols are referred to as interior routing protocols because they are used within an Autonomous System (AS) or a small group of routers privately managed.

RIP or the Routing information protocol comes in two versions. Both are suitable for small- to medium-sized networks where a large number of routers will not be used. By default, every 30 seconds RIP sends its entire routing table as a broadcast (under version 1, RFC 1058) or a multicast (version 2, RFC 2453) to other routers on the network. This information is added into other RIP routers routing tables, which will, over time, build our routing tables.

For a small network, the traffic generated by all of these RIP announcements is small, and there is little impact on the network. It's also easy to configure and manage (you install the protocol and that's it). For larger networks, however, the traffic generated by many routers can have a negative impact on the overall throughput of the network. Also, RIP has a distance limitation of 15 hops. If the network that I need to reach must pass through more than 16 routers, it is deemed too far away, and you get a *destination host unreachable* message.

OSPF or Open Shortest Path First (RFC 2328) is suitable for larger organizations and is a more flexible solution, as it calculates routes based not on hop count, but on other metrics such as the speed, MTU, and metric of the link. It also will not send its entire routing table in a broadcast every 30 seconds. Instead, it will send only the changes that have occurred in the routing table when a change occurs.

These incremental routing table updates reduce network traffic, making it more suitable for larger enterprises. It also has a larger hop limitation. On the downside, OSPF requires more of your time for configuration and management than RIP does.

FROM THE CLASSROOM

Routing Solutions

A big question that will appear in class is "which routing solution is best for my organization?" Many companies farm out router configuration and maintenance to an outside organization or telephone company. Frankly, they don't have any idea what routing protocols they are using, let alone which would be best for them. One way to find out what kind of router protocol you are using is to monitor traffic with Network monitor. If you are using RIPv1, you will see an advertisement in 30 seconds. If you are using OSPF, however, you will have to wait for a change in the routing tables to occur, and you must be using the full version of Network monitor that comes with SMS to monitor the packets on the router interfaces. If the routes are static, you will receive no traffic, as static routes do not announce themselves to other routers.

After you have determined which type of protocol you are using, you can begin to make some decisions as to which one to use. There are a considerable number of routing protocols not covered here as well. Cisco, for example, also has IGRP and EIGRP as proprietary routing protocols; other companies may have EGP and BGP, among others.

I would recommend using Dynamic routing (using routing protocols) to ease administration. It is much simpler to let the routers add the routing entries than to manually configure all of them yourself. Which one to use depends on your organization. As a rule of thumb, I tell my students that if you have ten or fewer networks, or 50 or fewer servers, RIP may be a good selection because of its simplicity. So long as network traffic is relatively light, the impact of the advertisements is low. The only other concern would be propagation delays where entries in a routing table have not aged out when a router goes down. If your routers rarely go down (as is the case with most hardware routers), this also should not be a problem. However, if your organization is larger than this, you may want to use OSPF for its advanced capabilities and can afford the extra time required for configuration and management.

While I would caution against using static routes, there are some uses for them. The static entries will not be sent to other routers, and all updates must be manually configured, greatly increasing your workload. However, they will not add traffic to your network in the form of table updates. They will also be the most useful in dial-on-demand routing situations.

—Neil MacMurchy, MCP, MCP+I, MCSE, MCSE+I, MCT, CCNA, A+, Networking+

The following exercise will take you through the steps of creating and configuring a RIP solution in RRAS.

Here is a brief explanation of what's on this page. The operation mode can be set to either *auto-static* or *periodic*. The auto-static mode will send updates only when requested by another router. The entries added in on the other router will be treated as static entries on that router. This means that the entries will be kept in the routing table even if the router is rebooted. When auto-static updates are requested, existing auto-static routes are deleted before the update is received.

CertCam 4-4

EXERCISE 4-4

Installing and Configuring RRAS for RIP Routing

Your customer has decided to implement routing for their two new subnets, but do not wish to purchase a hardware router. You have recommended that they use software routing through RRAS to meet their needs. They also have an existing hardware router that uses RIP.

To complete this lab will require two network cards each on a separate network. If you do not have two network cards install the Microsoft loopback. Each adapter should have a static IP address.

1. Install RRAS and then open RRAS in the administrative tools. Right-click on your server and choose Configure and Enable Routing and Remote Access Server.

2. At the RRAS setup wizard welcome screen, click Next and in the common configuration screen select Network Router and click Next. Verify that TCP/IP is on the list of routable protocols and click Next.

3. On the Dial-on-Demand Connections page, choose No and click Next and then Finish to exit the wizard. This may take a moment as RRAS starts.

4. Expand your server and the right-click on the IP Routing node and click on the General tab. Select New Routing Protocol and select RIP v2 for Internet protocol and click OK. RIP will be added under the IP Routing Protocol node in the left pane. Right-click it and choose New Interface and select your network interface card.

This will take you into the configuration properties of RIP. You may also open the properties of the interface after it has been configured to change these settings. Here is the General tab of the property sheet.

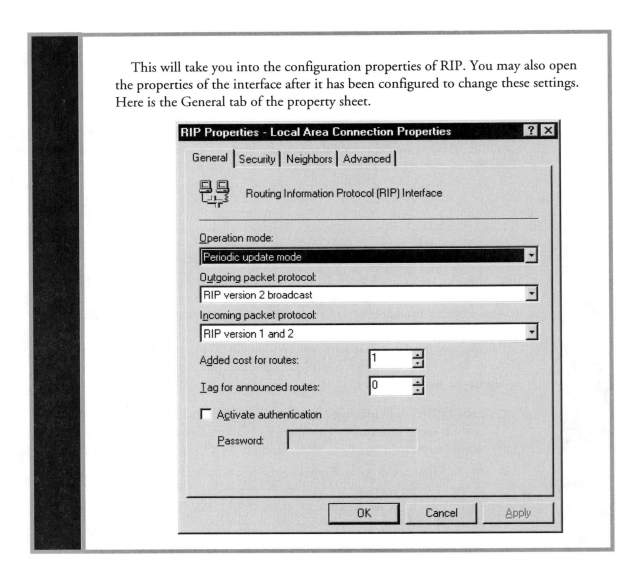

Auto-static routes may be useful in Demand-Dial situations. Keeping the line open for a RIP broadcast every 30 seconds is not an efficient use of the dialup connection. But, static routes may be difficult to manage. If the remote RRAS machine is also a RIP v2 system using auto-static updates, the remote routes are sent during the Demand-Dial session and can then be used on the local side to initiate Demand-Dial connections to the remote location. This eases administration by allowing the routers to create the "static" routes for possible multiple remote routes that can be contacted through this dialup connection. It also means that there will be no periodic updates every 30 seconds. Auto-static updates are supported under RIP for IP, RIP for IPX, and SAP for IPX, but not OSPF.

The periodic mode will operate as a normal RIP router sending updates based on the periodic announcement interval that you set in the advanced tab. Under the outgoing packet protocol, you may choose RIP v1 broadcast, RIP v2 broadcast, RIP v2 multicast, or silent RIP. If your environment contains only RIP v1 routers, then use RIP v1. If the network contains RIP v1 and v2, using RIP v2 broadcast will send to both types of routers. Use RIP v2 multicast in a RIP v2 only network (it will cut down on broadcast traffic, but RIP v1 will not see the announcements.) Silent RIP will disable outgoing RIP packets, but allow for incoming packets. This would be a good choice if you want to learn other networks routes, but keep your routing table private.

In the outgoing packets we have RIP v1 and v2 which will accept either type of packet, RIP v1 which will only accept RIP v1 packets, and RIP v2 which will only accept v2 packets. You may also assign a cost (from 1–15) to this interface if a lower cost interface to the same network exists that would become the preferred route. There is also the ability to activate authentication here. If the incoming RIP announcement does not use the appropriate password, the route entries will be dropped. All RIP routers must use the same passwords, and it must be manually assigned. Also, the password is sent *clear-text*, so this is only rudimentary security.

The second tab contains the Route filter where you can determine which routes you will add into your routing table. The choices are Accept All Routes, Accept All Routes in the Ranges Listed, or Ignore All Routes in the Ranges Listed.

The Neighbors tab allows you to specify routers to which you will send announcements. The choices to use here are broadcast or multicast only, neighbors in addition to broadcasts or multicasts, or neighbors instead of broadcasts or multicasts.

The Advanced tab shown in Figure 4-9 allows you to configure some of the more detailed aspects. The defaults are normally acceptable for this, but you may want to change your periodic announcement interval to decrease the amount of broadcast traffic if you are using RIP v1.

FIGURE 4-9

RIP Properties
Advanced tab

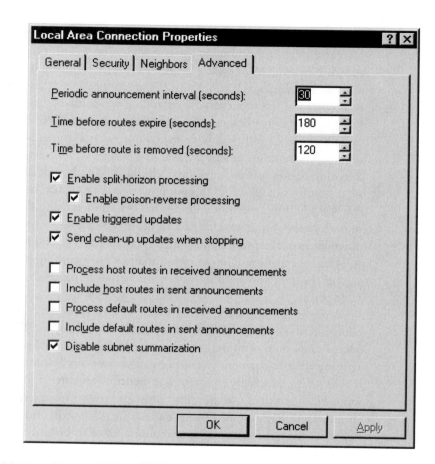

CERTIFICATION OBJECTIVE 4.07

Integrating TCP/IP with Existing WAN Requirements

Although it may be easier in some instances to create a fresh networking infrastructure, most organizations will have some connection mechanism in place with which you must work. As we put an additional strain on the available bandwidth, it will be important to use a design that will leverage the existing infrastructure. Here are some WAN environments in which you may find yourself and some thoughts that you should consider for the design.

T Carrier

T carrier systems are by no means new. They first appeared in the early 1960s as a digital carrier technology in the Chicago area. The system uses a time division multiplexing (TDM) technique to carry a 24-digital signal (DS0) into a single, larger system capable of speeds of 1.544 Mb/s. This is referred to as DS1, although we know it by the name of T-1. The DS levels have become synonymous with the T carrier level of the same speed. DS1C combines two T-1 circuits and provides a 3.154Mb/s service. DS2 uses 4 T-1s and runs at 6.312 Mb/s. DS3 is 28 T-1 channels with 672 voice circuits and a digital rate of 44.736 Mb/s. We know it as T-3. Europe has equivalent systems (E1 runs at 2.048 Mb/s).

Channel Service Unit / Data Service Units (CSU/DSUs) will be used to connect the customer premises equipment (CPE) to the telephone company's central office (CO).

The benefit of T carrier systems is the large amount of bandwidth that they provide and the fact that that bandwidth is constantly available. The drawback is the cost. Although competition has greatly reduced the cost of T carrier systems, it is still a major investment for a monthly recurring charge.

Although these systems provide high-speed access at significant distances, they are a high-priced solution. As emerging technologies such as DSL and cable begin to appear, consider them as an alternative. Use the T Carrier as part of a new design if it requires high-speed access at or above T-1 speeds or DSL is not available in your area.

If the T carrier is already in place and you plan on using it as part of your design, make sure that a sufficient amount of bandwidth exists for the additional load you will be placing on the line. Make sure that you maximize what you have as well. Schedule Active Directory replication, for example, to occur during off hours when the line is least busy. If the company is using fractional T-1, consider adding additional fractions to accommodate for the increased load.

ISDN

ISDN is a digital technology that is available in most North American markets. It supports data, voice, fax, and video. It incorporates OSI Layers 1-3 and is a suite of protocols in itself.

There are two categories of ISDN: Basic Rate Interfaces or BRI and Primary Rate Interfaces or PRI. The BRI uses two data channels, referred to as B channels (each channel may be purchased separately), and one channel for control information, known as D channels. The B channels operate at 64 Kbps while the D channels operate at 16 Kbps. Each B channel requires a phone number, though both channels can use the same number, and a Service Profile ID or SPID, which will differentiate the two channels. PRI uses 23 B channels and 1 D channel and provides a much higher bandwidth (1.544 Mbps), but is not as widely available.

When designing for ISDN, investigate which type you have. The limited bandwidth of BRI may require the use of both channels. If you do upgrade to a second channel, consider using BAP to give you better bandwidth, management. As with T carrier, a big issue will be bandwidth, so determine how much will be available and do all that you can to minimize traffic during working hours (scheduling replication traffic).

Frame Relay

Frame Relay has a distinct advantage over other WAN technologies. Instead of allocating a fixed amount of bandwidth, Frame Relay is capable of giving you the bandwidth you need when you need it. This is done by allocating a fixed amount for your use, called a Committed Information Rate or CIR, and allowing you to grow above that amount when your network requires it.

For example, you could contact a Frame Relay provider and request a CIR of 256Kbps, and that provider would guarantee a minimum bandwidth of that amount. During regular communication, the bursty nature of your traffic demands 512K at 9:00 a.m. as remote users log on. This is no problem whatsoever as the Frame Relay cloud allows you to grow your bandwidth to what you require at that time to whatever is available on the Frame Relay cloud. But you are not guaranteed that. If the cloud is already saturated, you will only receive the 256K as part of your CIR.

Frame Relay circuits are defined by Data-Link Connection Identifiers or DLCIs. The provider of your Frame Relay connection will assign you this DLCI, which operates like a MAC address for the system. You will have to manually map IP addresses to the DLCI as ARP is incapable of understanding Frame Relay directly. Many routers have this ability as well as the option of creating subinterfaces on the connections. Make sure you read the router's documentation to see what it is capable of doing.

Unlike T carrier or ISDN, bandwidth is not of the same concern when using Frame Relay. However, you will have to make the mappings from IP to DLCIs manually. Make sure that the CIR is sufficient for regular business data and that the total shared bandwidth of the frame will accommodate even the most taxing of traffic. Also, note that these circuits tend to be slightly more expensive than some other solutions, particularly when you exceed your CIR on a regular basis.

If Frame Relay is already in place, consider having the organization increase its CIR to accommodate the additional traffic. Also, keep replication traffic to off hours, as there will be less likelihood of a saturated cloud during those times.

Analog

Modems are a common, inexpensive solution for network connectivity. They provide a very limited bandwidth and should be used as part of a Windows 2000 design only if no other alternative is available. The bandwidth requirements of a routed TCP/IP network would be too great for the underlying analog infrastructure. There may be uses for them, however.

Consider using Multilink PPP with multiple modems to increase the available bandwidth. Using this in combination with BAP can be a solution where other WAN connectivity is either too costly or unavailable.

Secondly, consider using modems as a redundancy solution. For example, having a Frame Relay as a primary route with a metric of 1 and using the modem as a dial-on-demand device with a metric of 14 will cause routing traffic to use the Frame Relay connection the majority of the time and use the modem only if the Frame Relay connection becomes unavailable.

on the **job**

When using Dial-on-Demand routing, use static routes or auto-static updates whenever possible. Certain routing protocols like OSPF require an acknowledgment of packets. When the dial-up device is down, you could be subsequently removed from the remote routers routing table.

The following exercise will show you how to use dial-up devices for dial-on-demand routing.

EXERCISE 4-5

Configuring RRAS for Demand-Dial Routing

You have been asked to provide a routing solution for a small three-office company. They have asked you to use the existing infrastructure to accomplish this. To your dismay, you find that the existing infrastructure is a 56K modem. You have decided to use RRAS to configure the Demand-Dial routing.

For the following exercise will require a computer with a modem to simulate the set up of one end of the dial-on-demand configuration.

1. Open the RRAS MMC and select your server. Right-click the server and choose properties from the context menu. On the General tab, select both LAN and Demand-Dial routing. Click OK. You will receive a warning that RRAS must be restarted. Click Yes to restart RRAS.

2. Right-click Ports and select Properties. In the port properties, select your modem and click Configure. Ensure that the Demand Dial Routing Connections Inbound and Outbound are selected and type in the phone number for this device. Click OK twice to exit the port configuration.

3. Right-click routing interfaces and click new demand-dial interface. This will start the Demand-Dial interface wizard. Click Next on the welcome screen, give your interface a name, like "other end of town," and click Next.

4. Click connect using the modem, ISDN, or another physical connection, and click Next. Select your modem and click Next, then enter the phone number of the modem you will be calling and click Next. On the Protocols and Security page, ensure that Route IP Packets on This Interface is selected and click Next. (In a real configuration, at this stage we may want to create a user account that the other side would use to dial in to us.)

5. Enter the username and password that you will use to connect to the remote route on the dial-out credentials page and click Next, then Finish.

6. Right-click your server and click Properties. Select the IP tab to configure an IP pool. When the other device contacts you, it may not have an IP address assigned to it and will be expecting one from you. Creating a static IP address pool in the same range as your router will ensure that routers connecting to you will receive an address if they don't have one. Click OK.

7. Click Routing Interfaces in the left pane, and in the details pane, right-click your interface (the other side of town). Note part way down the context menu the Set IP Demand-Dial filter and the dial-out hours. The filters allow you to specify which type of traffic should initiate the Demand-dial port based on the source network, destination network, or protocol. The dial-out hours allow you to specify when the route can and cannot be active.

CERTIFICATION SUMMARY

As you may be aware, there are currently no plans for a TCP/IP exam for the Windows 2000 track. It would appear that all exams will be littered with TCP/IP questions, as IP is such a critical piece of the product. As you saw in the first section, your previous knowledge of TCP/IP will be grossly insufficient for Windows 2000 since so much has been added in. The good news is that if you do have the Windows NT 4.0 TCP/IP, and you have a solid understanding of the technology, you will have less of a learning curve than those that don't.

As with previous Microsoft exams, you should have a good hands-on knowledge of the product as well. Do more than just kick the tires of TCP/IP, test drive it—repeatedly. The shear mass of Windows 2000 going from 12 million lines of code to 24 million lines of code means that there is much to learn in the product. TCP/IP is a fundamental piece of that.

This chapter has covered the core components and new features of TCP/IP and has tried to point out some design concepts that you may wish to keep in mind not only for certification, but also in the real world. If anyone says "what should I use for a design," I hope you have seen from this chapter that the answer is "it depends." The goals and expectations of one company may be vastly different from another. A strong knowledge of the underlying features of TCP/IP should, however, point you in the right direction for each given situation.

TWO-MINUTE DRILL

Overview of Designing TCP/IP Networking Strategies

❑ TCP/IP is a stable, routable suite of protocols for multi-platform communications.

❑ The core components of TCP/IP have been enhanced with additional security and performance.

Analyzing IP Subnet Requirements

❑ Geography and politics will play a part in your design. Deal with it.

❑ Active Directory Replication can be controlled, but only between sites.

❑ DNS primary zones can be made part of the Active Directory structure.

Designing a TCP/IP Addressing and Implementation Plan

❑ $2^n - 2$ will calculate a subnet mask where n is the number of networks or the number of hosts.

❑ Use VLSM to subnet your subnet and to hide the underlying structure of your network from the outside world.

❑ Use CIDR to simplify routing calculations, but only use CIDR and VLSM on routers that support them.

❑ Watch out for MTU fragmentation when routing between LANS.

Measuring and Optimizing a TCP/IP Infrastructure Design

❑ Gather a baseline using performance monitor logs.

❑ Design redundant links for your network to ensure constant communications.

❑ Use QoS to reserve bandwidth in networks that support QoS.

Integrating Software Routing into Existing Networks

❑ RRAS provides inexpensive software-based routing.

❑ Use RIP in smaller organizations that do not have excessive traffic already.

❑ Use OSPF when you have a large inter-network, when to reduce traffic and when to spend the time on configuring and maintaining it.

Integrating TCP/IP with Existing WAN Requirements

❑ T-1 has high bandwidth at 1.544 Mbps and constant availability.

❑ ISDN has lower bandwidth at 64Kbps to 128Kbps on BRI and up to 1.544 Mbps on PRI.

❑ Frame Relay allows you to use more bandwidth if you need it, but only guarantees your CIR.

❑ Schedule replication to maximize bandwidth.

SELF TEST

The following questions will help you measure your understanding of the material presented in this chapter. Read all of the choices carefully, as there may be more than one correct answer. Choose all correct answers for each question.

Overview of Designing TCP/IP Networking Strategies

1. Which protocol will allow you to have an IP address assigned to you without a DHCP server?

   A. BAP

   B. APIPA

   C. BACP

   D. QoS

2. Your company is a financial institution that regularly transmits confidential information across the network. Which new feature of Windows 2000 would be most beneficial to your company?

   A. Use the APIPA to assign private addresses that will be inaccessible to the outside world.

   B. Disable NetBIOS on all systems to ensure that no Windows 9.x machines can communicate on the network.

   C. Use IPSec to authenticate and encrypt the data as it travels across the network.

   D. Use large TCP windows to ensure that the data is not on the WAN link for very long.

Analyzing IP Subnet Requirements

3. How many network IDs would be required in a configuration that had just two geographically separate offices connected by a WAN link?

   A. At least two

   B. At least three

   C. At least four

   D. At least five

4. You have been asked to configure a Windows 2000 DNS environment. The company already has a DNS server and would like to continue to use it. How would you install DNS to accommodate this?

   A. Install DNS on the new Windows 2000 server and set it up to be an Active Directory integrated zone.

B. Install DNS on the new Windows 2000 server and set it up to be a standard secondary zone. Ensure that the other DNS server is at BIND v4.2.

C. Install DNS on the new Windows 2000 server and configure it as a standard primary zone.

D. Install DNS on the new Windows 2000 server and set it up to be a standard secondary zone. Ensure that the other DNS server is upgraded to BIND v8.2.

Designing a TCP/IP Addressing and Implementation Plan

5. You are using a simple subnet mask of 255.255.240 and have an address of 145.145.68.7. What is your address class and how many networks and hosts does this mask accommodate?

   A. You have a class C address with 14 networks and 14 hosts.

   B. You have a class B address with 14 networks and 14 hosts.

   C. You have a class A address with 32 networks and 16.77 million hosts.

   D. You have a class B address with 14 networks and 4094 hosts.

6. Your company has been given an IP address of 162.15.64.0 with a subnet mask of 255.255.192.0. You would like to divide this into four subnets internally. How do you accomplish this?

   A. Verify that your routers support CIDR and create a supernet of all available hosts.

   B. Verify that your routers support VLSM and assign the internal networks the subnet mask of 255.255.248.0. Assign address ranges of 162.15.64.1–162.15.71.254 in net 1, 162.15.72.1–162.15.79.254 in net 2, 162.15.80.1–162.15.87.254 in net 3, and 162.15.88.1–162.15.95.254 in net 4.

   C. Verify that your routers support VLSM and assign a subnet mask of 255.255.224.0. Assign net 1 the addresses of 162.15.64.1–162.15.79.254, net 2 the address of 162.15.80.1–162.15.95.254, net 3 the address of 162.15.96.1–162.15.111.254 and net 4 the address of 162.15.112.1–162.15.127.254.

   D. Verify that your routers support VLSM.

7. You are working for an Internet service provider and they would like to reduce the number of entries in their routing table. How can you do this?

   A. Use private IP addressing and assign all customers an address from this range.

   B. Use private addressing and assign all customers the same address.

   C. Use CIDR and allow customers to maintain their current IP address.

   D. Use public addresses and assign all customers the same address.

8. You have an address of 26.133.12.5 with a subnet mask of 255.255.254.0. Which of the following is true? Choose all that apply.

   A. You have a public address.

   B. You have a private address.

   C. You have a class A address.

   D. You have a class C address.

   E. Your prefix is /15.

   F. Your prefix is /23.

Measuring and Optimizing a TCP/IP Infrastructure Design

9. Your organization has decided to increase security on the network. The servers on the network are underpowered and processing power is at a premium. How could you best improve security by encrypting and authenticating the data at a minimum of processing power?

   A. Configure IPSec to use the 3DES encryption and the SHA authentication.

   B. Configure IPSec to use the 40-bit DES encryption and the SHA authentication.

   C. Configure IPSec to use 56-bit encryption and the MD7 authentication.

   D. Configure IPSec to use 40-bit encryption and MD5 authentication.

10. When creating a Security Agreement (SA) authentication, what type of authentication can be provided? Choose all that apply.

    A. Pre-shared keys

    B. Kerberos v5

    C. X.509 certificates

    D. X.400

11. You have been asked to set up a system monitor of the server over a week of normal activity so that it can be used for future reference. What is the best way to do this?

    A. Run System Monitor to gather the information in a chart.

    B. Open a performance monitor log and gather the information in a log for one week. Set the log to gather the information at 10-minute intervals.

    C. Open a performance monitor log and schedule the monitor to gather statistics between 8 a.m. and 5 p.m. Set the log to gather information at 10-minute intervals.

    D. Run Network Monitor for one week to gather the statistics.

12. Which two commands of the QoS protocol RSVP are used to have the sender and recipient agree on the parameters for their communication path?

    A. SBM and QoS ACS

    B. PATH and RESV

    C. SMB and NCP

    D. TCP and UDP

Integrating Software Routing into Existing Networks

13. Which of the following protocols are not implemented in Windows 2000 RRAS?

    A. OSPF

    B. IGMP v2

    C. RIP v2

    D. IGRP

14. You have implemented RIP routing and are using only v2 routers. You have also decided to reduce network traffic of routing as bandwidth is at a premium. Which of the following will reduce network traffic? Choose all that apply.

    A. On the general page of the RIP properties, choose RIP v2 multicast for the "outing packets protocol."

    B. On the advanced page of the RIP properties, increase the value of the "periodic announcement interval."

    C. On the neighbors page of the RIP properties select "use neighbors instead of broadcast or multicast."

    D. On the general page of the RIP properties, choose the "activate authentication" and type in a password.

Integrating TCP/IP with Existing WAN Connections

15. You have been asked to install a Windows 2000 server. As part of the installation, you have been asked to create a redundant network link as a failover for this net environment. The company currently has a T-1 link and an ISDN link in place. How would you configure this system?

    A. Configure the Windows 2000 computers to only use the T-1. If the link goes down, you will reconfigure the systems to use the ISDN line.

B. Configure the Windows 2000 computers to use both the T-1 and ISDN lines by setting up different metrics for each link on the routers. Set the T-1 line for a metric of 1 and the ISDN line for a metric of 14 to ensure that the T-1 line will be used the most and the ISDN line only if the T-1 is down.

C. Configure the Windows 2000 computers to use both the T-1 and ISDN lines by setting up different metrics for each link on the router. Set the ISDN line for a metric of 1 and the T-1 line for a metric of 14 to ensure that the ISDN line will be used the most and the T-1 line only if the ISDN is down.

D. Configure the Windows 2000 computers to use only the ISDN line. If the link goes down, you will reconfigure the systems to use the T-1 line.

16. Which technology allows you to grow your bandwidth as required?

A. T Carrier

B. ISDN

C. Frame Relay

D. Analog

17. In which of the following situations should bandwidth not be a consideration when using an existing WAN?

A. T Carrier

B. ISDN

C. Frame Relay

D. Analog

E. None of the above

LAB QUESTION

As a consultant for BCD systems you have been called in to reconfigure VWX Corp's TCP/IP network. They have been running a Unix network for over ten years now and would like to eventually migrate to Windows 2000. As part of this migration, they will be ordering some Windows 2000 servers as part of a pilot project. Your task is to propose a design that will accommodate the existing network and allow for the addition of the Windows 2000 systems. VWX has provided you with the following information:

- Internet access will be required by all computers for e-mail and Web access.
- VWX has three locations (Boston, Chicago, and Los Angeles) with the head office in Chicago. The Los Angeles office is connected via T-1 and the Boston office is connected to the Chicago office via ISDN.
- Chicago has mission-critical applications that require 7/24 access.
- New routers have been purchased in the last 90 days to support new IETF protocols.
- All LANs are running Ethernet at 100Mb/s.
- The Chicago office has 800 hosts, Boston has 87 hosts, and Los Angeles has 680 hosts.
- The Boston connection is running at 78 percent utilization. The T-1, however, is only running at approximately 30 percent utilization.
- Security is a must because many confidential pieces of data are transmitted over the network. Access to this information from the Internet would be unacceptable. Both authentication and encryption will be required.
- They currently have no connection to the Internet, but have contracted with an ISP and will be using a fractional T-1 line at 128K. The ISP has allotted a class C address range of 207.134.222.x–VWX for their access.
- Chicago and Los Angeles are both subnetted using private addresses. There are currently two subnets in Los Angeles and three in Chicago.
- DNS is to remain under the control of the current Unix administrators. However, they are willing to upgrade the DNS servers if necessary.
- VWX will not buy servers unless it is an absolute requirement, but are willing to use servers as software routers.

Additional network information you have learned:

- The routers they have purchased are in two configurations. The Chicago office has a higher-end router that has three WAN interfaces and four LAN interfaces, and supports up to 254 users per segment on each port. The router in Los Angeles has a single WAN interface and two LAN interfaces. This router will support 127 hosts per segment. Boston is using an older router that has been in place for five years.

- Additional fractions may be added to the T-1 line, but only at 128k increments.

- The T-1 line is using an MTU of 1500, but the ISDN line has an MTU of 256.

- The current private address in Los Angeles and Chicago are in the 10.x.x.x range and you may reconfigure this as part of your design.

- VWX expects to hire approximately 200 new people for an office in Dallas next year.

- Although the router in Boston is not new, it has been upgraded and supports IPSec, QoS, CIDR, and VLSM. It may also be used as a VPN-tunnel end-point.

Your design must maximize working hour traffic, and you are able to recommend new or redundant equipment where it is warranted. You may offer any design that meets these criteria.

SELF TEST ANSWERS

Overview of Designing TCP/IP Networking Strategies

1. ☑ **B.** The Automatic Private IP Addressing (APIPA) feature of Windows 2000 will automatically assign you an address of 169.254.x.x if a DHCP server cannot be reached.
   ☒ **A**, BAP, is the Bandwidth Allocation Protocol, which dynamically allocates or deallocates bandwidth on multi-link PPP devices. **C**, BACP, is the Bandwidth Allocation Control Protocol and is another name for BAP. **D**, QoS, is the Quality of Service protocol and allows you to reserve bandwidth for specific applications.

2. ☑ **C.** Use IPSec to authenticate and encrypt your data.
   ☒ **A** is incorrect. Using APIPA would remove your ability to easily access the Internet. **B**, Disabling NetBIOS, would not keep traffic from being monitored as it traveled across the network and neither would **D**, using large TCP windows.

Analyzing IP Subnet Requirements

3. ☑ **B.** This would require at least three connections, one for each office and one for the WAN.
   ☒ **A, C,** and **D** are incorrect because at least three connections are required.

4. ☑ **D.** Setting up the server as either AD integrated or as a standard primary will create a new DNS zone and prevent using the existing DNS server.
   ☒ **A, B,** and **C** are incorrect. Creating a standard secondary zone will obtain the zone file from the existing DNS server, but BIND v4.2 will not accommodate the SRV records required with Windows 2000.

Designing a TCP/IP Addressing and Implementation Plan

5. ☑ **D.** The address of 145.145 is within the class B address range and its default subnet mask is 255.255.0.0. Using the additional four bits for subnets gives us 2^4-2, or 14, networks and leaves us with 12 bits for hosts, or $2^{12}-2=4094$.
   ☒ **A, B,** and **C** are incorrect because your address class is B and you have 14 networks and 4094 hosts.

6. ☑ **B.** VLSM will be required to subnet an already subnetted network. Assigning a subnet mask of 248 would use an additional three bits on top of the bits already taken and would give us six additional subnetworks. The ranges of the hosts in the same network must be in the ranges specified to be valid hosts.
   ☒ **A, C,** and **D** are incorrect because the proposed answers would not accommodate the need.

7. ☑ **C.** Classless InterDomain Routing (CIDR) allows you to make a large number of network segments appear to the routing table as a single network.

   ☒ **A** is incorrect because private addressing packets are dropped from routers on public addressed networks like the Internet. All hosts must be assigned a unique number, so **B** and **D** are incorrect.

8. ☑ **A, C, F.** You have a public address, a class A address, and a prefix of /23. The 26.x.x.x is not part of the RFC 1918 private address range. RFC defines the 10.x.x.x, 172.16.x.x to 172.31.x.x, and 192.168.x.x ranges for private addresses. The 26 number is within the class A address range as defined by RFC 791. Since 23 bits are being used for the network/subnetwork address, your prefix will be /23.

   ☒ **B, D,** and **E** are incorrect because they are not true.

Measuring and Optimizing a TCP/IP Infrastructure Design

9. ☑ **D.** Configuring IPSec to use the lowest authentication and encryption will reduce the overhead associated with processing the information.

   ☒ **A, B,** and **C** are incorrect. SHA will authenticate using 160-bit keys while MD5 uses only 128-bit. 3DES uses 128-bit encryption, while the other forms of DES encrypt at 40- or 56-bit. MD7 is a red herring.

10. ☑ **A, B, C.** Pre-shared keys, Kerberos v5, and X.509 certificates are all correct types of authentication.

    ☒ **D** is incorrect because it is a mail protocol.

11. ☑ **C.** This method would provide the data for normal business hours and would keep the data file smaller. The network monitor will only show us network activity to and from the server, and the capture file would be very large. System Monitor charts are in real time and will not provide you with a reusable log. Generating a log for the entire week and not just business hours would also generate too much data.

    ☒ **A, B,** and **D** are incorrect because the best approach to take would be to open a performance monitor log and schedule the monitor to gather statistics between 8 a.m. and 5 p.m. You would then set the log to gather information at ten-minute intervals.

12. ☑ **B.** The PATH and RESV are used to set up the communication parameters for QoS.

    ☒ **A, C,** and **D** are incorrect because the PATH and RESV are used to set up the communication parameters for QoS.

Integrating Software Routing into Existing Networks

13. ☑ **D.** The Interior Gateway Routing Protocol (IGRP) is a Cisco proprietary routing protocol.
☒ **A, B,** and **C** are incorrect because OSPF, IGMP v2, and RIP v2 are not implemented in Windows 2000 RRAS.

14. ☑ **A, B, C.** Activating a password will drop packets sent from routers that do not use your password, but the traffic is still sent across the network.
☒ **D,** on the general page of the RIP properties, choose the "activate authentication" and type in a password, is incorrect.

Integrating TCP/IP with Existing WAN Connections

15. ☑ **B.** Making both lines available, but with differing metrics means that you will not have to manually reconfigure for the other line should one go down. T-1 is a higher bandwidth line and should be used most of the time, as it is a constantly available bandwidth that would be wasted if we did not use it.
☒ **A, C,** and **D** are incorrect because you would configure the Windows 2000 computers to use both the T-1 and ISDN lines by setting up different metrics for each link on the routers. Set the T-1 line for a metric of 1 and the ISDN line for a metric of 14 to ensure that the T-1 line will be used the most and the ISDN line only if the T-1 is down.

16. ☑ **C.** Frame Relay gives you a base amount of bandwidth with the CIR and allows you to grow to whatever is available on the pipe at that time.
☒ **A, B,** and **D** are incorrect because although BAP and multi-link PPP allow you to increase the bandwidth you have to another line, it is not inherently part of the technology design of either ISDN or analog to do so.

17. ☑ **E.** None of the above. You should always consider bandwidth as part of your design and maximize whatever you have for the existing infrastructure. It is more critical with analog and ISDN than with T carrier or Frame Relay, but using off-hour replication to maximize working-hour bandwidth will give your customer more productive use of the WAN links.

LAB ANSWER

This is the type of scenario where almost too much information is presented all at once. The best way to deal with the above request for this design is to break it up into workable pieces. Here are some questions that you should think about as you are looking at the criteria:

- How many networks/hosts will I need today/in 18 months?
- What addresses/masks do I use?
- What will I need to do to integrate Windows 2000 with the existing DNS server?
- Do I need to add routers to the design? Software or hardware?
- Do I need to modify the existing WAN connections?
- What do I do for Internet access/security?

Let's answer them one by one. First, the question of how many networks. The Chicago office has 800 hosts and a hardware-based router that can accommodate 250 users per segment and four interfaces on the router. Here we will need four networks of approximately 200 hosts each with about 50 hosts worth of growth in each network segment.

The Los Angeles office has 680 hosts and a router that supports 127 hosts per segment with two LAN interfaces. Here we will need additional routers on top of the one in place. If we recommend the same router, we will need to break up this network into six networks of approximately 115 hosts in each network.

The Boston office will require only a single LAN network ID for the 87 hosts. The 200 new users in the Dallas office will require the same infrastructure as the Los Angeles office, so we may assume two networks of approximately 100 each. The final piece will be the number of WAN network IDs. Boston to Chicago, Chicago to Los Angeles and Los Angeles to the future Dallas office will give us a grand total of three WAN IDs. Altogether, we will require 16 network IDs with each network requiring no more than 250 hosts.

Since the Chicago and Los Angeles offices are currently using private IP addresses, it would be logical to follow this through to the rest of the organization. Since private IP addresses will not be passed through to the Internet, we will require some type of network address translation device. Although Windows 2000 does come with NAT in the RRAS component, it would be preferable to use a more complete product that would also have proxy and advanced firewall capabilities.

Once we have this in place, it will give us a secure network connection and we can worry about the addresses. Since we have determined that we will use private IP addresses, the unused addresses in the block that we have obtained from the ISP may be used for VPN sessions or future considerations.

The private addressing structure should be as uncomplicated as possible. We will require no more than 250 users in each subnet, and we have a 10.x.x.x range in place. If we use a subnet mask based on the number of hosts, we will use eight bits for the hosts, which leaves us with a simple 10.x.x.x with a mask of 255.255.255.0. This will give us 65,534 networks, which should leave enough room for growth in the foreseeable future.

Since the Unix administrators wish to maintain control of the DNS server, we will ask them to upgrade the DNS server to BIND 8.2 to support the SRV, dynamic updates, and IXFR, which will then support Windows 2000.

We see from the first bullet that two additional routers will be required in Los Angeles, or we may wish to implement that as part of an RRAS solution. The key point here will be budgeting. If the budget is in place, we will be allowed to purchase additional hardware routers that will perform better and off-load server load to another device. If the budget is not there for the hardware router, we will have to create the routes through RRAS, which will negatively impact the performance of the server. One way or another, four new subnets must be created. We will also need routers for the Dallas office when it comes online.

The connection between Boston and Chicago is currently running at 78 percent utilization; therefore, this WAN connection should be reconsidered. A fractional T-1 or full T-1 may improve the design and the ISDN connection could then be used as part of a redundancy design. This could then become the corporate standard for network redundancy by adding the same links into the Los Angeles and future Dallas offices. This will also eliminate the potential problem with fragmentation of traffic with the smaller MTU of the ISDN connection. The other connection in Los Angeles may be a bit much, so reducing this connection to a fractional T-1 and increasing the Internet fractions might be a wise idea. We are really just shifting costs, but it will be a better use of the connections we have.

The last piece of the problem requires us to look at IPSec. We will be using a firewall for our Internet connection, but using IPSec will give us the added authentication and encryption required in the design. Port and protocol filtering would not encrypt or authenticate—it would only block. Since all the routers can support IPSec, it should be implemented for internal use so long as it is not a drain on the servers that process the encryption.

5

Designing a DHCP Strategy

CERTIFICATION OBJECTIVES

D ynamic Host Configuration Protocol (DHCP) is an integral part of any network strategy and Microsoft has taken steps to enhance the Windows 2000 implementation of DHCP. In order to design a DHCP solution for your network, you must completely understand DHCP. Toward that end, it is important to learn the reasons such a specification was developed, what the current implementation looks like, and some of the changes that Microsoft has made in its latest development of DHCP for the Windows server platform.

CERTIFICATION OBJECTIVE 5.01

Overview of the Windows 2000 DHCP Server

An overview of Windows 2000 DHCP server will begin with a short history and a look at the vast changes Microsoft has made to this release. A good design must be built on a solid understanding of the system and, often, familiarity with some of the less frequently used features provides the perfect solution.

History

DHCP's predecessor was called the bootstrap protocol (BOOTP). BOOTP is an Internet standard defined by Request for Comments (RFC) 951 (BOOTP) and 1084 (BOOTP Vendor Information Extensions). It was designed mainly for the same reason we use DHCP today: network administrators grew overwhelmed at the idea of assigning static IP addresses to every workstation they put on their networks. BOOTP solved the problem by specifying a central source (server) that would assign and keep track of IP addresses for machines that request an address. The downside to this protocol was that IP addresses were reserved on the server for a particular physical network address. This meant that although the server would assign an address to the machine that requested it, the network administrator had to make sure that a machine's physical network address was entered into the BOOTP table on the server and manually correlated to an address before the workstation would receive the assignment. Assignments in this way mandated that one IP address is assigned to every machine, even though some machines may only access the network intermittently.

Experiencing the limitations of BOOTP, the Internet community reacted, and the result was RFC 2131 (DHCP), and later, RFC 2132 (DHCP Options and BOOTP Vendor Extensions). These RFCs defined the operating specifications for the DHCP servers we have today. DHCP solves several of the limitations of BOOTP by allowing the dynamic assignment of addresses to clients on a network. Addresses are leased to clients for a limited amount of time, then recovered when the lease expires. This allows the server to service more workstations than it has IP addresses to lend. DHCP is basically maintenance-free when it comes to assigning addresses. In contrast to BOOTP's high maintenance physical address-to-IP address table, the network administrator only has to set a scope of addresses that the DHCP server can assign and the server assigns the addresses to each client as it responds to client requests.

Windows 2000 BOOTP Support

Before you say, "What, no BOOTP support?", let me assure you that Microsoft's implementation of DHCP does support BOOTP. So if you have a large UNIX environment, you can still use a Windows 2000 Server for DHCP support. DHCP will allow administrators to assign addresses to machines based upon their MAC (media access control) address in the same way that BOOTP did. In addition, Microsoft took it a step further by providing dynamic BOOTP addressing. This means that if you choose, you can allow DHCP to assign addresses to BOOTP clients without retaining a BOOTP table making reference to the physical address to the IP address. No change to the client is necessary for this functionality. DHCP is fully functional, and can be configured to respond to DHCP clients alone, to BOOTP clients alone, or to both.

Diskless Workstations

Another function of BOOTP is its capability of integrating itself into a diskless workstation environment. The diskless workstation would notify the BOOTP server and request the IP address of a Trivial File Transfer Protocol (TFTP) server from which it retrieves a small boot-image file with which to boot. Although DHCP does not provide the TFTP service, it will allow you to configure the server with an address of a TFTP server that it will use as a redirect address for BOOTP clients.

on the **job**

Windows 2000 takes advantage of TFTP when implementing installations using the Remote Installation Service. The boot image is stored on an RIS Server.

System Requirements

As with all network services, it is important to always evaluate the necessary system requirements and take them into account in your design plan. As to hardware requirements, DHCP will run on any machine that meets the Microsoft-recommended hardware requirements for the Windows 2000 server. There are, however, many items to consider before deciding on the hardware requirements for DHCP. Consider:

- The number of clients that the DHCP server(s) will support
- The number of scopes (subnets) serviced by the DHCP server(s)
- The length of the lease for assigned addresses
- The other services running on the DHCP server(s)
- The network bandwidth available

Microsoft contends that with Windows NT 4.0 or later versions, a single DHCP server supports up to 10,000 clients comfortably. This is, of course, a theoretical boundary, for network conditions and configuration changes play a major role in the validity of this limit.

Addressing System Requirements

Let's take a large network of 10,000 hosts, for example. You have one multi-processor machine with 512MB RAM running Windows 2000 and DHCP alone. Let's say you have configured your standard lease length at eight days. We will talk more about leases later, but for now, you should understand a lease as the amount of time a client can use an IP address. In this scenario, the server will most likely handle the load well. However, if the administrator were to change the standard lease length to one day or less, the network would very likely slow to a crawl due to the DHCP traffic that is generated. In this situation, an eight-processor server, or even a sixty-four-processor server, is not going to help with this problem, for it is a limitation of bandwidth, not hardware. When considering system requirements, always look at the whole picture, not just the hardware.

exam

ⓦatch

As you study for the exam, be sure to fully understand the implications of changing configurations such as the lease length of a server or scope. Microsoft's new testing model includes many scenario-type questions for which you need to be prepared.

Many DHCP implementations use one or two large servers to service the entire enterprise. This makes management of your DHCP scopes easier, but forces all traffic on the network that is destined for DHCP servers to travel through wide area links, which is usually an asynchronous or Frame Relay connection, limited in bandwidth compared to the local LAN. This can occupy precious bandwidth that may be needed for other applications. So be sure to consider all aspects of your network before deciding where to place your DHCP servers.

Changes in Windows 2000 DHCP

The following list specifies the new and improved features in Windows 2000's DHCP service.

- Integration of DHCP with DNS
- Enhanced monitoring and statistical reporting of DHCP servers
- Vendor-specific and class-ID option support
- Multicast address allocation
- Rogue DHCP server detection
- Windows clustering support
- Improved DHCP Manager

Integration of DHCP with DNS

Domain Naming System (DNS) is a name-to-IP address resolution service for networks. If you have used the Internet, you have used DNS, for the entire Internet-naming infrastructure is based on DNS. DNS allows you to set an IP address such as 4.21.78.15 to a hostname in a domain such as microsft.com. This is valuable to the Internet, because it allows you to assign names such as **www** to a domain and to use it as the address of your Web server. This is much easier than typing the IP address manually, and much easier to remember.

Microsoft's new implementation of DNS for Windows 2000 includes dynamic update, and is referred to in Windows 2000 as Dynamic DNS, or DDNS. This means that machines (Windows 2000 and Windows 98 only) on the network that start will notify the DNS server of their name and IP address and dynamically create a record for that machine on that domain (operating as WINS clients have done in the past).

This is a strategic move that has a large impact on Windows 2000 design issues. The functionality that was provided through the WINS service is now being provided through DDNS, virtually eliminating the need for WINS in the LAN.

Not all operating systems support the new client registration functionality of dynamic DNS. For the exam, be sure you know that currently only Windows 2000 and Windows 98 support client registrations.

DHCP now integrates with dynamic DNS to offer registration services for clients that don't support dynamic updates of records. If a Windows NT 4.0 machine comes up on the network and requests an IP address from the DHCP server, the server will pass an address on to it. Then the server will tell DNS that it has assigned the address to that machine so that DNS can create a record for the machine. DHCP can also be configured to delete the record of machines that have expired leases. This makes name resolution with DNS completely dynamic and provides a solid networking platform for even the largest networks.

Be sure to know how each operating system integrates with the new features of the DNS service. With the advent of Dynamic DNS, the way that some clients interact with the DHCP and DNS server has changed.

Enhanced Monitoring and Statistical Reporting of DHCP Servers

The Microsoft Management Console (MMC) DHCP snap-in has replaced the DHCP Manager as the administrative console for DHCP and offers more granular and flexible monitoring of DHCP status information, including statistical reporting and console-alerting features.

Vendor Specific and Class ID Option Support

Windows 2000 DHCP adds the capability of tailoring the DHCP options the server assigns based on vendor specific classes, or user-defined classes. This means that if you have two machine types within the same scope that need different DNS addresses, you can group one collection of machines using a particular class ID, and leave the other collection of machines to receive the standard options defined within the scope. This can also be helpful with RAS clients who sometimes need a different configuration than the standard workstation options.

Vendors of certain networking products define vendor-specific options. The server recognizes the need to deliver vendor-specific options based on a data stream that determines whether an option class is standard or vendor specific. Vendor classes are described in detail in RFC 2132.

Multicast Address Allocation

Microsoft has included in the Windows 2000 release of DHCP server support for multicast address assignment. The standard DHCP client will not retrieve a multicast address. To utilize this feature, you must have an application written to request multicast addresses from the DHCP server.

Rogue DHCP Server Detection

A rogue server is an unauthorized DHCP server. Unauthorized DHCP servers that are active on a network can cause large problems by assigning invalid addresses to DHCP clients, causing the client to lose access to network resources.

Windows 2000 DHCP now includes rogue-server detection in the form of Active Directory authorization queries so that administrators can be informed of unauthorized DHCP servers on the network.

Windows Clustering Support

Used in conjunction with Microsoft Cluster Server (a service included with Windows 2000 Advanced Server), DHCP server can be set up to provide **fail over** between two servers. If one server were to fail, the other server would take over where the other left off. And because Microsoft Cluster Server uses common storage space, they work in tandem to keep the database consistent.

Improved DHCP Manager

The DHCP manager, with every other tool you were familiar with in Windows NT 4.0, is replaced by the Microsoft Management Console in Windows 2000. There is now a plug-in for each management tool, and DHCP is no exception. This new console is much easier to use, provides more statistical reporting, and includes many wizards to help you with difficult tasks.

Client/Server Communication

Understanding the process where a client on a network obtains an IP address assignment from a DHCP server will assist you in designing a Windows 2000 network and troubleshooting any problems along the way. The details of how DHCP works is covered in the Syngress MCSE study guide *Implementing and Administering a Windows 2000 Network Infrastructure* and tested on Exam 70-216. You should study the core Implementation and Administration topics prior to preparing for the Design exams, and be sure you are familiar with the process of a DHCP client communicating with the server and receiving a lease.

It is important to note that the DHCP process takes place as soon as the card is initialized, so network equipment such as switches that perform spanning-tree algorithms to check for loop conditions on initialization will prevent clients from communicating with the DHCP server. These types of loop checks are not required for user workstations and can be safely disabled.

DHCP Options

In addition to assigning IP addresses, DHCP servers can assign over 30 predefined options to clients (if the clients support them) as defined by RFC 2132. Options can be assigned to the entire server or to scopes individually. Options that are applied as a server option apply to all scopes serviced by that server. This is helpful if you have one server serving ten scopes and all scopes use the same WINS settings or DNS settings.

When designing your DHCP service, think clearly about how you will use options and whether they will be applied globally or based on individual scopes.

Note that even though DHCP supports over 30 options, Windows-based DHCP clients only support the following options:

- **Domain Name**   This is the domain name assigned to all hosts in this scope.
- **DNS Servers**   This is the address of the DNS server(s) that clients within this scope should use.
- **WINS/NBNS Servers**   This is the address of the WINS server(s) that the clients within this scope should use.
- **WINS/NBT Node Type**   This is the node type for all NetBIOS-enabled machines in the network and determines how clients locate hosts using WINS or broadcasts.

- **Router**   This is the router address or gateway address that should be used by clients on this subnet.

- **NetBios Scope ID**   This is a string that specifies the NetBIOS over TCP/IP Scope IP for the client, as specified in RFC 1001/1002. On computers with more than one network card, the scope ID is assigned to the machine, not to the individual card.

To define any of these options, select it from the list and then define a host name and/or IP address for the selected device, as shown in Figure 5-1. When designing a DHCP service for a large network, options are essential. Every scope that you create must have a set of options that specifies the location of DNS servers, WINS servers, NBT node types, and gateway (router) addresses.

on the
Job   *Try to avoid assigning a router address as a global variable. Rather, use a scope variable. Even if your network is small and you only have one subnet (and consequently one gateway), your network is sure to grow. Different segments cannot share the router address because they would need different gateway addresses. Alternatively, global options can be good for DNS entries when you want your entire enterprise to always use the same DNS servers.*

FIGURE 5-1

Assigning option values

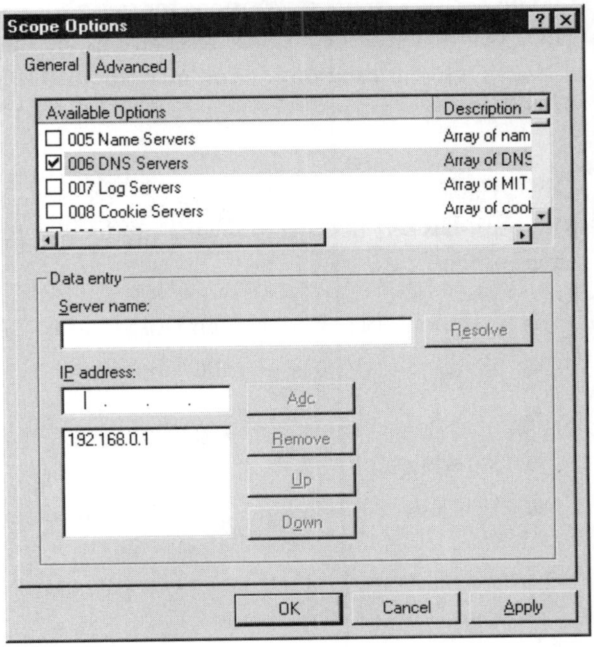

Planning for Reservations

Within any network it is necessary to assign static IP addresses to machines that perform a particular function. DNS servers, WINS servers, and printers are all good examples of devices that typically are assigned static IP addresses.

Reservations allow you to predefine what machines will not participate in DHCP as part of your planning process. Once your DHCP server is implemented, you can create the reservations for the machines you have decided to include within this group.

When planning for reservations, keep the following rules in mind.

- The MAC address is a physical address related to the network card, so if you swap the machine or change the network card, you will have to update the reservation. Don't plan to add reservations for machines that may be upgraded frequently.

- The IP address assigned through a reservation must be within a defined scope, so be sure to leave room for them in your scope.

- Even though a reservation address must be within a defined scope of addresses, it does not have to be between the start and end address of that scope. It just needs to be part of the subnet defined by that scope.

The decision to use reservations for static address assignments is really up to you, but if you do choose not to use reservations, be sure to keep track of the addresses you assign to workstations or you may run into IP address conflicts with your DHCP server.

DHCP Client Planning

Microsoft has certified the following products as functional in a DHCP environment:

- Windows NT Workstation (All versions)
- Windows NT Server (All versions)
- Windows 95
- Windows 98
- Windows for Workgroups 3.11 (with Microsoft 32-bit VxD)

- Microsoft Network Client version 3.0 for MS-DOS (with real-mode TCP/IP driver installed)
- LAN Manager client version 2.2c

There are other clients that will use DHCP for network address assignment, but you must check with the manufacturer for details on their compliance with the DHCP specification.

exam
ⓦatch

Although the exam covers the implementation of DHCP networking on the Windows 2000 platform, there will most likely be questions related to DHCP clients of different operating systems. Be sure you are familiar with the DHCP client setup for all supported clients.

In the ideal networking environment, you should set up your DHCP server to service all clients on your network, then set all of your workstations to retrieve addresses and configuration options from DHCP. Manual configuration of workstations should be limited as much as possible.

Always build your network plan based on what your network will be, not the way that it is currently. Plan for growth.

CERTIFICATION OBJECTIVE 5.02

Integrating DHCP into a Routed Environment

As technological innovations increase, networks become more and more sophisticated. The size and complexity of the typical network can range from a small workgroup network consisting of five to ten machines, to a large enterprise network containing thousands of machines. Many networks start small and due to company growth, increase in size exponentially, sometimes faster than networking professionals can implement solutions.

DHCP is user friendly and lightweight enough to be used on the smallest of networks, and robust and scalable enough to be used on large enterprise networks. With this in mind, it is always a good idea to implement a DHCP strategy early in your network's development. Beginning with a different protocol and migrating to TCP/IP with DHCP can be a difficult task. Implementing DHCP early will prevent this headache.

The implementation of DHCP can be done in several different ways, depending on the needs of your network, particularly the size and routing. In this section, we will look at the implementation of DHCP in three different scenarios:

- DHCP for Workgroups looks at the planning considerations for implementing DHCP in a small non-routed network of machines.

- DHCP for Small Networks reviews the implementation of DHCP in a small routed network contained within one location.

- DHCP in the Enterprise covers the placement of DHCP in a large enterprise network, characterized by thousands of machines across different geographical locations

DHCP for Workgroups

DHCP fits well into small workgroup (peer-to-peer) networks. A small workgroup network typically consists of one physical network segment supporting one server and three to ten workstations.

DHCP is dependent upon broadcasts for proper functionality and, aside from configuring a router to retransmit broadcasts or relay the data, the traffic created by a DHCP server will not leave the local physical segment. In a small single-segment network, the implementation of DHCP is quite simple and should be installed on the Windows 2000 server and configured with one scope. In a small workgroup it may be desirable to run DHCP on a server that is part of a network workgroup and not configured as a domain member. DHCP supports this configuration and will behave similarly to the installation of DHCP on a domain member server. There are, however, a few minor differences.

DHCP on a server that is part of a workgroup, rather than a domain, performs rogue server detection similar to its counterpart. How the workgroup DHCP server responds to the detection of a rogue server is slightly different from the way a domain member server would. If the workgroup server locates another DHCP server on the network, it will determine whether that server is a workgroup server or part of a domain. If the server is part of a workgroup, the event is logged in the event log and the server continues to function. If the server detected is a domain controller, the workgroup server will assume it is not authorized to service requests and cease to function until that domain controller is taken offline or the DHCP service is shutdown. This quick reference will help you remember the action of a workgroup DHCP server during rogue detection.

SCENARIO & SOLUTION

What happens if rogue detection does not detect a DHCP server on the network?	The workgroup DHCP server begins servicing requests.
What happens if rogue detection locates another workgroup DHCP server?	The workgroup server will log the IP address of the rogue DHCP server and continue to service clients.
What happens if rogue detection locates a domain member DHCP server on the network?	The workgroup server will log the event in the event viewer and cease responding to client requests.

DHCP for Small Networks

In a small network, DHCP should be a required service. Manually tracking IP address assignments, even for a small network, can be a burden. Most small networks consist of 10–300 machines and are all contained within one location.

Before Ethernet switches became popular, small networks were often routed using a network router. Physical segments would be limited to 30–60 nodes. Ethernet switches have made it possible to build large Virtual Local Area Networks (VLANs) that can contain hundreds of machines on the same segment. This can present difficulties for simple DHCP implementations due to the number of machines on the same physical segment. For instance, if you are using a 10.1.1.0/24 network, you have 254 addresses that can be assigned out of that scope (10.1.1.1–10.1.1.254). What if you have 300 machines on that segment? You could reconfigure your TCP/IP subnetting model for your entire network to allow for more addresses in the subnet, but this can be a difficult process in some networks.

Superscopes   DHCP offers another solution called *superscopes*. Windows NT has supported superscopes since the application of Service Pack 2 on Windows NT 4.0. Superscopes allow you to offer more than one defined scope to the same physical segment. This type of network is often referred to as a *multinet*.

In the scenario we just mentioned, you could add a second subnet of 10.1.2.0/24 to your DHCP configuration, and then group the 10.1.1.0/24 and the 10.1.2.0/24 into a superscope. This informs the DHCP server that it is acceptable to hand out addresses from both scopes to machines on the same physical segment. You will also have to inform the routers servicing the segment that a new network was added. This will add a small amount of overhead to the routers, but the performance hit is not substantial, and it is much easier than re-subnetting your entire network.

CertCam 5-1

Implementing DHCP in a Small Network

Your network is in the middle of a migration from Token Ring to Ethernet, and you have been given the task of implementing TCP/IP for all hosts on the network. Your network consists of two segments. One of them is a Token Ring segment of 15 workstations running Windows 2000. The other is an Ethernet VLAN of 80 machines also running Windows 2000. A new Cisco router separates the two networks and routes traffic from one segment to the other. You have been assigned the 192.168.0.1 network address space with a 26-bit mask (255.255.255.192). How would you implement DHCP in this environment?

Answer: Install a DHCP server on the Ethernet segment. (You could have installed it on the Token Ring segment, but since you are migrating to Ethernet, that would not be wise.) Set up the following scopes on the server:

1. 192.168.0.1–192.168.0.62 (255.255.255.192)
2. 192.168.0.65–192.168.0.126 (255.255.255.192)
3. 192.168.0.129–192.168.0.190 (255.255.255.192)

Join the first and second scope together in a superscope and assign the addresses 192.168.0.1 and 192.168.0.65 to the router interface serving that segment. Assign the address 192.168.0.129 to the router interface serving the Token Ring segment, then create an IP helper address on the router to point to the DHCP server so that all BOOTP/DHCP broadcast requests are forwarded to the DHCP server.

DHCP Relay Agent   Superscopes can solve many IP address limitations when working with large network segments. In some networks, however, there is still a need for routers in the local network, for the size of a VLAN is not unlimited. How would you implement DHCP in an environment where two physical segments are separated by a router?

In Windows NT 4.0 the DHCP Relay Agent can be installed on a Windows NT 4.0 server or Windows NT 4.0 Workstation machine; however, in Windows 2000, the DHCP relay agent service is only available in the Windows 2000 server. The DHCP relay agent acts as an agent for the DHCP server, listening on the local segment for any DHCP/BOOTP broadcast requests. Once a client broadcasts the first request for an IP address on the segment, the DHCP relay hears the broadcast and relays the request directly to the DHCP server on the other segment. The DHCP server then responds to the request by issuing an IP address assignment to the relay agent, which in turn relays the address to the client. All communication in the scenario between the DHCP relay agent and the client is the same as the communication between a DHCP server and client in a typical workgroup scenario. All communication between the DHCP relay agent and the DHCP server is point to point. No broadcasts are used for that communication, since they are on different subnets.

In this scenario, the DHCP server would be using two separate scopes, one for the local segment that the server is on, and the other for the network segment that the relay agent is on. The DHCP server knows the difference between clients that request addresses on the local subnet and addresses that are requested by relay agents, and assigns addresses appropriately, based on the subnet of the requesting machine.

on the Job

The DHCP relay agent uses the same TCP/UDP ports as the DHCP service and is intended to run on a separate subnet than the DHCP server. In no way should you ever install the DHCP relay agent on a server running the DHCP service, nor should you ever place a DHCP relay agent on the same physical network segment with a DHCP server.

DHCP for the Enterprise

With DHCP relay agents and superscopes, it is possible to build a sizeable network in one particular location, possibly even across remote locations. Dealing with an enterprise network is slightly different due to its size, the physical geography, and the administration involved. The implementation of DHCP in an enterprise raises several questions.

- How do remote users get IP addresses?
- How do I assign addresses across the Wide Area Network (WAN)?
- Do I need a DHCP server on each segment?
- What bandwidth is necessary to implement one DHCP server for everyone?
- How do I make my server fault tolerant?

Although this is just a sample of the questions that should be asked while planning your DHCP implementation, all of these questions are valid.

Implementing DHCP in an enterprise can be done using the features we have already discussed, but it is not very practical. One could place a DHCP relay agent on every network segment across the enterprise, but the cost of placing one server on each segment to serve only as a DHCP relay agent is outside of the budget for many IT groups, and it simply does not make sense.

e x a m
Ⓦa t c h
Microsoft's new testing model will include many scenario-based questions. Their intent is to test your knowledge of the content in real-world situations. Although there may be several ways to solve a particular problem, make sure you know the impact of each solution. It is likely that you will be asked to pick the best solution for a particular problem, not just a solution that works.

BOOTP Forwarding   For a sizeable network, DHCP relies upon network routers for relay services. Most routers support BOOTP Forwarding, a specification defined by RFC 2131 (DHCP) and RFC 951 (BOOTP). The BOOTP Forward address is often referred to as a **helper** address, and specifies to the router the destination address of the DHCP server(s) on the network, where all DHCP/BOOTP requests should be forwarded.

The BOOTP Forwarding feature of the routers allows large networks to build one primary DHCP server and direct all clients in the enterprise to that DHCP server via the router's helper address. This may not be practical if your WAN bandwidth is limited, but it does offer central administration of the DHCP server for all scopes in the enterprise. A more practical solution might be to designate one DHCP server for each location and direct all routers in each location to the DHCP server that is local (geographically).

So which solution is the best solution? Each situation is different based on the environment, so it is not possible to say that in all cases one solution is the best solution. However, the reference provided here will give you an idea of which solutions are best for which scenarios.

SCENARIO & SOLUTION

What if I have a small office network of three machines and there is no server and no connectivity outside of the office?	Use APIPA for your IP addressing. Machines will assign themselves non-conflicting addresses. (This does not provide name resolution!)

SCENARIO & SOLUTION

What if I have a network of 15 machines, all on the same segment, and there is no connectivity outside of the office?	Install a DHCP server with one scope to dynamically assign addresses.
What if I have a local network of 60 machines on two segments, separated by a router and there is no other connectivity outside of the office?	Install a DHCP server on one segment. If your router supports BOOTP forwarding, enable it for the other network segment. If not, install DHCP relay agent on the non-DHCP segment.
What if I have an office of ten machines on one segment and we are connected to the corporate office (that has a DHCP server) via a leased 256KB Frame Relay circuit?	Set up a scope on the corporate DHCP server to service the small segment. Configure the router to forward all requests for DHCP to the DHCP server in corporate, or install a DHCP relay agent on the local segment. In both cases, make your lease length high.
What if I have four offices of 200 machines each and all offices are connected by a T-1 Frame Relay circuit?	Set up a DHCP server in each location to service the needs of that site.

These are just a few examples of how an engineer might design a DHCP-enabled network in a networked environment. Next we will take a look at how DHCP integrates with other Windows 2000 services to provide an enterprise-networking environment.

CERTIFICATION OBJECTIVE 5.03

Integrating DHCP with Windows 2000

The strong point of Microsoft's new implementation of DHCP is the integration with the other Windows 2000 network services. Integration with remote access services, dynamic naming services, Windows Internet naming services, and the Active Directory makes DHCP more valuable than the standard DHCP network service, and gives the administrator much more flexibility in designing a Windows 2000 Network.

Integration with RRAS

If you have ever dialed an Internet service provider to gain access to the Internet, then it is likely that you acquired your IP address through DHCP. Windows 2000, building upon the Windows NT 4.0 remote-access service, includes the routing and remote access service that allows clients access to the network from remote locations. Although RRAS can be used with several different solutions such as virtual private networking, ISDN, and Internet routing, the most common implementation of RRAS is based on asynchronous dial-up connections.

In this configuration, the RRAS server (running as a service on Windows 2000) is configured to answer incoming calls and the client is configured to use a modem to dial into the server. When the client dials in to access the network, the first thing that must take place is the IP address assignment. Remember, a client cannot communicate with other devices on a TCP/IP network without an IP address. This is where DHCP's integration with RRAS is helpful.

Although RRAS allows you to assign a scope of IP addresses for assignment to dial-in clients (see Figure 5-2), it is recommended that you configure the RRAS service to acquire addresses from the DHCP server for assignment to dial-in clients. This allows the address assignments to be consistent with the DHCP scopes and minimizes administration tasks. However, when integrating DHCP with RRAS, there are a couple of issues to keep in mind.

RRAS Integration Planning Issues

The RRAS service in Windows 2000 behaves a little differently than its Windows NT 4.0 predecessor when it comes to address assignment. In Windows NT 4.0, the RAS server would access the DHCP server and lease enough addresses for every RAS device port on the server plus one. Therefore, if you had ten modems on a Windows NT 4.0 RAS server, the server would acquire 11 addresses from the DHCP server for assignment to its clients. Windows 2000 is different in that it will automatically obtain ten addresses from the DHCP server regardless of the ports on the RRAS server, and will request more addresses in blocks of ten as needed. This could be frustrating in some situations where your IP addresses are limited, so Microsoft does allow you to edit the size of the block of addresses that the RRAS server will acquire from the DHCP server by editing the following registry entry:

```
HKEY_LOCAL_MACHINE\SYSTEM\CurrentControlSet\Services\RemoteAccess\
Parameters\IP
Value Name: InitialAddressPoolSize
Data Type: REG_DWORD
Default: 10
```

FIGURE 5-2

RRAS IP address assignment properties

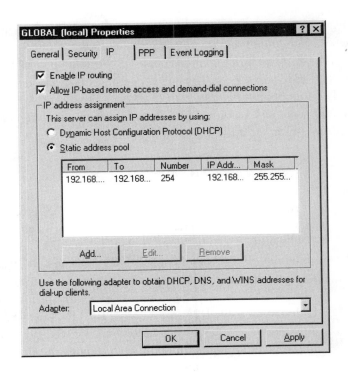

FROM THE CLASSROOM

Scope Options for RRAS and DHCP Clients

You must realize that although the RRAS server will acquire addresses from the DHCP server for assignment to clients, it does not pass along scope options that are defined on the DHCP server. The scope options the client receives will be identical to the settings of the RRAS server itself. You can get around this in two ways to ensure that the options assigned to the RRAS clients are the same as the options assigned to DHCP clients on the network. The first would be to make a reservation for the RRAS server in DHCP so that it is forced to use the options defined by

the RRAS server. This will ensure that the RRAS server passes along the correct options to the client. Secondly, you can force RRAS clients to receive options directly from the DHCP server by installing the DHCP relay agent on the RRAS server. The relay agent will function as expected in regard to your local network, so if you choose this option, make sure that your DHCP server is not on the same physical segment with the RRAS server and that there are no other devices on that segment listening for DHCP/BOOTP requests.

—Joseph Lamb

Also, if you have your Windows 2000 RRAS server set to retrieve addresses from a DHCP server and one is not available, it behaves differently than it did in Windows NT 4.0. In Windows NT 4.0, if a RAS server is configured to hand out addresses to RAS clients using DHCP and the DHCP server is unavailable, no address is assigned and the client is denied access to the network. In Windows 2000, if the RRAS server fails to communicate with the DHCP server, it will use the Automatic Private IP Addressing (APIPA) feature in Windows 2000 to assign an address from the private-address subnet 169.254.0.0/16 and generate an error in the event log. This could cause the client to be unable to communicate on the network (depending on what addressing you are using on your network), or it could cause problems if your internal network uses that subnet.

on the **job**

Windows 2000 server does include two related services that allow the sharing of Internet connections, the Internet connection-sharing service (configured via network and dialup connections), and Network Address Translation, (NAT,configured via RRAS). Both allow a machine to act as a gateway to another network (such as the Internet). ICS can be thought of as "NAT Lite." It uses its own DHCP scope of private addressing and cannot be edited. For this reason, you cannot run ICS and DHCP on the same machine. You can, however, run the RRAS NAT component in conjunction with a DHCP server to provide a gateway to the Internet. Windows 2000 Professional includes ICS but does not include RRAS NAT.

Integration with DNS

Dynamic Domain Naming System (DDNS) is one of the most advanced features of Windows 2000 and is the name resolution model around which all Windows 2000 networks will be built. DDNS allows clients to dynamically enter and update their own resource records within DNS.

The integration between DHCP and DDNS is new to Windows 2000. In the past, if you needed to have DNS track name-to-IP-address records, you had to configure WINS to update DNS. This was helpful in some situations, but was not a widely used solution because of the dependence most network clients have on the WINS service. But now, not only are some Windows clients DDNS aware (Windows 98 and Windows 2000), the DHCP server can now update records in DDNS for clients that don't support DDNS.

When a client on the network receives an IP address from the DHCP server, it may (if it is a Windows 98 or Windows 2000 client) register an "A" (address) record with the DDNS server, or the client may allow the DHCP server to act on its behalf by registering either an **A** (address) record, a **PTR** (Pointer) record, or both, with the DDNS server. The DHCP server will then keep track of the records for the client, and remove it from the DDNS server if the client loses the lease for the designated IP address it was assigned.

The new feature that allows clients to register themselves with DDNS is called the Fully Qualified Domain Name (FQDN) option and is detailed in RFC 2136

(Dynamic Updates in the Domain Name System). This new feature is currently used in Windows 98 and Windows 2000. It allows the client to communicate to the DHCP server the level of service it requires. If the client requests the right to register its resource records with the DDNS server, it must generate the dynamic update statement to add a record to the DNS server. Once complete, the DHCP server will register a PTR record with the DDNS server on the client's behalf. This is the default behavior.

exam
<table><tr><td>⚙️atch</td></tr></table>

DDNS is the core of the Microsoft networking offering. You can be assured that the exam will contain questions to verify your complete understanding of DDNS in Windows 2000 networks.

For clients that do not support FQDN, the DHCP server is responsible for registering their name and address with the DDNS server. The DHCP server also monitors the use of the address, and upon lease expiration, cleans the previously created records from the DDNS server. The DHCP server is dependent upon the dynamic domain name service and cannot be integrated on pre-Windows 2000 DNS servers that do not support dynamic updates.

When planning your DHCP implementation, be sure to work closely with the individual responsible for the DDNS setup, for the interaction of these services is critical to your network stability. If you are also tasked with the DDNS rollout, be sure you take into consideration the continued communication that the DHCP server will have with the DDNS server. If you are placing many DHCP servers in several different regional locations, you will want to ensure that the necessary bandwidth exists between the DHCP server and the DDNS server. The traffic between the two machines is minimal, but can be a problem across slow WAN links.

CertCam 5-2

EXERCISE 5-2

Integrating DHCP with DDNS

You are the network administrator for a Windows NT 4.0 network that has six regional locations. Your network is planning to upgrade all workstations and servers to Windows 2000, but they need to implement DNS first (currently WINS is the only name resolution service). Every location has its own DHCP server with scopes to serve that office.

Four of the locations are connected to the main office by T-1 lines, one office is connected to the main office by a leased 128KB ISDN line supporting 40 users, and the last office is using a demand-dial 128KB ISDN connection to support 30 users who access the line only for e-mail replication between exchange servers. Describe how you would place DNS servers in this environment to fulfill the following priorities. They are in order from most important to least important.

1. Service stability

2. Low administration costs

3. Minimal bandwidth utilization

4. Fast name resolution for clients

Answer: One DNS server should be placed in the main office to serve the four locations connected by T-1 lines. The traffic generated between the DHCP servers and the DNS servers (once upgraded to Windows 2000) will consume some of the bandwidth of the T-1 lines, but the administration will be minimal due to the centrally located DNS server. The office on the leased 128KB ISDN line would also be configured to use the DNS server in the corporate office. Even though this will increase the traffic on that leased line, it will provide for the number one priority—low administration costs. The location connected by dial-up ISDN should have its own DNS server installed. Since the remote office only uses the demand-dial connection for e-mail, the connection is most likely not continuous and would not provide a stable name resolution environment for the clients. A local DNS server would give them fast name resolution, minimal bandwidth use, and service stability.

The integration of DHCP with DDNS is a powerful new feature that will reshape the way name resolution is done in Windows networks, leading to the eventual removal of WINS from most networking environments.

on the !ob

DHCP servers integrated with DDNS and providing name registration services for clients, need to be placed in a special Active Directory security group called the DNSUpdateProxy Group, which makes updates from the DHCP server to the DDNS server unsecured. For this reason, do not install the DHCP server on a domain controller.

Integration with WINS

The Windows 2000 DHCP service, like Windows NT 4.0, integrates well with the Windows Internet Naming Service (WINS) by providing WINS server addresses and WINS service node type settings in the DHCP scope/server options. By setting these addresses, all computers retrieving addresses from the DHCP server will register their name and address with the same WINS server for central name resolution services.

Integration with the Active Directory

DHCP integrates with the Active Directory by storing a list of authorized servers for each domain. Upon startup, all DHCP servers check to see if they are part of a domain, then attempt to locate the Active Directory for the domain. If successful, they query the domain to determine whether they are authorized to service client requests in the domain.

This function allows the server to notify administrators of servers on the network that are not authorized to assign addresses, also called rogue DHCP servers. When planning your network, be sure to only provide one agent or server per segment that will respond to BOOTP/DHCP requests. Otherwise, your clients may receive incorrect addressing information.

on the
Job   *Yes, it is possible to have two DHCP servers on a particular segment if they have been set up as a DHCP cluster, or designed to function within a distributed scope, but that is an exception for fault tolerance and is discussed later.*

CERTIFICATION OBJECTIVE 5.04

Automatic Private IP Addressing (APIPA)

In an attempt to make networking simpler for busy professionals, Microsoft decided to add a new feature to the Windows 2000 family called Automatic Private IP Addressing (APIPA). It is likely that you will never use APIPA in a DHCP environment, but it is a good idea to have a grasp of the service and how it functions so you will know how to troubleshoot DHCP and name resolution issues that arise because of it.

How It Works

A machine straight out of the box is installed with Windows 2000. During setup, all default settings in the network properties are retained. This sets the machine to be a DHCP client. Upon boot up, the machine's first networking task is to locate a DHCP server and request an address. If the machine cannot find a DHCP server, the machine implements APIPA and assigns itself an address in a range between 169.254.0.1–169.254.255.254. This is a private address range reserved by the Internet Assigned Numbers Authority (IANA) for private networks, and will not be in conflict with any known Internet addresses.

This makes setting up a network without the knowledge of DHCP simple. Just build each workstation one at a time and, as you bring them on the network, they will pick a private, non-conflicting address. The downside is that clients that are on a subnet supported by DHCP and, for whatever reason, don't receive a requested address, self-assign an address and register that address with WINS and DNS (if applicable). If your machine is a server, that can cause a name resolution nightmare until you figure out what has happened.

Although it may seem as if machines will be grabbing these addresses all of the time, there is a bit of constraint built into the process. If a machine has never received an IP address from a DHCP server, it will use an APIPA address. If a machine has a leased address from a DHCP server, and the DHCP is not available to renew the lease, the client will first ping the gateway, as specified in their DHCP options or local configuration. If the machine receives a response from the gateway, it assumes that it is still on the same network and uses the previously leased address. If the machine fails to receive a response from the gateway, it assumes it has been moved to a different network and uses an APIPA address. It will then continue to query for a DHCP server every five minutes.

Disabling APIPA

In a networked environment based on DHCP, APIPA can present a problem. A well-planed Windows 2000 network will be using DNS (and maybe WINS) for name resolution on the network. If a machine cannot locate the DHCP server, but can locate the DNS (or WINS) server, it will use APIPA for automatic addressing and register addresses with DNS (or WINS) that will not be accessible by other machines on the network (because it will be a different subnet).

Microsoft fortunately had the foresight to recognize this issue and allow administrators to disable the service by editing the registry. Disabling the service on

Windows 2000 servers in your network is highly recommended and easy to do, as shown in Exercise 5-3. To disable APIPA on a large number of workstations, you could use a start-up script to run a .reg file, rather than manually edit the Registry of each machine.

EXERCISE 5-3

Disabling APIPA

1. Open the registry editor (regedt32.exe).

2. Navigate to the following key: HKEY_LOCAL_MACHINE\SYSTEM\CURRENTCONTROLSET\SERVICES\TCPIP\PARAMETERS\INTERFACES*adaptername,* where *adaptername* is the name of the adapter you want to disable. (This will be an object ID, not the actual adapter name. This means you will have to look at each object parameter to determine which key represents the adapter you want to select. You can do that by reviewing the IP address listed in each key.)

3. Make sure the *adaptername* that you want to disable is selected.

4. Select Edit | Add Value.

5. Type the value name **IPAutoconfigurationenabled** and select the REG_DWORD value type. Then select OK, as shown here:

Add Value	☒
Value Name:	IPAutoconfigurationenabled
Data Type:	REG_DWORD
	OK Cancel Help

6. In the DWORD Editor, type the value **0** and make sure the Radix radio button is set to Hex:

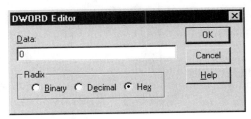

7. Select OK and the entry will be added. Reboot the machine for the changes to take effect.

Multi-homed Machines

If you choose to use APIPA for anything, it is important that you keep in mind that although the address is assigned automatically, it is a TCP/IP address and is constrained by the same standards as those assigned by DHCP. On a multi-homed system or a machine with more than one network card, APIPA cannot be used on both cards unless they are in the same physical network segment. TCP/IP requires that all network adapters from the same subnet be located on the same physical segment.

So, how do you know whether to use APIPA or DHCP? This reference will give you insight into what situations call for APIPA.

SCENARIO & SOLUTION

What do I do if I have two machines I need to network together? Don't I need name resolution?	Perfect for APIPA.
What if I have five machines that I need to network? There is no server.	Another good example. Use APIPA.
What if I have 15 machines and I need to share printers and files between them?	Use DHCP. You could use APIPA if you had a WINS/DDNS server running for name resolution, but if you are running WINS/DDNS on a server, you might as well put DHCP on it, too.

CERTIFICATION OBJECTIVE 5.05

Security Issues Related to DHCP

As with any network service, security is always an issue. DHCP is based upon UPD and IP protocols, which are inherently insecure. With the implementation of the Windows 2000 DHCP service, security is even more of an issue, due to its integration with DDNS and the Active Directory. In this section we will look at some of the security concerns related to designing and planning a DHCP service.

DHCP Groups

One of the newest features of DHCP is the addition of two built-in groups, the DHCP Administrators group and the DHCP Users group. These groups allow you to give certain access to users by placing them in the group, as shown in Figure 5-3.

DHCP Users

The DHCP Users group implies that you need to be a part of this group in order to obtain an address from the DHCP server, but this is not the case. Remember, the DHCP service is a network service that is independent of network security and will offer an address to any client that asks for one. The DHCP User group is meant for users who need to view DHCP configuration information, but do not need to edit it. Maybe you have regional LAN administrators that need to access the DHCP

FIGURE 5-3 DHCP groups

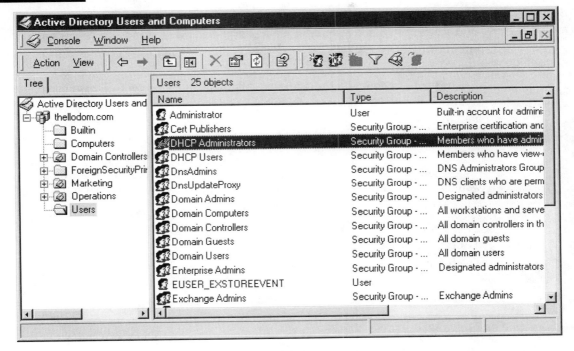

server configuration when making changes to their local IP addressing scheme. Placing them in the DHCP users group gives them rights to view your DHCP server configuration, but does not allow them to make changes.

DHCP Administrators

The DHCP Administrators group is intended for users that are designated as the administrators of the DHCP server. Domain administrators and local administrators on the DHCP server have full rights to the DHCP server configuration by default, but if you want to limit a person to only DHCP server administration, you can place that user in the DHCP Administrators group. This allows for full rights to the DHCP server configuration, but does not grant any other administrative privileges in the domain.

DNSUpdateProxy Group

The implementation of Dynamic DNS and its integration with DHCP is a great advancement to name resolution services in the world of Windows networking, but unfortunately, the relationship between DHCP and DDNS comes with a price—security.

The premise behind DDNS is simple. Allow clients to register their own name records in their DNS zone, thus simplifying name resolution services and minimizing administrator involvement. To allow a client to register with DDNS, the service has to allow just about anyone to register a record. The DDNS server that is not Active Directory integrated accepts all dynamic updates from all sources. DDNS servers that are integrated with Active Directory can be set to only allow secure updates, which would limit the individuals that can add and update records based on Active Directory access lists.

Secure Updates-Only Environment

The behavior of the DDNS server in a secure, updates-only environment is as follows: the client that adds a record to the DDNS server becomes the owner of that record, and after it is created, it can only be updated by the owner. This is where the integration with DHCP presents a security problem. Consider the following scenario: A DHCP server adds a record to DDNS for a Windows NT 4.0 workstation that does not have the capability to add the record itself. A month later, the network administrator upgrades that Windows NT 4.0 workstation to Windows 2000 Professional. The workstation now has the capability to update its record with DDNS because it is running Windows 2000, but lacks the rights to do so because the DHCP server, which has become the owner of the record, added the original record. The problem is even clearer in this example: Say you run a DHCP server within a network of Windows NT 4.0 workstations and, due to a server failure, you have to replace your DHCP server. You build the server, migrate the DHCP database, and start the services, but the server is now unable to make changes to the DDNS records for clients on the network, since it is not the server that originally added the records. In this scenario, all records in the DDNS zone would have to be deleted and repopulated by the DHCP server or the DDNS clients. This could cause a loss of connectivity between all clients on your network until they reregister their names and addresses in the database.

Solving the Ownership/Updates Problem

To solve this problem, Microsoft created a built-in security group called the DNSUpdateProxy group. Members of this group are limited by the incapability of owning a record in DDNS. So, by placing your DHCP server in this group, all records created by your DHCP server will not be owned by any particular workstation. This means that if a workstation is upgraded from Windows NT 4.0 to Windows 2000, it will have the capability to update its own record immediately and will become the owner of the record in DDNS. This also solves the other problem mentioned. If the DHCP server is replaced, the new DHCP server will be able to update all the records because the owner of the records will not be defined.

CertCam 5-4

EXERCISE 5-4

Utilizing the **DNSUpdateProxy** Group

You are an independent consultant working with a small company to design a Windows 2000 network. They have two network segments, separated by an old, non-BOOTP forwarding router. There are 30 clients on each segment. You have been given a budget to purchase three servers to place on the network. Describe how you would set up these services to provide domain authentication, DHCP, and DDNS on both network segments while ensuring that the security of your domain controller's host record in DDNS is not compromised.

Answer: Set up the first server as a domain controller and DDNS server (because domain controllers require DDNS to construct the Active Directory). Then build the second machine as a domain member (not a domain controller) and install the DHCP service. Place the DHCP server into the DNSUpdateProxy group for the domain (so that entries made by the server are not owned by the server). Next, build the third server as a domain controller on the second network segment. Install the DHCP relay agent on that machine and direct it to send requests to the DHCP server on the first segment. This will allow clients on that segment to authenticate to the server on the local segment (because it is a domain controller) and provide DHCP to clients on that segment by relaying requests to the DHCP server on the other segment.

Planning for Security Issues with DNSUpdateProxy

As with many technical solutions, solving one quandary opens the door to other potential problems. Placing a DHCP server in the DNSUpdateProxy group compromises the security of the machine running the DHCP server. All records registered by the DHCP server through dynamic update are insecure, including the record for the DHCP server, itself. This causes a large security risk if the server on which you are running DHCP is a domain controller, because it makes the address of the domain controller, as it is registered in DDNS, open to unwanted edits by third parties. And, since a domain controller has full rights to DNS objects in Active Directory, you must avoid installing a DHCP service on a domain controller unless you are not using DHCP to do dynamic updates for the client.

on the **Job** *Although it is possible to install and run the DHCP server on a domain controller, avoid it. The problems that will arise later from this decision can be catastrophic to your network and a large security risk.*

Rogue DHCP Server Detection

If you have ever managed a network using DHCP, then you know the frustration of having your network clients cease to function due to the presence of an unauthorized DHCP server on the network. This is called a **rogue server**. A rogue server on a network can cause all clients loss of access to network resources.

Windows 2000 DHCP services will not keep rogue servers from coming online, but there are several features included with the service that can prevent certain rogue servers, or locate them once they are brought online. Two main tools do this—Active Directory server authorization and rogue server detection.

Active Directory Server Authorization

As a security feature, DHCP requires that the server be authorized within the active directory before it will begin servicing clients. So, not only must you install the server and define scopes, you must also go the extra step of authorizing the server with the Active Directory for the domain. The downside to this feature is that nothing will prevent someone who builds a Windows 2000 server in its own domain from installing DHCP and authorizing it in the domain, since they will have admin rights over that domain. This only prevents DHCP servers from being run within your own domain. Nonetheless, Active Directory server authorization is a feature enhancement over previous versions of the DHCP service.

If for any reason you ever have to change the IP address of the server that is running DHCP, be sure to un-authorize the server in the Active Directory before changing the IP address. Once the IP address is changed, go back into the DHCP Manager and authorize the server once again.

Rogue Server Detection

When a Windows 2000 DHCP server starts, it polls the network, pretending to be a DHCP client, searching for DHCP servers. If one is found, it queries the Active Directory for the domain to determine if the server is authorized within the Active Directory. If it is not, it logs an event in the event viewer of the DHCP server specifying the IP address of the rogue server. This is called **rogue server detection**.

The addition of rogue server detection is a vital part of Windows 2000 DHCP services, and a security enhancement that is destined to save administrators significant time in tracking down rogue servers.

CERTIFICATION OBJECTIVE 5.06

Designing an DHCP Service for Remote Locations

Implementing DHCP in a large network environment will most certainly require a solution for remote locations. Often, remote locations are connected to the main network through dial-up networking or other limited-bandwidth connections. To make sure these clients receive the addresses to function on the network, you must carefully plan how DHCP will relay addresses to these clients.

Before making such a decision, you must take the following questions into consideration.

- How many clients are in the remote location?
- How is the remote location connected (dial-up or leased)?
- What is the bandwidth of the connection?

Let's look at these considerations individually, and then we will look at some solutions we can derive from our analysis.

exam

watch

Be sure to study RRAS thoroughly. An IP address is necessary for connectivity on a network, and RRAS is essentially a connectivity service. A study of Windows 2000 networking is not complete without a thorough understanding of RRAS.

Remote Location Size

The first question you must ask when implementing a DHCP solution for remote sites is, how many clients are located at each remote location? Some companies have small one-to-three-person offices numbering in the hundreds or even thousands all over the world. Those companies having only one or two remote locations with possibly up to 50 people choose not to purchase a high-bandwidth leased line to support the clients, preferring a demand-dial connection.

When considering size, keep in mind that the solution has to make sense, not only from a technical perspective, but also from a business perspective. If your remote office only has two machines, then it would not be cost effective to place a machine acting as a DHCP relay agent in that site, especially if you have hundreds of those sites.

If you have a large remote site of ten or more, you may consider placing a DHCP server on site. Even though it may be harder to administer in a remote location, it is not nearly as difficult as it would be to maintain static IP addresses for all of those machines. You need to think about not only existing machines, but also new machines that will be brought online in the future. If you have inexperienced personnel, the existence of a DHCP server would make their job much easier (and it would keep them from calling you every time they need a new IP address).

Remote Connectivity

The second consideration is the type of connectivity you have to the remote location. There are many different ways to connect remote offices, especially now that Windows 2000 has been released, providing easy routing and remote access services, as well as NAT. Here are some of the items you may run into:

- **Network 1** Company A has 42 remote location,; all with fewer than five machines each. For connectivity, each machine has an external modem that they use to dial in to the network as needed to access network services.

- **Network 2** Company B has three remote locations, all with roughly 15 machines each. For connectivity, they have configured a Windows 2000 server to perform demand-dial networking through an ISDN line. Once connected, the Windows 2000 server acts as a router between the local network and the remote network.

■ **Network 3** Company C has 30 remote locations, all with an average of 35 machines each. For connectivity, they have a Cisco Router routing traffic to and from the corporate network using a leased ISDN line.

This gives you an idea of the different types of remote connectivity you encounter when designing Windows 2000 networks.

Bandwidth Considerations

The bandwidth of a connection to a remote site is just as critical as the type of connection. DHCP is not an extremely bandwidth-intensive service, but machine start up times can be affected if the machine has slow response time from the DHCP server.

Certainly, the ideal bandwidth would be a T-1 to the corporate office, but this is not typical of remote locations (and if you find it, the location is considered a regional office, not a remote location). You will most likely be evaluating bandwidth speeds between 56KB and 256KB when dealing with remote access. Don't make the mistake of assuming that because you have a leased line, you can relay all of your DHCP traffic to the corporate office efficiently.

Solutions to DHCP in Remote Locations

When considering how to implement DHCP for remote locations, remember that DHCP is critical to the proper operation of the machine. There is no more critical service in terms of network communications. If a machine does not get an IP address, it won't matter that everything else is working fine—the workstation will not be able to access anything! So design with fault tolerance in mind.

Let's take the previous examples as real world scenarios and discuss the proper way to implement DHCP in each of these environments.

Scenario 1 Company A has 42 remote locations, all with fewer than five machines each. For connectivity, each machine has an external modem that they use to dial in to the network as needed to access network services.

Solution: This is actually a simple one. Because each machine is dialing in on its own, DHCP can be provided through RRAS. If the machines in each office need connectivity to the other machines in their office, then you have a different problem. RRAS would still work for their dial-up needs, but connectivity to the machines in each office would require that each machine use another protocol (such as NetBEUI), or that each machine be configured to use a static IP address. DHCP would not be able to assist in this scenario because there is no direct link to the corporate office—only individual links from each machine.

Scenario 2   Company B has three remote locations, all with roughly 15 machines each. For connectivity, they have configured a Windows 2000 server to perform demand-dial networking through an ISDN line. Once connected, the Windows 2000 server acts as a router between the local network and the remote network.

   Solution: The network in this scenario is using a Windows 2000 machine with two network connections (one local Ethernet and one dial-up) to route traffic between the corporate office and the remote location. There is a higher risk when using dial-up networking rather than a leased line, due to "ring, no answer," connection problems. For a machine on the network to contact the DHCP server, the Windows 2000 server would need to be configured as a DHCP relay agent so that broadcasts on the local network could be routed to the DHCP server.

   Because it is a dial-up connection and there are 15 machines on each network, the DHCP relay agent would not be the best choice for this network. Although the solution might function, the risk is great because the functionality of the machines on the network is dependent on the dial-up connection. The better solution would be to configure another machine on each remote network as a DHCP server to provide addressing for the local network. That would create three more DHCP servers in the network, but would ensure that the machines on the remote networks always have an IP address. If the number of machines in each remote location was as small as two or three, then this would not be a cost-effective solution. The remote location would most likely need to use static IP addressing to meet the IP addressing needs.

Scenario 3   Company C has 30 remote locations; all with an average of 35 machines each. For connectivity, they have a Cisco router routing traffic to and from the corporate network using a leased ISDN line.

   Solution: This network is easier to configure because it has a leased line to the corporate office. Because they are using Cisco routers, you can set an IP helper address (BOOTP forwarder) to direct all BOOTP broadcasts on the network to the DHCP server over the leased line. To minimize the network traffic being sent across the leased line, you would want to set the lease time for the remote scope to 15 or more days.

EXERCISE 5-5

Remote DHCP Placement

You have an organization with one main office and 15 remote locations that need dynamic TCP/IP addressing. The smallest location has 30 workstations and the largest location has 100 workstations. Ten of the locations are connected to the main office by a 256KB frame relay circuit. Three of them are connected via ISDN (leased) and two of them are connected with demand-dial 56KB dial up. All routers are non-BOOTP forwarding routers. How would you place your DHCP servers to provide dynamic addressing to the remote locations?

Answer: First set up your DHCP in the main office. In every location connected by a 256KB frame relay circuit, place a DHCP relay on that segment to relay DHCP requests to the DHCP server in the main office. In the three offices that are connected via leased ISDN, place either a DHCP relay agent or a DHCP server to provide dynamic addressing to machines on those segments. Finally, install a DHCP server in each location that is connected by demand-dial 56KB dial up. This will ensure that a DHCP server is always available on that segment.

The remote-location DHCP needs can be met, but must be approached carefully. An understanding of the size, connection type, and the connection bandwidth of your remote location will assist you in designing a solution that provides addressing to your remote location.

CERTIFICATION OBJECTIVE 5.07

Measuring and Optimizing a DHCP Infrastructure Design

Aside from designing and implementing a Windows 2000 network with DHCP, the network administrator must learn how to measure DHCP performance, optimize DHCP implementation, and build fault tolerance in the DHCP servers.

DHCP Lease Length

One of the most important configuration options in setting up DHCP scopes is the lease length. The lease length is the amount of time that the DHCP server will allow a client in a particular scope to retain an IP address before renewing the address.

Understanding Lease Lengths

The default lease length value for newly created scopes is eight days. To understand the best lease length for your environment, you must learn how it affects your clients.

Every client on the network that receives an address from DHCP receives a lease length. Every time the client starts after receiving that address, the client will query the DHCP server to make sure it is acceptable to continue using the address. Once half of the lease duration has expired, the client will begin asking the DHCP server for a renewal. If the DHCP server is available, it will grant the request and the lease length will be set once again.

exam
ⓦatch

Be sure to understand the effect that a lease length has on a network. Many scenario questions are likely to be asked that will require you to determine the optimal lease length for different environments.

Planning for Lease-Length Factors

When considering the traffic generated, keep in mind that the client will begin requesting a renewal after half of the lease has expired. If all your clients are set to a lease length of three days, they will begin asking for a renewal after one and a half days. To minimize traffic, set the lease length long. To provide for constant changes to location (such as traveling salespeople) or high client turnover, set the lease length short.

on the
ⓙob

It is possible to set the lease length shorter than one hour, but this is intended for testing purposes only and should never be used in a production environment due to the traffic that would be generated.

Fault Tolerance

The most essential network service should have the most fault tolerance. If your DHCP server is down, your clients will begin losing connectivity to everything as soon as their leases expire.

There are several ways you can make DHCP more fault-tolerant, including distributed scopes and clustering.

Distributed Scopes

Distributing scopes is a method of spreading the load and responsibility of DHCP to two or more servers on your network. Before clustering became popular, distributed scopes were the preferred method of load balancing and fault tolerance.

To create a distributed scope, build two DHCP servers on the same physical network segment. Create the same scope on both machines, then exclude the range of addresses on each machine that the other server will service. For example, say you have a subnet of 192.168.0.1/24 that you need to distribute between two servers. First you would create a scope on DHCP server 1 with the address range of 192.168.0.1–192.168.0.254 and a subnet mask of 255.255.255.0. Then create an exclusion for addresses 192.168.0.128–192.168.0.254. This gives the first server addresses 192.168.0.1–192.168.0.127 to assign to clients. Build the second server and create the same scope of 192.168.0.1/24 with an address range of 192.168.0.1–192.168.0.254 and exclude 192.168.0.1–192.168.0.127. This gives server 2 an address range of 192.168.0.128–192.168.0.254 to assign to clients.

This creates a distributed scope, where both servers can respond to and assign addresses to clients on the network segment. The exclusions are meant to prevent a server from attempting to assign the same address as another server.

on the **job**

It is essential when creating distributed scopes that you create the entire range of addresses on both DHCP servers, rather than creating half on one and half on the other. If you do, your DHCP servers will not know how to respond to a client that asks for an address outside of its listed scope.

CertCam 5-6

EXERCISE 5-6

Planning a Distributed DHCP Scope

You have been asked to set up DHCP service for a VLAN of 200 machines. The DHCP servers need to be load balanced and fault tolerant. Using a 10.1.1.1/24 network address space, describe how you would implement a distributed scope DHCP model across three machines. Provide the address ranges used, the exclusions used, and the step-by-step process necessary to bring the solution online. (Make sure to exclude the first ten addresses for static assignments and routers.)

Answer:

1. Install Windows 2000 Server on three servers.

2. Install the DHCP service on all three servers.

3. Authorize all servers in the domain.

4. Create a scope on the first server using 10.1.1.1–10.1.1.254 with a subnet mask of 255.255.255.0.

5. Exclude 10.1.1.1–10.1.1.10 from this scope. (This is for the static address assignments and routers.)

6. Also exclude 10.1.1.81–10.1.1.254. (This is the address space that the other two DHCP servers will use to assign addresses.)

7. Create a scope on the second server using 10.1.1.1–10.1.1.254 with a subnet mask of 255.255.255.0.

8. Exclude 10.1.1.11–10.1.1.80 and 10.1.1.161–10.1.1.254 from that scope as well. (This is the address space that the other two DHCP servers will use to assign addresses and for the static assignments.)

9. Create a scope on the third server using 10.1.1.1–10.1.1.254 with a subnet mask of 255.255.255.0.

10. Exclude 10.1.1.11–10.1.1.160. (This is the address space that the other two DHCP servers will use to assign addresses and for the static assignments.)

11. Activate all scopes.

DHCP Server Clusters

Clustering technologies have become popular in recent years, and have served to provide a great deal of fault tolerance when building enterprise resource planning application server farms or e-commerce server farms.

Understanding the Clustering Concept   The premise behind the cluster is simple: to provide a service to the network by using more than one machine, yet make the service appear as if it was running on one machine.

In a Web server farm, the servers are typically configured to balance the load of client requests between all Web servers, while accessing their data on clustered database servers. The clustered database runs on two or more machines that share a common data storage medium, such as an external drive array, and are acting as if they are one machine with one IP address.

Planning the Clustering of DHCP Servers   Clustering DHCP servers has not been popular in the past, mainly due to a lack of native clustering support in DHCP and the high cost of clustering solutions. That could be changing. Microsoft's Windows 2000 Advanced Server includes a two-node clustering service that can be used with DHCP to increase its fault tolerance. Clustering DHCP is superior to using distributed scope because it uses IP addresses more efficiently, and the loss of a server does not cut the available address pool in half. Clustering is intended to provide fail over so that if one server ceases to function, the other server will take over the responsibility. Because the data is in a shared medium, the servers can be created with the same scope and address range.

Monitoring DHCP

As with any network service, it is important to monitor the service for proper functioning to correct performance problems or errors before they affect your service level. DHCP offers three ways to monitor the DHCP service:

- Microsoft Management Console (MMC) monitoring
- Performance monitoring
- DHCP Logs

MMC Monitoring

In Windows 2000, the MMC has replaced the DHCP manager that was used in Windows NT 4.0 to manage the DHCP service. This console allows you to add snap-ins that will control the services you wish to administer. The DHCP snap-in for the MMC has been enhanced to include not only configuration data, but also monitoring alerts.

Understanding the DHCP Snap-In   A small icon next to the DHCP server name in the console now provides a visual flag of the server's status, as shown in Figure 5-4. Servers that are authorized and running, for example, have a green arrow pointing up, next to the server name. This icon changes, based upon the status of the server, and actually alerts you to problems that you would not recognize without looking further into the console. For instance, if you run low on available addresses,

FIGURE 5-4   MMC DHCP alert icons

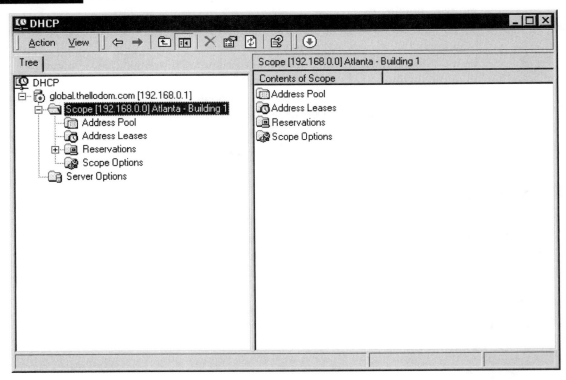

the icon will turn into a yellow arrow to alert you of the problem. If you run out of addresses, the arrow will turn red.

The Role of the DHCP Console in Planning a DHCP Design   When you are planning your DHCP implementation, make sure that every administrator can view every server in your enterprise (even if they cannot configure it). By allowing every administrator to view every server, they can add the server to their DHCP MMC snap-in and be instantly alerted if a DHCP server has a problem. This gives you greater odds on recognizing a problem early and being able to correct the issue before is causes downtime to your network.

Performance Monitor

The Windows NT 4.0 performance monitor has always been a very powerful tool for monitoring and troubleshooting performance problems on NT servers. The performance component in Windows 2000 has been divided into two parts: the system monitor and the logs and alerts. The interface for the performance component is now a snap-in to the MMC, and several new counters have been added that will help you monitor the performance of the DHCP server. Table 5-1 shows the available counters and their significance. These explanations are also included in the DHCP server help files for easy reference.

Using a performance monitor will give you insight into the workload of the DHCP server and help to pinpoint problems in the DHCP configuration.

e x a m
ⓦ a t c h

Be sure to know the value of each performance monitor counter, including what it means, what problems it may indicate, and what resolutions you may implement to correct it.

DHCP Logs

DHCP logging features can be a valuable asset when troubleshooting network problems with DHCP. DHCP logs are written in ASCII format to the c:\winnt\system32\dhcp directory. They are stored in a file called DhcpSrvLog.###, where ### represents the three-letter abbreviation for a day of the week. For example, Friday's log would be DhcpSrvLog.Fri. This logging is done by default and the files are overwritten weekly. Figure 5-5 gives an example of a DHCP log.

TABLE 5-1   Performance Monitor Counters

Counters	Meaning
Packets Received/Sec	Indicates the number of message packets received per second by the DHCP server. A large number indicates heavy DHCP message traffic to the server.
Duplicates Dropped/Sec	Indicates the number of duplicated packets per second dropped by the DHCP server. This number can be affected by multiple relay agents or network interfaces relaying the same packet to the server. A large number here indicates that either the network clients are timing out too fast or the server is not responding fast enough.
Packets Expired/Sec	Indicates the number of packets per second that expire and are dropped by the DHCP server. When a DHCP-related message packet is internally queued for 30 seconds or more, it is determined to be stale and expired by the server. A large number here indicates that the server is either taking too long to process some packets while other packets are queued and becoming stale, or traffic on the network is too high for the server to manage.
Milliseconds Per Packet/Avg.	Indicates the average time in milliseconds used by the DHCP server to process the data packets it receives. This counter is related to the I/O subsystem of the server and can indicate that the server hardware or I/O subsystem is not fast enough to process the requests.
Active Queue Length	Indicates the current length of the internal message queue of the DHCP server. This number equals the number of unprocessed messages received by the server. Some queuing is normal, but high amounts can indicate heavy network traffic.
Conflict Check Queue Length	Indicates the current length of the conflict check queue for the DHCP server. This queue holds messages without responses while the DHCP server performs address-conflict detection. A large value here might indicate that Conflict Detection Attempts has been set too high or that there is unusually heavy lease traffic at the server.
Discovers/Sec	Indicates the number of DHCP discover messages (DHCPDISCOVERs) received per second by the server. These messages are sent by clients when they start on the network and request a new IP address lease. A sudden or unusual increase indicates a large number of clients are attempting to initialize and obtain an IP address lease from the server, such as when a number of client computers are started at any given time.

| TABLE 5-1 | Performance Monitor Counters *(continued)* |

Counters	Meaning
Offers/Sec	Indicates the number of DHCP offer messages (DHCPOFFERs) sent per second by the DHCP server to clients. A sudden or unusual increase in this number indicates a heavy workload on the server.
Requests/Sec	Indicates the number of DHCP request messages (DHCPREQUESTs) received per second by the DHCP server from clients. A sudden increase in this number indicates a large number of clients trying to renew their leases with the DHCP server. This might indicate that Scope Lease Length for a specific scope is set too short.
Informs/Sec	Indicates the number of DHCP inform messages (DHCPINFORMs) received per second by the DHCP server. DHCP inform messages are used when the DHCP server queries the Active Directory or when the server is performing dynamic updates to DDNS on behalf of clients.
Acks/Sec	Indicates the number of DHCP acknowledgment messages (DHCPACKs) sent per second by the DHCP server to clients. An unusual increase in this number indicates that the DHCP server is renewing a large number of clients. This might indicate that Scope Lease Length is set too short.
Nacks/Sec	Indicates the number of DHCP negative acknowledgment messages (DHCPNAKs) sent per second by the DHCP server to clients. A very high value might indicate potential network trouble in the form of incorrect configuration of either the server or clients. A server configuration mistake or a deactivated scope could be a cause. Computers moving between subnets, such as laptop portables or other mobile devices could cause a very high value as well.
Declines/Sec	Indicates the number of DHCP decline messages (DHCPDECLINEs) received per second by the DHCP server from clients. A high value indicates that several clients have found their address to be in conflict with other machines on the network. Enabling conflict detection on the server could be used to troubleshoot this situation.
Releases/Sec	Indicates the number of DHCP release messages (DHCPRELEASEs) received per second by the DHCP server from clients. This number only exists if a DHCP client sends a release to the server. This counter will typically return a low value, for clients do not often release their addresses unless manually commanded to do so.

FIGURE 5-5   DHCP log

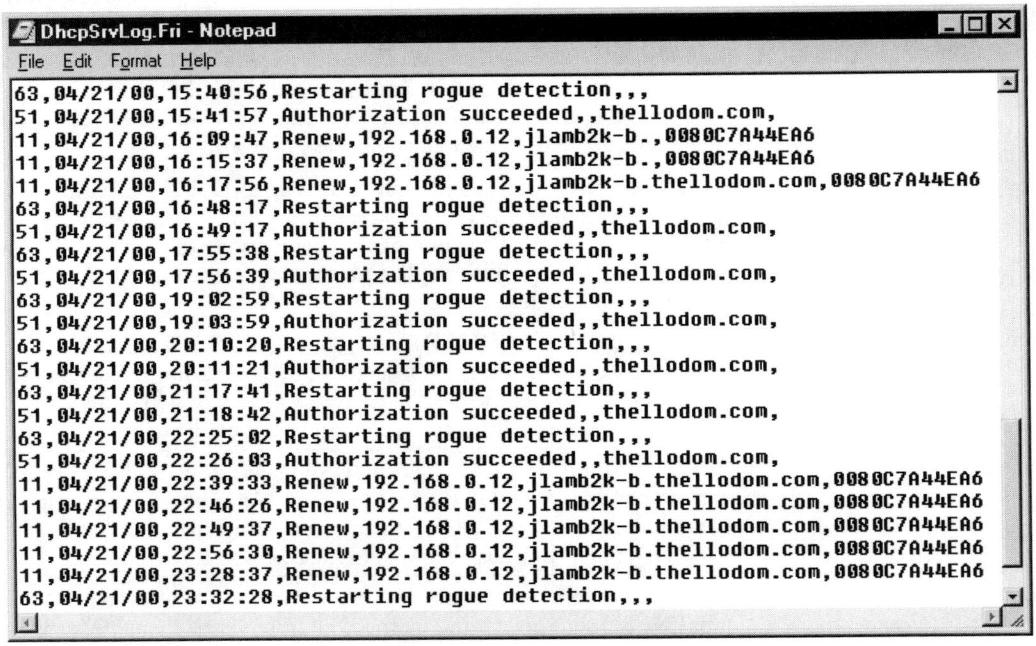

```
DhcpSrvLog.Fri - Notepad
File  Edit  Format  Help
63,04/21/00,15:40:56,Restarting rogue detection,,,
51,04/21/00,15:41:57,Authorization succeeded,,thellodom.com,
11,04/21/00,16:09:47,Renew,192.168.0.12,jlamb2k-b.,0080C7A44EA6
11,04/21/00,16:15:37,Renew,192.168.0.12,jlamb2k-b.,0080C7A44EA6
11,04/21/00,16:17:56,Renew,192.168.0.12,jlamb2k-b.thellodom.com,0080C7A44EA6
63,04/21/00,16:48:17,Restarting rogue detection,,,
51,04/21/00,16:49:17,Authorization succeeded,,thellodom.com,
63,04/21/00,17:55:38,Restarting rogue detection,,,
51,04/21/00,17:56:39,Authorization succeeded,,thellodom.com,
63,04/21/00,19:02:59,Restarting rogue detection,,,
51,04/21/00,19:03:59,Authorization succeeded,,thellodom.com,
63,04/21/00,20:10:20,Restarting rogue detection,,,
51,04/21/00,20:11:21,Authorization succeeded,,thellodom.com,
63,04/21/00,21:17:41,Restarting rogue detection,,,
51,04/21/00,21:18:42,Authorization succeeded,,thellodom.com,
63,04/21/00,22:25:02,Restarting rogue detection,,,
51,04/21/00,22:26:03,Authorization succeeded,,thellodom.com,
11,04/21/00,22:39:33,Renew,192.168.0.12,jlamb2k-b.thellodom.com,0080C7A44EA6
11,04/21/00,22:46:26,Renew,192.168.0.12,jlamb2k-b.thellodom.com,0080C7A44EA6
11,04/21/00,22:49:37,Renew,192.168.0.12,jlamb2k-b.thellodom.com,0080C7A44EA6
11,04/21/00,22:56:30,Renew,192.168.0.12,jlamb2k-b.thellodom.com,0080C7A44EA6
11,04/21/00,23:28:37,Renew,192.168.0.12,jlamb2k-b.thellodom.com,0080C7A44EA6
63,04/21/00,23:32:28,Restarting rogue detection,,,
```

Maintenance

Your network design plan must include planning for the maintenance of the DHCP service. DHCP is full of tools to assist you in the maintenance of the DHCP service and database. Using these tools and examples, you can devise a plan that will keep your database running efficiently and prevent data corruption.

Command Line Maintenance

If you are a network administrator who has been working with Windows NT for some time, then you have probably, at one point or another, used command line options to automate tasks or get you out of a bind when the interface tools were just not available. Microsoft did not lose sight of this need and included in DHCP the capability to perform just about every task from the command line, even remotely.

To access command line options, you must run a command line program called NETSHELL (NETSH). This program allows the command line control of several services in the Windows 2000 server suite. It can also be useful for building sophisticated scripts to perform scheduled maintenance on different services.

To access NETSH, type **NETSH** from a command line. To access a DHCP server, type **DHCP** and then **SERVER \\SERVERNAME** (or **\\IPADDRESS**). This will give you command line access to the DHCP context on the server selected. You must have local administrative rights on the server you are connecting to in order to access the server.

From within NETSH, you can view statistics or make changes to the configuration. For a full list of NETSH DHCP commands, see the DHCP Help library from within the MMC Administrator for DHCP.

Backup and Recovery

The DHCP service stores all of its information in the registry and a DHCP database. For proper functionality, the DHCP database and the registry keys must be reconciled. Occasionally, your database may become corrupted and need to be restored. It is important to know where the backup of the database is stored and how to plan for the repair or restoration of a damaged database.

Compacting the Database   The Windows 2000 DHCP database is based upon the Microsoft Exchange Storage Engine version 4. As with any database, it is necessary to perform maintenance to eliminate unused space.

CERTIFICATION OBJECTIVE 5.08

Dynamic Compaction

Since the release of Windows NT 4.0, the DHCP service has included dynamic database compaction, an automatic process of database maintenance that takes place on the server during idle times. Although dynamic compaction reduces the size of the database and fixes minor errors, it is not comprehensive enough to solely rely on.

CERTIFICATION OBJECTIVE 5.09

Manual Compaction Using the JETPACK.EXE Utility

Windows 2000 includes a command line utility called JETPACK.EXE that is used for database maintenance. Jetpack compacts the database, eliminating unused space and fixing any errors that it finds. Jetpack should be run on the server once a month for large databases supporting over 1000 users, and once every three months for smaller implementations.

The jetpack utility copies the dhcp.mdb database to tmp.mdb, runs maintenance on the tmp.mdb database, deletes the dhcp.mdb database, and then renames the tmp.mdb database to dhcp.mdb.

If jetpack encounters errors that it cannot repair, you will need to restore your database from a backup source.

FROM THE CLASSROOM

Windows 2000 DCHP Database

The DHCP database in Windows 2000 has a different structure than the Windows NT 4.0 DHCP database. If you perform an upgrade to Windows 2000 on a Windows NT 4.0 server running DHCP, the database will be upgraded. If you move the DHCP database from a Windows NT 4.0 server to a Windows 2000 server, the Windows 2000 server will attempt to convert the database upon startup. (Make sure you have imported the registry settings from HKEY_LOCAL_MACHINE\ SOFTWARE\Microsoft\DhcpServer\ Configuration before attempting the startup.) This will fail until you reconcile all scopes and verify all of the records in the DHCP Admin.

—Joseph Lamb

Planning for DHCP Backup   The DHCP database, as do all databases that contain vital information, needs to be backed up. Your design plan should include provisions for a regular backup.

Windows 2000 automatically backs up the database and configuration files to the %systemroot%\system32\dhcp\backup\jet\new folder every time the DHCP service is successfully shut down. Because the server is designed to run for long periods of time without a restart, it is best to make sure that backup software is getting a backup of the DHCP database nightly. The backup software will most likely not be able to backup the live database in the %systemroot%\system32\dhcp directory without the assistance of an open file agent because the DHCP service will have the file open. Many software vendors today include an open file agent add-on to their backup software.

If you do not have an add-on for your backup software, it is a good idea to restart the DHCP service manually or by automated scripts at least once a day. This will force the DHCP service to make a backup copy that you can use to restore your database in the event that it becomes corrupt.

DHCP Database Troubleshooting   If your database becomes corrupt, the DHCP service may stop, or it may just stop responding to client requests. Database corruption is typically indicated in the event log by jet database errors related to the DHCP service. The first thing to do is determine whether the DHCP service is still running. If it is, stop the service and restart it. If the service reports jet database errors on startup, you most likely have a corrupted database.

If you believe that your database is corrupt, you should run jetpack to determine if it can be repaired before restoring the database from a backup source.

If the jetpack utility reports errors that it cannot repair, you must restore your database from a backup copy. If no errors are reported, try starting the DHCP service again. If you still receive the jet database error messages, you will need to restore your database from a backup.

Restoring a DHCP Database   The easiest way to restore a corrupt database is to copy a non-corrupted version of the DHCP database into the %systemroot%\system32\dhcp directory. However, make sure that the DHCP database is not running and that you have copied the corrupted database out of that directory before restoring the backup copy. This is a safeguard in case you need that data.

Once you have restored the database, run the jetpack.exe utility to make sure the database is error free. Then start the DHCP service, reconcile, and verify the DHCP database with the registry using the DHCP Administrator.

Planning to Move a DHCP Database

In managing your DHCP database it may become necessary to move it from one server to another. Databases can be moved from Windows NT 4.0 servers to Windows 2000 servers or between Windows 2000 servers. However, DHCP databases cannot be moved from Windows 2000 servers to Windows NT 4.0 servers due to the difference in the database structure.

To move a database from one server to another, you must migrate the database and all of the registry entries for your scopes. It is important to always make a backup of your database before migration. This exercise assumes that DHCP is not installed on the destination server. If it is installed, uninstall it before proceeding. (The server will perform operations the first time you launch the MMC DHCP Admin that are essential to the conversion.)

This process assumes you are moving a database from Windows NT 4.0 to Windows 2000. Moving a database from Windows 2000 to Windows 2000 follows the same process, but the error messages mentioned will not be encountered.

Although the migration will convert all of your scopes and current leases in the database, the following server settings will not be migrated, and must be configured after the conversion.

- APIProtocolSupport
- BackupDatabasePath
- BackupInterval
- DatabaseCleanupInterval
- DatabaseLoggingFlag
- DatabaseName
- DatabasePath
- DetectConflictRetries
- RestoreFlag

Client Troubleshooting

The default installation for most client operating systems will set the client to "Obtain an IP address automatically," thereby enabling the DHCP client automatically.

Even though there are several tools you can use to verify TCP/IP connectivity, there is really only one tool to verify DHCP function. IPCONFIG (WINIPCFG in Windows 95/98) is a utility that runs from the command line and allows you to view the TCP/IP configuration of your workstation. The syntax is as follows:

```
ipconfig [/? | /all | /release [adapter] | /renew [adapter]
          | /flushdns | /registerdns
          | /showclassid adapter
          | /setclassid adapter [classidtoset] ]
```

Table 5-2 lists the parameters that can be used with IPCONFIG to return specific information about the configuration.

Using IPCONFIG with the /ALL parameter allows you to see detailed information about your TCP/IP configuration for each network card, including

TABLE 5-2	Parameter	Description
Parameters for IPCONFIG	/?	Displays the help screen for the utility as well as a list of all parameters that can be used with the program
	/ALL	Shows detailed information about all network adapters in your computer
	/RELEASE	Tells the adapter to release the address it is currently using. (Note: It does not automatically retrieve another address.)
	/RENEW	Tells the adapter to release the address it is currently using and acquire a new one from the DHCP server. (This does not mean that the DHCP server will not give the same address back to the client.)
	/FLUSHDNS	Purges the DNS resolver cache
	/REGISTERDNS	Refreshes all DHCP leases on the machine and re-registers all names with DNS
	/DISPLAYDNS	Displays the contents of the DNS resolver cache
	/SHOWCLASSID	Displays all of the DHCP class IDs that are allowed for the specified adapter
	/SETCLASSID	Modifies the DHCP class ID

whether you are receiving your TCP/IP address from a DHCP server. If your workstation receives its address from a DHCP server, the "DHCP Enabled" parameter will be marked "yes". You will also notice that the IPCONFIG utility allows you to see what WINS and DNS server addresses have been assigned to your workstation, as well as the NBT node type, which determines how your machine locates devices using NetBIOS over TCP/IP.

CERTIFICATION SUMMARY

Since the inception of the BOOTP specification, organizations have been striving to minimize the administration of network addressing and provide a low cost of ownership for networks. The Windows 2000 implementation of DHCP is the most advanced, flexible, and feature-filled implementation of DHCP to date.

Features, such as rogue detection, advanced monitoring, dynamic DNS integration, and Active Directory integration are sure to make Windows 2000 DHCP the chosen service for dynamic IP address assignment throughout networks worldwide.

Through the material covered in this chapter, you have learned the proper way to plan and implement a DHCP solution, including the integration of Windows 2000 DHCP in a networking environment, as well as its interaction with non-Windows 2000 devices and the security concerns related to implementing a DHCP strategy. You also learned the measurement and optimization of DHCP for networks from small to large and some of the necessary maintenance and disaster recovery procedures necessary to managing a DHCP network.

TWO-MINUTE DRILL

Overview of the Windows 2000 DHCP Server

❑ DHCP was created from a service called BOOTP, an Internet standard for IP address assignment which fully supports the functionality of BOOTP, including the existence of a BOOTP table and TFTP server redirection.

❑ DHCP includes the tailoring of DHCP options based on vendor-specific classes or user-defined classes.

❑ DHCP includes support for multicast address assignment.

❑ A scope is a logical sub-network of addresses grouped together for the purpose of assigning DHCP options.

❑ Reservations allow you to assign IP addresses to machines based upon their MAC or physical network address.

Integrate DHCP into a Routed Environment

❑ DHCP is dependent upon broadcasts for proper functionality.

❑ Superscopes allow you to offer more than one defined scope to the same physical segment. This is often referred to as a multinet.

❑ Windows 2000 servers can be configured as relay agents for the DHCP server, designed to relay broadcasts on one network segment to a DHCP server on another network segment.

❑ BOOTP forwarding is an option contained within most routers that allows them to forward broadcasts on one segment to a predefined DHCP server.

Integrate DHCP with Windows 2000

❑ DHCP integrates with RRAS to provide remote-access clients with dynamic IP address assignment.

❑ DHCP integrates with DDNS to provide name registration services for clients that do not support DDNS.

❑ Only Windows 2000 and Windows 98 workstation support the FQDN (Fully Qualified Domain Name) option that allows them to register their names with Dynamic DNS servers.

❑ DHCP integrates with WINS by providing WINS server addresses and NBT node-type settings to DHCP clients.

❑ DHCP integrates with the Active Directory by requiring Active Directory authorization before servicing clients.

Automatic Private IP Addressing (APIPA)

❑ APIPA is a feature in Windows 2000 that allows Windows 2000 workstations and servers to self assign a private IP address when DHCP servers are not available.

❑ Machines assigned with an address by APIPA will attempt to reach a DHCP server on the network every five minutes until successful.

❑ APIPA can be disabled by editing the registry.

❑ APIPA cannot be used on a multi-homed machine unless both network adapters are connected to the same network segment.

Security Issues Related to DHCP

❑ DHCP is based upon UDP and IP protocols, which are inherently insecure.

❑ Windows 2000 includes two built-in groups. They are the DHCP Administrators group and the DHCP Users group.

❑ The DNSUpateProxy group is intended for DHCP servers to limit their ownership capability when registering records in DDNS.

❑ DHCP servers perform rogue-server detection at startup and during idle times to locate unauthorized DHCP servers.

Design a DHCP Service for Remote Locations

❑ Lease lengths can be modified to reduce network traffic for remote locations.

❑ Relay agents should not be used on network segments that do not have leased-line access to the DHCP server.

❑ RRAS clients that access the network from a remote location will be assigned an address when they dial in and do not require a local DHCP server (unless they need to communicate on their local network as well).

Measure and Optimize a DHCP Infrastructure Design

❑ The lease length is the amount of time that the DHPC server will allow a client in a particular scope to retain an IP address before renewing the address.

❑ A distributed scope is a method of distributing the load and responsibility of DHCP to two or more servers on your network that reside in the same segment.

❑ DHCP supports Microsoft Clustering Services.

❑ DHCP is managed by the DHCP plug-in for the Microsoft Management Console.

❑ The Windows 2000 performance monitor can monitor DHCP server performance.

❑ DHCP logs are written to the %systemroot%\system32\dhcp directory in ASCII format.

❑ JETPACK.EXE is a command line utility used for compacting and repairing the DHCP database.

SELF TEST

The following questions will help you measure your understanding of the material presented in this chapter. Read all of the choices carefully, as there may be more than one correct answer. Choose all correct answers for each question.

Overview of the Windows 2000 DHCP Server

1. DHCP is derived from the following Internet standard protocol for IP address assignment:
   A. Dynamic Assignment of Internet Addresses (DAIA)
   B. Bootstrap Protocol(BOOTP)
   C. Enhanced Internet Gateway Routing (EIGR)
   D. Internet Address Assignment (IAA)

2. The following list specifies changes in the Windows 2000 DHCP service over the Windows NT implementation. Select the service that is not included with DHCP.
   A. Integration of DHCP with DNS
   B. Vendor-specific and class ID support
   C. Rogue DHCP server detection
   D. Enhanced IPX/SPX support

Integrating DHCP into a Routed Environment

3. The DHCP service can run on which of the following machines? Please select all that apply.
   A. Windows 2000 Server in a Workgroup
   B. Windows 2000 Professional Workstation that is part of a domain
   C. Windows 2000 Server domain controller
   D. Windows 2000 Professional Workstation that is part of a workgroup

4. In a large enterprise network, which of the following services can be used to forward DHCP requests across WAN links? Choose all that apply.
   A. DHCP relay agent service running on a Windows 2000 Server
   B. The Microsoft Relay Service for Windows 95/98
   C. BOOTP Forwarding service provided by a router
   D. The Microsoft Relay Service for DOS 6.22

Integrating DHCP with Windows 2000

5. You can configure Microsoft routing and remote access servers to assign IP addresses to clients using the following methods. Choose all that apply.

   A. Set up a predefined scope of addresses configured on the RRAS server.

   B. Set up RRAS to obtain addresses from the DHCP server.

   C. Set up RRAS to obtain addresses from the BOOTP server.

   D. Set up RRAS to assign addresses using APIPA.

6. You have a Windows 2000 network running DHCP (configured with one scope and scope options for the router, WINS addresses, NBT Node type, and DNS addresses) on Server1. You set up Server2 as a RRAS server to service dial-in clients. The clients dial in to get authenticated correctly and receive an IP address from the range specified on the DHCP server, but they do not receive DNS or WINS addresses. Why?

   A. RRAS clients must have static DNS and WINS addresses configured in their networking properties.

   B. The DHCP server is not working properly and should be rebooted.

   C. The RRAS server must be running DNS and WINS to assign those addresses.

   D. The RRAS server does not have DNS or WINS addresses defined in its network configuration.

7. Which of the following clients use the FQDN option to update DDNS upon startup, registering their names and addresses with the server? Choose all that apply.

   A. Windows 95

   B. Windows 98

   C. Windows NT 4.0

   D. Windows 2000

Automatic Private IP Addressing (APIPA)

8. You come into work one day to find that all 50 of your Windows 2000 professional workstations can no longer access network resources. After investigation, you find that every machine has an address in the range of 169.254.0.1169.254.0.30. What is likely to be the problem?

   A. Someone came in over the weekend and reconfigured your DHCP scope.

   B. Someone came in over the weekend and set static addresses on all of your workstations.

    C. DHCP ran out of valid addresses and began assigning private addresses from a random scope.

    D. Your DHCP server is not functional and all of your machines tried to renew their lease over the weekend.

9. APIPA has which of the following features? Choose all that apply.

    A. Automatic Private assignment of IP addresses

    B. Integration with WINS

    C. Integration with DDNS

    D. An advanced graphic interface management tool

10. What process disables the APIPA service?

    A. Disable the service in the control panel by accessing the Services icon.

    B. Access your network configuration by right-clicking Network Neighborhood, then Properties. Select the properties of the LAN adapter. Click TCP/IP, then properties. Select the Disable APIPA on this interface.

    C. Edit the registry key:

```
HKEY_LOCAL_MACHINE\system\currentcontrolset\services
\TCPIP\parameters\Interfaces\adaptername
```

    D. You cannot disable the service

Security Issues Related to DHCP

11. Which of the following built-in groups have been added to Windows 2000 as a result of installing DHCP? Choose all that apply.

    A. DHCP Database Administrators

    B. DHCP Users

    C. DHCP Power Users

    D. DHCP Administrators

12. What is rogue detection?

    A. A service that runs on each DHCP-enabled client PC that allows the PC to inform the DHCP server when unauthorized DHCP servers are found on the network

    B. A function of the DHCP server where the server poses as a client on the network searching for other DHCP servers

C. A function of the DHCP server by which it searches the network for clients without an IP address, and provides them with IP addresses upon discovery

D. A function of the client, which searches the network for clients without an IP address and relays their status to the DHCP server for IP address assignment

13. You run a small network of 50 machines. You run Windows 2000 on the servers and Windows NT 4.0 on the workstations. Over one weekend, you come in and upgrade all workstations to Windows 2000. Upon arriving on Monday, you find that all of the machines have error messages indicating the incapacity to update the host records on the DDNS server. What is likely to be the cause of this?

A. The DHCP server has the DDNS records for those machines locked. The server needs to be informed that the new clients can update their own DDNS records.

B. The DDNS server needs to be switched to dynamic mode to allow the clients to update their record in DDNS.

C. The DHCP server was never added to the DNSUpdateProxy group and now the records on the server are owned by the DHCP server.

D. The DHCP clients were never added to the DNSUpdateProxy group and now the records on the server are owned by the DDNS server.

Designing a DHCP Service for Remote Locations

14. Your employer informs you that your company has acquired a new sales office in Dallas. They have five Windows 2000 professional workstations and two Windows 2000 Professional laptops that need to access the corporate network. They currently have no network in their location. What is the best way to provide them with dynamic IP addressing for their machines so that they can access the corporate network?

A. Set up each machine as a RRAS client to dial in to your network via RRAS.

B. Install a small network HUB and an ISDN leased line to the corporate network. Then install a DHCP server in that location to assign addresses to the clients.

C. Install a small network HUB in their location, than configure a server for demand-dial access to your corporate network via RAS.

D. Install a router with a Frame Relay connection back to the corporate office. Then set the router with a BOOTP forwarding address so that it can relay requests for IP addresses to the DHCP server in corporate.

15. What is a lease?

    A. The time a client is allowed to use an assigned IP address

    B. The time a client will use an address assigned by a particular server before requesting an address from another server

    C. The time a DHCP server runs before dynamically updating DDNS

    D. The time a client will operate without a DHCP server being present

Measuring and Optimizing a DHCP Infrastructure Design

16. What is a distributed scope?

    A. The process of configuring two or more servers on different subnets to share the response to client requests for dynamically assigned addresses

    B. The process of configuring two or more servers on the same subnet to share the response to client requests for dynamically assigned addresses

    C. The process of configuring a DHCP server and a router in one location to share the response to client requests for dynamically assigned addresses

    D. The process of configuring a DHCP server and a router in separate locations to share the response to client requests for dynamically assigned addresses

17. You have decided to move your DHCP database from a Windows NT 4.0 server to a Windows 2000 server. You install DHCP on the destination server, export the registry entries from the source server, copy the database to the new server, import the registry entries into the new server and start the DHCP service on the destination server. Upon startup, you receive a jet database error 20036 in the event log, indicating a conversion process error. What did you do wrong?

    A. You forgot to upgrade the Window NT 4.0 server to Windows 2000 before doing the conversion.

    B. You forgot to run JETPACK.EXE /CONVERT on the database.

    C. You did not reconcile the database on the Windows NT 4.0 server before moving it to the new server.

    D. Nothing went wrong. This is a normal error message that will be corrected once the database has been reconciled and verified.

LAB QUESTION

You are a networking consultant. A new client approaches you and asks you to configure a DHCP infrastructure in their new network. The client has managed for years using manual processes, but now needs a computer network, as they have several locations. Analyze the following planned network infrastructure and determine the best way to implement DHCP in the client's environments. Please describe the scope of information for each location using the 192.168.0.0 network. You may subnet it however you would like.

The client has four regional locations and two small remote locations. All four regional locations have 100 employees who have desktop PCs running Windows 2000. Their LAN will be set up as a VLAN so that all machines are on the same segment. Frame Relay circuits running at 512KB connect all four regional locations. Each location uses new Cisco routers. One remote location has five users who use laptops. There is no connectivity to this office. The remote users need to access the corporate network, but only for e-mail and small file sharing. The other remote office has ten users, all using laptops on a local LAN. They are connected to the corporate office by a 128KB leased ISDN connection through a Windows 2000 server running RRAS.

SELF TEST ANSWERS

Overview of the Windows 2000 DHCP Server

1. ☑ **B.** Bootstrap Protocol (BOOTP) was the original industry standard defined by RFC 951 and 1084.
   ☒ **A,** DAIA, and **D,** IAA, are not correct because they do not exist. **C,** EIGR, is a routing protocol used within routers.

2. ☑ **D.** Enhanced IPX/SPX support. IPX/SPX is not a part of DHCP because DHCP is based upon the dynamic assignment of TCP/IP addresses, not IPX/SPX addresses.
   ☒ **A, B,** and **C,** integration of DHCP with DNS, vendor-specific and class ID support, and rogue DHCP server detection, specify services included in Windows 2000 DHCP.

Integrating DHCP into a Routed Environment

3. ☑ **A, C.** DHCP can be installed on any Windows 2000 server, whether it is part of a workgroup or a domain.
   ☒ **B** and **D** are incorrect because the DHCP service cannot be installed on the Windows 2000 Professional workstation platform.

4. ☑ **A, C.** To relay DHCP broadcast requests from any subnet, you must use the DHCP relay agent service running on a Windows 2000 server, or the BOOTP forwarding service provided by most routers.
   ☒ **B** and **D** are incorrect because they do not exist.

Integrating DHCP with Windows 2000

5. ☑ **A, B.** You can configure RRAS to assign addresses from DHCP or from a scope of addresses defined on the RRAS server.
   ☒ **C** is incorrect because RRAS will not acquire addresses from a BOOTP server to assign to RRAS clients. **D** is incorrect because RRAS cannot use APIPA to assign addresses to RRAS clients.

6. ☑ **D.** RRAS clients do not automatically receive scope options from the DHCP server, but rather obtain their options from the settings of the RRAS server. If the RRAS server is not configured with the options, the clients will fail to receive any settings.
   ☒ **A** is incorrect because it is not necessary for RRAS clients to set static networking properties.

This would defeat the purpose of using DHCP. **B** is incorrect because if the DHCP server were not functional, the client would not have received an IP address. **C** is incorrect because RRAS is not required to run WINS and/or DNS to deliver addresses for these services to clients–it only needs to have addresses assigned for these services in its own network configuration.

7. ☑ **B, D.** Both Windows 98 and Windows 2000 include the FQDN option and register their names and addresses with DDNS upon startup.

   ☒ **A and C** are incorrect because these clients do not support the FQDN option and must have DHCP register their names and addresses with the DDNS server.

Automatic Private IP Addressing (APIPA)

8. ☑ **D.** When a machine renews its lease and cannot contact the DHCP server, it will continue to try until the lease has expired. At expiration, it must give up the lease, so it uses APIPA to assign itself an IP address in the 168.254.0.1/16 range.

   ☒ **A and B** are wrong because, although it is possible for someone to reconfigure your machines over the weekend, it is not likely that someone would go to the trouble to visit every machine. Although someone could have reconfigured your DHCP server, it is more likely that your server is not functional. **C** is incorrect because DHCP ceases to hand out addresses once it has exhausted the address pool you specified

9. ☑ **A.** APIPA is a service that assigns IP addresses to a machine when DHCP fails to respond or a DHCP server is unavailable.

   ☒ **B, C, and D** are wrong because APIPA has no integration with WINS, no integration with DDNS, no scope options, and no administrative tool.

10. ☑ **C.** The only way to disable the APIPA service is to edit the registry.

    ☒ **A** is incorrect because the APIPA service is not a service in the conventional sense of the word as much as it is a system action. **B** is incorrect because you cannot disable the service from the network control panel.

Security Issues Related to DHCP

11. ☑ **B, D.** DHCP Users and DHCP Administrators. DHCP includes two security groups to the server in which it is installed. DHCP Administrators lets you add to DHCP individuals for whom you want to have full administrative rights, but grants no domain-wide administrative rights outside of DHCP. DHCP users lets you add users with read-only access to the DHCP configuration.

    ☒ **A and C** are incorrect because they do not exist.

12. ☑ **B.** Rogue detection allows the server to detect and locate unauthorized DHCP servers on the network by posing as a client machine sending DHCPDISCOVERY packets to the network.
☒ **A, C,** and **D** are incorrect because DHCP network clients do not have rogue detection.

13. ☑ **C.** By default, the DDNS server will make anyone who registers a name the owner of that name and no other machine will be able to edit it. DHCP allows registration of older clients with DDNS, such as the Windows NT 4.0 workstations in this example. Once the Windows NT 4.0 workstations are upgraded, they can update their record in DDNS, but the records are owned by the DHCP server. To correct this, the DHCP server should be placed in the DNSUpdateProxy group prior to serving clients. This limits the rights of the DHCP server, making the records registered by the server public to changes.
☒ **A** is incorrect because there is no such setting on the DHCP server. **B** is incorrect because there is no such setting on the DDNS server. **D** is incorrect because placing the Windows NT 4.0 machines in the DNSUpdateProxy group would not have had any value since Windows NT 4.0 workstations do not register their host name with DDNS.

Designing a DHCP Service for Remote Locations

14. ☑ **A.** The scenario does not mention any need for the machines to network with each other; they only need access to the corporate network. In this case, the best solution would be installing RRAS on each client. Once configured, the RRAS server would offer IP addresses to the clients as they dialed in.
☒ **B** is incorrect because, although the solution would work, it is not cost effective and installs a network that is not required. **C** is incorrect because a demand-dial connection will not access addresses for relay on the local network. **D** is incorrect because it is overkill. It is possible to make that configuration work, but a T-1 to a small sales office is not practical.

15. ☑ **A.** A lease is a time value assigned to each scope that defines how long a client can use an address before it will need to acquire a new lease.
☒ **B, C,** and **D** are incorrect because they describe functions of the server and clients that do not exist.

Measuring and Optimizing a DHCP Infrastructure Design

16. ☑ **B.** A distributed scope is the process of designing two or more DHCP servers to share a set of addresses to provide load balanced DHCP servers to a network.
☒ **A** is not correct because servers with a distributed scope must be on the same subnet. **C** and **D** are incorrect because DHCP and routers cannot be configured to share scopes.

17. ☑ **D.** It is normal to receive the jet database error when starting a Windows NT 4.0 database on a Windows 2000 server. Running Reconcile and Verify from the MMC DHCP admin will correct the problem.

☒ **A** is not correct because Windows NT 4.0 does not need to be upgraded to migrate the DHCP database from one server to another. **B** is not correct because jetpack does not support the /CONVERT option. **C** is not correct because reconciling the database on the Windows NT 4.0 server would not prevent the error message.

LAB ANSWER

The first step is to decide a DHCP solution for the four regional locations. Because the links between the offices are only 512 Kbps, it is best to implement a DHCP server in each remote location. Using the 192.168.0.0 network, the addressing is divided using a 24-bit (255.255.255.0) subnet. One scope is set up on the server in each location (192.168.0.0/24–192.168.1.0/24–192.168.2.0/24 and 192.168.3.0/24). This will provide DHCP for all four regional offices. The first remote office does not require a local LAN and its bandwidth needs are minimal, so it will be set up to dial into the network via RRAS. The RRAS server will be set up in the regional office closest to the remote office and configured to assign addresses for dial-in clients from the DHCP server in that location. The second remote site has a leased line and only a handful of clients. Because they do not have a router on site, a machine must be configured as a DHCP relay agent and placed on the local network. This agent will be directed to the regional office that is connected via the ISDN circuit. The DHCP server in that location will need to have an additional scope added (192.168.4.0/24).

6

Designing a
DNS Strategy

Threhe Domain Name System (DNS) is at the heart of Windows 2000. It is so essential to the function of a Windows 2000 network that you cannot install Active Directory until you have an appropriate DNS Server functioning on the network. The DNS service in Windows 2000 has gone through a major change since the release of Windows NT 4.0 Server. We will begin this chapter with an overview of DNS and a discussion of some of the new features in the product.

We'll continue with a thorough discussion of how to create a namespace that is suitable for both DNS and an organization's implementation of Active Directory. DNS and Active Directory naming are very closely related in Windows 2000, making this material essential to master. After this discussion, we will look in greater detail at some of the new features of DNS such as Active Directory Integrated Zones and DNS security. We will wrap up the chapter with a look at how to create a highly available DNS design as well as a solid look at the measurement and optimization you should be performing to keep DNS running at its best.

A strong knowledge of DNS is essential for anyone who will be planning or deploying Windows 2000 networks. Much of the functionality that used to be handled by WINS has been moved into DNS. WINS is now provided in the product primarily for backward compatibility. This means that DNS is now the primary service for locating services and computers on a Windows network. This chapter will provide you with the knowledge you need not only to pass a certification exam, but also to plan and deploy Windows 2000 DNS services in any size network.

CERTIFICATION OBJECTIVE 6.01

Overview of the Windows 2000 Dynamic DNS Server

Traditionally, DNS was designed to help computers find other computers. A DNS Server contained a static database (or databases) that was maintained by an administrator. In fact, it was often no more than a collection of text files. With the release of Windows 2000, DNS is now much more. Let's begin our look at DNS with a solid foundation of what it once was. The base functionality of DNS is still the foundation of the product.

The original purpose of DNS was to keep records of resources on a network. The most common use for DNS was to keep track of Fully Qualified Domain Name-to-IP address mappings. Each computer (host) on a network is typically provided with a user-friendly name such as computer1. Each host is also a member of a DNS domain (for example, syngress.com) or a subdomain (acctg.syngress.com). The combination of the host name and the domain or subdomain name is referred to as a Fully Qualified Domain Name (FQDN). In our examples, the domain names would be computer1.syngress.com and computer1.acctg.syngress.com. Host names are assigned by administrators because they are much easier to remember than a computer's IP address, which is a string of numbers that looks like this: 10.0.0.1. In addition, the name can tell the administrator something about the machine. For instance, accounting1 is most likely a machine that is located in the accounting department.

Although these names are helpful to humans, they don't mean much to computers communicating on a network. In order to communicate with another host, a computer needs the numeric address of the other machine. This numeric address is called the IP address in TCP/IP networks. DNS is the database where computers go to translate a FQDN name like computer1.syngress.com into the real IP address of that machine so that communication can begin. This process is the primary function of a DNS Server and is called a Forward Lookup.

This simple explanation belies the complexity underlying the Domain Name System. While it seems simple enough for an administrator to type in computer name-to-IP address mappings, and for another administrator to configure computers with the address of the DNS Server to look up those records as needed, consider the millions of machines that are connected to the Internet. Every time you type in http://www.syngress.com, your computer uses DNS to find the numeric address associated with the FQDN name you typed in. Imagine how many servers are needed to fulfill the requests from millions of Internet users each day. Then ask yourself, who maintains them? How does a machine know which one to ask to find the right record? The more you think about it, the greater the number of questions that will come to mind.

How Traditional DNS Works

The Internet has a series of root DNS Servers. You don't see it, but when you type **http://www.syngress.com** an extra dot (.) is appended to the end of your request. So http://www.syngress.com. is your actual request. That last dot represents a root server. Your computer is configured with the address of a DNS Server—possibly one maintained by the company you get your internet access through. This DNS Server probably contains only a small number of records for DNS domain names for which it is *authoritative*. Being authoritative means that it is in charge of all the records for that domain and any subdomains.

When your Internet provider receives a request for a domain for which it is not authoritative, it forwards the request to a root name server. A special file exists on the DNS Server that tells it where a root sever is located. It then goes out and asks the root DNS Server if it knows who http://www.syngress.com is. It most likely doesn't, but it should contain an entry for who is authoritative for the .com. domain. The DNS Server then asks the .com. DNS Server if it knows who http://www.syngress.com is. In this way the DNS Server at your Internet provider just keeps going out and asking who http://www.syngress.com is until it either finds out or determines that it will not be able to find out. Then it returns the result to your computer. This process is called a Recursive Forward Lookup.

Types of Traditional DNS Servers

As with any complex system, there are different types of DNS Servers. Perhaps a better way of thinking about this is that there are different roles that DNS Servers play in trying to resolve user-friendly names. The most important is the Primary DNS Server. A Primary DNS Server is authoritative for one or more domains. To be more accurate, it is authoritative for zones. A zone is a part of the DNS namespace that the server's administrators control. A zone might contain a domain, a subdomain, or a domain with subdomains. In traditional DNS implementations, a zone is really just a file that exists on the Primary DNS Server. In simplest terms, the file contains configuration information for the domain as well as resource records for the FQDN-to-IP address mappings.

As important as Primary DNS Servers are, they have a weakness. If they go down, all information about the domain they are authoritative for is unavailable until they come back up. Since there can be only one Primary DNS Server for each domain, this could be a major problem. Secondary DNS Servers are designed to provide fault tolerance. A Secondary DNS Server receives a *zone transfer* from the Primary DNS Server. A zone transfer is simply a copy of the information contained in the zone file on the Primary DNS Server. Because this contains all the records for a domain, a Secondary DNS Server can perform name lookups as reliably as the Primary DNS Server when it is properly synchronized. The zone information cannot be changed or updated on a Secondary DNS Server except through a zone transfer with a Primary DNS Server.

To further complicate matters, once a Primary DNS Server has a Secondary DNS Server that is configured to receive zone transfers from it, it gets a new title. It is still called a Primary DNS Server, but it is also now called a Master DNS Server. Secondary DNS Servers do not have to get their zone information directly from a Primary DNS Server. In fact, a Secondary DNS Server can get its zone information from another Secondary server, which received it from another Secondary server, which received it from the Primary DNS Server. Any server that a Secondary server gets a zone transfer from is also called a Master DNS Server. So, a server can be both a Secondary DNS Server and a Master DNS Server.

As if it isn't confusing enough, a server can be a Primary DNS Server, a Master DNS Server, and a Secondary DNS Server! Let's look at how this can be the case. If a server is authoritative for a zone, it is a Primary DNS Server. A server can be authoritative for any number of zones if configured that way by the administrator. In addition, a server can also be configured as a Secondary DNS Server for a zone it is not authoritative for. Finally, if any of the zones that are stored on it are transferred to Secondary servers, it will also be a Master DNS Server.

Until an administrator configures a server to be authoritative for a zone or to accept zone transfers, a DNS Server is neither a Primary nor Secondary DNS Server. Thus, most DNS Servers begin their existence as something called a Caching DNS Server. By default all Microsoft DNS Servers cache requests made by clients that they were able to successfully resolve. After a period of time the entries expire and are removed from cache. Let's look at what this means.

When a client requests http://www.syngress.com, the DNS Server goes out and finds its IP address. It then remembers this information for a period of time in case someone else asks for it. If another client makes the same request before the time expires, it will not go out to the Internet and try to look up the name again; it will simply return it from cache. If the time expires before the next person asks for it, it will be removed from cache and be forced to go out and look it up again.

Microsoft's DNS Features for Windows 2000

All of the features of traditional DNS just described are part of the Windows 2000 DNS service. They are, however, just the beginning. Microsoft has added a great deal of functionality to DNS. For starters, administrators no longer have to add and delete records in the DNS database manually. Windows 2000 computers and clients using the Windows 2000 DHCP service now have their records added and removed dynamically. Windows 2000 even incorporates new aging and scavenging parameters that help to keep the database clean and up to date.

In Windows 2000, DNS can be operated in a traditional way with Primary and Secondary servers and files that contain the zone database records. However, it can also be integrated with Active Directory. As we'll see later, this allows administrators to create a much more fault tolerant DNS infrastructure while still maintaining some backwards compatibility with traditional DNS implementations. When integrated with Active Directory, dynamic resource record updates can be secured to ensure that only the appropriate computers or administrators can alter them.

on the
ĵob

The ability to perform dynamic updates could pose a big security threat. Imagine what would happen if you ran a major online investment site and someone was able to get one of your DNS Servers to point to their Web server instead of yours. They could easily program their Web server to look just like your real Web site and begin collecting account IDs and passwords. Fortunately Microsoft has made it very hard for someone to do that by implementing some strong security options into the dynamic update features of the Windows 2000 DNS service. In order to use the additional security measures, you must be running the DNS Server service on an Active Directory domain controller.

Another major improvement in the Windows 2000 DNS service is the ability to have incremental zone transfers. When zone transfers occur in a traditional DNS environment, all of the records are transferred, not just the ones that changed since the last update. As you can imagine, for large zones with many records and numerous Secondary servers, this can take up considerable bandwidth, especially over slow WAN links. Windows 2000 DNS Servers do not do full zone transfers unless absolutely necessary. In most cases they transfer only the records which have changed since the last zone transfer occurred.

exam
ⓦatch

New features of the Windows 2000 DNS service include Active Directory integration, dynamic and secure dynamic resource record updates, and incremental zone transfers.

Configuring a Standard Primary Zone

EXERCISE 6-1

In this exercise we will configure a Standard Primary zone. You will need a Windows 2000 server with the DNS service installed.

1. Log on to the computer using an account with administrative rights.

2. Open up the Windows 2000 DNS administration tool by clicking Start | Programs | Administrative Tools | DNS.

3. Right-click DNS in the tree pane on the left side of the screen.

4. Select Connect to Computer.

5. In the Select Target Computer dialog box, select This Computer. Make sure that the Connect to the Specified Computer Now check box is selected.

6. Select OK. You will be returned to the main DNS administration screen and your computer will now have an icon in the tree pane under DNS.

7. Right-click the icon representing your computer in the tree pane.

8. Select New Zone.

9. Read the welcome screen and click Next.

10. Select Standard Primary and click Next.

11. Select Forward Lookup Zone and click Next.

12. Type **syngress.msft** in the Name text box.

13. Click Next.

14. Make sure the Create a New File With This Name text box displays syngress.msft.dns.

15. Click Next.

16. Review the information on the Completing the New Zone Wizard page and click Finish.

17. In the tree pane, click the plus sign to the left of your server's icon.

18. In the tree pane, click the folder labeled Forward Lookup Zones.

19. In the right pane, make sure your new zone is listed.

CERTIFICATION OBJECTIVE 6.02

Creating a DNS Namespace for the Organization

The DNS namespace is divided into domains and subdomains. Generally an organization has one root domain name that represents the entire organization (such as syngress.com) and several subdomains that further differentiate parts of the organization (such as acctg.syngress.com or europe.syngress.com). Active Directory also uses domains and can mirror the namespace of DNS. Because of this you will need to know not only how to design a DNS namespace but also how to integrate it with Active Directory for maximum effectiveness.

Determining the Scope of Active Directory Naming

On a network that utilizes Active Directory, the generally accepted way of creating a DNS namespace for your organization is to model it on an existing Active Directory design. In other words, it is recommended that you design your Active Directory structure first, and then fit your DNS implementation to it. There are several accepted methods to use when implementing Active Directory, each of which carries significant DNS design issues with it. In this section we will look at a series of best practices designed to take the various potential implementations into account.

You wouldn't want to have to modify your Active Directory design because it doesn't fit your business. An Active Directory design should always be as broad as possible so that it can accommodate change without needing major redesign. It should take into account a number of factors. The one that will affect DNS the most is whether or not your company will have an external Internet presence, or just an internal network.

Active Directory can only have one root domain, the Forrest Root. This root domain might be the same as your company's external Internet domain name, or it might not. In addition, you might have several divisions of your organization that operate as separate companies, each requiring its own external Internet domain name. These divisions would most likely be implemented as different Trees in your Active Directory Forest. Your DNS structure needs to accommodate all of these situations.

Remember that you must register your internal DNS domain names, such as syngress.com, with InterNIC if you intend to make resources from your network available on the Internet. InterNIC is charged with ensuring that no two organizations on the Internet are using the same domain name. DNS names that are not registered cannot be resolved from the Internet. Once you register your names, you will have full control over the subdomains and the hosts you create in them. In essence this means that your Active Directory structure will now exist inside of your Internet DNS structure.

The DNS/Active Directory Naming Hierarchy

It is important that you understand the difference between Active Directory domains and DNS domains. They are separate entities. DNS domains are a much older design and were originally used to store Resource Records for computers. These records were designed to help computers find each other, and thus communicate, on the network. The records stored human-readable names called Fully Qualified Domain Names (such as DNSServer1) and the machine's actual IP address. When a user typed in the name of a computer, his own computer would look up the name in DNS and obtain the IP address that was required for communication to take place. The new version of Microsoft's DNS service continues this base functionality while greatly expanding on it.

The DNS Naming Hierarchy

DNS is a hierarchical structure. For an organization, this means that it has a root domain and subdomains. The subdomains are designed to group computers together in a logical fashion. Subdomains are created by administrators and can be based on computer function (databases.syngress.com), the role of the computer's user in the organization (acctg.syngress.com), the computer's location (bldg1.syngress.com), the geographic region the computer is in (namerica.syngress.com), and a subsidiary the computer is assigned to (company2.syngress.com), to name a few possible criteria. These criteria can be combined to be even more descriptive. For example, a computer in France assigned to someone in accounting might be in the following domain: acctg.france.europe.syngress.com. If the computer's name was acctg10, its FQDN would be acctg10.acctg.france.europe.syngress.com. The namespace structure chosen should be easy for the network users to understand and navigate.

An additional benefit of using subdomains is that you can place them in their own primary zones. For instance, syngress.com can be contained in a primary zone on a server called DNSServer1. The subdomain acctg.syngress.com can be contained in a primary zone on a second server called DNSServer2. When a subdomain is in a different zone file than its parent domain, it is called a *delegated domain*. Zone delegation has many benefits including performance and availability.

Because the zone information for the delegated domain is stored on a separate server, it can be placed closer to the hosts that need to access its records. This can improve query response times and boost performance. It is also likely that any Secondary servers for the zone are located at the same site, thus reducing the effects of zone replication across WAN links and other parts of the network.

Because the server probably contains records for just one department or geographic region, if DNSServer1 becomes unavailable the impact will be minimized. Hosts in the delegated domain may not be able to resolve FQDNs for the syngress.com domain, but they will still be able to have their queries resolved for hosts in the acctg.syngress.com delegated domain. Under this scenario, if the DNS designers did their job properly, the resources that these hosts access most frequently are likely to be located in their delegated domain and still be accessible.

CertCam 6-2

EXERCISE 6-2

Creating a Standard Zone Delegation

In this exercise you will create a standard zone delegation. You will need two Windows 2000 servers with the DNS service installed. Complete the following exercise from the Windows 2000 DNS Server that contains the Standard Primary Zone for syngress.msft.

1. Log on to the computer using an account with administrative rights.

2. Open up the Windows 2000 DNS administration tool by clicking Start | Programs | Administrative Tools | DNS.

3. If there is no server listed in the tree pane, perform steps 4 through 7. Otherwise, skip to step 8.

4. Right-click DNS in the tree pane on the left side of the screen.

5. Select Connect to Computer.

6. In the Select Target Computer dialog box, select This Computer. Make sure that the Connect to the Specified Computer Now check box is selected.

7. Select OK. You will be returned to the main DNS administration screen and your computer will now have an icon in the tree pane under DNS.

8. In the tree pane, expand the folder labeled Forward Lookup Zone if this is not already done.

9. In the tree pane, right-click the zone labeled syngress.msft and click New Host.

10. In the Name text box, type the name of the DNS Server that contains the Standard Primary Zone for syngress.msft (this server).

11. In the IP Address text box, type the server's IP address.

12. Click Add Host.

13. In the Name text box, type the name of the DNS Server that contains the Standard Secondary Zone for syngress.msft (your other DNS Server).

14. In the IP Address text box, type the server's IP address.

15. Click Add Host.

16. Click Done.

17. In the tree pane, right-click the zone labeled syngress.msft.

18. Click New Delegation.

19. Read the Welcome screen and click Next.

20. In the Delegated Domain text box, type **delegated**. Notice that as you do so the Fully Qualified Domain Name box reflects the changes.

21. Click Next.

22. On the Name Servers page of the wizard, click Add.

23. Click the Browse button next to the Server Name dialog box.

24. Double-click the name of your server.

25. Double-click the Forward Lookup Zones folder.

26. Double-click syngress.msft.

27. Click the DNS Server that contains the Standard Secondary Zone for syngress.msft.

28. Click OK

29. Click Next.

30. Review the Completing the New Delegation Wizard page and click Finish.

31. Notice that the delegated zone shows up underneath the syngress.msft zone in the tree pane.

32. Close the DNS management console.

Complete the following steps from the second Windows 2000 DNS Server.

33. Log on to the computer using an account with administrative rights.

34. Open up the Windows 2000 DNS administration tool by clicking Start | Programs | Administrative Tools | DNS.

35. If there is no server listed in the tree pane, perform steps 36 through 39. Otherwise, skip to step 40.

36. Right-click DNS in the tree pane on the left side of the screen.

37. Select Connect to Computer.

38. In the Select Target Computer dialog box, select This Computer. Make sure that the Connect to the Specified Computer Now check box is selected.

39. Select OK. You will be returned to the main DNS administration screen and your computer will now have an icon in the tree pane under DNS.

40. In the DNS management console, right-click the icon representing your computer in the tree pane.

41. Select New Zone.

42. Read the Welcome screen and click Next.

43. Select Standard Primary and click Next.

44. Select Forward Lookup Zone and click Next.

The Active Directory Naming Hierarchy

Active Directory domains exist within the new Windows 2000 Active Directory service. They are administrator creations that help you to organize and manage accounts and resources logically. In addition to account management, Active Directory is designed for use by applications such as Exchange Server to store and manage user data centrally. For instance, future versions of Microsoft Exchange Server will be able to use groups in Windows 2000 as Distribution Lists. Active Directory primarily stores account and resource objects; DNS primarily stores computer name-to-IP address mappings.

Active Directory domains can also have subdomains. The first domain created in a forest is the highest domain in Active Directory. This domain is both the forest root domain and root domain for the first tree. Below the root domain are subdomains. These can be created for the same reasons subdomains are created in DNS. Thus, a great deal of symmetry can exist in an organization between its DNS and Active Directory domain structures. Syngress.com can function as both the name of the root Active Directory domain, and the DNS root domain name. Having a situation such as this can greatly simplify DNS planning, especially if the subdomains will be the same as well.

exam
ⓦatch

Remember that both DNS and Active Directory use the concept of domains and subdomains. DNS stores host name-to-IP address mappings in resource records. Active Directory stores account and resource objects such as users, groups, and printer objects.

Using an InterNIC-Registered DNS Domain Name for the Active Directory Root Domain Name

In the simplest case, you may elect to use your company's existing DNS name as your Active Directory domain name. Remember that the name of the first domain installed in your organization becomes your Active Directory forest root domain name. In this scenario, you will use your company's existing DNS zone to create a forest root domain with a name that matches it. Any subdomains created in Active Directory will correspond to an existing DNS subdomain. Microsoft points out several advantages and disadvantages of using this model. The advantages are:

- You do not have to modify your existing DNS structure.
- All of your current DNS host names and Resource Records will remain the same and will not require modification to match the Active Directory domain name.
- You will not need to register any additional domain names with InterNIC.

The disadvantages are:

- If you have resources that need to be accessed from the Internet, it is very likely that you will need to do additional work to protect Active Directory from unauthorized Internet access.

■ An existing DNS environment might not have DNS Servers capable of supporting service (SRV) records. Adding this support might increase TCO costs and/or add complexity to the DNS structure.

Using a Single DNS Domain Name for the Public and Internal Sides of the Network

Using an InterNIC-registered DNS Domain name for the Active Directory root domain name can complicate matters considerably if you are going to be using the same DNS Domain name for both the publicly accessible and internal (private) sides of your network. It is very important that you protect the DNS Server that is used by your Active Directory structure because it contains sensitive data about your network services, in addition to the standard host name-to-IP address mappings. Currently, there are two primary methods of achieving this separation: independent DNS zones separated by a firewall and separate DNS zones with public access allowed for internal clients.

Independent DNS Zones Separated by a Firewall

This solution involves two DNS Servers that are separated by a firewall. One is placed outside the firewall on the public network (such as the Internet), and the other is kept inside the firewall for use by clients on the internal network. The DNS Servers must be administered separately and each is authoritative for a zone that is named identically (for example, syngress.com). The server on the outside of the firewall contains records only for machines that are available to people accessing resources from the public network. This might include mail servers, Web servers, or FTP servers.

The internal DNS Server is the one that is used by Active Directory. It contains records for all internal clients and their associated services. Users are not allowed to access the servers that are on the public side of the network. Instead, the content provided by those servers is replicated on servers inside the network. Clients located on the internal network access the content on these internal servers. As you can see, quite a bit of work is required to keep things functioning optimally in this scenario.

Separate DNS Zones with Public Access Allowed for Internal Clients

This solution also involves two DNS Servers that are separated by a firewall. One is placed outside the firewall on the public network, and the other is kept inside the firewall for use by clients on the internal network. The DNS Servers are administered separately and each is authoritative for a zone that is named identically. The server on the outside of the firewall contains records only for machines that are available to people accessing resources from the public network.

The difference between this solution and the preceding one is that content from the external servers is not replicated to internal servers. Instead, the internal users are allowed to access the servers on the public side of the network by using the servers' public IP addresses. In order to maintain security, a great deal of work must be done to ensure the firewall only passes the traffic that is appropriate for such communication. When an internal client issues a DNS request for a server on the public network, the internal DNS Server will provide the requesting client with the public address of the host. Any connection from the client to this host will take place through the firewall.

Using a DNS Subdomain for the Active Directory Root

One alternative to using the organization's DNS name as the Active Directory root domain name is to create a DNS subdomain to hold the Active Directory information. If the subdomain is created in a separate zone, all administrative tasks for it can be delegated. Because the DNS root domain and this delegated domain exist in separate zones on separate servers, one can be exposed to the Internet while the other exists safely behind a firewall on the internal network. In this instance, the server containing the root domain's zone would sit outside the firewall and contain only records for hosts that were intended to be publicly accessible.

Another good example of why you might choose this design doesn't relate to the Internet at all. You might find yourself needing to design a DNS structure for a network that consists of a large number of UNIX hosts and only a few Windows 2000 machines. Because many UNIX hosts aren't designed to utilize the new features of Microsoft's Dynamic DNS (DDNS) implementation, it might be more desirable for them to continue to use the traditional DNS Servers that are already in place. In this situation, creating a subdomain for Active Directory and putting it in its own delegated zone might be the best solution. This is because you can then place this zone on a server that supports the SRV records that Active Directory requires. The name of this subdomain (for example, w2k.syngress.com) will become the name of the Active Directory forest root domain. By choosing this course of action, you have greatly simplified your DNS rollout because you did not have to alter any of the existing DNS Servers in the organization significantly.

Microsoft lists several advantages and disadvantages for using a DNS subdomain for the Active Directory root.

Advantages

■ It does not require existing DNS Servers to be upgraded to support SRV records. The existing DNS Servers can continue to function as they always have.

■ All of the Active Directory information is kept isolated in the delegated domain. This provides for greater security as in our example, in which the domain's root zone could be on a server that was exposed to the Internet while the Active Directory zone was kept safe behind a firewall. Even without a firewall, additional Windows 2000-specific security measures could be taken to further secure this server.

Disadvantages

■ A new DNS Server is required to host the new subdomain and zone that will be used for the Windows 2000 computers.

■ The name of the Active Directory forest root domain name is longer because it is now in the format of a third-level domain name (w2k.syngress.com as opposed to syngress.com).

on the
Job

One thing to note about creating domains in Windows 2000 is that there is no menu choice to create "subdomains." Even when you are creating a subdomain, you must select New Domain from the menus in the DNS snap-in.

Using a Reserved Private DNS Domain Name for the Active Directory Root Domain Name

It is possible that you will be called upon to design a DNS structure for an organization that does not have an Internet presence. Alternately, the organization might have an Internet presence that is hosted from another location by an outsourced Web site provider. If this is the case and the company is certain that they will not be in need of an Internet presence in the future that is hosted from their network, it might be best to use a reserved private DNS domain name for their Active Directory forest root domain name. In some instances, this might also be desirable if the organization has an Internet presence that is hosted from their network, but wants a separate and strongly differentiated DNS and Active Directory naming scheme for computers on the internal network.

Many organization use IP address ranges such as 10.x.y.z for their internal networks. These addresses are reserved for private use and are not allowed to be used on the Internet. Though much less known, there is also a reserved private DNS Domain name called .local. The .local DNS domain name is designed to be used internally in an organization and cannot be used for Internet access. Organizations wishing to use it internally can create subdomains that are more descriptive for their organization, such as syngress.local and acctg.europe.syngress.local.

Microsoft lists several advantages and disadvantages for this naming strategy.

Advantages

- This naming strategy does not require the organization to have an Internet domain name registered with InterNIC.

- Any combination of characters that is allowed for a DNS name can be used for the domain name and Active Directory forest root domain name. Because the network will not provide resources to the Internet, naming conflicts are not an issue.

Disadvantages

- Hosts configured with the .local reserved DNS Domain name cannot be resolved on the Internet

- If Internet resolution is ever necessary, a valid name will need to be registered with InterNIC. In addition, the forest will need to be completely reinstalled to make the name change in Active Directory.

Using a Different DNS Domain Name for the Public and Internal Sides of the Network

The final naming strategy we will discuss is using different DNS Domain names for the public and private (internal) sides of the network. This strategy makes a very clear distinction between internal and public resources. One example of such a strategy might be to use syngress.com for all public resources and syngress.local for all internal ones. Two different DNS Servers are required to maintain the separate namespaces, and administration also needs to be done separately. As in previous examples, a firewall would be used to separate the internal and public sides of the network.

SCENARIO & SOLUTION

Your organization wants its internal computers to be completely inaccessible from the Internet, but still needs to have some public computers that host their Web and FTP product support sites. What would be the best way to implement this?	The first place to start is obviously a design with a firewall separating the public and private networks. A valid domain name should be registered with InterNIC. DNS Servers should be placed on the public network that resolve the names required to access the public resources. Because the organization is so clear in their concerns that the internal network should not be accessible, in addition to the firewall this may be a situation where it is appropriate to use a reserved name for the internal network names. By doing so there is virtually no chance of the name being resolved.
Your company wants its registered domain name to be used for hosts on both the public and private sides of the network. They do not want to replicate content from public servers to private servers for internal hosts to access. What would be the best design for this network?	A firewall should be placed between the public and private side of the network. A DNS Server should be placed on the public side that contains records for all of the publicly available hosts. A second DNS Server should be placed on the private side of the network that contains records for all private and public hosts. Public content would be accessed through the firewall by private hosts.

Microsoft lists several advantages and disadvantages for this naming strategy.

Advantages

- The differences between what is on the public versus the internal network is very clear. This can help with management and security.

- There is no need to have resources on the internal network that contain replicated content from servers on the public side of the network. Internal clients would be free to access the public side of the network and all resources on it.

- The organization's internal naming structure (hierarchy) is not exposed to the Internet.

Disadvantages

- Resources on the internal network cannot be accessed from the public network by using their DNS names. While this might be a plus from a security standpoint, it can also be a disadvantage if you have resources you'd like to share from the internal to the public side of the network.

■ The two different naming standards might confuse users. This would be especially true for users that had to access company resources on both sides of the network.

CERTIFICATION OBJECTIVE 6.03

Creating an Integrated DNS Design

There are several different integration issues regarding Windows 2000 DNS. First, the DNS Server service can be integrated with Active Directory to yield substantial fault tolerance and security benefits. The DNS Server service can also be integrated with the Windows 2000 DHCP service on both servers and clients to greatly reduce the amount of administrative overhead involved in maintaining DNS resource records. Finally, even though it greatly expands the possibilities available in previous versions, Windows 2000 DNS still has all of the traditional functionality needed to work with standard DNS clients.

Integration with the Active Directory

DNS can be integrated with Active Directory. Active Directory only exists on domain controllers. Because of this, only domain controllers can serve as Active Directory integrated DNS Servers. This provides many benefits not available in previous versions of the Windows DNS service. By integrating DNS with Active Directory, you greatly increase fault tolerance because zone transfers occur as a normal part of the Active Directory replication process. Because the zone information is located on multiple Windows 2000 DNS servers, if one goes down another is available to take its place.

exam
ⓦatch

Be sure to remember that Active Directory integrated zones only exist on Active Directory domain controllers.

Security is also enhanced. All Active Directory replication is encrypted by default, making zone information more difficult to intercept in transit. In addition, all integrated DNS Servers must be registered in Active Directory. Servers that are not registered cannot participate in zone replication. Finally, the Window's 2000 version of DNS is dynamic which means clients and DHCP servers can update resource records. When DNS is integrated with Active Directory and secure dynamic updates are enabled (the default setting), only authorized clients can update their records.

Integration with DHCP

In the past, DNS required a great deal of manual administration. This is because every record in the database had to be created and maintained by hand. When DHCP started to be widely deployed in the enterprise, it caused some serious issues with DNS. DHCP is designed to distribute IP addresses to clients.

DHCP and IP addresses are leased to the client for a period of time. It is possible for the client to get a different IP address from one lease to the next. DHCP does not have a means of notifying the DNS administrator when it assigns a client a different address. Because of this, the DNS record would be wrong until the new address was discovered. Even though DHCP offers tremendous gains in management efficiency on IP networks, because of its conflicts with DNS, it has not seen wide deployment in traditional TCP/IP environments.

In Windows 2000, the DHCP client service runs on every machine. This is true even if the computer is not a DHCP client. It has also been extended to help make DNS administration much easier. The DHCP client service on Windows 2000 clients that are configured with static IP addresses will dynamically update its resource records on a Windows 2000 DNS Server every time it boots up, changes its per-adapter address, or changes its per-adapter domain name.

on the
job

Even some downlevel clients can take advantage of DDNS. For instance, Windows NT 4.0 clients that are DHCP clients cannot register their host name and IP address dynamically in DDNS. However, if they use a properly configured Windows 2000 DHCP server, the server will register and remove their address lease records dynamically for the client.

If the Windows 2000 computer is a DHCP client, the administrator can specify several different options. The administrator can choose to have various DNS resource records registered by the Windows 2000 DHCP server, the client or both. The server and client will also remove the record when the lease expires if configured to do so. This helps to keep the DNS database up to date.

Creating an Active Directory Integrated Zone

In this exercise we will create an Active Directory integrated zone. For the exercise you will need a Windows 2000 server functioning as an Active Directory domain controller. The server should have the DNS service installed.

1. Log on to the computer using an account with administrative rights.

2. Open up the Windows 2000 DNS administration tool by clicking Start | Programs | Administrative Tools | DNS.

3. If there is no server listed in the tree pane, perform steps 4–6. Otherwise, skip to step 8.

4. Right-click DNS in the tree pane on the left side of the screen.

5. Select Connect to Computer.

6. In the Select Target Computer dialog box, select This Computer. Make sure that the Connect to the Specified Computer Now check box is selected.

7. Select OK. You will be returned to the main DNS administration screen and your computer will now have an icon in the tree pane under DNS.

8. Right-click the icon representing your computer in the tree pane.

9. Select New Zone.

10. Read the welcome screen and click Next.

11. Select Active Directory-integrated and click Next.

12. Select Forward lookup zone and click Next.

13. Type **adsyngress.msft** in the Name text box.

14. Click Next.

15. Review the information on the Completing the New Zone Wizard page and click Finish.

16. In the tree pane, click the plus sign to the left of your server's icon.

17. In the tree pane, click on the folder labeled Forward Lookup Zones.

18. In the right pane, make sure your new zone is listed.

19. Close the DNS management console.

EXERCISE 6-3

Integration with Downlevel Clients and Downlevel DNS Servers

Microsoft uses *downlevel* to refer to pre-Windows 2000 operating systems. Even if integrated into Active Directory, the DNS service in Windows 2000 is capable of supporting all DNS clients in the enterprise. Windows 2000 clients will be able to take advantage of new features such as secure dynamic updates, but all clients will receive the level of support and name resolution that they require.

Downlevel DNS Servers also interoperate well with Windows 2000 DNS Servers. Downlevel servers can act as Secondary servers in both a Windows 2000 Standard Primary DNS and Active Directory integrated DNS environment. Conversely, Windows 2000 DNS Servers can act as Standard Secondary servers for a downlevel Primary DNS server. For BIND environments, Windows 2000 servers can be configured as BIND compatible.

CERTIFICATION OBJECTIVE 6.04

Creating a Secure DNS Design

There are important security concerns regarding DNS in a standard network environment. By default, zone transfers take place without using any form of encryption. This means that if a third party captures the packets, they can easily learn all about your entire DNS zone. To make matters worse, in standard DNS it is not difficult for someone to create a Secondary DNS Server that can receive unauthorized zone transfers from your current DNS Servers. In addition to this, remember that DNS now supports dynamic updates. Because of this it is very important that the appropriate security precautions be taken to ensure that only the correct clients update their corresponding host records. Windows 2000 addresses both of these concerns strongly.

Secure Zone Transfers

As was already mentioned, zone transfers are sent in clear text across the network. In high security environments, this can cause serious concerns on the local network. In environments where security isn't as important, if zone transfers take place over WAN or public network segments, your zone data may present a security risk.

Remember that any time your data leaves your local network, it is at a much greater risk of being intercepted by malicious third parties.

To secure your zone transfers, you should consider using the encryption tools available with Windows 2000. On the local network you might use IPSec encryption. For WAN and public network segments, you should take advantage of the strongest encryption level available or use VPN tunnels. Routing and Remote Access Service in Windows 2000 provide strong support for IPSec and highly secure VPN tunnels.

exam
ⓦatch

To secure zone transfers on the local network, use a Windows 2000-supported encryption technology such as IPSec. For zone transfers that take place over public or other types of insecure Wide Area Networks, use a VPN tunnel.

Another option to consider is implementing an Active Directory integrated DNS design. By default, all replication traffic involving Active Directory is encrypted. In addition, all Active Directory integrated DNS Servers are required to join Active Directory in order to participate in replication. This greatly benefits security because it makes it very difficult for a DNS Server to be impersonated. In an Active Directory DNS environment, each server is identified with a long and complex number called a Security Identifier (SID). Because the SID is difficult to guess, it is very hard to create a DNS Server that can pretend to be an authenticated server.

Secure Dynamic Updates

When you store zone information in Active Directory, by default the server requires secure updates. This means that only authorized users and computers can perform updates to the resource records that are stored in DNS. Clients can be configured in the registry to use dynamic updates in one of three ways:

- By only attempting a secure dynamic update
- By only attempting a non-secure dynamic update
- By attempting a non-secure dynamic update first and then trying to negotiate a secure dynamic update if they fail. This is the default configuration.

It is recommended that you use the default configuration so clients can interoperate in environments that contain DNS Servers that support dynamic updates, but not secure updates. For environments requiring greater security, however, secure dynamic updates might be the best option. Access Control Lists (ACLs) are used to determine who can and cannot update a record. ACLs can be specified for either an entire zone or individual records. Only users, computers, or groups specified in the ACL with write permission are allowed to alter a record.

Using Forwarders and Slaves

DNS Servers can only directly answer queries for which they contain zone information, or have stored in cache from a client query. When neither of these is the case, the DNS Server will communicate with other DNS Servers in an effort to resolve the query. Default DNS resolution was covered at the beginning of this chapter. Remember that in default resolution, a client queries a DNS Server for the

FROM THE CLASSROOM

DNSUpdateProxy Group

You may be wondering what would happen if one DHCP server initially creates the record in DNS and then becomes unavailable in a secure DNS environment. If the client then receives a lease from a second DHCP server, there could be a problem with updating the record. Generally, the owner of the record is the one that can alter it. In this case it would be the initial DHCP server and the second DHCP server wouldn't be able to alter the record even though its information needs to be changed.

Fortunately, Microsoft has considered this dilemma and has created a special group in Active Directory called the DnsUpdateProxy group. Any DNS object created by members of this group does not have any security associated with it. The first user or computer that is not a part of this group altering the record will become its owner. Therefore, if every DHCP server that registers records for clients is a member of this group, the problem is eliminated. On the down side, this group also introduces a security loophole. By default, any records that are created by a member of this group are unsecured. This security hole is especially important if the DHCP server is also a domain controller. In this case, all records registered by the domain controller with DNS dynamically are not secured. For this reason, Microsoft recommends that the DHCP service not be installed on a domain controller.

—*Jeffery A. Martin, MCSE, MCT, MCP+I, CCI, CCA, CAN, A+, Network+, I-Net+, CIW*

EXERCISE 6-4

Configuring a DNS Server to Use a Forwarder and Act as a Slave

In this exercise you will configure one of your DNS Servers to act as a slave by configuring it to use a forwarder in exclusive mode. For the exercise you will need two Windows 2000 servers with the DNS service installed. On one of your Windows 2000 DNS Servers, perform the following tasks:

1. Log on to the computer using an account with administrative rights.

2. Open up the Windows 2000 DNS administration tool by clicking Start | Programs | Administrative Tools | DNS.

3. If there is no server listed in the tree pane, perform steps 4–6. Otherwise, skip to step 8.

4. Right-click DNS in the tree pane on the left side of the screen.

5. Select Connect to Computer.

6. In the Select Target Computer dialog box, select This Computer. Make sure that the Connect to the Specified Computer Now check box is selected.

7. Select OK. You will be returned to the main DNS administration screen and your computer will now have an icon in the tree pane under DNS.

8. Right-click the icon representing your computer in the tree pane.

9. Click Properties.

10. Select the Forwarders tab.

11. Select the Enable forwarders check box.

12. Add the IP address for your other Windows 2000 DNS Server.

13. Click Add.

14. Select the Do Not Use Recursion check box.

15. Click OK.

IP address of a host. The DNS Server queried will then go out and ask any number of other DNS Servers until it either determines that it will never locate the information, or it has the IP address to return to the client.

On the surface, this seems like an excellent way of doing things. However, in practice problems arise, such as DNS Servers located on the other side of slow WAN links. Each time a client queries the DNS Server with a name it cannot resolve locally, it must cross the WAN link to resolve the name. As we've seen, a DNS Server generally has to communicate with a number of servers before it has successfully resolved the name. If there is a lot of DNS resolution going on, this can put a tremendous strain on the slow WAN link.

One way around such a problem is to configure the DNS Server on the other side of the WAN link to use a forwarder. Forwarders are DNS Servers that are designed to provide forwarding for other DNS Servers. When a DNS Server receives a query for a resource it cannot resolve it will send the query to the specified forwarder. That server then resolves the name.

By forwarding the request we are only sending traffic for one query to resolve the host name to an IP address across the slow WAN link. This might otherwise have taken many different queries. The forwarder that receives the query request becomes the DNS Server that issues as many queries as are necessary to resolve the name. When it has completed the task, it sends the resolved IP address back to the requesting DNS Server, which in turn sends it to the client.

A DNS Server can use a forwarder in nonexclusive or exclusive mode. In both modes, if the forwarder cannot resolve the name for some reason it will notify the original DNS Server. In nonexclusive mode, the DNS Server will make additional name resolution attempts if the forwarder is not able to resolve the request.

A DNS Server running in exclusive mode is also known as a slave. This is because it relies solely on the name-resolving ability of forwarders for queries it cannot resolve by using its local cache or zone files. In exclusive mode, if the forwarder fails to resolve the query, the original DNS Server will not attempt any additional methods of resolution. Instead, it will simply notify the client that the query failed.

CERTIFICATION OBJECTIVE 6.05

Creating a Highly Available DNS Design

Your DNS infrastructure is at the heart of your Windows 2000 network and possibly your network as a whole if you have many Unix type clients and servers. It is very important that you ensure that clients always have access to the information it contains. This is what creating a highly available DNS design means. Because of the new features of Windows 2000 DNS, more options are available to ensure DNS reliability than ever before.

The Windows 2000 DNS service continues support for Primary and Secondary DNS Servers. These servers have been the bedrock of DNS reliability for many years. Through integration with Active Directory, even more reliability becomes available because of Active Directory replication. In addition, DNS clustering becomes a viable option for high availability when Windows 2000 Advanced Server or Windows 2000 Datacenter Server are used.

Primary and Secondary DNS Servers

The traditional method of enhancing DNS reliability and availability was to incorporate Secondary DNS Servers and use zone transfers. Remember that the only writable (changeable) copy of a zone database resides on the Primary DNS Server. If your DNS strategy ends here and the server goes down, clients will not be able to resolve names to IP addresses using DNS.

To enhance the reliability in a traditional DNS environment, Secondary DNS Servers should be employed. Remember that a Secondary server receives zone transfers from the Primary or another Secondary DNS Server. The zone transfer includes all records for the domains contained within the zone. Each DNS client can be configured with more than one DNS Server for looking up names. If you have configured the clients with the address of the Primary and Secondary DNS Servers, and the Primary server becomes unavailable for some reason, the Secondary server will be used for name resolution, thus ensuring some fault tolerance and increasing reliability.

For DNS environments involving multiple locations, Secondary servers can be placed on the other end of the WAN connections. By doing this, the designer ensures that users in remote offices will still be able to resolve DNS names if the WAN connection becomes unavailable. In Windows 2000, Microsoft refers to Primary and Secondary servers and the zones they contain as Standard Primary and Standard Secondary.

Zone transfers in the traditional model can be full or incremental depending on the types of DNS Servers involved. Incremental zone transfers send only the records that have been updated since the Secondary server last received an update. This uses much less bandwidth than a traditional full-zone transfer. The Windows 2000 DNS service supports incremental zone transfer.

Creating a Standard Secondary DNS Zone

In this exercise, we will create a Standard Secondary DNS zone to provide fault tolerance for the primary zone created in the first exercise. Together, the two DNS Servers will form a standard zone replication topology. This exercise requires a second Windows 2000 server with the DNS service installed.

1. Log on to the computer using an account with administrative rights.
2. Open the Windows 2000 DNS administration tool by clicking Start | Programs | Administrative Tools | DNS.
3. If there is no server listed in the tree pane, perform steps 4–6. Otherwise, skip to step 8.
4. Right-click DNS in the tree pane on the left side of the screen.
5. Select Connect to Computer.
6. In the Select Target Computer dialog box, select This Computer. Make sure that the Connect to the Specified Computer Now check box is selected.
7. Select OK. You will be returned to the main DNS administration screen and your computer will now have an icon in the tree pane under DNS.
8. Right-click the icon representing your computer in the tree pane.
9. Select New Zone.
10. Read the welcome screen and click Next.
11. Select Standard Secondary and click Next.
12. Select Forward lookup zone and click Next.
13. Type **syngress.msft** in the Name text box.
14. Click Next.
15. In the IP Address box, enter the IP address of the Primary DNS Server for this zone.
16. Click Add.
17. Click Next.
18. Review the information on the Completing the New Zone Wizard.
19. Click Finish.

20. In the tree pane, click the plus sign to the left of your server's icon.

21. In the tree pane, click on the folder labeled Forward Lookup Zones.

22. In the right pane, make sure your new zone is listed.

23. Close the DNS management console.

You should always have more than one DNS Server that holds a given zone's data. In the traditional DNS environment, this means that you should have at least one Secondary DNS Server for each Primary DNS Server.

Active Directory Integrated Zones

As we've already mentioned, the Windows 2000 DNS service can be integrated with Active Directory. When you integrate DNS into Active Directory, the DNS service no longer uses zone files. Instead, all zone data is stored in Active Directory, so the information is not replicated using zone transfers, but rather is exchanged and kept up to date as a normal part of the Active Directory replication process. Because Active Directory replication is always encrypted, all zone updates are secure since they are transferred between DNS Servers.

Active Directory integration also has tremendous value in ensuring fault tolerance and high availability. Each Active Directory domain controller (which has the DNS service installed) in the domain hosting the zone is treated like a Primary DNS Server. This means that each domain controller that is running DNS contains all of the records that comprise the zone. These servers can also receive updates to the DNS zone database and will in turn replicate these changes to the other domain controllers that are running the DNS service. Because all the zone information is replicated to all domain controllers which are running the DNS service and each domain controller functions as a Primary DNS Server, there is not single point of DNS failure if one of the servers goes down.

Active Directory replication transfers information at the property level. An example of a property is the Last Name field in the user object. If an employee gets married and her last name changes, rather than replicating the entire object to the other domain controllers, only the Last Name property is sent. This benefits DNS replication as well. Because integrated zones use the Directory Replication process to update their zone information, only the property information that changes is sent to avoid an excessive amount of data being transferred.

Windows 2000 DNS Clusters

In environments that require an extraordinary level of availability, Windows 2000 clustering can be used. Clustering is only available on Windows 2000 Advanced Server and Windows 2000 Datacenter Server. In essence, clustering makes several Windows 2000 servers function as one machine. All of the clustered servers running the DNS service will contain the same DNS database. Clustered servers are required

SCENARIO & SOLUTION

You are in a mixed environment that consists of Unix and Windows clients. The Windows portion of your network is mixed between Windows NT 4.0 and Windows 2000 domain controllers. You are adding a new DNS Server to the existing DNS infrastructure. You are installing a new Windows 2000 DNS Server. How will you configure it?	Because you are in a mixed environment, it is reasonable to assume that you have a standard DNS environment consisting of at least one Primary and possibly some Secondary DNS Servers. We also know from the scenario that the Windows domain contains NT 4.0 and 2000 domain controllers and thus is not using Active Directory. Because Active Directory is not available, you cannot implement an Active Directory integrated DNS Server. This means that this server will need to be implemented with either a new Standard Primary or, more likely, a standard secondary zone configuration.
You are installing a new Windows 2000 DNS Server into a mixed Unix and Windows environment. The server is being installed to service only Windows 2000 clients. The domain it is installed in uses active directory. In what configuration should this server be installed?	Install the new DNS Server as an Active Directory integrated DNS Server. Because the server is designed to service Windows 2000 clients in an Active Directory domain this configuration will allow the clients to maximize the new Windows 2000 DNS features. It is important to remember that zone information should always be stored on more than one server.

to be on the same persistent high-speed network, so it is not appropriate to have servers in the cluster located at remote locations. Because this is a local solution involving multiple servers, the costs are higher and should be weighed against the level of availability.

Clustered servers provide some availability solutions that cannot be obtained elsewhere. If a clustered server goes down, there is an immediate fail-over to another server that is still up and running. In addition, when the failed server is brought back on-line, its restoration will be faster because the servers share the same DNS database. For this reason a zone transfer or zone database resynchronization is not required.

CERTIFICATION OBJECTIVE 6.06

Measuring and Optimizing a DNS Infrastructure Design

It is important to ensure that the DNS design matches the actual implementation as closely as possible. An effective analysis strategy will use a variety of tools to measure and optimize a DNS design. Alerts should be set up to notify the administrators of possible problems and variances from the design. In addition, a variety of troubleshooting tools come with Windows 2000 and can be implemented to assist in analyzing problems as they arise.

Important Events to Monitor

Microsoft recommends a series of events that should be monitored closely in a DNS Server environment. Where possible, administrators should set up automated methods that allow them to be notified of these events when they occur. The goal is to be able to fix a problem before it grows in significance. The events that should be watched closely are:

- **Unavailable DNS Servers**   Because a well designed network will have strong DNS fault tolerance in place, the failure of a DNS Server may not be immediately noticed. An automated procedure that detects server failure will assist in locating failed DNS Servers so that they can be rapidly returned to functionality.

■ **Unresolved DNS Queries**   DNS exists to resolve queries. Knowing about and correcting a loss in functionality is critical. Alerts should be generated for the DNS administrators when any DNS queries are not resolved.

■ **Slow Query Resolution**   DNS performance is measured in part by the speed of query resolution. DNS operations may not be affected by or notice slowdowns in query resolution for average network users, so it is important that alerts be generated when query resolution time exceeds the specifications that were built into the design.

■ **Increased Query Demands**   An increase in the number of queries indicates that demands on the DNS infrastructure are increasing. It is important that events be generated when the query demands exceed the amount specified in the original DNS design. This information is very important for capacity planning purposes.

■ **DNS Replication Not Occurring**   In environments with more than one DNS Server, system reliability depends on zone data replication. If zone data isn't replicated, DNS Servers may not contain the same information. It is important to generate alerts that allow administrators to know when replication is not occurring properly.

DNS Trace Logs

You can also use the DNS console to enable additional debugging by logging options to a trace file. When enabled, the text file, Dns.log, is created and stored in the *systemroot*\System32\Dns folder. All DEBUG logging options are disabled by default. When enabled, the DNS Server will perform additional trace-level logging of events or messages to assist in troubleshooting and debugging the server. Individual logging options must be selected by the administrator and include:

■ **Query**   Logs queries received from clients.

■ **Notify**   Logs notification messages received from other servers.

■ **Update**   Logs dynamic updates received from other computers.

■ **Questions**   Logs the contents of the question section for each DNS query message processed.

■ **Answers**   Logs the contents of the answer section for each DNS query message processed.

■ **Send**   Logs the number of DNS query messages sent by the DNS Server.

CertCam 6-6

EXERCISE 6-6

Configuring the DNS Trace Log

In the following exercise, we will configure all of the available options for the DNS trace log. We will then create a standard primary zone and view the entry it makes in the log. For the exercise you will need a Windows 2000 server with the DNS service installed.

1. Log on to the computer using an account with administrative rights.

2. Open up the Windows 2000 DNS administration tool by clicking Start | Programs | Administrative Tools | DNS.

3. If there is no server listed in the tree pane, perform steps 4–6. Otherwise, skip to step 8.

4. Right-click DNS in the tree pane on the left side of the screen.

5. Select Connect to Computer.

6. In the Select Target Computer dialog box, select This Computer. Make sure that the Connect to the Specified Computer Now check box is selected.

7. Select OK. You will be returned to the main DNS administration screen and your computer will now have an icon in the tree pane under DNS.

8. Right-click the icon representing your computer in the tree pane.

9. Select Properties.

10. Select the Logging tab.

11. Check the boxes next to: Query, Notify, Update Questions, Answers, Send, Receive, UDP, TCP, Full packets, and Write through.

12. Click OK.

13. Right-click your computer's icon in the left tree pane.

14. Select New Zone.

15. Read the welcome screen and click Next.

16. Select Standard Primary and click Next.

17. Select Forward lookup zone and click Next.

18. Type **logtest.msft** in the Name text box.

19. Click Next.

20. Make sure the Create a New File with this Name Text Box displays syngress.msft.dns.

21. Click Next.

22. Review the information on the Completing the New Zone Wizard page and click Finish.

23. In the tree pane, click the plus sign to the left of your server's icon.

24. In the tree pane, click on the folder labeled Forward Lookup Zones.

25. In the right pane, make sure your new zone is listed.

26. On the Start Menu, select Programs | Accessories | Windows Explorer.

27. Navigate to the systemroot\system32\dns directory.

28. Double-click the log file named dns.log.

29. View the contents. The final log entry should read something similar to "The DNS Server wrote version 1 of zone logtest.msft to file logtest.msft.dns."

30. Close dns.log.

31. Close Windows Explorer.

32. Close the DNS management console.

- **Receive**   Logs the number of DNS query messages received by the DNS Server.
- **UDP**   Logs the number of DNS requests received over a UDP port.
- **TCP**   Logs the number of DNS requests received over a TCP port.
- **Full Packets**   Logs the number of full packets written and sent by the DNS Server.
- **Write Through**   Logs the number of packets written through by the DNS Server and back to the zone.

Debug logging can be quite resource intensive. It can affect the overall performance of the server. In addition the log itself can consume considerable disk space on an actively used DNS Server. Microsoft recommends that trace logging only be used temporarily when more detailed information is needed about a server's performance.

DNS Log in Event Viewer

The DNS Log in Event Viewer contains messages that can warn you of problems that are occurring with the DNS Service. It will also contain informational messages such as events that notify you that the DNS service started or shut down properly. The DNS Log only contains records for the DNS Server service. DNS client messages are stored in the System Log.

on the **job**

Be sure to remember that the DNS Log in Event Viewer is for DNS Server service messages. DNS client messages are stored in the System Log in Event Viewer.

System Monitor

Performance monitoring for Windows 2000 DNS Servers is done with System Monitor. It is the latest evolution of the Performance Monitor tool that existed in Window NT 4.0. Though it is now integrated into the management console, the tool has not changed significantly. System Monitor is accessible through the performance console.

System Monitor allows you to create charts and graphs of server performance in real time. By using log files, you can also use the tool to graphically analyze trends over time. By measuring and reviewing server performance statistics over a period of

SCENARIO & SOLUTION	
Through alerts, trace logs, and event monitoring you have determined that your new DNS Server is not always performing queries in a timely fashion. Which additional tool could be employed to help you determine what might be wrong?	The next logical step is to begin logging server performance by using System Monitor. By keeping logs of server activity, comparisons of server resource usage can be made regarding times when query processing was and was not delayed.
You've used the following tools when trying to diagnose a problem: Event Viewer, Network Monitor, and Server Monitor. While they all provide some insight you still need an additional level of detail. What other tool would further analyze the problem?	Although you have tried many of the tools available to troubleshoot DNS, one major tool is still available. The additional debugging capabilities of the DNS trace log are your best additional resource. They are designed for troubleshooting situations such as this. Remember that because it can place a strain on system resources and disk capacity, it should not be enabled for routine monitoring.

time, it is possible to determine performance baselines and use them to decide if adjustments should be made to further optimize the system. When DNS is installed, it adds its own performance counters. Sixty-two different DNS counters allow you to monitor virtually any aspect of the DNS Server service.

Network Monitor

Network monitoring usually involves tracking server resource usage and measuring overall network traffic. System Monitor is typically employed to handle both of these tasks. Occasionally, though, in-depth network traffic analysis is needed. Network Monitor is a tool that is included with Windows 2000 that provides detailed network statistics and packet-level network analysis.

Network Monitor includes a protocol parser for DNS. The parser allows it to capture, filter, and display DNS related traffic. This can be a tremendous benefit in troubleshooting. Although the test does not require you to be familiar with the specifics of DNS network traffic, such knowledge is useful to greatly increase your ability to troubleshoot a DNS environment.

CERTIFICATION OBJECTIVE 6.07

Designing a DNS Deployment Strategy

In this chapter, we look at a DNS design through the eyes of a network consultant. The company that hired the consultant has a three-site network. We will refer to these sites as Site A, Site B, and Site C. Site A is the main company location and has 1,872 hosts. Site A also has a T1 link to the Internet. The internal network is isolated from the Internet by a firewall and proxy server.

Site B connects to Site A via a dedicated T1 WAN connection. Site C connects to Site A via a 256-Kbps–dedicated WAN connection. Site B currently has 1342 hosts and Site C currently has 357 hosts. Only minor growth is anticipated at each site.

The company wants its Intranet to be accessible to all employees at each site. It is currently hosted from Site A. All locations should also have Internet access. There should be no single point of failure in the DNS design. The company is in the process of migrating to Windows 2000 but is not currently using Active Directory.

The design should provide support for all of the hosts on the network as well as any networking devices (such as routers) that might need to make use of DNS. Initial testing indicates that the company's servers can support 1500 hosts at their desired performance level. Some of the company's mission-critical applications are Intranet-based and must be available around the clock, every day of the week. The DNS design should adequately address the above concerns regarding performance and availability.

The logical place to begin this design is at Site A. This is the main site of the company and is also where the primary technical staff is located. All the locations are linked by dedicated lines to this site. Because of these factors, it is the best location for the server that will host the company's primary DNS zone.

We know that each DNS Server can only support 1500 hosts at the desired performance level. Site A has over 1800 hosts so we should implement a Secondary DNS Server at this location for performance reasons. This will also enhance availability for this location if the Primary DNS Server becomes unavailable. The Primary DNS Server should be installed and configured first, followed by the Secondary DNS Server in this site. All clients in Site A would be configured to use these two servers as their Primary and Secondary DNS Servers.

We have several options concerning Sites B and C. We could elect to have the hosts at these locations utilize the DNS Servers in Site A. However, this would not meet the availability requirements for the design. If the WAN links between Site A and one of the other sites become unavailable, hosts in that site would be cut off from the DNS Servers and unable to perform name resolution. Performance requirements are also not met by this design. Site A only has two DNS Servers, each of which is capable of supporting 1500 hosts. Because of this, total DNS capacity for these two servers would be 3000 hosts, which is less than the total number of hosts in all sites (3571 hosts).

Another option would be to place a Caching Only DNS Server at Sites B and C. Hosts in these sites would be configured with the address of their local DNS Server and one of the DNS Servers in Site A. Remember that Caching Only DNS Servers keep resolved records in cache until they expire. This may produce a reduction in WAN traffic, but it does not adequately address either the performance or availability design requirements, for the same reasons mentioned in the previous paragraph. All DNS Servers by default are Caching DNS Servers.

A third option would be to implement Caching Only DNS Servers at Sites B and C and configure them as slaves. As in the previous option, hosts would be configured with the address of their local DNS Server and one of the DNS Servers in Site A. This would build on the previous design and further reduce the amount of DNS WAN traffic. Remember that a DNS slave sends queries it cannot resolve from its local zones or cache to a forwarder. In this case, the forwarder could be either DNS Server at Site A. Nothing in the design requirements mentioned the need to minimize the amount of network traffic used by DNS. Although this is an admirable goal, ultimately this design does not meet either of the performance or availability requirements.

The best option is to place a Secondary DNS Server in both Sites B and C. Because every DNS Server acts as a Caching DNS Server, all of the benefits mentioned above would apply. If the design had specified that DNS traffic on the WAN should be minimized, it would be appropriate to make each Secondary DNS Server a slave as well. Each of the Secondary servers in Sites B and C would take zone transfers from the Primary DNS Server in Site A.

This option fulfills the availability requirement by ensuring that a DNS Server with zone information is available at each site even if the WAN link to that site becomes unavailable. It also ensures that the performance guidelines are met. The DNS Server in each site is sufficient to handle the number of hosts each site contains. For additional availability and fault tolerance, each host would be configured with the address of its local DNS Server and a DNS Server from Site A. By configuring the hosts in this way, if the local DNS Server is unavailable, a server in Site A will be used.

Depending on the budget some additional steps can be taken to maximize this design for performance and availability. A third DNS Server could be implemented at Site A. This server would be configured as another Secondary DNS Server. Hosts in Sites B and C would be given this server's address as their second DNS Server. This way, if their local DNS Server failed and they were forced to resolve queries using a server in Site A, it would not exceed the capacity of the DNS Servers located in that site. This would ensure that the design performance requirements were met, even in the event of server failure at Sites B or C.

An alternative might be to place another Secondary DNS Server in each of the sites. This could be configured to obtain its zone information from either the original Secondary DNS Server in the site, or one of the servers at Site A. If the additional server obtained its information from the original DNS Server in the site, there would be no additional zone transfer traffic on the WAN. However, if the DNS Server it was using became unavailable, it would not receive updates even if the WAN link and servers at Site A were functioning properly.

Designing a DNS Infrastructure

In this exercise, you will be responsible for designing the DNS infrastructure for a network. The network specifications are the same as the ones we used above, except that the client is using Active Directory and wants an integrated DNS design. Take into account the following design requirements and then respond to the questions concerning how you would implement the design.

The company has a three-site network. We will refer to these sites as Site A, Site B, and Site C. Site A is the main company location and has 1872 hosts. Site A also has a T1 link to the Internet. The internal network is isolated from the Internet by a firewall and proxy server. Site B connects to Site A via a dedicated T1 WAN connection. Site C connects to Site A via a 256-Kbps–dedicated WAN connection. Site B currently has 1342 hosts and Site C currently has 357 hosts. Only minor growth is anticipated at each site.

The company wants its Intranet to be accessible to all employees at each site. It is currently hosted from Site A. All locations should also have Internet access. There should be no single point of failure in the DNS design. The company has just completed its migration to Windows 2000 and is currently using Active Directory.

The design should provide support for all of the hosts on the network as well as any networking devices, such as routers, that might need to make use of DNS. Initial testing indicates that servers the company is providing you with can support 1500 hosts at their desired level of performance. Some of the company's mission-critical applications are Intranet-based and must be available around the clock, every day of the week. The DNS design should adequately address the above concerns regarding performance and availability.

1. Where will you implement DNS Servers in this design?

   Answer: Because the DNS Servers are Active Directory integrated, there are no primary or secondary zones to implement. DNS Servers will be located on Active Directory domain controllers. For availability purposes, DNS Servers should be located at all of the sites.

2. How many DNS Servers will be implemented in Site A?

   Answer: Two servers are required in Site A to meet the performance requirements of the design. Each server can only support 1500 hosts. Site A has over 1800 hosts that require DNS access.

3. How many DNS Servers will be implemented in Site B?

   Answer: Only one server is required at Site B to meet the performance and availability requirements. Hosts in the site will be assigned their local DNS Server's address, and the address of one of the DNS Servers in Site A for additional availability fault tolerance.

4. How many DNS Servers will be implemented in Site C?

   Answer: Only one server is required at Site C to meet the performance and availability requirements. As in Site B, hosts will be assigned their local DNS Server's address and the address of one of the DNS Servers in Site A for additional availability fault tolerance.

5. Would you implement a Standard DNS design or an Active Directory integrated DNS design?

   Answer: Because the network uses Windows 2000 and Active Directory, all DNS Servers in this design should be Active Directory integrated.

6. Could you implement Standard Secondary DNS Servers at Sites B and C?

   Answer: Technically it would be possible to implement one Active Directory integrated DNS Server in Site A and to use Standard Secondary DNS Servers for the remaining servers. However, this would not meet the design requirements. In addition, you would not be able to take advantage of the additional benefits of a fully integrated design. These benefits include secure transfer of zone information as part of normal Active Directory replication and secure dynamic resource record updates.

If, instead, it was configured to obtain its zone information from one of the servers in Site A, traffic on the WAN would be increased, but it would still receive updates if the other DNS Server in its site failed. In either scenario, the hosts would be configured to use only the DNS Servers in their site for resolution. Because another local DNS Server would be available to service their query requests, hosts in Sites B or C would not burden the DNS Servers in Site A if one of their local DNS Servers failed.

Clustering could be used at the Site A to ensure maximum availability of the primary DNS zone information. If one of the DNS Servers at Site A went down, the other one could still accept updates to the primary zone database. In addition, any connections from hosts would be load balanced between the servers, allowing for maximum performance.

CERTIFICATION SUMMARY

As we have seen, DNS plays a very important part in a Windows 2000 network. DNS Servers that are implemented on Windows 2000 are capable of acting as traditional DNS Servers. They can be implemented as Caching, Standard Primary, and Standard Secondary servers in any DNS environment. Even in a Standard DNS configuration, the Windows 2000 DNS service supports advanced features such as incremental zone transfers and dynamic record updates.

In traditional DNS implementations, a zone transfer caused all records in the zone to be sent across the network. By using incremental zone transfers between DNS Servers, the amount of network traffic used to keep the zone databases synchronized between servers is greatly reduced. Dynamic DNS (DDNS) removes a great deal of the administrative burden of keeping records up to date. In a DNS environment, hosts and DHCP servers create and update DNS resource records, thereby automatically freeing up the administrator's time for other tasks.

When integrated with Active Directory, a number of additional benefits become available. Active Directory integrated DNS transfers zone information at the property level as a standard part of Active Directory replication. All Active Directory traffic is encrypted by default, which ensures secure transfer of zone information on the network. Further security is provided in an Active Directory integrated DNS design through secure dynamic updates. By default, only the owner of a dynamic DNS record can update it when the DNS service is integrated into Active Directory.

TWO-MINUTE DRILL

Overview of the Windows 2000 Dynamic DNS Server

❑ DNS is a database system that is designed to map Fully Qualified Domain Names to IP addresses.

❑ The four traditional DNS server roles are Primary, Secondary, Master, and Caching. In Windows 2000 DNS, Microsoft refers to the first two of these as Standard Primary and Standard Secondary.

❑ Traditional DNS servers require the administrator to add records to the database manually. Microsoft DDNS allows DHCP servers and the client machines to update their records dynamically.

Creating a DNS Namespace for the Organization

❑ The generally accepted way of creating a DNS Namespace for your organization is to model it on an existing Active Directory design.

❑ The design element that will affect DNS the most is whether or not your company will have an external Internet presence, or just an internal network.

❑ DNS is a hierarchical structure. For an organization, this means that it has a root domain and subdomains. The subdomains are designed to group computers together in a logical fashion.

Create an Integrated DNS Design

❑ Only domain controllers with DNS installed can serve as Active Directory integrated DNS servers.

❑ When using Active Directory integrated DNS servers, Windows 2000 DNS clients will be able to take advantage of new features, such as secure dynamic updates, but all clients will receive the level of support and name resolution that they require.

Create a Secure DNS Design

❑ By default, standard zone transfers take place without using any form of encryption.

❑ To secure your zone transfers, you should consider using the encryption tools available with Windows 2000. Routing and Remote Access Service in Windows 2000 provide strong support for IPSec and highly secure VPN tunnels.

❑ When you store zone information in Active Directory, by default the server requires secure updates for dynamically updated resource records.

Create a Highly Available DNS Design

❑ To enhance the reliability in a traditional DNS environment, Secondary DNS Servers should be employed.

❑ When you integrate DNS into Active Directory all zone data is stored in Active Directory and the zone information is replicated using the Active Directory replication process.

❑ Each Active Directory DNS Server hosting a zone is treated as a Primary DNS Server.

Measure and Optimize a DNS Infrastructure Design

❑ When enabled, the DNS Server service will perform additional trace-level logging of events or messages to assist in troubleshooting and debugging the server.

❑ The DNS Log in Event Viewer contains messages that can warn you of problems that are occurring with the DNS service. DNS client messages are stored in the System Log.

❑ System Monitor allows you to create charts and graphs of server performance in real time by using log files.

Design a DNS Deployment Strategy

❑ Ensure DNS availability by placing Secondary DNS Servers at remote sites.

❑ Deploy the Primary DNS Server first, then implement Secondary servers.

❑ When possible, utilize Active Directory integrated DNS Servers instead of Standard Primary and Secondary DNS Servers for increased security and fault tolerance.

SELF TEST

The following questions will help you measure your understanding of the material presented in this chapter. Read all of the choices carefully, as there may be more than one correct answer. Choose all correct answers for each question.

Overview of the Windows 2000 Dynamic DNS Server

1. What is the purpose of DNS?

   A. To map NetBIOS names to IP addresses

   B. To map FQDNs to IP addresses

   C. To map IP addresses to ARP addresses

   D. To map Host names to IPX addresses

2. What is the term for a server that is authoritative for a zone in DNS?

   A. A Master DNS Server

   B. A Primary DNS Server

   C. A Secondary DNS Server

   D. A Master Primary DNS Server

3. What roles can a Microsoft DNS Server fill? Choose all that apply.

   A. A DNS Server can be a Primary DNS Server for one or more zones.

   B. A DNS Server can be a Secondary DNS Server for one or more zones.

   C. A DNS Server can be a Master DNS Server for one or more zones.

   D. A DNS Server can be a Caching only DNS Server.

Creating a DNS Namespace for the Organization

4. You are creating your new DNS and Active Directory namespace. You do not want to modify your existing DNS structure. You want to ensure that all of your current DNS host names and Resource Records will remain the same and will not require modification to match the Active Directory domain name. You will not need to register any additional domain names with InterNIC. What type of naming scheme do you need to create?

   A. One that uses your InterNIC registered DNS Domain Name for the Active Directory Root Domain name

B. One that uses a DNS Subdomain for the Active Directory Root

C. One that uses a Reserved Private DNS Domain name for the Active Directory Root Domain name

D. None of the above

5. You are designing a DNS namespace for a nonprofit organization whose mission is to oppose all use of the Internet. As such, the organization does not have an Internet presence, nor do they intend to ever implement one. What DNS namespace will you implement in this organization?

A. One that uses an InterNIC registered DNS Domain Name for the Active Directory Root Domain name

B. One that uses a DNS Subdomain of an InterNIC registered DNS Domain Name for the Active Directory Root

C. One that uses a Reserved Private DNS Domain name for the Active Directory Root Domain name

D. One that uses a different DNS Domain Name for the Public and Internal sides of the network

Create an Integrated DNS Design

6. Which of the following are benefits of DNS integration with Active Directory?

A. Fault tolerance is increased if there is more than one Active Directory integrated DNS Server on the network.

B. DNS security is enhanced for DNS record updates between servers.

C. If configured properly, only authorized clients can update their records.

D. All of the above

7. You are using a static IP address on a Windows 2000 Professional computer. Which of the following is correct? Choose all that apply.

A. Windows 2000 Professional has a built-in DHCP service that will update the DNS record when its per-adapter domain name changes.

B. Windows 2000 Professional has a built-in DHCP service that will update the DNS record when the machine boots up.

C. Windows 2000 Professional has a built-in DHCP service that will update the DNS record when its IP address changes.

   D. Windows 2000 Professional has a built in DHCP service that allows it to get IP addresses dynamically assigned to it. The service does not provide any functionality when using static addressing.

8. You are in a mixed Windows NT 4.0 and Windows 2000 client environment. You have one Active Directory integrated DNS Server. Which of the following is true?

   A. All client computers will be able to use all of the functionality of this DNS Server.

   B. All Windows NT 4.0 and Windows 2000 computers will be able to use all of the functionality of this DNS Server.

   C. All Windows 2000 computers will be able to use all of the functionality of this DNS Server.

   D. None of the above

Create a Secure DNS Design

9. You have just upgraded your network to Windows 2000. You are operating in an environment where security is very important. Which of the following will you do to increase the security of your zone information as it is transferred between DNS Servers on the network?

   A. On the Windows 2000 DNS Servers, check the box for Secure Zone Transfers.

   B. Nothing. By default Windows 2000 DNS Servers use encrypted zone transfers.

   C. Create the DNS Servers on domain controllers and integrate DNS with Active Directory.

   D. B and C

10. You have a DNS Server that is on the other side of a WAN link. The queries that the server can't resolve using its local zones and cache are severely affecting the WAN bandwidth. What is the best remedy to this situation?

   A. Configure the remote DNS Server as a forwarder.

   B. Configure the remote DNS Server with the address of a forwarder that is located in an area of the network that has high network bandwidth.

   C. Configure a DNS Server at a central network location to act as a slave for the remote DNS server.

   D. A and C

Create a Highly Available DNS Design

11. You currently have only one DNS Server in your organization. Recently it went down and you realized that you needed to implement some fault tolerance in your DNS design. Which of the following should you do to increase your DNS fault tolerance?

    A. Install another Primary DNS Server.

    B. Install a new Master DNS Server.

    C. Install a Secondary DNS Server.

    D. All of the above

12. Which of the following is true concerning Active Directory integrated DNS zones?

    A. The zone information is stored in zone files on Active Directory domain controllers.

    B. Any Active Directory domain controller can serve as a DNS Server. It does not need the DNS service installed because this is only for Windows 2000 servers that will use DNS in a traditional manner.

    C. Zone information is replicated using the Active Directory replication process. This provides security because Active Directory replication is always encrypted.

    D. A and C

13. Your DNS implementation requires a very high level of availability and fault tolerance. Because of this, you are moving ahead with plans to implement Clustered DNS Servers at your organization's headquarters. Which versions of the Windows 2000 operating system could you implement that will provide clustering services? Choose all that apply.

    A. Windows 2000 Professional

    B. Windows 2000 Server

    C. Windows 2000 Advanced Server

    D. Windows 2000 Datacenter Server

Measure and Optimize a DNS Infrastructure Design

14. When monitoring events, it is important to use alerts to notify administrators of problems. You are setting up monitoring systems and using alerts to notify yourself of existing and potential DNS problems. Which of the following events will you implement?

    A. Alerts that notify you of DNS replication not occurring

    B.   Alerts that notify you of slow query resolution

    C.   Alerts that notify you of unresolved DNS queries

    D.   All of the above

15. You are having repeated problems with DNS resolution. The events written to the DNS Event Log are not providing you with enough information. What additional step can you take to learn more about what is wrong with your DNS Server?

    A.   Look in the DNS System Application Log.

    B.   Run the DNS Debug utility from the systemroot\DNS directory.

    C.   Run the DNS Debug utility from the command line.

    D.   Enable DNS Trace Logging.

16. You are trying to diagnose a problem that involves some DNS clients not being able to query a DNS Server. Which of the following tools might you use? Choose all that apply.

    A.   The System Log in Event Viewer

    B.   The DNS Log in Event Viewer

    C.   Performance Monitor

    D.   Network Monitor

Design a DNS Deployment Strategy

17. Your single domain network design calls for no single point of DNS failure. The network has two sites. Which DNS design best meets these criteria?

    A.   Place a Primary DNS Server in each site.

    B.   Place a Primary DNS Server and a Secondary DNS Server in each site.

    C.   Place a Primary DNS Server and a Secondary DNS Server in one site.

    D.   Place a Primary DNS Server in one site and a Secondary DNS Server in the other site.

18. You are implementing a Network design for a company with two sites. The company uses only Windows 2000 computers and Active Directory domain controllers. High DNS availability is important. What is the best DNS design for this company?

    A.   Implement an Active Directory integrated DNS Server at one of the sites, and a Primary DNS Server at the other site.

    B.   Implement an Active Directory integrated DNS Server at one of the sites, and a Secondary DNS Server at the other site.

C. Implement an Active Directory integrated DNS Server at one of the sites, and a second Active Directory integrated DNS Server at the other site.

D. None of these designs is appropriate for this situation.

LAB QUESTION

You have been called in to design a network for a company that is in the process of upgrading to Windows 2000. The upgrade process is expected to take the next eight months to accomplish. After the upgrade, the network will still contain a number of UNIX clients, which will require DNS support. DNS is one of the first items on the list to be upgraded. It will be upgraded before the domain controllers.

The company has three sites. The main one, Site A, contains a T3 to the Internet and is protected by a firewall. There are 5668 hosts at this site. Over 2000 users at this site require highly reliable, around-the-clock access to an Intranet-based application that provides core support to the company. The company has authorized you to spend whatever amount of money is necessary to ensure DNS support is available at all times to these users.

Site B is connected to Site A by a T1 link that operates at 35 percent of its capacity. There are 1445 hosts located at this site. Site C is connected to Site A by a 128-Kbps link that operates at 93 percent of its capacity. The company has asked you to find a way to reduce DNS traffic to and from this site. Site C has 377 hosts. Users at each of these sites need access to the company Intranet and to the Internet. They do not use the Intranet-based application mentioned above. The design requirements call for no single point of failure. They also specify that the DNS Servers that are being implemented can handle a maximum of 1500 hosts and still maintain their desired performance levels.

1. How many DNS Servers are necessary in Site A to meet the design requirements?

2. How should these servers be configured to meet the design requirements?

3. How many servers are necessary in Site B?

4. How many servers are necessary in Site C?

5. How will you meet the bandwidth reduction requirements for the link between Sites A and C?

SELF TEST ANSWERS

Overview of the Windows 2000 Dynamic DNS Server

1. ☑ **B.** The purpose of the Domain Name System is to map Fully Qualified Domain Names to IP addresses. DNS is designed for the TCP/IP networking environment. In order for a computer to communicate directly with another computer on a TCP/IP network, it must have the IP address of the machine it is trying to contact. One way in which it can find this address is by using DNS.

   ☒ **A** is incorrect. WINS, not DNS, is designed to map NetBIOS names to IP addresses. **C** is also incorrect. ARP is a protocol that is related to the hardware (or MAC) address of a computer. It has nothing to do with FQDN to IP address mapping. Finally, **D** is also incorrect because DNS does not relate to the IPX protocol; it resolves IP addresses.

2. ☑ **B.** A server that is authoritative for a zone in DNS is called a Primary DNS Server. A Primary DNS Server may be authoritative for more than one zone. A zone is a file that might contain information about a domain, subdomain, or domain with subdomains. Records that are stored on a Primary DNS Server in a zone that the server is authoritative for can be altered by the DNS administrator.

   ☒ **A and D** are incorrect. Although a Primary DNS Server might also be a Master DNS Server, it is not one by default. A Master DNS Server is a server that provides zone transfers to Secondary DNS Servers. It might be a Primary or Secondary DNS Server. **C** is also incorrect. A Secondary DNS Server received zone transfers from a Primary DNS Server. By default, the zone information it receives is Read Only and cannot be altered by an administrator.

3. ☑ **A, B, C, and D.** A DNS Server can function as a Primary server for one or more DNS zones. The same machine can also serve as a Secondary server for one or more DNS zones. A server with Primary or Secondary zones can provide zone transfers to other Secondary servers; therefore, a DNS Server can also be a Master DNS Server for one or more zones. Finally, by default a Microsoft DNS Server installs and always functions as a caching DNS Server regardless of other roles it fulfills, such as being a Primary DNS Server.

Creating a DNS Namespace for the Organization

4. ☑ **A.** A naming scheme that uses an existing registered domain name for the Active Directory Root Domain name is the answer which best meets the given criteria. Because you are using a name that is already registered, you do not need to register a new domain name with InterNIC. In addition, because you are using the organization's existing name, you will not have to change the current DNS structure or records to match a new one.

☒ **B** is incorrect. A naming scheme that uses a subdomain for the Active Directory Root is not appropriate because it will require modifying the DNS structure and records. **C** is also incorrect. Not only does it require changing the DNS structure and records, but it also uses a name that cannot be registered for Internet usage.

5. ☑ **C.** Because the organization will never require their local network to be accessed from the Internet, a Reserved Private DNS Domain Name can be used. The local domain name is set aside for such use and is not allowed to be used on the Internet. It can be used in a much more descriptive manner by adding subdomains to it such as syngress.local.

☒ **A** and **B** are incorrect. There is no reason for this organization to have an InterNIC registered domain name. Registered names are only required for organizations that will be accessed from the Internet. **D** is also incorrect. This organization does not make resources available on the Internet and therefore does not have a public side to their network.

Create an Integrated DNS Design

6. ☑ **D.** Active Directory integration with DNS produces all of the above benefits. Fault tolerance is increased because if one DNS Server goes down another one is always available which can receive record updates and answer queries. Because information transmitted as a part of Active Directory replication is encrypted, security is enhanced for record updates between servers. Finally, if configured properly only authorized clients can update their records in the DNS database.

7. ☑ **A, B, C.** All versions of Windows 2000 come with a built in DHCP service. One benefit that this service provides is the ability to update DNS records dynamically. If addresses are statically assigned, the service will update the computer's resource records in its specified DNS Server when the machine boots up, its per-adapter IP address changes, or its per-adapter domain name is changed.

☒ **D** is incorrect because answers **A, B,** and **C** are correct.

8. ☑ **C.** Only Windows 2000 computers will be able to take advantage of all of the functionality provided by the Active Directory integrated DNS Server. Windows 2000 computers will be able to use the secure dynamic update feature, for example, while the other clients cannot. The other Windows NT 4.0 clients could, however, benefit by Windows 2000 DHCP and DNS Servers. For instance, when a Windows NT 4.0 client obtains an IP address lease from a Windows 2000 DHCP server, the server will register the address in DNS for the client. It will also remove the record from DNS when the lease expires.

☒ **A** and **B** are incorrect. Only Windows 2000 computers can take full advantage of the new services provided by Active Directory integrated DNS. **D** is incorrect because **C** is the correct answer.

Create a Secure DNS Design

9. ☑ **C.** Active Directory integrated DNS Servers can only exist on Windows 2000 domain controllers. Once DNS is integrated with Active Directory, the transfer of zone information takes place as a part of the normal directory replication process. By default, Active Directory replication is encrypted. A further benefit is that Active Directory replication occurs on a property level, so only changes to the zone information are sent during the replication process, not the entire zone as in traditional DNS.

   ☒ **A** is incorrect. There is no Secure Zone Transfers check box. **B** is also incorrect. By default, DNS Servers transfer zone information in unencrypted form. Finally because answer **B** is incorrect, answer **D** is also incorrect.

10. ☑ **B.** One option when you have a DNS Server on the remote side of a slow WAN link is to configure it to use a forwarder. By doing so, you alleviate much of the DNS traffic on the WAN link. This is because the forwarder will do most of the work in resolving the query. Unless the forwarder cannot resolve the query, the only traffic that will pass over the WAN is the initial query request that is sent from the remote DNS Server to the forwarder and the completed response to the query that is sent from the forwarder back to the remote DNS Server. If the forwarder cannot resolve the query, the remote DNS Server may elect to attempt to resolve the query on its own.

   ☒ **A** is incorrect. Configuring the remote DNS Server as a forwarder will still result in it attempting to resolve non-local queries across the WAN. **C** is also incorrect. A slave is a DNS Server that is using forwarders in an exclusive manner. This means that if the forwarder that it is configured to use cannot resolve the query it will not make any additional attempts to do so. Placing a slave at a central location has no benefits in this situation. It would be more appropriate to configure the remote server as a slave and place a forwarder at the central location. **D** is incorrect because only **B** is correct.

Create a Highly Available DNS Design

11. ☑ **C.** The best and simplest way to increase your fault tolerance in this situation is to add one or more Secondary DNS Servers. Even adding just one will ensure that clients can continue to resolve their DNS queries should a DNS Server become unavailable. For added network efficiency, you should consider making sure that your DNS Servers are both capable of incremental zone transfers. Windows 2000 DNS Servers acting as Standard Primary and Standard Secondary DNS Servers are capable of incremental zone transfers.

   ☒ **A** is incorrect. Adding a second Primary DNS Server will only mean additional administrative overhead. Nothing in the question suggests this is warranted. **B** is also incorrect.

You cannot install a Master DNS Server. A DNS Server becomes a Master DNS Server when it has Secondary DNS Servers that it transfers its zone information to. Finally, **D** is incorrect because **C** is the only correct answer.

12. ☑ **C.** Integrating DNS zones with Active Directory has a number of benefits. Active Directory DNS Servers replicate zone information as a normal part of the Active Directory Replication Process. Active Directory integrated DNS Servers all function as do Primary DNS Servers. This means that they cannot only accept query requests, but can also have zone information updated on them through dynamic updates or direct administrator input. Because their changes are replicated to all other Active Directory integrated DNS Servers, if one server goes down another is always available to take its place.

☒ **A** is incorrect. Zone information on an Active Directory integrated DNS Server is stored in Active Directory, not zone files. **B** is also incorrect. In order for any Windows 2000 computer to function as a DNS Server, it must have the DNS service installed. Finally, **D** is incorrect because only **C** is the correct answer.

13. ☑ **C, D.** Only Windows 2000 Advanced Server and Windows 2000 Datacenter Server provide load balancing and clustering services. Clustered servers essentially act as one machine and offer a very high level of fault tolerance. Because they share the same database, restore time is reduced when bringing a failed server back on line in a cluster.

☒ **A** is incorrect. Windows 2000 Professional does not provide clustering services. **B** is also incorrect. Windows 2000 Server also does not provide clustering services.

Measure and Optimize a DNS Infrastructure Design

14. ☑ **D.** Microsoft recommends setting alerts for all these events. In addition to those listed, Microsoft also recommends setting alerts for unavailable DNS Servers and increased query demands. Events are important to set because administrators cannot depend on noticing DNS problems though common usage. By setting events that notify them when DNS performance is out of accepted ranges, they can quickly respond to problems and potential problems while minimizing the impact on users.

15. ☑ **D.** By default, additional debug logging is disabled in DNS. It can be quite resource intensive and should only be used temporarily when more detailed information is needed about a server's performance. When additional debugging options are enabled, the information they collect is placed in the *systemroot*\System32\Dns\DNS.log file.

☒ **A** is incorrect. There is no DNS System Application Log. **B** and **C** are also incorrect. There is no such thing as the DNS Debug utility.

16. ☑ **A, B, C,** and **D.** The System Log in Event Viewer might be used in this situation because it is where DNS clients store information and errors relating to the DNS service. The DNS Log in Event Viewer might also be used because it is where the DNS Server service stores information and errors. Performance Monitor can be used to track a number of DNS-related events. It could be used, for example, on the server to ensure that it wasn't overburdened, but simply incapable of filling more client requests. Finally, Network Monitor could be used at the packet level to ensure proper network functionality and also to analyze the DNS packet communication.

Design a DNS Deployment Strategy

17. ☑ **D.** The best design would be to place a Primary DNS Server in one site and a Secondary DNS Server for the zone in the other site. This design ensures a minimum of administrative overhead as records are entered into only one DNS Server, the Primary server. In addition, a Secondary server is available to resolve queries at the other site. This ensures that hosts in each site will be able to resolve DNS queries if the WAN connection becomes unavailable.

    ☒ **A** is incorrect. Placing a Primary DNS Server in each site will unnecessarily increase administrative overhead because the DNS administrator will have to enter resource records into two servers instead of just one. **B** is also incorrect. Although it increases fault tolerance within the site, it has the same administrative burden as answer **A**. **C** is incorrect because if the WAN link becomes unavailable, hosts in the site that do not have a local DNS Server will be unable to have their queries resolved.

18. ☑ **C.** The best DNS design in this situation would be to implement one Active Directory integrated DNS Server at each site. Because the network is comprised of all Windows 2000 clients, they will be able to take full advantage of advanced features such as secure dynamic updates. In addition, zone information will be updated as a normal part of Active Directory replication and will be transferred across the network in a secure manner.

    ☒ **A** is incorrect. It unnecessarily increases administrative overhead because the DNS administrator will have to enter resource records into both the Active Directory integrated DNS Server and the Primary DNS Server. **B** is also incorrect. Although this configuration would work, it is not the best answer. **B** does not allow the Windows 2000 clients on the site containing the Secondary Server to take full advantage of each of the new Active Directory integrated DNS features. **D** is incorrect because **C** is the correct answer.

LAB ANSWER

1. Four servers are required to meet the performance requirements. There are 5668 hosts in the site and each DNS Server will support 1500 hosts. It might also be appropriate to install an extra DNS Server in this site so that performance will not be degraded if one of the other servers becomes unavailable.

2. There are two possible answers to this question. Because of the need for very high availability, it would be appropriate to install them as a single DNS cluster.

    A second option would be to install the first one as the Primary DNS Server and install the additional three serves as Secondary DNS Servers. This option lacks the added advantages of load balancing. It also would not allow the zone records to be updated if the Primary DNS Server became unavailable. However, this design would technically meet the basic design requirements.

3. One server is required in Site B to meet the availability requirements. If a server is not located in this site and the WAN link between it and Site A becomes unavailable, hosts at Site B will be unable to have their DNS queries resolved. This would be a single point of failure that the design requirements do not regard as acceptable. The server should be implemented as a Secondary DNS Server.

4. One server is required in Site C for the same reasons given in question three.

5. The best method to use in reducing the DNS traffic between Sites A and C is to use a forwarder. Depending on the configuration, one of the DNS Servers or the DNS cluster in Site A should be specified as a forwarder on the DNS Server in Site C. This will ensure that recursive traffic from the DNS Server in Site C is handled by a DNS Server in Site A, therefore avoiding use of the WAN link. To avoid all recursive traffic over the WAN link, you might also elect to configure the DNS Server in Site C as a slave.

MICROSOFT CERTIFIED SYSTEMS ENGINEER

7

Designing a WINS Strategy

T his chapter will cover the basic principles of NetBIOS name resolution and will focus on how to effectively design a NetBIOS name resolution solution based on WINS.

Overview of NetBIOS Name Resolution

Solving NetBIOS name resolution problems is one of the most important goals of the Windows 2000 network architect. Even though Microsoft's ultimate aim is to completely eliminate NetBIOS from Microsoft networks, the legacy of all previous Microsoft network operating systems makes this change very slow to come.

The vast majority of network-aware applications written for Microsoft operating systems have been written to the NetBIOS interface. The endpoint of communications for NetBIOS applications is the destination computer's NetBIOS name. This presents a problem for operating systems and applications that are NetBIOS dependent and running on a TCP/IP-based network. The problem is that the endpoint of communications on a TCP/IP-based network is the destination IP address and port number.

NetBIOS applications must establish sessions with a destination computer via its NetBIOS name, and TCP/IP must establish a session with a destination computer via its IP address and port number. To solve this problem, a mechanism must be put into place that allows NetBIOS names to be translated into IP addresses before the request is passed to the Transport layer of the DoD model.

In this chapter, we will review the basics of NetBIOS name resolution and get to the business of designing a NetBIOS name resolution solution based on the Windows 2000 Windows Internet Name Service (WINS). The core design elements include taking into account what it is that you want to accomplish with your WINS network solution and matching those goals with the capabilities of the Windows 2000 WINS server.

Design decisions will focus on issues of security, availability, and responsiveness. After completing this chapter, you should have the requisite understanding of NetBIOS name resolution issues and WINS so that you can design a solution for an enterprise network and be well prepared to answer questions related to WINS issues on the Designing a Windows 2000 Network Infrastructure (70-221) exam.

NetBIOS Name Resolution

The history of Microsoft networking is the history of Network Basic Input/Output System (NetBIOS). A company named Sytek, Inc. developed NetBIOS in 1983 for IBM. The NetBIOS transport protocol was designed to accommodate small, single-segment LANs.

At its beginning, NetBIOS was created as a monolithic transport protocol. NetBIOS has matured over the years and now is implemented as a session layer interface that NetBIOS programs can access, in order to communicate on networks that use protocols other than NetBIOS. This allows programs written to the NetBIOS interface to function on installations that use network protocols such as IPX/SPX and TCP/IP as their LAN protocols.

The NetBIOS Extended User Interface

NetBEUI is an extension of the NetBIOS transport protocol. NetBEUI uses the instruction set provided with the NetBIOS standard and has extended it, hence the name NetBIOS Extended User Interface (NetBEUI). Windows NT actually used a more advanced version of the NetBIOS protocol called NetBIOS frames protocol or NBF. Although TCP/IP is the default protocol installed with Windows 2000, you still have the option to install NetBEUI as an additional protocol. You do not have the option of excluding TCP/IP.

Communicating via NetBIOS Names

Programs written to the NetBIOS interface use NetBIOS names as the endpoint of communication. Each computer on a NetBIOS network must have a different name. Each must be 16 bytes in length. Only the first 15 bytes of the NetBIOS name are user configurable. The sixteenth byte is used by the operating system to denote the availability of network services. Therefore, each computer using the NetBIOS interface will actually have multiple NetBIOS names.

NetBIOS programs must communicate with a destination computer via its NetBIOS name. For example, imagine we have two computers, CONSTITUTION and DS2000. CONSTITUTION wants to establish a session with, and access resources on, DS2000. CONSTITUTION will contact DS2000 via its NetBIOS name. To do this, CONSTITUTION will broadcast the name of the destination computer, DS2000. All computers on the segment will process the broadcast message to see if it is intended for them. Computers not named DS2000 examine the packet, assess that it is not intended for them, and drop it.

When DS2000 gets the packet, it recognizes that the packet was intended for it. DS2000 will return its MAC address to CONSTITUTION, and at that point, a session can be established.

See Figure 7-1 for a pictorial overview of this broadcast session.

FIGURE 7-1   NetBIOS computers establishing a session

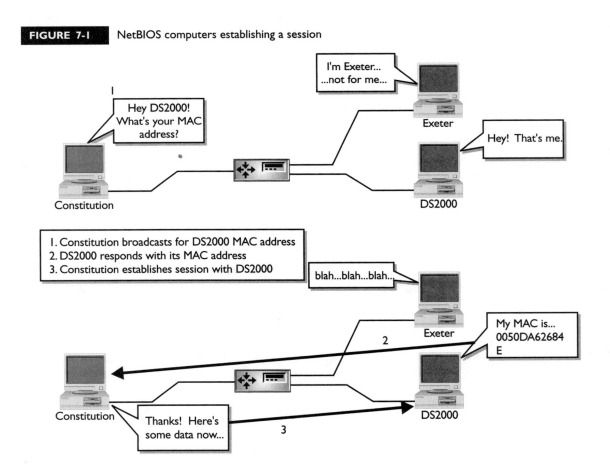

The Limitations of NetBIOS

This example highlights the main limitation of NetBIOS. NetBIOS was designed as a broadcast-based protocol. The NetBIOS broadcasts can generate a significant amount of traffic on a segment. In larger NetBIOS installations (for example, more than 40 computers in a non-switched segment), the volume of broadcast traffic will become so "loud" that network performance is adversely affected.

This is comparable to going out to eat at a noisy restaurant. People always seem to be yelling at each other in some restaurants. When the restaurant has only a handful of people, the total volume of the yelling is manageable, and you are able to communicate with your dinner partner. As a certain number of people enter the restaurant and start yelling at each other, you no longer maintain any reliable information exchange with your partner on the other side of the table, and you start yelling as well.

This limitation presents a significant challenge to NetBIOS programs that function on a TCP/IP-based network. But an even greater challenge to NetBIOS transport protocols is that they are not routable. There are no NetBIOS headers to support routing. A solution must be found not only for the broadcast nature of NetBIOS, but also its lack of routability.

Solving NetBIOS Limitations with NetBIOS over TCP/IP (NetBT)

The TCP/IP protocol stack was designed to work on large *Internetworks*. For our purposes, an Internetwork is comprised of two or more network segments connected by a router. Routers do not forward NetBIOS broadcasts. Because routers do not forward NetBIOS broadcast messages, applications are limited to communication with computers on the same segment. Even if we open the NetBIOS ports on the routers, we still have the problem of applications using only NetBIOS names as an endpoint of communications. Before a network request can be passed down the TCP/IP protocol stack, the NetBIOS name must be converted or resolved to an IP address.

Matching a NetBIOS name with an IP address is called *NetBIOS Name Resolution*. In order for the NetBIOS application to pass its request down the TCP/IP protocol stack, the NetBIOS name must be translated to an IP address. We must add something to TCP/IP so that it is able to perform this vital function. This "add-on" is called *NetBIOS over TCP/IP*, *NetBT*, or *NBT*. NetBT is implemented in the NetBIOS session layer interface. It provides an interface between the session layer components of the DoD Application layer and the DoD Transport layer.

Passing a Request to NetBT   When a request for network services is passed from the user application to the Application layer of the TCP/IP stack, NetBT intercepts the request and the NetBIOS name is resolved to an IP address. After the IP address of the NetBIOS host is discovered, the request is made using the destination computer's IP address, and it moves down the stack to the Host-to-Host (Transport) layer, then to the Internet layer, and finally to the Network Interface layer, and onto the wire.

Figure 7-2 displays this chain of custody.

Windows 2000 Methods of NetBIOS Name Resolution

Windows 2000 has several different methods for resolving NetBIOS names to IP addresses. If the NetBIOS name cannot be resolved to an IP address, the request cannot be passed down the TCP/IP stack, and no session can be established with the destination host. NetBIOS names can be resolved by the following mechanisms:

- NetBIOS Remote Name Cache
- NetBIOS name servers (NBNS)
- NetBIOS Broadcasts
- LMHOSTS file
- HOSTS file
- DNS server

Each of these methods resolves a NetBIOS name to an IP address. If one method fails, another one is used to resolve the NetBIOS name. Only after all methods fail does the attempt at creating a session with the destination computer fail.

Let's look at each of these NetBIOS name resolution methods in more detail.

NetBIOS Name Cache

The NetBIOS Remote Name Cache contains the IP address mappings of recently resolved NetBIOS names. This cache is searched before any other method of NetBIOS name resolution takes place. On Windows 2000 machines, an entry stays in the NetBIOS name cache for 600,000 milliseconds (ten minutes).

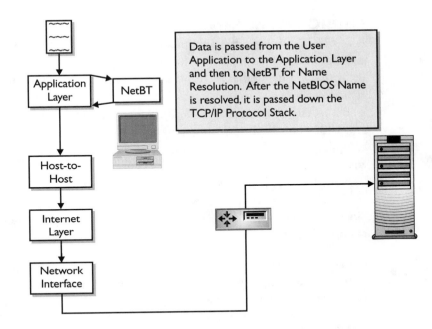

FIGURE 7-2

A request for network services moving down the TCP/IP protocol stack

Though the value is in milliseconds, you can change it to another value. The contents of NetBIOS Remote Name Cache is displayed in Figure 7-3. You can display the NetBIOS Remote Name Cache on a particular computer by typing **nbtstat –c.**

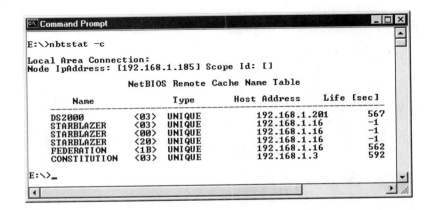

FIGURE 7-3

The NetBIOS remote name cache

NetBIOS Name Server

A *NetBIOS name server* maintains a database of NetBIOS names and their corresponding IP addresses. Its function is similar to that of a DNS server, with the difference being that the DNS server maintains mappings for host names and IP addresses.

Basic design parameters for NetBIOS name servers are delineated in RFCs 1001 and 1002. The NetBIOS name server supplied with Windows 2000 is RFC compliant, and contains many enhanced features to improve its value in a Windows environment.

NetBIOS is only in widespread use on Microsoft networks. The only popular NetBIOS name server is Microsoft's Windows Internet Name Service (WINS) server. Since it is unlikely that you'll ever run into any other implementation of NetBIOS name servers, from this point forward we will refer to them as *WINS servers.*

on the job

If you ever find yourself arguing with somebody about the name of the WINS server and dealing with the other person's reluctance to call it an Internet name server when it does not resolve Internet host names, keep in mind that the term Internet does not refer to the WorldWide Internet. It refers to the fact that a WINS server's main responsibility is to resolve NetBIOS names on Internetworks, and not on the Internet.

WINS servers provide two basic services: NetBIOS name registration and NetBIOS name resolution. NetBIOS clients automatically register names with a NetBIOS name server during system startup. WINS clients can query a WINS server to resolve NetBIOS names to IP addresses.

Broadcast

NetBIOS hosts can broadcast to obtain the IP address of a destination NetBIOS computer. The effectiveness of the broadcast method is limited because, by default, routers do not pass NetBIOS broadcast traffic over UDP ports 137 and 138 (the NetBIOS name service and the NetBIOS datagram services, respectively). NetBIOS name resolution via broadcast is effective only if the destination host is local.

LMHOSTS Files

The LMHOSTS file is a static text file containing IP address and NetBIOS name mappings. The LMHOSTS file is similar to the HOSTS file that is used for host name resolution for WinSock programs. The primary differences between the LMHOSTS file and the HOSTS file are:

- LMHOSTS contains NetBIOS names and HOSTS contains Internet-style host names
- LMHOSTS supports a number of tags that enhance its utility beyond that provided in the simple HOSTS file

The LMHOSTS file is easy to create. An example LMHOSTS file, which we use on our small office network, appears in Figure 7-4.

The LMHOSTS file resolves NetBIOS names by reading the file from top to bottom. The most frequently accessed computers should have their names placed on top, while less frequently accessed computers should have their names placed toward the bottom, or left entirely out of the file.

LMHOSTS Tags   There are a number of useful tags you can place in the LMHOSTS file. In Figure 7-4, for example, you see two of these tags, #PRE and #DOM. When you append the #PRE tag to an entry, its mapping is placed (or PRE loaded) in the NetBIOS remote-name cache at system startup. The #DOM tag indicates that the machine is a domain controller.

exam
ⓦatch

The entries with the #PRE tag are placed on the bottom of the list. There is no reason to place the entries with the #PRE tag above any of the other ones, since they have already been searched for when the NetBIOS Remote Name Cache was parsed.

FIGURE 7-4

An example
LMHOSTS file

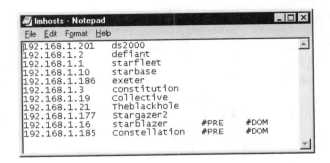

FROM THE CLASSROOM

LMHOSTS File Configurations

I have not taught a single class where students do not make errors in their LMHOSTS file configurations. Always check for misspelled names and incorrectly entered IP addresses in the LMHOSTS file. Another major error committed by less experienced (and sometimes experienced) administrators occurs when saving the LMHOSTS file using the GUI text editors. The LMHOSTS file has no file extension. Problems creep in if you edit the file with the default Windows 2000 text editor, notepad.exe. In order to save the file without a file extension, you must put quotation marks around the file name. If you don't use the quotation marks, the files will be saved as lmhosts.txt. If you save it as lmhosts.txt, Windows 2000 will not read it, and it will not be used for NetBIOS name resolution.

—Thomas W. Shinder, M.D., MCSE, MCP+I, MCT

The LMHOSTS file is placed in the %system_root%\system32\drivers\etc folder.

on the job

Information on the other available tags for the LMHOSTS file is contained in the lmhosts.sam file. Do not use this file as your LMHOSTS file by adding your entries to the end of the file. This will degrade performance because even though the lines that begin with a number sign (#) are read as comments (like the rem entry in batch files or the config.sys file), these lines are still parsed to assess whether they contain valid tags.

Remember that the LMHOSTS file must be placed on the hard drives of the machines that are *using* it for name resolution. There is no mechanism that allows you to create a central LMHOSTS file on a server, and then point the clients to this file, without first having an LMHOSTS file on the local machine. There are ways, described in the LMHOSTS.SAM file, that you can create central LMHOSTS files. However, the NetBIOS name to IP address mapping must exist on client LMHOSTS files, too.

HOSTS

The HOSTS file looks very much like the LMHOSTS file, except Fully Qualified Domain Names (FQDN) are mapped to IP addresses, rather than NetBIOS names. There are no tags used in the HOSTS file to denote any particular server role or network service. A major difference is that the number sign (#) is used *only* to denote comments in the HOSTS file, since there are no tags.

on the Job

One of the most common errors you'll see relating to host-name resolution problems is the use of LMHOSTS tags in HOSTS files. Remember that the tags used in LMHOSTS files can only be used on those files, and not in HOSTS files.

NetBIOS names can be resolved from the HOSTS file if traditional NetBIOS specific methods have failed. When the NetBIOS resolver uses the HOSTS file, the first 15 characters to the left of the first period are stripped from the FQDN and handled as a NetBIOS name. This provides a reason you might want to use the same naming convention for both NetBIOS and HOST names on your Windows 2000 network.

DNS Server

Domain Name System (DNS) servers provide host name-to-IP address resolution. This is similar to a WINS server, except that the WINS server provides NetBIOS name-to-IP address resolution.

Hybrid networks containing both WINS and non-WINS clients benefit from having a DNS server that is configured to perform WINS referrals. A non-WINS client is not able to query a WINS server directly. However, when the non-WINS client queries a Windows 2000 DNS server that has been configured to perform WINS referrals, the DNS server can obtain the NetBIOS mapping and return that information to the non-WINS client.

A DNS server can cache successful WINS lookups, which means that it can provide fault tolerance for WINS servers. In a situation where the WINS clients cannot access their configured WINS servers, they may be able to resolve a NetBIOS name by querying a DNS server that has cached entries for NetBIOS hosts. Although the DNS server itself may not be able to query an unavailable WINS server, the DNS server still contains cached WINS entries. This is another reason to configure DNS servers to provide for NetBIOS name lookups from a WINS server.

The following scenarios & solutions grid answers some common questions about NetBIOS and resolution of NetBIOS names.

SCENARIO & SOLUTION

Do I have to run NetBIOS applications on my network?	No. And you do not need to have the NetBIOS interface enabled on a Windows 2000 network. There are many advantages to disabling the NetBIOS interface, including the reduction of a significant amount of broadcast traffic.
Is there any way I can get LMHOSTS to automatically update itself?	No. LMHOSTS is a static text file that must be manually updated.
Do I have to have a WINS server on my network?	No. But a WINS server greatly simplifies and enhances NetBIOS name resolution on a segmented network. Your only other solution would be LMHOSTS files, which are unwieldy to maintain on a large NetBIOS installation.

CertCam 7-1

EXERCISE 7-1

Using LMHOSTS Files for NetBIOS Name Resolution

You are the system administrator for a small company that has 250 computers spread over four subnets. The subnets are designated by the letters A, B, C, and D. There is a domain controller on subnet B and a single WINS server on subnet A. You have noticed that when network access to subnet A is not available, none of the computers on the network can resolve NetBIOS name for remote subnets. How can you solve this problem?

Answer: You can use an LMHOSTS file to provide NetBIOS name resolution for your network clients. For a small network with a limited number of servers with static IP addresses, an LMHOSTS file represents a fault-tolerant method of providing NetBIOS name resolution for times when a WINS server becomes unavailable. Note that the LMHOSTS file solution will not work if servers obtain IP addresses dynamically via DHCP. When dynamic address assignment is used, each LMHOSTS file on each computer would need to be changed. Another option would be to include a central LMHOSTS file and use the #INCLUDE tag to designate the location of a central LMHOSTS file.

CERTIFICATION OBJECTIVE 7.02

Overview of WINS

WINS is the Microsoft implementation of the RFC-compliant NetBIOS name server. When planning a NetBIOS name resolution scheme for your enterprise, you must include WINS in that plan. All enterprise and the majority of smaller corporate environments exist as routed networking infrastructures. WINS is the only viable NetBIOS name resolution solution for multi-segmented networks.

To architect a cogent WINS design, you need to be aware of what problems need to be solved, and what functional components of WINS can aid in solving these problems. Consider the following problems that may benefit from a WINS networking solution.

SCENARIO & SOLUTION

What NetBIOS resources exist on the network?	You must consider what network devices and programs on your network are NetBIOS dependent. The legacy of Windows networking is the legacy of NetBIOS. It is likely that the vast majority of your network-aware applications are dependent, or have some element of dependency on NetBIOS calls. You should compile a complete inventory of NetBIOS-dependent network devices and applications and assess if there are WinSock equivalents. Your goal should be to move away from NetBIOS dependence.
What NetBIOS-related problems might require WINS?	The primary reason to implement WINS is to allow NetBIOS resolution on a routed network. NetBIOS Name Query Request broadcast messages do not cross routers. However, a WINS client avoids NetBIOS broadcasts for name resolution by issuing a directed datagram to the WINS server's IP address. WINS servers can also solve problems with excessive NetBIOS traffic on a single segment LAN when a large number of hosts exist in the same broadcast domain.

SCENARIO & SOLUTION

Are NetBIOS name resolution services required on a multiple-site enterprise network that is joined via multiple, relatively slow, WAN links?	The geographically dispersed organization has special NetBIOS name resolution needs. These companies may have hundreds, perhaps thousands of NetBIOS hosts distributed across the globe. In this type of situation, you must architect a NetBIOS name resolution solution that can provide fast and accurate services for all the computers on the network, regardless of location. This scenario is common for larger corporate entities, and requires a well-planned WINS network and WINS replication scheme.
Do you run a mixed NetBIOS and WinSock network?	While the history of Microsoft networks is NetBIOS, the Internet and Internet technologies have made large inroads into Microsoft corporate computing. These technologies, when introduced into a private network, are often referred to as *Intranet* technologies. In a mixed environment, leverage your existing NetBIOS name resolution infrastructure by using DNS servers configured to perform WINS referrals.
What networking services will require NetBIOS name resolution services?	Will your network deploy other networking services that are either dependent upon, or would benefit from, a WINS network infrastructure? For example, RRAS, DNS, Microsoft Exchange, and other networking services may benefit from your WINS architecture. Keep these other services in mind during development.

on the **job**

By first considering the NetBIOS name resolution problems that need to be solved by WINS, you will be in a better position to evaluate whether WINS capabilities and features will be able to solve them.

Becoming Architect of a WINS Design Plan

When becoming the architect of a WINS design, consider the components of a WINS infrastructure. These elements include:

- WINS servers
- WINS clients
- Non-WINS clients
- WINS proxy agents

- WINS replication network topology
- WINS network convergence time
- WINS server hardware

These elements usually exist on a routed or multi-segmented network, where networking devices such as routers and switches partition the broadcast environment. In such a partitioned network, NetBIOS name registration and name resolution broadcast messages cannot reach all the NetBIOS hosts on the network. WINS provides the most efficient and effective means of solving problems related to the broadcast limitations of NetBIOS.

Even if your network is not segmented, you may wish to deploy a WINS server to reduce the amount of broadcast traffic on the network by reducing and eliminating NetBIOS broadcasts. For a smaller network, the processor and disk resources required from a WINS installation are not significant. A WINS server in such an environment can co-exist on a server that is performing other functions, such as domain controller or DNS server, without impairing the overall performance of any of the networking services loading on that server.

WINS Servers

WINS servers represent the core NetBIOS name resolution server service for your network. The WINS server is responsible for NetBIOS name registration and NetBIOS name resolution. The server is also responsible for cleaning the database at periodic intervals to preserve WINS server performance.

WINS Clients

WINS clients are machines running operating systems that support the WINS client service. WINS clients are able to register their NetBIOS names with a WINS server, remove their NetBIOS names from a WINS server, and query a WINS server for NetBIOS name resolution.

All Windows operating systems are capable of being WINS clients.

Non-WINS Clients

Non-WINS clients are computers running operating systems that do not support being WINS clients. Non-WINS clients cannot register and query a WINS server directly. This is not problematic if the non-WINS client does not contain or need to access NetBIOS resources. However, if the non-WINS client does contain or access NetBIOS resources, mechanisms must accommodate the NetBIOS name registration and name resolution requirements of these non-WINS clients.

WINS Proxy Agents

WINS Proxy Agents provide a mechanism for non-WINS client to indirectly query a WINS database. The WINS Proxy Agent listens for NetBIOS Name Query Request messages on the local segment and forwards those messages to a WINS server for name resolution.

Note that the WINS Proxy Agent does not register NetBIOS Names for non-WINS client. Other methods must be used to enter the NetBIOS Names of non-WINS clients into the WINS database.

WINS Replication Network Topology

Large Internetworks separated by WAN links typically require multiple WINS servers for performance and fault tolerance reasons. Under normal circumstances, each WINS server needs to contain a complete copy of the WINS database. To ensure that the WINS database is consistent throughout the organization, the database entries are replicated among the servers. In order to ensure timely and efficient replication, you need to plan your replication scheme. There are a number of replication models from which you can choose. We will go into more detail regarding WINS network replication topologies later in this chapter.

WINS Network Convergence Time   WINS network convergence time
is a function of the WINS network topology. In designing a WINS replication topology, assess how long it takes a new WINS record registration on WINS server A to reach WINS server Z, where WINS A is the owner of the record and WINS Z is the last server to receive a replicated copy of the new WINS client registration.

WINS Server Hardware and Software Environment

The WINS server can take a significant amount of processor and disk resources on a large and dynamic NetBIOS network. You will need to take into account the hardware of the WINS server on a particular server through baselining. You will also need to consider the effect of running multiple server services on the same computer running the WINS service. Incompatibilities due to hardware resource limitations may lead to your planning more physical servers on the network to support WINS.

on the **Job**

Historically, WINS implementations on Windows NT 4.0 networks were done in a haphazard fashion. The guiding principle of WINS deployment in many organizations appeared to be "more is better." In fact, more is not better. The more WINS servers deployed in a company, the higher the likelihood that problems will arise in the replication network. Designing and planning WINS server networks is crucial to a safe and efficient NetBIOS name resolution for your network.

WINS Server Capabilities

Compared to many other Windows 2000 network services, configuration of a Windows 2000 WINS server is relatively straightforward and limited in the number of parameters you need to set. When architecting a NetBIOS name resolution solution with WINS servers as the central element, you should consider the following concepts and features:

- WINS client/server interactions
- WINS integration with DNS and DHCP
- Burst mode handling
- Replication partner configuration options

You should already be familiar with these concepts and features, but now is a good time to review them so that you can use them in your design plan. For more detailed coverage of this subnet, check out *MCSE Windows 2000 Network Administration Study Guide (Exam 70-216).*

WINS Client/Server Interactions

WINS is a client/server database application. The WINS server maintains a database of NetBIOS names and IP addresses. The WINS client and server participate in four basic activities:

- Name registration
- Name renewal
- Name release
- Name resolution

Name Registration WINS clients register their NetBIOS Names and IP addresses with either their *primary* or *secondary WINS server*. If the primary server is not available, the WINS client will register with the first available secondary. If none of the secondary WINS servers are available, the WINS client will move back to the top of its list of WINS servers and start with its primary WINS server again.

on the

(i)ob

Although the terms primary and secondary WINS servers are still used, the dedicated text boxes for entering the IP addresses of the Primary and Secondary WINS that existed on Windows NT 4.0 WINS clients are no longer there in Windows 2000.

After receiving the registration from the WINS client, the WINS server checks to see if the machine is already contained in the WINS database. If there is no other entry for that particular NetBIOS name, the WINS client will receive a *Positive Name Registration Response*. If the NetBIOS name is already in the WINS database, the WINS server sends the WINS client a *Wait For Acknowledgement (WACK)* message. Then WINS sends a challenge to the IP address of the requesting WINS client.

- ■ If there is no response to the challenge, then the WINS client receives a *Positive Name Registration Response*.

- ■ If the WINS server does receive a response to the challenge, the WINS client attempting to register the same name receives a *Negative Name Registration Response*.

exam

ⓦatch

*If the WINS client tries to register a name and IP address that are the same as one already contained in the WINS database, for example, its own name and IP address, the registration request becomes a **NetBIOS** name renewal.*

Renewal Along with a positive NetBIOS name registration response, the WINS server sends a *renewal interval* or *Time-to-Live (TTL)* for the registered NetBIOS name. The WINS client must renew its name in the WINS database before the expiration of the TTL in order to keep its record *active* in the WINS database.

A WINS client sends a *name-refresh request* to the WINS server to renew its NetBIOS name. The request is sent at 50 percent of the renewal interval. Once the name is refreshed, the WINS server may send the WINS client a new renewal interval.

exam
ⓦatch

WINS clients usually receive the same renewal interval after each name refresh. However, under certain circumstances the renewal interval may change. This might happen when the WINS administrator makes changes to the renewal interval or when burst handling mode *is active. We will discuss burst handling mode later in the chapter.*

Release　A WINS client sends a *NetBIOS name release* message when it is shut down properly.

- If the NetBIOS name and IP address of the machine requesting the release is the same as that contained in the WINS database, the WINS server will mark the record *Released* and the entry becomes inactive
- If the IP address is different than the WINS client that is seeking a release, then the release request is ignored

A record remains in the WINS database in the released state until the expiration of the *extinction interval.* While the record is marked released, if another computer wants to register the same NetBIOS name, the WINS server will issue no challenge.

After the extinction interval expires, the record becomes Extinct and is *tombstoned.* The record remains tombstoned for a period called the *extinction timeout.* After the expiration of the extinction timeout, the record is deleted or *scavenged* from the WINS database.

Figure 7-5 shows the WINS record lifecycle.

FIGURE 7-5

The WINS record lifecycle in the WINS database

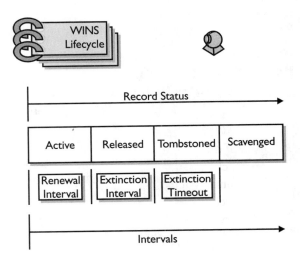

Resolution   An h-node WINS client will go through the following steps to resolve a NetBIOS name to an IP address:

1. A request is sent to the TCP/IP protocol stack from the NetBIOS application. The *NetBIOS Remote Name Cache* is checked first.

2. If the destination host's IP address is not contained in the NetBIOS Remote Name Cache, the WINS client will send a *NetBIOS Name Query Request* directly to its Primary WINS server. If the WINS server does not respond, it will query two more times. If the Primary WINS server fails to respond, Secondary WINS servers will be contacted.

3. When a WINS server is found, it will respond with either *Positive Name Query Response* or a *Negative Name Query Response*, depending on whether the server did or did not have a mapping for the requested NetBIOS name.

4. If a negative name query response is received, the WINS client will issue up to three name query request broadcasts to the local segment, 750ms apart. If this fails, the client may use other methods of NetBIOS name resolution, depending on client configuration and NetBIOS node type.

WINS Integration with DNS and DHCP

WINS can directly integrate with the Windows 2000 DNS server and indirectly interacts with the Windows 2000 DHCP server. By taking advantage of WINS ability to interact with these services you can streamline your NetBIOS name resolution solution for your network. We will discuss the interaction between WINS, DNS, and DHCP a little later in this chapter.

Burst Mode Handling

There are times when NetBIOS name registration requests may overwhelm a WINS server. This might happen after a system-wide power outage, or when the organization adopts the questionable policy of turning off all machines over the weekend and then having them all turned on simultaneously at 8:00 a.m. Monday morning.

When the WINS server receives more requests per unit time than it is able to register in the WINS database, it will queue the requests in memory until the registrations can be written to disk. If the number of pending registrations exceeds the available queue length, the registrations will be dropped. The WINS clients who had their registrations dropped will issue another registration request.

Repeated name registration requests from multiple WINS clients adds to overall network traffic, which can have a deleterious effect on network performance.

The Windows 2000 WINS server can switch to *burst mode* when large numbers of NetBIOS name registration requests arrive at the WINS server. When in burst mode, the WINS server will immediately acknowledge the request, but will *not* add the computer to the WINS database. The WINS server does not check the NetBIOS name against the WINS database and it does not issue a challenge against duplicate names.

Burst Mode and Short TTLs   The WINS server sends back to the WINS client a short TTL instead of the normal, longer TTL the client typically receives. This short TTL varies from 5–60 minutes depending on the number of pending registrations; compare this with the default TTL of six days. By returning a short TTL to the WINS client, the WINS client *believes* that its NetBIOS names have been registered and will not send another registration request. This reduces the amount of overall network traffic due to repeated NetBIOS name registration requests and also reduces the load on the WINS server during a period of excessive load. The WINS client renews its NetBIOS name at 50 percent of the short TTL, at which time the WINS server is, we hope, not preoccupied.

exam
Watch

Remember that once burst mode takes effect, no entries are recorded into the WINS database for those machines that are offered the short TTLs.

Burst handling allows the WINS server to accommodate WINS clients' attempts at name registration at times when the WINS server is too busy to write to the database.

on the
Job

Remember that burst handling is not new to Windows 2000 and is available on your Windows NT 4.0 WINS servers after they have been upgraded to Service Pack 3 or greater.

Replication Partner Configuration Options

There are several configuration options you should consider when configuring replication partnerships between WINS servers. WINS replication partners can be configured as

- Push partners
- Pull partners

■ Push/pull partners

■ Autoconfigured partners

Push partners are configured to send their changes to the WINS database after a set number of changes have been recorded. Pull partners send pull requests at set intervals. Push/pull partners send changes based on both number of records changed and time intervals. WINS servers can be configured to find each other automatically and autoconfigure their replication partnerships. Let's look a little more closely at how that works.

WINS Automatic Partner Discovery When *automatic partner discovery* is enabled, WINS servers use the *multicast* address 224.0.1.24 to discover other WINS servers.

The number of WINS servers found through autodiscovery depends on how the routers on your network are configured. If routers do not support IGMP forwarding, autodiscovery is limited to the local segment. Autodiscovered WINS partners become push/pull partners with a pull interval of two hours. The push parameter is set to zero, indicating that no push triggers will be sent.

Automatic partner discovery can be configured on the Advanced tab of the WINS server's Properties dialog box, as shown in Figure 7-6.

You must have a good understanding of the WINS client/server relationship and WINS capabilities to design an effective WINS solution.

WINS Interoperability

We touched on some of the WINS interoperability features earlier. Most significant is the capability of integrating with the Windows 2000 DNS and DHCP services.

Integrating WINS with the Windows 2000 Dynamic DNS

The Windows 2000 DNS server is able to accept dynamic host name and IP address registrations from Windows 2000 DNS clients. The Windows 2000 DNS server has some of the same characteristics as WINS. It is able to accept dynamic registrations and answer queries for dynamically registered hosts.

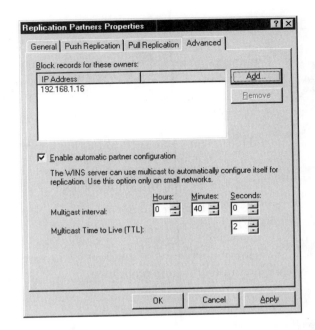

FIGURE 7-6

Configuration of WINS Partner Autodiscovery

However, down-level operating systems are not able to directly interact with the Windows 2000 DNS server. Down-level clients *are* able to dynamically register their NetBIOS names and IP addresses with the Windows 2000 WINS server. You can enable both WINS forward and reverse lookups on the Windows 2000 DDNS server to resolve NetBIOS names for computers throughout the enterprise.

If you plan to integrate WINS and DNS, you should create a dedicated WINS referral zone so that all WINS referrals are performed from lookups emanating from requests to that zone. In this way, all names resolved via WINS referrals have the domain name of the WINS referral zone appended to them.

Integrating WINS with the Windows 2000 DHCP Server

The primary value of WINS is its capability to dynamically register NetBIOS names with the WINS database. The dynamic aspect of the registration process is most important when NetBIOS hosts are also DHCP clients. These DHCP clients change their IP addresses at a variable frequency. When the NetBIOS clients obtain new IP addresses, these addresses are automatically entered into the WINS database.

The integration of WINS and DHCP is somewhat indirect. Unlike DNS, WINS servers do not directly communicate with DHCP servers. Rather, the following process takes place:

1. DHCP client requests IP addressing information from a DHCP server.

2. A DHCP server responds to the requests and assigns an IP address and other IP addressing information to the DHCP client.

3. The DHCP client can now register its NetBIOS name and IP address with a WINS server.

The following scenarios & solutions grid answers some common questions about WINS interoperability and replication.

SCENARIO & SOLUTION

Do I have to use WINS proxy agents to allow NetBIOS name resolution for my UNIX machines?	You only need a WINS proxy agent if you want to resolve remote NetBIOS names and choose not to open the NetBIOS ports on your routers (UDP 137 and 138). The UNIX NetBIOS hosts can broadcast for local NetBIOS name resolution requests.
Why should I create a WINS referral zone?	A WINS referral zone makes it possible to identify the names that have been resolved using WINS referrals by a DNS server. Many security and inventory programs use reverse lookups to identify machines on a network. Depending on your domain naming scheme, and how you have the DNS clients configured for resolving host names, the same computer can return different FQDNs on a reverse lookup. This could complicate your security and inventory assessments.
Why does WINS autodiscovery configure WINS replication partners to be both push and pull partners and then set the push parameter to zero?	In order to complete a pull operation, the pulling computer must be configured as a push partner in order to have its pull partner push the records after the pull trigger is sent. The push parameter is set to zero, which means that the pull partner will not send any records based on the number of changes made to the WINS database, and will only "push" records after a pull trigger is sent.

Planning Network NetBIOS Support

EXERCISE 7-2

You are planning a NetBIOS name resolution support infrastructure for a new company that has offices in Dallas, San Francisco, and Seattle. The corporate headquarters are in Dallas, where the majority of network support personnel are also located.

During your inventory of NetBIOS resources on the network you discover that you have the following:

- Microsoft Exchange Server 5.5 at each site

- Several workgroups using Microsoft Mail

- SQL Server 6.5 at each site

- An alert service dependent batch file used to monitor servers at the Dallas site

IP Addresses are managed via DHCP. The host environment is a mixture of Windows 2000, Windows NT 4.0, and Windows 9x computers. There are also a handful of UNIX workstations and servers using NetBIOS applications that share information with the other users of that NetBIOS application.

Given this basic background of the network architecture, what WINS capabilities can you bring into play to solve the NetBIOS name resolution problems?

Answer: This is an example of a multi-site organization separated by WAN links. Because of the WAN links, it is wise to include at least one WINS server, and preferably two, at each site. Because there are multiple WINS servers in the organization, you need to design a WINS replication network among the WINS servers in order to maintain database consistency throughout the organization.

The network clients are supported by DHCP. WINS-enabled network clients will be able to register their DHCP assigned IP addresses automatically with their configured WINS server. You will need to configure the network clients to receive a WINS server address via DHCP to simplify IP address administration and management.

Although no mention is made of a DNS server, you might plan DNS server integration between WINS and DNS because there are both Windows 2000 and UNIX clients on the network, both of which will likely require host name resolution services via DNS. The DNS server should be configured to perform WINS referrals for names not included in the DNS zone files.

Finally, you might want to consider including a WINS proxy agent to aid the UNIX clients in resolving NetBIOS names on the network.

CERTIFICATION OBJECTIVE 7.03

Integrating WINS into a Network Design Plan

After becoming familiar with WINS capabilities and limitations, you are ready to begin designing a WINS solution that integrates into your design plan. When planning your WINS solution, the following issues should be foremost on your mind:

- Are you designing for a single-segment environment?
- Are you designing for a multi-segment or enterprise environment?
- What client operating systems are you supporting and what level of support do you intend?
- Do you have non-WINS clients on the network and how can you provide a WINS solution for those clients?
- Will you have a distributed WINS database that will require a WINS network design?

These questions focus on key factors related to the networking infrastructure and the level of WINS client support you expect for your WINS network solution.

Creating a WINS Solution for the LAN Environment

NetBIOS name resolution on a single segment LAN is a simple affair. Normally, all the computers on the single logical segment will resolve NetBIOS names via NetBIOS broadcast messages. You have the option of installing a WINS server in this environment, but it is optional as long as no network device (such as a switch) blocks NetBIOS broadcasts.

If you have a large number of NetBIOS hosts on a single segment, or the logical segment is physically partitioned, it may be to your advantage to deploy a WINS server. Large amounts of NetBIOS broadcast traffic can have a detectable negative impact on single-segment networks. This can be avoided by deploying a WINS server.

NetBIOS Node Types

A good way to approach design decisions is to consider the different NetBIOS node types. There are four NetBIOS node types:

- b-node (Microsoft enhanced b-node)
- p-node
- m-node
- h-node

These node types determine how NetBIOS hosts resolve NetBIOS names to IP addresses. They determine what services are employed to resolve the NetBIOS names, and in what order. These node types focus on the *NetBIOS-specific* services used to resolve NetBIOS names.

b-node   B-node clients use broadcasts at the expense of WINS servers. Microsoft network clients that are not configured with an address for a WINS server are, by default, b-node clients. Microsoft has coined the term *Microsoft-enhanced b-node* to describe b-node clients that take advantage of the *#PRE* tag in an LMHOSTS file. When entries are made in an LMHOSTS file with the #PRE tag, those mappings are placed in the NetBIOS remote name cache on system startup.

The only environment where b-node is appropriate is the single segment network. Since b-node clients do not use WINS server, the only other solution for resolving NetBIOS names of computers on remote segments is an LMHOSTS file. If DHCP is in widespread use, an LMHOSTS file may become a cumbersome affair.

p-node   A p-node client uses a WINS server and excludes broadcast messages. If you wish to reduce the amount of NetBIOS broadcast traffic to an absolute minimum, consider configuring the NetBIOS hosts as p-node clients.

In order to make the p-node client solution work, WINS fault tolerance becomes a critical factor. Consider the example of two computers located on the same segment, computer A and computer B. There is a WINS server on this segment as well. What happens when the WINS server becomes indisposed? Computer A is no longer able to resolve the NetBIOS name of computer B, even though they are on the same segment! This is because the WINS server is not available, and the capability to broadcast has been disabled because of the p-node configuration.

The p-node solution is good if you have adequate hardware resources to back it up. In order to provide adequate fault tolerance for a single segment LAN using a p-node WINS client solution, you should have at least two WINS servers online. You also should configure the NetBIOS clients with the IP addresses of each server, or implement Windows clustering for real-time fail over for the WINS server.

Figure 7-7 illustrates the p-node situation.

FIGURE 7-7

Computer A and
computer B set
up as p-node
clients

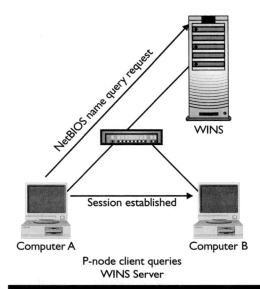

P-node client queries
WINS Server

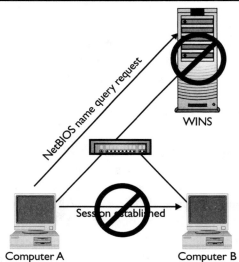

P-node client attempts to query failed WINS
Server. No session established because client
cannot broadcast on local segment.

m-node The m-node NetBIOS client can use both WINS and NetBIOS broadcasts to resolve NetBIOS names. The m-node will use broadcasts preferentially over WINS queries. At first glance, this might look like a less-than-efficient NetBIOS name resolution, but there are some situations where m-node might be ideal.

Imagine a situation where company Q has a main office in Portland and a satellite office in Beaverton. The two offices are connected via a dial-up routed connection using a 56 Kbps modem. There are about 300 machines in Portland and 15 machines in Beaverton. See Figure 7-8 for a diagram of how this setup works.

About 99 percent of the communications done at the Beaverton office are with the other computers in that office. Very rarely do the machines in Beaverton need to access any NetBIOS resources on machines in Portland.

Since the machines in Beaverton rarely need to communicate with the machines in Portland, and the Beaverton office is on a single logical IP network, you could configure the WINS clients to be m-node clients and avoid using WINS until necessary. The machines in the Beaverton office will broadcast to resolve each other's NetBIOS names, and if a NetBIOS resource is not available locally, the WINS server in Portland can be accessed via the slow dial-up line so that NetBIOS names for the Portland computers can be resolved.

h-node When a Windows 2000 network client is configured with a WINS server address, it is by default an h-node client. H-node clients can use both broadcasts and WINS queries to resolve NetBIOS names. The h-node queries a WINS server *before* issuing a broadcast message. This is the best solution for a segmented network where most of the NetBIOS resources accessed by WINS clients are located on remote segments.

Creating a WINS Solution for an Enterprise Network

An enterprise network consists of multiple subnetworks. Each subnet can be joined to the other via fast LAN connections or by relatively slow WAN connections. WINS is designed to provide a fast and efficient means of NetBIOS name resolution on such routed networks.

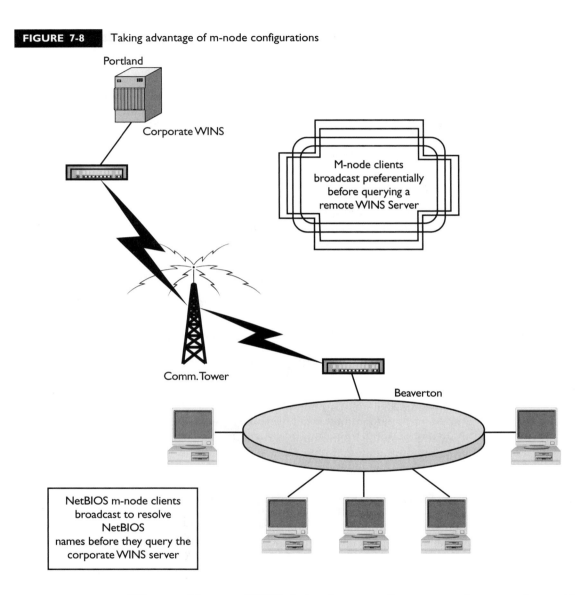

FIGURE 7-8   Taking advantage of m-node configurations

When working on a WINS design document for an enterprise network, consider several key implementation issues.

- Minimize the number of failed NetBIOS name resolution requests from WINS clients due to communication failures

- Keep the number of WINS servers to a minimum
- Decide upon an acceptable convergence time and have a design that assures that this value is met
- Minimize the number of registrations and queries that must cross physical segment boundaries

Each of these issues introduces important design considerations to be addressed in your implementation plan.

Minimize the Number of Failed WINS Communications Due to Network Link Failure

You should consider what the cost would be to productivity if WINS clients were not able to communicate with a WINS server. Failure to communicate with WINS servers can affect:

- NetBIOS name registration
- NetBIOS queries
- NetBIOS name releases

If a machine starts up and is not able to communicate with a WINS server at that time, it will retry every ten minutes to register its NetBIOS name. The failure of a NetBIOS name registration can cascade the amount of time required to complete WINS database convergence on the network and subsequently lead to failures of NetBIOS name resolution.

The potential incapability of a WINS client to contact a WINS server should lead you to include enough WINS servers on the network. The design should include WINS servers that are close enough to WINS clients so that occasional router outages do not disturb the WINS registration and resolution process. Include WINS servers on the most populated subnets and plan for redundant WINS servers on these segments. For segments that do not include WINS servers, redundant gateways should be available to WINS clients; if a single interface is not available, a backup allows communication with a WINS server.

Minimize the Number of WINS Servers

Each WINS server can support thousands of NetBIOS name registrations and thousands of NetBIOS name queries per minute. Because a WINS server has such capacity, give serious consideration to the number of WINS servers you place on your network.

exam
ⓦatch

Microsoft recommends that you never place more than 20 WINS servers on your network. If you feel the need to place more, you should consult Microsoft Consulting Services.

Microsoft is firm about their warning regarding an excessive number of WINS servers. A WINS network represents a single, distributed database. Although it is *distributed*, it is not *partitioned* like the DNS. The database is intended to be distributed as a whole. In order to maintain the integrity of the database, each WINS server should ideally have all the same entries as all the other WINS servers on the network. When WINS servers on a single network contain incomplete or invalid entries, the WINS network is considered *inconsistent*.

For a number of reasons, a WINS network can become easily inconsistent. Even when the WINS network works according to plan, the database is still considered *loosely consistent*. The loose consistency of the WINS database is related to issues such as convergence times and the frequency of changes to the WINS database. In Figure 7-9, see a typical example of a simple WINS replication network.

This is a common configuration in many corporations. The mesh-like configuration of the replication partnerships can sometimes lead to irreparable inconsistencies in the WINS database. At times the situation becomes so bad that the administrator must completely rebuild the WINS database in order to regain a reasonable level of consistency. On a large Internetwork, such a rebuilding process can be a laborious and unpleasant experience.

Design-Acceptable Convergence Times in the WINS Network

The *convergence time* is the amount of time it takes for a change registered on WINS server A to be replicated to WINS server Z. Server A is the *owner* of the record, and server Z is the point furthest away from server A in the WINS replication network.

In designing the replication network, the convergence times must be kept foremost in the designer's plan. How long does management consider a critical server running a NetBIOS application to be *unavailable* after it receives a new IP address, either via DHCP or because of a manual administrative change? This is a management decision, and after the management decision is made, you design the replication network to support the decision.

FIGURE 7-9

A typical example
of a WINS
replication
network

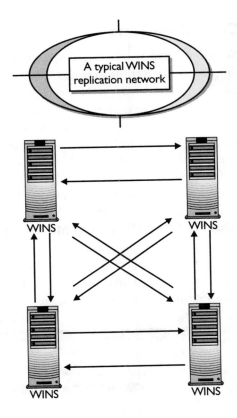

FIGURE 7-9

A typical example
of a WINS
replication
network

We will discuss WINS replication network design in more detail later in the chapter.

Minimize the Amount of WINS Traffic Crossing Routers

Your network routers have a lot to do, and adding more for the routers to process is
not something for which you should design. When designing your WINS solution,
try to make as many WINS clients as possible local to their configured WINS server.
In this way you take the load off the network routers and improve the accessibility of
WINS server services to your network clients.

exam
Watch

*When designing a WINS solution, issues of redundancy of WINS server services
on the network are important. If WINS clients cannot contact WINS servers,
all NetBIOS resources on the network will become inaccessible to those
WINS clients.*

WINS Client Considerations

The Windows 2000 WINS client supports up to 12 Secondary WINS servers. This is an improvement over the previous WINS client configuration, where you were limited to a single Primary WINS server and a single Secondary WINS server.

The capability to assign multiple secondary WINS servers to WINS clients provides a helpful fault tolerance mechanism for your NetBIOS name resolution scheme. If the Primary WINS server becomes unavailable for some reason, the WINS client can both register with, and query multiple Secondary WINS servers until it finds one available.

Figure 7-10 shows where you configure WINS server addresses for WINS clients.

The Double-Edged Sword of Multiple Secondary WINS Servers

While the capability to assign multiple Secondary WINS servers is a boon when considering issues of fault tolerance, multiple WINS Secondaries can become a double-edged sword. There are some situations that can lead to significant increases in NetBIOS name resolution times when multiple Secondaries are configured.

FIGURE 7-10

Configuring the WINS client with multiple Secondary WINS servers

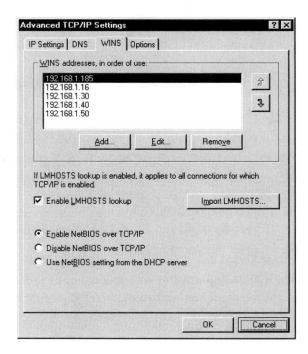

For example, imagine that a WINS client is located on subnet A. The WINS client is configured with a Primary and two Secondary WINS servers. There are no WINS servers on subnet A. All the Secondaries are located on remote subnets, one or more hops away from the WINS client. What happens when the single router interface to subnet A becomes unavailable and the WINS client is trying to resolve the name of a remote NetBIOS host?

The WINS client proceeds through the NetBIOS name resolution sequence. When it gets to the point of querying the WINS server on the remote network, it will make three attempts, 750 milliseconds apart, to contact the WINS server. Since the WINS server is not available, it tries the first secondary and repeats the process. When the first Secondary fails to respond, it tries the second Secondary. After the second Secondary fails to respond, it proceeds to try other methods of NetBIOS name resolution.

Each failed attempt at contacting a WINS server takes 2250ms. In this example, we added a total of 4.5 seconds to the NetBIOS name resolution process by failing to contact the two secondary WINS servers. If we had 12 Secondary WINS servers, none of which could be contacted, we might have added a total of 27 Secondary to the NetBIOS name resolution sequence.

on the **Job**

Even in situations where the local router interface is available, multiple WINS servers can be problematic. If you have 12 Secondaries and they are all located on non-available subnets, you will have to wait 27 seconds before the client moves on to another method of NetBIOS name resolution. If another method that is used after the WINS queries are completed is successful, you have added a lot of extra time to a successful NetBIOS name resolution request.

Microsoft WINS Client Support and Network Stability

All Windows operating systems support WINS client functionality. When configuring a WINS server, you should consider how often the WINS client will change its NetBIOS related information, such as logged on user or available NetBIOS resources. If the NetBIOS configuration of the network remains relatively stable, consider increasing the WINS renewal interval at the WINS server to longer than its default period of six days. This helps to reduce the total volume of WINS client/server traffic on the network.

NetBIOS Name Resolution for Non-WINS Clients

You need to support NetBIOS name resolution and registration services for non-WINS clients. For example, the network may contain UNIX servers that support NetBIOS applications, and those servers obtain IP addressing information dynamically from a DHCP server. When supporting NetBIOS name resolution and registration for non-WINS client, there are two Primary needs that should be addressed:

- How will non-WINS clients resolve NetBIOS names of remote NetBIOS hosts?

- How will WINS clients resolve NetBIOS names of non-WINS clients?

These problems can be addressed by using a WINS proxy agent and static WINS database entries.

WINS Proxy Agent

WINS proxy agents solve the problem of NetBIOS name resolution for non-WINS clients. A WINS proxy agent is a machine that is configured to listen for NetBIOS name query requests, which it then forwards to a WINS server.

When a non-WINS-enabled machine, such as a UNIX machine or b-node Windows client, issues a NetBIOS name query request, the WINS proxy agent intercepts the request and forwards it to a WINS server. If the WINS server contains a mapping for the NetBIOS name in question, it will send a positive NetBIOS name query response to the WINS proxy agent, which in turn sends the answer to the machine that issued the broadcast.

WINS Proxy Agent NetBIOS Caching   The WINS proxy agent caches query results. If another machine on the same segment as the WINS proxy agent issues a NetBIOS name query request for the same destination host that another machine within the last ten minutes had broadcast, the WINS proxy agent will be able to answer the query from its NetBIOS remote name cache, rather than having to query a remote WINS server.

You can adjust the timeout period for the NetBIOS remote name cache on the WINS proxy agent if you wish to allow the entries to remain in cache for a longer period of time. This might be of value if you wish to reduce the load on the WINS server and intervening routers. You can configure the CacheTimeout parameter in the Registry.

Figure 7-11 shows the registry key and the value configuration for the Cache Timeout. Note that the timeout period is configured in milliseconds.

WINS Servers Do Not Respond to Broadcasts   WINS servers do not respond to NetBIOS name query request broadcast messages. You should keep this in mind during your design for NetBIOS support for non-WINS clients. This may become an issue when a design includes non-WINS clients on the same segment as a WINS server. Even though the non-WINS client is on the same segment, you will still need to configure a WINS proxy agent on the same segment in order for it to communicate with the WINS server.

exam
⚠️atch

WINS proxy agents are configured by making a changed in the Registry. There is no GUI Interface that allows you to create a WINS proxy agent, but any Windows computers can be configured as one by editing the Registry as follows. To configure a computer as a WINS proxy agent, the value of the EnableProxy *registry entry must be set to 1 (REG_DWORD). This entry is located in the following registry subkey:* HKEY_LOCAL_MACHINE\SYSTEM\CurrentControlSet\Services\Netbt\Parameters

Static Mappings

The most significant and useful feature of WINS is that it is a *dynamic* rather than a *static* database. Unlike an LMHOSTS file that has to be manually updated, WINS clients automatically update their records. This is virtually required in an environment that uses DHCP.

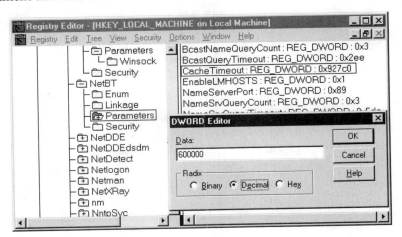

FIGURE 7-11

Configuring the cache timeout for the NetBIOS remote name cache

Non-WINS clients are not able to self-register with a WINS server. In order to solve the problem of NetBIOS name resolution for the names of these non-WINS clients, you can manually create entries in WINS for them. To do this, you must enter a *static mapping* for each non-WINS client into the WINS database, as shown in Figure 7-12.

Static mappings should only be used for non-WINS clients you intend to keep as non-WINS clients. Some administrators may import LMHOSTS files and create static mappings for computers that have the capability to be WINS clients in the future. If you do import LMHOSTS files that contain entries for computers that may become WINS clients in the future, you should enable the *Migrate On* setting at the WINS server. This is done as shown in Figure 7-13.

Issues with Static Mappings   Static WINS entries are not overwritten by dynamic name registrations. If you upgrade non-WINS clients, and then WINS enable them, they will not be able to overwrite the information configured in the static WINS database entry. However, if you enable *Migrate On* at the WINS servers, static entries *will* be overwritten by dynamic name registrations.

This is great when it works. However, there are circumstances when the static entries are not overwritten. One example is the <1Ch> entries in the WINS

FIGURE 7-12

Configuring a static mapping in the WINS database

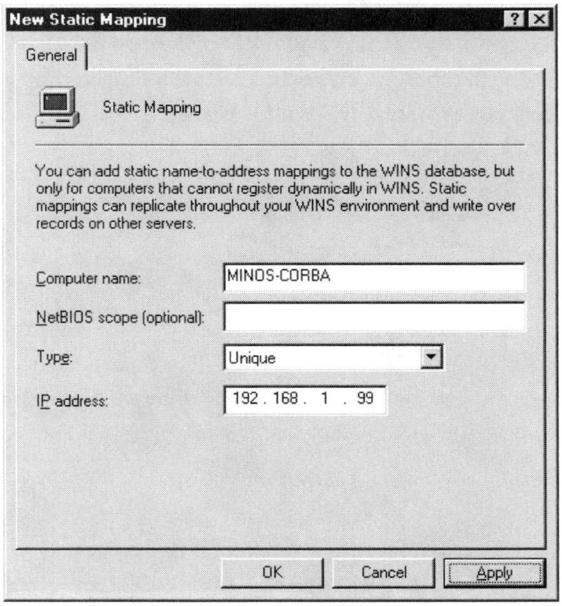

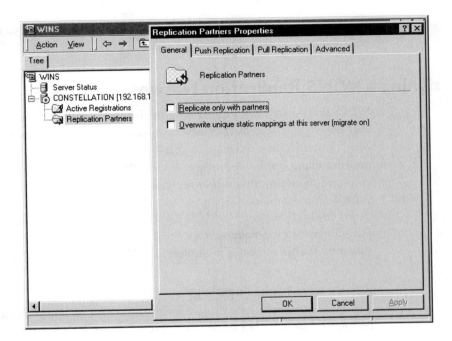

FIGURE 7-13

Enabling Migrate
On at the WINS
server

database. The <1Ch> entry designates a domain controller. This value is used by down level WINS clients to find machines with which they can authenticate. That means if you decide to change the IP address of a domain controller that has a static WINS database entry, even if you have subsequently enabled it as a WINS client, it will not update its IP address with the WINS database. If a WINS client queries the WINS database for a domain controller and finds that static entry and attempts to authenticate against the static entry no longer exist, bad things will happen.

Replicating Static Mappings   Static WINS database entries can cause more problems when they are replicated. When a static record is replicated, its status as a static record is replicated with it. This means that you must manually delete the record at *all* WINS servers in order to prevent it from being re-replicated back to a machine from which it had been deleted. So, if a machine that had been upgraded to be a WINS client creates its own dynamic entry at the WINS server, the static entry will overwrite the dynamic entry. Once overwritten as a static entry, the machine is no longer able to dynamically register its IP address.

Designing a WINS Replication Network

WINS servers are responsible for maintaining a distributed database. Although you may maintain several WINS servers on your network, all those servers must have the same entries in their database so that NetBIOS queries to any one of them, from any network client on the network, will yield the same result. In order to achieve this, you need to configure a WINS replication network that optimizes the consistency of your WINS database.

To ensure that your NetBIOS name resolution solution functions efficiently, a WINS network topology needs to be defined any time your design contains more than two WINS servers. The preferred WINS topology is the *Spoke and Hub* model.

Spoke and Hub Topology

The Hub and Spoke model includes a central *Hub* WINS server and several peripheral *Spoke* WINS servers. The Hub collects WINS database information from all Spoke WINS servers. After collecting the information from all the Spoke servers, the Hub then redistributes the collated information back to the Spoke servers.

A multi-site organization requires a design that includes a replication network for WINS servers contained within each geographic site separated by WAN Links. Each site should have a central Hub WINS server. After the intra-site replication scheme is designed, an inter-site replication network must be designed.

Intra-site replication should be based on the Hub and Spoke model. A single WINS server at each site is selected as a Hub WINS server. All other WINS servers are Spoke servers, and they are configured to be both push and pull partners of the Hub WINS server. By employing the Hub and Spoke Model you can simplify the replication partnerships, and be assured that all WINS servers will receive updates to changes in each WINS server's database.

Planning Replication Parameters

Configure WINS servers with both push and pull parameters when separated by fast LAN connections. When WINS servers are separated by relatively slow WAN links, you should design just pull parameters for the WINS replication partners.

Hub and Spoke Design Examples   For example, imagine that your company consists of 7500 computers distributed among three geographically separated sites. The main headquarters is located in Dallas where there are 3500 machines. There are also regional offices in Los Angeles and Portland. Each regional office has 2000 computers. All computers on the network are WINS clients.

At this time in your network plan, the company has not yet decided if all sites will be connected to each other via a WAN or if the regional offices will be connected just to the Dallas site, and not be connected to each other. Because there are different network architectures being considered, you should design alternative replication schemes to account for both possibilities.

Scenario 1—All Sites Linked Only to Central Office

First, consider how the WINS replication network might be designed if the sites are connected to Dallas only. In this case, you should design a single WINS server at each site to be a Hub WINS server for the site. All other WINS servers at each site should be designed as Spoke WINS servers to the site's central Hub. This configuration assures full replication of WINS database entries among all WINS servers within each site and ensures WINS database consistency for all machines within the site.

After designing the intra-site scheme, you should turn your attention to inter-site replication. Since the regional sites are both connected to Dallas, and not to each other, you should design Dallas as the central system-wide Hub. The remote sites are configured as pull partners so that you can configure the time and interval for replication. Pull replication settings give you more control over the impact replication might have on WAN link performance.

The design allows all changes to be pooled at the Dallas WINS server. The pooled information collected at the Dallas Hub is then redistributed to the site Hubs. The site Hubs are then able to replicate the complete database information back to the intra-site WINS servers.

This design is shown in Figure 7-14.

The major drawback of using a single central Hub server for synchronizing all the Hubs across the WAN is that there is a single point of failure. If the Dallas server becomes unavailable, no WINS database replication takes place across the WAN until it comes back online. This can have a major impact in destabilizing the WINS synchronization scheme; in order to bring all the WINS servers back into equilibrium, we have to take into account not only the time to bring the downed WINS back online, but also the convergence time for all the sites. We'll talk about convergence time later in this chapter.

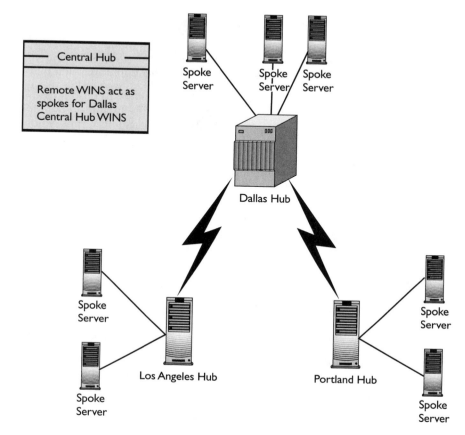

FIGURE 7-14

Hub servers replicating with a central server

Central Hub

Remote WINS act as spokes for Dallas Central Hub WINS

Scenario 2—All Sites Linked to Each Other

A second design can be considered when all the sites are connected to each other. Intra-site replication is configured in the same way as in the previous example. This design is shown in Figure 7-15.

Because all sites are connected to each other, we can configure the Hub servers at each site in a *Ring*, where each adjacent member in the Ring is configured as a pull partner. This design avoids a single point of failure. Also, in this three-site scenario, convergence of the WINS database takes place more quickly.

on the job

Although the Ring replication scheme may appear compelling because you obviate a single point of failure, there is a greater risk of database inconsistency when partners receive copies of replicated records from multiple partners. There is a trade-off between fault-tolerance and database integrity.

FIGURE 7-15

Each site hub replicates with adjacent hubs

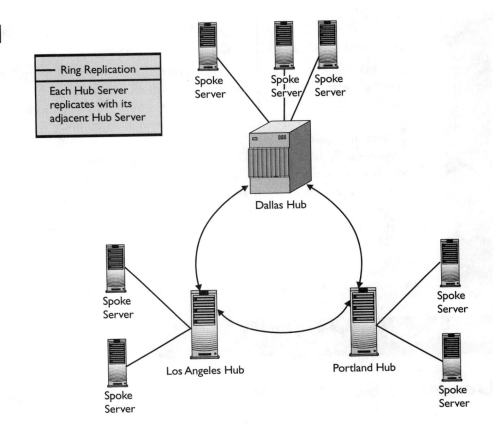

Ring Replication

Each Hub Server replicates with its adjacent Hub Server

Spoke Server

Spoke Server

Spoke Server

Dallas Hub

Spoke Server

Spoke Server

Los Angeles Hub

Portland Hub

Spoke Server

Spoke Server

SCENARIO & SOLUTION

What should I use, a Ring or a Hub and Spoke arrangement?	For most installations, the Hub and Spoke model works best and leads to fewer WINS database inconsistencies. To maximize this type of configuration, you should make sure that your inter-site hub is highly fault tolerant and available.
When should I use static entries?	The only time you should seriously consider using static entries is for servers that host non-Microsoft operating systems. You must also confirm that there is little or no chance that such servers will ever be upgraded to WINS clients.

EXERCISE 7-3

Supporting Non-WINS Clients

Your network contains several UNIX servers that host NetBIOS applications that must be accessed from Microsoft client computers. In addition, you have several engineers that run UNIX workstations that must be capable of accessing NetBIOS resources on several of the application servers on the network.

What technologies or methods would you use to resolve this?

Answer: To allow the UNIX workstations to access NetBIOS resources on remote subnets, you can use a WINS proxy agent to forward the UNIX workstations NetBIOS name resolution query broadcast messages. The WINS proxy agent will forward the requests to a WINS server for name resolution.

In order for the Microsoft client computers to access the NetBIOS resources on the UNIX computers on remote subnets, you can add static WINS database entries for those UNIX machines.

CERTIFICATION OBJECTIVE 7.04

Designing Security for WINS Communications

When planning a WINS network that spans WAN links, you will need to consider whether you should secure WINS-related traffic over the link. If your WINS replication network is entirely contained within the private LAN environment, there is little reason to incur the overhead of securing the communication, since all machines on the network have access to the WINS database in the normal course of NetBIOS name resolution.

Securing WINS Internet Traffic

If you do plan a WINS replication network that spans WAN links, you should consider securing the data if it is to be transferred over a public network, such as the

Internet. If your WAN links are dedicated lines, you may not wish to incur the overhead of adding security to the replication process. The design decision will depend on the level of security you require.

Businesses that use a public transit internetwork such as the Internet will use tunnels to secure data transfers. Tunneling technology accomplishes several things:

- Data is encrypted as it is passed through the tunnel
- Support for LAN protocols other than TCP/IP within the tunnel
- Authentication of tunnel endpoints

Each of these features contributes to your security solution.

Data Encryption Within the Tunnel

When you create a Virtual Private Network (VPN) tunnel, the goal is typically to allow for protected, encrypted information to move across a public network in a secure fashion. Note that when you create a tunnel, you do *not* have to encrypt the information moving inside the tunnel, but that is where the tunneling protocol finds its best application.

Windows 2000 provides two methods of tunneling that you can use to secure data as it crosses the Internet:

- PPTP with MPPE encryption
- L2TP/IPSec

When encrypting data inside a PPTP tunnel, the actual encryption of the data is done with Microsoft Point-to-Point Encryption protocol (MPPE). A PPTP tunnel can be created between two VPN servers that act as gateways between the internal network and the Internet.

The Layer 2 Tunneling protocol is a new tunneling method introduced with Windows 2000. Encryption of data inside the L2TP tunnel is accomplished via the IP Security Protocol, or IPSec. IPSec uses more sophisticated, stronger methods of encryption and authentication than MPPE, and is the preferred method of moving private data across a public network.

exam
ⓦatch

Although L2TP/IPSec is the preferred method of securing data traversing a public internetwork, there are some limitations. You cannot secure data end to end if you are using NAT on your internal network. If you are using NAT for your internal network clients, IPSec will not protect the data as it moves through the internal network, only as it moves from tunnel endpoint to tunnel endpoint. If you require end-to-end protection, you will need to encrypt the data by other methods.

If you are not using VPN tunnels and the WINS servers on the internal network use public IP addresses, you can configure the servers to communicate with each other directly, without having the data move through a tunneled connection. The replicated information would be secured via IPSec with specific IPSec policy parameters set to allow the safety of the data as it crosses the Internet.

CertCam 7-4

EXERCISE 7-4

Securing WINS Replication Traffic

Your organization has large offices in two locations: Seattle and Las Vegas. In the past, these two offices were self-sustaining and did not share a network connection. However, you have been called in to create a link between these networks using the most effective means at your disposal. One of your many goals is to create security for your WINS replication traffic. What can you do to ensure that your WINS replication and query traffic is secure?

Answer: Since you need to create a cost-effective solution, a virtual private network connecting the sites is the best solution. Because the data contained within a VPN is encrypted, you do not need to worry about Internet users accessing either NetBIOS name queries or WINS replication events. You can use either PPTP/MPPE or L2TP/IPSec to create the tunnel and perform the encryption of the data within the tunnel.

CERTIFICATION OBJECTIVE 7.05

Designing a Fault-Tolerant WINS Network

If your network uses mission-critical NetBIOS applications, then you must design fault tolerance and availability into your NetBIOS name resolution solution. We have discussed the most important aspect of fault tolerance for WINS networks: database replication. Since each WINS server ideally contains the complete WINS database, the database is considered fault tolerant. By configuring WINS clients to use Secondary WINS servers, they are able to automatically bypass a downed server and resolve a NetBIOS name by querying a Secondary.

However, while WINS clients consider all WINS servers equal, some are more equal than others. For example, if you are deploying a WINS network, some of the servers may require a higher level of fault tolerance than others. Typically, you will want your intra-site Hubs and your inter-site Hub to be highly fault tolerant in order to maintain maximum consistency of the WINS database.

Windows 2000 High Availability WINS Solutions

Windows 2000 Advanced Server and Datacenter Server include the Windows Clustering Service. The Windows Clustering Service provides a high level of fault tolerance and real-time fail over for your WINS servers.

A cluster contains two computers that, in addition to their connection to the production network, are also connected to each other, and only to each other, via a second, separate, high-speed (typically Ethernet) link. This can be best implemented by using a crossover cable to connect the network interface cards of the two servers directly to each other. This connection exists on a separate network. The WINS servers both have external connections to the network-at-large that allow WINS clients and WINS replication partners to communicate with them. The cluster shares an external hard disk that can be accessed by both computers.

The cluster is accessed via a single *cluster IP address*. When one member of the cluster is unavailable, WINS clients and replication partners access the WINS server that is still online. In this way, even if a single machine becomes totally disabled, the WINS server is still available.

Figure 7-16 shows how a cluster might be configured.

on the **Job**

Keep in mind that the Cluster provides fault tolerance for a single WINS server, even though there are multiple servers participating in the cluster. Clustering can be an expensive proposition, so you should design clusters into the plan for only those WINS servers that provide the most mission-critical services, such as the inter-site WINS Hub.

FIGURE 7-16

A clustered
WINS server

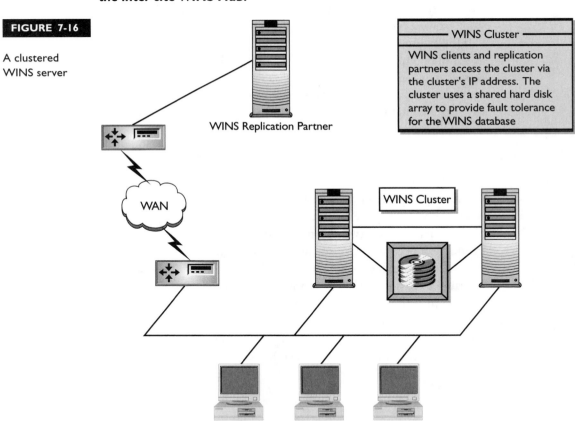

WINS Cluster

WINS clients and replication partners access the cluster via the cluster's IP address. The cluster uses a shared hard disk array to provide fault tolerance for the WINS database

WINS Replication Partner

WAN

WINS Cluster

WINS Clients

Tuning a WINS Network

Your primary goal in tuning your Windows 2000 WINS network is to improve the response time for WINS clients seeking to resolve NetBIOS names. You can break down the problem by approaching it from two directions:

- Improve the responsiveness of the server running WINS
- Improve the WINS network design

By focusing your tuning efforts on these two factors, you can improve the overall NetBIOS name resolution responsiveness for the entire network.

Improving Server Performance

To improve the server's response to NetBIOS requests, you need to address issues related to the machine's hardware and interface with the network. Some things that will help include:

- **Add processors to the server.** WINS is able to take advantage of a multiprocessor system and adding processors can result in up to a 20 percent improvement in performance.

- **Increase the amount of memory on the server.** Adding RAM to a server always helps performance of server services. Additional RAM can help circumvent the number of calls made to the page file during periods of system stress.

- **Improve the disk subsystem.** If you are using IDE drives, upgrade them to SCSI drives. If you are using simple volumes to house the WINS server and WINS database, move them to a striped array.

■ **Improve the network infrastructure.** If you are running an Ethernet 10 Mbps network, upgrade the WINS server, WINS clients, and transit devices to Ethernet 10/100. This may entail the purchase of new NICs, and perhaps, other network devices.

Improving the WINS Network Design

Improving the WINS network design is something that you can do before problems arise during the implementation phase. Some overarching issues you should keep in mind during the design process are:

■ **Load balance the WINS client assignments.** Don't assign all the WINS clients to the same WINS server. If you have two WINS servers that are of equal network cost from a group of WINS clients, assign half of them to the first server as their primary WINS server and assign the other half to the second as their primary WINS server. Load balancing in this way prevents a single WINS server from becoming overwhelmed by name registration and name resolution requests.

■ **Avoid allowing queries and registrations to cross a WAN.** Always design at least one WINS server on each end of a WAN link. Most WAN links lack the bandwidth to support the amount of traffic that can be generated during peak WINS interaction times and still provide bandwidth for other network services.

■ **Strategically place DNS servers on the same segment as WINS servers.** If your DNS servers will be performing WINS referrals, you should place those servers on the same segment as the WINS servers they refer to. This avoids network performance hits and decreased responsiveness that would ensue from congested routers or WAN links.

Optimizing WINS Convergence

When designing a WINS network that is highly reliable and available, you must create a replication scheme, which we talked about earlier in the chapter. When creating a replication scheme, you must consider the important matter of *convergence time.* Convergence time represents the total time it would take for a changed WINS record to be replicated to all the WINS servers on the network.

Convergence Time: Scenario 1

Consider the scenarios we were working with earlier. In the first scenario, all site hubs were connected to the central Dallas hub but were not connected to each other. If the intra-site pull interval is five minutes, and the inter-site pull interval is 15 minutes, what is the maximum time required to get an updated WINS record from a spoke WINS server in Portland to a spoke WINS server in Los Angeles?

The answer is 40 minutes. It would take five minutes to get the changed record from a spoke server in Portland to the port hub. Then it would take up to 15 minutes to get the record from the Portland hub to the Dallas hub. Then another 15 minutes could pass to get the record from the Dallas hub to the Los Angeles hub, and finally another five minutes to replicate the record from the Dallas hub to the Dallas spoke. The WINS intersite "hop count" was two: one hop to the Dallas hub, and a second hop from the Dallas to the Los Angeles hub.

Convergence Time: Scenario 2

What is the convergence time in the second scenario? All site hubs are only one *hop* away from any other site hub. For a changed WINS record to get to Los Angeles, it would take five minutes for the Portland spoke to get the information to the Portland hub, then 15 minutes for the Portland hub to the Los Angeles hub, and then five minutes from the Los Angeles hub to the Los Angeles spoke, for a total of 25 minutes. It would appear that the Ring model is more efficient, as well as being fault tolerant.

Convergence Time and Hop Count

The speed of convergence is related to the number of inter-site hops (assuming all intra-site hops are always equal to one and the pull interval is the same for all intra-site servers). A ring of 4 inter-site hubs would have a maximum hop count of two and a maximum convergence time of 40 minutes, as shown in Figure 7-17. The same would be true of a 5-node inter-site setup. So, the Ring replication model appears to be equal, or superior to the hub model for networks of up to five sites.

FIGURE 7-17 A four-node Ring has a maximum intersite hop count of two

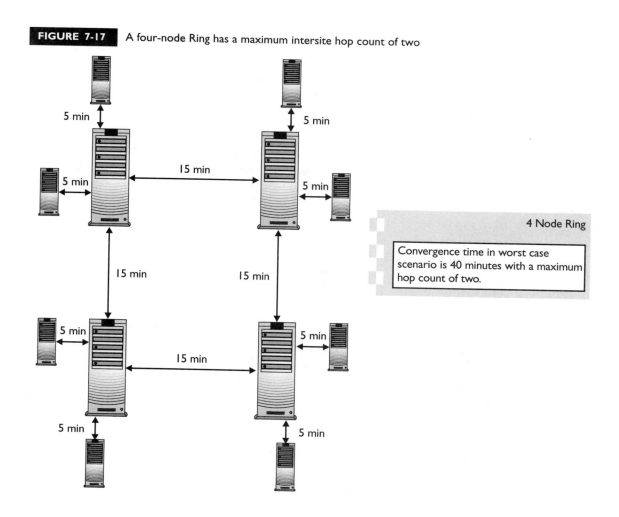

4 Node Ring

Convergence time in worst case scenario is 40 minutes with a maximum hop count of two.

What happens when there are five inter-site hubs and then one becomes unavailable? The maximum hop count is no longer two. It is now three, as shown in Figure 7-18.

The convergence time in the five inter-site hub model with one downed site is now 50 minutes and requires three hops! In the example in Figure 7-18, the convergence time is now 50 minutes.

FIGURE 7-18 A five-node Ring with one downed site has a maximum hop count of three

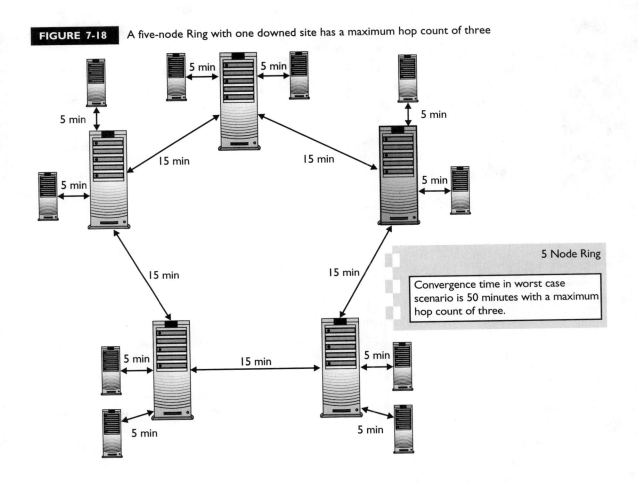

5 Node Ring

Convergence time in worst case scenario is 50 minutes with a maximum hop count of three.

From these examples it is clear that the more inter-site hubs that are included in the WINS network, the less effective the Ring model becomes, ensuring a reasonable convergence time. The drawback of the central inter-site hub concept is that if the central inter-site hub fails, or the link to the hub fails, no useful replication can take place. However, if you take measures to make the inter-site hub highly fault tolerant and available, it typically is your best solution.

CertCam 7-5

EXERCISE 7-5

Improving WINS Performance

During a performance monitoring session, you notice that the WINS server is dropping a good number of name queries and registrations during peak hours. What are some things you can do to improve WINS server performance and reduce the number of dropped events?

Answer: To improve server performance and reduce the number of dropped requests, you could increase the number of processors, add more RAM, change the disk subsystem to a SCSI array, and use a faster volume type, such as one of the stripe sets. You might also consider using hardware RAID rather than software RAID to improve performance.

CERTIFICATION SUMMARY

In this chapter, we reviewed important concepts involved with designing a WINS network and NetBIOS name resolution scheme. We continued with a review of NetBIOS name resolution and how they are resolved on single and multiple segment networks.

After a review of NetBIOS name resolution in general, you learned about how the Windows 2000 WINS server resolves NetBIOS names and the major elements of a Windows 2000 WINS network. Client/server issues and WINS interoperability were also discussed.

You learned some of the considerations you make in integrating WINS into your network design plan. Factors to consider included the NetBIOS node type, WINS server and client features, and WINS replication networks. WINS replication networks are the heart of a solid WINS design, and you saw a few examples of how to construct a WINS replication scheme.

The WINS database should be secured when it crosses public internetworks such as the Internet. We covered some ways you could secure WINS query and WINS replication by using either IPSec or tunnels using L2TP/IPSec or PPTP/MPPE.

Finally, you learned about important issues related to creating a fault tolerant and highly available WINS server solution. Microsoft Cluster Server provides real-time fail over capability to a single WINS installation, while a WINS network provides another way to add fault tolerance and availability to your NetBIOS name resolution scheme.

TWO-MINUTE DRILL

Overview of NetBIOS Name Resolution

❑ NetBIOS is a session layer interface that allows NetBIOS applications to communicate over a TCP/IP network.

❑ NetBIOS broadcast messages do not typically cross router interfaces.

❑ Microsoft network clients can resolve NetBIOS names to IP addresses by using a number of different methods. The method and the order of execution is determined by the NetBIOS client's node-type.

Overview of WINS

❑ WINS is a NetBIOS name server used exclusively on Microsoft networks.

❑ WINS is a client server application, where the network client must be configured to query a WINS server for NetBIOS name resolution.

❑ WINS uses a distributed database that allows WINS servers spread throughout the network to contain the same database entries.

❑ WINS client/server traffic consists primarily of NetBIOS name registrations, NetBIOS name queries, NetBIOS name releases, and NetBIOS name renewals.

Integrating WINS into a Network Design Plan

❑ NetBIOS clients on a single-segment network can be configured as WINS clients or use broadcasts to resolve NetBIOS names.

❑ Minimize the number of WINS servers on the network to reduce the chances of WINS replication errors.

❑ Do not use excessive Secondary WINS servers on WINS clients. This prevents excessive delays in NetBIOS name resolution when WINS servers cannot be contacted.

❑ A WINS proxy agent allows non-WINS clients to resolve NetBIOS names by querying a WINS server for a non-WINS client.

❑ Use static WINS database entries for non-WINS clients when those non-WINS clients share NetBIOS resources.

❏ Design a WINS replication network using the Hub and Spoke model to allow for the most reliable WINS database replication scheme.

Designing Security for WINS Communications

❏ WINS replication and name resolution traffic that crosses public networks should be secured to protect the internal network namespace from intrusion.

❏ If your internal WINS servers use public IP addresses, you can use IPSec to secure data communications between the servers.

❏ If you use private IP addresses for your WINS servers and clients, you can use L2TP/IPSec or PPTP/MPPE tunnels to secure your data.

Designing Fault-Tolerant WINS Networks

❏ WINS database replication provides a measure of fault tolerance for the WINS database when network clients are configured to use multiple WINS servers for NetBIOS name resolution.

❏ Microsoft Cluster Server provides a way to provide real-time fail over for WINS servers.

Tuning a WINS Network

❏ You can improve WINS server response by upgrading hardware components, including the disk subsystem, memory, and the network interface.

❏ You can also improve NetBIOS name resolution response times by improving the WINS network design architecture.

SELF TEST

The following questions will help you measure your understanding of the material presented in this chapter. Read all of the choices carefully, as there may be more than one correct answer. Choose all correct answers for each question.

Overview of NetBIOS Name Resolution

1. Which of the following are the greatest challenges to NetBIOS transport protocols on an enterprise network? Choose all that apply.

   A. NetBIOS transport protocols are not routable.

   B. NetBIOS transport protocols are broadcast-based.

   C. You cannot share resources on a NetBIOS network.

   D. You cannot run multiple-transport protocols on the same computer that has a NetBIOS transport protocol installed.

2. Your network runs many NetBIOS applications created by Microsoft. The transport protocol used on the network is TCP/IP. There are 20 segments on your network. What NetBIOS name resolution method should you use to most effectively provide NetBIOS name resolution for all computers on the network?

   A. LMHOSTS Files

   B. HOSTS Files

   C. DNS servers

   D. WINS servers

3. Most of the machines on your network are Windows 2000 professional or server machines. You have heavily invested in designing and implementing a DNS infrastructure for your organization. However, you still maintain a handful of Windows NT 4.0 servers that provide for file and printer services. How can you provide reliable name resolution for these downlevel clients without having to enter them manually into your DNS database?

   A. Allow the Windows NT 4.0 machines to automatically update records in the zone database files by using special LMHOSTS tags.

   B. Configure a WINS server to update the names of the Windows NT 4.0 machines in the DNS database.

   C. Configure the DNS server to provide for WINS referral.

   D. Create a dedicated WINS referral zone.

Overview of WINS

4. What characterizes the WINS network convergence time?

A. The longest time it takes for a newly registered WINS record to be replicated to all WINS servers.

B. The shortest time it takes for a newly registered WINS record to be replicated to all WINS servers.

C. The time it takes for a Secondary WINS server to replicate a record to a Primary WINS server.

D. The amount of time it takes for the WINS client to complete a new NetBIOS name registration.

5. You run a moderate-sized network that contains four segments and about 750 WINS client computers. Each segment is on its own side of a WAN link, where the sites are connected to each other via 768 Kbps DSL VPN connections. You would like to not have to come up with a detailed replication network plan until you have more time to think about it. What steps should you take to most easily configure WINS partnerships in the interim? Choose all that apply.

A. Manually configure push/pull replication partnerships between all of the WINS servers on the network.

B. Configure all WINS servers to be pull partners of each other.

C. Configure the Windows 2000 RRAS service to allow IGMP forwarding.

D. Configure the WINS server to perform autodiscovery of WINS partners.

6. You use WINS for NetBIOS name registration and resolution for your network. You also assign IP addresses to WINS clients using DHCP. You would like the WINS clients who receive the IP addresses from the DHCP server to automatically register their IP addressing information with their WINS server. How do you accomplish this?

A. Configure the DHCP server with the IP address of the WINS server on which it will register the IP addresses.

B. Configure the WINS server with the IP addresses of the DCHP server so that it can send a pull request to the DHCP server for NetBIOS name registration information.

C. Configure the DNS server to perform WINS referrals and then have the referral information sent to the DHCP server.

D. No configuration is required, as the DHCP client will automatically register its NetBIOS name in the WINS database.

Integrating WINS into a Network Design Plan

7. Which of the following node types could you effectively use on a multi-segmented enterprise network? Choose all that apply.

   A. b-node

   B. p-node

   C. m-node

   D. h-node

8. WINS clients support how many Secondary WINS servers?

   A. 1

   B. 3

   C. 9

   D. 12

9. You are the administrator of a company that has multiple subnets. On your network are multiple UNIX servers that host NetBIOS resources and require that they are able to contact other computers that host NetBIOS resources in a distributed computing environment. What can you implement to support the UNIX machines in their attempt to resolve NetBIOS names for computers located throughout the network ? Choose all that apply.

   A. DHCP server

   B. DNS server

   C. WINS proxy agent

   D. RRAS server

10. Your network is relatively stable and IP addresses change infrequently. Your DHCP server is configured to hand out leases of 60 days for machines that are file and print servers. What should you do to reduce the load placed by UNIX machines on a WINS server and still allow NetBIOS Name resolution for those non-WINS clients?

    A. Add several WINS proxy agents to the segments that contain UNIX machines.

    B. Open the NetBIOS ports on the network routers.

    C. Delete the LMHOSTS file on the WINS server.

    D. Increase the cache timeout value on the WINS proxy agent.

11. What can you do at the WINS server that will allow WINS clients to query the WINS server for non-WINS client IP address mappings?

    A. Create a static entry.

    B. Create a dynamic entry.

    C. Create a push entry.

    D. Enable Migrate On.

Designing Security for WINS Communications

12. What technologies can you use to protect your WINS database information during replication over the Internet? Choose all that apply.

    A. IPSec

    B. L2TP/IPSec

    C. PPTP/MPPE

    D. ISAKMP/Oakley

13. You wish to secure your internal network communications so that intruders that find their way into the company are not able to "sniff" NetBIOS name information on the network. Which technology can you use to encrypt NetBIOS traffic information as it traverses the internal network?

    A. PPTP/MPPE

    B. L2TP

    C. PGP

    D. IPSec

Designing a Fault-Tolerant WINS Network

14. Your organization encompasses ten sites within the continental United States. You have decided to use the Hub and Spoke model for your WINS network design. What single measure ensures that there is no system-wide failure of WINS database replication?

A. Use the cluster server software that comes with Windows 2000 Advanced server to create clusters of the spoke servers on each network.

B. Use the cluster server service on each intra-site hub.

C. Use the cluster server service on the inter-site hub.

D. Use high-speed links between all sites.

15. Your company does not have the resources to pay for a cluster server solution. What else could you do to ensure fault tolerance for your WINS server? Choose all that apply.

A. Buy a server with redundant power supplies.

B. Mirror the disk with the WINS server service and WINS database.

C. Deploy a network interface fail over solution that allows a second network interface card to take over for a failed card.

D. Plug the server into a UPS device.

Tuning a WINS Network

16. You have been receiving complaints from users about sluggish network performance. You run a network monitor trace and you don't find any evidence of bandwidth saturation. You run performance monitor and find that the WINS inter-site hub is having trouble keeping up with WINS registrations and NetBIOS requests. What could you do to improve the performance of the WINS server?

A. Add more processors.

B. Add more RAM.

C. Place the WINS database on a spanned volume.

D. Use IDE rather than SCSI Disks.

17. You are designing a WINS solution for a company that is situated in three geographic locations separated by 128 Kbps WAN links. Each site has three WINS servers. What type of replication topologies should you use to optimize NetBIOS name resolution for your geographically distributed network?

A. Ring

B. Hub and Spoke

C. Directory Replicator Service

D. XCOPY32 scripts to distribute the WINS database files

LAB QUESTION

You have been called to solve a problem with your WINS replication network. Your network spans several subnets and contains a variety of host operating systems, including Win3.x, Win9x, Windows NT 4.0, Windows 2000, and UNIX. All the host systems either share or access NetBIOS resources on other machines on the network. The UNIX computers included in the WINS databases are static records and they use WINS proxy agents to access information in the WINS database. All the machines on the network use DHCP, except the UNIX hosts, which have static IP addresses to support their static record assignment in WINS.

The NetBIOS applications that run on the UNIX machines now have Windows 2000 counterparts, and you want to upgrade those machines. The upgrade process goes smoothly, and the applications install without any serious events. You disable all the WINS proxy agents on the network to reduce the load on the WINS servers, and you have configured the former UNIX machines to be WINS and DHCP clients.

Later in the day, you start receiving calls from users telling you that they cannot access any NetBIOS resources on the machines that have been upgraded. When investigating the problem, you observe what is shown in Figures 7-19 through 7-22.

FIGURE 7-19

From the WINS
console I

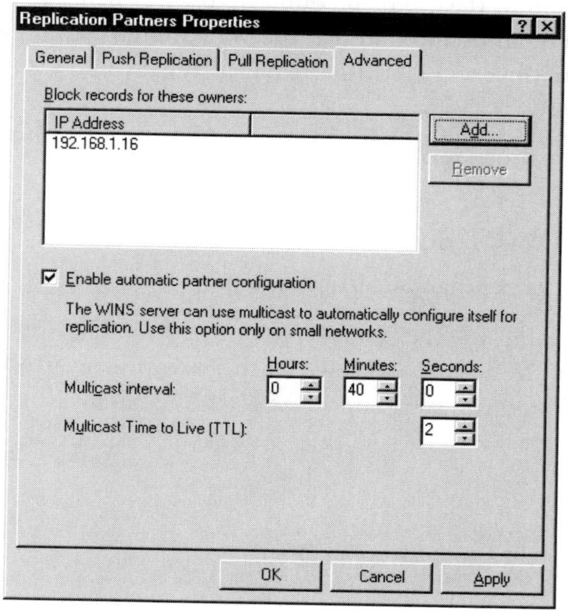

FIGURE 7-20

From the WINS
console 2

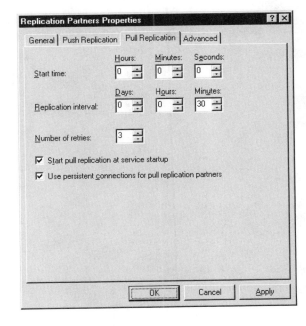

FIGURE 7-21

From the WINS
console 3

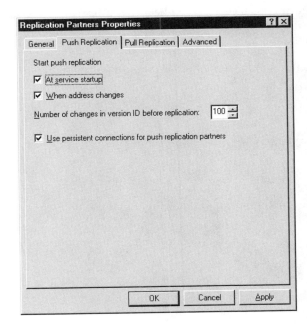

From the WINS
console 4

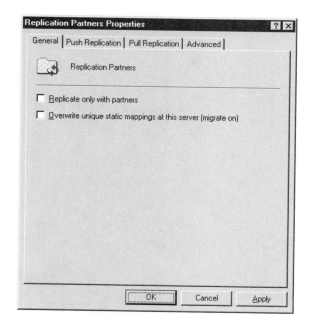

Given this information, what do you believe is causing the difficulty with connectivity to these devices?

SELF TEST ANSWERS

Overview of NetBIOS Name Resolution

1. ☑ **A, B.** NetBIOS headers do not support routing of NetBIOS transport protocols. NetBIOS transports are broadcast based, and enterprise networks are defined as spanning multiple physical segments separated by routers.

   ☒ **C** is incorrect because you can share resources when using a NetBIOS transport protocol. **D** is incorrect because when you use NDIS 3.0 or above you can bind multiple protocols to a single adapter. This includes any combination of protocols, even NetBIOS protocols.

2. ☑ **D.** WINS servers. WINS is designed to answer NetBIOS name resolution requests for large internetworks.

   ☒ **A** is incorrect because LMHOSTS files must be manually updated. On a large internetwork it becomes virtually impossible to update and keep current an LMHOSTS files and then distribute it to every computer on the network in a reliable manner. LMHOSTS files allow you to resolve remote NetBIOS names. **B** is incorrect because HOSTS files suffer from the same limitation as LMHOSTS files and must be manually updated. Also, if the NetBIOS name and host naming scheme are different, the hosts files may not be able to resolve NetBIOS names correctly. **C** is incorrect because DNS servers resolve host names and not NetBIOS names. (DNS servers can resolve NetBIOS names only if the NetBIOS and host naming schemes are the same, and the name of the destination client is the same as one contained in the zone for which a query is being sent. DNS servers can also query WINS server via WINS referrals.)

3. ☑ **C, D.** A DNS server can be configured to perform WINS referrals. It will make a WINS referral if it does not contain the name included in a host name query. **D** is correct because you should create a dedicated WINS referral zone on your DNS server that contains no host records, and disable WINS referrals for all other zones. All names returned from the WINS referral zone will have the FQDN indicating that it was resolved via WINS referral.

   ☒ **A** is incorrect because there are no tags that you can insert into an LMHOSTS file that will allow a Windows NT 4.0 machine to register itself in the DNS zone database. **B** is incorrect because a WINS server cannot be configured to query a DNS server.

Overview of WINS

4. ☑ **A.** Convergence time is the amount of time it takes for a newly registered WINS client record to be replicated from the owner of the record to the WINS server furthest away in the WINS replication scheme.

   ☒ **B** is incorrect because it is the longest time, not the shortest time that characterizes the convergence time. **C** is incorrect because in a WINS replication network, the servers are not characterized as Primary or Secondary. Those concepts are reserved for WINS client configurations. **D** is incorrect because the amount of time it takes for a WINS client to register its NetBIOS name with a WINS server is a reflection of response latency, and not a convergence issue.

5. ☑ **C, D.** WINS Partner Autodiscovery uses IGMP messages, and the routers must support forwarding of IGMP messages in order for WINS partners to find each other. **D** is correct because this is the easiest way to configure WINS partnerships when you lack the time or inclination to configure a detailed WINS replication scheme.

   ☒ **A** is incorrect because it is not the easiest way to configure the replication partnerships. **B** is incorrect because it is not the easiest way to configure the replication partnerships.

6. ☑ **D.** No configuration is required, as the DHCP client will automatically register its NetBIOS name in the WINS database. You do not need to make any special configurations in order for WINS clients that are also DHCP clients to register their IP addressing information with a WINS server. It happens automatically after the WINS client obtains an IP address from the DHCP server.

   ☒ **A** is incorrect because there is no way for you to configure a DHCP server with an IP address of a WINS server. DCHP and WINS servers do not directly communicate with one another. **B** is incorrect because WINS and DHCP servers do not communicate with each other, so a WINS server cannot issue a pull request to a DHCP server. **C** is incorrect because a DNS server will not send NetBIOS registration information to a WINS server.

Integrating WINS into a Network Design Plan

7. ☑ **B, C, D.** P-node clients will use WINS server at the expense of their ability to broadcast for resolving NetBIOS names. **C** is correct because an m-node client can query a WINS server for address resolution of remote NetBIOS hosts, but broadcasts first before querying a WINS server. **D** is correct because h-node clients can query a WINS server before broadcasting, and is typically the preferred node type for enterprise hosts.

   ☒ **A** is incorrect because b-node clients are limited to using broadcasts and LMHOSTS files as their NetBIOS-specific name resolution methods. Broadcasts are limited to the local segment, while LMHOSTS files are too unwieldy to manage in a large environment.

8. ☑ **D.** Windows 2000 WINS clients support up to 12 secondary WINS servers. However, you should be careful when configuring multiple Secondary WINS servers for WINS clients. In certain circumstances, multiple Secondaries can significantly increase the NetBIOS name resolution time.

   ☒ **A, B,** and **C** are incorrect because Windows 2000 WINS clients support up to 12 secondary WINS servers.

9. ☑ **B, C.** DNS server and WINS proxy agent. You can enable a DNS server to perform WINS referrals. The DNS server will query the WINS server and then forward the WINS server's reply to the UNIX client. **C** is correct because a WINS proxy agent can forward NetBIOS name resolution broadcasts to a WINS server and then forward the answer to the UNIX host.

   ☒ **A** is incorrect because a DHCP server does not help computers of any kind resolve NetBIOS names to IP addresses. **D** is incorrect because a RRAS server will not aid a UNIX host on the network in resolving NetBIOS names to IP addresses.

10. ☑ **D.** Increasing the cache timeout value will allow cached entries to stay in the NetBIOS remote name cache on the WINS proxy agent. Because the entries stay in cache longer, the WINS proxy agent does not need to query the WINS server as often.

    ☒ **A** is incorrect because adding more WINS proxy agents to the segment will actually *increase* the load on the WINS server. Each WINS proxy agent will forward the broadcast to the WINS server, increasing the amount of traffic by the number of WINS proxy servers added to the segment. **B** is incorrect because opening the NetBIOS ports will have no effect on reducing the load on the WINS server. **C** is incorrect because deleting the LMHOSTS file will have no effect on the UNIX server's requests for NetBIOS name resolution.

11. ☑ **A.** You can create static entries in the WINS database for non-WINS clients. WINS clients will be able to query the WINS server to resolve the NetBIOS name of the non-WINS clients.

    ☒ **B** is incorrect because you don't create dynamic entries. **C** is incorrect because you cannot create a push entry. **D** is incorrect because Migrate On only allows previously created static entries to be overwritten with dynamic registrations. It does not create new entries.

Designing Security for WINS Communications

12. ☑ **A, B, C.** IPSec, L2TP/IPSec, and PPTP/MPPE. You can use IPSec to secure information end to end. You do not need a tunnel to secure data using IPSec. **B** is correct because you can use IPSec in tunnel mode, using L2TP to create the tunnel to secure the data. **C** is correct because PPTP/MPPE will also secure your data.

    ☒ **D** is incorrect because the Internet Security Association-Key Management Protocol

(ISAKMP) and the Oakley protocols are part of the Internet Key Exchange (IKE). They do not represent a specific technology that you can use to secure data in and of themselves, but are used as part of IPSec.

13. ☑ **D.** IPSec can be used in Transport Mode to secure data as it moves from computer to computer on the internal network.

☒ **A** is incorrect because PPTP/MPPE is used to create tunnels. While you can create tunnels on the internal network, it would be unwieldy and unnecessary for every computer on the network to communicate via a tunneled connection. **B** is incorrect because L2TP does not provide encryption, just tunneling. **C** is incorrect because PGP cannot be used to encrypt all NetBIOS information as it traverses the network.

Designing a Fault-Tolerant WINS Network

14. ☑ **C.** Use the cluster server service on the inter-site hub. You need the inter-site hub to always be available for inter-site replication to take place. If the inter-site hub should become unavailable, then all replication between sites will stop.

☒ **A** is incorrect because providing fault tolerance for spokes will not provide fault tolerance for the entire replication network. If a single spoke server becomes unavailable, replication can still take place among all sites. **B** is incorrect. If a single intra-site hub should become unavailable, all the other sites could still continue with replication. **D** is incorrect because using high-speed links between the sites will not improve the fault tolerance of the network, although it will make replication more efficient.

15. ☑ **A, B, C,** and **D.** All of the above are correct. Each of these options provides hardware fault tolerance for a single server.

Tuning a WINS Network

16. ☑ **A, B.** Add more processors and add more RAM. WINS can take advantage of multiple processors. **B** is correct because adding RAM will reduce the processor and disk overhead of paging to disk and retrieving information from the page file.

☒ **C** is incorrect because there is no performance advantage conferred by using spanned volumes. **D** is incorrect because IDE disks are generally lower performing compared to their SCSI counterparts.

17. ☑ **A.** Ring. You can use the Ring replication method if all the sites are connected to each other. In this model, each inter-site hub replicates with adjacent inter-site hubs. In this Ring replication model, no inter-site hub represents a single point of failure in the replication chain.

However, this model may lead to more frequent WINS database inconsistencies than what you might find with other replication models. **B** is correct because, in most circumstances, the Hub and Spoke model is the preferred replication model. In the Hub and Spoke model, you designate a single inter-site hub as the central hub for all inter-site hubs, and the other inter-site hubs become pull partners with the central hub.

☒ **C** is incorrect because the Directory Replicator Service is a component of the Distributed File System (DFS) and would not be effective in replicating the changes in the WINS database. **D** is incorrect because the XCOPY32 command would not be able to maintain database consistency throughout the WINS network.

LAB ANSWER

The problem is related to the left-over static WINS database records for the upgraded UNIX hosts. After the UNIX hosts were upgraded to Windows 2000 and made WINS and DHCP clients, they began to receive their IP addresses dynamically and registered to those dynamic IP addresses in the WINS database. However, the static entries were not removed, and the Migrate On option was not enabled. Because the static entries remained in the database and the Migrate On option was disabled, the dynamic record registrations do not overwrite the static entries. When the former UNIX machines received a new IP address from the DHCP server, the static entries no longer accurately reflected the machines' NetBIOS name mappings.

To solve the problem, enable Migrate On at all WINS servers on the network.

8

Designing Distributed Data Access Solutions

In any network, reliability, stability, and high availability are primary concerns. As companies begin to deploy robust networking services such as Web server farms, Enterprise Resource Planning (ERP) applications, and enterprise client/server database applications, the need for distributed data access solutions within the network architecture grows. Designing a distributed data access solution is the process of determining what applications and services within a network are mission-critical and building an infrastructure to support applications that are distributed across an enterprise to provide reliability and availability.

Windows 2000 includes several services to assist you in your distributed access needs, including a robust clustering service, a network load balancing service, a distributed file system service, and native multi-protocol support. These tools can provide high availability, high performance, and a greater amount of scalability than any previous Windows platform.

In this chapter we will discuss design and planning considerations for deploying distributed data access solutions within your Windows 2000 network. We will look at services native to Windows 2000, including the Windows 2000 Advanced Server Clustering service, the Windows 2000 Advanced Server Network Load Balancing service, the Windows 2000 Distributed File System service, and Windows 2000's support for multi-protocol environments.

CERTIFICATION OBJECTIVE 8.01

Overview of Distributed Data Access Solutions

Every day companies around the globe experience data loss, network downtime, and a loss of productivity due to system failures. Many of these failures, however, could have been avoided by a well-planned distributed data access solution. The concept of a distributed data access environment is a simple one. Vital data should be accessible at all times. Since it is impossible to build a networking environment that is not subject to failure, the way that the applications are deployed must be designed to provide continued service, regardless of single component failures. There are two scenarios that make an application or service unavailable.

- A hardware or software component malfunctions leaving the application or service (or path to an application or service) in an unusable state
- The network load on the application or service is so great that the server fails to respond to client requests

To provide for these contingencies, a distributed data access solution seeks to apply the following methodology:

- Downtime due to a hardware/software failure does not affect the operation of the application or service that is being supported
- The application or service must respond in a timely manner to all requests, regardless of the number of clients requesting service

High Availability

Most organizations, from small to large, have mission-critical applications that serve as tools for their employees. These applications have a direct effect upon productivity and revenue generation. Designing a distributed data access solution includes the deployment of applications and services that guarantee high availability.

In the Windows 2000 server suite, many services are available to not only support the needs of small-to-medium–sized businesses, such as file and print sharing, but the needs of large data centers and e-commerce implementations. To empower this endeavor, Windows 2000 has robust hardware support, including: external RAID Arrays, enhanced two-to-four node server clusters (Windows 2000 Advanced Server and Windows 2000 DataCenter Server, respectively), up to 8GB (64GB is DataCenter Server) main memory support, and up to 8-way (32-way in DataCenter Server) symmetric multi-processing support.

The implementation of these features can assist your organization in deploying robust, highly available, applications and services.

on the

Job

It is important to note that no system can ever guarantee 100 percent uptime. The goal of a distributed data access implementation is to minimize unnecessary downtime due to failures or software upgrades as much as possible. Most vendors that market high availability products such as the clustering technology will use percentages such as 99.9995 percent. Although this percentage is impressive, it is not a guarantee of similar results in your own network. As the saying goes, always hope for the best and plan for the worst.

Load Balancing and Server Clusters

When deploying an enterprise application for a large organization or for high-volume Internet transactions, overworked servers can cause slow response times. Some Web sites receive several million hits per day. To provide for that type of service volume, a distributed data access solution must not only be protected from hardware/software failure, but must also provide the capability to balance the load across several different servers while making access to services provided by the cluster transparent to the user.

Using Windows 2000, administrators can take advantage of its load balancing and clustering capabilities and deploy enterprise applications on a cluster of servers working in unison rather than on a single machine. This allows scalability in your deployment because machines can be added to your load-balanced cluster as needed to field incoming client requests efficiently. The failure of one machine within your cluster does not adversely affect the operation of the application or service.

The most common implementation of load balancing is the deployment of a Web server farm—multiple machines running Internet Information Server to service one organization's Web presence. The site is distributed to all servers (in relatively static environments), and all servers are combined into one virtual server to respond to client requests.

Clustering is the method of grouping machines together to serve the same function. Windows 2000 allows administrators to build highly available applications such as SQL Server databases on clustered servers to provide guaranteed failover in cases where one machine experiences a failure. By sharing disk space among two to four servers, applications running on several machines can share data and provide transparent failover when a disaster occurs.

Distributed File Sharing

In addition to the deployment of high availability and load-balanced clusters, administrators can also architect distributed file sharing across large organizations. This allows the administrator to use the same file sharing namespace for users, regardless of their locations.

Distributed file sharing is vital to distributed data-access architecture, for it provides the following advantages:

- Assists the network administrator in managing file resources across a large enterprise
- Allows users to find files more easily by providing a single hierarchical view of the data on different servers within the enterprise
- Allow administrators to integrate two or more copies of a data collection to be presented to the client as one logical mapping to provide load balancing of file access

In a large networking environment, distributed file sharing can be used in conjunction with file replication to maintain multiple copies of a file share to provide every region with a local copy of the data. It can also be used as the data store for Internet or intranet servers, allowing each department to have its own share to which its members can publish data, while providing a unified appearance to users through a Web interface.

Benefits

The benefit of using a distributed data access architecture, as opposed to a standard deployment of applications and services, is clear. With Windows 2000, the integration of distributed data-access methodology into a new or existing network infrastructure is relatively easy and cost effective. Let's take a look at how Windows 2000 can help you to implement a distributed data-access environment.

Implementing a Distributed Data-Access Environment

As a network administrator, you have been asked to facilitate the building of an infrastructure to support an Internet SQL Server application that will be hosted in one location and will serve a combination of over 30,000 users on the network. Describe the technology you would use to deploy such an application infrastructure that would provide fault tolerance, failover, and the capability of upgrading the application without taking it offline.

Answer: This scenario is a perfect example of how a cluster should be used. Two servers running Windows 2000 Advanced Server would be clustered together, both running Microsoft SQL Server. The application would be installed on both machines so that a resource group could be created to provide database and application services to clients using a virtual server name and address. This scenario would provide fault tolerance, failover, and the capability to upgrade one node at a time so that the application stays online during an upgrade.

CERTIFICATION OBJECTIVE 8.02

Designing a Multi-Protocol Strategy

Networks today are *heterogeneous*, meaning they contain systems and services from different vendors, serving different functions within the network. Because no one vendor offers a product that has every network service for any environment, organizations often turn to a variety of vendors for software that fills in the gaps or better serves the organization's needs. This creates networks that are diverse, in many cases inconsistent, and difficult to maintain.

One of the greatest difficulties in diverse networks is a problem of protocol compatibility. Not every network device or service "speaks the same language" or follows the same set of rules (protocols). Although there are many standards being implemented, it is uncommon to find a network that has only one network protocol running across its wires.

Windows 2000 is designed with flexibility in mind, allowing you to not only implement a robust and "multi-lingual" network environment, but one that will integrate well with the systems you already have, assisting you to maintain your existing infrastructure. Consider Windows 2000 as a translator, with a wide diversity of different "languages" available. Windows 2000's multi-protocol support is wider than that of any Microsoft operating system, and the most recent implementation has added support for routing protocols and filtering typically only found within routers and network switches.

Integrating Multiple Network Protocols into a Single Network

When you are designing your Windows 2000 network, it is important to detail every aspect of your network and determine every "language" or protocol on your network (or will be on your network if you are building one from scratch). Networks typically pass more than just TCP/IP or IPX/SPX packets, but many administrators never realize it. Protocols such as IGMP, ARP, EIGRP, and SAP are often visible on a network if you use a network analyzer, but many operating systems and software packages don't participate in those conversations.

With Windows 2000, you not only have the ability to bind many routable and non-routable protocols to a network interface, but you can now implement sophisticated routing protocols and services that have been limited to routers and network switches in the past.

Multi-protocol support in Windows products began as early as Windows NT 3.51 (service pack 2), which included RIP for IP, RIP for IPX, and SAP for IPX. The release of the Routing and Remote Access Service for Windows NT 4.0 added support for many features including RIP (version 2) for IP, OSPF, ICMP router discovery, RADIUS, and PPTP. The latest implementation of RRAS in Windows 2000 has been enhanced to include IGMP and support for multicast boundaries, Network Address Translation (NAT), AppleTalk routing, and Layer Two Tunneling Protocol (L2TP) of IP. The integration of routing services and remote access services creates a variety of features for Windows 2000 that allows it to be used as a robust remote-access server for remote networking and/or a multi-protocol software router.

Design NetBIOS Protocols Integration

Network Basic Input Output System (NetBIOS) is an application-programming interface (API) originally developed by IBM to empower the communication of computers across a network. Many organizations, including Microsoft, have used this API to develop simple networking protocols for small networks.

A common protocol stack implementation of NetBIOS is termed the NetBIOS Extended User Interface (NetBEUI). This was one of the earliest protocols used within personal computer networks and functions well for small non-routed networks that need a simple protocol solution.

NetBIOS Frame (NBF) is the term Microsoft uses in their documentation to refer to the underlying implementation of NetBEUI installed on a Windows 2000 computer (even though the operating system components still refer to it as NetBEUI), which is designed around the NetBEUI version 3.0 specification. This protocol provides compatibility with existing implementations of NetBEUI on Microsoft and non-Microsoft products. Among the chief enhancements to the protocol are the implementation of an unlimited number of NetBIOS sessions (the original specification was limited to 254 sessions), support for dial-up connectivity using NetBEUI, and enhanced memory management features.

Because NetBEUI is a legacy protocol, its use in today's networks is not common. Small non-routed networks can benefit from the speed and simplicity of NetBEUI, but its implementation within the enterprise network should be limited to times when the protocol is warranted.

on the **job**

Although NetBEUI is a non-routable protocol, it can be used to span different Token Ring network segments when a network bridge or router is placed between the segments to offer source routing of Token Ring packets.

Natively, NetBEUI is not a routable protocol, meaning it cannot be routed across connected networks. However, there are many protocol implementations today that allow the encapsulation of NetBEUI within their frames. To provide this functionality, the NetBIOS standard has been built into protocols such as PPTP, L2TP, TCP/IP, and IPX/SPX, so that the standard would not be limited by an incapability to route the traffic across different network segments.

NetBIOS over TCP/IP (NetBT) is detailed in RFC 1001 and RFC 1002. The Windows 2000 Workstation service and the Windows 2000 Server service (as well as a few others) use NetBT for communication with other Windows clients, such as Windows 98 and Windows NT 4.0. Windows 2000 does support direct hosting, the ability for machines to complete name resolution based upon DNS rather than legacy NetBIOS conventions. In an environment where only Windows 2000 machines exist, the NetBT interface can be disabled to force clients and servers to use direct hosting.

When designing your Windows 2000 network, keep in mind the limitations of NetBEUI. NetBEUI is not a routable protocol, meaning that two separate network segments cannot communicate with each other if both of them are running NetBEUI alone. NetBT (NetBIOS over TCP/IP) is a better solution, providing the same naming functionality as NetBEUI, but using TCP/IP as the transport, allowing the communication between clients and servers to be routed over different network segments, as well as through the Internet.

Although Windows 2000 has complete support for legacy protocols such as NetBEUI and support for NetBIOS conventions through TCP/IP or IPX/SPX, design your network with the end goal of eliminating NetBIOS from your network. Because Windows 2000 now offers direct hosting (the ability to use DNS for name resolution rather than NetBIOS), networks can be implemented that do not rely upon the legacy NetBIOS specification.

exam
😀 a t c h

Eliminating NetBIOS from your network is definitely the goal that Microsoft is encouraging through their literature and their product development. But keep in mind that operating systems like DOS, Windows for Workgroups, Windows NT 4.0, and Windows 9x all depend upon NetBIOS for communication across the network, so if you have any of these machines in your network, you will still need to use NetBIOS on every network interface.

Design IPX/SPX Protocol Integration

Internetwork Packet Exchange/Sequenced Packet Exchange (IPX/SPX) is a routable protocol originally developed by Novell as their protocol of choice for their enterprise network operating system Novell NetWare. NetWare is still widely used within networks all over the world, sharing the network operating system market second only to Microsoft.

Windows NT has supported IPX/SPX since its creation in an attempt to integrate with Novell NetWare environments and to provide multiple protocol options for systems designers. Windows 2000 has continued that tradition by providing protocols and services that allow the Windows 2000 network operating system to work seamlessly with Novell NetWare and the IPX/SPX protocol specification.

When planning your network design, keep in mind that IPX/SPX is not only for running Novell services, and that it can be integrated into a Windows 2000 only environment. IPX/SPX is a robust routable protocol, and can be used independent of Novell to provide communication between computers on small to large networks. Many network designers use IPX/SPX for secured communication on subnets that need to be isolated from Internet traffic, or between a pair of computers that need an added measure of security.

The most significant enhancements in Windows 2000 with regard to its support for IPX/SPX are the added IPX routing capabilities within the Routing and Remote Access Service.

IPX/SPX Services

Whether your design goal is to eliminate Novell NetWare from your network or to integrate Windows 2000 into your Novell NetWare network, you will need to depend upon services provided by Windows 2000.

Although Novell NetWare in its recent revisions has implemented native support for TCP/IP, IPX/SPX is still widely used. To allow smooth integration with Novell NetWare, Windows 2000 supports IPX/SPX protocols as well as many tools and services to assist administrators in the task of integrating both network operating systems.

Windows 2000 includes Gateway Services for NetWare (GSNW), a service that allows a Windows 2000 server to connect to Novell file and print resources and share them as Windows file and print shares to Windows clients. By providing a gateway to the Novell Resources, it is easy to convert the workstations in your organization to a "Microsoft Networked" workstation as the first step in the migration of systems from a NetWare centric model to a Windows 2000 environment. The communication between the client and the Windows 2000 server can be any protocol you choose, while the connectivity between the Windows 2000 Server and the Novell NetWare server will be IPX/SPX.

File and print services for NetWare (FPSN) is an add-on component for Windows 2000, available from Microsoft, that allows you to configure Windows 2000 resources to make them available as Novell NetWare resources on a network. This may be useful in environments where many non-Windows workstations are in use on a Novell NetWare network. By providing the Windows 2000 resources as Novell-based services, you can easily migrate file and print services from Novell to Windows 2000 without removing the Novell NetWare client from the workstations.

Both of these services, along with several other conversion utilities included with Windows 2000, provide for easy integration of Windows 2000 into NetWare environments, or the migration of NetWare systems and services to Windows 2000.

IPX Routing

On traditional Novell NetWare networks, two different protocols were used to allow communication between Novell NetWare Servers and clients. The first is IPX (which is routed using RIP for IPX), which we have discussed, and the second is Service Advertising Protocol (SAP). SAP is a protocol that broadcasts a list of services available on the network and their corresponding IPX addresses, similar to the way that the browser service works within traditional Windows networks.

Microsoft provided protocol support for Novell NetWare with Windows NT 3.51 (service pack 2), adding protocol routing support for (RIP for IPX) Novell NetWare in Windows NT 4.0. Windows 2000 includes not only the previous supported options, but the addition of an IPX router, which includes the RIP for IPX routing protocol as well as a SAP agent for routing Novell NetWare routing advertisements across a network.

Table 8-1 lists the features that Windows 2000 IPX router includes.

With the inclusion of a wide array of support for IPX/SPX and Novell NetWare integration, it is easy to see how Windows 2000 could not only be easily implemented in a Novell NetWare environment, but could provide assets that are

TABLE 8-1	Feature	Description
IPX Routing Features	IPX Packet Filtering	The ability to filter incoming and outgoing IPX packets based on key fields within the IPX header.
	RIP for IPX	Support for the primary routing protocol used within Novell NetWare environments.
	IPX Route Filtering	The ability to filter routing advertisements.
	Static IPX Routes	The ability to create static IPX routes to be advertised on the network.
	SAP for IPX	Support for the SAP protocol, allowing the IPX router to route service advertisements on a network.
	SAP Filtering	The ability to filter incoming service name announcements.
	Static SAP Services	The ability to add static SAP service designations that are distributed using SAP.
	NetBIOS Broadcast Propagation	The ability to forward NetBIOS over IPX broadcasts.
	Static NetBIOS Names	The ability to configure static NetBIOS names searchable by the NetBIOS over IPX name query broadcasts.

not currently available to some organizations. IPX software filtering and SAP broadcasts across network segments when the use of a router is not cost effective is only one example of how a Windows 2000 server within an IPX/SPX environment could provide value.

Design SNA Gateways

Windows 2000 Server relies upon Microsoft's SNA Server, soon to be renamed "Host Integration Server," as the gateway for providing IBM Host and Mainframe connectivity for clients. SNA Server provides an easy and secure gateway for Microsoft and non-Microsoft clients to connect to resources on IBM Mainframe and AS/400 systems and services. Microsoft's SNA Server is a member of the Backoffice Server family of products and integrates with Windows 2000 in the same way it did with Windows NT 4.0.

When designing your Windows 2000 network, you can deploy SNA Server to provide access to host systems for clients using multiple protocols, including TCP/IP, IPX/SPX, NetBEUI, Banyan VINES IP, and AppleTalk. This offers more flexibility than some of the bridging and source routing solutions of the past, allowing clients to connect to SNA Servers via standard Internetworking protocols, while the SNA Servers connect to the Host systems via traditional means (channel attachment, Synchronous Data Link Control, X.25, etc.).

The steps to planning a deployment of SNA Server within your networking environment include determining how your SNA Server infrastructure will be deployed, integrating your SNA Server into a Windows 2000 domain, and selecting a SNA Server-to-Host connection method.

SNA Deployment Model

When designing your SNA Server implementation, closely review your WAN configuration, the location of your Host Systems, and the location of your users. Three different deployment methods can be considered:

- Branch Deployment
- Centralized Deployment
- Distributed Deployment

The deployment model you choose for your organization will be based on the current or planned network infrastructure, quantity of users, and the required fault tolerance of your SNA Services.

Branch Deployment Model   The Branch Deployment Model is the method of implementing a Microsoft SNA Server in each location that contains users who need access to host systems. This provides a decentralized deployment, allowing each region to manage its own SNA Server. In this scenario, each machine that needed access to the Host System would connect to the local SNA Server in their network. The SNA Server would then contact the Host System through a traditional connectivity option. The following list details some common connectivity options:

- **Synchronous Data Link Control**   SDLC was invented by IBM to replace the older Bisynchronous protocol for wide area connections between IBM equipment. SDLC is not a peer-to-peer protocol like HDLC, Frame Relay, or X.25. An SDLC network is made up of a primary station that controls all communications, and one or more secondary stations. When multiple secondaries are connected to a single primary, this is known as a multipoint or multidrop network.

- **X.25–X.25**   This is a packet switched data network protocol that defines an international recommendation for the exchange of data as well as control information between a user device (host), called *Data Terminal Equipment* (DTE), and a network node, called *Data Circuit Terminating Equipment* (DCE). X.25 provides a connection-oriented technology for transmission over highly-error prone facilities, which were more common when it was first introduced. Error checking is performed at each node, which can slow overall throughput and renders X.25 incapable of handling real-time voice and video.

- **Source-Routed Token Ring**   The source-route bridging (SRB) algorithm was developed by IBM and proposed to the IEEE 802.5 committee as the means to bridge between all local-area networks (LANs). Source Routing allows you to place a virtual bridge between two network segments so that traffic between the two segments is considered local to the same segment. This is often used on Token Ring networks to bridge SNA dependent segments.

The advantage to the branch deployment method is the limitation of network traffic. Connectivity between the client and the SNA Server requires more network bandwidth than connectivity between the SNA Server and the Host System. So this scenario would limit the traffic between the client and the SNA Gateway, constraining it to the local network. If your organization already has a large SNA network in place, with SDLC or X.25 connections to each location, then the implementation of the Branch Deployment Model would be advantageous, giving you the ability to leverage your current infrastructure. Another advantage is the decentralized support. If your organization has support personnel in each location, this model is ideal, allowing each administrator to manage their own SNA Server.

The disadvantage to this model could be response time, which would be caused by slow WAN links to the Host System, as well as sophisticated routing configurations that may be required on the routers to support the bridging of SNA traffic across a Wide Area Network.

Centralized Deployment Model   The centralized deployment model is the method of deploying your SNA Server near the host rather than the clients. This allows clients from anywhere in the WAN to connect to the Host System via the Gateway by using standard protocols such as TCP/IP, NetBEUI, and IPX/SPX. In this scenario, a server (or several servers) can be directly or indirectly connected (through a Front End Processor) to the Host System, providing one gateway for the entire organization to use. Clients would then connect to the SNA Server using whatever WAN protocols are being routed on the network and the SNA Server will communicate with the Host System on behalf of the client.

The advantage to this scenario is the efficiency of the connectivity (because the SNA Server can be directly connected to the Host System), as well as the flexibility of client access. Allowing the clients to connect to the Host System with whatever protocol they are already running minimizes implementation time. This scenario also offers a centralized management model, allowing all SNA Servers to be grouped together for easier management. If desired, efficient load balancing and fault tolerance can also be implemented by utilizing a second SNA server to serve as a secondary access point for clients.

The disadvantages to this model are minimal, but worth noting. If you centralize your SNA Servers in one location with the Host System, then those machines cannot be efficiently used for other network services. Some organizations may have limited budgets, requiring them to use existing servers in each region rather than purchasing new servers for the SNA implementation. Another disadvantage is the need for an efficient WAN architecture to support the traffic that will be generated by the clients accessing the SNA Server through the Wide Area Network.

Distributed Deployment Model   The distributed deployment model is a combination of the branch deployment model and the centralized deployment model. In this configuration, SNA Servers are placed local to the Host System and configured in the same way as they would be in a centralized deployment model. SNA Servers are also added at each branch office or location and configured to use Distributed Link Services, a component that SNA Servers use to share configured link services with other SNA servers.

This model is advantageous because it combines the best of both the branch and the centralized models, while supporting high fault tolerance and load balancing across the enterprise. This is the recommended configuration for medium-to-large organizations that wish to provide fault tolerant Host Connectivity to clients.

This model does, however, require the use of more servers than the other two models, which could be a disadvantage to a budget constrained organization.

SCENARIO & SOLUTION

I have an existing SNA infrastructure with X.25 connections to each location. I want to implement SNA Server. Which is the best deployment method?	For this situation, the branch deployment method would be the easiest way to implement SNA Server, providing a distributed deployment of SNA servers while relying upon the existing infrastructure.
I have a large wide area network with high-speed lines to each location. We just implemented a new Mainframe computer in our home office to which we need to provide connectivity, but the budget is running slim. What is the best way to deploy SNA Server?	In this scenario, the best solution is the centralized deployment. Your existing WAN infrastructure will provide the transport you need for clients to access the SNA servers in your home office. This method will be simple and cost effective.
I have a large organization with several remote offices. The remote offices want to be able to configure their own SNA server, but I want the ability to control the actual connectivity to the Mainframe. What deployment method is most appropriate in these circumstances?	For this situation, the distributed deployment model would be best. By placing SNA servers in the field, you give local administrators the flexibility to change configuration information for their site, without changing the configuration for the rest of the company. Using home office SNA servers for the connectivity gives you more control over direct connectivity to the Mainframe.

SNA Server Organization within Windows 2000

The deployment of SNA Servers within your enterprise is similar to planning and implementing your Windows 2000 Domain strategy. SNA Server is also implemented using a logical grouping of servers. In Windows 2000, this would be called a domain. Within SNA Server, they are implemented as *subdomains*. A subdomain is a logical grouping of SNA Servers that allows you to provide primary, backup, and stand-alone or member servers for your SNA Server deployment.

You can include up to 15 SNA Servers in any given subdomain. This allows you to configure one primary SNA Server (which holds the primary copy of the configuration), and up to 14 backup or member SNA servers. The primary SNA Server holds the master copy of the configuration for the SNA Server, while the backup SNA Servers contain a backup of the configuration information in the event of a primary SNA Server failure. The member servers do not contain a copy of the configuration file, but act as a part of the subdomain in the same way that the primary and the backup do, responding to client requests as needed.

exam
ⓦatch

Although the number of SNA Servers within a subdomain is limited to 15, the number of subdomains in any given Active Directory domain is unlimited. When configuring large SNA subdomains, try to configure a separate subdomain (with backup and member SNA servers) for each site where your users are organized into large groups. This will allow you to build your SNA Server implementation to scale for future growth. If you are using a centralized deployment method, and you need to add more than 15 SNA Servers, just configure another subdomain and configure the client software for large groups of users towards the new subdomain.

When designing your SNA Server implementation, try to implement all SNA Servers that belong to the same subdomain in the same location, due to the replication that must occur between the servers. The creation of subdomains should be consistent with your Active Directory Sites. If you find it necessary to implement two or more SNA Servers in the same subdomain across slow WAN links, you can modify the replication of the SNA Servers through the SNA Server Manager. This configuration parameter is referred to as the "Mean Time Between Server Broadcasts."

When a client is configured for SNA connectivity through an SNA Server, you can specify the subdomain, instead of the server itself. The client (if it is a Windows 2000 client) will negotiate with the Active Directory to determine the closest SNA Server in the desired subdomain that can service the request. This integration with Active Directory Sites and Services allows your clients to intelligently detect and utilize the server that will cause the least amount of traffic on your network.

The choice to specify a subdomain or a particular server is always yours. In some cases, it may be advantageous to configure the SNA client on each desktop to use a particular server, rather than a subdomain, but this is a change that must take place on the client and the administrative burden of having to reconfigure this option may be time intensive. In most environments, it is recommended that you configure your clients to use the subdomain rather than a particular server.

Another valuable integration with Windows 2000 is the use of security. Because SNA Server was written for the Windows Server platform, the security is integrated. This allows you to determine which users have access to which services provided by the SNA Server. You can use Windows 2000 users and groups to assign rights to certain SNA Server services so that your users can access the SNA Server without a second login.

SNA Server–to–Host Connectivity Options

Another important decision in the planning and deployment of SNA Server in your enterprise is how you will connect your SNA Server to your Host System. This is important because it determines the proximity of the SNA Server within your enterprise, and can often be an expensive endeavor.

If you are using a branch deployment model, then your connectivity options are limited due to the distance between the SNA Server and the Host System. Your options would include X.25 and SDLC, both of which are limited to 19,200 bps and only support 256 sessions over a single connection. You could also use (assuming your router supports it) a source routed Token Ring connection directly to the mainframe or front-end processor. This is often referred to as bridging, and is typically not recommended due to the excessive network traffic that is usually caused by bridging two separate networks.

If you are using a centralized or distributed deployment model, then connectivity from your branch office SNA Servers to your central office SNA Servers will be provided using whatever WAN protocols you have implemented (such as TCP/IP or IPX/SPX). Then your only decision is how to connect the SNA Server in the central office to the Host System. If you are using an FEP (Front-End Processor), you can connect to it using Token Ring, Ethernet, FDDI, SDLC, or X.25. If you are connecting directly to the Mainframe, you can use a Bus & Tag or ESCON Channel Attachment, Token Ring, Ethernet, or FDDI to make your connection.

If your Host System is an AS/400, the connectivity options are slightly different for direct connections. SNA Servers can connect directly to AS/400 systems using SDLC, 802.2/DLC (Token Ring, Ethernet, FDDI), X.25, Twinax, or Frame Relay.

Whichever option you choose, make sure to consider the amount of bandwidth needed for the connection, the number of users that will rely upon the server, and the cost involved in your decision. The best solution for your environment is not always the most expensive, and the price margin between the connectivity options can be great.

CertCam 8-2

EXERCISE 8-2

Designing a SNA Server Network

You have been tasked with the creation of a project plan to convert an existing network to Windows 2000. You must provide for no interruption of service during business hours (9–5). The current network consists of four locations connected by full T-1 lines. The network operating system is Novell NetWare 4.11 and an outdated version of the IBM SNA Gateway currently provides the connection to the Mainframe for the Windows 2000 clients that have already been deployed throughout the enterprise.

Describe the steps you would take (in general) to provide a Microsoft SNA Server infrastructure, along with a migration of all file and print services to Windows 2000 Server. Make sure to include the specifics about the SNA Server placement and subdomain design. For this exercise, assume you will be implementing a Windows 2000 domain controller in each location, separate from the SNA Servers. Your budget is limited to four servers for Windows 2000 domain controllers and four servers for SNA Server implementation.

Answer: The first step would be to implement the four Windows 2000 domain controllers, one in each location, all within the same Active Directory domain. Configure the Active Directory Sites and Services based on geographical boundaries. Install Gateway Services for NetWare on each domain controller and configure each client to make network connections using Microsoft Networking commands to the same file and print shares they were using on the NetWare server. Remove the NetWare client from all machines. During non-business hours, migrate all print queues from NetWare to Windows 2000. Then migrate all file volumes to Windows 2000 file shares. Remove NetWare from the environment. Build one SNA Server subdomain in the same office as the Mainframe using one server as the primary SNA Server, one server as the backup SNA Server, and two servers as member SNA Servers in the same subdomain. Configure all clients to use the Microsoft SNA Servers instead of the IBM SNA Server. Shut down the IBM SNA Servers.

Designing a Distributed File System (DFS) Strategy

The inclusion of the Distributed File System (DFS) service in Windows 2000 is beneficial to designing a Windows 2000 distributed data access solution. First implemented as an add-on to Windows NT 4.0, the Distributed File System service provides a unified namespace for all file shares within a network.

The advantage for the administrator is the ability to store any data on any server in the enterprise, and provide it to users on the network through one single namespace. The advantage for users is they no longer have to know where data is stored on the network to access it; all data will be presented to the user as a domain resource, listed in a hierarchical format much like a directory.

The Distributed File System service is automatically installed with Windows 2000 Server and Windows 2000 Advanced Server, and allows companies to:

- Provide high availability in their file sharing services
- Provided a unified namespace for all file sharing
- Provide load sharing of network file resources
- Expand capacity of volumes transparent to the user
- Create Intranet/Internet Publishing shares consolidated into one namespace for Web server retrieval

on the job

The Distributed File System service is managed by the Microsoft Management Console snap-in dfsgui.msc. DFS can be managed locally or remotely. There is also a scripting agent (dfscmd.exe) included that allows you to manage DFS roots through the command line or through scripting.

Design a Functional Dfs Solution

DFS is not a complicated solution, but one that does take careful planning. File sharing is one of the most basic of networking needs and must be provided to users in a way that is easy for them to navigate, allowing them to find the resources they need quickly and easily. Be sure to plan your DFS thoroughly before implementation, for a redesign of your DFS hierarchy will be difficult to accomplish and confusing for users once your DFS tree is in use.

Namespace Planning

When designing your DFS tree, make sure to develop a naming standard for the enterprise namespace that will be used by all administrators in your enterprise. Some administrators will seek to build one namespace—or DFS root for the entire organization—while others may prefer to build one DFS root for each department. However you decide to group your resources, make sure there is a standard structure and naming convention used by all DFS trees. This will ensure that the users do not lose productivity when moving from one DFS root to another. As you begin your design, ask yourself the following questions.

- How many DFS roots are needed?
- How many DFS links should be added to the tree?
- What is the namespace strategy?
- How deep should the directory structure be?
- How should the data be organized?

Domain Based or Stand Alone

DFS can be implemented as a domain-based service or as a stand-alone service. It is recommended that you implement DFS as a domain-based service to take full advantage of the file replication and active directory integration. The stand-alone

CertCam 8-3

EXERCISE 8-3

Designing a DFS Namespace

You need to design a DFS namespace for a company with seven regional offices, located all over the world. The company has six departments, each of which is represented in each location: Sales, Marketing, Development, Administration, Accounting, and Service. What is the best way to design your DFS root and DFS links so that each department has its own shared file storage and the management of the DFS is minimized?

Answer: Create a Dfs Root on one server and name the root share "shared." Then create a share for each department, each on a different server, linking the share into the Dfs Root. This will provide users with one logical namespace called \\domainname\shared that will contain a department folder for each department.

service is provided to supply backward compatibility with previous versions of DFS and is limited in functionality.

The version of DFS that was implemented under Windows NT 4.0 was DFS version 4.0. The version of DFS that ships with Windows 2000 is DFS version 5.0. These services can only be integrated together when running DFS version 5.0 as a stand-alone service.

The "brain" of Windows 2000 DFS is a sorted lookup table called the Partition Knowledge Table (PKT), which maps DFS roots and replica nodes to Active Directory Sites and Services. On domain-based DFS services, the PKT is stored in the Active Directory and replicated to all domain controllers in the enterprise. The stand-alone DFS service stores the PKT in the registry of the server hosting the service, making stand-alone DFS a poor choice for enterprise implementations of DFS.

Limitations of DFS

Although DFS is a robust service and provides a means for deploying a unified file sharing namespace across a network of any size, there are some limitations that should be considered. When designing a DFS strategy, keep in mind the following limitations of Windows 2000 DFS.

- The maximum number of characters in a path is 260
- The maximum number of domain replica members is 256
- The maximum number of Dfs roots per server is 1
- The maximum number of Dfs roots per domain is unlimited
- The maximum number of Dfs links within a Dfs root is 1000

Because the maximum number of characters in a path is limited to 260, be careful when you nest DFS roots inside of other DFS roots. Too much organization in a large complex DFS root can cause your path to extend beyond the maximum 260 characters, leaving those shares unreachable by the client.

Clients

The existence of Dfs is not new to Windows NT; however, the integration of Dfs with Active Directory is, so there are some client limitations when utilizing Dfs for your unified file sharing namespace that you should consider.

Windows 95 and Windows 98 machines cannot access DFS natively, and require an add-on utility from Microsoft to enable that functionality. Once it is installed, Windows 95 and Windows 98 clients can access a DFS root or a Dfs share by mapping a drive to that resource through a Net Use command or through the Windows Explorer interface. Windows NT and Windows 2000 machines can access Dfs roots and shares natively, and can even map a network drive to folders within DFS shares. For instance, if you have a DFS root in the domain Mercury called *dfsvolume*, and you have a DFS link to a share called "apps" that contains application installation files, with Windows NT and Windows 2000 clients you can map a drive to \\mercury\dfsvolume\apps\microsoft\msproject. This is called a *deep Net Use,* which can make it easier to provide short file paths for users that utilize folders deep within the Dfs file system. Unfortunately, Windows 9x clients do not support this functionality.

e x a m
ⓦ a t c h

Keep in mind that because DFS is integrated into the Active Directory, the DFS tree is an object within the Active Directory and can be located through Active Directory queries. The domain name that hosts the DFS root can also be used to address drive mappings. Therefore, \\domainname\dfsroot can be used in addition to \\servername\dfsroot.

Windows 2000 clients have an advantage over Windows NT clients, for Windows 2000 includes the ability to recognize which shares are DFS shares, and where they are physically located. To view this information, you can access the properties of a DFS link (share) within Windows Explorer. This can be helpful in troubleshooting DFS connectivity issues.

Design Security to DFS

With any network service, security must always be addressed, and DFS is no exception. The good news is that there are really no security concerns related to DFS outside of the standard NTFS file and share permissions that are applied to the DFS shares that are represented as links within DFS. Remember, DFS is just a namespace; it does not actually store any data, so there is really nothing to secure except access to the DFS mapping information itself.

To control access to the DFS mapping information (PKT), open the Microsoft Management Console DFS snap-in, select the DFS root you would like to modify, right-click, and select properties. Then select the Security tab to view the security that

FROM THE CLASSROOM

Replicating Files

Windows 2000 DFS does not contain its own mechanism for replicating files between DFS replica shares; it relies upon the Windows 2000 File Replication Service. FRS is installed by default on all domain controllers within an enterprise and uses multi-master replication to replicate data such as login scripts and domain information to domain controllers throughout the network. When designing your DFS namespace, do take note of what shares you will be adding to your DFS root and the NTFS share and file security that is applied to them. If you are going to use DFS replicas—a publication of one share that is actually contained in two or more places— it is necessary for you to apply the same security on one file structure that you do on another. Unfortunately, there is no utility within the DFS Administrative Console to accomplish this; however, if you are using File Replication Service (FRS) to synchronize your data between two places, the NTFS access control lists will be replicated by that service. If you do not use FRS for your replicas, you will have to set your access control lists on both volumes manually.

—*Joseph Lamb*

is applied to the DFS root object. (See Figure 8-1) Again, this controls access to the object, not access to the root or any links within the DFS tree. To control access to the links within the tree, you must modify the NTFS access control lists through traditional means (through Windows Explorer).

In most cases, it will not be necessary to modify these security settings; however, if you wanted to limit a particular group or user from attaching to the DFS root, you could modify this list to accomplish that purpose. This would *not* prevent them from mapping a drive directly to a server share using the UNC name.

Design DFS for High Availability and Performance

The integration of DFS with Active Directory has made DFS a valuable service essential to any distributed data access solution. Let's look at how DFS, combined with Active Directory, provides high availability and fault tolerant file shares.

FIGURE 8-1

DFS object
security settings

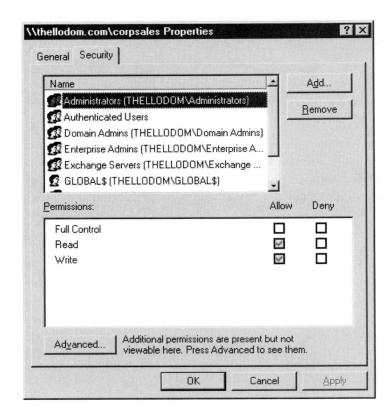

DFS with Active Directory Sites and Services

DFS works in conjunction with FRS and the Active Directory Sites and Services architecture to provide services to clients on the network.

When a domain-based DFS root is established on a server, the PKT is stored in the Active Directory and replicated through multi-master replication to all domain controllers in the enterprise. This gives all domain controllers knowledge of the DFS Root, its replicas and links. The advantage of this integration is simple; proximity in networking determines response time. When you deploy your Windows 2000 networking infrastructure, you will most likely have a Windows 2000 domain controller in each local area network to provide authentication services for users on that subnet. As your DFS infrastructure is built, your DFS mappings will propagate to all the domain controllers, giving users on every subnet quick access to the knowledge of DFS roots and links within the network.

Consider this scenario. John decides to implement DFS into his existing Windows 2000 network. He has four regional offices: one in Atlanta, one in Chicago, one in London, and one in Tokyo. His entire network is based on one Active Directory Forest with one domain. He has domain controllers in each regional office. John creates a DFS root named *DFS* on his server in Chicago, and creates a link called *Apps* within the DFS tree. He assigns four shares to the DFS link, each one named "applications," to correspond to the existing shares on his servers in each regional location. He then sends an e-mail to Jenny, the LAN administrator in Tokyo, requesting that she map a drive to \\domainname\dfs\apps to see if she can access the DFS tree. Jenny reads the e-mail an hour later and goes to a command prompt and types net use x: \\domainname\dfs\apps to map a drive to the share. Jenny's machine accesses the Active Directory in Tokyo, reads the DFS PKT (because it has been replicated automatically to the Tokyo domain controller), and sees that there are four share replicas that correspond to the Apps share. Using the IP address of her machine, the server determines the share that is local to her site and directs her to that share for the mapping.

As you can see, DFS works in conjunction with Active Directory Sites and Services to determine the proximity of resources on the network, allowing you to deploy replicated file shares across your enterprise that are both high performing and highly available.

High Performance DFS

DFS is designed for the enterprise with performance in mind. Several features of DFS work together to make DFS fast and efficient.

Client Caching   When a client contacts a domain controller to locate a DFS replica, the referral that the server gives to the client is cached by the client, allowing that resource to be accessed in the future without having to contact the domain controller for every session.

DFS uses a feature called Time To Live (TTL) to determine how long a client stores DFS referrals before accessing the domain controller to refresh the information. The TTL is an option applied to each DFS link by the DFS administrator and passed on to the client.

DFS Load Balancing   In addition to PKT replication to the domain controllers in your network, DFS provides load balancing by allowing administrators to add several network shares to the same DFS link in the namespace. When a client connects to the DFS namespace to request access to a DFS link, the client is sent all shares within the namespace that are associated with that link. The client then randomizes the shares and connects to one of them, giving preference to shares located in the same Active Directory Site.

This allows you to provide load balancing for high-volume file shares, distributing the load across several synchronized copies of the data.

DFS System Requirements

Even though DFS is a robust, powerful service, the system requirements are minimal. As always, make sure that any hardware you plan to use is on the Windows 2000 hardware compatibility list. Specific system requirements for DFS are determined by the amount of memory consumed by the PKT, which is only about 400 bytes per DFS link.

With that in mind, imagine a large DFS root with 500 different links. The DFS PKT would still be a slim 200K. Although that would cause large file replications of the PKT to all domain controllers in the network, because every change to the DFS root would trigger replication, it would still be manageable, and the likelihood of building a DFS root with 500 DFS links is low.

When you implement DFS, make sure that all Windows 2000 Domain Controllers in your network are running the DFS service. If not, workstations on the subnet where the DFS-less domain controller is located may have trouble locating the DFS resources.

CERTIFICATION OBJECTIVE 8.04

Designing a Network Load Balancing Strategy

If you have ever visited an online store, or other type of e-commerce site, then you have experienced the functionality and usefulness of an online application. Up to just a few years ago, only the largest organizations needed to build their applications to scale, for their "users" were only the individuals within their own organization. In an Internet age, even a small business that markets products online can have millions of users per day. The difference between designing applications for 1000 users and 1,000,000 users is significant, and can only be provided through a technology called load balancing.

What Is Network Load Balancing?

Load balancing is the process of distributing client requests for an application or service across multiple nodes (or machines) to minimize the chance of overworking one particular server. This has been referred to as a server cluster, server farm, or Web farm, but the methodology behind the technology is the same in all occurrences. To provide fast, reliable, scalable applications, distribute the application across multiple machines.

Windows 2000 Advanced Server includes the Network Load Balancing service, allowing you to deploy applications or services across several Windows 2000 Advanced Server machines. Once the Network Load Balancing software is installed on all machines, they form a "cluster" of machines that respond as a single host to all incoming client requests.

exam
⑩atch

The term "cluster" is often used to refer to a group of Network Load Balancing machines operating together to provide a virtual server, but don't confuse the use of this term with Microsoft's Windows 2000 Clustering Service, which is discussed later in this chapter.

Deploying applications or services using Windows 2000's Network Load Balancing service provides:

- Load balancing of incoming client requests
- High availability and automated recovery from single machine failures
- Scalability by adding machines to the Network Load Balancing cluster as needed

Installation and Management Planning

The Windows 2000 Network Load Balancing service can be installed on servers running Windows 2000 Advanced Server or servers running Windows 2000 DataCenter Server. The service is not included with Windows 2000 Professional or Windows 2000 Server.

System Requirements

The system requirements for Windows 2000 NLB are consistent with the system requirements for Windows 2000 Advanced Server. If Windows 2000 Advanced Server supports your server hardware, then your server will run in a Network Load Balancing environment. Always be sure to check the Windows 2000 hardware compatibility list before attempting to deploy Windows 2000 services.

The Network Load Balancing software is included with the purchase of Windows 2000 Advanced server, but you must purchase a copy of Microsoft Windows 2000 Advanced Server for each machine within your NLB cluster. Also, if you plan to load balance a third party product on the cluster, you must always check with the vendor of your software to determine the software licensing requirements for running the software on a cluster, as requirements vary from vendor to vendor.

When planning to implement Windows 2000 NLB service, keep in mind the following limitations:

■ NLB service does not support Token Ring networks

■ NLB will not function properly on a Layer 3 network switch. (Use a shared hub or Layer 2 switch instead.)

■ If you plan to use two network cards in each machine to make communication within the cluster more efficient, make sure you have the available slots for the extra card in each machine, and that both network cards are supported under Windows 2000

■ TCP/IP is required on all machines participating in the cluster. You cannot bind any other protocols to the cluster adapter

■ All hosts within a cluster must be installed in the same subnet

exam
ⓦatch

Although using two network cards in each machine to make communication between cluster nodes more efficient, the second card in each machine must be connected to the same network segment as the first. Using a crossover cable between machines is not supported on Windows 2000 Network Load Balancing (although it is supported by Windows 2000 Clustering Service).

In addition to the hardware limitations, there are software limitations. For one, the application you want to load balance must be "cluster aware." Check with the vendor to make sure the application will operate on a NLB cluster. Secondly, NLB and Microsoft Clustering Service can be configured together to provide a high level of fault tolerance and performance, but they must never be installed on the same machine. NLB and Microsoft Clustering Service cannot operate on the same machine.

Placement Considerations

When designing your Windows 2000 network, make sure to plan accordingly for the placement of load-balanced servers. As stated earlier, the only placement requirement is for the servers to be located on the same subnet.

Remember, load-balanced servers do not share hard disk storage like Microsoft Clusters, and therefore appear as many separate machines on a network. It is the software that allows the servers to act in unison as one virtual server.

exam
Watch

The Windows 2000 Network Load Balancing service supports up to 32 nodes in a load-balanced cluster. These machines do not need to be identical machines, but they do need to run Windows 2000 Advanced Server, have the NLB service installed, and run the same application or service that is being served by the cluster.

A typical configuration would be the design of a Web farm. A company running an e-commerce Web site might decide to build a server farm to host their Web site. To accomplish this, they would purchase as many machines as they would like placed within the cluster, and install Windows 2000 Advanced Server on each machine, along with the Internet Information Server service and the Network Load Balancing service. All servers would have two network cards, all plugged into a 24-port Layer 2 network switch. This switch would then be connected to the Internet via a router to begin servicing incoming requests.

on the
Job

It is important to note the difference between a Layer 2 network switch and a Layer 3 network switch. Layer 2 network switches read header information within a data packet to determine the destination Media Access Control (MAC) address and forward the packet to the appropriate port based on that information. A Layer 3 switch operates in the transport layer, reading packet information to determine the destination protocol address, such as IP address or IPX address, forwarding (or routing) the packet to the proper interface. Because a cluster creates a virtual MAC address that is not assigned to any particular port on the switch, traffic destined for that address (on Layer 2 switches) will be broadcast to all nodes on the switch. Clusters do not work properly in a Layer 3 switch because a virtual IP address will not be handled in the same way a virtual MAC address is handled on Layer 2 switches.

If you run a Web site that has several million hits per day, then you will need a robust solution. If you build a network load-balanced cluster with 32 machines, the limitation may be network traffic on that segment, not the ability to balance the load. Remember, each machine will have two network cards, which equals 64 connections to the same segment. If that works for you and traffic is not excessive, then great! But if you find that the network traffic is too high on that segment, or the 32 machines still do not balance the load efficiently, another Network Load Balancing cluster can be set up on a different subnet. Once the second cluster is online, you will then have two virtual addresses to which you can send clients for Web services. You can then load balance between the two clusters by enabling the "round-robin" parameter in your DNS server and adding another host record for the second virtual IP address. The ability to balance load in this scenario is limitless.

How Network Load Balancing Works to Balance Load

The core of the Network Load Balancing service is a driver called WLBS.SYS. This driver includes a statistical mapping algorithm that the hosts in the cluster use to determine which host is to handle each incoming request. This allows the machines within the cluster to operate as one. NLB does not use a central host to receive and distribute packets, for that would decrease the response time of the application. Rather, all NLB hosts receive every request, and decide whether or not the request should be handled based on port rules assigned by the administrator.

Cluster State

To maintain the "state" of the cluster, hosts within the NLB group exchange messages, sometimes called "heartbeat" messages. This allows all hosts to be informed whether a host is offline or not responding for any reason. Once a "dead node" is identified, the cluster performs a process called *convergence*, and dynamically removes the server from the cluster, redistributing the load across the remaining servers. When the server is brought back online, the cluster will dynamically recognize the machine and integrate it back into the load balancing group.

Port Rules

When a NLB cluster is built, the administrator defines "port rules" that specify to the cluster how traffic is to be managed by the cluster. This allows the administrator to load balance based on the TCP port the application uses to communicate. For instance, by default the World Wide Web Service uses port 80 for all HTTP (TCP) communications. To implement load balancing across multiple services for that service, the administrator would implement a port rule that tells the cluster to distribute all traffic on port 80 equally across all hosts. This allows you to not only configure load balancing for an equal distribution of the load across all servers in the cluster, but you can also use NLB for application failover.

In this scenario, two machines would be in the cluster, and both machines would have a port rule that directs all traffic on a particular port to be handled by a particular host (by setting a handling priority), but the primary host would have a higher handling priority than the other. This would force the first machine to handle all incoming requests. In the event of a failure, the second machine would begin servicing requests.

Affinity

For each port rule setting, you must also specify an *Affinity* setting. The affinity of a port rule setting defines the relationship between client requests from an IP address or from a class C subnet network of clients and one of the cluster hosts.

Affinity is used for managing *state*. Many applications, especially Web applications, manage user sessions as they navigate through a Web site. If you have ever logged into a Web site, then you have experienced this functionality. The server has the responsibility of keeping track of your actions and other vital variables (such as your user ID and password) for later use. These variables are typically stored in the RAM of the server. Since Network Load Balancing does not share RAM or Hard Disk space, the service needs to ensure that all users who start a session on one Web server continue their session on that machine. This is done by setting port rule affinity settings.

There are three affinity settings that define how the servers balance load:

- **None**   If affinity is set to none, the servers will distribute client requests evenly across the cluster. This speeds up response time to requests, but cannot be used when you need to manage state, because the server used for a session is not guaranteed to the client, and the client may access several different servers during any one session.

- **Single**   When affinity is set to single, the servers will manage state for particular IP addresses. For example, if you connect to the virtual server using IP address 4.22.72.11, then the server you connect to the first time will continue to service your requests for the entire session. This helps to manage state for individual machines, used mostly for corporate Intranets.

■ **Class C** This setting directs the server cluster to service client requests based on 24 bits of the clients IP address. For example, if a client connects to the virtual server using IP address 4.22.72.11, anyone during that session that connects to the virtual server using an IP address in the 4.22.72.0/24 subnet (4.22.72.0-4.22.72.254) will be serviced by the same server. This setting is used mostly for servicing Internet requests, and is necessary due to the way in which Firewall and Proxy Servers translate addresses for their clients, making the source IP address of the client different for each request.

Optimizing Network Load Balancing Performance

Even though a server farm using Network Load Balancing will perform better than single server machines running the same service, there are many things you can do to optimize the performance of your Windows 2000 Network Load Balancing implementation.

Network Switching

Using network hardware switches in combination with Network Load Balancing can increase the performance of the cluster. However, it is important to note that Layer 3 switches should not be used because they are designed to route traffic to a

SCENARIO & SOLUTION

I have a Web site that needs to be load balanced, but does not require management of state or sessions. How should I set my affinity setting?	Set your affinity setting to none. If you do not require the management of client or session state, the affinity is not required.
I have a Web-based application I use only within my organization. I do need to manage state. How do I set my affinity setting for this application?	Set your affinity setting to single. This will allow your servers to manage state for single users within your network.
I have a Web-based application that I am providing to Internet users. I do need to manage state. How do I set my affinity setting for this application?	Set your affinity setting to Class C. This will ensure that the state is managed for all clients, even those behind firewalls that may have variable IP addresses during the same session.

particular port based upon a destination IP address, and the virtual IP address of the cluster cannot be directed to a single port.

When using NLB with a Layer 2 switch, it is important to note that every client request that is received by the switch will cause a *switch flood*—the broadcasting of the request to all ports—because the incoming request will have the MAC address destination of the virtual server, not a real server. Because the switch cannot determine the location of the virtual server, it will broadcast the request to all ports. For this reason, it is recommended that you run clustered groups of servers on a dedicated segment or network switch.

Default Host

Using NLB service, it is possible to define a default host for a specific application or service. If you run applications or services on your clustered machines that do not need to be load balanced, specify a default host for that service. If your application or service does not require failover, you can use the actual IP address of the server hosting that application, rather than the virtual IP address, to bypass the load balancing services. Load balancing only applies to services requested using the virtual IP address. Client requests to actual IP addresses of the machines in the cluster are ignored by the NLB service.

Planning for Application Load

When planning your NLB service implementation, be sure to provide enough servers in the cluster to maintain adequate response time for the clients. Application requirements differ, so there is really no way to say how many servers you will need to support a specific number of clients. As a general rule, build the server cluster with just a few machines, and then monitor performance. As performance dictates the need for more servers, add them one at a time, monitoring the performance. Once you have enough servers to adequately serve the load, add one more server to the cluster. This will ensure optimal performance in the event that one server is not responding due to a hardware or software failure.

When your cluster reaches a point where your local subnet is saturated, consider building another cluster on another subnet and distributing the load between the two virtual servers using "round robin" DNS. This is an efficient way to scale your application, but it does have drawbacks. If for any reason the network subnet that the virtual server is on becomes unreachable, and DNS continues to forward requests to the address, clients will not be able to access the application. This is more of a router/circuit fault tolerance issue though, and does not imply a lack of fault tolerance in the load-balanced cluster.

on the
job

Keep in mind that throughout all the scenarios discussed, you need to have a plan in mind for synchronizing the data on all of the machines within the cluster. If you use round robin DNS to add additional load balancing, you will also need to consider the best way to synchronize data on different subnets. If the data is a Web site, or some other form of static data, then synchronization won't be necessary after you copy the application or files to each machine. However, if your application or Web site needs to access a database or other data source, you will need to maintain the database or data source separate from the load balancing cluster.

Network Speed

The Network Load Balancing service operates as a standard network driver under Windows 2000, and can be used on several high bandwidth solutions to optimize cluster performance. Windows 2000 NLB service will run on Fiber Distributed Data Interface (FDDI) or Ethernet based local area networks.

exam
watch

Windows 2000 Network Load Balancing service does not support Token Ring networks.

When planning your NLB design, consider using a FDDI or Gigabit Ethernet network for connectivity between nodes within the cluster. This will increase the efficiency of the cluster and improve response times.

Also, plan to implement a second network card in each machine that is a part of the cluster. Even though it is not required, it will greatly increase the efficiency of the cluster. In this configuration, the first network adapter is enabled for Network Load Balancing, handling the client-to-cluster network traffic and the second adapter provides communication between hosts on the network and the server itself. Both adapters must be connected to the same network segment.

on the
job

As with most network services, the Windows 2000 Network Load Balancing service requires the use of static IP addresses on all network interfaces. DHCP cannot be used for any server operating within a cluster.

EXERCISE 8-4

Implementing an Enterprise Load Balancing Solution

As a new employee with BuyEverything.Com, you have been asked to redesign the Web hosting environment in a way that provides fault tolerance, load balancing services, and the ability to scale to meet ever increasing demands. Currently, the company uses "round robin" DNS to direct customers to five different servers running their Web site and a copy of the database. There are many complaints of overworked servers, server timeouts, and "data not found" messages because of inconsistent database replication. The statistics say that the site receives over seven million hits per day. Describe how you would implement a solution to meet the company's needs. You will be given as many servers as you require for this endeavor.

Answer: To field the incoming requests efficiently, a load balancing solution using Windows 2000 Advanced Server should be implemented. The database should be migrated to one central source, not replicated across several machines. A Microsoft Cluster Server would be a good back end for the database and should be used to provide fault tolerance for the back end processing. Although the number of servers that you will need can vary based on load, you should purchase approximately 12 servers. Six should be placed on one subnet and configured for Microsoft Network Load Balancing, while the other six will be configured the same, but on a separate subnet. This will create two separate virtual servers (with two IP addresses). Once active, the Web site should be manually loaded to each server (because the pages are not dynamic) and the DNS entries for both virtual servers should be entered into DNS. "Round robin" DNS will still be used to balance the load between both load-balanced clusters. This will provide load balancing, fault tolerance, and data consistency within the cluster.

CERTIFICATION OBJECTIVE 8.05

Windows 2000 Server Clustering

Any network that provides mission critical applications must provide a measure of fault tolerance within the infrastructure and design of those applications. In most cases, designers seek to implement a system that has no single point of failure, providing a robust, efficient, stable computing environment to the end users with a virtual uptime of 100 percent. This is often the expectation of end users and executives alike. But how do you design an application offering that has practically zero downtime? How do you engineer an infrastructure that provides fault tolerance for every contingency?

This is never an easy task, and always requires the designer to utilize fault tolerant hardware or fault tolerant software, or a combination of both. Let's take a look at how a designer might approach the design of an application that needs to be accessible twenty-four hours a day, seven days a week, and then we will discuss Windows 2000 Clustering Service, and how it can assist designers in offering a fault tolerant application infrastructure reliable enough for even the largest of applications.

Overview

The first task in building a fault-tolerant infrastructure is to determine what the needs of your application are. Assuming that twenty-four hour, seven day per week access is required, what else may be required? In this case, the application is an Internet based application, so Internet access would be a requirement. It also stores data in a database, so the existence of a database is required as well.

If you were designing this application for fault tolerance, you would need to envision the hardware and software requirements of the application, and systematically trace the connectivity from the client to the server, listing each component that could fail and cause the application not to function.

For this scenario, we will look at the server hardware more in depth than the other components, because the example seeks to emphasize the value of a clustered server solution.

For our Internet application, let's start with the client. The client is an Internet user, and since you have no control over that workstation or the user's connection to the Internet, there is no controllable point of failure at that point. The first place that a client attaches to your network is through an Internet connection providing access to your network. This connection consists of a circuit provided by your ISP, a DSU/CSU, and a router. The router is then connected to the local network through a network hub or network switch with a CAT 5 cable. The server(s) hosting your application are also connected to the network hub or shared switch, providing services to Internet users. The server that runs the application is a standard Intel based server with a single SCSI hard drive.

Now that you have mapped connectivity from the client to the application, list your points of failure. In this scenario, the points of failure are:

- The Internet circuit
- The DSU/CSU
- Connectivity from the DSU/CSU to the router
- The router
- The cable connecting the router to the hub or switch
- The cable connecting the server to the hub or switch
- Server Network Card
- Server Power Supply
- Server Hard Drive
- Server RAM

Once you have determined your points of failure, you would then plan for the fault tolerance of each item. Because our topic is Windows 2000 Clustering, we cannot list the fault tolerance considerations of each item, but in most cases you will need to provide a secondary device for the devices listed (for a quick swap in the event of a failure), or purchase items that have fault tolerance built into the device (like a router with redundant power supplies).

When considering the fault tolerance of your server hardware, there are many changes that can be made to the design to provide a moderate amount of fault tolerance. For instance, a RAID Array Controller can be installed with three hard drives to provide fault tolerance for the data on the hard drive, or redundant power supplies can be installed to provide a backup power supply in the event of a power supply failure. There are many other examples of how that one machine can be made more fault tolerant, but it will never cover every contingency. What if the motherboard in the server fails? Then the redundancy in the power supply and hard drives will be useless.

To address these types of issues for high-end applications, Microsoft has included a service within Windows 2000 called Microsoft Clustering Service. This service allows the administrator to group independent servers into logical "clusters," working together to provide services for the same application while providing the image of a single machine to the client. This technology allows up to four machines to be configured as one logical group, sharing disk space and providing access to an application through one logical IP address. Although load balancing is an advantage of this technology, as discussed previously, the ability of one server to failover to another server in the cluster is the main asset. This means that an application running on one machine that fails can failover to another machine, (typically) transparent to the client running the application.

on the job

Although the cluster does failover transparently, some database applications will force you to authenticate to the second server, requiring another login. This behavior is by design, due to the enhanced security controls of the database application.

Most organizations deploy clustering technologies to ensure the availability of their application. And although buying two separate sets of hardware and software to run the same application may have a high price tag, the cost of having a mission critical application offline for a long period of time is typically much greater. Clustering offers the following benefits to an organization:

- Reduced system or application downtime due to failures
- Easy deployment of application upgrades
- Highly efficient applications and services
- More efficient use of equipment

SCENARIO & SOLUTION

I need to set up a large Web site that will receive several million hits per day. The Web pages are static and do not change. Which technology should I use?	For this situation, Microsoft Network Load Balancing is a clear solution.
I need to set up a large Web site that will receive several million hits per day. The content of the site changes daily. Which technology should I use?	Although a cluster would work for this scenario, it would not scale for the amount of traffic that is needed. Consider using Network Load Balancing with the File Replication Service to manage the dynamic content distribution.
I have a large SQL database that needs to be fault tolerant. Which technology should I use?	This would require Microsoft Clustering Service. Clustering two or more machines together would provide for premium fault tolerance.

Planning a Server Cluster

A successful cluster implementation must begin with a well thought out plan. To plan and deploy a server cluster, the following process should be observed:

1. Identify the specific needs of each application or service to be clustered.
2. Determine which clustering technology to use for each application.
3. Determine the necessary clustering model for your application.
4. Create an implementation plan.
5. Create a contingency plan.

Let's look at each of these steps in detail.

Identify Application Needs

Always be sure to identify what the specific needs of each application are before planning a clustering solution to house them. Be sure to consider:

- Software to be used by your application (Is it cluster aware?)
- Specific hardware requirements
- The amount of data to be stored by your application
- The number of users that will be accessing the data
- The required availability of the application

Determine the Appropriate Clustering Technology

Remember, even though the *cluster* is often used to refer to both Microsoft Network Load Balancing Service and Microsoft Clustering Service, these different services meet different needs. Network Load Balancing is designed to provide the balancing of client requests across multiple nodes. The data on a Network Load Balancing cluster is typically static and manually replicated to each node. Microsoft Clustering Service is designed to provide failover for dynamic applications, using up to four machines with shared disk storage.

Make sure to select the appropriate clustering technology for your application or service. Choosing the wrong clustering technology may not provide the functionality that you desire or require.

Determining a Clustering Model

Using Windows 2000 Clustering Service, there are several different models that can be used to meet the needs of different organizations and applications. Your goal should be to determine which applications will require the greatest demand, and then choose the model that will support the maximum total throughput and availability for the needed application.

Model 1: Single Node Server Configuration   This model is very simple, requires the use of only one server, and does not provide failover for applications. In this configuration, one server is used as a single node cluster, providing a virtual IP address to clients, by which they can access services on that machine.

This model is mainly used for administrative purposes (because the applications or services on the server would be managed through the Microsoft Clustering snap-in), or for organizations that want to implement one portion of a cluster first and then add a server to the cluster later to provide fault tolerance for the application. Some organizations may find this useful in situations where an application is rolled out in a beta mode, and limited to a restricted number of users. Setting the server up to provide the service or application as a single node cluster will allow the organization to add servers to the configuration later to increase the fault tolerance before deploying the application company wide.

Model 2: Dedicated Secondary Node   This model is the simplest form of a failover cluster. A cluster contains resource groups that are configured by the administrator. A resource group is an association of dependent resources that failover together in the event of a failure. Each resource group represents a virtual server that can provide services to clients and includes a network name, a disk resource (if applicable), and an IP address. Failover policies can be applied to any resource group to determine how the group behaves during a failure.

In the dedicated secondary node model, two servers are built and configured for the cluster. The first server provides all the applications and services necessary to clients, while the second server sits idle, waiting for a failure to occur. If a failure does occur, the ownership of the applications and services will failover to the secondary node so that the service is not interrupted.

This model provides reliability and is a good solution when a cluster is being built to provide a single application or service, or you are building your cluster with two sets of hardware that are very different (for example, one server is powerful while the other server is not).

Model 3: Distributed Cluster   The third model is similar to the dedicated second node model, except both nodes have the responsibility for servicing clients and responding to requests for different applications. Each server then provides failover for the other server.

For example, you may be running SQL Server on your cluster, as well as a POP mail server. To set up a distributed cluster with these two applications, you would configure one server as the owner of the SQL Server application and the second server as the owner of the POP mail server. Each one would be configured to failover to the other so that both servers can respond to client requests, and either server can shoulder the entire load of both applications, if necessary.

This model works well when you have multiple applications to support on your cluster, or the server equipment you are using for each server is equivalent and you would like to utilize the power of each for all of the applications in your cluster.

Creating an Implementation Plan

As with any system implementation, it is recommended that you carefully develop an implementation plan before attempting the deployment of a cluster. Make sure in your planning to determine what applications you will be using in your cluster, the placement of your cluster within your network, as well as secondary equipment that may be needed such as UPS, backup drives, or extra network cables.

Creating a Contingency Plan

To ensure that your network is not interrupted during the deployment of your cluster, make sure that any vital services that are being provided before you deploy the cluster can be brought back online quickly in the event of a failed cluster implementation. There are many variables that can cause your cluster not to function correctly, so try not to completely remove vital services from your network until they are successfully running on the cluster.

In many cases, it may be advantageous to build your cluster on a private network, isolated from your network, documenting the installation and configuration procedure as you do the implementation. Once you are pleased with the successful setup of the cluster, format both servers and attach them to the company network. Then rebuild the cluster, following the same procedure.

Make sure that you have a contingency plan in case your cluster does not function correctly so that you can bring necessary applications or services online quickly if the implementation fails.

Server Cluster Implementation

As you plan to implement your cluster, there are several items that you should review to ensure the proper operation of the cluster. The choice of hardware cannot be underestimated when dealing with clustering. Nor should you be ignorant of several clustering limitations. Review the following system requirements and clustering limitations before deploying your cluster environment.

System Requirements

To create server cluster, you must have the proper hardware, and although Windows 2000 supports a variety of hardware, Windows 2000 Clustering does not. Be sure to check the Windows 2000 hardware clustering compatibility list at Microsoft's Web site to confirm that the hardware you will be using is supported.

The following hardware requirements should be considered:

- Systems used must be Intel I386 based
- Network Interface Cards must have a PCI bus
- Systems must share a SCSI bus for disk storage
- Disks within a shared SCSI bus must be formatted NTFS
- Each system should have a minimum of 256MB RAM
- Shared storage should contain one disk partition for each application supported on the cluster
- Servers can be domain controllers or member servers, but must belong to the same domain

Most of the requirements are self-explanatory. The shared SCSI bus is used so that the data can be dynamic, and so that data is not lost when failover occurs.

exam
Ⓦatch

Microsoft's Clustering Technology uses a share nothing cluster methodology, where a particular machine owns every disk resource. During failover of a particular resource, the ownership of the resource is transferred to the remaining node.

When implementing a cluster, always be sure to use a RAID controller for the shared disk storage. RAID allows the shared storage used for the cluster to be fault tolerant so that one disk failure will not cause the data to be inaccessible. Although Windows 2000 includes the ability to use software-based RAID on dynamic disk volumes, only hardware-based RAID is supported under Windows 2000 Clustering Service.

When partitioning the shared storage, be sure to create a partition for the *quorum* resource. The quorum resource is the partition that the cluster service uses to communicate changes to the cluster configuration to all nodes within the cluster. This disk partition contains the cluster registry and the cluster transaction log. You will also want to create a partition for each application you plan to make available on your cluster. This will make configuring your resource groups easier, allowing you to make each application (and the data that it stores) an independent resource group.

Servers within a cluster must be in a domain. They can be domain controllers, but this is typically not recommended due to the overhead that domain controllers require. If you do decide to cluster domain controllers, make sure that the active directory information and system storage is on the local disk, for it cannot be clustered. If you build your cluster servers as domain members, make sure that your domain controller providing services for that site or segment is fault tolerant and always available. The Microsoft Clustering Service is dependent upon authentication. If no domain controller is present, the cluster will not function.

Server Clustering Limitations

As you plan your clustering implementation, consider the following limitations:

- Removable storage cannot be used for shared cluster disk storage
- You must use NTFS with basic disk configuration on all disks used for shared disk storage
- You cannot use Encrypting File System, Remote Storage, Mounted Volumes, or Reparse Points
- You cannot use Software RAID on any shared cluster storage
- The cluster service only supports TCP/IP
- You cannot cluster Microsoft Terminal Server on a Windows 2000 Cluster
- Network Load Balancing and Cluster service cannot be used on the same machine

CertCam 8-5

EXERCISE 8-5

Designing a Server Cluster

As the network administrator for FreeEmailbySnoopy.com, you have been asked to design a clustering solution for their POP mail server (which provides mail services to over 20,000 people) and for their Web site database (which contains just over 2GB worth of data). Describe how you would build a server cluster to run these two applications. Detail the clustering model you would use, as well as the hardware used for the cluster.

Answer: Two high-processor servers with a minimum of 256MB of RAM should be purchased, along with an external RAID array equipped with 6–36GB of hard drive space. Each server should have two network cards, both Ethernet PCI bus. Both machines should have Windows 2000 Advanced Server installed along with the Microsoft Clustering Service. A network interface from each machine should be connected to the Internet-enabled network segment, while the other network interface in each machine should be connected to a private network. The distributed cluster model should be used to provide failover for both applications and equal load balancing. Each server will own one of the applications and respond to client requests for that application. In the event of a failure, the second server will provide services for the failed application.

CERTIFICATION SUMMARY

As a part of any network, an administrator should always seek to implement solutions that are fault tolerant, easily accessible, and easy to manage. The implementation of Windows 2000 into networking environments offers a whole new range of services not available in earlier versions of Windows.

The multi-protocol support within Windows 2000 allows administrators to integrate Windows 2000 into any networking environment, and provides tools for enhanced features typically found only within expensive routing hardware. By using Windows 2000 Distributed File System, Network Load Balancing, and Clustering Service, you can deploy highly available, load balanced, fault tolerant applications for any size enterprise.

TWO-MINUTE DRILL

Overview of Distributed Data Access Solutions

❑ A distributed data access solution is a deployment solution that provides for highly available and fault tolerant systems and services

❑ Windows 2000 Server includes Multi-protocol support and Distributed File Sharing services

❑ Windows 2000 Advanced Server and Windows 2000 DataCenter Server includes Network Load Balancing and Clustering technologies

Designing a Multi-Protocol Strategy

❑ Windows 2000 allows you to implement sophisticated routing and filtering of network protocols on your network using the Routing and Remote Access Service

❑ Windows 2000 supports RIP (version 2) for IP, OSPF, ICMP Router Discovery, RADIUS, RIP for IPX, SAP for IPX, L2TP, PPTP, NetBEUI, IPX/SPX, TCP/IP, and AppleTalk

❑ Windows 2000 supports direct hosting and can be configured to run without NetBIOS support using DNS

❑ Windows 2000 includes Gateway Services for NetWare, a service that allows Microsoft clients to connect to NetWare resources as Windows 2000 shares

❑ Windows 2000 utilizes Microsoft SNA Server (Host Integration Server) for connectivity to IBM Host Systems

Designing a Distributed File System (DFS) Strategy

❑ The Distributed File System can be configured as a domain-based service or a stand-alone service

❑ DFS provides end users with a single unified namespace for all network file storage

❑ DFS security is based on the existing share and file system permissions set on network resources

❑ DFS clients use Active Directory Sites and Services to determine the proximity of resources on the network

Designing a Network Load Balancing Strategy

❑ Load balancing is the process of distributing client requests for an application or services across multiple nodes (or machines) to minimize the chance of overworking one particular server

❑ All nodes within a Load Balancing cluster must be connected to the same network segment

❑ Windows 2000 Network Load Balancing supports up to 32 machines within a cluster

Windows 2000 Server Clustering

❑ A fault tolerant system is a system that has no single point of failure

❑ Microsoft Clustering Service allows up to four machines to be configured to share hard disk space and work together to seamlessly provide a service to clients

❑ Microsoft Clustering Technology uses a share nothing cluster methodology in which a particular machine owns each disk resource. In the event of a failure, the ownership of an application can be transferred to surviving nodes. No disk resource is owned by more than one machine at any time.

SELF TEST

The following questions will help you measure your understanding of the material presented in this chapter. Read all of the choices carefully because there may be more than one correct answer. Choose all correct answers for each question.

Overview of Distributed Data Access Solutions

1. Which of the following features in Windows 2000 can be used to design and deploy a distributed data access environment? (Select all that apply.)

   A. Distributed File System (DFS)

   B. Network Load Balancing services (NLB)

   C. Connection Manager Administration Kit (CMAK)

   D. Clustering service

2. You need to deploy a high availability Web site for your Internet-based customers. What is the best service to use to deploy this application?

   A. The Distributed File System (DFS) would be used to replicate a copy of the Web site to several different Web servers connected to the Internet.

   B. The File Replication Service (FRS) would be used to replicate a copy of the Web site to several different Web servers connected to the Internet.

   C. The Network Load Balancing service will be used to cluster several machines together, offering a unified Web presence to Internet users.

   D. The Microsoft Clustering Service will be used to cluster several machines together, load balancing the incoming client requests across the entire cluster.

3. Which of the following Windows 2000 services can provide 100 percent uptime for applications and services?

   A. Multiple-Protocol Support

   B. Network Load Balancing

   C. Microsoft Clustering

   D. Distributed File System

   E. None of the above

Designing a Multi-Protocol Strategy

4. Which of the following Windows 2000 Routing and Remote Access Service multiple protocols are support? (Select all that apply.)

   A. RIP for IP and IPX

   B. EIGRP

   C. OSPF

   D. RADIUS

   E. PPTP

5. Which of the following are enhancements included in the Windows 2000 implementation of NetBEUI? (Select all that apply.)

   A. Support for native routing to multiple subnets

   B. Support for an unlimited number of NetBIOS sessions

   C. Support for dial-up connectivity

   D. Enhanced memory management features

6. You need to deploy an SNA Server infrastructure for your company. You plan to install six different SNA Servers for your 600 users. How would you best configure the clients to access the servers so that no one server becomes overworked?

   A. Configure each group of 100 clients to access a different server.

   B. Configure all clients to access a DNS name, and create a round robin DNS entry for the servers.

   C. Configure all SNA Servers to be a part of the same subdomain and configure the clients to access the subdomain rather than individual servers.

   D. Install Network Load Balancing service on all the SNA Servers to provide a clustered IP address for the SNA Service. Then configure the clients to access the SNA Server using the clustered IP address.

Designing a Distributed File System Strategy

7. DFS can provide many benefits to an enterprise organization. Which of the following are benefits provided by DFS? (Select all that apply.)

   A. Provides high availability of file sharing services

   B. Provides a unified namespace for file sharing

   C. Provides load sharing of network file resources

   D. Provides the ability to change access rights for many file volumes from one interface

8. What is DFS nesting?

   A. The process of creating a DFS root that is several subdirectories below a root drive

   B. The process of creating a DFS root on a temporary workstation before migrating it to a domain controller

   C. The process of placing a DFS link within a namespace that refers to another DFS root

   D. The process of placing a DFS link within a namespace that refers to a file share on another domain

9. You have created a DFS root with a DFS link that refers to two separate file shares to provide load balancing. The file shares are being replicated using the File Replication Service. What is the best way to ensure that changes made to the access rights of one volume is replicated to the other?

   A. Using the DFS API, create a custom application to copy the access control lists (ACLs) every time a change is made.

   B. Using the DFS administrator program, set the replication service to "synchronize all file permissions" and "synchronize all share permissions" for replicated DFS links.

   C. When making a change to the ACL of one share, manually make the same change to the other share.

   D. Replicated ACLs is native to the File Replication Service; no additional effort is needed to ensure their consistency.

Designing a Network Load Balancing Strategy

10. Which of these features are part of the Windows 2000 Network Load Balancing implementation? (Select all that apply.)

   A. Load balancing of incoming client requests

   B. Automatic replication of data between load balanced nodes

   C. High availability and automated recovery from single machine failures

   D. Scalability by adding machines to the Network Load Balancing cluster as needed

11. You have created a Network Load Balancing cluster of 32 machines servicing a large e-commerce Web site. Due to user load, the response time has been slowly declining. How would you change or add to the configuration of the cluster to increase response time?

A. Create another cluster on another network segment and use round robin DNS to load balance between two virtual IP addresses.

B. Add five more servers to the load balancing cluster.

C. Connect the 32 machines to a Layer 3 network switch.

D. Increase the affinity setting for each application in the cluster to improve response time.

12. Which of the following best describes Affinity?

A. A setting used within the Network Load Balancing service to determine the amount of sessions that a particular server can service before redirecting client requests to other servers in the cluster

B. A setting used within the Network Load Balancing service to manage state within a Web application, directing client requests to a particular server based upon IP address

C. The amount of time it takes for a failed node in a cluster to be removed from the cluster group

D. The amount of time it takes for a failed node in a cluster to be added back to the cluster group after coming back online

13. You have a Network Load Balancing cluster of six nodes running a dynamic Web application that needs to manage state. The individuals using the application are Internet users. How would you set the affinity setting for this application?

A. None

B. Single

C. Double

D. Class C

Windows 2000 Server Clustering

14. The Windows 2000 Clustering Service allows you to:

A. Group independent servers into logical clusters, working together to provide services for the same application while providing the image of a single machine to the client

B. Group Network Load Balanced groups into a logical group for maximum load balancing and failover support

    C. Configure several servers to respond to client requests at the same time, providing load balancing and fault tolerance

    D. Configure several workstations to work together as one cohesive unit, distributing the processing of applications for end users over many different machines

15. You need to deploy one application to your enterprise. You must cluster the application on two machines, but you have two machines with very different hardware configurations. One is very powerful, while the other is more of a workstation class machine. What clustering deployment model would work best for this implementation?

    A. Single Node Server configuration

    B. Double Node Server configuration

    C. Dedicated Node Server configuration

    D. Distributed cluster

16. Which one of the following is not a limitation of the Windows 2000 Clustering Service?

    A. Systems used must be i386 (Intel-based) computers.

    B. Network Interface Cards must be PCI–based.

    C. Disks within a shared SCSI bus must be formatted NTFS.

    D. Both machines must have two network cards to segment private and public data.

17. You need to create a cluster for two different applications: Microsoft SQL Server and a third-party POP server. How would you partition and format an external RAID array in preparation for this cluster?

    A. Make one partition, formatted NTFS.

    B. Make one partition, formatted FAT32.

    C. Make two partitions, formatted NTFS.

    D. Make three partitions, formatted NTFS.

LAB QUESTION

You are the system administrator of a large corporation. Your organization has recently purchased a smaller company and you have been given the task of deploying a network to their locations and integrating it with your corporate office. Your corporate office runs Windows 2000 and your Active Directory structure consists of one forest with one domain. Your corporate office also hosts a Mainframe computer, to which the new organization will require access. The new organization your company has purchased has locations in Atlanta, Chicago, and Houston. They have no existing network or communication links. Each office has about 50 people, all with computers on their desktop running Windows 2000 and Windows 98, but all independent of a network. Although members of this organization will require file sharing, it will not be necessary between the corporate organization and the subsidiaries.

The new organization is being transformed into a dot-com company and will need to host a large e-commerce Web application. A static front end with a SQL Database back end will be required.

Describe in detail how you would use the features of Windows 2000 to deploy a network in the newly purchased organization. All administrative control must reside in the corporate office (in New York), for they have no regional administrators.

SELF TEST ANSWERS

Overview of Distributed Data Access Solutions

1. ☑ **A, B, D.** The Windows 2000 Dfs, Network Load Balancing and Clustering Service are included (Clustering is included only with Windows 2000 Advanced and DataCenter Servers) to assist administrators in designing and deploying a Windows 2000 Distributed Data Access Environment.
   ☒ **C** is incorrect because the CMAK is used to create a graphical interface for remote users to connect to your network.

2. ☑ **C.** When designing an architecture for a Web hosting environment, deploy the Web site within a load-balanced cluster to provide failover and network load balancing of incoming client requests.
   ☒ **A** is incorrect because the Dfs service is used for distributing file volumes through an enterprise, not the load balancing of a particular application or service. **B** is incorrect because file replication does not provide load balancing services natively. **D** is incorrect because the Microsoft Clustering Service is for the provision of failover of dynamic content (such as databases), not Web sites that are typically static.

3. ☑ **E.** No system or service can ever guarantee 100 percent uptime. The purpose of a distributed data access solution is to provide high reliability and efficiency, not to make an application or service fail proof.
   ☒ **A, B, C,** and **D** are incorrect because, although several of them provide high reliability and efficiency, none of them guarantees 100 percent uptime.

Designing a Multi-Protocol Strategy

4. ☑ **A, C, D,** and **E.** The Routing Information Protocol (RIP) for both IP and IPX, Open Shortest Path First (OSPF), the Remote Authentication Dialin User Service (RADIUS), and the Point-to-Point Tunneling Protocol (PPTP) are all supported by Windows 2000 RRAS.
   ☒ **B** is incorrect. The Enhanced Interior Gateway Routing Protocol (EIGRP) is a routing protocol supported by Cisco routers, but is not currently supported by the Windows 2000 RRAS services.

5. ☑ **B, C,** and **D.** In Windows 2000, NetBEUI can support an unlimited number of NetBIOS sessions. Support for dial-up connectivity and enhanced memory management features are also included.
   ☒ **A** is incorrect; NetBEUI is still a non-routable protocol.

6. ☑ C. SNA Servers should always be grouped into subdomains to provide replication of configuration data, fault tolerance, and load balancing of the SNA Server load.
☒ A is incorrect because configuring clients to access individual servers is a very inefficient way to deploy SNA Server. B is incorrect because you cannot use a DNS name when configuring the SNA client. D is incorrect because the Network Load Balancing service cannot be used with SNA Server.

Designing a Distributed File System Strategy

7. ☑ A, B, and C. DFS makes file sharing services highly available to users, provides a unified namespace for file sharing, in which users need not know the physical location of files on the network, and provides for load sharing of network file resources.
☒ D is incorrect because DFS does not provide any mechanism that allows for changing of access rights on multiple volumes simultaneously.

8. ☑ C. The process of nesting can be used to integrate several DFS roots into one namespace, presenting a unified view to the clients.
☒ A, B, and D are incorrect because they do not refer to the process of nesting.

9. ☑ D. The File Replication Service automatically replicates ACL changes to replicated file folders and files.
☒ A is incorrect because Microsoft does not supply an API specifically for DFS. B is incorrect because the replication settings referenced are fictitious. C is incorrect because it is not necessary due to the automatic ACL replication of the FRS.

Designing a Network Load Balancing Strategy

10. ☑ A, C, and D. Windows 2000 Network Load Balancing allows for load balancing of incoming client requests and automated recovery from single machine failures. Scalability is provided, allowing you to add machines to the NLB cluster as needed.
☒ B is incorrect because automatic replication is not included in the Windows 2000 NLB service.

11. ☑ A. Once a cluster reaches 32 nodes, you must add a second cluster and load balance between the two to achieve greater response time and availability.
☒ B is incorrect because 32 is the maximum amount of servers that can be in a cluster. C is incorrect because a load balancing cluster cannot operate correctly on a Layer 3 switch. D is incorrect because the affinity setting has nothing to do with the response time of the cluster.

12. ☑ **B.** Affinity is used for managing state, allowing Web applications to manage the state of a user during the entire session.
☒ **A** is incorrect because applications in a cluster are (typically) equally load balanced across multiple nodes in the cluster. **C** and **D** are incorrect because the amount of time it takes for a cluster node to be deleted or added to the cluster group is called convergence.

13. ☑ **D.** For Web applications that need to manage state and response to Internet requests, the affinity setting should always be set to Class C. This allows clients residing with the same Class C address space to be handled by the same server.
☒ **A** is incorrect because it disables affinity. **B** is incorrect because it only manages state for a single IP address. **C** is incorrect because double is not a viable affinity setting.

Windows 2000 Server Clustering

14. ☑ **A.** Windows 2000 Server Clustering allows you to group independent servers into logical clusters (a virtual server), working together to provide services for the same application while providing the image of a single machine to the client.
☒ **B** is incorrect because the Clustering Service is not dependent upon the Network Load Balancing service for operation. **C** and **D** are incorrect because they do not correctly represent the definition of a Windows 2000 cluster.

15. ☑ **C.** A dedicated node server configuration would allow you to cluster your application to provide failover, but would grant ownership of the application to one particular machine (the more powerful one). The less powerful machine would only be used as a failover machine and would take ownership of the application as the first machine went offline.
☒ **A** is incorrect because it does not include two servers. **B** is incorrect because a double node server configuration is a fictitious clustering model. **D** is incorrect because it is used to support more than one application.

16. ☑ **D.** Although two network cards in each machine is recommended, it is not a requirement.
☒ **A**, **B**, and **C** are incorrect because they are all limitations of the Clustering Service.

17. ☑ **D.** To prepare for the cluster, you must create one partition for each application that will be used, as well as one partition for the quorum resource (the area the Cluster Service uses to communicate information to other nodes in the cluster).
☒ **A** is incorrect because it does not provide a partition for each application. **B** is incorrect because cluster partitions must be formatted with NTFS. **C** is incorrect because it does not provide a partition for the quorum resource.

LAB ANSWER

The first task would be connectivity within each of the remote offices. Network switches or hubs can be installed to network all workstations within each location into one segment per location. Routers should be purchased and placed in each location. A frame relay connection should be acquired for each location with a private virtual circuit linking the corporate office with each remote office. TCP/IP should be installed and routed between the corporate office and the remote locations.

A Windows 2000 domain controller for the corporate domain should be installed in each location and configured as a site within Active Directory Sites and Services.

A DFS root named *companyname* should be established in the corporate office and replicated to the regional offices. File shares can be created closest to the users that will be using them and linked into the DFS namespace that was created. Login scripts should be configured to map drives to the new DFS namespace.

An Internet circuit should be installed in the corporate office to host the new company's Web site. Four servers will be clustered together using Network Load Balancing service to provide Internet Information Server services to clients on the Internet, while two other machines will be clustered together using Microsoft Clustering Service to run the SQL Server service for the dynamic Web site interaction.

To provide Mainframe services, two new servers should be set up in the corporate office and configured with SNA Server directly connected to the mainframe. These servers should represent one subdomain. All clients in the new organization will have the SNA client installed and configured for the subdomain. Traffic to the SNA Server will be passed across the frame relay connection using TCP/IP.

MICROSOFT CERTIFIED SYSTEMS ENGINEER

9

Designing Internet Connectivity Solutions

CERTIFICATION OBJECTIVES

M icrosoft's primary focus in designing Windows 2000 was to create an operating system that provides comprehensive Internet support. In this chapter, we look at various features and components for Internet, intranet, and extranet connectivity. In order to implement successful Internet connectivity and remote access capabilities, you must plan your design solution carefully. Here we look at firewalls, what they do, and their impact on your network. We also talk about routing and remote access to your network. A component that is new with Windows 2000 Server, not previously available with Windows NT 4.0, is Network Address Translation, or NAT. Furthermore, included in both Windows 2000 Server and Professional is a relatively new feature called Internet Connection Sharing (ICS), a "lite" version of NAT. These two components allow multiple nodes to use a single IP address to connect to the Internet.

Other new features of Windows 2000 are IIS 5.0 and the Integrated Mail Server. In this chapter, we discuss how Exchange 2000 interacts with the Integrated Mail Server. After we learn about NAT and ICS, we examine a comparison to Microsoft Proxy Server to help you fully understand the capabilities and limitations of each.

CERTIFICATION OBJECTIVE 9.01

Designing Internet Connectivity Solutions

When it comes to designing a final solution for your Internet-based components, you should consider both best- and worst-case scenarios that can occur in conjunction with each possible solution. This foresight is very important for the security and safety of the information that travels on the company network. This is not an easy task. It is a big job to think of all the considerations that are necessary to provide the access your organization needs while protecting your network from outside intrusions or attacks. Internet connectivity design is a multiple-step process.

Audit your existing environment and make sure you know what you have in place. This will help you to understand the organization's needs when you are designing a method of connecting to the Internet or configuring remote access.

1. Take an inventory.

2. Finally, you can start putting a plan together.

Auditing Your Existing Environment

An audit of the existing environment can be a complicated task if you are not organized. You should consider some of the following issues in relation to your Internet connectivity solution:

- Which users need access to the Internet?
- Which applications need access to the Internet?
- Do any users require remote access to the network (from home or while on the road)?
- What data needs to be secure from malicious attacks, and where is that data physically located?
- How will you protect sensitive or mission-critical data?

This is a starting point for listing the items for which an administrator wants to have solutions before beginning the second phase of the audit. These questions are usually not difficult to answer, with a little research.

Taking an Inventory

Once you have determined the needs of the organization, you should inventory your existing hardware and software. An inventory will help you consider the big picture of how the hardware and software will affect the final solution. The initial step in the inventory process involves researching the applications and hardware that will need Internet access.

The easiest way to do this is to make lists detailing the hardware and software that are currently deployed. These lists will help you determine what hardware and software should be parts of your ultimate solution. A spreadsheet or database can be created to provide an efficient way to sort and manipulate the information. This database can also be used for documentation of your network and Internet solution.

Determining Who Needs Access

When designing your solution, make a list of which persons in the organization need access to the Internet. In many cases, it is not necessary for all users to have full Internet access, and universal access could even result in decreased productivity.

Consider each user's job duties and how (or whether) Internet access is necessary or desirable in performing those tasks.

Determining Which Applications Need Access

Along with the list of users who need access, you might need to determine exactly what Internet resources each needs to access. Ask yourself the following questions:

- Do users need e-mail?
- Do they need to browse the Web?
- Do they need to upload or download information via FTP?
- Do they need to connect to other private networks via a VPN?
- Are there special Internet applications they need to run?

Knowing what applications need access to the Internet can be vital to a successful implementation. Make a separate list. Include contact information for technical support in order to help you determine the proper configuration of the application.

Determining Remote Access Requirements

When determining remote access requirements, you must estimate the maximum number of simultaneous connections anticipated. This knowledge is the basis for ordering phone lines, modems or modem cards, and proper cabling and rack equipment. If you underestimate the number of dial-up connections needed, users will complain and management will not be pleased.

Determining Security Requirements

Adopting a security plan to keep your information safe from hacking attacks is vital when you connect your LAN to the public Internet. Once connected, the network is vulnerable to access from anywhere in the world—if you haven't established proper security measures. It is essential that you understand how to configure firewalls and packet filtering, along with proper implementation of access permissions.

SCENARIO & SOLUTION

What should you consider in determining which users and applications require Internet access?	Consider which users need access to Internet resources and services such as e-mail, the World Wide Web, FTP, Telnet, etc.
How can you provide private addresses on your network and share one IP address for Internet access?	Use NAT (in Windows 2000 Server) or ICS (in Windows 2000 Server or Professional), or consider a proxy solution.
What benefit does a hardware/software audit provide for you?	An audit gives you an inventory for planning deployment of existing hardware and software, as well as guidelines for upgrading or replacing hardware and software.
Why should you determine which applications will access the Internet?	This knowledge will allow you to configure security by opening or restricting specific ports on the firewall and will help you determine which access-sharing solution (NAT, proxy, or a routed connection) is most appropriate.

Making a Plan: Solution Diagrams

An important step in planning and designing your Windows 2000 solution is to create a diagram of your existing network and Internet connectivity solution. This diagram serves a two-fold purpose; it is also an essential component of documenting your network.

Several excellent applications are available for diagramming your network, such as Microsoft's Visio. Being able to visualize your solution will help you catch design flaws before they are put into practice. Figure 9-1 shows an example of a simple network diagram.

As you develop your Internet solution and your diagram expands, you should develop separate diagrams for your LAN/WAN and Internet connectivity. Figure 9-2 shows an example diagram.

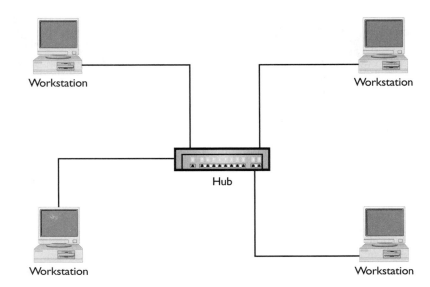

FIGURE 9-1

A simple network diagram

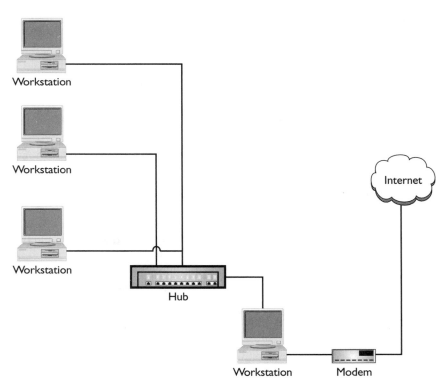

FIGURE 9-2

An example Internet diagram

Determining Physical Connectivity Requirements

When constructing your diagrams, you first need to determine your organization's physical requirements. This process includes asking yourself the following questions regarding the type of connection that is appropriate:

- What is the size of the company and how many users will need access? If yours is a small company, a dial-on-demand connection might be sufficient. If it is a large company, you could consider various leased-line solutions such as T1, T3, OC3, or a combination of these.

- What type of Internet traffic will be generated? If the organization must send or receive very large files or transmit streaming media, a high-performance connection is mandatory.

- What level of reliability is required? If your organization sends and receives time-sensitive data, an always-on, committed information rate is preferred.

Network Diagramming as Presentation Aid

Your completed diagrams will form the basis of the presentation of your final solution to management. The visual aids will make presentation and explanation to decision makers easier. If upper-management personnel are not technologically savvy, you should keep these diagrams simple and easy to understand.

Step-by-Step Network Diagramming

The following steps walk you through the process of diagramming your network. After reviewing these steps, you will complete an exercise that challenges your ability to create a coherent, usable network diagram. You can use a piece of paper (lined paper or grid paper is easiest to work with) or a network diagramming software tool such as Visio to complete your diagram:

1. Find the central part of your network, which will be either switches or hubs. Draw out each switch and hub in your network, keeping each wiring closet separate but connected as they are physically. Next, add devices that are connected to your wiring closets. These include each printer, workstation, server, and any other network device plugged into a hub or switch. If workstations are all the same, you can lump groups from a switch or hub into one area to save space on the paper.

2. Once you have your entire network diagrammed, step back and view the "big picture." Are all components properly connected? Are any components missing? Don't forget to indicate WAN links such as ISDN or frame relay connections.

3. On your diagram, determine where the entry point to the Internet should be. Then determine, based on this decision, whether you will need to add new servers. These could be proxy servers, Web servers, e-mail servers, FTP servers, remote access servers, VPN servers, or the like.

4. Consider whether you will need to add hardware devices such as routers, hubs, or switches. List these devices for future reference.

After you've determined the changes that need to be made, duplicate your diagram, incorporating the additions and changes. This process will give you both "before" and "after" versions to use for reference as you implement your solution.

EXERCISE 9-1

Network Diagramming

Read the following scenario and create a network diagram that reflects the information given.

You have just been hired to provide an Internet connectivity solution for a company called Tacteam, a consulting firm. The company has two locations, a headquarters office in Dallas and a small branch office in Houston. There are approximately 800 users at the Dallas location and 175 at the Houston office. Currently, the two offices are connected via a 56K frame relay connection.

The Dallas office has a 128K ISDN connection to the Internet, which is shared by the 120 systems in the research department. Some individuals, such as the company president and other executives, have dedicated phone lines for 56K modem dial-up connections. The Houston office does not have Internet access.

Each office has two domain controllers, a DNS server and a WINS server. The Dallas office has a file server that must be accessed occasionally from Houston. The Dallas office also hosts a Web server.

Prepare a diagram of the current network. (Later in this chapter, you will diagram your proposed changes to the company's setup.)

Designing an Internet and Extranet Access Solution

When designing an Internet and extranet solution, you must consider many factors that an isolated LAN or WAN would not have to face. These factors include firewalls, remote access, and Internet connectivity to the workstations as well as overall wiring layouts and design to ensure that throughput is adequate to support your needs.

Designing the Firewall

Your firewall solution must function with the outside world in mind, considering both the threat from external intruders and the exposure caused by actions of employees internally. If you don't keep in mind what applications will be used, it will be harder to determine what ports to open in your firewall. Some organizations open their firewalls based on IP address. If your organization does this, you have to know the IP address of all end users who need access to allow them connectivity to the outside world.

Designing Remote Access Solutions

Remote access can take multiple forms. Dial-up access is one of the most common. Allowing your users to dial directly in to your network is easy to set up with Windows 2000. Issues to keep in mind include the following:

- How many inbound ports do you need?
- Will the inbound ports be serial, dedicated, or virtual (or a combination)?
- What type of security will be used when authenticating?

We examine these questions in more depth later in this chapter.

With your Internet and extranet solution, you might consider using *Network Address Translation (NAT)*. NAT allows you to use private IP addresses on your internal network and still access resources on the public Internet. Using private IP address ranges significantly reduces the chance of intrusion by external users on the Internet. We look at how NAT works later in this chapter.

Other things that you should consider when devising your master plan are:

- Internet Information Server
- Exchange Server
- Other BackOffice products

At the end of this chapter, we take a look at the interactivity of Exchange and IIS in your design.

With these things in mind, we can start determining our final solution. Using the audit of your existing network, you can come up with "before" and "after" scenarios so that when your final proposal is presented, it will show the true benefit of your design. Once you have your diagrams in place, you can develop the necessary documentation for your end users as well. Documentation includes how to access the network remotely from satellite offices, hotels, or even from home.

EXERCISE 9-2

Creating a Plan

Your design plan should be in writing. As changes are made to the plan, you can replicate those changes to the documented information you have so far.

Referring to the network diagram you created in Exercise 9-1, consider the following additional information:

Tacteam has several executives who need to be able to connect to the network from their homes. These executives include approximately 10 people in the Dallas office and 2 in the Houston office. They primarily need access to the files on the Dallas file server; however, at times they also need to access the data on their office desktop computers' local hard drives.

1. Create a remote access solution that will allow the executives to access the data they need.

2. List any additional hardware that will be required to implement your solution.

3. Discuss alternative solutions, should management balk at the idea of purchasing additional hardware and should the executives who live outside the local calling area be unhappy with the idea of paying long distance charges to connect.

4. Discuss security issues involved in providing the solution and how you will address these issues.

Answer: One solution is to set up a Windows 2000 remote access server in the Dallas office. Allow access to the entire network over RAS, and set the user accounts of the executives to allow remote access. You need to purchase a modem or modem bank with at least as many ports as you expect simultaneous remote connections. You also need a phone line for each modem port. If management balks at purchasing hardware and/or the executives are unhappy at the prospect of long distance charges, you could configure their portable computers to connect to a VPN server at the Dallas office and allow them to access the LAN via a VPN. This solution requires that they have Internet access from home. If high security is an issue and the executives will always be calling from home, you can set up callback security with preset numbers so that when a RAS connection is made, the server will hang up and call the user back at his or her home number to complete the connection. You should also ensure that access permissions are set on the users' accounts to allow access only to authorized resources.

CERTIFICATION OBJECTIVE 9.02

Firewalls

When you hear the term *firewall* in computer and Internet terminology, you should picture a real firewall of the three-dimensional variety. This image will help you understand the function of a network firewall. A real firewall is a wall made of fireproof material, built between two buildings to keep a fire from spreading. In other words, it is built to keep something (the fire) out of something else (the building). If a fire breaks out in building A, the firewall prevents the fire from getting into building B. Figure 9-3 shows an example.

FIGURE 9-3

A three-dimensional firewall between two buildings

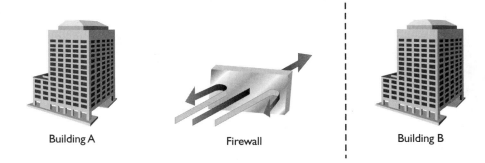

Building A   Firewall   Building B

With that image in mind, you can better understand that a network's virtual firewall is designed to keep information secure by keeping intruders out of your network, much like the physical firewall keeps fire out of the protected building. In a TCP/IP world, everyone communicates via IP addresses and routers. With this in mind, we can configure our firewall to serve as a barrier between our network's addresses and those of the outside world. We can allow traffic from only certain IP addresses, or we can block traffic from specific addresses. We can also allow or block packets based on port numbers. Table 9-1 presents a list of well-known TCP/UDP ports that can be opened or blocked.

When you open a port on the firewall, it is often referred to as "punching a hole" in the firewall. Figure 9-4 shows what a typical firewall configuration might look like.

TABLE 9-1

Well-known TCP/UDP Ports and Functions

Port Number	Protocol	Function
20/21	TCP/UDP	FTP
23	TCP/UDP	Telnet
25	TCP/UDP	SNMP
53	TCP/UDP	DNS
69	TCP/UDP	TFTP
80	TCP/UDP	World Wide Web
88	TCP/UDP	Kerberos
110	TCP/UDP	POP3
119	TCP/UDP	NNTP

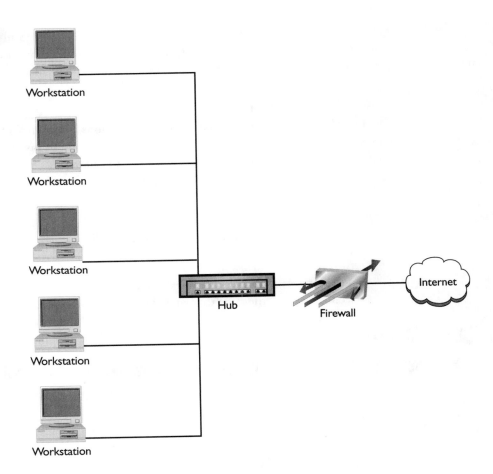

FIGURE 9-4

A typical network firewall configuration

Hardware-based Firewall Solutions

When you consider hardware-based firewall solutions, think of the word *appliance*. Internet appliances are becoming more and more common; these are dedicated devices that are limited to performing one or two tasks. The hardware firewall solution is a box specifically designed to do only one thing: be a firewall.

Firewall Administration

Most hardware solutions are programmable and can be administered. Sometimes you have to connect to a management port on the box; other firewalls have an

HTML interface that can be administered from a Web browser. Still others might have their own management consoles that can be used to administer the firewall. Figure 9-5 shows an example of a PIX firewall solution and its management interface.

Firewall Integration

The nice thing about hardware-based firewall solutions is that they offer you connectivity and configuration, all in one box. Often you can install the device in a rack and plug it in and go—the essence of Plug and Play. This system can make it easier for novice administrators to implement a simple firewall solution.

Implementation Considerations

Some things to keep in mind when implementing a firewall solution include:

- Ensure that the firmware or software is upgradable when future releases come out. If it is not and there are bugs, you could be in bad shape if there is a major security flaw in the code that runs the appliance.

FIGURE 9-5   A hardware PIX firewall solution

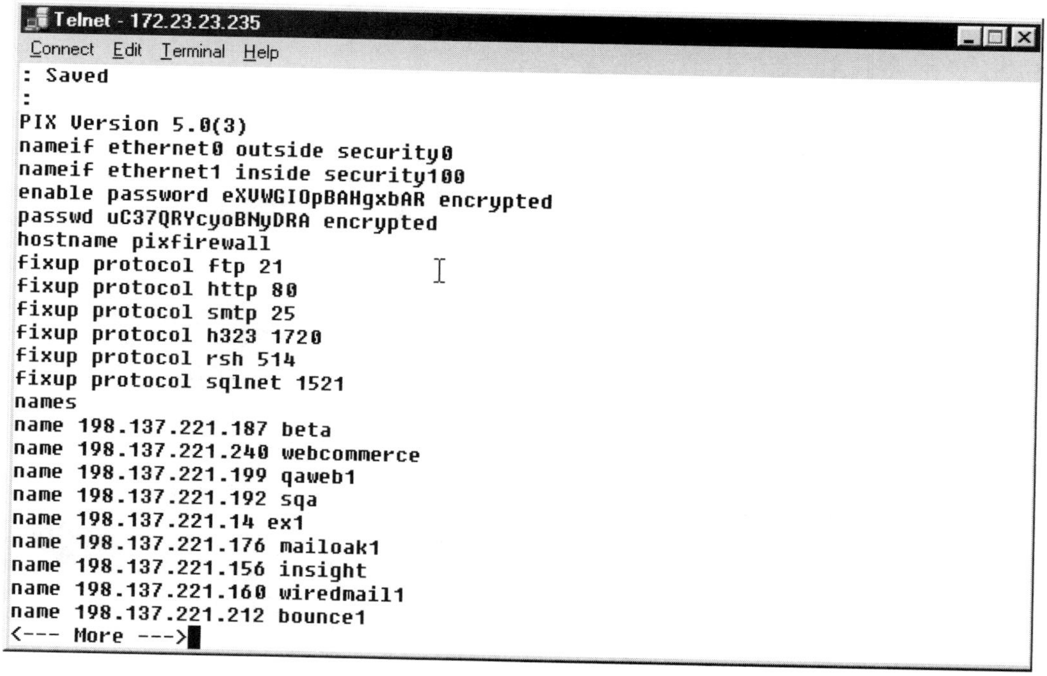

```
Telnet - 172.23.23.235                                    _ □ ×
Connect  Edit  Terminal  Help
: Saved
:
PIX Version 5.0(3)
nameif ethernet0 outside security0
nameif ethernet1 inside security100
enable password eXVWGIOpBAHgxbAR encrypted
passwd uC37QRYcyoBNyDRA encrypted
hostname pixfirewall
fixup protocol ftp 21                    I
fixup protocol http 80
fixup protocol smtp 25
fixup protocol h323 1720
fixup protocol rsh 514
fixup protocol sqlnet 1521
names
name 198.137.221.187 beta
name 198.137.221.240 webcommerce
name 198.137.221.199 qaweb1
name 198.137.221.192 sqa
name 198.137.221.14 ex1
name 198.137.221.176 mailoak1
name 198.137.221.156 insight
name 198.137.221.160 wiredmail1
name 198.137.221.212 bounce1
<--- More --->
```

■ Be aware of the firewall's interactivity with your network. Are there major compatibility issues in the operating system or with the applications you are running?

These are just a couple of the questions you should ask before implementing a hardware-based firewall. When it comes to administering these types of devices, you should determine how much of a learning curve your administrators will have to go through to successfully protect your network. Some firewall companies offer training and implementation assistance at purchase time. Depending on the brand, you might be able to get computer-based training or third-party documentation in the form of books, online support, or instructor-led training.

EXERCISE 9-3

Configuring Your Firewall

Consider the following scenario: You are the administrator of a small network (70 computers) for an accounting firm. You have connected to the management console of your firewall and disabled ports 25, 53, 69, and 119 to enhance network security. Based on your actions, answer the following questions:

1. A user reports to you that she is having problems with her e-mail while using Outlook Express. You explain to her that because of your security measures, her e-mail program will not be fully functional. What e-mail tasks, if any, should she still be able to perform?

2. A user reports to you that she is no longer able to browse the World Wide Web. You note that you did not disable port 80. Does your firewall have anything to do with her problem, and if it does, how can this user access Web sites?

3. A user wants to download files from a remote Web site using the file-transfer feature of Internet Explorer. Will he be able to do so, based on your security enhancements?

4. What complaints from users can you expect, based on your decision to disable port 119?

Answer:

1. Because you disabled port 25, used by Simple Mail Transfer Protocol (SMTP) to send mail over the Internet, the user will be unable to send e-mail. However, she should still receive e-mail messages via POP3, which is not disabled.

2. Although you did not disable port 80, used by the World Wide Web's HyperText Transfer Protocol (HTTP), you did disable port 53, used by the Domain Name System (DNS). Thus, if a user tries to access Web sites using a "friendly" DNS name, the name will not be resolved and she will not be able to browse. However, she should be able to connect to Web sites using their IP addresses.

3. Although you disabled port 69, used by the Trivial File Transfer Protocol (TFTP), the FTP function built into Internet Explorer uses FTP on port 20 (port 21 is the FTP control port).

4. Because you disabled port 119, used by the Network News Transfer Protocol (NNTP), you can expect users to complain that they are no longer able to access newsgroups.

Software-based Firewall Solutions

Most firewall appliances consist of firewall software that runs on top of a dedicated operating system. The operating system provides only those features necessary for running and configuring the firewall software. Another option for implementing a firewall is to install a firewall package that runs on top of a general purpose operating system, such Windows NT 4.0, Windows 2000, or UNIX. The advantage of this strategy is that you may be able to size the hardware better to fit your requirements.

An example of a software firewall is Microsoft Proxy Server. (Internet Security and Acceleration Server, or ISA, now in beta, will be the next release of Microsoft Proxy Server 2.0 and will include improved firewall options.) This software component can be installed and up and running relatively easily. There are also other third-party software solutions, such as Checkpoint Systems. Figure 9-6 shows the management console from Checkpoint.

One temptation you should resist with a software-based firewall solution is using the firewall system to provide additional services. Although this is quite possible since you are running the firewall software on a general purpose operating system, it is a bad idea from both security and performance standpoints, as any network security professional will quickly tell you.

on the

job

It is very easy to configure a firewall to allow appropriate access. The challenge is to make sure you have covered the ports that need to be covered. Some applications use more than one port, and some could be UDP transmissions; others could be TCP transmissions. Testing is always very important to ensure proper operation of applications going through the firewall.

FIGURE 9-6   A Checkpoint Software firewall solution

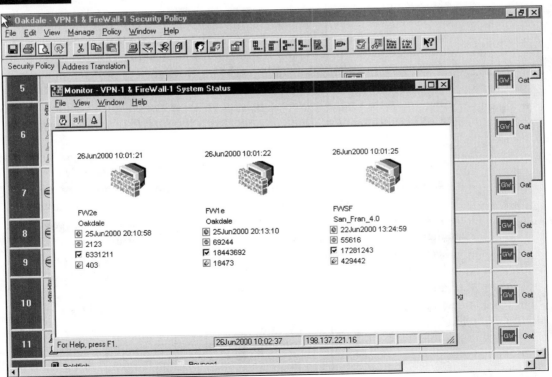

Software solutions require hardware to go along with them. You might need to purchase at least one server, and in many cases two, for redundancy. You also have to buy the operating system on which the software solution will be installed. Because Windows 2000 is relatively new, you could have difficulty finding a firewall solution that is on the certified software list. This potential roadblock should be considered, as should compatibility with the operating system. Previously, we talked about making sure your applications will function through your firewall solution, but ensuring that the operating system and the hardware you buy can support a software product can actually be the most challenging part of getting your firewall up and running.

CERTIFICATION OBJECTIVE 9.03

Routing and Remote Access Strategies

Remote access to your network can be a necessity if you don't have a VPN configured. Routing and Remote Access Services (RRAS) are fully integrated into Windows 2000. With Windows NT 4.0, many of the crucial aspects of the RRAS were implemented in the "steelhead" add-on, also known as the RRAS upgrade.

exam
⑳atch
RRAS will more than likely be a subject you will see on the exam in one fashion or another. Being familiar with the interface will be useful in answering the case study questions.

When it comes to configuring RRAS in Windows 2000, there is no need to install it. RRAS is installed by default. A new feature from the administration standpoint is where you configure RRAS. All configuration of RRAS can be done from a single MMC console. The network connections themselves are configured via the Network and Dial-up Connections applet in the Settings menu.

Security and authentication are stronger and there are more options available with the Windows 2000 version of RRAS. Microsoft Challenge Handshake Authentication Protocol (MS-CHAP) was supported in Windows NT 4.0, but a new version, MS-CHAP v2, comes with Windows 2000; it provides a higher level of security for logon authentication. Also supported are Remote Authentication and Dial-In Services (RADIUS) and Extensible Authentication Protocol (EAP). NAT is implemented as a component of RRAS and is considered one of the RRAS

Routing Protocols. ICS, on the other hand, is configured through Network and Dial-up Connections. Configuration for ICS is minimal; there is more flexibility in configuring NAT options. We discuss NAT/ICS in more detail later in the chapter.

CertCam 9-4

EXERCISE 9-4

Installing Routing and Remote Access Services

In this exercise we configure a Windows 2000 server as a RAS server. This exercise requires that a modem be installed.

1. Click Start, go to Programs | Administrative Tools and select Routing and Remote Access.

2. You will see a server icon in the left pane. Right-click the server icon and choose Configure and Enable Routing and Remote Access.

3. You will see a warning about stopping existing services. Acknowledge that you have done so, and let the Configuration Wizard start. Click Next.

4. The Routing and Remote Access window will allow you to enable Remote Access. Select this option only.

5. Click Next. You will see the Dial-in or Demand Dial Interfaces dialog box. This is where you determine what devices will be used for remotely connecting.

6. Click Next. You will see the Authentication and Encryption dialog box. Here you can select the authentication options you want to use. Select the options that are appropriate for your organization.

7. Click Next, which brings you to Access Rights. Your choices are Access This Server Only or Access Entire Network. Choose Access Entire Network.

8. Click Next. You can now specify information in the TCP/IP addressing settings. You can configure DHCP or a static pool of addresses. This series of addresses is the one that workstations use upon renewing their leases. For this exercise, let's use DHCP.

9. Click Next. You should see a summary screen, and then you can click Finish.

10. The changes will be made, and then the system will offer to start the appropriate services.

Integrating Remote Access Services in a Routed Network

When routing and subnets are involved in your network design, you should make the RRAS network its own network segment. If the network adapter on the RRAS server is on a 192.168.0.0 network, make sure the dial-up connection that is established is on a different network. There should be a route between the RAS network and the local area network to make sure communication works between the two.

Remote Access Services Security Implementations

When configuring your RAS options, you must consider how you want your users to access the internal network. Some of the simple options include how the initial connection is made. For example, you can choose whether you want a user to receive a call back to verify that he or she is a legal user on the network. There are a couple of ways to do this. You can have the Callback Control Protocol either dial a predetermined number or let the caller set the number to call back. Figure 9-7 shows the dialog window to set this configuration item.

There are different forms of authentication as well. The dial-up user must log on with username and password. The following is a list of protocols supported with RRAS:

- Password Authentication Protocol (PAP)
- Shiva PAP (SPAP)
- Challenge-Handshake Protocol (CHAP)
- Microsoft CHAP (MS-CHAP)
- Microsoft CHAP version 2 (MS-CHAP2)
- Extensible Authentication Protocol (EAP)

PAP is not very secure, because passwords are sent across the wire in clear text. The other methods use some sort of encryption or a challenge token when sending information across the wire. EAP is a way for third-party vendors to develop other authentication methods compatible with Windows 2000.

exam
ⓦatch

The various authentication protocols could be an exam item, so study them as you get ready for the exam.

Specifying
Callback Mode

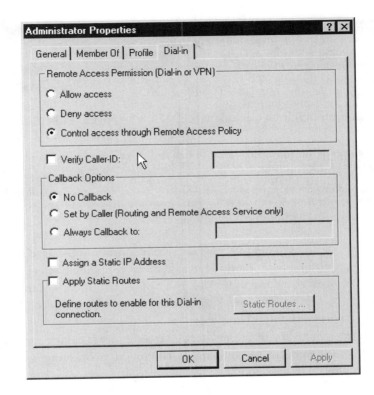

Improving Remote Access Service Accessibility

To make your RRAS server available, you must have the required number of access ports to support your organization. If you will provide direct modem dial-up to your remote access clients, you can install a multiport serial device, such as a Digiboard.

To install a modem or other connection device, use the Computer Management console. To get to the Computer Management console, you can right-click the My Computer icon on the desktop and select Manage from the menu, or select Computer Management from the Administrative Tools menu.

Now that you have a basic understanding of RAS, review some of the highlights shown in the following Scenario & Solution box.

SCENARIO & SOLUTION

What protocols are supported for authentication with RRAS?	PAP, SPAP, CHAP, MS-CHAP, MS-CHAP version 2, EAP
What options are available for Callback Mode?	No Callback, Callback Set by Caller, Predetermined Callback
Where are all network connections, local or remote, administered?	The Network and Dial-Up Interface Connection window
What piece of hardware is required for RRAS?	A modem or multiport modem-type device

In the Computer Management console, you can select Device Manager and see a list of devices already installed and configured. If you right-click the computer icon at the top of the list, you can select Initiate a Scan for Hardware Changes. If you have Plug-and-Play modems or multiport devices installed, the drivers will be installed automatically for you.

The key to successful RAS accessibility is having enough dial-in ports for your organization. A company of 100 to 150 people might be able to get away with eight ports, if you do not have many people who connect remotely. If you have a large staff of traveling sales people, you might need a modem bank of 20 to 30 modems for a company the same size. The easiest way to determine the number of modems you'll need is to know your users. The best plan of attack is usually to start with a small number and work your way up until you know you are successfully handling the number of dial-in users. You will be able to tell that you need additional modem ports when users complain about busy signals and not being able to connect.

on the
job

An important part of configuring your RRAS is to test all configurations thoroughly. It is possible for RRAS to work one day and not the next, because connectivity can be affected by numerous elements. If you have multiple lines, be sure that each one works with the rollover configuration. You should also ensure that lines are disconnecting the way they should. I saw a case in which lines were shown as "in use" several hours and sometimes even days after disconnection, which prevented new dial-in users from connecting. It cannot be repeated enough: test, test, test.

Windows 2000 Network Address Translation

Network Address Translation (NAT) is a new feature of Windows 2000. In Windows NT 4.0, NAT required third-party add-on software; that's no longer the case with Windows 2000. NAT allows for secure connections behind your firewall, using one public IP address to access the Internet for every workstation on your network. The addressing scheme behind the NAT server can be whatever you want it to be. However, you should use the range of addresses set aside as nonroutable on the Internet. These addresses are:

- Class A: 10.0.0.0–10.255.255.255
- Class B: 172.16.0.0–172.31.255.255
- Class C: 192.168.0.0–192.168.255.255

Every packet that leaves the network appears to other computers on the Internet to be coming from the one designated public IP address on the NAT server. The public address is assigned by the Internet service provider (ISP). Workstations accessing the Internet remain anonymous and secure because you are translating to the "live" or "shared" IP address. Figure 9-8 shows how NAT would be drawn in a diagram.

There are two ways to install and use NAT with Windows 2000 Server. The first, called *manual method*, is configured through the RRAS console. This method requires an administrator with some knowledge of the functionality of NAT and routing and remote access. This method requires more configuration and is designed for larger environments.

The other option is the *automatic method*, set up through the Network and Dial-up Connections applet. This method uses Internet Connection Services (ICS), which we cover later in this chapter. This method doesn't require nearly as much configuration as the manual method and does IP address assignment, DNS, and other configuration items as well.

Installing Windows 2000 Network Address Translation

Installing NAT is an easy process. It is done from the Routing and Remote Access Console, as shown in Figure 9-9.

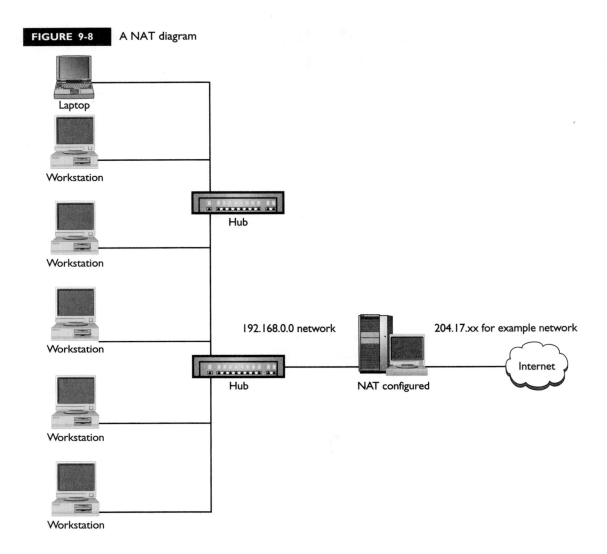

FIGURE 9-8   A NAT diagram

NAT is considered a routing protocol and can be added from the Routing and Remote Access Console. Once it is added as a protocol, you must add interfaces that will be loaded with the NAT configuration. When selecting NAT, you will see a window entitled New Interface for Connection Sharing (NAT). Once the interface is added, you can view the properties of NAT from the RRAS Console, which is shown in Figure 9-10.

FIGURE 9-9

The Routing and
Remote Access
Console

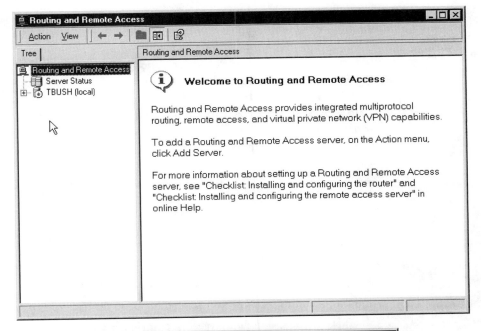

FIGURE 9-10

Network
Address
Translation
Properties

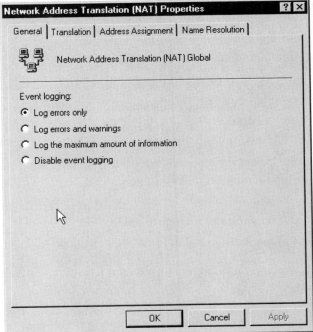

After these items are configured, NAT is installed and you can close all windows. We cover additional configuration items in the next section.

NAT can be complicated to understand. Just remember that there are two worlds to consider when thinking in terms of NAT. One is the public world; the other is the private world. The public world is the Internet; the private world is your network. Separate the two on your network diagrams. This separation makes it easier for others to understand and will be invaluable when you are training new engineers.

CertCam 9-5

EXERCISE 9-5

Installing Network Address Translation

In this exercise we add NAT and choose an adapter to load the protocol.

1. Go to the Routing and Remote Access Console (Start | Programs | Administrative Tools | Routing and Remote Access).

2. Click the plus sign (+) next to the Local Server icon to expand the tree.

3. Click the plus sign (+) next to IP Routing to expand the tree.

4. Right-click the General icon and choose New Routing Protocol.

5. From the New Routing Protocol window, select Network Address Translation (NAT) and click OK.

6. Single-click the IP Protocol icon. NAT will be in the list of items at the right.

7. Once you have NAT installed, you must select an adapter with which it will load. If you right-click the NAT icon in the console pane, you can select New Interface from the menu.

8. Select the interface you want from the New Interface for Network Address Translation (NAT) and click OK.

9. A window entitled Network Address Translation Properties will open. Close all windows when finished.

FROM THE CLASSROOM

NAT and ICS

As new features in Windows 2000, NAT and ICS are likely to be the focus of exam questions. When combined with a firewall, NAT provides an Internet solution for your network that will help protect your workstations, clients, and users from the outside world. It is important to become very familiar with NAT. In addition, be sure to take the opportunity to observe how IIS and Exchange operate behind a NAT configuration.

—Brian Frederick (MCSE, MCNE, Network+)

Configuring Windows 2000 Network Address Translation

Once you have NAT installed and running using the default settings, you can use some configuration items to tweak how NAT is utilized. One thing you can configure is static port mapping. Static ports are used for Exchange or IIS servers behind your NAT server. You can assign an incoming port and a private address and port in your NAT table so that outside users who need access to the resource can access it via the live public port.

A good example involves an IIS on your network that you want to use to host a Web site. In this situation, you have to know the port number that IIS uses. Generally, this will be port 80. Using NAT, you set up port 80 on your outside network to "redirect" requests from the outside network to the IP address and port number of the actual IIS server running on your internal network. The following exercise will take you through the steps necessary to do this.

exam
ⓦatch

Questions about static port mapping are likely to appear on the exam. Be sure to complete the exercise to become familiar with static port mappings and how to configure them.

EXERCISE 9-6

Configure Static NAT Ports

1. On your Windows 2000 Server machine, first complete the previous exercise and have NAT installed. Open the Network Address Translation Properties window by right-clicking on Network Address Translation in the console pane and selecting Properties.

2. In the Network Address Translation Properties window, select the Special Ports tab.

3. In the Special Ports tab, click the Add button. The Add Special Port window should open.

4. For our example, we assume you have a Web server with the address of 172.16.21.6. In the Add Special Port window, enter the incoming port of 80.

5. In the Private Address field, enter the IP address of our Web server.

6. For the outgoing port, we use port 80 also, since we are using the standard port number for a Web server HTTP request.

7. Click OK. This action will show you your entry added to the list in the NAT Properties window.

8. Click OK to close the window.

This exercise should have added a port mapping to a Web server with the address 172.16.21.6 and a port mapping of 80. If you have a Web server or another server configured with IIS, you can try to connect to your Web server via the Internet using this method.

Network Address Translation Implementation Considerations

When implementing NAT, you must keep a few things in mind. First, what range will you use for your internal addressing, and how will it correlate to your external addressing? You must also consider the need for assigning static internal addresses to ports. This would apply, for example, if you have Exchange or IIS deployed on the internal network and want to keep it off the live, outside network. To do this, you must map an external port to an internal address. The following is an example of statically mapping an address: The DNS MX record of 204.71.151.23 for syngress.com is mapped to port 25 for SMTP. Your Exchange box is at the IP address of 172.16.21.5. Anything addressed to 204.71.151.23 will translate to your exchange box, and vice versa, on the internal segment. If you address something to the Internet coming from 172.16.21.5, the network will translate the address to the external address in the NAT table.

With some software that accesses the Internet, you need to make sure that NAT will not interfere with the functionality of the software. Some applications do not function properly—or at all—using address translation. If this is the case, you might need to make a configuration change on your final Internet implementation plan.

These are just a few of the things to think about when you are designing a solution. Later in the chapter we look at other components that could enter into the final solution as well. Network environments can vary tremendously; it is beyond the scope of this chapter to discuss every possibility, but we cover common scenarios that affect most networks. Because NAT is a new feature with Windows 2000, you could see some exam questions that address the scenarios listed in the following Scenario & Solution box.

SCENARIO & SOLUTION

When configuring NAT with a Web server on your network, what should you have added to your configuration?	Static NAT port mappings
From what management console do you install NAT?	The Routing and Remote Access Console
What is the name for the "lite" version of NAT that is automatically installed using Network and Dial-up Connections?	Internet Connection Sharing (ICS)

CERTIFICATION OBJECTIVE 9.05

Windows 2000 Internet Connection Sharing

As mentioned earlier, there are two ways to configure and install address translation in Windows 2000. The automatic method is called Internet Connection Sharing. This feature is the same in Windows 2000 as in Windows 98 second edition (Windows 98 SE). The whole reason for Internet Connection Sharing is spelled out in its name. To be able to share one Internet connection can be a major cost benefit for a small office/home office (SOHO) or a relatively small company (fewer than five servers). Instead of bringing in costly T1 or ISDN lines, you could get a DSL or cable modem and share one connection throughout your company. This sharing can provide a cost-effective way for your users to get to the Internet.

When ICS is installed, a process takes place that you should understand for the exam. When ICS is installed on the machine that will host the Internet connection, the private IP address of its internal adapter is set to 192.168.0.1. There is no choice but to accept this value. (If you need to use a different internal address, you need to deploy NAT via RRAS on a Windows 2000 Server instead of using ICS.) If you are using a different IP addressing scheme and still want to use ICS, you should consider changing the addressing scheme, because you cannot change the private IP address on your server running ICS. Along with ICS come some preconfigured AUTODHCP and DNS settings. The AUTODHCP hands out addresses for the 192.168.0.0 network. The ICS computer is called a *DHCP allocator*.

Installing Windows 2000 Internet Connection Sharing

To install ICS, use the Network and Dial-Up Connections window. Select the adapter, whether it is dial-up or a network adapter that will be the shared card for ICS. Be aware that the IP address of the card you select will change. If the machine is currently connected to a network, this means you might lose communications. The default address of the card will be set to 192.168.0.1.

If you are using a modem to dial up and connect, you need to deal with another configuration item. This is the on-demand dialing feature; you must decide whether you want demand-dial to be enabled. This feature allows the ICS computer to dial up and connect only when a workstation or server tries to access the Internet. It

EXERCISE 9-7

Installing Internet Connection Sharing Services

For this lab, you need two workstations, each configured with Windows 2000 Professional. One of the workstations needs two access devices. They can be either two network adapters, with one connected directly to the Internet, or a network adapter and a modem that can dial an ISP. This setup is required for the test phase of the exercise.

1. On the workstation that has the two network devices, open the Network and Dial-up Connections window.

2. Right-click either the dial-up connection or the network adapter that is on the Internet. Select Properties from the menu.

3. Select Internet Connection Sharing from the available tabs. Under Shared Access, select Enable Internet Connection Sharing for This Connection. The On-Demand Dialing option becomes available.

4. If you are using a modem as your Internet connection, select the On-Demand Dialing option.

5. Click OK. You should see a warning about the local connection being changed to 192.168.0.1. This step will lose the local connection temporarily, but once the configuration is complete, you can have your workstation retrieve a new IP address via DHCP. Click Yes to acknowledge the warning.

6. The updates will take effect, and then you can use IPCONFIG to check the IP addresses assigned to your adapters. Open a DOS window and type **IPCONFIG /ALL** and look for the 192.168.0.1 address.

7. At your other workstation, make sure your network adapter is set to obtain an address automatically. After confirming this is the case, open a DOS window and type **IPCONFIG /RENEW**. If you are running Windows 9x, you can run the WINIPCFG utility and click Renew on the appropriate adapter.

8. When the adapter has been assigned a 192.168.x.x address, you can try to access the Internet via a browser or by opening a command-line window and typing **PING www.syngress.com**.

9. If you have a dial-up device, you might hear it connecting. If you have a standard network adapter connected to a cable modem or ADSL line, the response should be almost immediate.

doesn't keep the modem line tied up 24 hours a day. When a request is made, the ICS server dials up, accesses the Internet, and makes the real request once the connection is made. When data stops streaming across the wire and after a certain threshold is reached, the connection is dropped.

You can test your configuration by going to a workstation on the network. At the workstation, make sure you have TCP/IP bound to your network adapter. You can try to obtain an address using one of the following commands. On Windows NT 2000:

```
IPCONFIG /RENEW
```

Or, on Windows 9x platforms:

```
WINIPCFG
```

Click Renew in the WINIPCFG window.

You should see an address received using the simple DHCP setup on the ICS server that starts with 192.168.x.x. The xs are based on your DHCP lease from the ICS server. Now you can try to ping a server on the Internet. For example:

```
PING WWW.MICROSOFT.COM
```

You should see this command resolve to an IP address and then give you four replies. If you are using a dial-up connection, you might hear the ICS computer dialing when an attempt is made to access the Internet.

Configuring Windows 2000 Internet Connection Sharing

Configuring ICS is like configuring any other component in Windows 2000. If you right-click the shared connection and choose the Internet Connection Sharing tab, you can configure some items. For example, if you click Settings, you can then specify services for Web servers or DNS servers internally. Figure 9-11 shows the Sharing tab.

As you did with NAT, you can assign static ports for servers behind your main ICS server. To do this, open the Properties window of the adapter configured for ICS and then select the Internet Connection Sharing tab. Here you can select the service, as it is called with ICS. You can select the name of service, the port number, the IP address, and DNS name of the machine you want to access behind the firewalls.

FIGURE 9-11

The Sharing tab

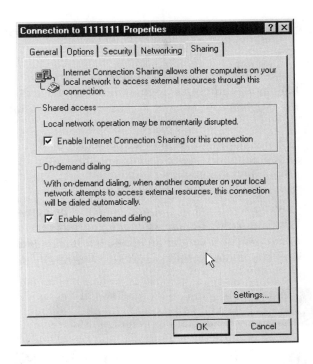

Now that you know a little about ICS, see the scenarios and proposed solutions listed in the following box.

SCENARIO & SOLUTION

You are configuring ICS on your network; what IP address will your ICS server have?	192.168.0.1
How will your clients obtain an IP address to function on the network for Internet access?	The ICS computer becomes a DHCP allocator to hand out internal IP addresses to client computers.
After installing ICS, what should you do at your client machine to obtain the IP address?	In Windows 2000/NT: Type **IPCONFIG /RENEW** at the command line. In Windows 9x: Run WINIPCFG and click Renew.

Internet Connection Sharing Implementation Considerations

ICS is very simplistic and really requires no administration. That is one big consideration when implementing ICS services on your network. If you already have an IP addressing scheme, you might have to change it if you are not on the 192.168.0.0 network. Making this change could be a major project if you are a medium-sized company. In most cases, however, ICS is used in small organizations.

Another consideration involves caching of Web pages. Caching isn't included with an ICS configuration; if your organization needs caching, consider implementing Microsoft Proxy Server instead.

exam
Watch

Questions related to ICS and NAT will be common since they are new to Windows 2000. Be sure to make yourself comfortable with the interface. This exam will focus on design issues, but it is necessary to be thoroughly acquainted with the implementation process to properly design a NAT solution.

CERTIFICATION OBJECTIVE 9.06

Integrating Windows 2000 with Microsoft Proxy Server, Internet Information Server, and Exchange Server

Designing an Internet solution for a Windows 2000 network often includes deployment of various Internet services. Your organization could require the Web page caching and filtering capabilities of a proxy server. You might want to provide a Web presence via a Web server. Furthermore, it is almost certain that you will need to provide e-mail for your users. Microsoft products such as Microsoft Proxy Server, Internet Information Server, and Exchange Server are easier to integrate into your Windows 2000 network if you plan for their deployment.

In this section, we briefly discuss each of these products and how they will impact your overall Internet strategy and design.

Integrating Microsoft Proxy Server 2.0

Microsoft Proxy Server has been around for a while and is a viable solution for connecting a LAN to the Internet. With the introduction of Windows 2000, Microsoft provides other options: NAT and ICS. The functionalities of Proxy

Server, NAT, and ICS are related, but the feature sets differ, and you should be aware of the limitations and capabilities of each.

How Proxy Server Works

Proxy Server uses address translation to provide Internet access to a private network, much as NAT and ICS do. However, the address translation method used does not comply with the RFCs that define the specifications for NAT.

A proxy server is configured with one Internet address and one LAN address. The Internet requests are transmitted by the clients to the server through the internal LAN address and then out to the public or Internet address.

Firewall Functionality   Microsoft Proxy Server adds firewall functionality to address translation. Using Proxy Server's filtering feature, you can block or allow IP traffic from specified domains or IP addresses.

You can also filter packets based on ports. For example, you can prevent network users from receiving Network News Transfer Protocol (NNTP) packets.

Caching   Proxy Server also provides caching of Web pages and FTP objects. This reduces the amount of Internet traffic and speeds access by internal users to frequently visited Web sites (see Figure 9-12).

Whether or not to enable caching, which speeds Web page access for frequently used pages but also consumes hard disk space on the proxy server, is a consideration in planning your proxy solution design.

Proxy Server Features and Characteristics

Proxy Server provides three basic services:

- Web Proxy, which supports HTTP, FTP, and Gopher for TCP/IP computers
- WinSock Proxy, which supports Windows Sockets applications on client computers and works with either TCP/IP or IPX/SPX
- SOCKS Proxy, which is used as a cross-platform mechanism to provide secure communications between clients and servers using TCP/IP

All this functionality comes with a price: Microsoft Proxy Server is a relatively expensive solution, whereas ICS and NAT are built into the Windows 2000

Proxy Server allows you to enable and configure Web page caching

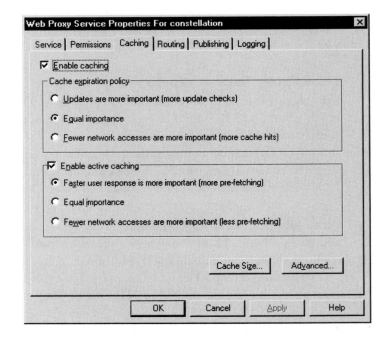

operating system. The correct solution for your organization depends on its size, security needs, and budget.

Compare and Contrast: Proxy Server, NAT, and ICS

In determining which connection sharing option is most appropriate for your organization, ask yourself the following questions:

Is Web performance an issue?

- Do you need advanced filtering capabilities?
- Is cost a major factor?
- Will you be using IPSecurity?
- Do you need to access Internet applications for which NAT filters are not available?
- Do you need to use a range of IP addresses other than the 192.168.0.0 range?
- Is there a DHCP or DNS server on your network?

| TABLE 9-2 | A Comparison of Connection Sharing Solutions |

Requirement	Supported by ICS	Supported by NAT	Supported by Proxy Server
Share one IP address among several computers	Yes	Yes	Yes
No additional software purchase	Yes; built into Windows 2000 Server and Professional	Yes; built into Windows 2000 Server	No; Microsoft Proxy Server must be purchased separately
Web caching is needed to increase performance	No	No	Yes
An IP address range other than 192.168.0.0 must be used on the internal network	No	Yes	Yes
There are DHCP or DNS servers on the network	No	Yes	Yes
Advanced filtering and firewall capabilities are required	No	No	Yes
You must use IPSecurity	No	No	Proxy Server's Web caching and filtering can be used, but its address translation feature cannot; you need a routed connection

Table 9-2 illustrates how the answers to these questions will affect your choice of connection sharing solutions.

Integrating Internet Information Server 5.0

If you want to include Web servers in your Internet environment, you can do so easily with Windows 2000; IIS 5.0 is integrated with the operating system. IIS 5.0 is more powerful and takes advantage of multiprocessor machines and memory better than IIS 4. The surface similarities are apparent, so if you are familiar with IIS 4, you should be able to use IIS 5.0 with relatively little training.

Configuration Considerations

When you have a Web server on your network, you must make sure that your configuration supports the various ports that are used by IIS. Two common ports are 80 and 443. Port 80 is the standard Web server, or HTTP, port. Port 443 is used for Secure Sockets Layer (SSL). Figure 9-13 shows a screen from the MMC and the IIS snap-in. This screen can be opened by clicking Start | Programs | Administrative Tools | Internet Services Manager.

You also must consider your firewall and ensure that IIS can receive and send data through your firewall configuration. If you have virtual sites set up, there is a good chance that your Web server is serving multiple IP addresses.

If you are using NAT on the network, you need to have static mappings set up, as discussed earlier. It is possible to use ICS in conjunction with IIS, but NAT is a better choice in terms of configurability and functionality. Static port mappings might be needed for both 443 and 80, depending on your configuration.

FIGURE 9-13

The Internet Information Services window

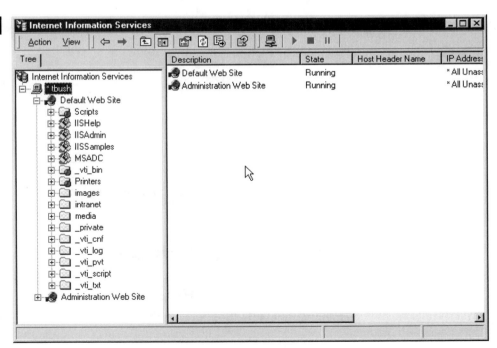

Internet Information Server Services and Features

Internet Information Server 5.0 supports four popular application-layer protocols from the TCP/IP suite: HTTP (for World Wide Web pages), FTP, SMTP to provide e-mailing for Active Server Pages (ASPs), and NNTP. With IIS 5.0, you can implement a Web server, an FTP server, a news server, or all three.

Lightweight Directory Access Protocol (LDAP) is supported for the purpose of allowing the SMTP service to access data that is stored in an LDAP directory service (such as Active Directory). Bandwidth throttling allows you to limit the amount of network bandwidth used by IIS; if your network runs over a slow connection or the server functions in multiple roles, you will want to consider bandwidth allocation in designing your Internet solution.

Internet Information Server Security Features

An important consideration in implementing a network that includes IIS is how it will impact overall network security. IIS 5.0 uses a multilayered security model, which protects network data from unauthorized access via the Web, FTP, or news servers.

Security features include the following:

- **IP address and domain name filtering**   Administrators can easily configure IIS to block traffic from specific addresses and/or domains.

- **Authentication settings**   Web sites can be configured to require a specified type of authentication.

- **IIS permissions**   Access and application permissions can be configured for Web sites or FTP sites, including virtual directories.

- **NTFS permissions**   Specific user accounts or groups can be denied access via NTFS permissions on the resource.

The Permissions Wizard makes it easy to configure permissions in IIS. The wizard is accessed via the IIS MMC (see Figure 9-14).

As part of your design plan, you should consider the security needs of the organization and how you will provide protection for sensitive data while opening up your network to the world via your presence on the Web.

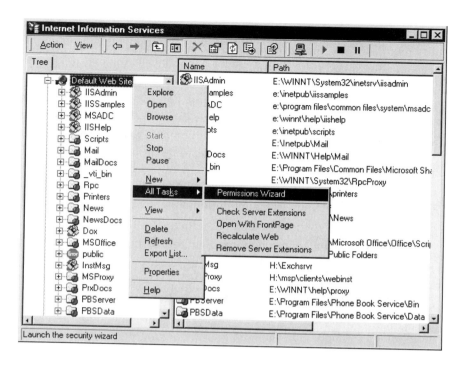

FIGURE 9-14

The IIS 5.0
Permissions
Wizard makes it
easy to configure
access

Integrating an E-mail Solution with Exchange Server 2000

E-mail is the most popular Internet application, and almost every company, large or small, that is connected to the Internet wants to have e-mail access. Exchange Server 2000 is the latest incarnation of Microsoft's corporate mail server, designed specifically to work with Windows 2000. In fact, Exchange 2000 runs only on the Windows 2000 operating system. This is because Exchange is tightly integrated with Active Directory, using the Windows 2000 directory services instead of maintaining its own directory, as was the case with previous versions.

Another difference involves the internal protocols used by Exchange. Older versions used the X.400 standard, whereas Exchange 2000 relies on the SMTP Internet standard.

E-mail Protocols: SMTP, POP, and IMAP

You may be familiar with SMTP as a member of the TCP/IP protocol suite. Most often, SMTP is used for sending mail, and POP is used for downloading the mail to the local computer from a mail server on which it is stored. Of course, SMTP and POP can both run on the same server, or they can run on separate servers. A more sophisticated protocol for receiving e-mail is the *Internet Message Protocol (IMAP)*. IMAP allows users to manipulate messages and folders on the server and search or delete them without first downloading them to the local machine.

If your organization will have e-mail on your network and you are planning for Internet connectivity, you must ensure that the proper ports are available for the e-mail messages to get through the firewall. SMTP uses port 25, whereas POPv3 uses port 110. IMAP uses port 143. If the server uses SSL, you might also need to open port 995 for secure POP3.

E-mail Security Considerations

As with other aspects of your Internet connectivity design, security is a primary concern when you deploy an e-mail solution. Because e-mail messages (like all Internet traffic) pass through multiple nodes on the way to their destinations, they are inherently vulnerable to diversion, unauthorized access, or alteration.

Exchange 2000 provides the means to protect the integrity of e-mail messages by integrating mail services into the Windows 2000 Public Key Infrastructure (PKI). You can encrypt the folders in which client-based mail messages are stored. Exchange provides for encryption of RPC messages used by Outlook to communicate with the Exchange Server, and public key cryptography can be used to encrypt messages sent over the Internet. Consider the security needs of the organization and the sensitivity of data sent via e-mail when you design your e-mail solution.

Exchange 2000 Features and Capabilities

Exchange 2000 provides multiprotocol support, including native support for SMTP, POP, LDAP, IMAP, HTTP, NNTP, Secure MIME, and X.509v3. This breadth of support makes it easier to incorporate the mail server into almost any environment for use with a variety of mail clients.

Another consideration in designing your e-mail solution is the need for collaboration, such as group scheduling, discussion groups, and folders that can be shared. Exchange supports all these collaborative activities. The Web storage system and integration with Office 2000 make group tasks easier to organize.

If your organization includes personnel who travel or work off site, you will want to consider Exchange 2000's Outlook Web Access support, which allows users to access their e-mail, contacts, calendars, and the like via a Web browser. For real-time communication, instant messaging and chat services are provided and data conferencing is supported using Microsoft NetMeeting or other T.120-compliant client software. This communication includes application sharing, file transfer, whiteboard sharing, and audio and video conferencing. As you design your Internet solution, be sure to consider your users' communications needs.

E-mail Planning Considerations

Questions you should answer as you consider the deployment of an e-mail server in conjunction with your Internet/intranet strategy include these:

■ How many users will need e-mail access, and will e-mail volume be low, medium, or high?

■ What e-mail client software is currently deployed or planned for deployment?

■ Do users need sophisticated collaborative tools such as conferencing and document sharing?

■ What are your organization's e-mail security requirements?

The answers to these questions will guide you in making the decisions necessary to integrate an Exchange Server (or servers) into your Windows 2000 network.

EXERCISE 9-8

Planning Internet Access Methods

You run a consulting company that specializes in connecting businesses to the Internet. At this time, you have two companies with which you are working:

■ Ajax Modeling Agency needs to connect its 15-computer LAN to the Internet. All the client computers are running Windows 95 or 98. They do not have a server at this time but would like to connect all the computers to the Internet without changing their network client software. The owner is only mildly concerned about security, but he would like to make sure that personnel and payroll records are not accessible to others. A part-time LAN administrator comes into the office about twice a month to make sure everything is working correctly.

■ The small municipality of Townville has an established network with 120 client computers running a mix of Win9x, Windows NT 4.0 Workstation, and Windows 2000 Professional. Two Windows NT 4.0 servers run a Windows NT 4.0-based single domain network. The city requires a high level of security on its servers because of the sensitive nature of law enforcement and legal data. The city employees access the Internet via modems connected to each computer, and the users access the Internet via their personal America Online (AOL) accounts. They want you to review their Internet access scheme and come up with a more cost-effective and secure solution. They also have a part-time network administrator who visits City Hall once a week to review the network status and take care of outstanding network issues.

What recommendations would you make to these two companies?

Answer: In the first scenario, the best solution for Internet access is to install a Windows 2000 Server machine and then connect that machine to a dial-up ISDN line. Dial-up ISDN is cost effective and relatively secure because the IP address assigned to the modem changes with each dial-up. On the Windows 2000 server, you would configure Internet Connection Sharing and make all the client computers DHCP clients so that they get their IP addressing information from the ICS DHCP allocator. You can place the files that require security on the Windows 2000 Server and take advantage of both NTFS permissions and the Encrypting File System to make sure that no one is able to access the secure data.

In the second scenario, the city has a network administrator who can handle the more complex security and Internet access scheme required in such an environment. First, you must eliminate the modem access from the client computers; it represents a significant security breach for the network. Users should not be using personal AOL accounts to access the Internet because that practice represents a security risk as well.

The best solution in this scenario is to upgrade the Windows NT 4.0 servers to Windows 2000, making sure to upgrade the PDC first. After upgrading the servers, install Proxy Server 2.0 and configure access controls, such as domain filters and packet filters. This step will prevent the city from potential ethics problems related to Web surfing to less than savory sites. You should place all confidential data on the second server that is not connected to the Internet and implement Share, NTFS, and EFS to secure the data.

The network technology to access the Internet could be dedicated ISDN, or better, DSL. In either case, it is important that you configure security on the proxy server to prevent inappropriate access from external and internal users.

CERTIFICATION SUMMARY

Devising an Internet connectivity solution can be a monumental task. The first step in planning your design is to audit your existing network and start diagramming the current and planned components. This process will give you a visual aid in determining the correct solution for your environment. It is much easier to make additions and deletions and move devices around on the diagram rather than in the physical world.

Some new features in Windows 2000 that will play into your Internet strategy include Network Address Translation (NAT) and Internet Connection Sharing (ICS). NAT, included in Windows 2000 Server, allows users to share one or more IP addresses for accessing the network. ICS is a simplified form of NAT, included with both Windows 2000 Server and Professional. The ICS component includes DHCP to send out addresses to client workstations. NAT can also use the DHCP allocator, or it can be disabled so that NAT can be used on a network with a DHCP server.

Routing and Remote Access Service (RRAS) is also expanded and improved with Windows 2000, making remote access easier to implement and control. More and stronger authentication protocols are supported. The configuration of network connections has been integrated into a single interface for simplified handling. When considering your final solution, you must determine the services you will provide. Will you deploy a proxy server? Will you have Web servers? Will you have e-mail servers? If the answer to any of these questions is yes, proper configuration of firewall components and NAT or ICS components is vital to successful implementation. Knowing the standard and nonstandard ports is also important, to ensure that users can connect remotely and get to the resources they need both in and out of the network. Always keep the organization's security needs in mind as you design your Internet connectivity plan.

This chapter provided an overview of the basic design considerations involved in creating an Internet/intranet connectivity solution and gave you a look at some of the ways in which Windows 2000 will enable you to give your network access to outside resources while still maintaining the integrity of the internal data.

TWO-MINUTE DRILL

Designing Internet Connectivity Solutions

❑ An audit of your existing network is important in putting together a solution for Internet connectivity. Things like applications, user needs, e-mail, and Web servers are some of the things you have to consider in devising a design plan.

❑ Creating diagrams helps organize the thought process and planning steps. It is also helpful in providing network documentation after your solution is in place. The documentation can serve as a foundation for proposals and presentations as well. Diagrams assist the nontechnical management personnel in understanding the solution.

Firewalls

❑ There are two types of firewalls: software firewalls and hardware firewalls. Advantages of hardware firewalls include out-of-the-box readiness (most of the time), with no extra hardware needed. Advantages of software firewalls include seamless integration with the OS; disadvantages include the fact that hardware must be purchased separately and both software and hardware configuration is required.

❑ Firewalls can allow access via IP address or IP port number. When configuring your network, you may use a combination of these two. This will generally make your environment that much more secure.

Routing and Remote Access Strategies

❑ Authentication protocols include Password Authentication Protocol (PAP), Shiva PAP, Challenge-Handshake Protocol (CHAP), Microsoft CHAP (MS-CHAP), MS-CHAP version 2, and Extensible Authentication Protocol (EAP).

❑ Another security area is Callback Mode. Callback Mode can be set to No Callback, Callback Set by Caller, or Callback Preset. When you use Callback Preset, you enter a preset number entered, with callback set by the caller. The dial-in user enters a phone number at which he or she will be called back by the server.

Windows 2000 Network Address Translation

❑ Dynamic NAT translation uses different ports based on the workstation sending the information. The NAT-configured server keeps track of its clients using these port numbers.

❑ You can configure static NAT ports for specific machines behind your NAT server. For example, you could use port 80 for a Web server or port 25 for a mail server. You would assign the static port to the address of the server on your network.

Windows 2000 Internet Connection Sharing

❑ Little configuration and administration are required for ICS. When installed, the simple DHCP allocator uses network addresses in the 192.168.0.0 Class C network. The address of the ICS-bound adapter gets changed to 192.168.0.1.

❑ As with NAT, you can set up static mapped ports for your ICS services. This allows you to have servers behind your ICS connection for specific purposes, such as Web servers, FTP servers, or mail servers.

Integrating Windows 2000 with Microsoft Proxy Server, Internet Information Server, and Exchange Server

❑ Internet Information Server version 5 is included with Windows 2000 Server. When designing your Internet solution, you should consider whether you will be running IIS on your network. If you will be, you must consider security factors and integration with other network components.

❑ Port 80 is the common HTTP port used by IIS for Web services. IIS also uses port 443 for Secure Socket Layer (SSL) connections. If you use NAT or ICS for your Internet connectivity, static port mappings should be used for these types of services.

❑ When using the Exchange mail server, you must make sure your firewall is configured to allow the different ports used (typically 25 and 110) to communicate with other mail servers.

❑ If using NAT or ICS in conjunction with Exchange, you must make sure you have the appropriate static port mappings in place to allow communication through the NAT server to the mail server on your network.

SELF TEST

The following questions will help you measure your understanding of the material presented in this chapter. Read all of the choices carefully, as there may be more than one correct answer. Choose all correct answers for each question.

Designing Internet Connectivity Solutions

1. When laying out your Internet design, which of the following are items to consider? Choose all that apply.

   A. Network Address Translation

   B. Firewall

   C. Hubs

   D. Switches

2. What is the first thing you should do when starting to plan your Internet access solution?

   A. Rewire your existing network.

   B. Diagram your existing network.

   C. Do a complete audit of your network.

   D. Convert workstations to Windows 2000.

3. Why should you construct a diagram of your network? Choose all that apply.

   A. It gives you a visual framework for your network to help plan its design.

   B. It allows for easier explanations to nontechnical upper management.

   C. It provides network documentation for future reference.

   D. It can give you a before and after look at the network for comparison purposes.

4. Why is a firewall important in your final solution when designing your plan?

   A. It gives you the ability to share addresses for Internet use.

   B. It allocates IP addresses for you so that you don't have to configure DHCP.

   C. It helps secure your network from potential intruders.

   D. It is required for Internet connectivity.

Firewalls

5. You are configuring your firewall and are trying to determine how to open access to your remote users. The applications that are being used require a wide array of TCP/IP ports to be opened. What is the best way to give access only to certain users?

   A. Open the appropriate ports for any IP address.

   B. Open the appropriate IP addresses only for all ports.

   C. Open the appropriate ports for users' IP addresses.

   D. This cannot be accomplished when a firewall is used.

6. Which of the following is true of the typical firewall configuration? Choose all that apply.

   A. Packets can be blocked based on IP address.

   B. Packets can be blocked based on protocol.

   C. Packets can be blocked based on port number.

   D. Packets can be blocked based on subject matter of the message.

7. You are designing a firewall solution for your network. You do not want users to be able to upload or download files from between their computers and other computers. Which of the following ports should you block to accomplish this goal?

   A. Port 80

   B. Port 119

   C. Port 20

   D. Port 21

Routing and Remote Access Strategies

8. Where do you go to install Routing and Remote Access Services?

   A. Winnt\i386

   B. Winnt

   C. I386

   D. None of the above

9. When designing your RRAS solution, you determined that a dial-up solution will fit your needs and budget. You know you need phone lines, and you must configure RRAS on the server. What other key component do you have to consider when designing your RAS solution?

   A. Modems for connectivity between the phone line and server

   B. Adapters to convert the digital signal to analog for use on the phone lines

   C. Third-party software to allow the Windows 2000 Server to receive incoming calls

   D. Nothing; the phone lines and RRAS are all that are needed

Windows 2000 Network Address Translation

10. Which of the following is true of Network Address Translation (NAT) but not of Internet Connection Sharing (ICS) in Windows 2000? Choose all that apply.

    A. It is included in both Windows 2000 Professional and Windows 2000 Server.

    B. It can be used in conjunction with a DHCP or DNS server on the network.

    C. It must use addresses from the range 192.168.0.0.

    D. It is configured via the RRAS console.

11. You are designing a NAT solution for your network. You have an IIS 5.0 Web server and an Exchange Server on your network. Which of the following should you do to ensure that these servers continue to work properly after NAT is implemented?

    A. Configure NAT to be a DHCP allocator, and configure the Web and mail servers as DHCP clients.

    B. Configure static ports with the IP addresses of the Web and mail servers.

    C. Use ICS instead of NAT.

    D. No address translation solution is possible when you have Web and mail servers on the network.

12. You want to use the automatic method of configuring a shared Internet connection. What should you choose?

    A. Network Address Translation

    B. OSPF

    C. Internet Connection Sharing

    D. Microsoft Proxy Server

Windows 2000 Internet Connection Sharing

13. You are configuring your authentication protocol for your RAS server. Which of the following are options? Choose all that apply.

    A. Microsoft CHAP

    B. Shiva PAP

    C. EAP

    D. Shiva CHAP

14. Your organization requires Internet access, and you do not want to purchase multiple IP addresses. Your organization has 15 people, 10 workstations, and one file server. What would be the easiest service to use to accomplish this task with little administration?

    A. Network Address Translation

    B. Dynamic Host Configuration Protocol

    C. Domain Name Services

    D. Internet Connection Sharing

Integrating Windows 2000 with Microsoft Proxy Server, Internet Information Server, and Exchange Server

15. You are setting up a Web server behind your NAT-based server. What should you also do to your NAT server to ensure the outside world can reach your Web server? Choose all that apply.

    A. Static map port 25 to the IP address of your Web server.

    B. Static map port 110 to the IP address of your Web server.

    C. Static map port 443 to the IP address of your Web server.

    D. Static map port 80 to the IP address of your Web server.

16. You are configuring your ICS-enabled server to handle sending mail requests to and from your mail server. What do you have to do on your ICS box to ensure that the outside world can communicate with your mail server?

    A. Static map port 25 to the IP address of your Web server.

    B. Static map port 110 to the IP address of your Web server.

    C. Static map port 443 to the IP address of your Web server.

    D. Static map port 80 to the IP address of your Web server.

17. You want to integrate an e-mail server into your Windows 2000 network Internet strategy. Users need to be able to read and delete their mail messages on the server without downloading them to their local hard disks. Which of the following e-mail protocols will allow this activity?

A. POPv2

B. POPv3

C. IMAP

D. SMTP

LAB QUESTION

You are the network engineer who is considering connecting an organization with the following characteristics to the Internet:

- You have 40 workstations running a mix of Windows 98 and Windows NT Workstation.

- You have three servers: a Pentium 200 file server with 256MB RAM; a Pentium 200 mail server with 512MB RAM and three 18GB drives in RAID 5; and a communications server with a four-port modem board. The communications server is a 486 with 256MB RAM and a 4GB hard drive.

- You have six printers using HP Jet Direct Cards.

- The company is in one location, but a few remote sales people need dial-in capabilities.

Design a plan that incorporates the following:

- Sales people need dial-up access to the office/domain.

- The mail server will be used for Internet mail as well as internal mail.

- The organization wants secure connectivity with minimal administration and investment.

- Users need to be able to browse the Internet as well as FTP to specific sites.

- Users take advantage of online ordering, which has access to the Internet, versus dial-up with proper configuration.

The Internet connectivity is already present; all that has to be done is hook the users up and roll. Draw up a plan to meet the requirements. This plan should bullet the key considerations and provide a diagram.

SELF TEST ANSWERS

Designing Internet Connectivity Solutions

1. ☑ **A and B.** Network Address Translation and firewall. These are correct because they impact your total Internet solution and design layout.
   ☒ **C and D** do not apply because hubs and switches are already in place and do not directly impact the final solution.

2. ☑ **C.** Do a complete audit of your network. This step ensures you have a complete handle on your network details for properly implementing your final solution.
   ☒ **A** is incorrect because rewiring the network should not be necessary and in any event is not part of the planning process. **B**, diagramming the existing network, is incorrect because it should be the second step, based on your audit or inventory. **D** is incorrect because the conversion of workstations to Windows 2000, although possibly desirable, is part of implementation of an overall Windows 2000 rollout, not part of an Internet/intranet design.

3. ☑ **A, B, C, D.** All the answers are good reasons to diagram your network. The more diagrams and the more documentation you have, the better off you are in terms of planning and maintaining your network.

4. ☑ **C.** It helps secure your network from potential intruders. A firewall does packet filtering and will allow only packets that you tell the firewall to let through.
   ☒ **A** is incorrect because the firewall does not provide address sharing; this is accomplished by NAT. **B** is incorrect because the firewall does not replace a DHCP server. **D** is incorrect because a firewall is not necessary for Internet connectivity, although it is certainly desirable when your private network is connected to the public Internet.

Firewalls

5. ☑ **B.** Open the appropriate IP addresses only for all ports. This is the easiest and a very secure solution.
   ☒ **A** is incorrect; it opens the network to hackers because it allows the most access. **C** would be an administrative nightmare, requiring an unreasonable amount of time and effort. **D** is incorrect because firewalls do allow for opening specific ports for remote use.

6. ☑ **A, B, and C.** You can configure the firewall to block packets based on IP address, or you can block specific ports. Because each protocol uses a different port, this effectively allows blocking based on protocol.

☒ **D** is incorrect because filtering is typically done based on information in the packet headers rather than the data inside the packet.

7. ☑ **C and D.** TCP and UDP ports 20 and 21 are used by the File Transfer Protocol (FTP) and thus should be blocked in this situation.
☒ **A** is incorrect because port 80 is used for HTTP (Web services). **B** is incorrect because port 119 is used for NNTP (newsgroups).

Routing and Remote Access Strategies

8. ☑ **D.** None of the above. RRAS is installed automatically when Windows 2000 Server is installed. Since this is the case, you don't need to install this component, but you do need to configure it.

9. ☑ **A.** Modems for connectivity between the phone line and server. A modem for each incoming phone line (or a multiport modem/modem bank) is required to connect the phone line to the server.
☒ **B** is incorrect because the modem itself modulates and demodulates the signal (converting from digital to analog and back), so no additional device is needed. **C** is incorrect because Remote Access Services are built into Windows 2000, so no additional software is required. **D** is incorrect because there is no way for the server to communicate with the phone line without a modem.

Windows 2000 Network Address Translation

10. ☑ **B and D.** It can be used in conjunction with a DHCP or DNS server on the network, and it is configured via the RRAS console. NAT, unlike ICS, can be used in conjunction with DHCP or DNS on the network. Although ICS is configured via Network and Dial-up Connections, NAT is configured as a routing protocol in the RRAS console.
☒ **A** is incorrect because, although ICS is included in both Windows 2000 Professional and Server, NAT is available only in Windows 2000 Server. **C** is incorrect because, although the default address range is 192.169.0.0, NAT allows you to change the address range, whereas ICS does not.

11. ☑ **B.** You should configure static ports with the IP addresses of the Web and mail servers.
☒ **A** is incorrect because the servers should have static IP addresses to be mapped to the static port. **C** is incorrect because ICS will not allow you to configure static ports. **D** is incorrect because address translation can be deployed with Web and mail servers on the network.

12. ☑ **C.** Internet Connection Sharing is considered the automatic method of configuring shared Internet access.

    ☒ **A** is incorrect because NAT is considered the manual method. **B** is incorrect because Open Shortest Path First (OSPF) is a dynamic routing protocol that has nothing to do with connection sharing. **D** is incorrect because Microsoft Proxy Server requires manual configuration.

Windows 2000 Internet Connection Sharing

13. ☑ **A, B, and C.** The remote access server can be configured to use Microsoft Challenge-Handshake Authentication Protocol (MS-CHAP), Shiva Password Authentication Protocol (SPAP) or the Extensible Authentication Protocol (EAP).

    ☒ **D** is incorrect because there is no such protocol as Shiva CHAP.

14. ☑ **D.** Internet Connection Sharing offers the easiest installation and configuration and is appropriate for a small network that has no DNS or DHCP server.

    ☒ **A** is incorrect because, although NAT could be used if the server is running Windows 2000 Server, it would require quite a bit of configuration and administration. **B** is incorrect because DHCP assigns IP addresses; it does not provide IP address sharing or address translation. **C** is incorrect because DNS is used for name resolution, not connection sharing.

Integrating Windows 2000 with Microsoft Proxy Server, Internet Information Server, and Exchange Server

15. ☑ **C and D.** Port 80 and 443 are the default ports for HTTP and HTTP SSL connections. The static mapping of the ports ensures that your Web server is accessible behind your NAT-enabled server.

    ☒ **A and B** are incorrect because port 25 is for SMTP and port 110 is for POP3, which are both for mail servers.

16. ☑ **A and B.** Mapping ports 25 and 110 is important because these are the two main ports for mail transfer. Port 143 is also used for e-mail messaging by IMAP.

    ☒ **C and D** are incorrect because ports 80 and 443 are for a Web server.

17. ☑ **C.** The Internet Message Access Protocol (IMAP) provides the ability to manage mail on the remote server without downloading it to the local disk.

    ☒ **A and B** are incorrect because the Post Office Protocol (POP), both versions 2 and 3, does not allow this capability. **D** is incorrect because SMTP is used for transferring mail across the Internet from one point to another.

LAB ANSWER

First we need to determine what the company has:

- Three servers: two Pentium 200 and one 486. With this in mind, we have to ask if we have enough servers to incorporate a solution. Ideally, we would need to either upgrade the 486 or add another server for Internet connectivity so that the communications server could be used strictly for dial-up.

- Forty users. We need to see how many of these 40 people are going to be taking advantage of Internet access. Ten of these could be customer service reps taking phone calls, which means that only 30 would potentially be accessing the Internet. Then again, 20 could be technicians in an automotive shop, for example. These 20 most likely would not be accessing the Internet. There is a mix of NT and Windows 98, so workstation configuration could be a little different between the two; documenting this difference can aid in ensuring that all are set up correctly.

- At least one application needs to communicate across the Internet. We should be sure that there are no other apps to worry about. We know for sure that we will have browsing, e-mail, and FTP. Knowing the port numbers for the firewall is important.

- The company wants a simple firewall solution. A hardware firewall, a small one, is the best solution here. Something economical with little administration is important.

The diagram would look similar to the one shown in Figure 9-15. The Internet server would be using NAT; we would have static mapping for the mail server so that Internet mail could get in.

FIGURE 9-15 A sample diagram for the Lab Question

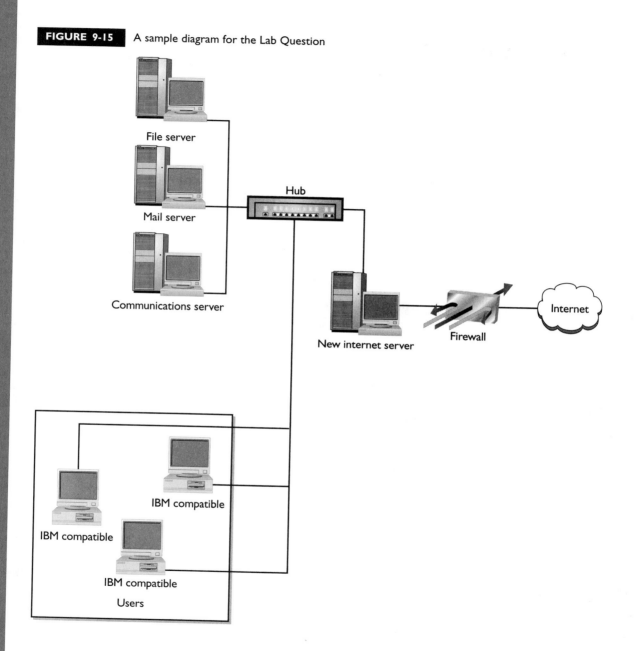

10

Designing Internet Connectivity Using Microsoft Proxy Server 2.0

CERTIFICATION OBJECTIVES

T his chapter will focus on several key factors you must consider when designing a proxy solution for your Windows 2000 network. These factors include:

■ Designing a proxy solution based on the extant network infrastructure

■ Designing a security scheme utilizing proxy services access controls

■ Designing a fault tolerance plan for the proxy server network

■ Designing a proxy server network that optimizes performance

CERTIFICATION OBJECTIVE 10.01

Introduction to Proxy Server 2.0

Microsoft Proxy Server 2.0 is a full-featured proxy server and firewall product. Proxy Server 2.0 is not included with Windows 2000, but can be purchased separately. When you integrate Proxy Server 2.0 into your Windows 2000 network design, you can provide Internet connectivity for your internal network users, and protect the internal network from Internet users while still providing Internet users with controlled access to internal resources.

The second version of the Microsoft Proxy Server was not designed specifically for Windows 2000, but rather for Windows NT 4.0. However, there is a patch that can be downloaded from www.microsoft.com/proxy that will allow you to run Proxy Server 2.0 on a Windows 2000 Server (Proxy Server will *not* run on Windows 2000 Professional computers).

Proxy Server 2.0 will provide your organization with a secure Internet access solution for your internal network clients and also protect your internal network from Internet intruders. In addition, Proxy Server 2.0 provides a mechanism for Internet access for internal networks that do not have public IP addresses, using Network Address Translation (NAT). The proxy is able to accomplish this by processing a proxy client request for an Internet object. Only the proxy server requires a public IP address, and only the proxy server's external interface is exposed to the Internet at large.

exam
ⓦatch

Remember that private IP address ranges are not accessible over the Internet because Internet routers do not include these IP addresses. All requests for resources located on machines with private IP addresses will be dropped by Internet routers.

Installing and Configuring Proxy Server 2.0

For Microsoft Exam 70-221, Designing a Microsoft Windows 2000 Network Infrastructure, you will be expected to understand some of the basic concepts of Microsoft Proxy Server 2.0. Although this was not a requirement in the Windows NT 4.0 MCSE certification series, Proxy Server 2.0 is an elective exam that counts toward both the Windows NT 4.0 and Windows 2000 MCSE certification. It is highly recommended that you study Microsoft Proxy Server 2.0 and even take the certification exam on the topic. Proxy or firewall services are used in just about every organization connected to the Internet and it will stand you in good stead to understand how they work. Take some time to learn the basic concepts of Proxy Server 2.0 and how to properly configure it.

on the
!
Oob

To install Microsoft Proxy Server 2.0 you need to have Internet Information Server 5.0 installed on the Windows 2000 Server first. Microsoft Proxy Server 2.0 is essentially an ISAPI extension to Internet Information Server, and therefore requires IIS as a platform on which to run. After installing Internet Information Server 5.0, download the patch file from Microsoft. You will do the actual installation of Proxy Server 2.0 by using the patch file. Go to www.microsoft.com/proxy/Support/win2kbeta3.asp? to download the patch file.

There are two main scenarios you will encounter when installing the Microsoft Proxy Server 2.0: Installing Microsoft Proxy Server 2.0 fresh on Windows 2000, and upgrading Windows NT 4.0 with Proxy Server 2.0 already installed.

Performing a Fresh Installation of Microsoft Proxy Server 2.0 on Microsoft Windows 2000

If you have installed Windows 2000 as a fresh installation on a new computer, Microsoft Proxy Server 2.0 will not yet be installed. To install Proxy Server 2.0 follow these steps:

1. Close the Microsoft Management Console prior to running the Update Wizard that you have downloaded from the Web site.

2. Double-click on the Update Wizard file (msp2wizi.exe) that you downloaded. During the installation process you will be asked for the Proxy Server 2.0 source media. You can point the wizard to either the original CD-ROM or to a network share point that contains the Proxy Server 2.0 installation files.

Upgrading Microsoft Windows NT Server 4.0 to Microsoft Windows 2000 with Microsoft Proxy Server 2.0

If you are upgrading your Windows NT 4.0 Server with Proxy Server 2.0 installed, you are likely to run into one of two scenarios:

■ You have planned the upgrade with the Proxy Server installation in mind.

■ You forgot about the Proxy Server installation and have already upgraded the machine.

The following procedures will guide you in how to proceed in either situation.

CertCam 10-1

EXERCISE 10-1

Upgrading a Windows NT 4.0 Computer with Proxy Server 2.0 Installed

Part One: Upgrading a Windows NT 4.0 Server with Microsoft Proxy Server 2.0 Installed:

1. Use the proxy server configuration interface to back up your Proxy Server 2.0 settings, as seen here:

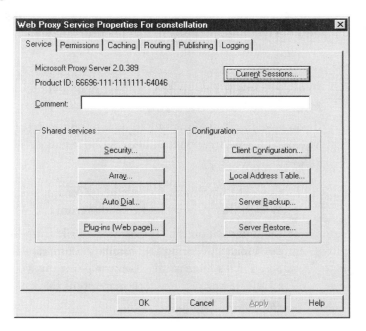

2. To back up the Proxy Server 2.0 configuration, select the Server Backup button and select a location to store the proxy configuration files.

3. After backing up the Proxy Server 2.0 configuration, you need to uninstall the proxy server. Go to the Start | Programs | Microsoft Proxy Server and select the UNINSTALL command. During this process, be sure to leave the proxy server log files, Web cache, and backup configuration files in place. The uninstall program will ask if you want to save these components.

4. Perform the Upgrade of the Windows NT 4.0 Server to Windows 2000 Server or Advanced Server.

5. After the machine has been upgraded, confirm that the upgrade was successful by letting the machine run for a short shakedown period. If the installation is stable, install Microsoft Proxy Server 2.0 Server according to the above instructions.

6. Once the Proxy Server is installed, use the Server Restore button in the proxy server Properties dialog box to restore your previous configuration. You must remember the location of your stored configuration files!

Part Two: Perform the following steps if you upgraded your Windows NT 4.0 Server to Windows 2000 and forgot to uninstall Proxy Server 2.0 prior to the upgrade:

1. Run the Update Wizard that you downloaded from the Microsoft Web site. Be sure that the Internet Information Server 5.0 Management Console is closed before you start the update.

2. During the installation process, you won't be given the option of updating the proxy server installation already installed. You will need to perform a fresh installation. Be sure to choose all the same installation locations that you did when you first installed Proxy Server 2.0 on the Windows NT 4.0 installation. If you place the files in the same location, your previous configuration should remain intact.

Once the Microsoft Proxy Server 2.0 is installed on your Windows 2000 computer, you can access it via the Administrative Tools menu by clicking on the

INTERNET SERVICES MANAGER command. You will see the Internet Information Services console:

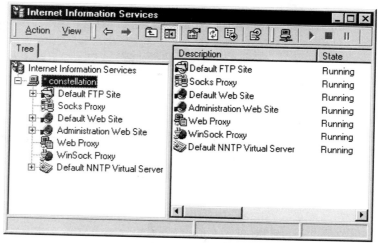

After you have installed Proxy Server 2.0 there will be three new nodes in the left pane of the Internet Information Services console, the Socks Proxy, the Web Proxy, and the WinSock Proxy. To access the configuration of any of these proxy services, right-click on any one of them and click on the PROPERTIES command.

Design Considerations in a Proxy Server Infrastructure

When you first set forth to design a proxy server solution, there are some overarching concerns you need to consider. After making the following assessments, you should have a good starting point for constructing your Proxy Server 2.0 network. Ask yourself these questions:

- Does your organization center around a single physical site, or is it spread across multiple geographical sites separated by WAN links?

- Is the network segmented? If so, will different segments need to have different degrees of exposure to the Internet? Will Internet-based users need access to each of these segments are well?

- Do you plan to use access controls to limit what users can do with their Internet connection, or will users be free to access whatever they like, whenever they like?

- Will users on the Internet require access to any internal resources on your network?

When answering these questions, you will begin to have a good general idea of what will be required of the proxy design solution.

Single Versus Multiple Sites

If the organization is housed at a single geographical location, all machines on the network are likely to be connected via fast links using LAN or MAN connections. The placement and configuration of proxy servers on a network connected by fast links will be different than one where the company is geographically displaced over a wide region and requires slower WAN links for internetwork communications.

When you have a geographically dispersed network, you are more likely to use more aggressive caching schemes in order to reduce the amount of WAN utilization. You may choose Active Web Caching at remote sites to reduce the amount of WAN traffic during busy daytime hours. We'll look further at Web caching later.

Segmented Networks

If your network consists of a single physical and logical segment, your proxy server solution is simple. You may install a single proxy server or proxy array to allow access to Internet resources. Internet users will also access the internal network with this single connection.

However, the vast majority of networks you will encounter will have multiple physical and logical segments delineated by routers. This will introduce a higher level of complexity to your proxy server solution.

For example, you may want to open up selected segments of the network to users on the Internet. These segments are often referred to as the DMZ (Demilitarized Zone). By their very nature, those segments will be less secure than those subnets that are not open to Internet users. You will need to place and configure your proxy servers appropriately for this kind of network configuration.

Another example might be when you want to maintain selective control over what users on different segments can access on the Internet. In this case, you can place proxy servers on the edge of selected segments and place access control and filters that are appropriate for users on the particular segment.

on the
ⓘob

Proxy Servers can be used not only to protect the internal network from Internet users, but can also be used to protect selected segments from users on other segments. In this way, the proxy server can act as a segmental-level firewall and limit access to segments that may contain sensitive information.

Access Controls

Proxy Server 2.0 provides a number of ways to control what your internal users can access on the Internet. Controlling users' activities has become increasingly important in a litigious environment where employees may seek restitution from employers who allow their users to view objectionable content that creates a hostile work environment, even inadvertently. In addition to filtering objectionable material, it is important to consider the bandwidth impact of the Internet applications to which users have access. America Online, ICQ, and IRC all have the potential for saturating your network with non-work-related network traffic. You can use Proxy Server 2.0 to block access to these network services, and many more. This allows you granular control over users' Internet access.

Internet User Access

Do Internet users need access to your internal network? What type of access do they require? It is important to consider these questions before setting forth on a proxy server design plan.

For example, you may want Internet users to gain entry to your network via Virtual Private Network (VPN) connections. If this is the case, you may prefer to have them access the network via a different interface than that used by the proxied connections. Most often, VPN users will need to make SMB connections via NetBIOS calls to resources on the internal network. While Proxy Server provides packet filters that allow access to VPN connections, you may prefer to segregate these connections for bandwidth or performance reasons. In this scenario, you would plan on using different network interfaces that are exposed to the Internet to allow for VPN and proxied connections, respectively.

Proxy Server contains filters that will allow VPN (PPTP) and NetBIOS connections through the proxy server. However, if you are using packet filtering, these ports will be closed until you manually configure them and open them. Note that proxy server does not have a filter for VPN tunnels that use L2TP/IPSec. If you choose to use L2TP/IPSec, you will need to create your own filters.

If Internet users access internal resources in the form of Web sites and FTP sites, then a proxy server makes an ideal intermediary. Reverse hosting and reserve proxy capabilities of Proxy Server 2.0 optimize and secure Internet access to internal resources.

For most organizations, security is a top priority for a proxy server solution. When you put together your proxy server design document, make security considerations and solutions your foremost objective.

This grid provides a quick reference for common questions about Proxy Server design considerations.

SCENARIO & SOLUTION

When should I use more aggressive caching schemes, such as active Web caching?	When the network is widely dispersed geographically, these caching schemes will help reduce WAN traffic.
What if I want to maintain selective control over what users on different segments can access on the Internet?	Place proxy servers on the edge of selected segments and place access control and filters that are appropriate for users on the particular segment.
How can I block user access to objectionable material on the Internet?	Use Proxy Server's domain and packet filtering features.
Does Proxy Server allow access to VPN connections?	Yes, filters are provided to allow access to VPN connections, but you may prefer to segregate these connections for bandwidth reasons or performance reasons.

Proxy Server Advantages

One of the main advantages of using proxy servers on your network is to isolate your network from the Internet. When internal network users access the Internet via a Proxy Server, at no time do users make direct contact or establish a session with Internet hosts. The proxy server intercepts all requests from the internal network clients on its internal network interface and forwards those requests through its external interface. Only the external interface of the proxy server is directly exposed to the Internet.

Another plus to using a proxy server is that you do not need public IP addresses for your internal hosts. There is a severe shortage of public IP addresses due to the extraordinary growth in Internet use over the last several years and those given out are done so reluctantly by Internet Service Providers. Most ISPs impose an extra cost for each additional IP address. Internal networks that lie behind a proxy server can use all private IP addresses that fall into the Class A, Class B, or Class C private IP address ranges. Those ranges are:

- 10.0.0.0–10.255.255.255
- 172.16.0.0–172.31.255.255
- 192.168.0.0–192.168.255.255

Because Internet routers do not recognize these private IP address ranges, it is very difficult (although not impossible if a NAT or Proxy intercedes) for Internet users to establish direct connections to machines that have these private IP addresses. The proxy server must first process any connection request coming from the Internet, then either forward or reject it based on rules that you have defined.

High Security

Another method the proxy server uses to protect the internal network is via *access controls*. These access controls can be used to control access by internal network users attempting contact with Internet hosts, and can also control which communications are allowed from Internet clients trying to access internal network resources.

Access can be limited based on the user account or group membership. You may wish to allow certain groups, such as Marketing, full control of Internet resources, but you want clerical group members to have access only to Internet e-mail. You can control access to these external resources based on user or group membership just as you would control access to any other resource.

Firewalling with Packet Filters   A particularly powerful method of controlling data that flows in and out of your network is by filtering via protocol and IP addresses/Port numbers. In this way you get granular control over what Internet applications and what sites internal and external users can access.

Secure Hosting of Web Material on the Internal Network   Web-based technologies are a mainstay in corporate computing. Internet users can access Exchange e-mail via a Web-based interface, files can be uploaded or downloaded, and documents can be shared and edited using HTTP.

Traditionally, Web hosting is done on the server with the direct connection to the Internet. You have this option when using Proxy Server. However, you have even more options with Proxy Server 2.0. Public-access Web sites can be hosted on the Proxy Server via *Web Publishing*. You can take advantage of reverse proxy and reverse hosting and make resources on your internal network available via the proxy server as well.

Dedicated subnets should be defined to provide resources to Internet users. In this way you can focus your attention on security issues pertaining to these segments and route traffic as appropriate to these Internet-accessible subnets. This reduces the risk of attack on subnets that do not offer Internet-accessible resources and should not be accessible to Internet users.

exam
ⓦatch

When using reverse hosting and reverse proxy, you will want to place those resources on segments that are dedicated as DMZs. It is considered a security risk and poor security practice to place resources that are accessible to Internet clients on segments that contain information not intended for Internet access.

Performance

Proxy Server can significantly improve network performance via its Web and FTP caching abilities. When users request objects from the Internet, these objects are placed in the proxy server's Web cache. When another user makes a request for the same Internet object, the proxy server can retrieve it from cache and deliver it to the private network client without incurring the time and expense of the proxy server retrieving it from the Internet server hosting the information.

The proxy server also caches requests from Internet users. When the Internet user requests an object from a Web server that the proxy server hosts, the proxy will cache this object as well. When the next Internet user attempts to access the same object, it will be retrieved from cache rather than from the internal server. This will have the positive effect of reducing internal network traffic due to Internet-based requests and improve the internal network users' computing experience.

Application Compatibility

The Microsoft Proxy Server 2.0 has three primary components:

- The Web proxy
- The WinSock proxy
- The SOCKS proxy

Each service can provide access for your existing Internet applications, regardless of the type of WinSock application you may have on your network.

This grid will help you to understand the different functions of Proxy Server's three primary components:

The Web Proxy   The Web proxy service provides CERN-compliant Web browsers access to Internet objects via the HTTP, Secure HTTP (https), FTP (FTP read, not FTP put), and Gopher protocols. CERN-compliant Web browsers are created to be proxy aware, and you configure the browser with the host name or IP address of the Proxy Server running the Web proxy service.

SCENARIO & SOLUTION

What is the function of the Web proxy?	Allows CERN compliant browsers to access the Internet via HTTP, HTTPS, FTP (GET command), and Gopher.
What is the function of the Winsock Proxy?	Allows Windows Sockets applications that are not proxy aware to connect to the Internet (requires client software).
What is the function of the SOCKS proxy?	Allows access for non-Windows applications, such as those written for UNIX and Macintosh (supports TCP connections, *not* UDP).

FROM THE CLASSROOM

CERN

The Conseil Européen pour la Recherche Nucléaire (CERN) is the European Organization for Nuclear Research, a high-energy particle physics laboratory in Geneva, Switzerland. This is where Dr. Tim Berners-Lee is credited with having "invented" the World Wide Web in 1991. Berners-Lee is recognized for developing the idea of combining hypertext with modern high-speed networks. He and his small team developed the Hypertext Transfer Protocol (HTTP) on which the Web is based. CERN compatibility is the industry standard that defines applications (for example, Web browsers, the Real Audio player, and others) that are written to be proxy aware and do not require any additional external software to operate with a proxy server.

—*Thomas W. Shinder, M.D., MCSE, MCP+I, MCT*

The Web proxy is very easy to enable on compliant browsers, and processing takes place completely in the background. When objects are accessed via the Web proxy service, they are placed in the Web cache. *Only objects accessed via the Web proxy service are cached.* This is something to consider if you find that you must use non-CERN compliant browsers and access Internet resources via the WinSock proxy or the SOCKS proxy.

exam
Watch

Only objects accessed via the Web proxy service will be placed in the Web cache. For network clients that use the WinSock proxy service, you must be sure to configure the browsers on the WinSock proxy clients to use the Web proxy service.

The WinSock Proxy   The WinSock proxy service allows WinSock applications to connect to Internet resources via the proxy server without the WinSock applications needing to be aware of the proxy server. All applications written specifically for TCP/IP networks are written to the WinSock interface. However, not all WinSock applications are written to be proxy aware. If you have WinSock applications that are not proxy aware, you can take advantage of the WinSock proxy to help integrate these applications into your proxy server solution.

Figure 10-1 shows how the WinSock application interacts with the WinSock proxy service.

The WinSock proxy client can use either TCP/IP or IPX/SPX as its LAN protocol. There may be circumstances when you prefer to use IPX/SPX as your LAN protocol, such as when you have a number of legacy NetWare servers which require use of IPX/SPX. An advantage of using IPX/SPX as your LAN protocol is that when combined with Proxy Server 2.0, you can protect your network via *protocol isolation*. Since Internet users cannot use IPX over the Internet, all resources on the Internet network are stopped cold.

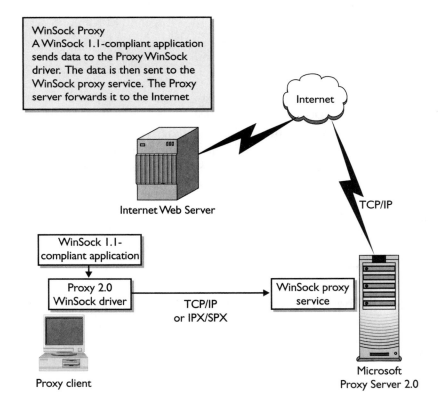

FIGURE 10-1

How a WinSock client application interacts with the WinSock proxy service

WinSock Proxy
A WinSock 1.1-compliant application sends data to the Proxy WinSock driver. The data is then sent to the WinSock proxy service. The Proxy server forwards it to the Internet

Internet

Internet Web Server

TCP/IP

WinSock 1.1-compliant application

Proxy 2.0 WinSock driver

TCP/IP or IPX/SPX

WinSock proxy service

Proxy client

Microsoft Proxy Server 2.0

You can secure your network using IPX/SPX by binding only IPX/SPX to the network interfaces of all the network clients and IPX/SPX and TCP/IP to the internal network interface of the Proxy server. This isolates the client interfaces from non-proxied Internet connections while still allowing network clients to find the Proxy server via its IP address.

Unlike the Web proxy, you must install the WinSock proxy client software on the internal client machines that will use the WinSock proxy service. This client software replaces and renames the native WinSock .dll files and replaces them with its own files. The WinSock proxy .dlls intercept WinSock calls and either send them to the renamed native WinSock .dlls or processes these calls itself.

The SOCKS Proxy Service   The SOCKS proxy service provides proxied Internet access to non-Windows Internet applications. The SOCKS proxy service supports SOCKS version 4.3a and *not* version 5.0. Internet protocols supported by the SOCKS proxy services include HTTP, FTP, Telnet, and Gopher. One important consideration in choosing a SOCKS proxy design is that the SOCKS proxy service supports no UDP applications. In addition, access control is implemented in a *kludgy* fashion that makes security somewhat more difficult when applied to SOCKS proxy clients.

The SOCKS proxy service is somewhat limited when compared to the capabilities of the Web and WinSock proxy services. The SOCKS proxy service is aimed primarily at providing limited Internet access to UNIX and Macintosh machines, with a small handful of SOCKS applications running on the Windows platform.

Integrating Proxy Server with Windows 2000

Although Proxy Server 2.0 was not designed with Windows 2000 in mind, after you upgrade it with the Windows 2000 installation wizard, it can fully integrate with other networking services available in Windows 2000.

If you choose to use Proxy Server with your VPN solution, you can take advantage of Active Directory integrated access controls. Microsoft Proxy Server 2.0 also works seamlessly with your routing and remote-access server's capability to create Virtual Private Networking interfaces, RRAS policies, IP address filters, and Demand-Dial connections.

If you seek optimal security for your VPN tunnels, you will want to use L2TP (Layer 2 Tunneling Protocol) with IPSec as your tunneling protocol of choice. However, there are some limitations in what IP addresses you can use in this circumstance. By running Microsoft Proxy Server 2.0 in a Windows 2000 environment, you can take full advantage of the security benefits of IPSec and its enhanced authentication and encryption capabilities.

Figure 10-2 shows how Proxy Server 2.0 integrates with other Windows 2000 networking services.

When implementing a proxy server solution with IPSec, you can use Active Directory and the Kerberos protocol to provide the highest level of authentication and data security for your network access.

FIGURE 10-2

Proxy Server 2.0 integrates with popular Windows 2000 networking services

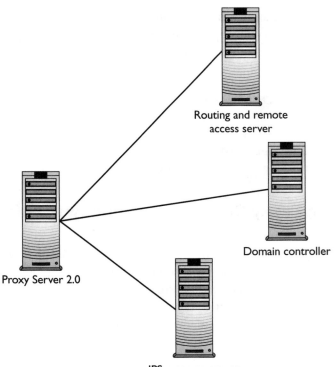

Routing and remote access server

Domain controller

Proxy Server 2.0

IPSec secure server

Designing a Proxy Server Networking Implementation

Now that we've covered some of the basic proxy server features, let's turn our attention to the actual process of designing a proxy server network. When we design a proxy server networking implementation, there are three basic areas to address:

- Where are you going to locate your proxy servers?
- How will the proxy server network interact with the extant network infrastructure?
- What applications and services will be required in order to support Proxy Server clients on the network?

By answering these questions, we are well on our way to designing a viable proxy server networking implementation.

Where to Locate Proxy Servers

Proxy servers can be placed at the edge of the internal network, where there are network interfaces with both the internal network and the Internet. These proxy servers are at higher risk of Internet intrusion because of their direct interface with the Internet.

Another location for proxy servers is within the confines of the corporate network, where all interfaces are connected only to local network connections and no interface on the proxy server is directly connected to the Internet.

Let's look at the advantages and disadvantages of each strategy.

Locating Proxy Servers Within the Corporate Network

There are some advantages to placing a proxy server completely within the confines of your corporate network, far from any direct connection to the Internet. One of the major reasons to place a proxy server internally is to take advantage of its Web caching features. All Web proxy clients that are pointed to the proxy server inside the corporate network can use the Web cache built on the internal proxy server.

Internally placed proxy servers allow you to fine-tune your security and help isolate subnets from each other. Internet users are not the only source of potential risk. You can use the same filters to protect one subnet from another by using a proxy on each subnet.

Multiple proxy servers are also placed internally to form a *proxy chain*. Proxy chaining allows you to control the amount of bandwidth consumed on a busy network backbone and can reduce the number of Internet network accesses. In many cases, the chain is contained entirely within a single site on the corporate network.

on the
Job

Proxy chaining is commonly performed on large corporate networks to reduce the congestion at a central Internet-access interface. The proxy servers that are downstream in the chain can answer queries for Web objects from their own Web caches and reduce the stress on the Internet access link. In addition, many organizations suffer from excessive bandwidth use on their backbone networks, and proxy chains are especially useful in reducing the burden on the backbone as well.

A proxy server can contain network cards to support different network signaling infrastructures. You can place an ATM, Ethernet, and Token Ring card into a single proxy server and allow communication between segments using different signaling technologies.

Placing Proxy Servers on the Edge of the Corporate Network

Placing a proxy server on the edge of the public network offers all of the advantages of internally placed proxy servers. This strategy also allows your network to have access to the Internet. The proxy server can act as a firewall between the internal network and the Internet because of its packet filtering abilities.

On a large corporate network, proxy servers, or *proxy arrays*, can be placed on the edge of the corporate network to provide company-wide Web caching. All Internet objects accessed on the corporate network can be cached on the edge, which allows other, internally placed proxy servers (proxy chains) to take advantage of this cache and place the objects in their own caches. This reduces Internet traffic, which can provide significant savings if you are paying packet charges on your Internet access.

Figure 10-3 displays a corporate proxy network consisting of three proxy servers, all of which are located on the edge of either the corporate or branch networks. Notice that on the branch networks the proxy server is directly connected to the

Internet. At Branch Office 2, the proxy server has a dedicated connection to the Internet and therefore is always exposed. At Branch Office 1, the proxy server uses a demand-dial interface via an ISDN modem to connect to the Internet.

FIGURE 10-3

A corporate proxy network

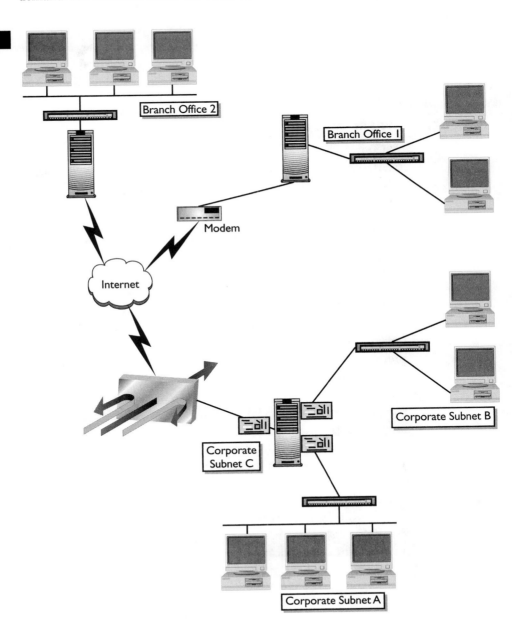

Note that the corporate network proxy server has three network interfaces. Multiple interfaces allow us to segregate traffic, leaving and arriving, from and to the corporate network. Each segment may have a different network architecture that allows ATM, Ethernet, and Token Ring segments to communicate with the proxy server transparently. Finally, note that the proxy server is located behind a firewall. This is done to further secure the corporate network, as the firewall can be configured to provide additional security, over and above that provided by the proxy server.

Introducing Proxy Servers into an Existing Network Infrastructure

When introducing a proxy server to your network, you should start at the network interface layer in determining how to integrate it into the existing network. How many network interfaces will the proxy server have? Will they all be connected to the internal network, or will some of them be connected to the Internet?

As mentioned earlier, you can configure a proxy server with a single network interface card. These proxy servers will receive all requests for Internet access and forward these requests in the same fashion as a multi-homed proxy server with a direct connection to the Internet. However, the proxy forwards the request to another network device that acts as the default gateway for the segment.

As shown in Figure 10-4, a single-homed proxy server can receive requests from network clients and forward the requests to the gateway. The single-homed proxy server solution is best used when you want to take advantage of Web caching and protocol isolation. Protocol isolation will protect your internal network from Internet intruders.

In the example shown in Figure 10-4, the network client computers would be configured with only IPX/SPX bound to their NICs. The proxy server internal interface must have both TCP/IP and IPX/SPX because the network clients must connect to the internal interface via an IPX address rather than a DNS host name. The network clients are protected via protocol isolation because no Internet intruder can establish a session with the network clients running only IPX/SPX.

Regardless of whether the proxy server is single- or multi-homed, you must be sure that the TCP/IP settings on each interface are correctly configured. Be sure that the IP address, subnet mask, and default gateway settings are correct for the subnet on which the card is located.

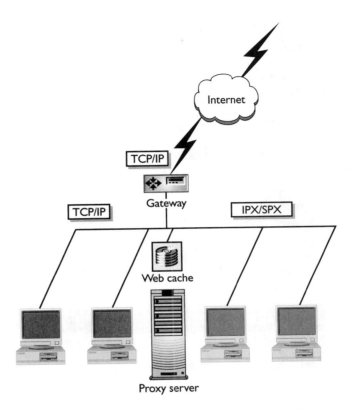

FIGURE 10-4

Single-homed
proxy server

e x a m
ⓦ a t c h

*In order to use IPX/SPX on the internal network, you must have the client
machines run the WinSock Proxy Client software. Note the web cache on the
proxy server is accessible only to Web proxy clients. Client machines running
IPX/SPX cannot use the Web proxy service because IPX/SPX connectivity is
limited compared to TCP/IP installations. Although the Web cache is in place
on the proxy server for the Web proxy clients, network clients that run
IPX/SPX only will not be able to use it.*

Network Interface Hardware

An important consideration is what type of network interfaces you will use on your
proxy server connections. In determining the type, you must consider what speed
you need and whether or not you will use a dedicated connection to the network to
which it interfaces.

Internal Network Interfaces   For the internal network interfaces, your options include:

- ATM
- Ethernet
- Token Ring

The advantage of using ATM interfaces is the increased speed and reliability of the ATM network architecture. ATM is not a broadcast-based technology and uses MARS (Multicast Address Resolution Server) servers to eliminate the broadcast element for ATM adapter addresses. Ethernet networks have the advantage of being relatively cheap and available. You can choose either 10 or 100 Mbps speeds with Ethernet LAN adapters, although Gigabit Ethernet looms on the horizon. For legacy networks, Token Ring adapters can be placed in the proxy server.

LAN adapter connections are dedicated connections; however, you can still create virtual dial-up interfaces on the dedicated LAN connections. Using VPN connections within the internal network creates these virtual connections. This is often done to secure selected segments of the internal network from other segments at large.

External Network Interfaces   There is a wide variety of choices for your external network interfaces. These include:

- ISDN
- DSL
- Frame Relay
- Cable
- T-Carrier
- PSTN (POTS)

ISDN BRI (Integrated Services Digital Network–Basic Rate Interface) provides up to 128 Kbps of bandwidth and is a popular solution for branch offices that do not have large bandwidth requirements. ISDN is widely available and can be a reliable, affordable solution, depending on your location. In some areas, ISDN lines are metered and you are charged based on data transfer. In such a case, ISDN is a less-than-ideal solution.

DSL (Digital Subscriber Line) is a recent technology that provides very high bandwidth at very reasonable prices. There are a number of different DSL implementations, including ADSL, SDSL, VDSL, and IDSL. DSL technology can provide network speeds of up to 6 Mbps. DSL access is somewhat limited at this time, and there are a wide number of line provisioning options.

Frame Relay is very reliable but traditionally has been relatively slow. However, Frame Relay technology is alive and well and a viable alternative for those who require dedicated, point-to-point connections via permanent or switched virtual circuits.

Cable access is relatively new and there have been reliability concerns. Also, most cable implementations work on a shared access basis that can pose a security risk for your organization. Another major disadvantage is that the cable company is the ISP and they have a reputation for not providing the expert service that most dedicated ISPs can deliver.

T-Carrier connections provide fast, reliable access for your external Internet connections. The major drawback for T lines is their expense. The advantage is that you are guaranteed the amount of bandwidth you have contracted for, which is not the case for other high-speed access solutions such as DSL.

PSTN (Public-Switched Telephone Network) connections are slow in comparison to the other technologies discussed. The great advantage of POTS (Plain Old Telephone Service) is that it is universal and very inexpensive. You can order either a dial-up or dedicated POTS account. A dedicated POTS connection is somewhat of a misnomer, since it is not dedicated, but rather a dial-up connection. The difference typically is that you are assigned a dedicated IP address when you dial up. These types of connections are useful when you contract with an ISP that will provide dial-up routing to your modem when a communication comes in from over the Internet.

The following grid summarizes the features of these WAN link options.

on the **job**

X.25 is another WAN solution available to allow external network access. However, the X.25 protocol has a lot of built-in error checking which leads to a lot of protocol overhead. It was developed during a time when the public telephone network could not offer reliable connectivity, so X.25 provided its own. The reliability of the X.25 connection leads to its tardiness and in general it has fallen out of favor, although there are still numerous X.25 networks in operation today.

SCENARIO & SOLUTION

If T-carrier lines are the fastest and most reliable connection type, why would I use anything else?	T-1 and T-3 lines provide high-speed and guaranteed bandwidth, but have a couple of drawbacks. First is cost; T-carriers are much more expensive than the other WAN links listed. Also, T-carrier connections are dedicated point-to-point lines. If you have a need to connect to multiple locations, such as several different ISPs at different times, you should select a different connection type.
What is the advantage of PSTN, plain old telephone service? Isn't it obsolete as a data transfer carrier?	On the contrary, PSTN/POTS enjoys a couple of huge advantages: it's cheap and it's literally everywhere. Many locations do not yet have DSL or other high-speed services available.
I hear a lot of comparison between DSL and cable modem. Which is better?	Better is a subjective term. A better question might be: which is available? If you're lucky enough to be located in an area that offers both, consider such factors as shared vs. dedicated bandwidth (your DSL connection is a switched circuit connection like any phone line; cable access is shared with everyone on your subnet), service (phone company vs. cable company), and cost (usually similar for the two services).

Dedicated or Dial-up Interfaces   POTS and ISDN offer the option of dial-up interfaces to the Internet. When the machine dials up the ISP, it connects to the ISP's server as a remote-access client and is assigned an IP address via DHCP. Each time the machine dials up it will most likely receive a different IP address. Dial-up access has the advantage of being cheaper than the typical dedicated access line. Dial-up access is especially important for ISDN clients that might be metered based on time online.

on the
Job

ISDN also has an advantage over POTS because call setup time is much quicker over the digital interface.

The other public interface technologies discussed use dedicated connections and typically maintain the same IP address over time, with the possible exception of cable modem. These dedicated connections offer faster access because the architectures themselves offer higher bandwidth and there is no call setup time.

You can create a virtual dial-up interface on a dedicated connection. This can be accomplished via a demand-dial VPN network interface. During the VPN interface call setup an exchange of credentials is performed for authentication purposes. When the tunnel times out, the virtual connection is torn down.

exam
Watch

If you don't have experience with VPN call setup you should be aware that the VPN connection is established after the link to the ISP is made. After the link is established you set up a VPN call to either a destination IP address or host name. If you choose a destination host name, you must be sure that the IP address of the host is in the DNS. Remember that the VPN call is dependent on the initial Internet connection being made first.

Proxy Server Clients

Proxy server clients must be made aware of which destination IP addresses should use a proxied connection and which IP addresses are contained within the internal network. Proxy Client computers that run the WinSock Proxy Client software are made aware of which machines should be considered local via the **Local Address Table** (LAT). The LAT contains a list of IP address ranges that are part of the local network.

Figure 10-5 shows the local address table on a proxy server.

The local address table consists of IP address ranges that should not be proxied. The non-proxied hosts are not subject to processing via the proxy server and are not subject to the security or access controls that may be set on the proxy server. Direct sessions are established with network clients contained in the LAT. The LAT is downloaded to WinSock Proxy clients on a periodic basis.

Web Proxy and Non-proxy Clients

When network clients only use the Web proxy service, the default gateway should be set to the proxy server's internal IP address if you do not wish the client to use any non-proxied connections. Access controls will not be enforced except for the Web proxy service components in this case. Remember, whenever you configure a proxy client's default gateway to be anything other than the proxy server, you allow the proxy client free access to Internet resources (unless there is a firewall interceding between the proxy client and the Internet).

Planning Services for Existing Network Applications

You have a simple single-segment network with 30 workstations and a Windows 2000 Server computer with two network interfaces. One of the network interfaces is connected to the local network and the second interface is connected to the Internet via a dedicated routed ISDN connection.

You would like to provide Web-browsing capabilities to your internal users and also need them to have access to corporate FTP sites at other locations. What proxy server solution would you use to provide the required services?

Answer: As shown next, all network clients can connect to the single dual-homed proxy server that runs only the Web proxy service to allow for Web and FTP access to Internet sites.

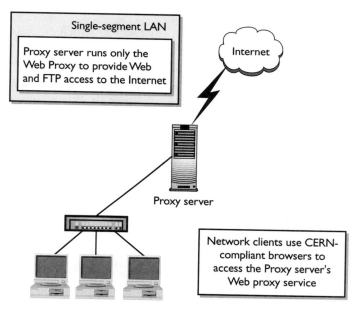

Because the clients are configured to communicate only with the Web proxy, they will not be able to use any other WinSock application such as IRC or Internet e-mail. If other Internet related services are required, the WinSock proxy service client would need to be installed on the Network Clients and the WinSock proxy service enabled on the proxy server.

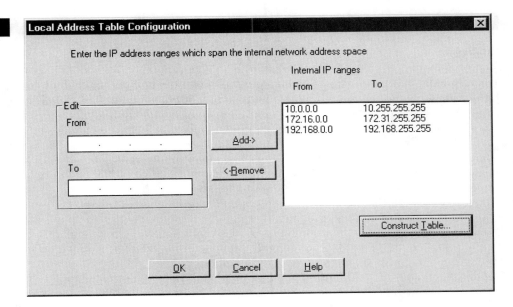

FIGURE 10-5

The Local
Address Table
Configuration
interface

Non-proxy network clients should not use the proxy server as a gateway. In order for non-proxy clients to successfully use the proxy server as their default gateway, the Windows 2000 RRAS server would have to be configured to allow IP forwarding. This is a major security breach on a proxy server and you should *not* enable IP forwarding on the proxy server. Non-proxy clients should have another network device forward their requests for remote resources. No security will be applied to these network clients via proxy server services. However, you may have other devices, such as hardware firewalls, apply security to non-proxy clients.

Figure 10-6 displays the configuration sheet for disabling IP forwarding on the Windows 2000 proxy server computer. Just remove the checkmark from the Enable IP routing check box to disable IP forwarding:

There are disadvantages to making all network clients use the proxy server as their default gateway, the most signifcant being the increase in network traffic incurred at the proxy server interface. Non-proxy server clients should be set to use another network device as their default gateway if this is at all possible.

Client Software

When implementing a proxy server solution for the network, you need to look at the client software environment. It is a good idea to inventory all software in your organization that accesses any Internet-related service. After you have inventoried

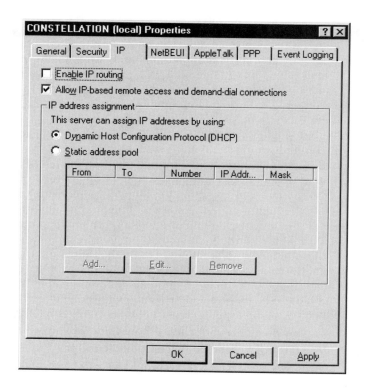

the software, you will be ready to assess which Proxy Server 2.0 service will be used to provide access and access controls for each application.

In order to take advantage of the Web caching service provided by the Web proxy service, you should ensure that all browsers on the network are using the latest version of Microsoft Internet Explorer. Internet Explorer is a core operating system application, so there are myriad advantages to using IE for your browser.

on the ***job*** *If there are political reasons why you cannot implement Internet Explorer as your preferred browser, you can use any CERN-compliant browser to connect to the Web proxy service.*

Figure 10-7 shows the GUI interface for configuring IE as a Web proxy client.

If you have other Internet applications such as ICQ, IRC, e-mail, and others for which you want to provide both access and access controls, you should make sure that they use the standard WinSock Version 1.1 interface. WinSock-compliant applications will be able to use the WinSock Proxy Client software to access the WinSock client service.

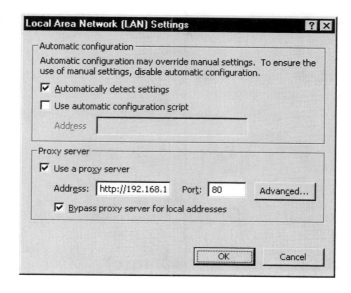

FIGURE 10-7

Configuring
Internet Explorer
as a Web proxy
client

For network applications that are not WinSock or CERN compliant, you may
be able to use the SOCKS proxy service. Remember that this service is designed
primarily for UNIX and Mac applications that are not able to use the Web Proxy
or WinSock proxy services.

exam
ⓦatch

*Remember that any IP address range that is included in the LAT is considered
a non-proxied subnet and any connections to hosts on those subnets will not
be secured via any of the proxy server services. It is critical to not include IP
address ranges that you wanted accessed via the proxy server to be on the LAT.*

CERTIFICATION OBJECTIVE 10.03

Proxy Server Security

After completing your analysis for integrating a proxy server solution into your
network, configure proxy server security parameters. Some organizations may forego
security configuration and install Microsoft Proxy Server 2.0 for its Web caching
capabilities only, and leave the security configuration to other devices such as
hardware-based solutions from Cisco and similar vendors.

Your primary security focus will aim to answer the following questions:

- Do you want to control internal network user access to Internet resources?
- Do you want to take advantage of domain filtering to control Internet user access to the Internet?
- How do you want to control Internet user access to your internal network resources?
- Do you want to make Web-based resources available to Internet users?

After answering these questions, you will be in an excellent position to construct a proxy-based security plan that attends to both internal and external users and how internal and external resources are accessed.

Proxy Server Client Access Control

Most organizations will be interested in controlling internal user access to Internet resources. Organizations that have historically allowed unfettered access to the Internet have found this can result in significantly reduced employee productivity, as many employees find themselves searching out stock quotes, sports scores, AOL-like chat rooms, and other drains on employee time and motivation. In order to prevent loss of productivity from non-work related Internet activity, you must institute access control over Internet resources.

You can control access to Internet service on a:

- Per-user basis
- Per-group basis
- For everyone on a per-server basis

It is far easier to manage security groups than to manage on a per-user basis. This is the recommended approach to access control.

Proxy Server 2.0 integrates with the Active Directory and therefore can take advantage of user and group accounts stored in the Active Directory database. If your network is not Active Directory enabled, you can still allow access via the Guest Account, but this is not good practice because you forfeit granular control and monitoring of Guest users. The Guest account should be disabled in any Active Directory domain.

If you are not using Active Directory, you can set up accounts on a Windows 2000 stand-alone server that is running Proxy Server. Users will pass security credentials to the stand-alone server's local security database for authentication. This is especially helpful if you are working in a mixed environment that includes downlevel operating systems such as NetWare, UNIX, and Apple.

Figure 10-8 shows how to set access controls based on Active Directory membership for Web proxy-mediated protocols. In this case, it is the FTP Read Protocol that is being controlled via Active Directory Group Membership.

Other proxy services can be configured in a similar fashion.

exam
Ⓦatch

You can configure the Web proxy and WinSock proxy services to allow and deny access via user and security group permissions. You cannot control access to the SOCKS proxy via user- or security group-based access controls. Per-server security that extends across all users and security groups can be set for domain filtering and packet filtering.

FIGURE 10-8

Setting access controls based on Active Directory membership for the Web proxy services

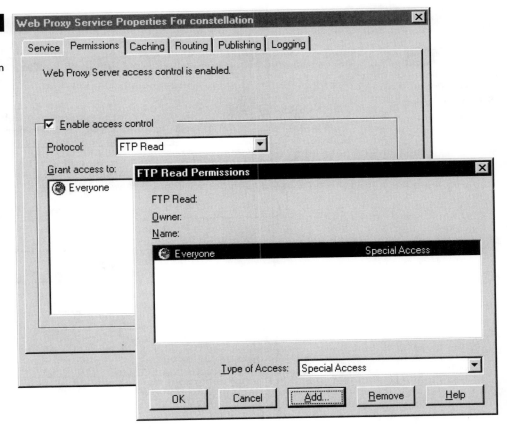

Controlling Access via Packet Filtering

You can control inbound and outbound information transfer by defining **packet filters** on your Proxy Server installation. Packet filtering allows you to determine which packets should be examined and which should be immediately dropped, based on which filters you have defined. In order to enable packet filtering, you must have at least one adapter connected directly to the Internet.

Packet filters allow you to control access based on protocol and direction that stretches across all three of the proxy server services. The inbound or outbound packets are examined as they arrive at the external interface and they are compared to existing protocol filters before further processing takes place on the proxy server.

You can access the Protocol Filters dialog box via the Properties page of any of the proxy services. Figure 10-9 shows what the Properties dialog box for the Web Proxy service looks like.

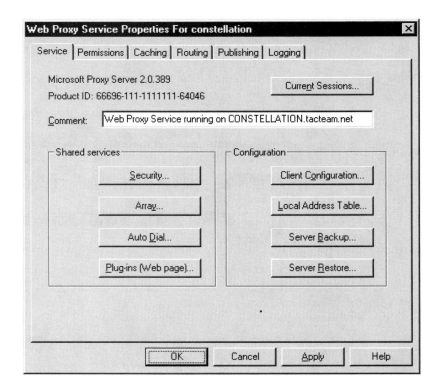

FIGURE 10-9

The Web Proxy Service Properties dialog box

The Service page will look the same for all of the proxy server services. In order to access the packet filters that affect all proxy services, select the Security button in the Shared Services frame on the left side of the dialog box. You will see the dialog box that appears in Figure 10-10.

When the *Enable packet filtering on external interface* checkbox is checked, it automatically filters out all packets that are received at the proxy server external interface. The packet filters evaluate packets arriving from either the Internet or the internal network.

By default, the *Enable dynamic packet filtering of Microsoft Proxy Server packets* is enabled. This is done to allow the proxy server to open and close ports as needed when it is issuing requests to Internet hosts. When the proxy server sends an outbound request, it must include in the request an IP address and port number to which the reply should be sent. Once the reply is received on a particular communication, the proxy server will close the open port. This is called **dynamic packet filtering**.

FIGURE 10-10

The Packet Filters tab in the Security dialog box

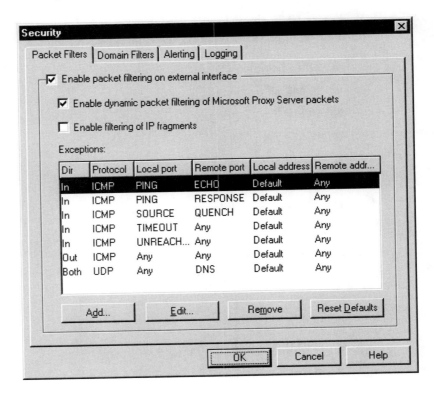

Many students have been confused by the concept of filtering. This is because the students' common sense tells them that if you add a filter, you must be interested in filtering something out. For example, if you add a coffee filter, you filter out the coffee grounds. If you don't add the coffee filter, everything comes through. However, it is the exact opposite with Microsoft Proxy Server 2.0; you add filters for the protocols and ports you want to allow through. Any protocols without filters will be blocked.

Note that you can also *Enable filtering of IP Fragments*. This is useful for protecting the proxy server from certain Internet attacks including SYN and FRAG attacks.

Adding Packet Filters

When adding a new packet filter, you can choose to add a predefined filter. Microsoft Proxy Server 2.0 comes with a number of predefined filters, right out of the box. If none of the predefined filters meet your needs, you can create a new packet filter for your custom application that may require one.

Figure 10-11 shows the Packet Filter Properties dialog box.

The list of predefined packet filters includes:

- DNS Lookup
- ICMP all outbound
- ICMP Ping Response
- ICMP Ping Query
- ICMP SRC quench
- ICMP timeout
- ICMP unreachable
- PPTP Call
- PPTP Receive
- SMTP
- POP3
- Identd
- HTTP Server (port 80)
- HTTPS Server (port 443)
- NetBIOS (WINS client only)
- NetBIOS (all)

FIGURE 10-11

The Packet
Filter Properties
dialog box

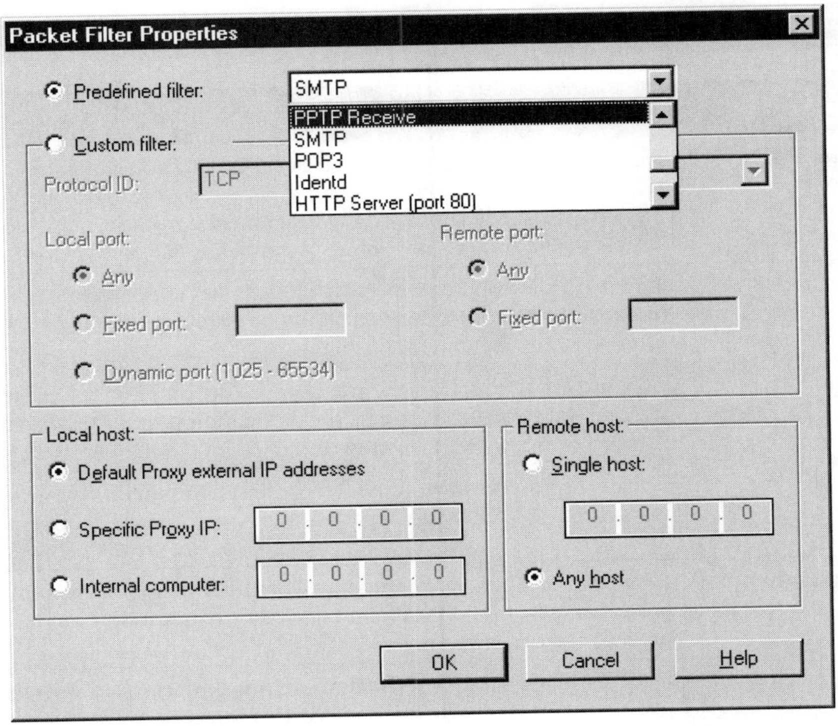

You can use one of these, or define one of your own. You can create custom combinations of packet filters and apply them to each interface as required by the security needs of your network. Table 10-1 includes the basic criteria and requirements for defining your own packet filters.

Packet Filtering is a powerful method for improving the security of your proxy server and confers to the proxy server functionality similar to that of a hardware-based firewall product.

Limiting Visibility with Domain Filters

In earlier days, companies would allow their employees to "surf the Web" without a care in the world. Then the first lawsuit hit. An employee happened to sit down in front of a computer that had a Web page open with objectionable content and felt the company was to blame for damage suffered.

| TABLE 10-1 | Configuration Settings for Custom Packet Filters |

Setting	Configuration
Protocol ID	This is the protocol ID as defined by RFC 791. You can get a complete list of protocol IDs at: http://www.isi.edu/in-notes/iana/assignments/protocol-numbers This is also known as the Protocol Number.
Direction	This is the direction to which the filter applies and therefore is subject to examination by the filter processes. You can choose to examine outgoing packets, incoming packets, or packets moving in either direction.
Local Port	This is the UDP or TCP port number for the source if the packet originates from the internal network. It can also be the destination port if the packet originates from the Internet or other external network.
Remote Port	This is the port number of the remote host computer. It can be a UDP or TCP port number for the source if the packet originates from an external network, or the destination, if the packet sources from inside the private network.
Local Host	This is the IP address of an internal computer that exchanges packets with a remote host. While typically it is the proxy server's IP address, it can represent any host server on your internal network.
Remote Host	The remote host that is allowed to exchange information with the proxy server or the internal network service's designated IP address.

Employees also enjoyed using the Web for finding technical information about subjects they needed to research. Back then, the Web was used primarily as a way to disseminate meaningful information and was a great research tool. Now, even unsophisticated employees are able to use the Web for their own kind of research: searching out basketball scores and real-time stock quotes—or worse.

In order to save your company the costs of frivolous lawsuits and lost productivity from abusive browsing habits, you need a way to control what employees can and cannot access on the Internet. One excellent way to accomplish this is to use Proxy Server 2.0 domain-filtering capabilities.

Figure 10-12 shows the Domain Filters tab in the Security dialog box.

When you Enable filtering by domain, you choose whether to allow access to all domains and then add a list of forbidden domains, or you can choose to deny access to all domains and include a list of approved domains.

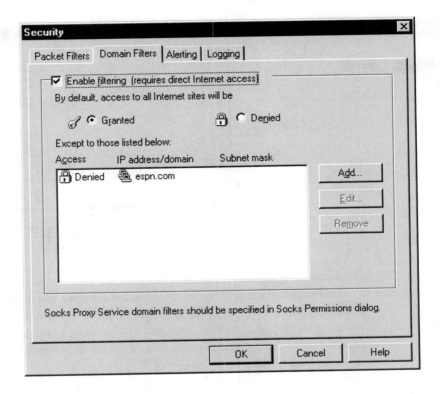

FIGURE 10-12

Controlling
Internet access
using domain
filters

To add a list of exceptions, click the Add button. You will see the dialog box that appears in Figure 10-13.

In this example, all domains are permitted except for those on the list, which are added by the administrator. In this case, we are adding a domain filter to prevent access to resources in the aol.com domain.

on the **Job**

Practical application of domain filtering of objectionable and time-wasting material can be a full-time occupation for a network administrator who has many other tasks to complete other than playing gendarme for Internet access. Companies such as Websense or surfCONTROL offer excellent plug-in software for Proxy Server 2.0 that automatically updates itself with the latest URLs and integrates smart features that allow you fine-tuning of domain access control.

While the most common method of site access control is by using domain names, you do have the options of filtering access to individual computers via IP address or groups of computers via their Network ID.

FIGURE 10-13

Adding a
domain filter

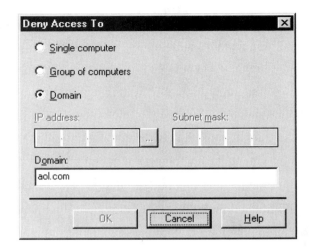

In designing a security solution based on domain access you should always keep in mind that restricted access based on domain names can become a very political affair, and you should not make such decisions in a vacuum. IT and other departments will have to agree on an access plan and enforce it as a unified force. You might propose that users submit requests to access certain domains that must be available to get their work done. This kind of polling is very helpful at reducing or eliminating corporate network usage dedicated to retrieving personal e-mail and chat activities.

Web Publishing and Reverse Hosting

Web publishing allows you to control the proxy server and Web server response to Internet requests for Web or FTP-based resources. Remember that, when implemented on a Windows 2000 server, Proxy Server "sits on top" of Internet Information Server 5.0. If your proxy server is on the edge of the network, it is open to direct requests from the Internet for IIS-related services.

Figure 10-14 shows the Publishing tab in the Web Proxy Properties dialog box. When you enable Web publishing, you must make one of three choices:

- Discard all incoming requests for Web or FTP resources
- Send Web and FTP requests to the local Web server, which is the Web server on which the proxy server is installed
- Forward Web and FTP requests to another Web server

FIGURE 10-14

The Publishing
tab in the Web
Proxy Service
dialog box

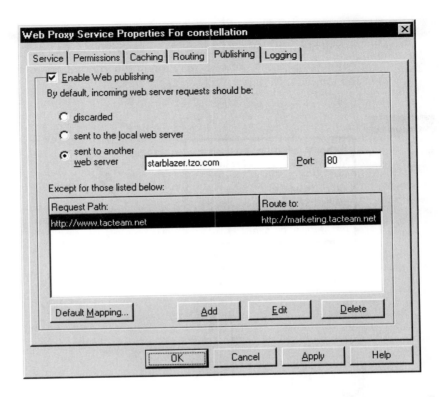

The first option is straightforward: all requests for HTTP or FTP objects will be dropped without further processing by the server. The *Sent to local server* option allows IIS-related services to evaluate the request and act on it according to the IIS configuration. The last option allows you to forward any requests to another Web server for processing.

You do have the option of creating exceptions to the choice you made. If you wish to maintain Web resources on your intranet, you can redirect requests for certain URLs to internal Web server installations for processing. For example, if a request from the Internet arrives at our edge proxy server for www.tacteam.net, we can configure the proxy server to reroute this request to an internal Web server at http://marketing. The marketing Web server will service all requests from the Internet for www.tacteam.net. In this way, we can allow Internet users access to resources contained on the internal network, without allowing them to establish sessions with any of our internal machines. All connections are via the edge proxy server.

It is a good policy to place Web resources that will be accessed by Internet users on a dedicated internal subnet, as shown in Figure 10-15. This makes securing and monitoring Internet sourced activity on the internal network much easier, efficient, and effective.

FIGURE 10-15

Positioning internal Web resources for Internet access

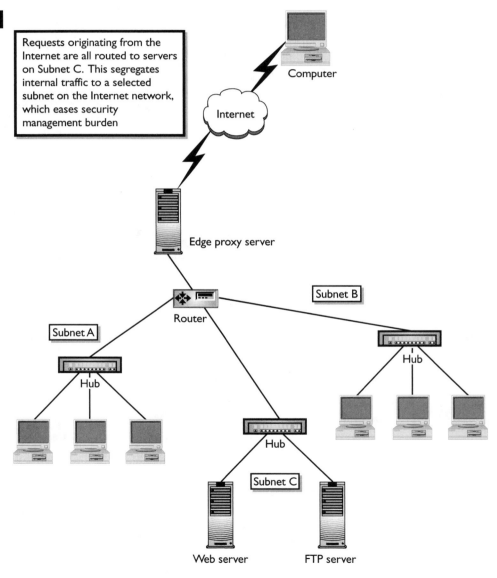

Requests originating from the Internet are all routed to servers on Subnet C. This segregates internal traffic to a selected subnet on the Internet network, which eases security management burden

Keep in mind that the most secure option is to not use Web publishing and discard all Web-related requests from the Internet.

on the

Job

In the example in Figure 10-15, Subnet C could represent a DMZ subnet. Subnets A and B would use private IP addresses, and Subnet C would use public IP addresses. IP forwarding would be enabled and packet filters would be used to protect the DMZ. This is most commonly used when Subnet C contains servers that are not Windows computers, such as Apache Web servers, that cannot use the reverse-publishing capabilities of Proxy Server 2.0. The other subnets are protected by virtue of their use of private IP addresses.

CertCam 10-3

EXERCISE 10-3

Using Proxy Server 2.0 to secure internal resources

You are the administrator for a corporate network that has approximately 1200 client computers. The company has a good number of temporary clerical personnel that need intermittent access to Internet sites in order to perform research for their jobs.

You have noticed that the network has become less responsive in the last couple of weeks. During a monitoring session you noticed a lot of traffic directed to aol.com addresses. Upon investigating this further, you find out that many of the temporary workers have been using AOL Web chat rooms during office hours.

What would you do to improve network performance to its previous level?

Suggested Solution:

Since your monitoring sessions captured a large amount of monitored traffic identifying AOL domain addresses and your further investigation shows employee usage of AOL Web chat rooms, it is important to take quick and decisive action.

First, you should confer with IT management regarding the situation. As we have discussed, any time you consider a change in the security infrastructure of the organization, you need to make sure that all decision makers are on the same page. This type of problem lends itself well to a network usage policy (which, since you brought up the issue, will probably have to be written by you).

After everyone has agreed that AOL domain access is not required for employee job duties, you can use domain filtering to prevent access to any aol.com site by adding a domain filter. If you find that there are other sites that are problematic, you should consider using a third-party add-on such as surfCONTROL.

CERTIFICATION OBJECTIVE 10.04

Designing a Fault-Tolerant Proxy Network

Because the proxy server is central in your Internet access and security solution, it is important to ensure consistent and reliable availability of proxy server services around the clock. Windows 2000 allows you several methods to increase the reliability of your proxy services.

The main methods used to enhance availability of proxy services are:

■ Proxy server arrays

■ Multiple DNS entries to accommodate DNS round robin

■ Windows 2000 network load balancing

You can use these methods individually or in tandem to increase the fault tolerance of your proxy network.

Proxy Server Arrays

Proxy server arrays provide an excellent method of fault tolerance and load balancing for Web caching and proxy server access. When you configure a proxy array, you join several proxy servers together to act as a single proxy server. Requests are automatically routed to the proxy server that contains the cached information. If any single proxy server in the array fails, the requests are automatically rerouted to a functioning server in the array.

Proxy server arrays are configured via the Shared service frame on the properties dialog box of any of the proxy services. After selecting the Array button, you see a dialog box similar to Figure 10-16.

This example shows that there are two machines in the array. If we wanted to add a new machine to the array, the Leave Array button on the new machine would say Join Array instead. Then you would type in the name of the existing array.

exam
ⓦatch

Note that the array name is not the name of any particular computer on the network. The array name is specific to the array only. The array name is stored in the Active Directory along with the array configuration.

FIGURE 10-16

Configuring a
proxy array

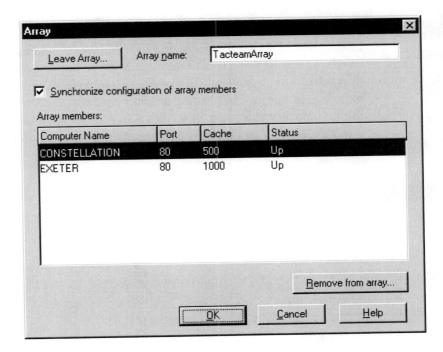

Proxy server clients can use a client configuration script that enhances the speed of resolution for cached Web pages. The client must be configured with these settings either via Group Policy or manually at the client workstation.

Round Robin and Network Load Balancing

Proxy server arrays alone provide a good method for load balancing, but a connection from the proxy client to an array must be specified at the client. The connection can be made to either an IP address or DNS host name, but still it must be specified. In order to provide fault tolerance, you should have the proxy clients connect to the proxy server via a DNS name so that you can take advantage of DNS round robin to add fault tolerance to the proxy array.

A more sophisticated method of providing fault tolerance for an array is to take advantage of network load balancing (clustering) and make each member of the array a cluster member.

Let's look at each of these methods.

DNS Round Robin

DNS round robin is a method that allows multiple IP addresses to be sent to a client based on the host name sent to the DNS Service. This is a method for commonly used services, such as Web sites that need high levels of availability. DNS round robin is accomplished by creating multiple entries in the DNS for a single name, in this case, the one you create in the DNS and use for members of the proxy array.

Figure 10-17 shows how the DNS round robin process works when the DNS client requests name resolution.

FIGURE 10-17 DNS client requesting name resolution via DNS round robin

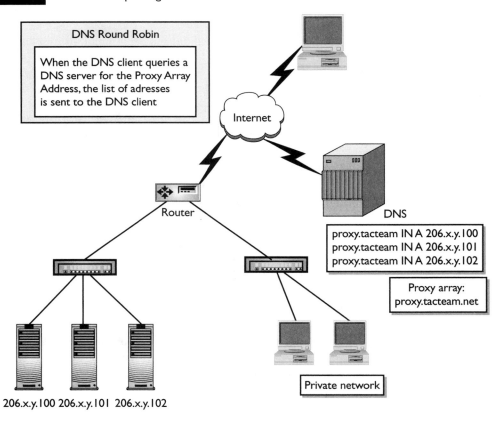

Figure 10-18 provides an example of how multiple entries are made for a single host name in the DNS.

In this example we have two entries in the DNS for **tacteamarray.tacteam.net.** Each entry points to a machine that is a member of the proxy server array. When a DNS client queries the DNS Service, a list of IP addresses is sent to the DNS client. You can confirm this by doing an nslookup for the array entry in the DNS. You will see something like what appears in Figure 10-19.

Be sure that DNS Round Robin is enabled on your Windows 2000 DNS Service if you plan to use this technique. You can do this at the Advanced tab of the DNS Service's Properties dialog box.

Network Load Balancing

Network Load Balancing (NLB) provides a method that represents true fault tolerance and load balancing for proxy services. NLB is coupled with the

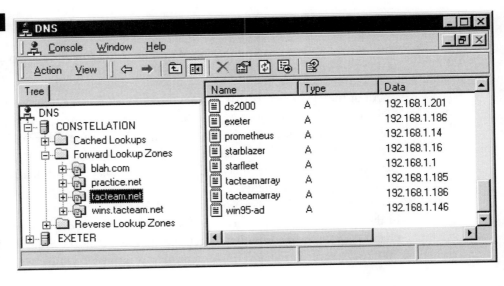

FIGURE 10-18

Multiple Entries for a single host name for DNS round robin

Performing an
nslookup on the
array name

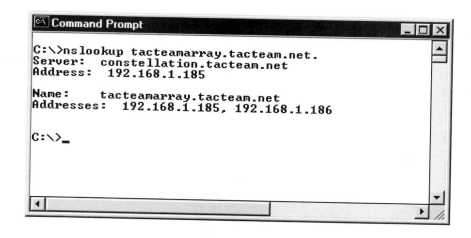

```
C:\>nslookup tacteamarray.tacteam.net.
Server:   constellation.tacteam.net
Address:   192.168.1.185

Name:     tacteamarray.tacteam.net
Addresses:   192.168.1.185, 192.168.1.186

C:\>_
```

Windows 2000 Cluster Service and provides a method to provide truly transparent and real-time failover of proxy server access.

exam

ⓦatch *The cluster service is available on Windows 2000 Advanced Server. Clustering is not included with Windows 2000 Server.*

All of the proxy servers that are members of a cluster share the same IP address when using NLB. All client requests are routed to the cluster. If a single member of the cluster becomes unavailable, the other members of the cluster quickly take over for the failed client. The primary advantage of using NLB over DNS round robin is that when servers become unavailable in a cluster, they are automatically excluded from access by proxy clients.

When a DNS client requests name resolution for the array's address, the address of the cluster is returned. Network load balancing is outside the scope of this chapter. For more information, check the Syngress Osborne Study Guide for Exam 70-216, Administering and Implementing a Windows 2000 Network Infrastructure.

EXERCISE 10-4

Improving Proxy Server 2.0 Fault Tolerance

All network clients in your organization use a proxied connection in order to access Internet resources. There are 500 client machines at your site and the proxy server goes down periodically because of some intermittent hardware problems. You have contacted the hardware manufacturer about the faulty item and they told you that the item is temporarily out of stock, but that they should have it available in two weeks.

What could you do to improve Proxy Server 2.0 fault tolerance in this situation and prevent problems with a single proxy server from disabling your network client's access to Internet resources?

Suggested Answer:

The problem this administrator has is with fault tolerance rather than load balancing. Remember that proxy arrays allow for load balancing and increase the size of the available Web cache by spreading the cache over multiple servers. However, since proxy clients must connect to a particular server, proxy arrays alone do not provide for fault tolerance.

In this situation you should employ either DNS round robin for name resolution of the proxy array, or better yet, network load balancing for a Windows 2000 cluster. First, the administrator should add at least another computer to act as a proxy server for his network. After adding the second server, he should have the second server become a member of an array. After the array is created, add DNS entries for the array name to point to the IP address of each server. Alternatively, you can create a proxy cluster and then create a DNS entry for the cluster IP address.

CERTIFICATION OBJECTIVE 10.05

Maximizing Proxy Server Performance

There are a couple of technologies you can apply that will improve the user experience after installing Proxy Server 2.0. These include:

- Web content caching
- Configuring chains of proxy servers

Web content caching can significantly improve the user's Web experience by caching objects that are accessed from Web servers. Proxy chaining allows you to distribute responsibility for answering Web requests across multiple proxy servers or arrays.

Configuring the Web Cache

Microsoft Proxy Server 2.0 allows you to cache virtually all Web objects that are accessed via the proxy server. When the proxy server's Web caching function is enabled, all content that is not secure will be placed on a reserved part of the proxy server's hard disk. When the proxy server receives the next request for the same object, it can return the object to the requestor by receiving it from the cache, rather than having to obtain the object again from the server on the Internet.

There are two ways you can implement Web caching: passive or active.

Passive Caching

With passive caching, each object that does not have security attached to it is placed in the Web cache. The object stays in cache for a time based on how you have configured the Advanced properties of the cache itself. You access the Web cache configuration via Caching in the Web Proxy Properties dialog box. Figure 10-20 shows what this looks like.

Note that the Cache expiration policy has three options. Choose the option that fits your requirements based on what is more important: faster user response or fewer Internet accesses. Your decision should be based on factors such as costs related to Internet access and whether or not there are periods of time when you have excess bandwidth to spare.

The primary advantages of passive caching over active caching are that there is less use of the Internet bandwidth and a small overall decrease in processor use on the proxy server machine.

Active Caching

Active Caching differs from passive caching in that it will proactively seek out Web content and updates the content cache for popular URLs. The algorithm for updating the content cache takes into account how frequently and often sites are accessed and the proximity to the end of the object's TTL. Note that when Active Caching is enabled, all objects without security are still added to the Web cache

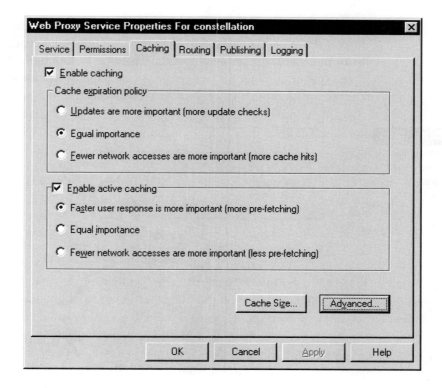

FIGURE 10-20

Configuring the
Web cache

when accessed. The only difference is that the proxy server will also perform automatic refreshes of some of the information in the cache.

The main advantages of active caching are that user response is much better because fresh objects are already located in cache and the user does not have to wait for the objects to be accessed from Internet servers before receiving them. Some disadvantages of active caching are overall increase in processor use, a larger Web cache, and more bandwidth use of the Internet access channel. These can be important issues if you pay per-packet charges on your Internet access, or if you are running a VPN on the same interface and the VPN users must compete with the proxy server as it updates its Web cache.

Chaining Proxy Servers

You can chain proxy servers to distribute the load and improve perceived end-user performance. A chain should be configured in a hierarchical manner, with the proxy servers with the fastest link at the top of the chain and successively slower links further down on the chain. An example of such chaining appears in Figure 10-21.

In this chain the national headquarters has a T4 link to the Internet. All Internet access for the corporation takes place via the national headquarters Internet connection. A proxy array caches all Web objects received from the Internet.

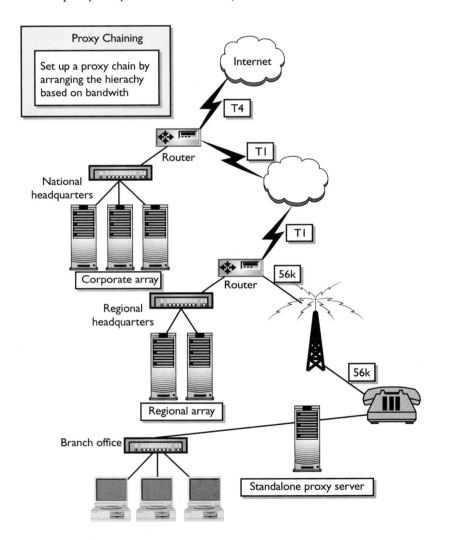

FIGURE 10-21

Chaining proxy servers and arrays

The regional headquarters has a T1 link to the national headquarters and also has a proxy array. When a proxy client at the regional headquarters attempts to access a Web object from the Internet, the regional array will be checked first. If the object is not contained in there, the corporate array will be checked. If the corporate array does not have the object cached, that array will retrieve the object from the Internet.

After the corporate array retrieves the object, it places the object in cache and returns the object to the regional array. The regional array places the object in its cache, and then returns the object to the proxy client at regional headquarters.

A similar sequence of events will take place when a client tries to access Web resources from a branch office that is connected to its regional headquarters via a dial-up 56k line. Notice what happens when all Web resources are accessed from a central Internet connection at national headquarters. *All* Web requests in the organization are cached there, and all unfulfilled local requests are ultimately routed to the national array. In this way, all users in the organization benefit from the cached objects requested from all other users and in the process, all user requests for Web objects are accessed more quickly.

CertCam 10-5

EXERCISE 10-5

Configuring the Web Cache

In this exercise you will configure the Web cache service that is part of the Web proxy service. Do not perform this exercise on a live production network without the permission of your network administrator.

1. Log on as Administrator.

2. Click the Start menu, point to Programs, then point to Administrative Tools. Click on the Internet Services Manager shortcut.

3. In the Internet Services Manager, right-click on Web Proxy in the left pane and click Properties. Click on the Caching tab.

4. On the Caching tab make sure that the Enable caching check box it is checked, and then select the Cache Size button. You will see the following dialog box.

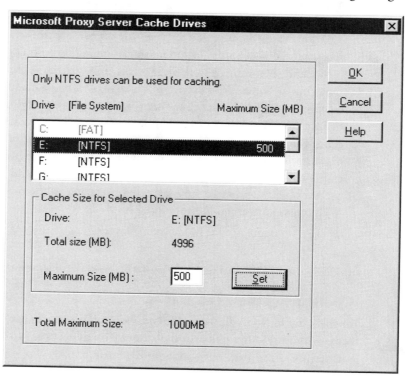

5. In the Maximum Size text box, type in a value for the number of MBs you wish to use for the Web cache, then click Set. Note in Figure 10-25 that the C: drive is grayed out. That is because it is a FAT partition and you cannot place the Web proxy cache on a FAT partition.

6. Click OK and click Apply. The Web proxy cache size is now set.

CERTIFICATION SUMMARY

Microsoft Proxy Server 2.0 provides an organization a way to access the Internet in a secure fashion, protecting the network from both outbound and inbound attacks. With proxy server, you can control what internal network users access on the Internet, and you can limit the level of access to internal network resources for Internet users.

Proxy Server 2.0 is comprised of three services: the Web Proxy Service, the WinSock Service, and the SOCKS Service. Each of these services provides a means to access particular applications and content on the Internet using slightly different technologies.

When planning your proxy network solution, start with considering the functionality you wish to provide to your network clients. Ascertain what type of Internet access they require, the level of access controls, the speed of the internal and external interfaces, the network architecture, and signal requirements for your network.

After basic functionality plans are created, start on a security analysis. When planning for security, remember that you must consider security controls on both outgoing and incoming data. You can control what internal network users access on the Internet using Web Proxy and WinSock Proxy user and group permissions. You can also use domain filtering and cache filtering to control the type of content users can access.

Packet filtering is an especially powerful method of protecting your internal network from Internet attacks. You must determine the type of network traffic that needs to enter your internal network, then enable packet filtering to reject all packets that do not meet your specifications.

Fault tolerance is addressed next. If Internet access is vital to your organization, devise methods to allow the proxy server network to be available even after proxy server crashes. Methods of fault tolerance include network load balancing and DNS round robin. Proxy arrays provide a measure of fault tolerance via load balancing and allow for distribution of Web cache requests across members of the array.

Finally, consider how you can increase the performance of the proxy server solution. Methods you can employ to improve performance include increasing the size of the Web cache, using a proxy chain across sites, and enabling active caching. Hardware upgrades almost always improve the performance of your proxy server solution as well.

TWO-MINUTE DRILL

Introduction to Proxy Server

❑ Microsoft Proxy Server 2.0 provides a way to secure the internal network from Internet intruders and provide access controls over what content internal users can access on the Internet.

❑ Microsoft Proxy Server 2.0 was not designed with Windows 2000 in mind. However, you can download a setup program from the Microsoft Web site that will allow Proxy Server 2.0 to install and integrate with Windows 2000 services, including the Active Directory.

❑ If you are upgrading a Windows NT 4.0 machine that already has proxy server installed, you should first save your Proxy Server 2.0 settings to a file, then perform the Windows 2000 upgrade. Install Proxy Server 2.0 into the same location that previous installation was located.

❑ When preparing to design a Proxy Server 2.0 infrastructure, you should consider the number of geographical sites, whether or not you will be dealing with routed networks, whether or not you will need access controls for inbound or outbound requests, and to what types of access controls you want to subject internal users.

❑ Microsoft Proxy Server 2.0 is installed "on top of" Internet Information Server 5.0.

❑ Proxy Server 2.0 includes three separate and distinct services: the Web proxy Service, the WinSock Proxy Service, and the SOCK Proxy Service.

❑ The Web Proxy Service is used by CERN-compliant browsers and provides access to resources via HTTP, HTTPS, Gopher, and FTP protocols.

❑ The WinSock Proxy Service is used to replace the native WinSock driver on the proxy client's TCP/IP protocol stack. All WinSock calls are then redirected to the new driver and sent to the WinSock Proxy Service. The WinSock Proxy Service requires that the WinSock Proxy Client software be installed on the client, but it allows access to a full range of WinSock applications. These applications do not need to be proxy aware and access the proxy WinSock driver as they would the native WinSock driver.

❑ The SOCKS Proxy Service is for Sockets applications that run primarily on UNIX and Mac systems that do not support the WinSock session layer interface.

❑ Microsoft Proxy Server 2.0 integrates into the secure structure of Windows 2000 Servers and takes advantage of accounts that are contained in the Active Directory. In addition, proxy array information is also contained in the Active Directory.

Designing a Proxy Server Networking Implementation

❑ When designing a proxy networking implementation, you need to consider where to locate, and the implications of locating proxy servers on your network.

❑ A proxy server can be located on the "edge" of a network. These edge proxy servers have at least one interface exposed to the Internet. This interface will have a public IP address that is accessible from any host location on the Internet.

❑ A proxy server can also be located internally, and have no interfaces exposed to the Internet. These proxy servers are used primarily to manage Web caching. However, you can also use these for security purposes, on the edges of subnets, for increased security for particular segments.

❑ Consider the hardware you require for your proxy servers. Most important, what network architecture is in use for the segments that the server will interface with? Ethernet, Fast Ethernet, Gigabit Ethernet, ATM, and Token Ring are just some of your options.

❑ Along with hardware considerations are bandwidth requirements. External interfaces will have slower interfaces that are dependent on the WAN technology being used.

❑ Decide whether you will use dedicated or on-demand connections, such as dial-up. Dedicated connections are faster and more reliable, but dial-up solutions are typically cheaper.

Proxy Server Security

❑ Proxy Server 2.0 provides both inbound and outbound security for the internal network.

❑ Outbound security can be enforced for all three proxy services in a slightly different manner. Access controls based on user or group membership allow you to control which users can access what particular content on the Internet.

❑ Inbound security can be enabled by firewall-like capabilities of Proxy Server 2.0 via packet filters. Packet filtering allows the proxy server to examine all packets coming to the external interface prior to any further processing. If the packet is not of an allowed protocol or port type, it is rejected without further processing.

❑ You can limit the visibility of potentially harmful domains on the Internet by using domain filters. Certain well-known domains are prime targets for domain filters. For more sophisticated domain filtering, you should consider a third-party product that plugs into a proxy server that allows for up-to-date domain filtering and elegant reporting capabilities.

Designing a Fault Tolerant Proxy Network

❑ Proxy Server arrays provide a measure of fault tolerance and also load balancing. An array allows groups of proxy servers to function as a single server entity for a number of server-related functions. All servers share the same Web cache. Clients are directed to the appropriate server that contains the sought after object in the cache.

❑ DNS round robin can be used to provide fault tolerance for proxy server arrays. You enter the name of the array in the DNS for each server in the array. When clients query DNS, they will receive a randomized list of IP addresses to access the proxy service required.

❑ Network load balancing is an extension of the Microsoft Cluster Service, which allows the entire server cluster to share a single IP address. When a client request is made for proxy services located on a cluster, a member of the cluster will respond. If a member of the cluster becomes disabled, the remaining cluster member automatically handles requests.

Maximizing Proxy Server Performance

❑ You can improve user experience when accessing Web objects by implementing the Web proxy caching capability. The Web cache on the proxy server will automatically place all objects accessed via the proxy server into the cache. Only objects that are not secured by a password or via SSL will be placed in the cache for security reasons.

❑ Passive caching is when the proxy server places objects in the Web cache after they have been requested by a proxy client. No matter what type of caching you implement, passive caching is always in effect.

❑ Active caching improves the speed of Web object access for end users. Not only does it take advantage of the passive caching capabilities of Proxy Server 2.0, but the proxy server will also seek out popular and frequently accessed Web objects on its own during times of low processor use on the proxy server.

❑ While Active Caching does provide a speed advantage for the end user, it does consume more bandwidth on the Internet connection. It also requires more disk space for the Web proxy cache, and there is an overall increase in the amount of processor use.

SELF TEST

The following questions will help you measure your understanding of the material presented in this chapter. Read all of the choices carefully, as there may be more than one correct answer. Choose all correct answers for each question.

Introduction to Microsoft Proxy Server 2.0

1. Your organization is in the process of upgrading its Windows NT 4.0 Servers to Windows 2000. Several of the Windows NT 4.0 Servers have Proxy Server 2.0 installed. You tell your assistant to proceed with the upgrade of these servers that have Proxy Server installed. After the completion of the upgrade, you note that Proxy Server 2.0 no longer works on these servers. What must you do in order to get Proxy Server 2.0 to work properly again on these upgraded machines?

    A. When a Windows NT 4.0 computer with Proxy Server 2.0 installed is upgraded, the proxy settings are saved in the registry. You must re-enable these settings in the registry.

    B. The first time the upgraded computer starts, the Proxy Server 2.0 services do not start automatically. You must open the Internet Services Console to manually start the Proxy Server services the first time the Windows 2000 computer is started after the upgrade.

    C. After the computer is upgraded to Windows 2000, you must reinstall Proxy Server 2.0 with the updated installation program. You must then reinstall Proxy Server 2.0 into the same location it was installed in with the Windows NT 4.0 installation.

    D. You must install the WinSock Proxy Client on the Windows 2000 Server computer in order for proxy services to work correctly.

2. You manage a network with three physical segments that have been partitioned into three logical subnets. These subnets are referred to as Subnet A, Subnet B, and Subnet C. All users on Subnet A are managers or executives and all users on Subnet B are clericals or other lower-level functionaries. Subnet C is reserved for servers that are open to Internet user access. You wish to allow the managers and executives full access to the Internet, but you want to implement domain filters on the clerical segment. How could you accomplish this?

    A. Place an edge proxy server that all segments will use to access Internet resources. Set access controls based on the user account to limit access to certain domains to particular users or groups.

    B. Place a proxy Server on Subnet C and limit access from Internet users to those machines located on that subnet.

C. Place a single proxy server on the edge of Subnet A and set access controls based on user account or group to control access to particular domains.

D. Place proxy servers on the edges of Subnet A and Subnet B. Do not configure domain filters on the proxy server on Subnet A. On the proxy server on the edge of Subnet B, configure the domain filter to prevent access to objectionable sites.

3. The private IP address ranges include the following:

A. 10.0.0.0–10.255.255.255

B. 172.16.0.0–172.31.255.255

C. 192.168.0.0–192.168.255.255

D. 206.215.60.0–206.215.60.255

4. You want to provide basic Web and FTP services to your internal network users. However, you do not want your users to be able to access all Internet sites because the management is concerned about loss of productivity related to abusive Web surfing. What proxy service would provide you with the type of access you need and also provide you with a method of controlling what internal users can access on the Internet?

A. WinSock

B. Web

C. SOCKS

D. Windows

Designing a Proxy Server Network Implementation

5. What type of proxy server has the lowest liability of Internet intrusion?

A. A proxy array located on the edge of the private network

B. A proxy server located inside a DMZ, where the proxy server is located between the firewall and internal network.

C. A proxy server with three network cards that are all connected to internal segments

D. A proxy server using a dedicated ISDN connection as a backup route in a proxy chain

6. You would like to take advantage of protocol isolation to secure your internal network. How would you accomplish this task using Proxy Server as part of the solution?

A. Install NetBEUI on the internal interface of the proxy server and TCP/IP on the external interface. Install only NetBEUI on the internal interfaces of the proxy clients on the internal network.

   B. Install TCP/IP and IPX/SPX on the internal interface of the proxy server and install TCP/IP and IPX/SPX on the internal interfaces of the proxy client computer. Change the binding order so that IPX/SPX is on top for the proxy server's internal interface and also change the binding order so that IPX/SPX is on top of the proxy client's internal interface.

   C. Install IPX/SPX on the internal interface of the proxy server and TCP/IP on the external interface of the proxy server. Install only IPX/SPX on the internal interfaces of the proxy client computers.

   D. Install TCP/IP and IPX/SPX on the internal interface, and only TCP/IP on the external interface of the proxy server computer. Install only IPX/SPX on the internal interface of the proxy client computers.

7. You have installed Proxy Server on the edge of the private network. You have configured all the network clients to use the proxy server as the default gateway for all the proxy clients as well. You have configured the WinSock and the Web Proxy services with access control to prevent abuse of the Internet connection. However, when you run some network traces, you see connections being made to AOL domain names. What might be the explanation for this problem?

   A. You cannot filter out AOL connections.

   B. You must set the default gateway to be the external interface of the proxy server computer.

   C. You must disable IP forwarding on the proxy server since you have set the default gateway to be the proxy server computer. If users decide to disable the WinSock client, they have unfettered access to Internet sites and resources.

   D. You must enable IP forwarding to prevent unauthorized access to Internet resources.

Proxy Server Security

8. What methods can be used to control access to Internet resources using Microsoft Proxy Server 2.0?

   A. On a per-user basis

   B. On a per-security group basis

   C. On a per-server basis

   D. On a per subnet-ID basis

9. You have been having problems with hackers bringing down your Web server that is directly connected to the Internet. You are running Web Publishing on the proxy server that is installed on the same installation of Internet Information Server that the Web sites are located. After performing a network analysis, you have ascertained that the hackers are using FRAG attacks to bring down the server. What can you do to reduce the risk of crashing the Web server from hackers using FRAG attacks?

A. Add a packet filter for the TCP FRAG protocol.

B. Disable dynamic packet filtering for the external interface of the proxy server.

C. Enable filtering of IP fragments.

D. Add a packet filter for the PPTP (Call) protocol.

10. You would like to allow your internal users access to virtually all Internet material. However, you are concerned about exposing the company to risk of litigation. What would be the most efficient way for you to allow users free access to legitimate Web sites, but prevent them from comparing the artistic merits of various porn sites?

A. Perform a Web search based on key words that you believe will uncover the majority of objectionable Web sites.

B. Have the proxy server perform an autodiscovery of objectionable material on the Internet and place that material in a dedicated Web cache that you can view at your convenience.

C. Purchase a third-party plug-in program that will configure domain filters automatically and create reports for you that you can present to management.

D. Ask the users on the network what URLs they have found offensive in the past and record these so that you can enter them manually into the domain filter list.

11. You would like to allow Internet users to download documents stored on your internal network but maintain a high level of security. You do not run a Web site, but you have data stored in the form of .pdf files and word documents that you want them to be able to access. What is the best way for you to accomplish this task?

A. Enable NetBIOS by creating packet filters for NetBIOS port numbers.

B. Share the folders on the hard drive of the computer that contains the files and then let users access those files via SMB file-sharing protocol.

C. Copy the files to the FTPROOT folder on the Internet Information Server on the internal network, and then use mappings so that users can request files via FTP on the FTP Server on that IIS computer.

D. Open all ports on the proxy server and allow all traffic to move through the proxy server and directly to the internal computer via mapped network drives. Enable IP forwarding and use public IP addresses on the internal servers.

12. When enabling Web publishing, what three options do you have?

A. Discard all incoming requests for FTP or Web resources

B. Send Web and FTP requests to the local Web server

C. Forward Web and FTP requests to another Web server

D. Forward all Web and FTP requests as an e-mail attachment to the proxy server administrator for future analysis

Designing a Fault Tolerant Proxy Network

13. You want to use a proxy server array to improve the fault tolerance of your proxy server solution for your network. Your network clients will only use the Web Proxy service and they have been informed on how to configure their Internet Explorer application to connect to a proxy server by its DNS name. You have created an array of five proxy servers. One of the proxy servers goes offline, but the other machines continue to run normally and the majority of the users have no problems. However, about 20 percent of the users of the proxy array complain that they can no longer access Web resources on the Internet. What is the most likely reason for this?

A. You need to resynchronize the array.

B. After a server failure on the array, you must restart all the participating machines in the array in order to properly answer queries for all users.

C. You have not properly configured the dedicated array IP address, so when one server fails, there are intermittent failures on requests to the array.

D. You must configure DNS round robin for all the array members.

14. What are the primary methods of fault tolerance for your proxy server solution?

A. Network load balancing

B. DNS round robin

C. Offline spares

D. Online spares with daily mirroring

15. You notice that proxy server performance has degraded significantly after a recent merger. What can you do to improve proxy server performance?

    A. Configure a proxy array.

    B. Enable DNS round robin.

    C. Add more RAM into each proxy server.

    D. Upgrade the processor in each proxy server machine.

16. Your company has a national office in Dallas. It also has a regional office in Tombstone, AZ and a branch office in Albuquerque, NM. The Tombstone office is connected to the Dallas office via a T1 line and the Albuquerque office is connected to the Tombstone office via a dedicated 56k Frame Relay. The Company has a T3 connection to the Internet at the Dallas location and it's the company's security policy that no computer may connect to the Internet other than by connecting via the T3 line. What would help all employees at all locations take advantage of a centralized Web caching solution and also reduce the amount of bandwidth consumed on each of the WAN links?

    A. Implement a proxy chaining solution.

    B. Install a proxy array at the Dallas office.

    C. Install a proxy cluster at the Dallas office.

    D. Install a proxy server on each network segment at the Dallas office.

17. You are upgrading your Proxy Server 2.0 to completely new hardware. You have created a very complex set of cache filters, packet filters, permissions for the Web Proxy and WinSock Proxy, and SOCKS permissions, as well. If you had to reconstruct the entire proxy server configuration it would take you at least an entire day to complete. How can you avoid manually reconfiguring the proxy server on the new computer hardware that you will be installing proxy server on?

    A. Use the Server Backup button on the Properties dialog box of any of the proxy services to back up the configuration on the original proxy server.

    B. Use the Server Restore button on the Properties dialog box of any of the proxy services to restore the server configuration file on the new server.

    C. Copy the proxy-related registry entries on the original server and then restore those registry entries on the new server.

    D. Copy the entire proxy server folder and its subfolder to a network location, then copy the entire folder hierarchy to the new machine. Restart the new machine and everything will work as it did previously.

Maximizing Proxy Server Performance

18. Which of the three proxy services is responsible for maintaining the content cache of Internet sites that have already been visited by network users?

    A. Web

    B. WinSock

    C. SOCKS

    D. WINS

19. Users complain that it takes too long for them to access content on the Web during business hours. The company does not do much business in the evenings and most of the work is done during daylight hours. What could you do to improve the users' Web experience during the day?

    A. Enable Turbo browsing in the Web proxy service.

    B. Configure the registry to increase the priority of the Web proxy service.

    C. Enable active caching.

    D. Enable passive caching.

LAB QUESTION

You have been consulted to help a small office connect to the Internet. This office is in a location where the only high-speed Internet access is ISDN. There are packet charges for data transfer using ISDN in this region. There are 15 network clients and they have one Windows 2000 Server computer. They are willing to pay for new software, but want to keep hardware costs to a minimum.

What would you suggest to this company for their Internet access solution?

SELF TEST ANSWERS

Introduction to Microsoft Proxy Server 2.0

1. ☑ **C.** If you upgrade a Windows NT 4.0 machine with proxy server already installed, and then just upgrade that machine to Windows 2000, the Proxy Server 2.0 server will not be migrated to Windows 2000. You will need to install Proxy Server 2.0 as a fresh installation, because no upgrade options will be available to you during the installation with the updated Windows 2000 install file. Be sure to install Proxy Server 2.0 into the same location in which it was installed with the Windows NT 4.0 installation. Your settings should be carried over when you install to the same location.

   ☒ **A** is incorrect because there are no registry settings that you have to configure in order to allow Proxy Server 2.0 to work correctly in Windows 2000 after the upgrade has been completed. **B** is incorrect because the proxy services should start automatically after the correct Proxy Server 2.0 installation has been performed. That being said, there are times when a proxy service may "hang" and you will need to start the process manually after the server is brought online. **D** is incorrect because you do not need to install the WinSock Proxy Client on the proxy server to make it work correctly.

2. ☑ **D.** You can place proxy servers on the edge of each subnet and create custom domain filters for each subnet. Since the filter on each proxy server applies only to those users located on the particular proxy server's subnet, you gain some control as to whom domain filters apply.

   ☒ **A** is incorrect because cache filters apply across all services and cannot be applied to a particular user or group. Therefore, a single proxy server on the edge of the network will not provide granular domain filtering for the subnets. **B** is incorrect because Subnet C is used only for servers that provide content for Internet-based users. Any access controls or domain filters placed on that proxy server will have no effect on users on Subnets A and B. **C** is incorrect because domain filters are system-wide and are not subject to per-user or group-access controls.

3. ☑ **A, B, C.** These represent groups of IP addresses that have been reserved for private networks. These private network IP addresses are not included in Internet routing tables and therefore Internet routers drop any requests for these addresses. This confers a great security advantage because Internet users cannot directly interface with internal machines that use these private IP addresses. However, the same applies to the internal machines and their ability to access Internet resources such as Web site and mail servers. In order for the internal machines to access public sites, they must use an intermediary such as a proxy server or a network address translator (NAT) service. In both of these cases, the internal network client makes a request for

a public resource and the proxy or NAT server intercepts that request. The intercessor then makes the request itself using its external interface's IP address as the source of the request. When the Internet computer responds to the request, it sends it to the proxy or NAT server's external interface. The proxy or NAT server then forwards the reply to the internal network client that issued the initial request.

☒ **D** is incorrect because that is a public Class C network address block.

4. ☑ **B.** You can use the Web Proxy Service to provide the basic Internet services that are required in this scenario. You can control access via users and groups using the Web Proxy Service, and you can also take advantage of domain filtering to control even further what you want your users to access on the Internet.

☒ **A** is incorrect because the WinSock Proxy Service will provide more than basic Internet services for your internal network Internet clients. This may be an undesirable situation if your network is bandwidth challenged and you have users that might abuse other Internet applicatons. **C** is incorrect because you would not want to use the clumsy SOCKS Proxy Service when the Web Proxy will work better and meet your needs. The SOCKS Proxy Service provides basic SOCKS Version 4.3a support for UNIX and Mac users that must access Internet resources. **D** is incorrect because there is no Windows Proxy Service.

Designing a Proxy Server Network Implementation

5. ☑ **C.** All adapters interface only with the internal network and so are at the lowest risk for Internet intrusion.

☒ **A** is incorrect because an edge proxy server is wide open for Internet intruders. You can decrease the risk of intrusion by enabling packet filtering on the external interface of the edge proxy server. **B** is incorrect because, although the proxy server is located behind a firewall, it is closer to the edge of the network than some of the other possible choices; the use of a DMZ is common in proxy implementations. **D** is incorrect because a dedicated ISDN connection will have a public IP address attached to it, which increases its liability to scanning and subsequent attack by Internet intruders.

6. ☑ **D.** In order to successfully implement protocol isolation on the network, you install only IPX/SPX on the internal clients, and IPX/SPX and TCP/IP on the internal interface of the proxy server and only TCP/IP on the external interface of the proxy server.

☒ **A** is incorrect because you cannot use NetBEUI and Proxy Server together to create a protocol isolation solution for network security. In order to take advantage of protocol isolation using Microsoft Proxy Server 2.0, you must use IPX/SPX and have the WinSock proxy client installed on the proxy client computer. **B** is incorrect because if you have TCP/IP installed on both the internal interface of the proxy server computer and also have TCP/IP installed on the internal interface of the proxy client computers, you will have no protocol isolation, since TCP/IP exists on all links in the path from the Internet. You must remove TCP/IP from the client computers in order to isolate them from Internet intruders. **C** is incorrect because you must have TCP/IP installed on the internal interface of the proxy server. Because of limitations on how the IPX/SPX protocol stack functions with the WinSock client software, it cannot use IPX numbers or NetBIOS over IPX/SPX to connect to the internal interface via a computer name; you must use an IP address in the client configuration to connect to the proxy server internal interface.

7. ☑ **C.** You must disable IP forwarding on the proxy server computer to prevent unproxied connections to the Internet. It is relatively easy for users to disable the WinSock and Web Proxy configurations on their local machines. After those client configurations are disabled, users who have the default gateway set to the internal interface of a proxy server with IP forwarding enabled will be able to directly access any Internet content they like.
   ☒ **A** is incorrect because you can filter out AOL domains and protocols by using packet filters on the external interface. This is a common access control because most organizations have no requirements for AOL access in order to allow employees to accomplish their work. **B** is incorrect because you should not set the default gateway for the proxy clients to be the external interface of the proxy computer since the proxy server's external interface will have a public IP address, and the default gateway of any machine must be on the local segment. It is very unlikely that any proxy client will be local to the network ID of the external interface of the proxy server. **D** is incorrect because you want to disable IP forwarding, not enable it. Enabling IP forwarding on a proxy server is a significant security breach.

Proxy Server Security

8. ☑ **A, B, C.** You can control access to the Internet using per-user, per-security group and per-server mechanisms.
   ☒ **D** is incorrect because there is no method to control access on a single proxy server to give you per-subnet access controls.

9. ☑ **C.** When you enable filtering of IP fragments, you can protect the server from a number of hacker attacks, including the FRAG and SYN attacks.
   ☒ **A** is incorrect because there is no FRAG protocol of either the TCP or the UDP type. **B** is incorrect because dynamic packet filtering applies only for ports that are opened on the external interface of the proxy server so that the proxy server can receive replies for requests that it has made; these ports are closed immediately after the Internet server has replied to the

request, hence the name *dynamic*. **D** is incorrect because the PPTP (Call) protocol filter is used to allow outbound PPTP connections from the internal network to an external location. Filtering the PPTP (Call) protocol will not protect the server from FRAG attacks.

10. ☑ **C.** There are several excellent plug-in programs that you can integrate with Microsoft Proxy Server 2.0 that will update your domain filter cache and also keep the filter list current with frequent updates.

☒ **A** is incorrect because performing your own searches would not be the most efficient use of your time. Plus, you would have to update your list everyday, as these kinds of sites are quite mobile. **B** is incorrect because Microsoft Proxy Server 2.0 does not have an Autodiscovery utility that searches out objectionable Web content and places it in the filter list of domains. **D** is incorrect because asking users which Web sites they find objectionable would not be the most efficient way to build a filter list. In addition, the list would not update itself automatically and most users would be reluctant to share with you objectionable sites they have visited.

11. ☑ **C.** You should place the files in the FTPROOT directory on an IIS installation in the internal network. Configure access controls for the directory and via IIS. Then use the Web publishing feature of Proxy Server 2.0 and map a path to the internal server. Use private IP addresses for the internal server to prevent Internet users from establishing unproxied connections and disable IP forwarding on the proxy server.

☒ **A** is incorrect because NetBIOS ports should always be closed on the proxy server. NetBIOS is inherently insecure and can allow Internet users to browse the folder structure of all accessible machines. **B** is incorrect because sharing files via SMB requires that you open up the NetBIOS ports and then have users access the files via mapped network drives or via browsing or via a UNC path. This is very insecure and a poor security practice. **D** is incorrect because you never want to open all ports on the external interface of the proxy server and you never want to enable IP forwarding on the proxy server. By enabling IP forwarding, you allow packets to move through the proxy server without being examined by packet filters.

12. ☑ **A, B, C.** You can have the proxy server's external interface examine all requests directly toward the IIS server for HTTP or FTP resources. When the proxy server examines those requests, it will drop them. You can also configure the proxy server to forward all HTTP and FTP requests directed to the local Web server to the local Web server to be answered. IIS and NTFS provide security in this circumstance. **C** is correct because you can configure the proxy server to intercept Web requests and forward those requests to another Web server. This server can be either internal or external.

☒ **D** is incorrect because Proxy Server 2.0 provides no mechanism for forwarding Web requests to the administrator for further evaluation.

Designing a Fault Tolerant Proxy Network

13. ☑ **D.** You must configure DNS round robin for all the array members. The users are connecting to the array via manual configuration of their Web browsers and using an individual machine name to establish a connection to the array. When users of the Web Proxy service connect to the array via a DNS host name for a particular machine, if that machine should become unavailable, they will no longer be able to connect to the array. To solve this problem, create a name dedicated to the array, and then create a DNS entry for each of the IP addresses in the array with this array name. When network clients attempt to connect to the host name for the array, they will receive a list of IP addresses in random order, and are not dependent on a single machine being online in order to connect to the array.

☒ **A** is incorrect because you do not need to resynchronize the array after a machine becomes unavailable. You need to resynchronize the array if you make changes to one of the server's configurations when another server is not available. **B** is incorrect because you do not need to restart all members of an array after the failure of one of the array members. Other members of the array will automatically handle requests for Web objects that were located on the failed array member. **C** is incorrect because an array does not have a dedicated IP address; each member of the array has its own IP address.

14. ☑ **A, B.** You can use Network load balance as a superior method of fault tolerance. NLB, used together with Microsoft Cluster Services, provides virtually real-time fault tolerance for proxy services via a single, clustered IP address. You can use DNS round robin, together with multiple proxy servers in an array, to provide fault tolerance for proxy services.

☒ **C** and **D** are incorrect because, while you can use offline and online spares, they represent poor fault tolerance solutions because of configuration and synchronization limitations.

15. ☑ **A, B, C, D.** Each of these options can improve proxy server performance. A proxy array is an ideal way to distribute the load of answering queries for Web objects from the distributed cache. DNS round robin allows a different proxy server to be delivered on a random basis to machines seeking to make an initial connection to a proxy array. Adding more RAM always improves performance of services. And upgrading the processor is especially useful for busy proxy arrays in helping the array calculate on which proxy server the cached object is located.

16. ☑ **A.** You can implement a proxy chain to reduce the amount of bandwidth consumed on the Internet links and on interlinks among sites. You would install a proxy array at the Dallas office, a proxy array at the Tombstone office, and a lone proxy server at the branch office. You would then configure the proxy server at the branch office to query the Tombstone proxy array if the Web object is not in cache, and you would configure the Tombstone array to query the Dallas array if the Web object is not in its cache. By creating a proxy chain, you limit the number of network and Internet accesses required for retrieving Web objects.

☒ **B** is incorrect because you must do more than just install an array at the Dallas office to provide a viable solution. **C** is incorrect because a proxy cluster, while fault tolerant, will not improve bandwidth use for any of the locations. **D** is incorrect because it will not solve bandwidth use issues for remote sites. It may improve network performance at the Dallas location by removing some network traffic off the Dallas backbone.

17. ☑ **A, B.** You can back up and restore the proxy server configuration easily by using the Server Backup and Server Restore buttons in the properties dialog box of any of the proxy server's services dialog boxes.

☒ **C** is incorrect because backing up the registry can be a complicated and error prone affair; it is much better to use the server backup and restore buttons. **D** is incorrect because restoring the proxy files to the new location will not make the required registry entries on the new computer's proxy server installation.

Maximizing Proxy Server Performance

18. ☑ **A.** The Web proxy service is responsible for maintaining the Web cache. The cache stores objects obtained from the Internet.

☒ **B** is incorrect because the WinSock proxy service does not maintain the Web cache. WinSock proxy clients do not use the Web cache and WinSock proxy clients must have their browsers or other CERN-compliant software configured to use the Web cache. **C** is incorrect because the SOCKS proxy does not use the Web cache and SOCKS proxy clients cannot use the services of the Web Cache. **D** is incorrect because a WINS proxy has nothing to do with the Proxy Server services. A WINS proxy intercepts NetBIOS Name Resolution requests and forwards them to a WINS server for NetBIOS name resolution.

19. ☑ **C, D.** Active Caching allows the proxy server to retrieve popular Web objects in advance and place them into the proxy cache during periods of reduced processor utilization on the proxy server. Since the company does not conduct business in the evenings, the proxy server can retrieve Web objects throughout the evening and have them ready for the network clients by morning when they return. Passive caching is better than no caching at all. The passive caching feature allows the proxy server to cache all Web objects that have been accessed by Web proxy clients. However, the passive cache will not proactively retrieve popular objects, and therefore Web access will not be as quick as the users see with Active Caching.

☒ **A** is incorrect because there is no turbo browsing function in the Microsoft Proxy Server 2.0. **B** is incorrect because configuring the registry to increase the priority of the Web proxy service will not likely improve the Web object access times for the network Web proxy clients.

LAB ANSWER

Since this company is small and you do not want to add any new hardware, you could suggest that they purchase Proxy Server 2.0 and install it on their Windows 2000 Server machine. You want to take advantage of the Web Proxy Caching service, to minimize the packet charges from ISDN access. In addition, you would not want to use Active Caching, since that would increase the amount of data transferred over the ISDN line. So, in this instance, you would choose Passive Caching. Another method you can use to reduce packet charges is to suggest that they use packet and domain filtering. Discuss with the management what Web sites they need to access most. Alternatively, you could suggest the installation of plug-in software that will block access to graphics intensive, objectionable Web sites.

MICROSOFT CERTIFIED SYSTEMS ENGINEER

11

Designing a Wide Area Network Infrastructure

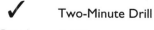
CERTIFICATION OBJECTIVES

W e may look back on today's technologies for connecting remote locations and see them as technological advances that changed the way we lived. The day that our CEO in Los Angeles was able to access the hard drive of his business associate in Tokyo, at a speed that was comparable to accessing it from one on the LAN in Los Angeles, was also the day that remote access became integral to the world.

In today's corporate environment, it is quite common to have branch offices, distribution centers, and other locations that need to be connected to the corporate network. Having the speed and bandwidth to do this has changed the way in which we do business and in many ways, how we live. We are sure to see the continued growth of trends that the enterprise environment brings, like the board meeting that is held via video conferencing from all parts of the globe, and the increase in users that work from home. These sometimes-complex network structures will bring many a challenge to the network administrator of the future, but are sure to afford many opportunities for success.

In this section of our text, we will look into some of the key aspects of remote access, and how Windows 2000 and Active Directory play a role in making these work. We will cover all of the key points of discussion, like that of Dial-Up Remote Access, Remote Authentication Dial-in User Service (RADIUS), Virtual Private Networks (VPNs), and Routing and Remote Access Routing Solutions. We will also attempt to share with you the importance of these technologies to all types of business environments. The ability to successfully link remote users to corporate network resources will surely become one of the most required tasks of tomorrow's network administrators, and those that have that ability will have many doors open to them.

CERTIFICATION OBJECTIVE 11.01

Overview of Designing a WAN Infrastructure

Let us begin our look at the design of a WAN infrastructure with an overview of the Wide Area Network itself. This will allow us to have a firm foundation of understanding from which to work. The traditional definition of a Local Area Network (LAN) is a network that exists at a single geographical location. The traditional Wide Area Network (WAN), which consists of any number of LANs connected via WAN networking technologies, is the most common. Let's begin our overview with these.

Two or more georgraphically separated LANs, connected via a full-time, direct physical link, constitute a WAN. These physical links can take on many forms. They can be made using slower services, such as Integrated Services Digital Network (ISDN) or the Public Switched Telephone Network (PSTN, i.e., a dial-up modem that is always connected). Those companies needing higher-speed, full-time access solutions have typically purchased costly T-Carrier lines (T-1, T-2, and T-3), but newer technologies such as Digital Subscriber Line (DSL) and cable modems that actually rival or exceed the capabilities of T-1 lines are making high-speed access an affordable possibility for smaller companies.

Another form of wide-area connectivity is a Virtual Private Network, or VPN. A VPN allows you to have secure communications over a public network, such as the Internet. When considering using VPN communication versus the more traditional direct link, we start to see big dollar savings. VPNs in some situations cost considerably less than a direct link, especially over vast distances. If this is the case, why isn't VPN already the standard for WAN connectivity? Many people share the fear that once their information is accessible to the Internet, it will be read by other people. With today's VPN protocols and increasing levels of security, this is becoming little more than a psychological barrier. However, this fear does have some basis in reality. Without continually upgrading security standards, your VPN communication will eventually become public knowledge.

When designing WANs, we must also consider the other aspects of connectivity that are needed to complete our network infrastructure. When we connect LANs to create WANs, there must be more than just a physical connection present. WAN links must also contain a remote access protocol to encapsulate the LAN protocol. Though more protocols exist, Windows 2000 requires either Serial Line Internet Protocol (SLIP) or Point-to-Point Protocol (PPP) for dial-up accounts. SLIP is an older protocol that is used primarily with UNIX servers. The Windows 2000 RRAS service does not support being a SLIP server, although it can be a SLIP client. The Windows 2000 RRAS server can be both a PPP server and client. PPP itself supports DHCP, encryption, and compression. VPNs need to use an additional set of protocols. VPN connections are typically made over Point-to-Point Tunneling Protocol (PPTP) or Layer 2 Tunneling Protocol (L2TP). Any network wanting to communicate with another over a VPN must have a server running one of these protocols and Routing and Remote Access.

exam
ⓦatch
Microsoft exams often times scrutinize your understanding of IT terminology. For this exam it is important to fully understand what sets VPNs apart from virtual networks. You can use a virtual networking protocol such as L2TP and create a virtual link between your LANs that are separated over the Internet. However, it will not be a VPN until you add an encryption protocol that protects the data as it moves through the virtual link.

CERTIFICATION OBJECTIVE 11.02

Designing a Remote Access Solution that Uses Routing and Remote Access

As the network administrator of a large corporation, you have many responsibilities. One of these is undoubtedly ensuring that the upper management pet projects are implemented. Imagine the following scenario: You approach the CEO's office. It's time to deliver your new proposal. Things are not looking good. He's upset because productivity is down, the branch office computers cannot communicate with the ones in the corporate office, and worst of all, he had to cancel a trip because the current network infrastructure does not allow a safe way for him to work on the road. So, you deliver your proposal. Through Windows 2000 and Routing and Remote Access you can increase productivity, establish quality WAN links between the corporate office and it's subsidiaries, and best of all, the CEO can now work while on the road.

For any server that is either a member server or domain controller to become a remote access server, the server must have Routing and Remote Access installed on it. RRAS is a collection of networking services that allows you to control remote access and routing services via a Windows 2000 computer. Whether the server is routing dial-up information or routing between two or more network cards, it is handled by RRAS.

In this section, we will discuss RRAS. When using RRAS it is important to understand how to properly enable and manage it. Optimization is also an important part of RRAS. If you learn how to enable RRAS, but not how to optimize it, your systems may work incredibly sluggishly. Finally, you will need to understand what monitoring options are available to you and how you can make use of them.

The Installation of RRAS

RRAS installation is a simple process since it is installed by default with Windows 2000. RRAS is by default disabled. To enable RRAS, you must first open the MMC RRAS console. You can locate a shortcut to this in Administrative Tools in the Start Menu.

With simple access to such a powerful tool, there must be a great deal of planning and design prior to its implementation. Before beginning the installation process, you, as an administrator, must decide what the role of this RRAS server is going to be. When configuring the computer you need to decide whether it is going to become a dial-up server or a multihomed router. These are important decisions that will be covered in more detail later in this chapter.

Once you have decided on its role, installed it, and the RRAS console has been started, you must enable the RRAS service. To do this, right click on **Server Status**, click on **Add Server**, and then choose **This Computer,** as shown in Figure 11-1. Once you have added your current server, you need to right click on the computer icon in the console window. After that, choose the **Start Routing and Remote Access** button and you are ready to go.

FIGURE 11-1

RRAS server
installation

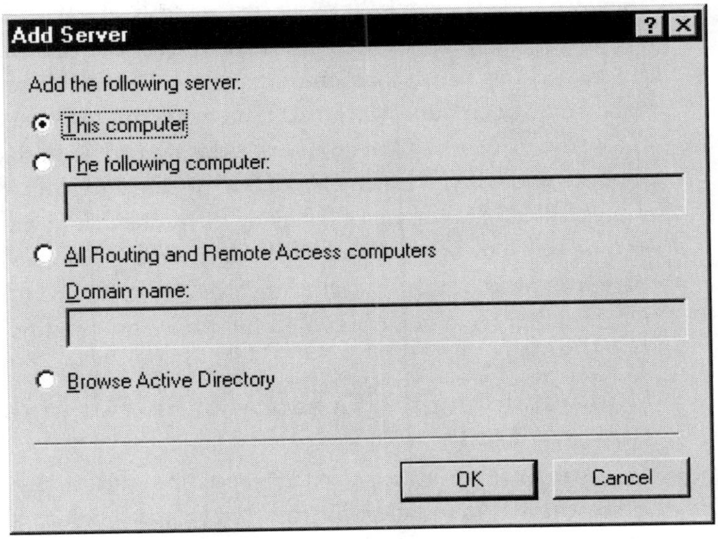

You will find that material found in this book will be very useful in the real world. As you get started in the world of networking, you will find that the definition of a WAN and a LAN will be quite different, due to the advancement of Fiber Optics. LAN used to be thought of as a site at one location, but in today's world, a LAN could be a campus of different sites, or even a city.

Optimizing Router Design for Availability and Performance

When designing a Windows 2000-routed environment, there are many considerations for optimizing your router to provide the most availability and best performance. While hardware performance is important in accomplishing this, a proper setup and configuration is much more important. There are many times when a high-end server can have its performance improved tenfold by improving its configuration. And, to provide a more stable routing solution, it is of the utmost importance to properly establish your method of connectivity at all levels, including those that involve routing protocols.

Proper communication between routers is one of the most important aspects to consider when planning for optimum up-time. For example, which routing protocol is required for your environment, or is a protocol required at all? There are a number of protocols that aid in router configuration. RIP versions 1 and 2 and OSPF are all provided with Windows 2000. These protocols all transmit router status and tables. How they transmit this information, and the benefits to each one, needs to be understood before deciding which solution is best for you. There is also no reason to use extra bandwidth when none is required. You may want to consider static routing, especially for smaller networks. One drawback to be aware of with static routing, however, is just that: it's static. If you experience a failed or congested link, those routers using static routes will have no means of detecting the problem and will not be able to intelligently reroute traffic to a functioning link. Static routing becomes a less viable option for larger networks because the effort involved in keeping routing tables up-to-date and synchronized can quickly become a full-time responsibility.

Understanding the Creation of Entries in the Windows 2000 Routing Table

There are a couple of ways to add an entry into the routing table of a Windows 2000 server with RRAS installed. First, and by far the easiest, is to set up dynamic routing. At times, however, static routing is the best choice.

Most administrators have used the command-line process of entering and editing routes using the ROUTE command; however, there is a much easier method—using RRAS. To accomplish this, right click on the Static Routes in the RRAS console. Then select New, followed by Static Route. This method gives you the same options as the command line version does, but with the added convenience of using the MMC in the GUI.

CertCam 11-1

Adding Static Entries to the Routing Table Using RRAS

EXERCISE 11-1

1. Open the RRAS console.

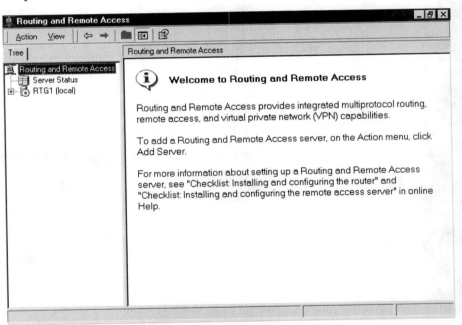

2. Expand the server to which you want to add the entry.
3. Expand IP Routing and click on Static Routes.
4. Click in Action, followed by New Static Route.

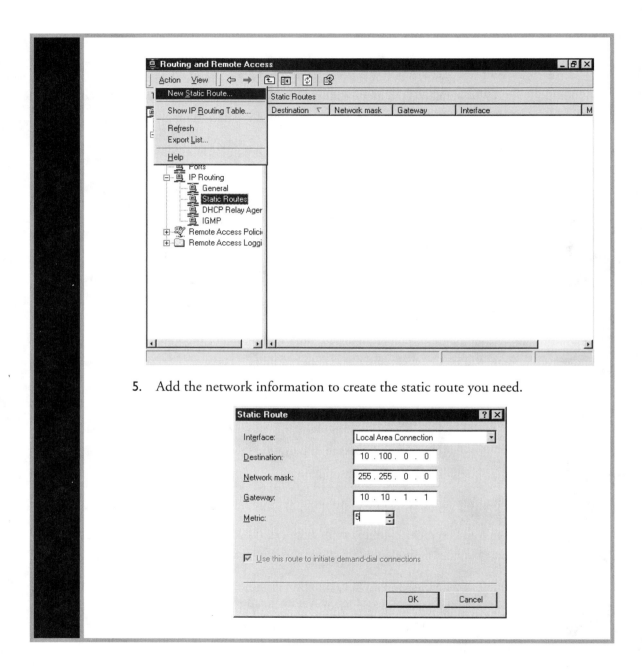

5. Add the network information to create the static route you need.

6. Click OK.

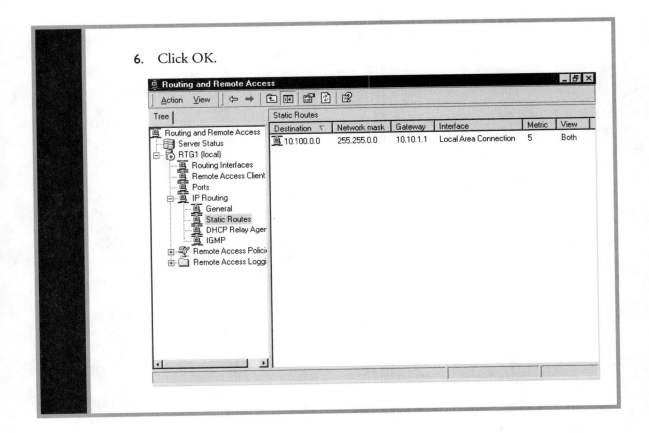

RIP

Designing a RIP routed environment raises many considerations. For example, the maximum diameter of RIP internetworks is 15 routers. However, the Windows 2000 router considers all non-RIP-learned routes to be at a fixed hop count of two. Static routes, even static routes for directly connected networks, are considered non-RIP learned routes. When a Windows 2000 RIP router advertises its directly connected networks, it advertises them at a hop count of two, even though there is only one physical router to cross. Therefore, a RIP-based internetwork that uses Windows 2000 RIP routers has a maximum physical diameter of 14 routers.

RIP uses the hop count as its means of determining the best route for a packet to take. Using the number of hops as the basis for choosing routes may lead to undesired route choices. For example, if two sites were connected together by using a T1 link and a 56K dial-up link as a backup, both links have the same value. When a router is given a choice between two routes of the same value, the router is free to choose between them. You can use custom costs to indicate link speed, delay, or reliability factors; however, the cost between any two endpoints on the internetwork cannot exceed 15.

Due to security improvements, you should use RIP version 2 in your RIP environment. Keep in mind that if there are older routers in your network that do not support RIP version 2, you need to implement an environment of both RIP version 1 and version 2. RIP version 1 does not support classless inter-domain routing (CIDR) or variable-length subnet masks (VLSM).

If you have support for CIDR and VLSM in one part of your internetwork, but not another, you may experience routing problems. If your network is using RIP version 1 and RIP version 2 routers, then you must configure the Windows 2000 router interfaces to advertise by using either RIP version 1 broadcasts or RIP version 2 broadcasts and accept either RIP version 1 or RIP version 2 announcements.

I have mentioned earlier that RIP version 2 has security improvements over RIP version 1. With these improvements come many considerations with respect to implementation. For example, if you use RIP version 2 with simple password authentication, then you must configure all of the RIP version 2 interfaces on the same network with the same case-sensitive password. You can use the same password for all the networks or you can vary the password for each network.

Remember that if you use RIP to perform auto-static updates across demand-dial links, you must configure each demand-dial interface to use RIP version 2 multicast announcements and to accept RIP version 2 announcements. Otherwise, the router on the other side of the demand-dial link does not respond to the RIP request for routes sent by the requesting router.

OSPF for Single and Multiple Areas

When designing a larger routed network, remember that Open Shortest Path First (OSPF) is a much more robust routing protocol for complex environments than RIP. However, as mentioned earlier, proper configuration is the key to high performance. For this reason, when you are planning an OSPF environment, keep in mind that there are three levels of OSPF design. The first level is planning an autonomous system design. When designing an autonomous system in OSPF, it is recommended that you first subdivide your system into areas that can be summarized. Although not all structures are going to be organized similarly, try dividing your IP addresses into areas of network, area, subnet, and host. It is also makes sense to ensure that the backbone is a single, high-bandwidth network.

When designing OSPF areas, make sure to assign them network IDs so they can be expressed as a small number of summary routes. Keep an eye out for areas that can be summarized as a single route, as these should be advertised. If you run into a situation where multiple area border routers (ABRs) are present, make sure that they are summarizing the same routes.

It is extremely important to the structure of your network that you make sure there are no back doors for packets to sneak through, so as not to needlessly tie up your backbone's bandwidth. For simplicity's sake, try keeping your network under 100 areas. When designing the overall network, remember that you need to assign router priorities so that the least busy routers are the designated routers and backup designated routers. For proper data flow, it is important to designate link costs to reflect bit rate, delay, or reliability characteristics. However, you can design the most structured network in the world and have it all come crumbling down without proper security. Make sure that throughout the design phase, you don't forget to assign a password for your OSPF routers.

We already know that an OSPF routed network can be subdivided into areas, which are collections of contiguous networks, and that all areas are connected together through a common segment called the backbone. However, a router that connects an area to the backbone is called an area border router (ABR). Normally, ABRs have a physical connection to the backbone area. When it is not possible or practical to have an ABR of an area physically connected to the backbone area, you can use a virtual link to connect the ABR to the backbone.

Evaluate Hardware Versus Software Routing Solutions

There are many aspects to consider when evaluating the differences between hardware and software routing solutions. The primary consideration is cost. There is a tremendous difference in cost between software and hardware routing solutions. For the most basic solutions, all that is required for a software solution is a modem or second NIC. Since the software is included with Windows 2000, there are no more added expenses. However, these solutions can begin to bog down a server. If a server is routing between three of four different subnets, it is definitely not a good idea to install Exchange or SQL on it, as this would put enough strain on the computer's resources to impede its overall performance.

Hardware solutions, which include routers and Layer 3 switches, can be much more expensive. Hardware routers and switches can be much faster than their software counterparts. Configuration programs can vary greatly between manufacturers; however, with all Windows 2000 RRAS-enabled computers, you always have the same management interface.

A Windows 2000 router can rival the performance of a hardware router. However, to do this, the machine should be a dedicated device and should not run other services that would use machine resources. If you factor in the cost of the hardware and the Windows 2000 software, you may find that a dedicated hardware router is a better option, especially in very high-bandwidth environments. Although RRAS works fine, it requires resources that you may not have without spending more money than you intended to spend.

A high-end hardware solution will be able to handle a bandwidth load that only a very expensive server devoted exclusively to routing could handle. Software-based routing solutions, such as the Windows 2000 router, are best used on small-to-medium-sized networks with moderate throughput requirements via the router interfaces.

FROM THE CLASSROOM

Routing Solutions for Companies of all Sizes

Most courses we find today only discuss the hardware solutions for routing, yet many companies (especially small-to-medium-sized companies) have implemented software solutions because of the initial investment. It is however, advantageous to study this material so that we are able to work together with companies of all sizes when it comes to routing solutions. This will also allow us to offer our input when selecting solutions.

There are also often questions regarding the different uses of RIP and OSPF, both for exams and in the field. It is important to remember that RIP works well for those environments that are less complex, and OSPF works well for those larger, more complex, enterprise environments.

Review Technology Group
—*Russell Thomas, A+, MCP + I, MCSE, MCT*
—*Jerrod Couser, A+, MCP +I, MCSE + I, CCA*
—*David Blue, MCP + I, MCSE*

Optimizing and Monitoring Routing and Remote Access

Now that we have considered the pros and cons of software routing and understand the protocols, we are now able to set up a RRAS router. One of the most critical design considerations when looking at the optimization and monitoring of RRAS deals with security. As network administrators, we must realize that someday a hacker may send out a "rogue RIP packet" and begin receiving information about all the routers on our network. Even though we have decided to use OSPF, or RIPv2, and our security is tighter than most, eventually this password could also be cracked if no action is taken to stop hackers.

When looking at router security we should consider the following:

- Authentication
- Authorization
- Data Encryption
- Remote access dial-in permissions
- Caller ID and callback
- Security hosts
- Account lockout

If you monitor RRAS on your system, you can receive forewarning of any unauthorized attempts to access your systems. As I am sure you are aware, monitoring is critical even if you are unconcerned about unauthorized entry attempts. It is through monitoring that we are able to become aware of additional performance and operational concerns.

Monitoring Remote Access

It is always a good idea to monitor unauthorized access attempts. Many other events are also important, such as CPU and NIC use. These and other performance monitors are important in determining whether to upgrade a system or even switch to a hardware solution. Of course, the choice to make changes to our network based on monitoring criteria is subject to the requirements of our users; however, the key to making these decisions is in setting up monitoring baselines.

The Routing and Remote Access MMC Snap-in (see Figure 11-2) provides much of the information an administrator needs to make these decisions, such as the server

FIGURE 11-2

Monitoring
remote access

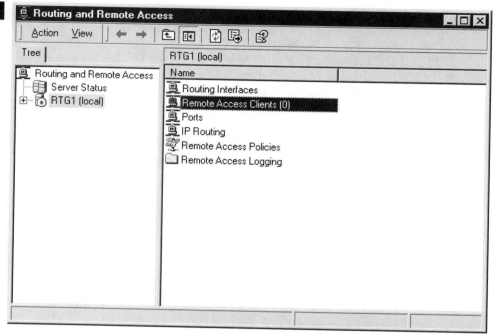

name, the state of the service (started or stopped), total ports on the server, ports in
use, and amount of time that the server has been up since the service was last started.

on the
Job *Keep in mind that the passwords exchanged between routers are not encrypted.*
This free-text password exchange represents a potential hole in your security
design. Consider using IPSec to secure communications between your routers.

CERTIFICATION OBJECTIVE 11.03

Integrating Authentication with Remote
Authentication Dial-In User Strategy (RADIUS)

After taking part in the RRAS implementation covered above, you are definitely in
line for a promotion. The CEO now thinks the world of your technical expertise.
The CEO informs you that he will be traveling to Los Angeles for a meeting. While

he is there, he wants to use a dial-up connection from the Los Angeles branch office to retrieve files from his New York headquarters. Trusting no one else but you, he has given you the task of personally setting up his account with RAS authentication rights in Los Angeles.

Time to take a trip to the West Coast? Not exactly. With Windows 2000, this trip is no longer necessary. By using Remote Authentication Dial-In User Service (RADIUS), you can set the CEO up with RAS authentication rights from the New York office. In Windows 2000, the RADIUS server components are configured in the Internet Authentication Service (IAS) console. RADIUS lets us centralize our RAS accounting and RAS policies, and allows for a tighter control over RAS authentication. Using RADIUS, you are not dependent on the authentication infrastructure of the local ISP that the user may be dialing into.

In this section, we will look further into this process known as RADIUS and attempt to better understand its inner workings, including functionality, security, optimization, fault-tolerance, and monitoring.

Designing a Functional RADIUS Solution

For some Internet service providers and corporations with remote access environments, the remote access equipment consists of multiple remote access devices of different types from different manufacturers. In a heterogeneous remote access environment, a single standard must exist for providing authentication of remote access user credentials and accounting of remote access activity. In many of these environments, the Remote Authentication Dial-In User Service (RADIUS) is used. RADIUS is a client/server protocol where RADIUS clients send authentication and accounting requests to a RADIUS server. The RADIUS server checks the remote access authentication credentials on the user accounts and logs remote access accounting events.

Internet Authentication Service is a service that runs on Windows 2000 to allow for centralized administration of all RAS servers, or devices, throughout the network. Through IAS, it is possible to eliminate much of the administrative overhead involved in implementing a RAS solution within your network. Remote RAS servers that are managed by local ISPs can be configured to send authentication requests to a RADIUS server, who in turn sends the request for authentication to a domain controller under your control. The RADIUS server will keep accounting information regarding the connection, which allows you direct access to this information, and allows you to avoid having to query the ISP for RAS accounting information.

When designing a functional RADIUS solution on your network, you must first install IAS on a centralized, secure server. With IAS, we can then work with the RADIUS protocol.

Securing the RADIUS Server

IAS servers manage the Remote Access information for your entire network, so it is important to keep them secure. There are a number of ways to secure such a system. First, use physical isolation. It is helpful to be able to limit the number of people

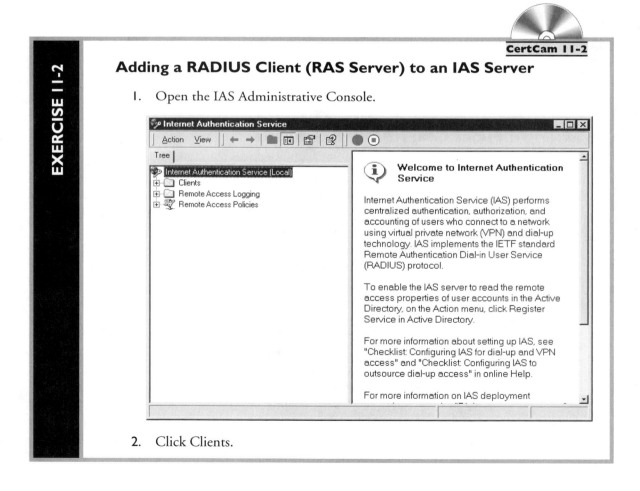

EXERCISE 11-2

CertCam 11-2

Adding a RADIUS Client (RAS Server) to an IAS Server

1. Open the IAS Administrative Console.

2. Click Clients.

3. Choose Action | New Client.

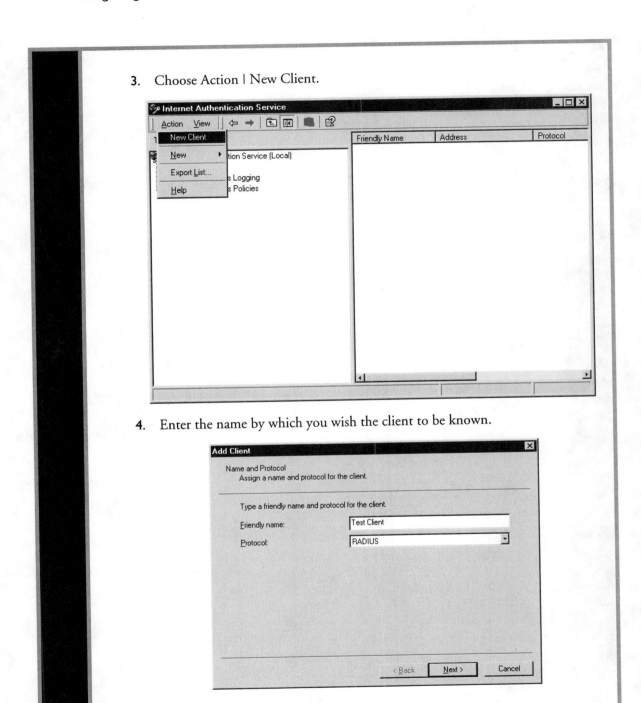

4. Enter the name by which you wish the client to be known.

5. Click Next.

6. Enter appropriate information for your client.

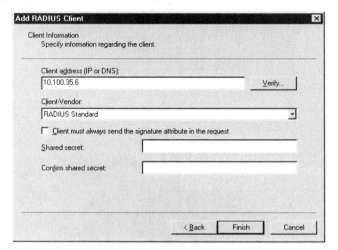

7. Click Finish.

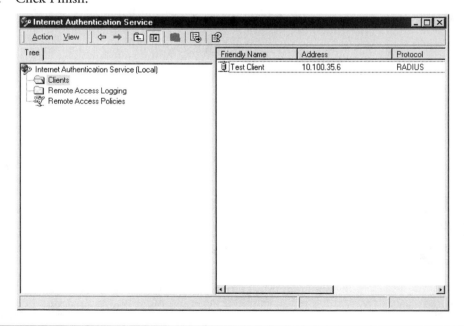

who have access to the server. Second, place your RADIUS server behind a firewall to keep unwanted packets away from your server. Make sure that you are using the most secure communications, such as TCP/IP with IPSec policies. IPSec will be discussed in more detail later in this chapter; however, you should know that using it in conjunction with RADIUS allows you to maintain end-to-end security.

While IPSec provides secure data transfer, you should also implement a secure authentication protocol, such as Microsoft-CHAP version 2. By implementing a secure authentication protocol, you are assured that only designated users will be able to access the servers. In addition, you must use an authentication protocol, such as Microsoft CHAP version 1 or 2 in order to encrypt data if you choose to implement tunneling protocols such as PPTP.

Improving RADIUS Server Accessibility

As you just learned, you should limit the number of server services installed on the IAS server to improve security. Another benefit of limiting the number of services on the IAS server is improved performance. If a server is running nothing other than IAS, it will have the entire system's resources available to manage the RADIUS servers on your network. It is also possible to increase the number of concurrent authentication calls (the number of people that can concurrently be validated by the IAS server), by editing the registry. Select HKEY_LOCAL_MACHINE\SYSTEM\CurrentControlSet\Services\Netlogon\Parameters and edit the REG_DWORD to a value between two and five. Although it may seem wise to do this, do not put too high a value here, as it will cause an excessive load on your domain controller.

RADIUS Fault Tolerance and Performance Solutions

While RADIUS is still in the design phase, keep in mind that there is one way in which to increase IAS performance and create a fault-tolerant solution. If you are running Windows 2000 Advanced Server, you can implement load balancing with another advanced server. With Windows 2000 Advanced Server Network Load Balancing, you can create a server cluster. This will allow two or more servers to share the work, and if one of these computers happens to go down, the other one will continue to operate. If you set up your servers in this way, you not only allow for more than one computer to accept authentication calls, but also have a second server running IAS if the first should fail. You'll therefore be increasing performance and fault-tolerance at once.

Load balancing is a great idea in that it accomplishes its goals—increased fault tolerance, and increased performance. However, there are other ways to improve performance that may not simultaneously accomplish fault tolerance. For example, placing the IAS server near the server on which the Global Catalog resides will improve performance. Since IAS validates logon requests via queries to the Global Catalog Server, a lower response time from this server would greatly improve RADIUS performance.

Hardware upgrades can also improve the performance of RADIUS on your network. Upgrading the processor, RAM, or NIC in your IAS server will provide a performance increase. However, if you recall why being closely located to the Global Catalog Server was important, you should also understand that upgrading the Global Catalog Server can be just as important to the IAS server.

Important RADIUS Events to Monitor

A preventive approach to network maintenance is always the preferred method for network administrators, and the key to this is always in monitoring our network resources. Windows 2000 supports three types of logging for its remote access servers.

■ **Events**   One location in which a network administrator can look for information about his remote access server's activities is in the Windows 2000 system event log. Here he will find helpful information, critical for troubleshooting and alerts.

■ **Accounting and local authentication**   By enabling Windows accounting or authentication, network administrators can create local logging files that will store important information about both of these activities. They can then track information like authentication attempts and remote access usage.

■ **RADIUS-based accounting and authentication**   More specific to the monitoring of our Remote Authentication Dial-In User Service, Windows 2000 can identify and log accounting and authentication that is unique to its activities. These can then be used to assist in troubleshooting. Internet Authentication Service (IAS) will result in the log files residing on the IAS server.

Designing a Virtual Private Network (VPN) Strategy

Arriving at work, you receive a memo from the accounting department stating that the long distance charges to connect the branch offices to the corporate headquarters have become too much of a burden for the company to handle. It is now up to you. Without a less expensive method of connecting your offices, your company could easily find itself in financial difficulty. Upon researching the situation, you come across a solution. Running the numbers by the accounting department, your solution is approved: Connecting via the Internet would be much less expensive, significantly reducing the amount spent on long distance charges.

VPNs allow remote networks or users connectivity to another network through the Internet, or other large networks. VPNs securely provide channels through larger internetworks, allowing users to view them as private dedicated links. VPNs provide remote access and routed connections to private networks.

In this section, we will be discussing the choices we have to make when designing a VPN in a routed environment. We will cover both demand-dialing and persistent configurations, and we will discuss the reasons we would choose one over the other. We will also discuss ways in which we can maximize our VPN's availability through some administrative best practices. We will also discuss how to use PPTP, IPSec, and L2TP to enhance the security and stability of our virtual networks.

exam
ⓦatch

Virtual Private Networking technology is high on Microsoft's list of networking services. Because of the significant cost savings afforded to businesses that implement VPNs, Microsoft wants its engineers to be thoroughly versed in the concepts and practice of VPN implementation. Be sure you thoroughly understand how VPNs work, and how to design efficient and cost-effective VPN solutions before tackling the Microsoft exam.

Designing a VPN in a Routed Network

The key to the planning and designing of our VPN is in the decision to use on-demand or persistent connections for your routed network. This choice is usually based on a number of criteria. Decide whether you will use dedicated or dial-up access to the Internet. A dedicated link to the Internet significantly improves performance, but suffers from high cost. A dial-up, or non-persistent, link is typically slower, but more reasonably priced.

The decision a network administrator must make between a persistent or demand-dial connection requires her to understand both the requirements of the organization's connectivity, the financial resources available, and the availability of persistent connections at each remote site. When cost is a deciding factor, analog or ISDN is most often selected. This is also the choice, of course, when other methods of Internet access are unavailable. These companies and organizations will have to be satisfied with demand-dial connections. Others that have the ability to afford the consistent connectivity will select the speed and availability of persistent connections, but will have to pay the price financially (this scenario is changing every day with the availability of high-speed, persistent Internet access).

Maximizing VPN Availability

When so much of the company's productivity is dependent on a consistent VPN link, it becomes increasingly important to properly plan your VPN design to allow for the maximum amount of up-time of the link. One major concern is whether to implement one-way or two-way connections.

With one-way initiated connections, one router is the VPN server and one router is the VPN client. The VPN server accepts the connection and the VPN client initiates the connection. One-way initiated connections are well suited to a permanent connection, spoke-and-hub topology where the branch office router is the only router that initiates the connection. With two-way initiated connections, either router can be the VPN server or the VPN client, depending on who is initiating the connection. Both routers must be configured to initiate and accept a VPN connection. You can use two-way initiated connections when the router-to-router VPN connection is not up 24 hours a day and traffic from either router is used to create the on-demand connection.

In a larger corporate environment, you should keep in mind that the default number of VPN ports may not be sufficient. The default number of PPTP and L2TP ports is five. The default value of VPN ports can be changed through the RRAS console to any value between 0 and 1,000.

Keep in mind that both routers on a router-to-router VPN connection must have the appropriate routes in their routing tables to forward traffic across the connection. Routes can be static or dynamic. You can add static routes to the routing table either manually or through an autostatic update. You can add dynamic routes to the routing table by adding the VPN connection demand-dial interface to a routing protocol. However, enabling a routing protocol on the VPN connection demand-dial interface is only recommended when the demand-dial interface is permanently connected.

Use PPTP to Secure the VPN

You can use Windows 2000 remote access to provide access to a corporate intranet for remote clients who are making PPTP connections across the Internet. In order for the remote access server to properly forward traffic on the corporate intranet, you must configure it as a router with either static routes or routing protocols so that all of the locations of the intranet are reachable from the remote access server. With this use of the Internet to transmit corporate data, security measures need to be taken.

Microsoft dial-up networking clients typically use MS-CHAP authentication. For smart card support, you need to enable EAP authentication. Non-Microsoft dial-up networking clients use CHAP, SPAP, and PAP authentication. For encrypted PPTP connections, you must use MS-CHAP or EAP-TLS as the authentication method. You can verify the credentials of dial-up clients by using Windows 2000 security or a RADIUS server. If RADIUS is selected, you need to configure RADIUS server settings for your RADIUS server or RADIUS proxy. You may also record dial-up client activity for analysis or accounting purposes by selecting and configuring an accounting provider with PPTP.

To secure the corporate router from sending or receiving any traffic on its Internet interface except PPTP traffic from branch office routers, you need to configure PPTP input and output filters on the interface on the corporate router that correspond to the Internet connection. Because IP routing is probably enabled on the Internet interface, if you do not configure PPTP filters on the Internet interface of the corporate router, any traffic received on the Internet interface is routed, which may forward unwanted Internet traffic to your intranet.

Use IPSec/L2TP to Secure the VPN

Previously we reviewed the design considerations involved in securing a network using PPTP. However, PPTP is an older protocol now, and it is not as secure as the newer L2TP. Much of the new security features with L2TP are the result of a close tie-in with IPSec. When beginning to plan your L2TP over IPSec connection it is important to keep in mind that a properly installed computer certificate must be installed on the corporate router. To secure the corporate router from sending or receiving any traffic on its Internet interface, except L2TP over IPSec traffic from branch office routers, you need to configure L2TP over IPSec input and output filters on the interface on the corporate router that corresponds to the Internet connection. Because IP routing is enabled on the Internet interface, you do not configure L2TP over IPSec filters on the Internet interface of the corporate router.

It is important to note that the default setting for L2TP allows various levels of encryption. To require encryption, clear the **No Encryption** option and select the appropriate encryption strengths on the **Encryption** tab of the remote access policy profile that is used by your calling routers.

Important VPN Related Events to Monitor

When monitoring VPN communication, it becomes important to understand how the communications take place. Monitoring these communications requires the use of a number of tools, including the following:

- Event logging
- PPP logging
- Network Monitor

Let's discuss each of these briefly to identify how they can play a role in keeping our VPNs operational.

The logging of events in Windows 2000 allows us to record many of the critical processes that make up our VPN communications, and record them in the system event log. With event logging, we can record remote access server errors, remote access server warnings, and other detailed information. In order to enable event logging, we go to the Event Logging tab on the properties of a remote access server.

Logging of PPP information keeps track of the programming functions and PPP messages that take place during a PPP connection, and it is a valuable resource when troubleshooting the failure of a PPP connection. In order to enable PPP logging, we must select the Enable Point-to-Point Protocol logging option on the PPP tab that is on the properties of a remote access server.

The use of Network Monitor is common for most that administer LANs; however, they also capture the network traffic between dial-up networking clients and remote access servers. By using Network Monitor to analyze remote traffic, we can find answers to remote access problems and design possible solutions for them. The important events that take place with VPNs happen on the wire. To view packets that deal with authentication and encryption, you should monitor TCP/IP port 1723. Port 1723 is the port on which PPTP communicates. It is also important to be able to monitor Generic Route Encapsulation (GRE) packets for use in debugging VPN issues.

exam
ⓦatch

Network Monitor has always been on NT 4.0 exams, and there is a strong possibility that you will see questions on it in the Windows 2000 exams. It is very important that we actually use the tools we are speaking of and not just read about them. It is often difficult to find ways to actually have access to wide area connectivity for our studies. If necessary, you may also want to explore the many companies that have developed simulations for us to work with. These applications depict actual networking activities without the cost of intensive network resources.

CERTIFICATION OBJECTIVE 11.05

Designing a Routing and Remote Access Routing Solution to Connect Locations Via Demand-Dial Routing

Demand-dial connections represent the actual opening and closing of a link from one remote site to another for the purpose of passing data or routing information. This process involves the creation of a connection that is established over a specified amount of time. With that in mind, let us also define demand-dial routing as a demand-dial connection that links networks across WANs. This means that we can have remote networks dial each other when they require a connection to send data. By only using our connections when necessary, it assists greatly in reducing telephone costs.

Configure Demand-Dial Routing

In this section, we will spend some time considering the decisions we must make when designing a network environment that includes the demand-dial processes, from configuration to monitoring.

EXERCISE 11-3

The Processes Involved in Installing and Configuring Demand-Dial Routing

1. Open network and dial-up connections.

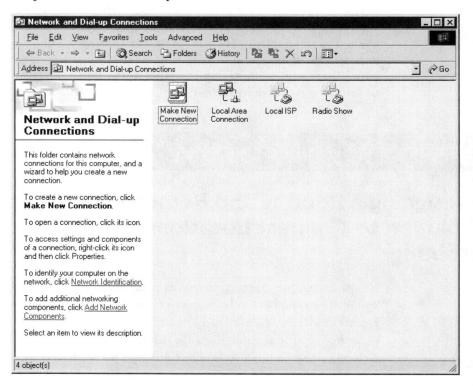

2. Right-click the dial-up, VPN, or incoming connection you want to share and click Properties.

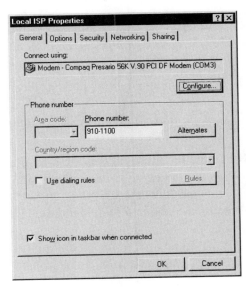

3. On the Sharing tab, select the "Enable Internet Connection Sharing for this connection" check box.

4. If you want this connection to dial automatically when another computer on your home network attempts to access external resources, select the "Enable on-demand dialing" check box.

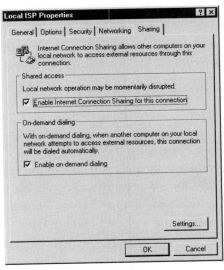

Some important points to remember:

- This feature should not be used in a network with other Windows 2000 Server domain controllers, DNS servers, gateways, DHCP servers, or systems configured for static IP.

- When enabling Internet connection sharing, the network adapter connected to the home or small office network is given a new static IP address configuration. Existing TCP/IP connections on the Internet connection-sharing computer are lost and need to be reestablished.

- To use the Internet connection-sharing feature, users on your home office or small office network must configure TCP/IP on their local connection to automatically obtain an IP address. Home office or small office network users must also configure Internet options for Internet connection sharing.

- If the Internet connection-sharing computer is using ISDN or a modem to connect to the Internet, you must select the "Enable on-demand dialing" check box.

Demand-Dial Routing Considerations

As discussed in the section on VPNs, when designing a plan to implement demand-dial routing, there are a number of options to consider. The first option is whether to create an on-demand or persistent connection. When making this decision, it is important to ask yourself this question: What are the costs of keeping the link up? If packet charges are getting out of hand, you may need to use an on-demand connection, allowing you to save the extra phone charges. If you are using a dedicated line or making a local call, you would probably be a good candidate for a persistent connection, saving yourself the connection time.

Another option is to set up a one-way or two-way initiated environment. When making this decision, you need to take into consideration your current topology. If you have one office that always makes the calls to the other office, save yourself the administrative headache and just create a one-way connection. However, if both servers will be making equal calls, you need to just go ahead and install a two-way connection.

If money is a concern, try restricting the initiation of demand-dial links. You can keep a server from incurring excessive charges on an expensive connection by either filtering the packets, or restricting the time the connection can be made. The capability to configure dial-out hours will be useful if your connections are made over a long-distance telephone line with which you will have better rates during the phone company's reduced rate hours.

exam
Watch

When using a demand-dial connection to establish the link, use ISDN rather than analog devices if possible. The link establishment time is much quicker than analog, and the link tends to be more stable. The slightly higher cost of ISDN can be offset by the stability of the link and the increase in employee productivity.

Monitoring and Configuring Demand-Dial Routing

To view the current connection status of a demand-dial interface, use the Routing and Remote Access snap-in in the Microsoft Management Console. If you want to view more detailed information, however, you will need to make use of the Windows 2000 Resource Kit. With the Resource Kit comes a program called RASMON (rassrvmon.exe). This program will allow you to view such objects as the line speed, device statistics, connection statistics, and device errors. Identifying the proper tools you will need to monitor your remote network environment is critical even during the early designing stages.

CERTIFICATION SUMMARY

Never before in the history of humankind has there been a time that has given so many the ability to be connected in so many ways. Through remote networking, people from all cultures and areas of the globe now have the ability to share ideas and information. This remote connectivity has only begun to make changes to the way in which we do business and live our lives. Throughout the next few years, we are bound to be influenced by increased speeds and accessibility, but along with this ability to connect come new challenges and concepts. In this chapter, we have attempted to share information about a few of the key features with which you are sure to be confronted when considering WAN connectivity.

Our initial section spoke to the most common method of remote access, namely, that of dial-up connectivity. This method has been in existence for years and will probably continue to be the most common, due to its ease of use, accessibility, and cost. Yet, as the demand for increased speeds and bandwidth continues to grow, we are sure to see increased use of higher-speed methods like that of ISDN, T1, DSL, cable, and the like.

We have also discussed the various dial-up protocols, or languages, that allow us to communicate, like that of the Point-to-Point Protocol, or PPP. Next, we spent some time discussing remote authentication with Remote Authentication Dial-in Service, or RADIUS. RADIUS allows administrators the ability to use logon validation via remote, dial-up connections, an integral part of remote security. Here we were introduced to Virtual LANs and various other aspects of WAN protocols like PPTP and L2TP.

Moving forward in our discussions, we talked about a growing method of linking users and networks to other users and networks, known as Virtual Private Networks (VPNs). With the unbelievable growth in use of the Internet, it is completely understandable that VPNs are slowly becoming one of the fastest growing methods of remote access.

Our final section dealt with the requirements necessary when we are working on joining two separate networks via a WAN connection. In doing so, it is necessary for us to be able to configure our routers to communicate with one another. Whether we are connecting via a 56K line or DSL, the future is sure to hold great opportunities for those that have taken the time to learn of the inner workings of remote access.

✓ TWO-MINUTE DRILL

Designing a Remote Access Solution that Uses Routing and Remote Access

❑ Dial-Up Remote Access can be set up either through the Internet or dial-up accounts for remote users.

❑ Windows 2000 does not support SLIP. It supports Point-to-Point Protocol (PPP) for dial-up accounts.

❑ Wide Area Network (WAN) consists of any number of LANs connected together.

Integrate Authentication with Remote Authentication Dial-In User Service (RADIUS)

❑ VLAN connections are typically made over Point-to-Point Tunneling Protocol (PPTP) or Layer 2 Tunneling Protocol (L2TP).

❑ Routing and Remote Access (RRAS) is a program that manages all routing of packets that a server would perform.

❑ RRAS is installed and is disabled by default with Windows 2000 server. To enable RRAS, you must first open the MMC RRAS console in Administrative Tools in the Start Menu.

Designing a Virtual Private Network (VPN) Strategy

❑ RADIUS works over TCP/IP and requires an IP or a DNS address to communicate with the RADIUS client. RADIUS is a protocol that IAS uses to communicate with RAS clients. This protocol is what IAS uses to facilitate communication between itself and the RAS servers throughout your network.

❑ Virtual Private Networks (VPNs) allow remote networks or users to connect to another network through the Internet or other large networks.

❑ Layer 2 Tunneling Protocol (L2TP) is another VPN communications protocol that is included with Windows 2000. However, L2TP relies on (IPSec) to create a secure tunnel for VPN communications.

❑ It is always a good idea to monitor unauthorized access attempts. Other concerns are also important, such as CPU or NIC use. Monitoring is done through Performance Monitor.

Designing a Routing and Remote Access Routing Solution to Connect Locations via Demand-Dial Routing

❑ Routing Information Protocol (RIP) is the basic protocol routers use to communicate. One of the major concerns about RIP has always been a lack of security. This is fixed with RIP version 2, which supports password authentication.

❑ Open Shortest Path First (OSPF) is a much more robust routing protocol. Speed is one of the major improvements that is made with OSPF, because it finds and uses the quickest path to transmit data.

❑ Routing hardware solutions, which include routers and Layer 3 switches, can be very expensive, but hardware routers and switches can be much faster than software routing.

SELF TEST

The following questions will help you measure your understanding of the material presented in this chapter. Read all of the choices carefully, as there may be more than one correct answer. Choose all correct answers for each question.

Designing a Remote Access Solution that Uses Routing and Remote Access

1. Your company's campus network consists of 10 buildings. Each building is connected by a high-speed fiber-optic connection to a central network operations center. Each building also has an older wireless connection that is now used as a backup link. With a Windows 2000 router in each building, and both links active, which routing protocol would be best used?

   A. None. Use static addressing.

   B. OSPF

   C. RIP version 1

   D. RIP version 2

Integrating Authentication with Remote Authentication Dial-In User Strategy (RADIUS)

2. You are a network administrator for a large Internet Server Provider (ISP) that has approximately 75,000 users. After implementing a RADIUS solution in your network, your company has become worried that it has spent too much money on a server that only runs IAS. What can you tell your fiscal depart is acceptable to run on your IAS server?

   A. SQL

   B. Exchange

   C. SMS

   D. Active Directory

3. After implementing a RADIUS solution for your organization, what steps should be taken to improve security on your RADIUS server?

   A. Place the IAS server and an authentication server on the same segment..

   B. Secure communications between the IAS server and the authentication server using IPSec.

   C. Place the IAS server on a screened subnet.

   D. Install PCAnywhere so you can administer the server from home.

4. After implementing RADIUS, you receive complaints that logons are taking longer than they did before the RADIUS implementation. After monitoring the IAS server, you realize that you may need to increase the Maximum number of Concurrent logons. What impact would such a change have on the RADIUS solution?

   A. By increasing this value, fewer people will be able to login in the office.

   B. By increasing this value, you may put an excessive load on the domain controllers.

   C. By increasing this value, the Exchange server may no longer function properly.

   D. By increasing this value, you may no longer be able to login locally to the IAS server.

Designing a Virtual Private Network (VPN) Strategy

5. Planning the security of a VPN is of the utmost importance. Your corporate VPN will use all Windows 2000 VPN servers and all Windows 2000 clients. With the possibility of sensitive corporate data crossing the Internet, and considering your choice in operating systems, which VPN protocol would be best to use to communicate with your other VPN servers?

   A. Use IPX/SPX. Since everyone connects to the Internet using TCP/IP, they will be unable to read these packets.

   B. Use PPP. Since this protocol supports encryption and compression, you will have safe, fast communications across the Internet.

   C. Use PPTP. Since this protocol was used with Windows NT 4.0 and is still included with Windows 2000, it will be your best choice for secure communications.

   D. Use L2TP/IPSec. Using this means of communication will allow much more secure links when communicating with your other server.

6. While designing the corporate VPN, your financial department has decided that your VPN servers should take on multiple roles. Being reluctant to run any more services on these servers for fear of overloading them, what other roles can these VPN servers perform other than VPN routers?

   A. SQL 7.0 Server

   B. Direct Dial-up server

   C. WINS Server

   D. OSPF router

7. While designing your corporate network, it has been decided that employees must be able to connect to the corporate office when they are on the road. The employees in question need to be able to connect from client offices without incurring any expense to the client. The financial

department has suggested that you implement a VPN solution to allow the remote employees to dial a local ISP and connect via a VPN link. However, Management has expressed concern that some clients may not have a local number to the ISP that you wish to use, and has also expressed that it is very important not to create extra cost for clients. Since your concern is that any solution be secure, which of the following answers would work best?

A. Have the employees connect to the client's network, and have them establish a VPN connection via the client's Internet access link.

B. Allow employees to connect to an ISP, and then create a VPN connection.

C. Use a toll-free number to connect to your RAS server, and then implement the dial back feature to allow for better security.

D. Use a toll-free number to connect to your RAS server, and use EAP-TLS with smart cards for security.

8. Your company has just finished the installation of a VPN. Your branch offices are still using Windows NT 4.0, however, your main office is using Windows 2000 on its VPN servers. After VPN implementation, it is a good idea to monitor your VPN servers to ensure proper performance. Since monitoring traffic is important in maintaining secure communications, how would you establish the monitoring required to keep your system running smoothly?

A. Turn on your VPN task monitors.

B. Review the server Event Logs in Event Viewer.

C. Review the AT commands.

D. Use Network Monitor.

Designing a Routing and Remote Access Routing Solution to Connect Locations Via Demand-Dial Routing

9. When designing your Windows 2000 routing solution, you need to ensure proper routing across various WAN connectivity devices. How can you program a router to determine which route offers the best performance for its packets?

A. Render a three-dimensional image of the routing table, and enter the coordinates into RRAS.

B. Have RRAS issue a local broadcast to assess local network conditions.

C. Manually assign values, or have a routing protocol assign values to each link (the slower links get higher values and the faster link gets lower values), and RRAS will use the cheapest link available.

D. Filter out all traffic on router interfaces, except for messages delivering routing information.

10. When designing your Windows 2000 router, you must decide which routing protocol to use. Since your internal network already consist of a Windows NT 4.0 router without RRAS, which protocol can you use to communicate without reprogramming your old router?

    A. Point-to-Point Tunneling Protocol

    B. OSPF

    C. RIP version 2

    D. RIP version 1

11. Your company has decided to use RIP as its routing protocol. Since your employer didn't specify which version, what is the benefit of using RIP version 2 over RIP version 1?

    A. Version 2 supports Variable Length Subnet Masking.

    B. Version 2 incorporates SQL server.

    C. Version 2 supports password authentication.

    D. Version 2 uses IPSec.

12. You have decided to use OSPF in your routed network. However, after reading your report on it, a corporate administrator has questioned your reasons for doing so. The Administrator does not understand the concept of a "Rogue RIP Packet." How can you explain this to him?

    A. A RIP packet from a RIP router not authorized in the Active Directory

    B. A RIP packet originating from a router that has a DHCP installed on it, and that is not authorized in the Active Directory

    C. A OSPF packet

    D. A RIP packet originating from a RIP router that advertises false or inaccurate routes

13. While determining the layout of your corporate network, you have decided that using OSPF is the best solution. Your supervisor is not so sure. She would like some information regarding the benefits of using OSPF instead of RIP. Which of the following would you give her as reasons?

    A. OSPF uses a more efficient routing algorithm.

    B. OSPF has a faster convergence time than RIP.

    C. OSPF uses less bandwidth than RIP.

    D. OSPF has less security, allowing it to process packets more quickly.

14. After reviewing your plans to implement Windows 2000 routers throughout your network, your company has decided to attempt to use their servers more efficiently. In an effort to do so, the company has decided to run SQL server and SMS from the RRAS server. The RRAS server

is currently routing for four segments of the network as well as a dial-up server. What advice would you offer under these circumstances?

A. Not a problem. Those added applications shouldn't add too much of an extra load.

B. Let's make this the WINS server as well.

C. Add an extra processor and we will be fine.

D. That is too much of a load. Let's remove the applications or buy a Layer 3 switching device to do the IP routing.

LAB QUESTION

Your company has decided to use a router to connect its 20-workstation network to the Internet. You need to implement a routed solution that will be powerful, but also affordable. Your company has just upgraded to Windows 2000, has one server, and cannot afford to spend more than $100 to connect its network to the Internet. What would be the best solution for this? Note: Assume that Internet access has already been paid for.

SELF TEST ANSWERS

Designing a Remote Access Solution that Uses Routing and Remote Access

1. ☑ **B.** OSPF can be configured to communicate with selected routers and is not broadcast or multicast based. This would not be an optimal routing protocol to use for links such as the slow wireless connection.

   ☒ **A** is incorrect because maintaining a static routing table would not be cost effective or efficient in a network of this size. However, in some circumstances, you may wish to include static entries into the routing table. **C** and **D** are incorrect because RIP version 1 is broadcast dependent, and RIP version 2 uses either broadcasts or multicasts, neither of which would be efficient in a network of this size.

Integrating Authentication with Remote Authentication Dial-In User Strategy (RADIUS)

2. ☑ **D.** In environments that contain a large number of users, you should place IAS and Active Directory on the same computer. This will improve response times significantly, and reduce the number of retries attempted for authentication. In smaller environments, you can consider using other programs, such as SQL or Exchange, on the same computer as the IAS server, but the overall performance of these services will suffer because processor and memory resources will be divided among the services.

   ☒ **A, B,** and **C** are incorrect because running programs on an IAS server may degrade IAS server performance.

3. ☑ **A, B, C. A** is correct because placing the IAS and authentication server on the same segment will reduce the risks inherent in cross-segment communications, and it is easier to monitor the activities on a single segment. **B** is correct because IPSec will protect data as it moves across the network, preventing its interception by third parties. **C** is correct because you should isolate the IAS server from both the internal network and the Internet. This will allow you to more easily focus on protocol and port filters that should be configured for the IAS server's network segment.

   ☒ **D** is incorrect because PCAnywhere, Symantec's remote control software, will open an unacceptable security hole for you network.

4. ☑ **B.** By editing HKEY_LOCAL_MACHINE\SYSTEM\CrrentControlSet\Services\Netlogon\Parameters, you may put too high a load on domain controllers in your network because

of the increased number of concurrent logon requests. You will need to strike a balance between the number of concurrent logon requests and the authentication related server load on the domain controller. The optimum balance will provide a faster logon experience for the end users.

☒ A, C, and D are incorrect because properly increasing the maximum concurrent users should not create these problems.

Designing a Virtual Private Network (VPN) Strategy

5. ☑ D. Using L2TP with IPSec gives the highest level of encryption to transmit data across the Internet. The Layer 2 Tunneling Protocol (L2TP) provides the tunnel in which data encrypted by IPSec can travel. The primary limitation of L2TP/IPSec is that you must use Windows 2000 on the clients and servers to implement this solution. If you have downlevel clients that must utilize the VPN, then PPTP would be the VPN solution of choice.

☒ A is incorrect because IPX/SPX represents transport and network layer protocols. IPX/SPX alone will not allow you to create the virtual link required for tunneling. You can use IPX/SPX as your LAN protocol after the tunnel has been established. B is incorrect because PPP is a datalink layer protocol used to create a point-to-point connection. Clients can use PPP to establish the physical link, but a tunneling protocol must be used to create the virtual link between the client and the VPN server. C is incorrect because it does not provide the highest level of security for an all-Windows 2000 environment. If you have downlevel clients that need to connect to the VPN server, then PPTP would be the correct solution.

6. ☑ B and D. It is not uncommon, and may be considered a best practice, to have both virtual and direct connect RAS services handled on the same server. Modem banks can be installed on the same machine that has the dedicated Internet connection, which is used for the VPN services.

☒ A is incorrect because the VPN server typically has an interface directly connected to the Internet or DMZ. This places the server at increased risk of Internet intruders, and therefore you may not wish to have your corporate data placed on the same server. SQL 7 is also disk- and processor-intensive, and therefore may impair RAS services handled on that machine. C is incorrect for similar reasons. It is not good practice to place a WINS server in a location where intruders may be able to access the WINS database (which contains the NetBIOS name structure of your internal network). WINS also has the potential of being processor- and disk-intensive, and may impair RAS service performance.

7. ☑ D. This is the only option that allows for tight security without incurring any extra cost to clients. Although VPNs are designed to avoid the additional costs of 800 numbers,

direct dial-up links still have their place, as seen in this scenario. The VPN Server would be configured with additional hardware that would allow multiple direct dial-up connections to the server.

☒ A is incorrect because you should not place the cost or administrative burden of providing Internet access and security protocols on the client just to accommodate your dial-up network requirements. B is incorrect because it places the cost of long distance charges on the customer. C is incorrect because call-back security is not the highest level of security mentioned in the possible answers to this scenario.

8. ☑ B and D. B is correct because useful information regarding the RRAS service and error conditions related to the service can be found in the Event Viewer. D is correct because you can monitor activity of your VPN server connection, and all other connections on a particular machine, by using the Network Monitor.

☒ A is incorrect because there is no dedicated "VPN Task Monitor." C is incorrect because the AT service is used to schedule events, and is not directly used to monitor a VPN connection.

Designing a Routing and Remote Access Routing Solution to Connect Locations Via Demand-Dial Routing

9. ☑ C. The most efficient method of routing packets involves selective route assignments to more efficient paths. You can manually assign relative costs to routes, or have a routing protocol, such as OSPF, assign these values.

☒ A is incorrect because this sort of routing is only done on Star Trek, and is not seen with present routing technologies. B is incorrect because routers do not use this technique to establish routes. D is incorrect because if you filter out all packets except those contained in the routing protocols, you effectively filter out all user and application data. This would make the network unusable for the network clients.

10. ☑ D. Windows NT 4.0 without the RRAS add-in only supports RIP version 1. You can use the RRAS add-in to confer OSPF and RIP version 2 functionality to a Windows NT 4.0 router.

☒ A is incorrect because Point-to-Point protocol is a datalink layer protocol used to create links via telephone lines, and is not used as a routing protocol. B is incorrect because OSPF is not supported on Windows NT 4.0 routers that do not have the RRAS add-in. C is incorrect because Windows NT 4.0 routers without the RRAS add-in do not support RIP version 2.

11. ☑ **A** and **C**. **A** is correct because RIP version 2 supports Variable Length Subnet Masking. This is not supported with RIP version 1. **C** is correct because password authentication of routers is supported by RIP version 2, and is not supported by RIP version 1.

☒ **B** is incorrect because RIP version 2 is not dependent on the services of a SQL server, and **D** is incorrect because RIP version 2 is not dependent on IPSec.

12. ☑ **D**. A rogue RIP packet originates from a RIP router that contains false or inaccurate routing information. A Rogue RIP router can be used to manipulate the routing tables on a network in order to send information to a hacker's destination network ID. A Rogue RIP router can also be used to collect routing information about the network's routed infrastructure.

☒ **A** is incorrect because a RIP router does not need to be authorized in the Active Directory. **B** is incorrect because a Rogue RIP router has nothing to do with DHCP or DHCP Authorization. A DHCP server that is not authorized in the Active Directory is sometimes *referred* to a Rogue DHCP server; but Rogue DHCP servers on a network can hand out false or inaccurate IP addressing information to DHCP clients. **C** is incorrect because OSPF is a legitimate routing protocol.

13. ☑ **A**, **B**, and **C**. **A** is correct because OSPF uses a link state routing algorithm, which creates more efficient routing tables and RIP, and which uses a distance vector routing algorithm. **B** is correct because OSPF does have a faster convergence time than RIP, and therefore all OSPF routers on the network will have accurate routing information more quickly than a RIP router. **C** is correct because RIP is dependent on either broadcast or multicast messages. OSPF routers can be configured with partners, which eliminates the broadcast element.

☒ **D** is incorrect because OSPF does allow for security of routing table information.

14. ☑ **D**. Those applications create too much of a load to run on a heavily used RRAS system. However, that system may be too heavily used for even RRAS.

☒ **A**, **B**, and **C** are incorrect because you shouldn't be adding any more applications to this system. Another processor may not help much either, because your system may become bottlenecked with all the NIC and MODEM use.

LAB ANSWER

1. Buy a modem and place it in your server.

2. Configure RRAS to create an on-demand connection to the ISP.

3. Create a demand-dial router interface.

4. Test connection to assure proper operation.

MICROSOFT CERTIFIED SYSTEMS ENGINEER

12

Designing an IPSec Implementation Strategy

CERTIFICATION OBJECTIVES

I t is a testament to IP flexibility that it has survived long enough for its weaknesses to become such a threat. The protocol has always emphasized redundancy and survivability over integrity or privacy. It would be unfair to condemn TCP/IP for these priorities, since they were valid architectural choices for its original audience.

However, the purposes for which the protocol was designed are no longer aligned with the requirements of the marketplace. First-year computer science students have the skills to disguise the origin of TCP/IP packets and network sniffers (once available primarily to legitimate network administrators) are easy to acquire and configure. In an information economy where information itself has become the product, the disruption or manipulation of packets can cost companies billions. Security has been added to IP using protocols such as SSL, but because these protocols occur at a higher OSI level, the work done developing a protocol for one application cannot be easily leveraged.

With the deployment of Windows 2000, though, there is a valuable new tool to help provide this security: IPSec. (Although you can use third party tools to apply IPSec into legacy networks, Windows 2000 is the first version of Windows to incorporate IPSec directly into the operating system.) IPSec is implemented at the network level and is therefore considered an OSI Layer 3 encryption technology. Because of this, in the years to come it should be easier for application vendors to integrate this security into their products.

This chapter describes the components of IPSec, the benefits and impact it can have on your network, and how it fits into your network design plan.

CERTIFICATION OBJECTIVE 12.01

Overview of IPSec

While IPSec will not solve all IP-related security issues, it can provide significant protection against denial of service attacks, replay attacks, and spoofing.

As defined in RFC 2401, IPSec offers two main categories of functionality via the two IPSec protocols:

- Authentication Header (AH)
- Encapsulating Security Payload (ESP)

These are discussed in greater detail next.

IP Header	TCP Header	Payload

Packet before
applying AH

Authentication Header

Imagine that a packet has arrived at your Network Interface Card. The IP Header
indicates that it came from your friend Bob. However, you know it is easy to fake
the bytes in an IP header to disguise its origin, so how can you tell if the packet
really came from Bob?

IPSec uses an additional series of bytes, called an "Authentication Header,"
to provide this assurance. The contents of the packet have been hashed using an
agreed-upon hashing algorithm and an agreed-upon key. (While the details of
this negotiation are beyond the scope of this chapter, for the test you may want
to be able to recognize this process as either "ISAKMP/Oakley" or "IKE.")

on the
job

*Note that AH does not encrypt the data and so does nothing to protect the
data from being read by unauthorized users. However, absence of
confidentiality can actually be a "feature," because encryption is illegal in
many countries, and therefore AH may be more suitable for international
operations.*

Observe the two packets shown in Figures 12-1 and 12-2. They can deliver the
same payload, but the second represents the output after AH is applied to the
packet. (For simplicity, we are ignoring the difference between configuring AH in
tunneling mode or transport mode. This distinction is described in greater detail
later in this chapter.)

Notice that even though both packets contain the same data payload (TCP
Header and TCP Payload), the second packet is longer. Most of the performance
loss due to IPSec, though, is due to the process of generating and negotiating
keys, and not to the increased number of bytes transferred.

Because the result is a "normal" IP datagram, it can be routed through network
devices that do not directly support IPSec. Although the source and destination

IP Header	AH Header	TCP Header	Payload

Packet after
applying AH

IP Header	TCP Header	Payload

computers must both support IPSec, one advantage of IPSec is that the devices that route the packet do not need to recognize this protocol.

Encapsulating Security Payload (ESP)

Because of AH, you now have confidence that the packet actually originated from Bob. However, how do you know that no unauthorized users have observed the packet en route?

This assurance can be provided using Encapsulating Security Payload. Observe the difference between an unencrypted packet and the same packet after ESP has been applied, as shown in Figures 12-3 and 12-4.

The information in these additional segments correspond closely to the information in the AH header. Table 12-1 compares the two.

exam
Watch

Although you will not need to know the contents of the headers in your day-to-day administration, you should be familiar with them in case they show up on the exam. Table 12-1 shows a list of the contents of these additional fields added by AH and ESP.

on the
Job

Data cannot be effectively compressed after it has been encrypted. Compression algorithms identify semantic patterns in the source data and compress them into larger logical units. The encryption process eliminates these patterns. Therefore, when planning your network architecture, it is important to remember that any encryption should occur after all outbound compression, or the compression will become ineffective. Note that Windows 2000 does not allow you to set both file encryption and file compression attributes on a file simultaneously.

IP Header	ESP Header	TCP Header	Payload Data	ESP Trailer	ESP Auth.

TABLE 12-1	Information	Length	Location in AH	Location in ESP
AH Headers vs. ESP Headers	Next Header	1 byte	AH Header	ESP Trailer
	Payload Length	1 byte	AH Header	n/a
	Reserved	2 bytes	AH Header	n/a
	Security Parameters Index	4 bytes	AH Header	ESP Header
	Sequence Number	4 bytes	AH Header	ESP Header
	Authentication Data	variable	AH Header	ESP Auth.
	Padding	variable	n/a	ESP Trailer
	Pad Length	variable	n/a	ESP Trailer

If ESP provides a superset of the functionality that AH provides, why would you ever use AH? The following Scenario & Solution box discusses this in more detail.

SCENARIO & SOLUTION

Will IPSec work with my existing firewall?	Firewall software often analyzes packet payload data, so if you use ESP, this software may not work properly. In general, this would be less of an issue when using AH.
Can I use IPSec across international boundaries?	It may be illegal to use ESP in some countries where the jurisdiction does not allow encryption without a formal key escrow system. AH may cause fewer international issues.
Will implementing IPSec slow down my router?	AH requires less computation because no data encryption is required. If you choose to use ESP for data encryption, more processor cycles will be dedicated to IPSec communications.
I am performing compression at the hardware level. Will IPSec affect my performance?	If you are compressing data at the hardware level, this compression may not be successful if it occurs after ESP encryption. Using AH would be less likely to interfere with the effectiveness of the encryption.

Defining the Goals of IPSec on Your Network

While IPSec has some uses on internal networks, it is most useful for defending the "seams" between your internal network and external users. In this section, we will observe how this security applies to Virtual Private Networks and remote access.

VPN Integration

In Windows 2000, you can choose between two VPN tunneling protocols, Point-to-Point tunneling Protocol (PPTP), and Layer 2 tunneling Protocol (L2TP). These protocols do not encrypt data themselves, but provide for data encryption in the following ways:

- When you use PPTP, you can use the RSA/RC4 based MPPE protocol to encrypt data
- When you use L2TP, you can use IPSec to encrypt data

In both of these cases, the encryption of the data is optional; however, a non-encrypted tunnel over the Internet would not be considered a Virtual *Private* Network, because without the encryption, there is no privacy.

The primary difference between tunneling provided through IPSec and that provided by PPTP on NT 4.0 is that IPSec operates at the network level (Layer 3) of the OSI model. IPSec in tunnel mode requires another protocol to establish a virtual link.

on the **job**

There are two very different ways of implementing IPSec tunneling, namely using Layer Tunneling Protocol (L2TP) or IPSec tunneling. IPSec tunneling can only be used on your internal network, because IPSec tunneling in and of itself does not include a link protocol that can establish a VPN connection. If you wish to establish a virtual link for an Internet tunnel after creating the initial PPP link, you must use L2TP as the virtual linking protocol to create the tunnel.

Remote Access Integration

The integration of IPSec and remote access is very similar to its integration with VPNs. The default settings for configuring a Windows 2000 server for remote access or as a VPN are done in the first step of the "Routing and Remote Access Server Setup Wizard". You get to this screen from START/PROGRAMS/ADMINISTRATIVE TOOLS/ROUTING and remote access. The first time you configure RRAS, this will invoke the wizard. Click Next and you will be presented with five different options:

- Internet connection server
- Remote access server
- Virtual private network (VPN) server
- Network router
- Manually configured server

Think of these options as "templates," and not as mutually exclusive functions. If you wanted the server to function both as a VPN server and a remote-access server, you could start with one of these two options and change the options as needed, or you could start with "Manually Configure Server" and configure the options individually.

on the job *The use of IPSec for Remote Access will become more important in the near future, but is currently relatively limited in Microsoft networks. This is because Windows 2000 is the only Windows operating system that supports IPSec, and if your users are using Windows 95 or 98, they will not be able to use this protocol directly.*

Data Confidentiality

The implementation of IPSec does not mean that your data cannot be compromised. Here are some risks even after deployment:

- IPSec simply confirms that the receiving computer is using the correct private key, which provides no assurance if the key has been compromised. Each of the three ways that Windows 2000 distributes keys has an associated risk. A static key could be intercepted if it is distributed via unencrypted e-mail; certificate revocation is frequently not grandfathered; and Kerberos authentication provides its own risks if server passwords are not adequately secured

- If policies on Windows 2000 servers are configured to request but not require IPSec for communication, it is a trivial matter to retrieve unencrypted data from these machines

- If you are using DES, a dedicated and skilled data thief can decrypt your messages without your key

- If you use IPSec to protect your network from external connections but not on your internal servers, you remain exposed to threats from within the organization, such as the inappropriate use of Network Monitor by employees or on-site consultants

Analyzing IPSec Risks and Benefits

IPSec provides many advantages, but it is not yet suitable for every organization. While the benefits of IPSec are clear, below are five issues you can use to analyze whether the risks outweigh the benefits on your network:

- **Internal risks**   Do you depend upon short-term consultants to manage your security? If internal risks are a significant concern, then your immediate focus should be organizational and not technological, and the integration of IPSec may not be the best investment of time and resources. However, if you have confidence that internal risks have been minimized, then implementing IPSec may be the next appropriate step in maximizing security on your network.

- **Workforce mobility**   IPSec requires identification of IP addresses at the connection endpoints. While there are software solutions to accommodate this mobility, much of the software is new, and if you require reliability above security, then it may be appropriate to delay implementation of IPSec until these tools mature.

- **Failure preferences**   Your users will need to decide which they consider to be a higher risk—not having data transferred at all, or having data transferred with sub-optimal security? IPSec tends not to degrade gracefully, so if your users cannot tolerate outages while the new technology is incorporated into your network, you may want to begin your implementation of IPSec with less mission-critical systems.

■ **Traffic capacity**   IPSec requires significant server resources to provide encryption, decryption, and key generation, so if your infrastructure is close to being bottlenecked, you should work on resolving those issues before stressing your system further. (Note that with Microsoft's Network Driver Interface specifications, it may be possible to offload some of these processes to the NIC if the card supports those functions.)

■ **International issues**   The government of the United States recently eased legal restrictions associated with encryption, but other governments still equate encryption technology with munitions and the use of AH and ESP can violate the laws of these jurisdictions. These laws are evolving very rapidly, so unless you have supreme confidence in the timeliness and accuracy of your international legal resources, you may want to use extreme caution when deploying IPSec internationally.

EXERCISE 12-1

Using IPSec in Different Environments

To examine how these issues could affect your environment, we will look at a few different scenarios, and examine how these issues could affect that implementation. By using these scenarios, we can help illustrate and extrapolate some issues that could arise. Contrast the following three organizations:

■ A public university, where most network traffic is generated by students and most of the students access the network while physically connected to the computer network.

■ A Big Five accounting firm, where there is a great deal of sensitive material stored on internal servers, and there is significant internal communication among branch offices, and workers want to access firm resources from the Internet connections at client sites.

■ A small consulting company, where the only network resources accessible to the public are the Web site, the FTP site, and employee e-mail.

Would you recommend that any or all of these organizations adopt IPSec? If so, how aggressively? While it is not possible to reduce any of these scenarios to a black-and-white decision, analyzing the probable needs of these organizations can help clarify the issues involved and assist you in designing your own company's IPSec solution.

Look at the potential internal security risks. The accounting firm may have the highest risk because of the risk to clients if the internal working products were inappropriately exposed. The small consulting firm would be less likely to have conflicts of interest, and the data inside the university network would be less likely to be sensitive if it was generated by undergraduates.

Analyze workforce mobility. The accounting firm probably has the most mobile workforce, especially if they need to connect to internal resources from network connections at client sites. While students are very mobile at a university, they will be frequently moving among defined locations, such as a dorm room or computer lab, offering less variety and risk. A small company might have very mobile employees, but they would not necessarily need to connect to company resources while working at a client site.

Look at the tolerance for and preferred behavior during network failures. The university and accounting firm are probably more sensitive than the small consulting company. However, it is likely that the accounting firm would rather have their data be inaccessible temporarily rather than have unencrypted data transmitted.

Analyze how close the organization is to overwhelming their capacity. The university is probably the largest consumer of bandwidth, because their network is more likely to be used for streaming media and other purposes that might be considered "inappropriate" in a corporate environment. The network traffic at the accounting firm would not be quite so bad, but it would still be busier than the small consulting firm. The amount of traffic must then be compared to the bandwidth limitations of the network infrastructure. Although the university network generates far more traffic, it may have multiple T-1 or T-3 lines, while the small consulting firm's WAN link is a single 56K-modem connection.

Investigate international issues. The university and accounting firm are both at a very high risk of transmitting packets to countries where encryption is tightly regulated. However, because of the lack of corporate policies and repercussions, it is more likely that students would be transmitting secure data internationally than employees of an accounting firm. The small consulting company, on the other hand, probably has minimal international communication.

While this is only a starting point in weighing the benefits and costs of implementing IPSec, these criteria can be a helpful start in making these decisions.

CERTIFICATION OBJECTIVE 12.03

Installing and Configuring IPSec

Because it is built into Windows 2000, installing and configuring IPSec is simple enough to conceal some of the organizational complexities associated with this technology. Later in this chapter, we will discuss some of the configuration options in more detail, but in this section, we will just focus upon the issues involved in using IPSec in end-to-end or transport mode.

Configuring End-to-End Security

exam
ⓦatch

End-to-end security is also called transport mode. You should be prepared to recognize either term on the exam.

When operating in transport mode, IPSec leaves most of the packet unchanged. Some bytes in the header are altered (such as the Time To Live and size indicators) and the new headers are added, but the rest of the packet is left intact. The process of decrypting the packet on the receiving end is therefore relatively simple and requires less time than in the past.

Configuring IPSec for Tunneling

Tunneling mode requires more computational power than transport mode, but it is more flexible. Tunneling simply redefines that the original TCP/IP packet as just another kind of generic data, no different from ASCII text in an e-mail. The whole packet is encapsulated as the payload in a new TCP/IP packet, headers and all. This new packet then travels through the network until it arrives at the receiving end, where the original packet is then "unloaded" and the original payload is delivered to its destination.

In general, transport mode is more appropriate for fixed endpoints that are used inside your internal network. Tunneling is more appropriate when the data needs to be transmitted across an external network. Some of the differences between using tunneling and transport mode are discussed in the following Scenario & Solution box.

To configure IPSec for tunneling, you set the options on the tunnel setting tab of the policy rule. (Policy rules are discussed in more detail under *IP Security Policies*.)

SCENARIO & SOLUTION

Which approach is more secure?	Transport mode can be used with either AH or ESP. When ESP is used, the data is encrypted, but not authenticated. AH performs authentication, but does not provide confidentiality of the data. AH and ESP can also be used together for maximum security.
Which approach is faster?	Transport mode is used to secure communications from end-to-end from the source to the destination computer. Tunnel mode is used to protect data at tunnel endpoints. Because the tunnel endpoints can handle large amounts of traffic, transport mode requires less overall processing on a per-computer basis.
Does the function of the Windows 2000 server make a difference?	It is better to use transport mode when transmitting traffic between two Windows 2000 computers within the confines of your corporate network. When communicating between Windows 2000 routers, it is better to use tunnel mode.
What if I am using Network Address Translation (NAT)?	You cannot use NAT with IPSec when using transport mode because the IP headers are concealed. You can use IPSec in tunnel mode.
What if I have firewall software on the Windows 2000 server?	You will have to open the appropriate ports to allow IPSec traffic through the firewall, but otherwise, the firewall should remain unaware of IPSec-encrypted packets.

The following options are available on the tunnel setting tab:

■ This rule does not specify an IPSec tunnel. When this is selected, IPSec tunneling is disabled.

■ The tunnel endpoint is specified by this IP address. If you select this option, you need to confirm that the defined server has a fixed IP address (for example, it cannot be receiving its address dynamically from DHCP).

Figure 12-5 shows the Rule Properties Tunnel Setting tab.

FIGURE 12-5

The Rule Properties Tunnel Setting tab

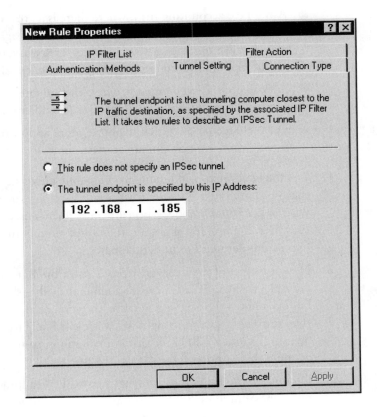

EXERCISE 12-2

Choosing Between Transport or Tunnel Mode

There are many tradeoffs involved in determining the right way to implement IPSec.

In this section, we will extend Exercise 12-1 and we will see how these three previously defined scenarios might be impacted. For context, here are the three scenarios again:

- A public university, where most network traffic is generated by students and most students access the network while physically connected to the computer network.

- A Big Five accounting firm, where there is a great deal of sensitive material stored on internal servers, and there is significant internal communication among branch offices, and workers want to access firm resources from the Internet connections at client sites.

- A small consulting company, where the only network resources publicly accessible are the Web site, the FTP site, and employee e-mail.

For each of these scenarios, which might be more appropriate—IPSec transport or tunnel mode? What issues might affect these choices?

1. List the issues that could apply to the public university. (One possibility is that you have relatively little trust of users inside your network, so you may want to use tunnel mode, especially on segments used by undergraduates. However, because this is slower, this could have an impact upon the high bandwidth demands of undergraduates.)

2. Now list some of the issues that could affect the Big 5 consulting firm. For example, the data is much more valuable than that shared by undergraduates, but by contrast the people generating the content are much more trustworthy than university students might be. It is more likely that the employees would be using Windows 2000 for their workstations, so transport mode would be more of an option there than at the university.

3. Finally, list the issues that apply to the small consulting company. If they are not using Windows 2000, then transport mode is not even an option. If they are, then consideration should be given to where the work is done. Because little work spans the internal and external network, a stronger firewall would be called for, so you may want to consider using tunneling mode for updates to the Website, and put the Internet-enabled resources on a domain not "trusted" by your primary domain.

CERTIFICATION OBJECTIVE 12.04

IPSec Security Policies

To help manage the behavior of IPSec in your organization, Windows 2000 supports policies that alter the following behavior:

- Does this computer request secured data? Does it require secured data?
- Does this computer use Authentication Header? Encapsulating Security Payload? Both?
- Should IP packets be filtered by IP address for inbound traffic? For outbound traffic?

Windows 2000 supports the ability to combine these options in hundreds of different ways, but to simplify the administrative process, it provides the following template security policies that many organizations need (seen in Figure 12-6):

- Client (Respond Only)
- Server (Request Only)
- Secure Server (Require Security)

FIGURE 12-6

Built-in IPSec
policies

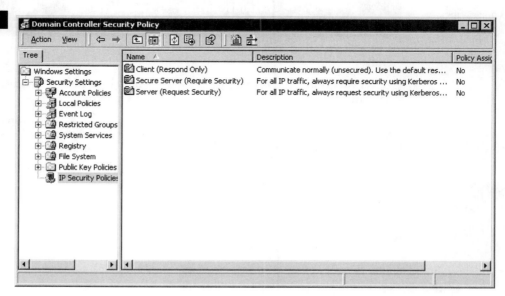

Table 12-2 lists a comparison of these policies.

These policies are accessible in a number of locations including the Local Security Policy, the IPSec Stand-Alone Snap-In, and Group Policy.

You can create your own security policy, or you can assign one of the three default policies to a GPO. To assign one of these policies, right click on the policy and click Assign. The Policy Assigned field should then read Yes for that policy, and No for all other policies.

exam
⚔️atch

The Client Template should be used only on machines where IPSec security is not required. The choice between Server and Secure Server depends on which is more critical—security or accessibility for users with older Windows operating systems.

After the policy has been added, you can configure the rules associated with the policy using the following five tabs shown in Figure 12-7:

- Authentication Methods
- Tunnel Setting
- Connection Type

TABLE 12-2		Respond to Request for Secured Data?	Accept Non-Secured Transmissions?	Secure outgoing transmissions?
Built-in IPSec Policies	Client (Respond Only)	Yes	Yes	No
	Server (Request Security)	Yes	Only with systems not supporting IPSec	Sometimes
	Secure Server (Require Security)	Yes	Only as initial step in creating secured connection	Always

FIGURE 12-7

The Edit Rules
Properties dialog
box

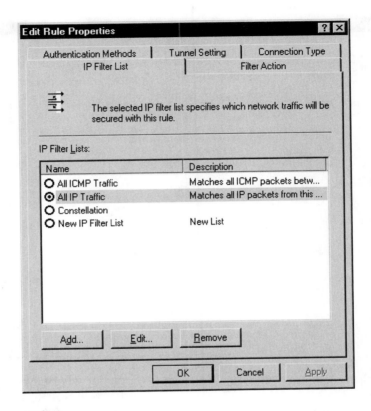

- IP Filter List
- Filter Action

The tunnel setting was discussed above. Connection type, shown in Figure 12-8, is just a simple radio button selection (distinguishing whether the rule should apply to all network connections, LANs, or remote access).

The other three tabs offer most of the functionality managing your IPSec policies, and are the focus of the remainder of this section.

The Connection Type tab in the Rules Properties dialog box

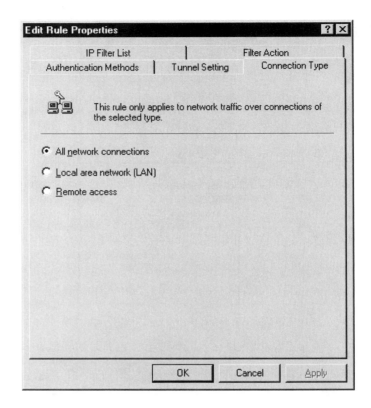

Authentication Schemes

Before two machines can generate a key to share, both computers have to agree on a technique to authenticate each other's identity. The Authentication Method tab, shown in Figure 12-9, offers the following three options to do this:

- Windows 2000 default (Kerberos V5 protocol)
- Use of a certificate from this certificate authority (CA)
- Use of a string to protect the key exchange (pre-shared key)

on the *Job*

The first option is only appropriate if the client is inside a trusted Windows 2000 domain. The second option requires that the client and server share a trusted certificate authority. The third option requires a manual text string that serves as the pre-shared key. (Clearly, you should NOT distribute this key by e-mailing it, because if you do, the key will be visible to every server routing this e-mail.)

FIGURE 12-9

The
Authentication
Method
Properties dialog
box

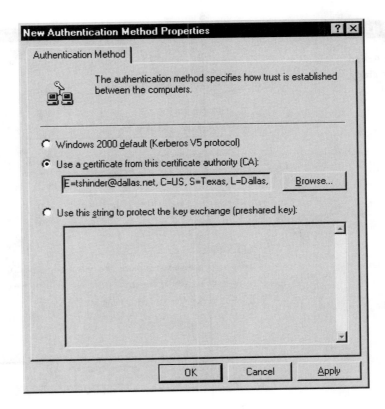

These three options define the methods for authentication, but not the hashing algorithms. These hash algorithms are defined in the properties of a defined filter action (shown in Figure 12-10). These are the two primary hashing algorithms used to provide integrity:

- SHA1
- MD5

These algorithms are described in more detail under *Planning Considerations*.

Encryption Schemes

As with Authentication Header, when using Encapsulating Security Payload, you define the algorithms on the Rule Properties dialog box. However, in addition to

FIGURE 12-10

The Filter Action
Properties dialog
box

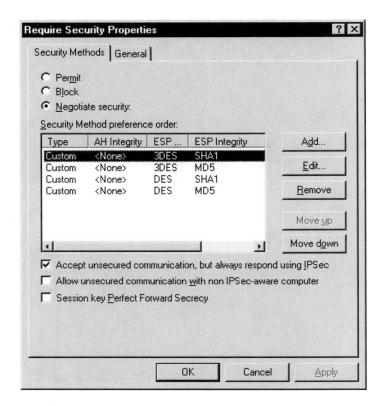

defining the integrity algorithm, you must also define an encryption algorithm. The
two most common encryption algorithms are:

- DES
- 3DES (called "triple DES")

These algorithms are described in more detail under *Planning Considerations.*

IPSec Filter Rules and Filter Actions

The other two tabs are IP Filter List and Filter Action. These tabs allow you to
define when the rule is applied, and what happens when it does.

IP Filter List

In the Filter Properties dialog box there is a three-tab dialog box restricting the application of the rule either by IP address or by Protocol (as shown in Figure 12-11).

The IP Addressing options are:

■ My IP Address (no parameter required)

■ Any IP Address (no parameter required)

■ A specific IP Address (for example, 207.46.130.14)

■ A specific IP Subnet (This could be used to restrict application of the rule to a single sub-network)

FIGURE 12-11

The Filter Properties dialog box

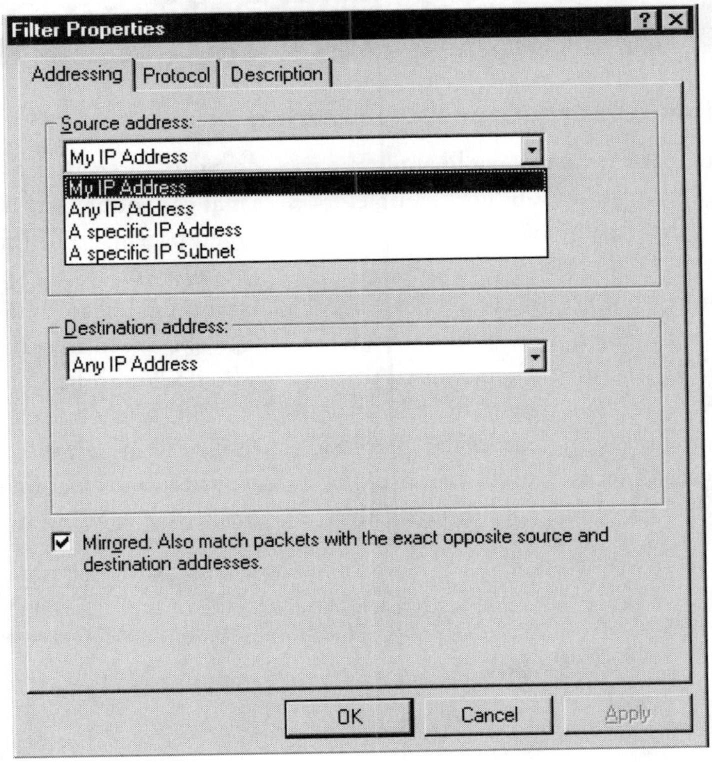

You can specify these options for the source address or destination address (or both). By selecting the Mirrored check box, you can also accommodate a transposition of the source and destination without requiring an additional rule.

Filter Actions

All of the previous steps define when a rule takes effect, but the Filter Actions tab defines what the rule actually does when it is applied.

After you click Edit, you see the Filter Action dialog box. On the top section you can specify whether you want to permit, block, or negotiate security. This last option allows you to define a set of behaviors associated with a single rule.

FROM THE CLASSROOM

Applying Rules to Your Organization

There are many ways you could apply these rules in your organization. For example, imagine you want the information you are publishing to your Web server to be authenticated but not encrypted (after all, the information is going to be public anyway, so why sacrifice performance to conceal that data?). However, you may want to have all of the information from your legal department authenticated and encrypted. You may also want to distinguish the application of the security filters to define what to do with data that cannot be validated. For e-mail, you may want packets to be transmitted anyway, because you have aggressive internal virus scanning, but for Human Resources, the data may be so sensitive that no unsecured data should go through.

This is just one example of how these policies can be a valuable resource in turning your business requirements into networked reality using Windows 2000.

—*Michael F. Martone, MCSE, MCSD, MCP+Internet*

The following three check boxes are at the bottom of this dialog, shown in Figure 12-12.

- Accept unsecured communication, but always respond using IPSec
- Allow unsecured communication with non IPSec-aware computer
- Session key Perfect Forward Secrecy

FIGURE 12-12

The Filter
Actions dialog
box

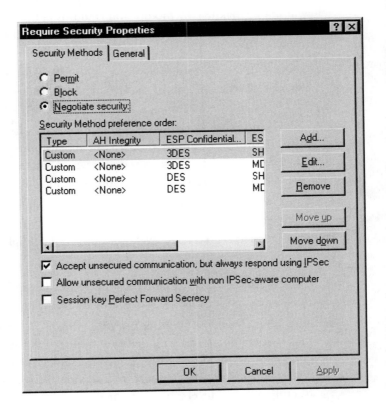

CertCam 12-3

EXERCISE 12-3

Reviewing the Configuration of the Client Policy

When learning how to use a new technology, it is common to rely upon the default settings, sometimes at the expense of understanding how they work. In this exercise, we will look at the details of how one of the default policies is configured.

1. Click Start, point to Programs, and then point to Administrative Tools. In the Administrative Tools menu, click Local Security.

2. Click once on the Server policy. Then right click and select Properties. (We will not be making any modifications to this policy, but we will learn more about what a policy looks like if we examine one with a meaningful configuration.)

3. The screen you see should have two tabs: Rules and General. On the Rules tab, observe the contents of the IP Security Rules section. Click once on All IP Traffic and click Edit.

4. You should now see a dialog box with five tabs on it: IP Filter List, Filter Action, Authentication Methods, Tunnel Setting, and Connection Type. Click on the connection type and observe whether this policy applies to all network connections. Observe the other options.

5. Click on the tunnel-setting tab. You should see that the rule does not specify an IPSec tunnel. (Remember that this just refers to the tunneling implemented at the IPSec level, not tunneling configured using a VPN.)

6. Click on the authentication method tab and observe the default value.

7. Click on the IP filter list tab. You will see all the configured IP filter lists for that machine. Click the list named All IP Traffic and then click Edit.

8. This takes you to the IP Filter List dialog box. Click the Edit button in this dialog box. You should see a dialog with three tabs: Addressing, Protocol, and Description. Observe the options for source address and destination address, then go to the protocol tab and view the protocols available for filtering. Click Cancel twice to return.

9. Click on the Filter Action tab. Click on the first item visible under Filter Actions and click Edit. Observe the settings for this filter action.

10. Click Cancel to close the dialog.

CERTIFICATION OBJECTIVE 12.05

IPSec Planning Considerations

In the section above, we covered many of the issues involved in implementing IPSec. In addition to these issues, we will be analyzing three considerations in this section:

- Which integrity algorithms should you use with AH and ESP?
- Which encryption algorithms should you use with ESP?
- Under what circumstances is IPSec undesirable?

These issues are described in more detail in the sections below.

Which Integrity Algorithms Should You Use with AH and ESP?

The biggest difference between the two integrity algorithms is how many bits are used to generate the hash:

Integrity Algorithms	Number of Bits in Hash
MD5	128-bit hash
SHA1	160-bit hash

As you might anticipate, MD5 will operate more quickly than SHA1, but SHA1 is more secure. The specifications for MD5 are available in RFC 1321 and were developed by R. Rivest in 1992. This algorithm was developed to be very concise and quickly executed. Although the length of the bit hash is longer for SHA1, the actual SHA1 algorithm is very similar to MD5's predecessor, MD4.

Which Encryption Algorithms Should You Use with ESP?

The two most common ESP encryption algorithms are DES and 3DES.

- **DES (Data Encryption Standard)**   56-bit key. This protocol is popular, well defined, and part of the IPSec standard. Unfortunately, due to the relatively small key length, it is no longer considered secure, and amateur hackers can crack it in less than a day. (It was included in the IPSec RFC because DES was first compromised while the standards were close to being finished.) However, due to inertia and due to the relatively low processing overhead this protocol requires, DES will probably remain in use for quite a while.

- **3DES (Triple DES)**   One approach to address the weakness of DES is to use it three consecutive times with three different keys. (After all, the weakness of DES is not due to any architectural flaw, but rather due to the power of modern computers that now makes it possible to crack DES using brute force.) As you might anticipate, this takes longer to encrypt and decrypt than simple DES.

 Although 3DES applies three different 56-bit keys, do not confuse the power of 3DES with that of a 168-bit key, which would provide much more security than 3DES. The additional key possibilities are multiplicative, not exponential. However, 3DES is much more secure than DES, and if you require the extra level of security, you should consider using it.

Under what Circumstances Is IPSec Undesirable?

After you alert your manager to the security issues associated with sending unencrypted packets across a public network, it may be difficult to explain why IPSec should be avoided in certain contexts. However, IPSec can cause technological and legal issues when used indiscriminately. Here are some examples of where you should use extreme caution.

- **Routing Protocols**   Some protocols are incompatible with IPSec, such as NAT (when using IPSec transport mode).

- **International Communication**   If you are setting up a network that is communicating across international boundaries, you may want to use extreme caution in configuring IPSec, especially ESP. The encryption supported by ESP is illegal under many foreign jurisdictions. While AH does not encrypt data, it is best to check with the local authorities before implementing any type of encryption or authentication scheme.

- **Streaming Media**   Because streaming media is extremely time sensitive, and because of the time required to encrypt and decrypt these packets, you should probably delay application of IPSec for these purposes until you have successfully managed its deployment on other parts of your network. (Unlike the other two exceptions above, this concern may fade over time, and is due to the intersection of IPSec and current technology limitations. However, you should be aware that because of wire tap laws that require real-time access to data, the legal issues associated with encrypting voice are usually even more complicated than those associated with encrypting text, and you should anticipate the need for legal consultations as you proceed.)

CertCam 12-4

EXERCISE 12-4

Additional Implications of IPSec

For this exercise, we will analyze the issues discussed in this section and apply them to the three scenarios discussed in Exercises 12-1 and 12-2 (the public university, the Big Five accounting firm, and the small consulting company).

1. List additional implementation issues that might arise when using IPSec at a university. One issue could be the popularity of streaming media at universities (not only to receive pre-recorded video and audio, but also to make toll-free long distance calls). If the university intends to support these uses of bandwidth in the future, implementing IPSec could have a very negative impact upon performance for all users.

2. Consider how these issues could affect the Big Five accounting firm. It is quite likely that they are not directly supporting significant streaming media because they are using external resources to provide teleconferencing connectivity. However, the potential for these firms to be vulnerable to litigation and industrial espionage will only increase over time. As the technological hurdles associated with IPSec telephony are reduced, the firm may want to investigate the appropriate legal tradeoffs.

3. Note how these issues could impact the small consulting company. If the company has limited resources, it may be using the same servers to perform multiple tasks, and there is a higher risk that they are using the same server both as a multi-homed gateway and the Web server. (Of course, this is not a recommended configuration regardless of IPSec, but it is more likely to be the case at a small company than at a large one.) If this is the case, there is a greater risk that IPSec could conflict with the administrative protocols on that computer.

CERTIFICATION OBJECTIVE 12.06

Monitoring and Optimizing IPSec

Even after you have successfully implemented IPSec, your job is not over. As the volume of IPSec traffic in your organization starts to increase, you may observe performance degradation, or possibly total failure. Therefore, it is important to understand the use of the tools you can use to diagnose and monitor IPSec. The remainder of this section describes these tools.

Important IPSec Events to Monitor

Below are four tools that are among the most valuable in diagnosing issues related to IPSec.

- IPSECMON
- Network Monitor
- System Monitor
- Event Viewer

The order in which you would use these tools should depend upon the kind of problems you are having. If you are having no problem transmitting unencrypted IP packets but cannot transmit IPSec packets, you should start with the IPSec Monitor (IPSECMON) utility. However, if you are having global connectivity issues, there is a very good chance that the problem has nothing to do with IPSec, and you may want to begin your investigation at a higher level.

These tools are discussed in more detail in the next section.

The IPSECMON Utility

If you believe the communication issue is IPSec related, the first diagnostic tool you should use is the IPSec Monitor. This tool allows you to monitor the operation of IPSec in real time, on either a local or remote machine. It does this by displaying the active security associations, and by providing metrics on the successful and unsuccessful transfer of secure data.

The IPSECMON application is not visible from the Start menu, so to initiate it you need to open the RUN command and type **IPSECMON** in the RUN command's text box.

As shown in Figure 12-13, there are three panes. The top pane lists every active security association. (The fields displayed are: Policy Name, Security, Filter Name, Source Address, Destination Address, Protocol, Source Port, and Destination Port.)

This tool has no flags and no logging ability, and the only option you have is to change how often the data refreshes (15 seconds by default). However, by observing the ratios among packets, you can use it to manually derive real-time data on the successes of your secure transfers.

Network Monitor

Network Monitor allows you to observe the data sent in the protocol headers, but it can be hard to find the information, due to the very nature of IPSec. Below is a comparison of how AH and ESP are reported in Network Monitor.

FIGURE 12-13	
The IPSECMON Console	

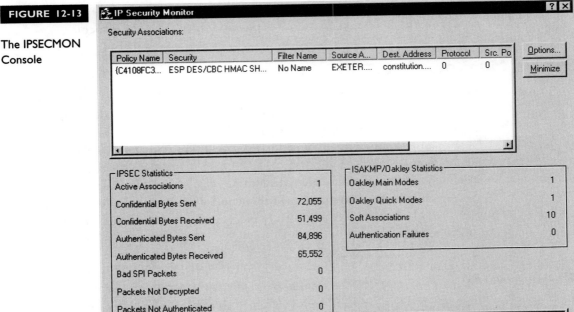

- **Encapsulating Security Payload** ESP packets are labeled as being transferred with the ESP protocol, so they are easy to filter and monitor. However, because contents are encrypted, only the header bytes are identifiable, so if you are sending significant ESP traffic on that computer, sniffing for particular text strings will probably be fruitless and very inefficient. Below is a Network Monitor excerpt reporting an ESP frame:

  ```
  + ESP: SPI = 0xE422BEDC, Seq = 0x1
  ```

- **Authentication Header Packets** Unlike ESP packets, the individual bytes in an AH packet should be easy to observe and analyze in Network Monitor. However, it is harder to filter for these packets, because they are not labeled as "AH" packets, but rather they are labeled as the lower-level protocol (TCP, UDB, or ICMP). The AH header is visible, however, when the individual packet is opened up inside Network Monitor. Below is a Network Monitor excerpt showing how this is reported.

  ```
  AH: Protocol = ICMP, SPI = 0x7C4BD8FA, Seq = 0x1
  ```

Remember—ESP Packets are shown in Network Monitor under the ESP protocol, but AH packets are not reported under the AH protocol.

System Monitor

The System Monitor is useful for providing longitudinal analysis of a server and of network conditions. However, just as a doctor can better diagnose your illness if he or she has a baseline of your vitals when you are well, as an administrator you can better maintain your network if you have a baseline of satisfactory performance to use for comparison.

The diagnostics available are far too numerous to list here, but as you examine these options it should become clear that you have the ability to keep dividing your problem into smaller and smaller pieces until you can identify where the bottlenecks are.

Event Viewer

There are actually three different logs where an administrator can identify diagnostics for IPSec.

- System

- Security

- Application

The most frequently checked of these is the system log. It should be the default, but if it is not, select System under the Log menu.

If you are lucky, you will mostly see blue entries. There are three levels of severity logged in the system log: "Error" (red), "Warning" (yellow), and "Information" (blue).

Here are some of the IPSec-specific events that can occur in each of these logs:

- **System Log**   When the IPSec policy agent starts, it writes its configuration parameters to the system log

- **Security Log**   The Oakley protocol updates its status and logs failure warnings

- **Application Log**   Additional ISAKMP/Oakley messages are logged here

In Figure 12-14 you see an example of the properties of an event contained in the security log.

The full contents of the description can be copied to the clipboard and pasted into Notepad or another text processor. Figure 12-15 shows the full description of this event.

Full description of the IPSec security event

```
Untitled - Notepad
File  Edit  Format  Help
Description:
IKE security association established.
 Mode:
Data Protection Mode (Quick Mode)

 Peer Identity:
Preshared key ID.
Peer IP Address: 192.168.1.3

 Filter:
Source IP Address 192.168.1.186
Source IP Address Mask 255.255.255.255
Destination IP Address 192.168.1.3
Destination IP Address Mask 255.255.255.255
Protocol 0
Source Port 0
Destination Port 0

 Parameters:
ESP Algorithm DES CBC
HMAC Algorithm SHA
AH Algorithm None
Encapsulation Transport Mode
InboundSpi -1254146648
OutBoundSpi -2120217315
Lifetime (sec) 900
Lifetime (kb) 100000
```

The following Scenario & Solution box summarizes some of the issues discussed.

SCENARIO & SOLUTION

I am trying to set up two Windows 2000 servers in a test environment and I am trying to see if I have successfully created the Security Association. Where is the best place to confirm this?	In IPSECMON, you can observe all currently active Security Associations, as well as seeing the real-time diagnostics of the secure data that has been processed.
Communication with an IPSec-enabled server was working fine when only my department was accessing it, but now that the entire business unit is reading information from that server, performance has slowed to a crawl. Where is the bottleneck?	Because each inbound and outbound connection to a secure server is protected via IPSec, the amount of processor overhead increases with the number of active data transfers to and from the secure server. There is a good chance that IPSec is beginning to take a larger toll on the server that is accessed by a larger number of users.
I believe that I have set up my communication so that all packets would be protected using ESP encryption. How can I confirm that these packets are unreadable to sniffers?	By using Network Monitor, you can investigate the specific contents of a packet sent to that computer, and you can confirm that a clear text message is unreadable on that destination workstation. (Of course, this doesn't itself confirm that ALL packets are encrypted—THAT behavior is dictated by the policy filters.) You should also check the Event Monitor to see if there have been any failures in IPSec policy negotiation.
I received a page from one of my users complaining that they were not able to view an IPSec-protected server. I went to that user's machine and everything seems fine. I can't recreate the problem, so how can I find out what happened?	By using the Event Log on the user's computer (and possibly on the protected server) you can see the messages created by the IPSec service. If there are failures, you should see them listed in the Event Monitor.

EXERCISE 12-5

Archiving a Simple IPSec Baseline

The goal of this exercise is to establish some baseline data about the operation of IPSec on your network. The value of baselining is not specific to IPSec. You would probably want to extend this to other operations and perform it on multiple machines.

1. Open the RUN command from the Start menu.

2. Type **IPSECMON** in the RUN command text box. Take a screenshot of the screen that appears and paste it into a WordPad document.

3. If you have a workstation with IPSec installed, go to that computer and open a command prompt. At the command prompt, type **PING <IP_ADDRESS_OF_SERVER>**. Return to your server, observe how the screen has changed, take another screenshot, and paste it into your WordPad document.

4. From the Administrative Tools menu, open the Services applet. Stop the IPSec Policy Agent and restart it.

5. Open the Event Viewer. Observe the events that have been added when the event was stopped and restarted. Use View/Filter Events to restrict the display to the events of the last five minutes.

6. Export all of the events into a TXT file by using Save As. Open up this text file and paste the records into your master WordPad document.

There are, of course, much more sophisticated network monitoring utilities than just copying diagnostics into WordPad, but even having a simple baseline of behavior can be very helpful in diagnosing issues in the future.

CERTIFICATION SUMMARY

IPSec is an extension to IP that allows packets to support authentication and encryption, while still being able to be routed through servers that do not directly support IPSec. The two components of IPSec are Authentication Header and Encapsulating Security Payload. Both of these can be configured in tunnel or transport mode.

By editing the security policies, you can determine which packets get through and which packets will support or require IPSec. While Windows 2000 comes with default policies, you also can edit your own policies to define these behaviors. If there are errors caused by these policies, or other issues caused by IPSec, the best tools to investigate the issues are IPSECMON, Network Monitor, System Monitor, and Event Viewer.

TWO-MINUTE DRILL

Overview of IPSec

❑ IPSec has two primary components. Authentication Header (AH) verifies the origin of content while Encapsulating Security Payload (ESP) encrypts data.

❑ Authentication Header adds an extra series of bytes after the IP Header, but routers that don't support IPSec can still handle these packets just like any other payload data.

❑ ESP is primarily associated with encryption, but you can also support authentication directly within ESP.

Defining the Goals of IPSec on Your Network

❑ There are two primary ways to configure IPSec—tunnel mode or transport mode.

❑ Tunnel mode is more taxing on the server because it requires that all data passing through the gateways be secured via IPSec tunneling.

❑ If you choose to use IPSec tunneling, you must specify the destination endpoint of the tunnel.

Installing and Configuring IPSec

❑ If you use L2TP to provide your VPN, you can use IPSec to provide your security, but if you use PPTP, you must use the MPPE protocol for this purpose.

❑ When using L2TP, the IPSec protection is optional, but if you do not use any encryption on your VPN, then your network resources will be vulnerable.

❑ Even after IPSec is operating on your network, there are still security risks with IPSec—for example, DES vulnerability and improper transmission of keys.

IPSec Security Policies

❑ The settings for IPSec are defined in Security Policies. While you can create your own policies, Windows 2000 also provides the following three templates: Client (Respond only), Server (Request only), and Secure Server (Require security).

❑ You can define the specific hashing algorithm used (such as SHA1 or MD5) or encryption algorithm (such as DES or 3DES) depending upon your security needs.

❑ By defining filter rules and filter actions, you can determine which packets require IPSec processing and which packets can travel through unaltered.

IPSec Planning Considerations

❑ The tool that provides the most specific IPSec diagnostics is IPSECMON. This tool displays security associations, IPSec statistics, and ISAKMP/Oakley statistics, but it offers very little configuration flexibility.

❑ Using Network Monitor, you can observe whether ESP or AH packets are transmitted over the network, but you will not be able to read the contents of packets protected via ESP.

❑ IPSec events can be found in all three sections of the Event Viewer (the system log, security log, and application log).

Monitoring and Optimizing IPSec

❑ When selecting an integrity algorithm, selecting SHA1 will provide more security but MD5 will provide faster performance.

❑ DES is an industry standard encryption algorithm, but it has been compromised by hackers. 3DES is another algorithm that applies DES three times in a row with separate hashes.

❑ Some additional scenarios where it is inappropriate to use IPSec are international communication and streaming media.

SELF TEST

The following questions will help you measure your understanding of the material presented in this chapter. Read all of the choices carefully, as there may be more than one correct answer. Choose all correct answers for each question.

Defining the Goals of IPSec on Your Network

1. You are configuring a Windows 2000 server. In which of the following scenarios would it be appropriate to use Authentication Header for all direct communication with that server? Choose all that apply.

   A. All transmitted data must be encrypted.

   B. Some encrypted data may be encrypted with a higher-level protocol such as SSL.

   C. All of the workstations in your organization are running Windows NT 4.0.

   D. All of the routers in your organization are running Windows NT 4.0.

2. You have implemented IPSec on one of your primary file servers. During the first week of the implementation, there were no problems associated with IPSec or any other problems reported. After the week of testing, you decide to open the server to all users on the network, and all users are IPSec enabled. You then begin to receive calls regarding problems connecting to the server. What may cause some of the problems?

   A. The users are using Windows 2000 Professional, and they should be using Windows 95 and 98 computers to access the secure file server.

   B. The additional connections to the file server increase the processor load due to IPSec on the server.

   C. The clients and the server are using different authentication methods.

   D. The increased network traffic could be causing an increased demand on the network segment on which the server is located.

3. Which of the following represent valid choices for implementing security and tunneling in a VPN? Choose all that apply.

   A. PPTP for tunneling and IPSec for encryption

   B. PPTP for tunneling and MPPE for encryption

   C. L2TP for tunneling and MPPE for encryption

   D. L2TP for tunneling and IPSec for encryption

4. Of the following choices on the first step of the routing and remote access wizard, which options should you select if you wanted to set up a server to support a VPN? Choose all that apply.

   A. Remote access server

   B. Virtual Private Network

   C. Network router

   D. Manually configure server

Installing and Configuring IPSec

5. Which of the following best describes the impact upon the headers when you are using transport mode security with AH?

   A. No bytes in the IP header are altered.

   B. A new IP header is added in front of the old IP header.

   C. The old header is completely discarded and replaced with a new header generated by AH.

   D. Most of the fields in the IP header are unaltered. Those that are will be excluded from the hash.

6. Your boss informs you that he read something about VPNs in the newspaper over the weekend and that he wants you to create one for the company as soon as possible. He also read that since the data typically moves over the Internet, it is not safe from hackers. But, he tells you, there are ways to make the data very safe. What combination of protocols would you use to make the data as safe as possible when it travels over the Virtual Private Network?

   A. IPSec

   B. L2TP

   C. PPTP

   D. IKE

7. You are using two Windows 2000 servers as internal routers. Which of the following is true in this situation?

   A. Transport mode is more appropriate than tunnel mode.

   B. Tunneling is more appropriate than transport mode.

   C. Both transport mode and tunneling would be equally appropriate.

   D. Neither transport mode nor tunneling could be used.

8. You are configuring IPSec tunneling to share a key with somebody who is not in your network. The user gets the IP address from DHCP. Which of the following statements is the best option?

   A. This rule does not specify an IPSec tunnel.

   B. This rule does not specify an VPN tunnel.

   C. The tunnel endpoint is specified by this DNS name.

   D. The tunnel endpoint is specified by this IP address.

IPSec Security Policies

9. Which of the following are appropriate options to share a key between two servers if one of them is running Windows 2000 and the other server is running Linux? Choose all that apply.

   A. Windows 2000 default (Kerberos US protocol)

   B. Windows 4.0 default (Kerberos US protocol)

   C. Use a certificate from this certificate authority (CA).

   D. Use this string to protect the key exchange (preshared key).

10. You believe you have a spy in your company that is using SMS inappropriately. Because of performance concerns, you don't want to implement IPSec across your entire internal network, but you do want to implement it in between the router endpoints that separate the network segments your suspect is listening to. If you only wanted to modify the policy options in one rule on one Windows 2000 server, which of the following options could accomplish your goals?

    A. A Specific IP Address

    B. A Specific IP Address and Mirrored

    C. My IP Address

    D. My IP Address and Mirrored

11. Which of the following options is selected in the default rule in the Secure Server policy?

    A. Accept unsecured communication, but always respond using IPSec.

    B. Allow unsecured communication with non IPSec-aware computer.

    C. Do not accept unsecured communication.

    D. Session key Perfect Forward Secrecy.

IPSec Planning Considerations

12. Which of the following best describes the difference between MD5 and SHA?

    A. SHA uses a longer bit-length hash than MD5 and therefore provides better encryption.

    B. MD5 uses a longer bit-length hash than SHA and therefore provides better encryption.

    C. SHA uses a longer bit-length hash than MD5 and therefore provides better authentication.

    D. MD5 uses a longer bit-length hash than SHA and therefore provides better authentication.

13. Imagine that a new encryption protocol was developed that was exactly like DES but had a 120-bit key. Which of the following protocols would provide the most security for your data?

    A. DES

    B. 3DES

    C. This new 120-bit key protocol

    D. They would all provide the same security.

14. Which of the following protocols would be appropriate to use in conjunction with ESP in transport (End-To-End) mode? Choose all that apply.

    A. AH

    B. HTTP

    C. NAT

    D. Telnet

Monitoring and Optimizing IPSec

15. You have configured your users to use IPSec for communication with the legal department, but not for any other departments. The legal department is having difficulties getting to the network and every other department is operating normally. You know of no other significant difference between that department and the other departments. Which of the following tools would be the most useful for beginning your investigation?

    A. IPSECMON

    B. Network Monitor

    C. System Monitor

    D. Event Viewer

16. Which of the following describe ways in which you could use IPSECMON to troubleshoot communication? Choose all that apply.

A. Compare "Packets not Authenticated" to "Authenticated Bytes Sent" to see if any data is getting through.

B. Use IPSec to generate a log file and use this log file to compare results with a previously created baseline file.

C. Monitor the top pane to see if the needed Security Associations are being created.

D. Use IPSECMON with the Ping flag to put it into diagnostic mode.

17. Which of the following protocols might you see in Network Monitor when using IPSec?

A. ESP

B. AH

C. TCP

D. ICMP

LAB QUESTION

Over the weekend, you have implemented IPSec on your network, using Kerberos authentication. On Monday morning, one of your users is complaining that they can no longer get to their departmental file server. You have applied the "Secure Server (Require security)" to this server. What steps should you take to diagnose the problem? Identify the correct actions to take from the list below, and then place a number to the left of each step indicating the correct order of completing the step. Some steps may not be valid, and there is not necessarily a single correct order to perform these steps.

___ Confirm that the user's workstation is successfully logged in to the same domain as the server (or a trusted domain).

___ Confirm that the workstation can communicate with other servers that do not require IPSec.

___ Determine if other workstations in that department can access the server.

___ From the server, run IPSECMON, then have the user try to PING the server and see if the security association is being created.

___ From the user's workstation, turn on the IPSECMON automatic logging utility, and use TRACERT to view the path to the server.

___ Go to Event Viewer and see if IPSec events have been recently logged in to any of the three logs.

___ Physically walk to the server and see if you can TRACERT the user's workstation.

___ Remove all filter actions from the Security Policy used by both computers.

___ Try to PING 127.0.0.1 to confirm that the user's TCP/IP stack is operating correctly.

___ Use Network Monitor and observe the headers being set.

SELF TEST ANSWERS

Defining the Goals of IPSec on Your Network

1. ☑ **B, D.** Some encrypted data may be encrypted with a higher-level protocol such as SSL is correct because even though AH does not encrypt data, it is not incompatible with encryption provided by other protocols such as SSL. **D.** All of the routers in your organization are running Windows NT 4.0 is correct because IPSec packets can be routed through servers that do not support IPSec.

   ☒ **A** is incorrect because AH doesn't guarantee that data is encrypted (though ESP can provide this functionality). **C** is incorrect because NT 4.0 does not support IPSec.

2. ☑ **B, C, D.** The additional connections to the file server increase the processor load due to IPSec on the server, the clients and the server are using different authentication methods, and the increased network traffic could be causing an increased demand on the network segment on which the server is located. The additional encryption and authentication load placed on the server's processor may lead to increased response latency. The clients and server use the same authentication protocols. Finally, an overburdened segment could slow down responsiveness of the file server.

   ☒ **A** is incorrect because Windows 2000 Professional does support IPSec and downlevel Windows clients do not support IPSec.

3. ☑ **B, D.** The PPTP protocol supports MPPE to provide encryption, and L2TP supports IPSec for the same purpose. (Using L2TP without encryption is possible, but not recommended.)

   ☒ **A** and **C** are both incorrect. It is not possible to use the encryption protocols independent of the protocols used for tunneling.

4. ☑ **B.** In order to create a tunnel server for a VPN, you can use the wizard option to create a Virtual Private Network Gateway.

   ☒ **A, C,** and **D** are incorrect.

Installing and Configuring IPSec

5. ☑ **D.** When using transport mode security, most of the existing IP header is leveraged, and the few bytes that are changed (for example, the size and Time-To-Live) are excluded from the hash algorithms that are used to confirm the identity of the sender of the packet.

   ☒ **A** is incorrect because there are bytes that are altered. **B** is incorrect because there is not a new IP header added (although there is a new AH header added.) **C** is incorrect because most of the existing IP header information is preserved, and this is part of the reason transport mode requires less network resources than tunneling.

6. ☑ **A, B.** IPSec provides the strongest level of encryption and authentication for your Virtual Private Network. In order to create the virtual link, you need to use a tunneling protocol compatible with IPSec, and that protocol is L2TP.
☒ **C** is incorrect because PPTP uses MPPE as its encryption protocol, which is not as secure as IPSec. **D** is incorrect because IKE is not a tunneling protocol.

7. ☑ **A.** Transport mode is more appropriate than tunnel mode. When using the Windows 2000 servers as routers, you could use IPSec in either transport mode or tunnel mode, but transport mode will be faster and will cause fewer conflicts with administrative protocols.
☒ **B** and **C** are both incorrect because while it would be possible to use tunneling IPSec, it would be better to use transport mode. **D** is incorrect because both transport mode or tunneling could work in this scenario.

8. ☑ **C.** Because this IP address could vary, the tunnel endpoint should be identified by a DNS name so that no matter what the current IP name is the packet can be transmitted properly.
☒ **A** is incorrect because this option would result in IPSec tunneling not being enabled. **B** is incorrect because this option does not exist. **D** is incorrect because the IP address could change for the tunnel endpoint, and therefore the IPSec traffic would not be able to be transmitted.

IPSec Security Policies

9. ☑ **C and D.** Both of these are valid approaches for sharing a key across platforms. While the certificate authority is a much more scalable solution, the use of a string to protect the key exchange can be established more quickly and with less overhead.
☒ **A** is incorrect because you can only use this option when both computers are running Windows 2000 and are in a trusted domain. **B** is incorrect because this option does not exist.

10. ☑ **B** is correct because the traffic could be intercepted in either direction, so by checking the Mirrored check box you could force the data to be encrypted both ways. By using ESP on the packets, the user with an unauthorized installation of SMS would not be able to read the contents of the packets.
☒ **A** is incorrect because the data would only be encrypted in one direction. **C and D** are both incorrect because the My IP Address option would not successfully define the relationship between the two routing endpoints.

11. ☑ **A** is correct because even though the Secure Server policy is the most stringent of the default policies, it still accepts unsecured requests for secured communication.
☒ **B** and **D** are both incorrect because they are not the default option for the "Secure Server" policy. **C** is incorrect because this option does not exist.

IPSec Planning Considerations

12. ☑ **C.** SHA uses 160-bits to generate the authentication header, while MD5 only uses 128 bits.
☒ **B** is incorrect because MD5 uses fewer bits to generate the authentication header than SHA. **C** and **D** are both incorrect because SHA and MD5 are used to provide authentication, not encryption.

13. ☑ **C.** This new 120-bit key protocol would be much more secure than the 56-bit key used by DES. The 3DES protocol uses three different 56-bit keys, but this is not the same as a 168-bit key and is only marginally stronger than DES.
☒ **A** is incorrect because DES is weaker than 3DES. **B** is incorrect for the reasons articulated in the correct answer above. **D** is incorrect because these protocols would provide significantly different levels of security.

14. ☑ **B** and **D.** Both HTTP and Telnet are compatible with ESP in either transport or tunnel mode. (In fact, most of the protocols designed to initiate end user communication with a public Internet resource will be successful when used with IPSec.)
☒ **A** is incorrect because you would not use ESP and AH on the same packets (although ESP can be used to provide functionality that is quite similar to what AH provides). **C** is incorrect because this protocol requires information about the contents of the packets that are concealed when using ESP (although NAT can be used with IPSec when in tunnel mode).

Monitoring and Optimizing IPSec

15. ☑ **A.** IPSECMON is correct because the binary partitioning performed has indicated that it is very likely that the failure is occurring with IPSec and is not due to other failures on the network or the failure, and this tool will provide the most specific diagnostics of the issue.
☒ **B, C,** and **D** are all incorrect because they are general purpose diagnostic tools that would provide only high-level information about the connectivity issues. (If the initial thumbnail analysis that led to the investigation using IPSECMON is not helpful, the next most useful tool is probably Network Monitor, followed by Event Viewer. System Monitor is most useful in diagnosing degradation of performance, rather than total failure.)

16. ☑ **A, C.** The value of the IPSECMON lies largely with the capability to observe what is happening in real time, to identify ratios that seem out of line in the diagnostic statistics, and to observe how the Security Associations are created.

    ☒ **B** is incorrect because IPSECMON cannot create log files. **D** is incorrect because there is no Ping flag and no diagnostic mode. (IPSECMON is an optional parameter that identifies which machine to observe, and the only option available from within the application is to alter the refresh rate of the statistics.)

17. ☑ **A, C, D.** You might see ESP because packets encrypted with Encapsulating Packet Header are labeled with this protocol, and you might see TCP or ICMP because packets authenticated with AH are labeled with their underlying protocols.

    ☒ **B** is incorrect because packets authenticated with AH are not displayed as being sent with the AH protocol in Network Monitor. However, it is possible to observe the AH header inside these packets when you "unfold" the packets in Network Monitor.

LAB ANSWER

Diagnosing issues with IPSec can be very similar to diagnosing other network issues—you want to cut the problem into smaller and smaller pieces until you can isolate the exact location of the issue. Below is a list of steps you might use to diagnose the problem. It is not the only sequence possible, but it is organized to achieve this binary partitioning.

1. Determine if other workstations in that department can access the server. (This would be the first step to identify if the problem is with the workstation or with the server.)

2. Try to PING 127.0.0.1 to confirm that the user's TCP/IP Stack is operating correctly. (If the problem can be isolated to the workstation, network connectivity is frequently the next most common problem.)

3. Confirm that the workstation can communicate with other servers that do not require IPSec. (If the workstation does have network connectivity, the problem may be IPSec specific.)

4. Confirm that the user's workstation is successfully logged in to the same domain as the server (or a trusted domain). (Because you are using Kerberos, you must be in the same domain or a trusted domain.)

5. Physically walk to the server and see if you can TRACERT the user's workstation. (If the failure is closer to the workstation than to the server, switching directions can be a useful tactic to identify the point of failure.)

6. From the server, run IPSECMON, then have the user try to PING the server and see if the security association is being created. (If TRACERT confirms connectivity, then you can get clues from IPSECMON when attempting to initiate the authentication from the server.)

7. Go to Event Viewer and see if IPSec events have recently been logged in to any of the three logs. (If there were errors that you've missed, you might be able to find information here.)

8. Use Network Monitor and observe the headers being set. (If the steps above do not isolate the issue, you can start tracing the issue on a byte-by-byte basis. However, this is much more difficult and requires specific expertise.)

The following two steps would not be applicable to the debugging process:

■ From the user's workstation, turn on the IPSECMON automatic logging utility, and use TRACERT to view the path to the server. (There is no automatic logging utility associated with IPSECMON.)

■ Remove all filter actions from the security policy used by both computers. (Even if you were willing to compromise security on a production machine in this way, you can't remove all filter actions from a security policy.)

13

Network Management Strategies

A ll networks, including your Windows 2000 network, require a well thought-out design for the management of their networking services. And along with this well thought-out design, it is imperative that you develop reliable ways of comparing the current state of your network services with those in your original network management design plan.

CERTIFICATION OBJECTIVE 13.01

Understanding Network Management Processes and Procedures

With a well-executed network management design, you will be able to continually assess and respond to variances in your network design specifications. Therefore, it is vitally important that you work on your network services management strategy during the design phase of network implementation.

In this chapter, you will learn how to approach the management of networking services on your Windows 2000 network. Your primary goal during the design phase is to map out what networking services you wish to implement, and then determine how those networking services should perform. The design must also contain a mechanism to inform you what normal performance is, and a method to determine if a service is not performing to specifications. Finally, you should have in place a mechanism to correct problems and issues with networking services when they arise.

Creating the Network Services Management Plan

A functional network management plan will include procedures that your staff can use to quickly find and respond to network conditions that fall outside of what you consider acceptable in terms of functionality and performance. These management designs should include parameters for defining key aspects of the network management plan, and management policies and procedures that the administrative staff can use to detect and correct network services variances.

Network Management Strategies

In order to complete a cogent and effective network management plan, you need to consider the available strategies you can use to manage your networking services. These strategies will include methods for monitoring, reporting, analyzing, and acting upon the data collected on network behavior.

For example, a DNS server is of critical importance in Windows 2000 networks, and you need to be sure that the service is running efficiently. You must, in advance, determine what you believe defines an adequate level of performance for the DNS service. You then determine a method to detect when the DNS service fails to perform to the level of efficiency you defined, and come up with a plan to return the DNS service to the level of performance defined in your design. One way to measure this level of performance is to use the System Monitor, as seen in Figure 13-1.

Assigning Levels of Importance to Management Strategies

The most important consideration for your network management plan is how your staff will detect and respond to failures and variances in mission-critical services.

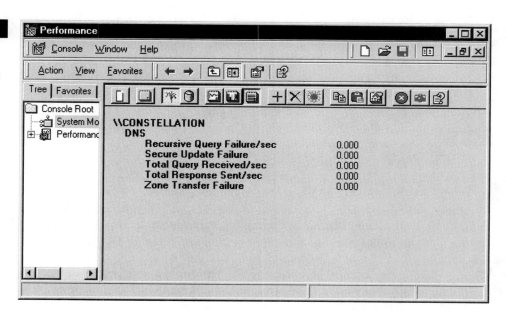

These mission-critical services are those services that, if they fail, could cost your company significant sums of money because of network downtime.

on the

Oob

Timely response to failure of mission-critical services is one of your foremost responsibilities as a network administrator or architect. Fault tolerance for all critical network services should be built into the network design, and not left as something for "someone else" to figure out after the rollout is completed.

An example of such a mission-critical situation would be the failure of the WWW service to start on your IIS 5.0 server. If you company runs an e-commerce site, the failure of the WWW service would mean that you would not be able to process any orders during the time the service is unavailable. You should therefore include a mechanism to inform you of this service's failure to start. The plan should also include what type of response, and the latency of the response, when this type of failure occurs.

After you have designed methods of detecting and responding to faults in your mission-critical services, your next step is to put in place a system of monitoring network services for *design compliance*. Design compliance refers to whether the actual performance of networking services matches what you set forth in your design. If the service is performing at a lower level than included in your design, the network service's performance is considered *noncompliant* or *variant*.

When putting together your network management plan, you need to consider how you will respond when network services deviate from design parameters. There are several ways you can design response strategies, including:

- ■ Reactive
- ■ Proactive
- ■ Manual
- ■ Automatic

Typically, when putting together your response strategy, you will use a combination of these approaches.

exam

Watch

Pay careful attention to the various types of response strategies. You will be presented with scenarios that will require an appropriate response strategy, and it will be up to you to know which strategy fits the network management solution best.

For example, suppose you include in your design a requirement that the WINS Server service should drop no more than one query/second. Any value over that would be considered noncompliant or variant. A proactive approach would include scheduling regular monitoring sessions to assess the performance of the WINS server. You could automate this process, and have the WINS service monitored once a week. You could accomplish this programmatically, rather than doing it manually, by starting the monitoring session interactively. You then would include in the design your response to when the WINS server starts dropping more than the expected number of queries.

Although we are focusing on network services management in this chapter, keep in mind that networking services do not exist in a vacuum. Your organization is likely to use a number of network-enabled applications, and those applications will depend on and influence the functionality of your network services. Therefore, you will also need to consider how different network-enabled applications will affect the performance of your network services.

Elements of Network Service Management Strategies

When putting together your network services management design document, you should include some basic elements in each design. Each management plan should include methods for:

- Responding to situations in which networking services behavior or performance falls outside of design tolerance.

- Monitoring the present status of the network, so that you can determine if networking services fall within the parameter of your design plan.

- Assessing when networking services will require modification or upgrade. This is usually accomplished via trend analysis.

Response to Service Noncompliance

A service variation is when the network service's level of performance falls outside the range of performance that is compliant with your design parameters. If the WINS Server service should stop responding to queries, you need to decide if someone should be informed, who should be informed, and when they should be informed. Should the response be automated? You can have the operating system attempt to restart the service automatically. Or, should you let the service remain stopped, and wait for an administrator to manually restart the service? The latter option could also have the administrator investigate the cause of the service interruption while at the machine.

Scheduled Monitoring and Comparison with Network Services Performance Design Parameters

The plan should include schedules and procedures for measuring the performance of network services. This will allow you to assess whether service performance is falling below the level you specified in your design.

For example, if you require the Web server to be able to respond to 5000 requests per minute, you will need to monitor the WWW service's performance on a regular basis, and compare the performance with what you expected the desired performance to be.

Projecting Network Service Performance and Trend Analysis

The design documentation needs to include specifications for measuring trends in network service performance, and a method to predict when resources will not meet design specifications. For example, if the WWW service on your IIS server is designed to handle a maximum of 5000 concurrent sessions, you will need to be able to project when the average or absolute number of sessions will exceed this value.

Putting It All Together

To implement these strategies, put together a list of procedures that will allow you to do the following:

- Acquire current status information about network services.
- Analyze the data you collect about the network services.
- Detail how and when responses to network service variances should be handled.
- Define trend analysis procedures that will allow you to respond proactively to situations that could lead to failure of network services.

For example, you might choose to use SNMP to monitor network service performance. The Simple Network Management Protocol provides you with a means to collect information on the current status of network services and devices. You will need to obtain SNMP network management software. Prior to purchasing the software, your team will need to review the SNMP Management products available and determine which one meets the requirements of the organization, based on monitoring and reporting features and the cost of the software. After obtaining SNMP Management software that can analyze your network data, include in the design the appropriate response to variations in network service performance. Finally, include a method of taking the collected data and performing a trend analysis to help identify potential weaknesses of service performance.

Designing Your Response Measures

As we discussed earlier, you will need a method to assess the current status of your network services. Examples of such status assessments would include whether a particular network service is offline, or if the service is being overwhelmed by requests that it cannot handle efficiently or on a timely basis. Some examples of situations that need some form of response include:

- Networking services fail to start, or becoming corrupted after successfully starting.

- Network services are available, but other network conditions make it impossible for service clients to communicate with the required network services.

- Network services are online, and network clients can access the network services, but the services fail to perform at the level predicated in the design documentation.

- Composite calculations of network services performance fail to meet design parameters.

What would be an adequate response plan for the failure of a mission-critical networking service? For example, you want to get immediate notification if power goes out on a network server. You can configure the server to notify users when it is on battery backup, and to provide information when the power is restored and the server is back on AC power again.

Each of these response measures should be included in your network management design plan. Each response methodology has a place where it is best applied. Remember that real-time processing and notification take more processor cycles and network bandwidth than proactive measures and trend analysis and disaster prevention.

How would you handle failures in client access to networking services? For example, you would like to be notified if clients on a particular subnet are not able to contact the SMTP server they use to send e-mail. You could configure rules on the e-mail clients to forward to you messages regarding failure to connect to the server. You may not want to do this on all stations, but you might select key stations on particular segments for forwarding this information.

You need to include response actions to cover the eventuality that network services fail to perform at the level stated in the design documentation. If your Web server has been optimized to provide service for 2500 concurrent connections, you need to be notified if average or total concurrent connection values exceed this number.

How will you respond to situations in which composite or "combined values" are exceeded? You may have a Web server farm that consists of three Web servers that use network load balancing. You want to make sure the average number of active sessions on each server is less than 2500. There is no System Monitor counter that allows you to measure this directly, so you need to schedule monitoring sessions on the servers and come up with the composite value. You can then take appropriate actions after making these calculations

Be aware of the most common and useful System Monitor counters, and in what circumstances they find their best use. Also know how to calculate indirect values based on the common System Monitor counters. The Windows 2000 Professional Resource Kit provides valuable information regarding performance monitoring.

The ultimate goal is to include methodologies in your design that will allow you to prevent service interruptions. This should be the primary concern during the network management design process.

Automate Service Responses to Fault and Performance Variations

In the event that a network service fault does occur, there should be a mechanism in place that will allow someone to know quickly that the fault has occurred, so that the issue can be quickly investigated.

While it is useful to have systems automatically respond and correct failures in system services, if no one is informed of the failure, a similar failure in the future cannot be prevented. Failure to notify reduces overall system fault tolerance and should be avoided. Make sure that there is a method in place that allows the system to inform someone—via e-mail, pager, or fax—that a fault condition has occurred.

Monitoring Network Services to Assess Variance from Design Specifications

In order to assess whether network services are performing at the level designated in your design document, you must have a monitoring infrastructure in place to assess design compliance. When you create the specifications for acceptable network services performance, you should include levels of exception.

The first level of exception would be considered the "warning" level, where network services performance begins to fall short of design compliance. The second level would reflect a more emergent situation, where immediate action needs to be taken to prevent a catastrophic event that would lead to major service disruption. As mentioned earlier, there are a number of different ways you can assess for design compliance. You can choose to measure network services performance on a manual basis, or you can automate the collection of network services performance data.

For example, in the manual approach, you would need to monitor the performance of the WINS server, and the number of dropped queries per second. You could schedule an administrator to manually start the System Monitor console once a week, and have him save a log of the monitoring session that can be analyzed later. Alternatively, you might want to automate the process, and schedule the Performance Logs facility to automatically start a monitoring session once a week, and then send an e-mail message to you after the process is complete.

on the **job** *Manual starting and stopping for performance monitoring and assessment is rare on an enterprise network, unless a specific fault has been identified and real-time analysis of data is required. In your network management design document, focus primarily on automated approaches and supplement the automated approaches with manual assessments.*

Both approaches have their advantages and disadvantages. The manual approach has the disadvantage of dedicating administrator time to the manual configuration and monitoring of the WINS server. However, an advantage of this method is that if there are severe variances apparent during the monitoring session, the administrator is able to respond to them immediately. The automated approach has the advantage of not requiring administrator time and attention, but has the disadvantage of allowing for the possibility that a critical situation is in development and may go unnoticed until it's too late.

In your network management design plan, you should include specifications for monitoring your network services, and for performing trend analysis on the data you collect. A trend analysis can provide valuable information regarding when a particular service needs to be reconfigured, or if hardware or software upgrades will be required in the future.

For example, when performing routing monitoring of your Web server, you configure the monitoring program to send you an alert when the number of concurrent connections is more than 2500 users. This is your threshold value. In addition, in your design plan, you estimate that the Web site will increase by 10 users/day over the course of six months. In order to assess the average increase in users/day, and to predict what the number of users will be in six months, you will have to analyze the accumulated data and create projections from it.

Methods of Monitoring for Design Compliance

There are three primary methods you can use to assess overall design compliance for network services and network devices:

- Manual testing methods with real-time network administrator or technician interaction with the network services software or network device
- Scheduled monitoring of selected network services
- Continuous monitoring of network services and devices

Interactive Testing   There are some aspects of the design and configuration of your network services and supporting network devices that cannot be tested in any way other than manually. In these circumstances, you will have to include manually testing routines to check on the health and status of these devices.

For example, you may have created a server cluster. In order to test whether the clustering software is working properly, you will need to manually disable one of the servers and then test whether the other server was able to take over processes assigned to the server cluster.

Scheduled Monitoring of Networking Services and Access Controls

You will need to include in the network management design plan a security configuration that determines who has access to configuration parameters of the network services and devices. It is extremely important that you consider who has access, and develop methods in advance to record who has access to the network services and devices on your network. This information is crucial in assessing who might be responsible for network failures and security breaches.

Because security configuration will change over time, you will need to include in your design who initially has access to configuration controls, and a method of tracking what changes take place in the security infrastructure over time. You can use tools such as showacls.exe (Figures13-2 and 13-3) or perms.exe that are included in the Windows 2000 Resource Kit, which will allow you to automate the process of auditing permissions on file, folders, registry key, or network services.

Other issues that should be in your network management design plan include:

- Service uptime

- Continuous service performance assessment

- Interservice communications performance assessment

The Microsoft Windows 2000 Server Resource Kit includes tools such as svcmon.exe and smconfig.exe to help monitor services. Figure 13-4 shows the Service Monitor Wizard Welcome page.

To assess the availability of a service, design your strategy to measure the uptime of both individual servers and services. The performance of a server providing a service begins to degrade as the client query rate increases. Monitoring

---

FIGURE 13-2

The showacls.exe program displays the permission to a folder

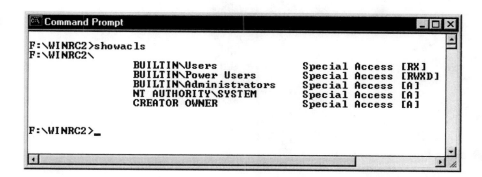

FIGURE 13-3

The showacls.exe program results can be piped to a text file for later analysis

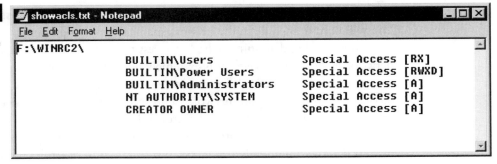

client-to-service interaction and processor performance gives an indication of when the specifications are being exceeded.

You must monitor interaction between services, such as replication between multiple WINS servers, or DNS-to-WINS query traffic, to ensure compliance with specifications. Your plan must include analysis of replication schedules, replication traffic, and service interaction traffic.

To measure service uptime, you can use the event logs and manually determine how long a service has been running by observing the times services start and stop

FIGURE 13-4

The smconfig.exe program is used to configure the Service Monitor (svcmon.exe) program

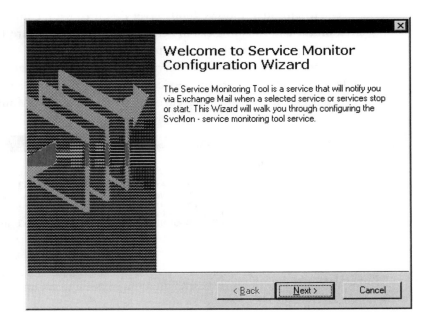

and ascertaining the percentage of the time the service was "supposed" to be up, based on when the service was supposed to start in relation to when the server starts and stops. You should also make a note of how long servers remain up in relation to the total amount of time the server should be in service.

In addition to the built-in tools such as Event Viewer, you may want to become familiar with some of the Windows 2000 Resource Kit tools such as uptime.exe, which can give information regarding how long the server and network services have been up.

The relationships between the networking services and the network clients they service should also be monitored and evaluated. This relationship may not be as straightforward as you might expect. For example, when a DNS server performs a WINS lookup, the DNS server becomes a client to the WINS networking service. You should monitor these interactions and typical network service client interactions, such as the DNS client and DNS server interactions.

Using Network Management Data for Trend Analysis

The data you collect is useful in determining which network services need immediate attention, and which ones need attention in the near future. These assessments are typically based on an initial comparison of the gathered performance with the parameters delineated in the network management design plan.

You should also include in the network management design a protocol to follow that allows you to see trends in network performance. For example, you find that average network utilization has been running about 19 percent, which is within your network design plans. With the value alone, you might think that there are no significant issues related to network utilization. However, if you were to chart the data in a way that would allow you to see trends in network utilization, you might find that the network would reach a saturation point within six weeks. If you could predict this circumstance, you could prevent downtime and poor network performance.

Trend Analysis

A variety of methods can be used to measure and anticipate changes over time. For example, the WINS database is a disk-based file that requires disk space. As time passes, this database will grow in size. You can perform weekly audits of the size of the WINS database, and include this information in an Excel workbook or Access database. You can then analyze the rate of change of the database size and easily project when the size of the database will reach a point where you'll either need to move it to another drive or volume, or replace the drive itself.

It may be wise to include in the design document parameters regarding the expected rate of growth for various networking services, and then set warning and critical levels of growth parameters. When acceleration of these parameters reaches a warning stage, you may want to monitor the service more closely and assess whether the projections are accurate. You should also consider what is a critical rate of acceleration, and include in the design a method of dealing with potentially limited resources quickly, before they run out.

Designing Event Notification Procedures

The design documentation needs to include explicit policies and procedures regarding how event notification will be carried out. You should include different methods of event notification depending on the level of importance of the event. For example, you need to be notified immediately, using all possible contact methods, in the event a server experiences a system STOP error. On the other hand, a more leisurely approach can be taken with events such as network utilization intermittently exceeding 30 percent. The more emergent the event, the more intrusive the notification process should be.

In order to get the kind of feedback you need, you should shape your management plan with the following objectives in mind.

How Will You Obtain the Current Status of Networking Services?

You could use the svcmon.exe program from the Resource Kit. It provides real-time monitoring of network services. When there is an interruption in service, a message will be sent to an account with an Exchange server. You can also use the services MMC snap-in to view the status of services on any machine on the network.

How Will You Analyze the Collected Data, and Ensure that Potential Fault Situations Are Recognized and Reported?

After collecting data from performance-monitoring sessions and log files, you can import the information into a spreadsheet or database engine. For example, you can use the database engine to query for the frequency of DNS name resolution failures, and compare that with the values in your design document.

EXERCISE 13-1

Collecting and Analyzing Data

You are the Help Desk Manager, and need to check the usage levels and capacity of disk drives on several servers in your computer room. You need this information to prepare documentation that supports your annual growth budget requirements. How would you collect the data, over what period would you collect data, and how would you analyze the data?

Suggested Answer:

One possible solution would be to run an instance of automated Performance Logs and Alerts on each server to collect data continuously, and to start a new file for every 500 kilobytes of collected data. You can write the data to files in .csv format, and then import the collected files into an Excel spreadsheet to produce the required report. For this type of report, data collected every 5-10 minutes would be sufficient.

How Will the Notification System Be Implemented? For real-time response requirements, you will need an automated notification system. Network management packages such as CA Unicenter or HP OpenView can provide these types of real-time assessment and notification via FAX, pager, telephone, and e-mail. Microsoft Systems management server can provide similar data. The design should include what applications you will use to collect and report the information, who will receive this information, and what that person should do with it.

CERTIFICATION OBJECTIVE 13.02

Understanding Service Reports and Data Analysis

Status reporting is a cornerstone of the network management plan. You must have a reliable method that will allow you to compare the current state of network services with those in the network management design plan. Any significant or nominal variation from that plan should be reported and assessed.

At a minimum, you should consider the following in your network management design plan:

1. Include a methodology for collecting information about the status of devices and services. Examples of a service would include the WINS Server service or the Browser service. The services infrastructure includes any hardware or software component on which the proper functioning of the service depends, such as computer hardware, hubs, bridges, switches, or routers.

2. An analysis protocol should be selected that works with the type of data collected, and the protocol should include ways to measure trends in the data. For example, you may be running the Folder Redirection service to redirect particular folders from the users' local machines to a central server. This service is highly dependent on available disk space on the servers that store the users' data. You can monitor the disk space usage on these server computers, bring that data into a spreadsheet or database, and predict when you should upgrade the storage capabilities of the server.

3. Include a standard response methodology for when network service performance falls outside of the values included in the network management design plan. Service variations include when a particular network service fails to start, or performs at a level lower than specified in your design documentation. An example would be when DNS queries are not being resolved reliably. The design documentation would include parameters such as processor usage, throughput on the network interface, and memory usage that should be checked to assess whether those components need to be upgraded or adjusted. The design document would also include steps to take if one or more of these components need to be changed.

Generating Information on the Status of the Services

The network management design plan should be thorough in its coverage of how information about network devices should be obtained. The network administrator's job will be to carry out the procedures and policies in this design. This process requires you to obtain information about individual network services and network conditions, and verify that client systems are able to properly communicate with the network services and devices. The design may need to include multiple tools in order to get an accurate picture of the network service's current status.

The following table describes some of the methods you can use to monitor and detect status information.

Information Source	Overview
Data collection strategies	There are two primary data collection strategies: centralized and distributed. In this chapter, we will investigate the advantages and disadvantages of each.
Tools and utilities	There are a number of tools and utilities that come with Windows 2000 that you can use to monitor and report on network activity. We will cover several command-line tools such as nbtstat, netstat, and pathping. You will also learn about GUI-based tools such as Network Monitor and System Monitor.
Performance Logs and Alerts	You can use the Performance console to access the System Monitor and Performance Logs and Alerts. These tools allow you to record the results of your monitoring sessions, and alert you when service performance falls outside of the accepted range.
Simple Network Management Protocol (SNMP)	You will learn about how you can use SNMP Management software and SNMP agents to collect and report data about network devices.
Event logs	Event logs provide you with a method for checking on service failures and abnormal service behavior after the fact. You will see how to use these in your network management design.
Scripting and programming solutions	You will get a high-level overview of some of the technologies included with Windows 2000 that allow you to automate data collection and response activity.
Windows Management Instrumentation (WMI)	Windows Management Instrumentation allows a programmer to create applications that can gather data and reports on it automatically. WMI is very helpful to application developers when they wish to design and create third-party network management software.

Network Data Collection Policies

The design of a network management data collection policy includes several different strategies the network administrators can use to collect data about the condition of network services. When designing the network services management data collection policies, keep in mind that this process can be very network and hardware intensive. The typical data collection session can generate large amounts of data. Normally, this data is not processed during collection, and systems must be in place to organize and give meaning to the collection data.

The goal is to provide meaningful information so network administrators can react appropriately to changes or variations in network services. The reaction may be immediate, such as when a server goes offline unexpectedly. Alternatively, the reaction may be planned, based on projections made from studying long-term trends. In either scenario, the data is first collected via logs or monitoring utilities. These tools and utilities must be configured to provide the appropriate data for analysis, and ideally, provide a means of initiating a response in the event of a fault.

Collecting Data

In a large networking environment, you are going to need to include in the design a way to collect data from locations far from the central point of IT management. Data in remote centers may or may not need to be collected and analyzed locally before being sent to the central network information center for your organization. You will also need to consider how data will make it to individuals responsible for taking real-time action for fault situations.

If you are designing a network management plan for an organization that spans multiple physical locations, you will need to consider how to get the data from remote locations to your network information center:

- **Collecting data via established network infrastructure**   In this scenario, the data is transferred from the site at which it is collected to a central network management facility. This setup uses the established network infrastructure; therefore, any bandwidth dedicated to these functions will impact network performance as a whole. This is sometimes referred to as *in-band* data collection.

- **Collecting data via external network connections**   In this scenario, you create network connections that are outside of the normal data transfer network. An example of this might be an ISDN RAS connection between the data collection points and the central data collection facility. This is sometimes referred to as *out-of-band* data collection.

Centralizing the Collected Data

In a centralized data collection scheme, all data collected at all sites is transferred to a centralized data collection center. This location can be a single computer or group of computers running network management software—it is typically a network management station that runs a set of network management tools and programs. The advantage of a centralized network data collection system is that all network management data is collected and analyzed at a central site, which simplifies access. The primary drawback of such a technique is that if the data travels in-band, it has the potential for adversely impacting network performance. In addition, if the in-band infrastructure fails, you cannot collect any more data. In the event of a network failure, it is even more critical that you have access to network management data, which would not be available when the in-band channels are down.

Because of the mission-critical nature of network management data collection during these periods of network failure, it is important to include in the design an out-of-band solution, such as an analog or ISDN connection that is outside of normal network communication channels. You would use these alternate access schemes to collect data that would be otherwise inaccessible because of in-band network failure. This type of configuration would be employed when you have multiple sites for which you want to collect data. Information is gathered at each site and sent to a central monitor location via this dial-up interface, rather than being returned to the central location via normal data network connections.

Decentralized Data Collection

Instead of using a centralized data monitoring solution, you may decide that a decentralized data collection approach would fit your organization better. In this model, data is collected and stored at the remote locations, and would be analyzed and acted upon at the remote locations. Remote locations may provide data on a periodic basis to a central data clearinghouse facility, but the majority of the data collection, analysis, and response is done at the remote site, with perhaps only summarized data sent to the central facility.

The decentralized model has the advantage of allowing local engineers the chance to collect and analyze the data on a timely basis. Since local personnel have a more intimate understanding of their local infrastructure, the insight they can lend to the data analysis provides a powerful advantage. Remember that, in general, a decentralized approach is much more efficient for most business processes, and also leads to lower overhead and increased efficiency. The disadvantages of this option are that there may not be local engineers to work with the data, and that there would be costs to add them if they were not already in place.

Notification of Fault Situations

There are several types of network management data that you can collect. Data that you collect for long-term trend analysis can be collected on a continuous or periodic basis. Data that you collect on an ongoing basis may need to be acted upon immediately in order to prevent a costly service or network failure.

There are several ways you can collect data and allow for event notification:

- Performance logs and alerts
- Individual application service event notifications
- SNMP Management solutions

Performance Logs and Alerts Events

In the Performance console, you can use the Counter Logs and the Alerts node to track and report on network service and general network conditions in real time. Figure 13-5 shows the Alerts node with several Alerts configured for network reporting.

Figure 13-6 shows some of the configuration options available in one of the configured Alerts on this server.

Application-Specific Service Monitoring

Individual applications may include tools for monitoring the health and status of the services they provide. You can take advantage of these built-in service monitors to collect real-time data and event notification. Application-specific server monitors can also perform actions such as restarting the service and starting other programs in the event of a service fault situation.

You can also use the svcmon.exe program that comes with the Windows 2000 Server Resource Kit. Using this utility, you can monitor any service you like, on any computer on the network. When an interruption of service occurs, the svcmon.exe program will send an e-mail message to an Exchange Mail account.

An example of event generation after a change in status of a network service might include sending an administrative alert when a computer on the network experiences a Critical Stop Error (bluescreen). This event is generated automatically, and allows support personnel to respond to the error condition in real time.

Unprocessed information is data that has not been sent through any sort of filter. For example, you can use Network Monitor to collect information about all packets that traverse the network segment. If you run the monitoring session for an extended period

FIGURE 13-5

The Alerts node
and several
configured alerts

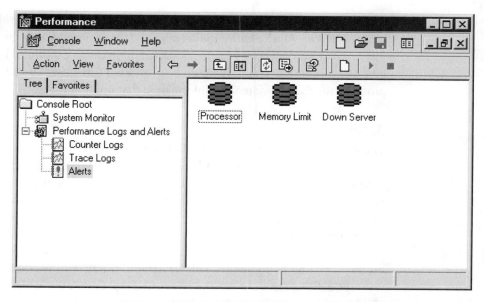

FIGURE 13-5

The Alerts node
and several
configured alerts

FIGURE 13-6

Details of a
Down Server
alert

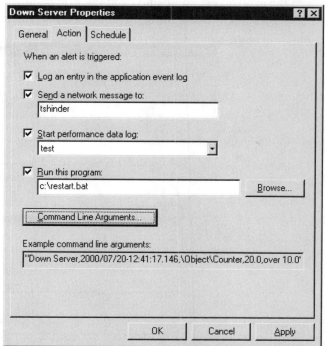

of time, you will collect an enormous amount of data, only some of which you may be interested in. An alternative to this might be to use filters during the data collection phase, where you only collect network packet information exchanged between a defined group of computers. This data would be considered "processed" because the filter processes the data and filters out information that is not of interest.

SNMP Events

You can use the Simple Network Management Protocol to assist in notification of significant network events. When you use an SNMP Agent and Management Station combination to collect and report information about network events, you can design a very effective network management plan. You can use Trap Messages to have the Agent automatically inform the Management Station in the event of a critical event. Figure 13-7 shows an example of Trap configuration.

An SNMP trap is a message initiated by the SNMP Agent software that resides on the computer being monitored. By default, the Windows 2000 SNMP Agent has no traps defined. You can use the Event to Trap Translator, which can be accessed via the evntwin.exe command from the Run command. Figure 13-8 shows the configuration interface for the Event to Trap Translator.

FIGURE 13-7

Configuring trap destinations

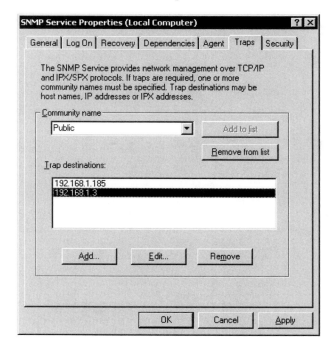

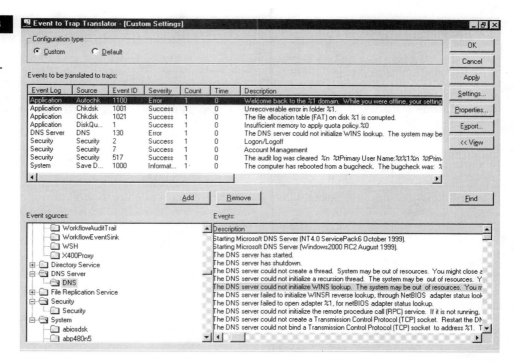

Windows 2000 "Out of the Box" Utilities

Windows 2000 comes with a number of programs and utilities that you can use
to perform basic network management and analysis. The following table describes
some of these tools.

Tool	Function
Network Monitor	Network Monitor allows you to evaluate packets as they travel across the network. NetMon is a network analyzer that can also assess the level of network utilization and analyze traffic patterns. The version of NetMon that comes with Windows 2000 out of the box allows you to assess traffic coming into and leaving the monitoring stations. The full version of NetMon is available with Systems Management Server, and this version allows you to put the NIC in *promiscuous* mode. In promiscuous mode, the NIC will be able to assess all traffic on the network.

Tool	Function
Netdiag	Netdiag is an all-purpose tool for assessing the current TCP/IP and general network configuration of a particular computer. Netdiag is the "Swiss army knife" of troubleshooting a PC's network configuration. The tool can run many different tests and save the results to a file. You must install netdiag by extracting it from the .cab file in the Support Tools folder on the Windows 2000 CD-ROM.
Ping	The ping tool allows you to check basic connectivity information between computers. Ping sends out an ICMP Echo Request message to a destination computer, and if the destination computer is able to receive it and send it back successfully, then you know that you have basic connectivity.
Tracert	Tracert allows you to assess characteristics of the routers in the path from the source to the destination computer. This tool sends a series of ICMP Echo Request messages to routers along the path to the final destination. By examining the Round Trip Times for these PINGS, you can assess congested or failed routers along the path.
Pathping	The pathping tool allows you to assess the state of the routers in the path from the source to destination, and to characterize the link between the routers. The pathping tool uses an algorithm that tests both the "fast path" and the "slow path" for packet handling by routers. Using this algorithm, the pathping command can assess the current status of routers and the links that separate them.
Nslookup	Nslookup provides a way to assess the integrity of a DNS zone database, and to troubleshoot host name resolution on the network or on the Internet.
Netstat	The netstat utility allows you to assess the nature of all inbound and outbound connections on a particular computer. You can see what ports are open and which ones are currently active.
Nbstat	Nbtstat provides statistics centered on NetBIOS over TCP/IP. Use this tool to assess problems with NetBIOS applications and connectivity problems.

Collecting Network Data

There are many different applications you can use to collect network data. The Windows 2000 built-in tool, System Monitor, provides a couple of options for collecting network service data on your network.

One way you can use System Monitor is to run the System Monitor application on each machine you wish to monitor. You would save the log files, or configure alerts on each of these machines. Another option is to use a central System Monitor computer, and monitor all machines and devices you are interested in from a single machine.

Remember, using a centralized collection system will have a negative impact on your network performance. You should assess the impact of a centralized collection process prior to implementing it. Network monitoring can provide valuable network utilization data to aid you in your assessment.

Server Data Collection

There are hundreds of different counters available that allow you to assess the current performance of your servers. You must include in your design document what performance parameters are worth measuring, and then how those counters should be configured in terms of logging and alerting.

Windows 2000 includes several logs that you can use "out of the box," one of which is the System Overview log. Figure 13-9 shows some of the characteristics of this log.

Collecting Network Data

Collecting network performance data can be done with either Network Monitor or System Monitor. In order for System Monitor to collect network performance data on

FIGURE 13-9

The System Overview Properties dialog box

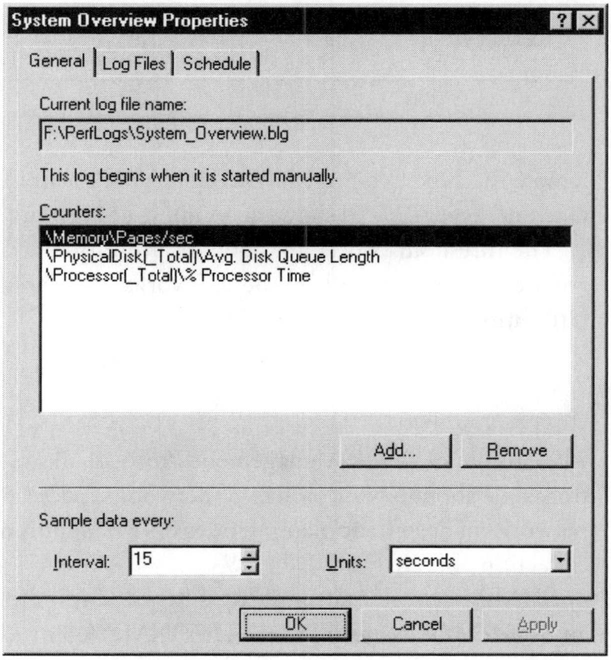

FIGURE 13-10

Using Network Monitor to collect network statistics

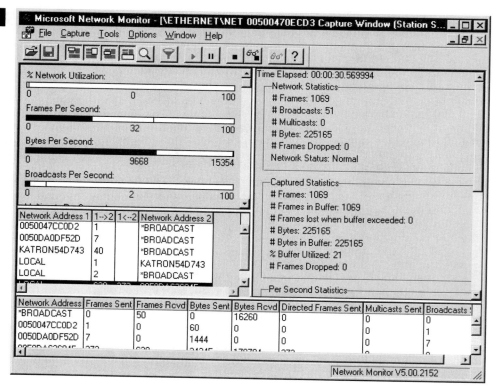

remote machines, you must have the Network Monitor Agent installed on that machine. Figure 13-10 shows an example of Network Monitor collecting network data.

The threshold you set on network utilization is dependent on your network architecture. On most Ethernet networks, you should keep the %Network Utilization down to less than 30 percent.

SNMP

The Simple Network Management Protocol allows you to collect voluminous data from and about a wide variety of network services and devices. Every enterprise-level network management plan includes SNMP solutions as a way to automate data collection and analysis.

SNMP network management is dependent on the services of an *SNMP Agent* and an *SNMP Management system.* The SNMP Agent software is installed on the network devices and computers that you wish to monitor. The SNMP Management station collects information gathered by the SNMP Agent. The SNMP Agent uses *Management Information Bases (MIBs)* to determine what information is collected from the network device or computer.

The SNMP Agent gathers information, but does not send this automatically to the SNMP Management system. The SNMP Management system must send queries to the SNMP Agent to access the collected data. The only time an SNMP Agent will initiate an unsolicited communication with an SNMP Management system is when the SNMP Agent sends a trap message. You must manually configure the SNMP Agent to send trap messages, and you must configure what events should trigger a trap message.

Using the Event Log to Collect Services Data

You can use the Event Log to collect information about network services running on a particular computer or group of computers. From a single management station, you can attach to any computer on the network and access the entries in its Event Log.

Event Logs, by their very nature, are difficult to analyze in their "raw" state. You can export Event Log entries into a file, and then import that file into a spreadsheet or database program. A superior approach would be to purchase third-party solutions that automate the process of Event Log data collection and analysis.

Figure 13-11 shows an example of raw Event Log data.

Event Viewer allows the examination of logs for information about hardware, software, system problems, and security events. Event Viewer can export the logs as files in various formats for analysis with tools such as Microsoft Excel. Figure 13-12 shows some data imported into an Excel spreadsheet.

Analyzing the Collected Data

After you collect data using either an SNMP Management station or the Windows System Monitor, you need a way to analyze that data. You can collect the data via log files that store the results of your monitoring session. However, the log files alone contain data in an unorganized and random arrangement. In order for you to turn data into information, you need to process it and give it a logical structure that is easy to view and interpret.

There are several ways to do this. You can take the log files saved by the monitoring application and manually import them into a spreadsheet or database

FIGURE 13-11

Event Log
information

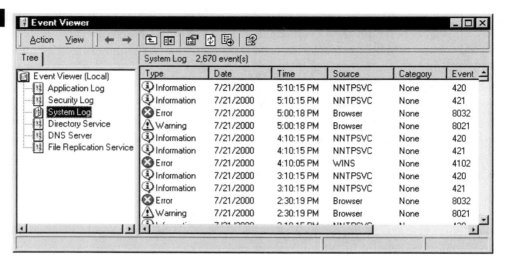

application. Or, you could use a program that will be able to scan the data in the log files, and automatically organize it for you.

Data Analysis

After collecting data, you will need to select a method to analyze it. Data analysis options vary from the very simple, such as the manual inspection of data, to the very complex, such as an industrial-strength SNMP-based management solution such as HP Overview or CA Unicenter.

FIGURE 13-12

Event Log data
imported into
Excel

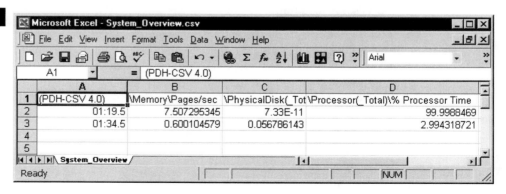

CertCam 13-2

EXERCISE 13-2

Monitoring Critical Systems

You are a consultant hired to provide a monitoring system for critical services for an organization with five locations. The organization has support staff only at the head office. WAN link usage between the sites is a major concern. How would you monitor remote sites and collect the data?

Suggested solution:

This situation requires out-of-band data collection. One possibility is to poll the remote sites by using a demand-dial routing modem connection. This could be automated by using a script. By using an out-of-band mechanism, such as a dial-up or dedicated ISDN line, you can collect data at each site without having an adverse impact on in-band network performance. You can use a centralized monitoring model by implementing an out-out-band ISDN dedicated connection that collects data continuously and reports it to a central network information center. You could also implement a decentralized reporting system, where the data is collected and processed locally, and then use an out-of-band dial-up connection to receive the processed data.

Manual Inspection of Status   The low-tech way to analyze data is to "eyeball" it, or submit it to manual inspection. An example of such manual inspection would be to examine the raw log files, such as shown in Figure 13-13.

FIGURE 13-13

Manual inspection of a log file

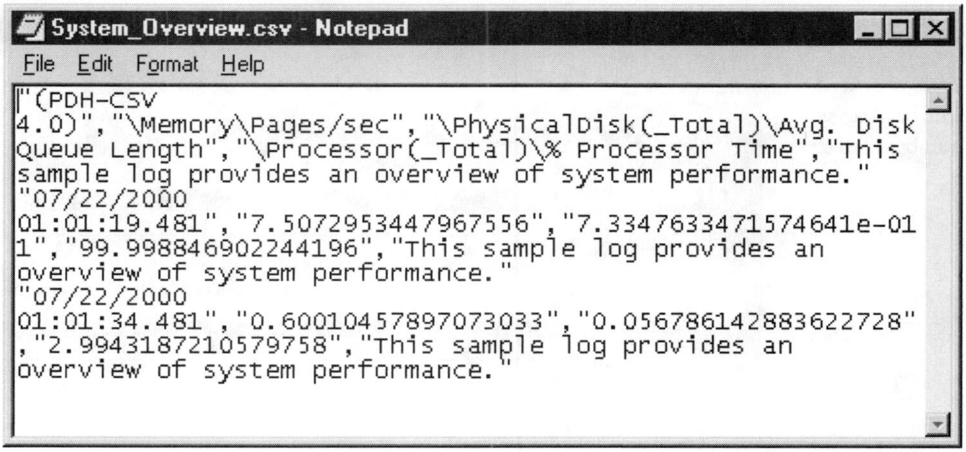

```
System_Overview.csv - Notepad                          _ □ ×
File  Edit  Format  Help
"(PDH-CSV
4.0)","\Memory\Pages/sec","\PhysicalDisk(_Total)\Avg. Disk
Queue Length","\Processor(_Total)\% Processor Time","This
sample log provides an overview of system performance."
"07/22/2000
01:01:19.481","7.5072953447967556","7.3347633471574641e-01
1","99.998846902244196","This sample log provides an
overview of system performance."
"07/22/2000
01:01:34.481","0.60010457897073033","0.056786142883622728"
,"2.9943187210579758","This sample log provides an
overview of system performance."
```

Excel   Microsoft Excel is a spreadsheet program that allows you to import delimited text-based data files into a spreadsheet format. You can even create charts and graphs based on the data contained in the spreadsheet.

Microsoft Access or Microsoft SQL Server   Database programs offer the highest level of flexibility and power for your data analysis tasks. Programs such as SQL Server or Microsoft Access allow you to import data collected by a management station, and then analyze it depending on the tools available to the database program. Figure 13-14 shows raw text data imported into an Access table.

Third-Party Solutions   The richest set of features will be found with third-party products that can provide detailed data collection and reporting capabilities. The are a number of excellent network management suites available. Figure 13-15 is an example of the Tivoli Enterprise Network Management Station.

Choosing a Response Strategy

The time it takes to return a network service or device to normal operation is dependent upon the time taken to detect and complete your response to the failure. Your design goal is to keep at a minimum the time it takes to detect and respond to service variations. You can meet this goal by designing into your plan automated and manual response approaches.

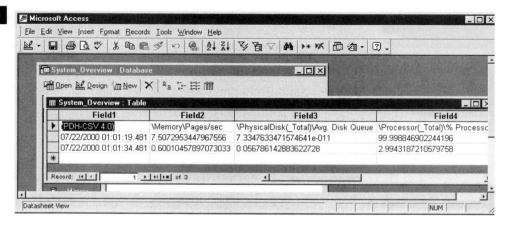

FIGURE 13-14

Data imported into an Access database table

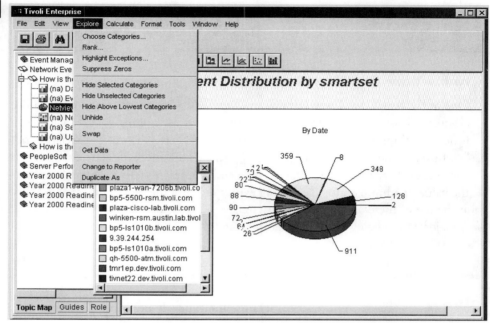

FIGURE 13-15

User interface for the Tivoli Enterprise SNMP Management station

The status information collected can contain data on service variations ranging from critical failures to capacity-planning information or trend analysis with noncritical response requirements.

You can configure services to respond automatically to failure in a number of ways. You can have the service notify an available technician, or have the service restart itself. The services can even be installed on a Microsoft server cluster, so if one of the servers fails, the other server in the cluster will take over.

Reactive Response Strategies

Reactive response strategies depend on the variation or failure of the monitored service before eliciting action. For example, if the WINS server fails to answer WINS database queries, you must wait for someone to notice that he or she is unable to resolve NetBIOS names, or for the service to notify you that something is awry.

The following event notifications can be thought of as reactive, because notification takes place after the fault or variation has occurred:

■ Review of Event Logs or Performance Logs

FROM THE CLASSROOM

Know Your End-User Applications

One of the issues that I often deal with in the classroom is new administrators who know little or nothing of what they consider to be "end-user" applications, such as Excel, Word, and Access. I try to reinforce the purpose and the value of administrators becoming expert at the use of these office productivity tools. A major part of being a network administrator and network architect is creating and delivering reports of network data and performance. There is a strong correlation between an administrator's success at documenting and presenting information in a compelling way and the rate of upward mobility of that administrator's career.

—Thomas W. Shinder, M.D., MCSE, MCP+I, MCT

- End-user complaints about poorly performing services
- Automated notification systems via e-mail

Responding Proactively to Analyzed Data

Proactive management strategies define procedures aimed at preventing variances or faults. Proactive network management strategies aim at prevention, rather than response. In order to accomplish this goal, data is collected over a long period of time, and trend analyses are carried out in order to determine patterns or trends in the data.

The following status information would be suitable for proactive responses:

- **Server performance monitoring**   Performance analysis can be performed using a tool such as System Monitor. When conducting a monitoring session, you can save the information to a log. After the log data is collected, you can create projections for what the expected performance will be at some future date.

- **Network device or service analysis**   Service analysis is related to performance of a specified service, rather than a computer component such as processor load or memory status. You can analyze the performance of a service, such as the WINS Server service, by using System Monitor to collect data about how efficiently the service is performing certain tasks, such as NetBIOS name queries and NetBIOS name registrations.

- **Network traffic analysis** You can use a protocol analyzer, such the Microsoft Network Monitor, to assess the status of segment traffic patterns. If it appears that the average network utilization is over 30% on a particular segment for an extended period, you will need to consider infrastructure upgrades.

- **Interface overload** You can use an SNMP Management station and Agent to collect data regarding server and router congestion status. If it appears that the network devices' interface is working at its limit for an extended period of time, you should consider upgrading the network interface, or adding more interfaces.

- **Capacity planning trends** Trend analysis takes advantage of historical data collected in the log files from monitoring sessions. As you collect your data, you should import the data into a spreadsheet or database application that will allow you to map out your data and assist you in trend analysis. By viewing consistent trends, you will be able to avoid disasters.

- **Service workload simulation** You can test how services will respond to a defined load by simulating high stress conditions and then measuring how the server or services respond.

Which Strategy to Use?

The following table elaborates on the similarities and differences between reactive and proactive strategies.

Use a Proactive Response Strategy If:	Example
Prior warning of capacity limitations and performance failures is essential.	You have a database file that must be limited to a certain size. If it exceeds this maximum optimal size limit, database queries will suffer. You can use trend analysis to predict when the database will exceed its optimal size, and take action before the event actually takes place.
Downtime must be minimized.	The DNS Server service is critical on a Windows 2000 network. You should proactively perform network-monitoring sessions on a regular basis in order to assess that the DNS Server service is performing within acceptable performance parameters.

Use a Reactive Response Strategy If:	Example
Some downtime can be tolerated.	Some system services, such as the Exchange Chat service, are not mission critical. There can be a period of downtime that will not adversely affect the company business. A reactive strategy would include an automated notification when services become unavailable.
Redundancy is built in to the services.	Some services, such as Microsoft Cluster Server, have redundancy built in. When one server becomes unavailable, another computer takes over. A message should be sent automatically to an administrator who can investigate the problem.

CERTIFICATION OBJECTIVE 13.03

Planning Service Interaction and Resource Strategies

Network services such as WINS, DNS, and DHCP must often communicate important information with one another over the network. For example, when a WINS client receives new IP addressing information from a DHCP server, that WINS Client must register its new IP addressing information with a WINS server. A DNS server may need to communicate with the WINS server to obtain IP addressing information about that same client.

These networking service interactions are common on Microsoft networks. In this section, we'll look at some methods you can employ that optimize their interaction.

Combining Network Services

You can effectively combine network services to improve networking service performance and reduce overall network traffic due to networking service interactions. Combining network services should be part of the network management design plan.

For example, a common interaction between network services is seen between the Dynamic DNS Server and the DHCP server. On Windows 2000 networks, a DHCP server can be configured to automatically update the Host (A) Record and

Pointer (PTR) record of computers that receive IP addressing information from the DCHP server. When the DHCP and Dynamic DNS services are on different computers, a delay will occur as the communication is conducted over the network.

If you were to place both DNS and DHCP services on the same computer, there would be no delay due to network lag times. The services will communicate with each other directly on the same machine. This has the combined effect of increasing the speed of Interservice communications and reducing the amount of bandwidth required for the services to interact.

You can also benefit from placing the WINS Server service and the DNS Server service on the same computer. DNS often needs to communicate with WINS in order to perform WINS lookups. When these two services are on the same computer, the delay and network bandwidth utilization that would otherwise be required is obviated!

Caveats to Combining Networking Services

While there are advantages to combining networking services, you also must be careful regarding how you combine these services. If you install networking services that compete for the same hardware resources, they can significantly slow down the entire system's functioning, and lead to a performance degradation to the extent that no gains would be realized by combining the services.

You can categorize these services as: Disk Bound, Memory Bound, or Processor Bound. Each of these categorizations reflect the primary hardware resource a particular network service demands in order to function optimally. WINS is a Disk Bound network services, DHCP is primarily a Processor Bound service, and DNS is a RAM and Disk Bound service. Network applications such as Exchange Server and SQL Server demand high utilization of RAM, Disk, and Processor cycles.

If you install networking services and applications that compete for the same hardware resources, the effect of the contention will be to reduce the performance and reliability of the contending networking services. In order to circumvent this, you should install more RAM, more processors, or faster disk subsystems. For network applications such as Exchange or SQL Server, placement on separate computers is the best plan of attack.

Designing a Network Management Resource Strategy

Closely aligned with the subject of combining network services is the concern over planning your network management resource strategy. The primary reason that you would want to combine networking services on the same machine is to conserve networking and computing resources.

You network management resource strategy should be based on the results of monitoring sessions you have carried out over multiple monitoring sessions. After completing these sessions, you need to move the data into a database or spreadsheet program that can perform a trend analysis. This allows you to assess whether or not the measures you have taken have led to a salutary result. It will also allow you to assess whether you need to upgrade devices or services.

EXERCISE 13-3

Designing a Network Resource Strategy and Combining Network Services

You are the network administrator for a growth company that has been challenged to keep up with the hardware and software requirement to maintain its network infrastructure. You have noticed during your monitoring sessions that network resources appear adequate to meet the demands of the organization, but then after a few weeks or months, network bandwidth becomes challenged, and WINS, DNS, and DHCP performance parameters begin to suffer and fall outside of tolerance levels included in the network management design document.

How would you approach this problem and prevent network utilization issues from becoming a focal point of user complaints?

Suggested Answer:

You should assess the networking services infrastructure on a periodic basis, and then after several monitoring sessions, put together a trend analysis graph. Check to see if there are any reliable or predictable trends to the growth of network service utilization. After determining the growth rates of network services demands, determine the day or week where they will fall out of tolerance. Then, proactively make changes to the networking environment. When you make these proactive changes, the issues will never have a chance to come to fore, and the infrastructure will always be up to the extant challenges.

After several months of monitoring and planning, create a document that can be incorporated into the yearly budget so that the costs of upgrading and reconfiguring networking services can be included in the overall cost design for the organization.

CERTIFICATION SUMMARY

In this chapter, you learned about methods you can use to manage your network infrastructure. Network management procedures should be built into your design plan. In order to optimize network performance, you need to consider what your acceptable level of performance is for the variety of network services you have deployed. You learned that after the basic requirements for network performance have been established, your job is to develop a means to monitor networking services. You saw that this can be done in real time using a program such as svcmon.exe, or with a variable degree of latency using performance monitoring sessions.

You learned how to create a response plan for when network service performance falls outside the boundaries of acceptable performance. In addition, you learned that you can forestall problems related to limited computer resources for following trends, and then project when resources will need to be augmented to support your network design. You learned that a proactive approach included in the design documentation will prevent problems with network functionality, and will prescribe an efficient response protocol when error conditions do arise.

You also learned about strategies you can use to collect and analysis network data. By knowing these strategies and how they are implemented, you can work them into your network design plan.

You learned about the differences, advantages, and disadvantages of centralized and distributed data collection and analysis techniques. You saw what some of the valuable tools are that you can use to collect and analyze network data, and how performance logs and alerts can help in the data reporting and response design.

We discussed some aspects of the Simple Network Management Protocol, and how you can use it to collect and analyze large amounts of network data in an automated fashion. You saw how SNMP Management solutions offer the richest collection of options available for network management.

TWO-MINUTE DRILL

Understanding Network Management Processes and Procedures

❑ In order to assess a network service's compliance with design specifications, you must include methods to measure performance in the network management design document.

❑ The network management design plan must include a list of parameters that are considered acceptable for all network services. This list is compared to measured values.

❑ A network management design document must include methods used to respond to variances from acceptable performance as defined in the design document.

Understanding Service Reports and Data Analysis

❑ Be sure to include a series of response measures in your network management design. Administrators should be able to follow instructions on how to respond to situations based on information contained in the network management design plan.

❑ Remember that responses can be reactive and proactive. The ideal design will contain both types of response measures.

❑ Learn how to use office productivity applications. Tools such as Excel or Access can analyze data collected during routine monitoring sessions.

Planning Service Interaction and Resource Strategies

❑ One way to improve network performance is to combine networking services. This can reduce the amount of time it takes for networking services to communicate with each other, and reduce the amount of network bandwidth required for services intercommunication.

❑ Be careful when combining network services. Avoid combining networking services that compete for the same hardware resources.

❑ Your network management resource strategy design plan should include methods for assessing whether your networking services performance parameters fall within tolerance levels. Use trend analysis to make this assessment and plan to proactively correct problems.

SELF TEST

The following questions will help you measure your understanding of the material presented in this chapter. Read all of the choices carefully, as there may be more than one correct answer. Choose all correct answers for each question.

Understanding Network Management Processes and Procedures

1. You are the network architect in charge of designing a Windows 2000 network that includes network services such as WINS, DNS, and DHCP. Because each of these network services is pivotal to your network operations, you need to include in your design document acceptable service performance and notification of variations in service performance. Which of the following might be included in a well-designed network management plan?

    A. The WINS Server service will be monitored once a year using the Performance Monitor. The results of the monitoring session will be saved to an Excel workbook. If there is a failure of the WINS Server service, you should look at the results gathered in the Excel workbook and decide what to do about the problem at that time.

    B. The DHCP service will be monitored in real-time using an SNMP Management program. The data will be stored in a database maintained by the SNMP Management program, which will automatically generate charts and graphs for later review. The program has been configured to flag error conditions in the DHCP Server services it is monitoring so that when a network administrator reviews the logs, he will be able to easily find the problem machines. If a problem is found, the administrator will investigate the issue and come up with a response based on his personal experience.

    C. The DNS service will be monitored by an administrator who periodically runs the Task Manager. If the administrator finds that the DNS service appears to be using too much memory or a large amount of processor time, he should confer with the administrator one level up in seniority to assess what the appropriate response might be.

    D. All network services will have predetermined levels of performance included in the design documentation. An SNMP Management system will be used to provide virtually real-time monitoring of all networking services. The program will be configured to log events that fall outside of the predetermined performance levels, and an e-mail and pager message will be sent to at least two administrators. The design will also include the procedure the administrators will use to resolve problems with networking services. In addition, if there is no resolution to the problem in the design document, a procedure will be defined regarding the process of escalating the problem for resolution.

2. Your network is becoming bogged down due to excessive status reporting information being delivered over a WAN link. What solution would help correct this situation?

   A. Use QoS to give priority to the network management traffic.

   B. Install additional routers between the network management station and the monitored devices.

   C. Use an ISDN line to connect directly to the monitored stations.

   D. Use an e-mail solution to collect network data.

3. Which of the following would you would include in your network management design plan? (Choose all that apply.)

   A. Simple Network Management Protocol

   B. AOL Instant Messenger

   C. The Windows 2000 Performance Monitor

   D. Microsoft Access 2000

4. Your network is being overtaxed, and monitoring sessions show that excessive data is being transferred from the aol.com domain. What can you do to solve this problem?

   A. Create a newsletter and let users know how to efficiently use AOL.

   B. Make an addition to the corporate network policy that states that AOL use on the network will not be tolerated and will be grounds for dismissal.

   C. Install a firewall and filter out AOL port numbers and domain names.

   D. Do nothing. AOL is part of key business functions, and all employees should have unlimited access to AOL.

5. You have been hired to assess the network management design of a medium-sized company spread across five locations. The central office is in Laramie, Wyoming. There are four regional locations in Carson City, Nevada; Roseburg, Oregon; Las Cruces, New Mexico; and Redding, California. All of the company's technical support and engineering personnel are located at the central office in Laramie. All the remote sites are connected to the main office via 128k dedicated ISDN lines in a Virtual Private Network (VPN) configuration. The company is growing, and these dedicated WAN links are now at capacity for data transfer around the clock. What sort of network management design would you recommend to this company?

   A. Set up network management stations at all sites. Have the data processed and analyzed locally at each site. After local analysis, have the data sent to the central office for trend analysis and archiving.

B. Set up a central network management station in the Laramie office, and then collect data for all sites via the established WAN Links in real time. Process and analyze the data as it is received from the remote sites.

C. Set up RAS Servers at each network location and maintain an open connection to each site via a 28.8Kbps link so that you can gather network management information in real time. You can then process and analyze the data as it is received from the remote sites in real time.

D. Set up RAS Servers in each network location and schedule a 28.8Kbps dial-up session to obtain network statistics that can be processed and analyzed at the central office.

6. Your business consists of two offices in cities located about 150 miles apart. You would like to connect these offices in the most cost-efficient way possible. You have been able to obtain two computers, both Pentium II 300 machines with 128MB of RAM. You wish to install Windows 2000 on each machine and make them gateways for each network. What is the best solution for this company?

A. Make each gateway a VPN server and use L2TP/IPSec as the tunneling and security protocol.

B. Make each gateway a VPN server and use PPTP/MPPE as the tunneling and security protocol.

C. Use demand-dial routing and configure the servers to dial up a direct connection to the other server when requests for the remote network ID are received.

D. Install an ISDN line to recreate a dedicated connection between the offices.

7. You run a consulting business that services small offices of fewer than 100 computers. You are currently working with one office that is interested in network management and would like you to devise a network management scheme. This company is located about 60 miles from your office. They are connected to the Internet using a 128Kbps dedicated ISDN connection. The office is divided into two network segments, using a Windows 2000 server as the router between the segments. They run WINS, DHCP, DNS, and a mission-critical database application. How would you implement a network management solution for this organization?

A. Install PCAnywhere on the machine that is connected to the Internet. Make the machine that is the Internet gateway the network management station. Use PCAnywhere to connect to the gateway and network management station and collect data in real time throughout the day.

B. Install Terminal Services on the network gateway machine. Designate a second server on the network to be the network monitoring station. Connect to the Terminal Server and maintain that connection around the clock. Configure the System Monitor and Performance Logs and Alerts on the Terminal Server to connect to the network management station. Configure Alerts to be sent to you when fault conditions arise.

C. Install a 56Kbps modem on the machine you designate as the network monitoring station. Use the System Monitor and the Performance Logs and Alerts nodes to configure monitoring to take place in response to events that fall outside of your design parameters and on a regular basis. Dial in to the network monitoring station twice a day to collect this performance data. Configure svcmon.exe to send you e-mail alerts when critical services fail.

D. Configure a machine on the network to be a network management station. Assign the office manager to be the site administrator in charge of network monitoring. Have the office manager check the network management statistics periodically throughout the day, and e-mail you when she notices that things are "not right" with the network.

8. You would like to be able to perform remote administration on servers on the network. Which of the following would be the least processor and bandwidth intensive?

A. Use Terminal Server in Administration mode.

B. Install PCAnywhere32 on all the servers and manage them via PCA.

C. Install RRAS on all the servers, and then dial in to them as a network client.

D. Install admt.exe and remotely manage the servers via that utility.

Understanding Service Reports and Data Analysis

9. You are a consultant hired by a company to design a management plan. The plan must reduce the time taken for help desk staff to respond to problems with file servers and critical services. The company has a head office and two distribution centers that are maintained by a help desk in the head office. LANs exist in each location and high-speed persistent links exist between the head office and the two distribution centers. Help desk staff currently drive to the distribution centers only when a problem is phoned in. Which of the following could be included in a response strategy that will reduce response time from the help desk?

A. Collect performance and status data for networking services for each location *at* each location.

B. Periodically collect the data collected at each site, and return it to the main office for analysis.

C. Deploy an automated data collection system, such as an SNMP Management program at the head office, so that administrators there can be informed in real time when service interruptions and variances occur at any site.

D. Set up a weekly newsletter that is sent to all employees. In the newsletter, you inform employees of things they should watch out for, and what issues might come up that would need to be reported to their local help desk. The local help desk would collate the results of the employee's observations, and prepare a monthly report detailing the observations of the organization's employees.

10. Which of the following are examples of SNMP Management systems?

A. Tivoli

B. HP Openview

C. Microsoft Systems Management Server

D. AOL Instant Messenger

11. You are the network administrator for a small real estate agency that employs 65 workers. The company uses a Windows 2000 Server as a FAX server, to which all faxes are sent for all employees in the organization. All faxes are stored on disk. What could you do to ensure that the server always has an adequate amount of disk space for the stored fax images?

A. Install the SNMP Agent on the Windows 2000 FAX server.

B. Configure a SNMP Management system to collect data on the available disk space on the FAX server.

C. Assign an employee to periodically check on the free space on the FAX server's disks.

D. Configure a System Monitor Log that runs automatically once a day, in which the log records the amount of available disk space on the FAX server. Have the System Monitor send a network message to an administrator when the amount of available disk space falls below a threshold value.

12. You have been called to consult with a small company that has 15 computers and a single Windows 2000 Server. All the user data is stored in the My Documents folder on each client machine, and the office manager has mapped a network drive on the server for each of the user's My Documents folder. During backup, the network becomes very slow. What can you recommend to reduce the network congestion during backup time?

A. Have all the users save their data to the server.

B. Configure backups to take place only at night.

C. Use folder redirection.

D. Do nothing.

13. You wish to restrict your performance analysis for the DNS server to events that represent a "fault" state in your DNS server. Which of these counters would provide you with the information you need to detect fault status information for your DNS server?

A. All the WINS-related counters

B. All the zone transfer-related counters

C. All the counters that indicate failure information for Query, Zone, and Secure Update

D. All the TCP-related counters

14. You wish to have real-time fault tolerance for your WINS database in the event of a server failure. Which is the best way to accomplish this?

A. Terminal Server

B. Server Clustering

C. Manually back up the database daily.

D. Automate the daily backup of the WINS database.

15. When designing a monitoring solution for your network services, under what circumstances would you use a distributed data collection strategy?

A. Distributed data collection is most suitable when you wish to have all data sent to a central monitoring facility in real time. Engineers located at the central facility will monitor the status of local site performance. In the event of a fault, someone at the central facility will inform a local technician to correct the fault.

B. Distributed data collection is most suitable for situations in which a large number of servers and counters must be monitored, no out-of-band data collection facilities exist, frequency of data collection is high, and in-band data collection may impact network performance.

C. Distributed data collection is most suitable when you have an out-of-band infrastructure such as dedicated ISDN lines at each site. Using the ISDN infrastructure, you can collect data periodically during the day, and inform local site administrators of the status of network services as needed.

D. Distributed data collection is most suitable for organizations that have a large centralized network information center that uses multiple computers that access network services status information from all sites via in-band network connections. Quality of Service parameters are configured on network devices that are interposed between the network operation center's computers and the data collection devices at each site in order to provide priority bandwidth to data collection channels.

16. You have collected data from five remote servers locally at each site. What tool could you use to analyze the data and spot trends after multiple monitoring sessions?

A. Excel

B. Access

C. Internet Explorer

D. mIRC

Planning Service Interaction and Resource Strategies

17. You are planning on combining network services to optimize network bandwidth and Interservice communication. Which of the following two services would be best to combine to maximize service performance?

A. WINS

B. DNS

C. Exchange 2000

D. SQL Server 2000

18. You network has been running sluggishly since a recent IPO. NetBIOS and host name resolution seems to get getting slower and slower. What are some things you can do to assess and prevent network services outages due to network growth?

A. Perform a Trend Analysis.

B. Consider combining networking services.

C. Wait until services fail and then fix the problem.

D. Place all network services on different subnets.

LAB QUESTION

You are the network administrator for a company that has six sites located all over the United States and Canada. All the sites are connected via dedicated IDSL 144 Kbps links. There are approximate six servers that you must monitor at each site. Intersite network bandwidth has been an ongoing issue, and you have requested on several occasions that the WAN infrastructure be upgraded to a higher bandwidth solution. However, you have been told that the company has a contract with the telecommunications provider and will not be able to upgrade the WAN connections for at least a year.

You have been using a centralized monitoring scheme with a SNMP Management station location at your office. You have been collecting data in real time for the past four weeks, and during this time you have noticed that overall WAN performance has degraded significantly. What could you do to help solve your monitoring and bandwidth problems?

SELF TEST ANSWERS

Understanding Network Management Processes and Procedures

1. ☑ **D** is correct. All the elements of a good design are included in this answer. A baseline is defined, and then monitoring of networking services is included in the design. A mechanism is included so that if services fall out of tolerance, a notification is sent. A response procedure and a "back-door" response plan are also included for those circumstances that are not foretold in the documentation.

   ☒ **A** is incorrect because yearly monitoring of a network service is inadequate and will not provide useful information in terms of design compliance, nor will it provide a means of analyzing trends. The response mechanism is also inadequate, since the entire responsibility for resolving issues is placed on the personal recognizance of the network administrator. **B** is incorrect because there is no notification of network service variations. The response latency is dependent on when an administrator may "get around" to viewing the log files. **C** is incorrect because it lacks procedures for regular assessment of networking services, and the Task Manager is not an appropriate tool to use to monitor and assess the performance of the DNS Server service.

2. ☑ **C** is correct. The problem is related to excessive in-band data transfer due to network monitoring. In order to get around this problem, you can create an out-of-band solution using ISDN or related technologies.

   ☒ **A** is incorrect because QoS will not solve this problem; in fact, it may make it worse for data transfer for other important network activities. **B** is incorrect because adding additional routers will not solve this problem, and may end up making it worse because of the added processing required at each router. **D** is incorrect because an e-mail solution is likely to be in-band, and therefore will not solve the primary problem of in-band network saturation.

3. ☑ **A, C, and D** are correct. **A** is correct because you can use the Simple Network Management Protocol, together with the Microsoft SNMP Agent and a Network Management program, to automatically collect data on network services and devices. The SNMP Management system can collect and organize the data, and can be configured to provide immediate or delayed notification via e-mail, telephone, fax, or pager. **C** is correct because you can use the Windows 2000 Performance Monitor to collect information about network service performance, and save that information to log files. You can even schedule performance-monitoring sessions to take place automatically, and configure the system to send an e-mail or network message to you when threshold values have been exceeded. **D** is correct because you can save the results of your

monitoring sessions to a database, such as Microsoft Access 2000. You can then use the database program to create charts and graphs that display trends and can be used in forecasting dates when resources will be outstripped by the requirements of a particular network service.

☒ **B** is incorrect because AOL Instant Messenger does not collect useful performance or status data, and represents a security hole that should not be introduced into the networking environment.

4. ☑ **C** is correct. The best action to take is to remove accessibility to AOL ports and domains. Since AOL traffic is rarely, if ever, part of network business communications, it is important to block access to the service. Before implementing such a policy, you must be sure that it is approved by IT design and security.

☒ **A** is incorrect because you do not want to encourage employees to use AOL. The service is typically a portal for viruses and large amounts of unsolicited e-mail, which could choke network bandwidth. **B** is incorrect because a network policy will not eliminate the problem. Although such a policy is good to institute from a security and network management point of view, you must actually block access in order to prevent adverse events from taking place. **D** is incorrect because AOL is rarely pivotal to a business's performance, and the service is typically used for entertainment reasons only.

5. ☑ **D** is correct. This situation requires an out-of-band solution. Since the ISDN VPN links that connect the offices to each other are saturated, you do not want to add to in-band stress by burdening the normal data network with the additional load of the network management information gathered from each site. A periodic collection of data from each site using a 28.8Kbps modem that is scheduled to retrieve the data will hold down costs and allow you to gather the requisite data required to assess network performance at each location.

☒ **A** is incorrect because this solution requires you to have support personnel at each site who are capable of doing the data collection and analysis. Since all support personnel are located in the central office, this is not a viable solution. **B** is incorrect because this represents an in-band data collection solution. By using in-band data collection, you will add the stress of the network management data to the already overtaxed WAN links. This could cause critical delays in the normal data-processing activities of the organization's employees. **C** is incorrect because this solution would be cost prohibitive. Although this solution does present an out-of-band solution, the costs realized by keeping a telephone line open to the remote sites would be too high to justify.

6. ☑ **B** is correct. This is the most cost-effective solution, and is optimized for the extant hardware. The machines on which the VPN server will be run are somewhat underpowered. A Pentium II 300 with only 128MB of RAM running Windows 2000 Server may be overtaxed,

and the additional stress of using L2TP/IPSec may not lead to a functional solution. The best VPN solution for these computers would be to use PPTP because of its lower processing overhead. One work-around for this might be to buy network interface cards (NICs) that perform IPSec calculations for the operating system. This would offload the processing overhead from the machines' CPU, and make IPSec a more viable, albeit somewhat more expensive, solution.

☒   A is incorrect because L2TP/IPSec would lead to excessive processor overhead, making PPTP a superior solution in this context. C is incorrect because demand-dial routing to create a direct connection with a server that far away would be more expensive than a VPN solution. D is incorrect for similar reasons. A dedicated direct-dial connection between the two servers could be prohibitively expensive.

7. ☑   C is correct. This scenario requires an out-of-band solution. There are 100 computers on the internal network using the 128Kbps ISDN line. This averages 1.28Kbps/user. Any additional stress on the Internet connection would have an adverse impact on the office's Internet connectivity performance. By installing a 56Kbps modem on the network management station that is also configured as a RAS server, you can schedule calls to the server, and download the log information on a periodic basis without negatively impacting the company's Internet access solution. You can also have the exchange server forward e-mail to your ISP mail account when critical events take place. While this would take place in-band, critical faults are not too frequent, and a plaintext e-mail message will not consume excessive bandwidth.

☒   A is incorrect because when you connect via PCAnywhere over the Internet, you will be using in-band resources, and will adversely impact the Internet performance for the entire organization. In addition, PCAnywhere can be a security risk, and should not be used to manage mission-critical resources over Internet connections. You might consider using PCAnywhere via a RAS connection to the network management station. B is incorrect because remaining connected to the Terminal Server over the Internet also represents an in-band solution and will adversely impact the Internet experience for the office personnel. Data collection over this in-band connection has the potential of making Internet access impossible for the internal network users. D is incorrect because you should not use nontechnical personnel as part of your network monitoring solution. While the office manager might be well intentioned, there is an excellent chance that she will be occupied with her other duties in the company and will forget to check the network management station on a regular basis. In addition, the office manager will not be able to accurately assess the meaning of the data gathered. This can lead to you not being informed of important network events, or lead to you being called several times a day for noneventful recordings for which the office manager has questions or concerns.

8. ☑ **A** is correct. Terminal Server in remote administration mode offers the lowest bandwidth alternative. It is also more cost effective since it comes with Windows 2000 Server.
☒ **B** is incorrect because PCAnywhere consumes a significant amount of bandwidth and processor cycles. It is an inferior solution compared to Terminal Services. **C** is incorrect because when you dial in as a network client, you do not take control of the server; you are merely a client on the network. **D** is incorrect because admt.exe is used for migration, not for remote administration.

Understanding Service Reports and Data Analysis

9. ☑ **A, B,** and **C** are correct. **A** is correct because collecting data at each location can be an efficient use of network bandwidth. If a reliable schedule of collating the gathered data were defined, it would fit well into a network management design plan. **B** is correct because returning the data to a central location for analysis can be an efficient way to bring issues to the attention of most senior administrators and prevent them from having to travel to each site to analyze the data separately. **C** is correct because an SNMP Management system designed to collect data on only the most mission-critical services and report that information to the central office would be an efficient use of bandwidth. By implementing such a system, the most senior administrators can respond in real time to failures of mission-critical services.
☒ **D** is incorrect because you should not rely on user input in your network management scheme. In addition, a monthly compilation of users' observations would take a significant amount of administrative time and effort, and likely would have little salutary effect on improving network performance.

10. ☑ **A, B,** and **C** are correct. Tivoli Enterprise Manager, HP Openview, and Microsoft Systems Management Server are all examples of SNMP Management stations.
☒ **D** is incorrect. AOL Instant Messenger is a chat program.

11. ☑ **D** is correct. This solution will allow the small company to know, in advance, of potential problems with limited disk space that could prevent the server from receiving any more faxes. This is also a cost-effective solution that would work well for a small company such as the one in this scenario.
☒ **A** is incorrect because it involves using an SNMP Management station to record and analyze the data. SNMP Management software is often prohibitively expensive, and therefore would not be the best solution for this small company. Since the network monitoring

requirements for the company are minimal, the built-in solution provided by Windows 2000 will satisfy their network monitoring requirements. **B** is also incorrect for the same reasons. **C** is incorrect because depending on an employee to make periodic checks is an unreliable and error-prone plan. It is too easy for an employee to forget about "checking the computer," and by the time the problem has come to the attention of management, many valuable faxes might have been lost.

12. ☑ **C** is correct. Folder redirection would be the most cost effective and easiest to implement.
☒ **A** is incorrect because users cannot be relied upon to understand the file system to the extent that they will be able to reliably save their data to the server. **B** is incorrect because configure backups can take place at times other than at night. **D** is incorrect because the network is experiencing periodic slowdowns, and some decisive action needs to be carried out.

13. ☑ **C** is correct. In order to measure fault states, or failures in the DNS service's activity, you should select all failure-related counters. The other counters provide valuable information about the status of the DNS service as a whole, but do not give you information about the fault status of the DNS Server service activity.
☒ **A** is incorrect because if you select all the WINS-related counters, you will obtain information other than just the fault status. **B** is incorrect because if you select all of the zone transfer-related counters, you will receive information other than just the fault status. **D** is incorrect because if you select all of the TCP-related counters, you will receive information other than just the fault status.

14. ☑ **B** is correct. Server Clustering provides real-time failover for networking services. If a single server should become unavailable, the other member of the cluster will be able to take over for it.
☒ **A** is incorrect because Terminal Services do not afford any degree of fault tolerance. **C** is incorrect because this does not provide real-time fault tolerance. **D** is incorrect for similar reasons; this solution does not provide real-time fault tolerance.

15. ☑ **B** is correct. A distributed data collection model should be used when there is a large amount of data collected at each site that needs to be processed and acted upon locally. In this model, local engineers would be responsible for collecting and analyzing data that is collected in their location. Data can be transferred to a central location at some future time via in-band or out-of-band methods, but the priority is for local analysis and action. You would also use the method when there is no established out-of-band infrastructure, such as dedicated or dial-up ISDN, that would allow a central monitoring facility to access data in a timely basis that would not negatively impact in-band data transfers.
☒ **A** is incorrect because this concept of centralized monitoring and data collection is not part

of the distributed model. This is an example of centralized data collection and analysis, where data is collected and analyzed centrally. **C** is incorrect because it represents a mix of central and distributed data collection and analysis. In this scenario, data is collected in a distributed fashion, and then collected to a central site via an out-of-band infrastructure. Data analysis is performed centrally as well. **D** is incorrect because this represents a pure centralized model of data collection and analysis. Note that when QoS parameters are configured to provide bandwidth priority to the network operations center's machines, this comes at the expense of other data transfer activities on the in-band network.

16. ☑ **A** and **B** are correct. You can use both Excel and Access to analyze data that has been collected via text files by importing the data into each of these program's native formats. You can then create trend analyses and graphics to assess when the network service may reach a fault state.
 ☒ **C** is incorrect because Internet Explorer is a Web browser. **D** is incorrect because mIRC is an IRC chat client.

Planning Service Interaction and Resource Strategies

17. ☑ **A** and **B** are correct because these two services must often communicate with one another. WINS is a Disk Bound service while DNS tends to be a Memory Bound service. Since these two networking services do not compete for the same hardware resources, they would be ideal candidates to combine on the same computer.
 ☒ **C** and **D** are incorrect because both Exchange 2000 and SQL 2000 are very hardware intensive on all fronts, and therefore should be placed on computers dedicated to running Exchange 2000 and SQL 2000, respectively.

18. ☑ **A** and **B** are correct. **A** is correct because a trend analysis can foretell when problems with networking services might arise. By predicting when problems might occur, you can take decisive action in advance and prevent network outages from ever taking place. **B** is correct because you can improve the performance of networking services, and the network as a whole, by combining network services on the same machine.
 ☒ **C** is incorrect because you should not wait until there is a problem before fixing something, and **D** is incorrect because placing interacting networking services on different subnets can slow down the performance of those services.

LAB ANSWER

The primary problem in this situation is that of limited in-band resources to support network monitoring in real time. A couple of possible solutions would be to reduce the level of monitoring so that information is collected in-band on a periodic basis. Another possible solution would be to connect to each site using an out-of-band solution, such as a dial-up 56 Kbps modem link. The best solution would be to upgrade the WAN infrastructure or to obtain dedicated out-of-band links to the destination sites. This would allow you to continue your real-time data collection scheme.

A

About the CD

This CD-ROM contains the CertTrainer software. CertTrainer comes complete with ExamSim, Skill Assessment tests, CertCam movie clips, the e-book (electronic version of the book), and Drive Time. CertTrainer is easy to install on any Windows 98/NT/2000 computer and must be installed to access these features. You may, however, browse the e-book directly from the CD without installation.

Installing CertTrainer

If your computer CD-ROM drive is configured to autorun, the CD-ROM will automatically start up upon inserting the disk. From the opening screen you may either browse the e-book or install CertTrainer by pressing the Install Now button. This will begin the installation process and create a program group named "CertTrainer." To run CertTrainer use Start | Programs | CertTrainer.

System Requirements

CertTrainer requires Windows 98 or higher and Internet Explorer 4.0 or above and 600MB of hard disk space for full installation.

CertTrainer

CertTrainer provides a complete review of each exam objective, organized by chapter. You should read each objective summary and make certain that you understand it before proceeding to the SkillAssessor. If you still need more practice on the concepts of any objective, use the "In Depth" button to link to the corresponding section from the Study Guide or use the CertCam button to view a short .AVI clip illustrating various exercises from within the chapter.

Once you have completed the review(s) and feel comfortable with the material, launch the SkillAssessor quiz to test your grasp of each objective. Once you complete the quiz, you will be presented with your score for that chapter.

ExamSim

As its name implies, ExamSim provides you with a simulation of the actual exam. The number of questions, the type of questions, and the time allowed are intended to be an accurate representation of the exam environment. You will see the screen shown in Figure A-1 when you are ready to begin ExamSim.

When you launch ExamSim, a digital clock display will appear in the upper left-hand corner of your screen. The clock will continue to count down to zero unless you choose to end the exam before the time expires.

There are three types of questions on the exam:

- **Multiple Choice** These questions have a single correct answer that you indicate by selecting the appropriate check box.

- **Multiple-Multiple Choice** These questions require more than one correct answer. Indicate each correct answer by selecting the appropriate check boxes.

- **Simulations** These questions simulate actual Windows 2000 menus and dialog boxes. After reading the question, you are required to select the appropriate settings to most accurately meet the objectives for that question.

FIGURE A-1

The ExamSim opening page

Saving Scores as Cookies

Your ExamSim score is stored as a browser cookie. If you've configured your browser to accept cookies, your score will be stored in a file named *History*. If your browser is not configured to accept cookies, you cannot permanently save your scores. If you delete this History cookie, the scores will be deleted permanently.

E-Book

The entire contents of the Study Guide are provided in HTML form, as shown in Figure A-2. Although the files are optimized for Internet Explorer, they can also be viewed with other browsers, including Netscape.

CertCam

CertCam .AVI clips provide detailed examples of key certification objectives. These clips walk you step-by-step through various system configurations and are narrated by Thomas Shinder, M.D., MCSE, MCT. You can access the clips directly from the CertCam table of contents (shown in Figure A-3) or through the CertTrainer objectives.

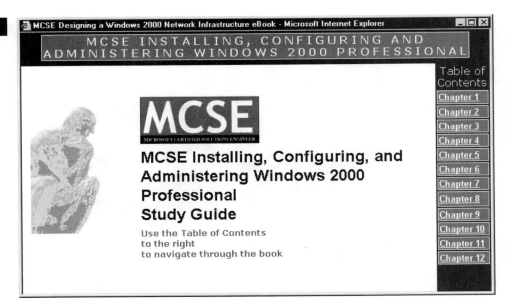

FIGURE A-2
Study Guide contents in HTML format

The CertCam .AVI clips are recorded and produced using TechSmith's Camtasia Producer. Since .AVI clips can be very large, ExamSim uses TechSmith's special AVI Codec to compress the clips. The file named tsccvid.dll is copied to your Windows\System folder when you install CertTrainer. If the .AVI clip runs with audio but no video, you may need to re-install the file from the CD-ROM. Browse to the "bin" folder and run TSCC.EXE.

DriveTime

DriveTime audio tracks will automatically play when you insert the CD-ROM into a standard CD-ROM player, such as the one in your car or stereo. There is one track for each chapter. These tracks provide you with certification summaries for each chapter and are the perfect way to study while commuting.

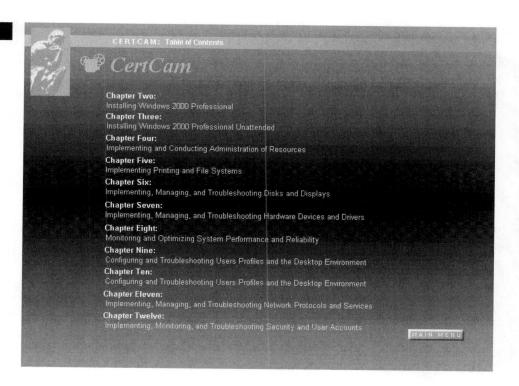

FIGURE A-3

The CertCam Table of Contents

Help

A help file is provided through a help button on the main CertTrainer screen in the lower right-hand corner.

Upgrading

A button is provided on the main ExamSim screen for upgrades. This button will take you to www.syngress.com where you can download any available upgrades.

MCSE
MICROSOFT CERTIFIED SYSTEMS ENGINEER

B

About the Web Site

A t Access.Globalknowledge, the premier online information source for IT professionals (http://access.globalknowledge.com), you'll enter a Global Knowledge information portal designed to inform, educate, and update visitors on issues regarding IT and IT education.

Get *What* You Want *When* You Want It

At the Access.Globalknowledge site, you can:

- Choose personalized technology articles related to your interests. Access a news article, a review, or a tutorial customized to what you want to see, regularly throughout the week.

- Continue your education, in between Global courses, by taking advantage of chat sessions with other users or instructors. Get the tips, tricks, and advice that you need today!

- Make your point in the Access.Globalknowledge community by participating in threaded discussion groups related to technologies and certification.

- Get instant course information at your fingertips. Customized course calendars show you the courses you want, and when and where you want them.

- Obtain the resources you need with online tools, trivia, skills assessment, and more!

All this and more is available now on the Web at http://access.globalknowledge.com. Visit today!

Glossary

Account Lockout Policy   The Account Lockout Policy dictates the behavior for locking and unlocking user accounts. There are three configurable parameters: Account lockout threshold determines how many times users can attempt to log on before their accounts are locked. This can range from low (five attempts) to high (one or two attempts). The Account lockout duration parameter controls how long an account is locked after the Account lockout threshold parameter is triggered.

ACPI   *See* Advanced Configuration and Power Interface.

Active Directory   The Active Directory is implemented on Windows 2000 domain controllers, and the directory can be accessed from Windows 2000 Professional as an Active Directory client. The Active Directory arranges objects—including computer information, user and group information, shared folders, printers, and other resources—in a hierarchical structure in which domains can be joined into trees (groups of domains that share a contiguous namespace). Trees can be joined into forests (groups of domain trees that share a common schema, configuration, and global catalog).

Active Directory Service   This service provides the means for locating the Remote Installation Service (RIS) servers and the client computers on the network. The RIS server must have access to the Active Directory.

Add Printer Wizard   All clients running a version of the Windows operating system (Windows 2000, Windows NT, Windows 98, and Windows 95) can use the Add Printer Wizard to create a printer entry on the client. This Add Printer Wizard can create and share a printer on a print server. The Windows 2000 version of the Add Printer Wizard has more options than the wizard in other versions of Windows, but many of the same methods can be used to get the printer set up on the client.

Address Resolution Protocol (ARP)   The Address Resolution Protocol (ARP) is used to resolve Internet Protocol (IP) logical addresses to Media Access Control (MAC) physical hardware addresses. ARP uses broadcasts to discover the hardware addresses, and stores the information in its arp cache.

Administration   The word *administer* is generally used as a synonym for *manage,* which in turn means to exert control. One of the many enhancements to Windows 2000—both the Professional and Server incarnations—is the ability Microsoft has given administrators to apply the degree of control desired, in a flexible and granular manner.

Advanced Configuration and Power Interface (ACPI)   ACPI combines Plug and Play (PnP) capability with Power Management, and places these functions under complete control of the operating system.

Advanced Power Management (APM)   An Intel/Microsoft application programming interface (API) allowing programs to indicate their requirements for power to regulate the speed of components.

Alerts   Alerts allow some action to be performed when a performance counter reaches a particular threshold. A common action is to log the event in the application event log. You can also send a network message to a specified computer. You can have the alert start a performance log to start logging when the alert occurs. And finally, you can configure the alert to start a program.

Algorithm   A procedure or formula used to solve a problem.

Analysis   Analysis is the process of comparison, contrast, diagnosis, diagramming, discrimination, and/or drawing conclusions.

Answer file   An answer file is a file containing the information you would normally have to key in during the setup process. Answer files help automate the installation process as all the queries presented to you during installation are answered by the answer files. With careful planning, you can prepare answers that eliminate the possibility of incorrect answers typed in by the person performing the installation, thus reducing the chances of setup failure. You can use the Setup Manager wizard to create a customized answer file. This technique minimizes the chances of committing syntax-related errors while manually creating or editing the sample answer files.

APIPA   *See* Automatic Private Internet Protocol Addressing.

APM   *See* Advanced Power Management.

AppleTalk   The AppleTalk protocol suite was developed by Apple Computer for use in its Macintosh line of personal computers. AppleTalk is a local area networking system that was developed by Apple Computer Inc. AppleTalk networks can run over a variety of networks that include Ethernet, FDDI, and Token Ring as well as Apple's proprietary media system LocalTalk. Macintosh computers are very popular in the education and art industries, so familiarity with the way they communicate using their native protocol is very useful.

AppleTalk printing device   Another type of remote printer is the AppleTalk printing device. Like a Transmission Control Protocol/Internet Protocol (TCP/IP) printer, an AppleTalk printer can be connected directly to an AppleTalk network or shared across the network through an AppleShare print server. Like the TCP/IP printers, a large number of modern, high-capacity PostScript printers can be configured to communicate with an AppleTalk network as well as a TCP/IP network. In fact, many Hewlett-Packard LaserJet printers have JetDirect cards that will speak TCP/IP and AppleTalk at the same time.

Application   The process of choice, demonstration, performing a procedure, solving, plotting, calculation, changing, interpretation, and operation.

Application Software   A program designed to perform a specific function directly for the user or for another application program. An application would be, for example, word processors, database programs, graphics/drawing programs, Web browsers, and e-mail programs.

Application Service Provider (ASP)   ASPs are companies that manage applications and provide organizations with application hosting services. Analysts expect the ASP market will be a six billion-dollar industry by the year 2001. The application-hosting model offers organizations the option of outsourcing application support and maintenance.

Application System Border Router (ASBR)   An AS Border Router is a router that connects together different ASs. When the ASBR exchanges routing information with an external network – the routing information received from outside the AS are referred to as external routes.

ARP   *See* Address Resolution Protocol.

ARPAnet   ARPAnet, the predecessor of the Internet, was begun by the U.S. Department of Defense (DoD) in conjunction with major universities. The DoD developed the nation-wide system (which then was extended throughout the world) to provide highly reliable, redundant communication links that could withstand even a nuclear war.

ASBR   *See* Application System Border Router.

ASP   *See* Application Service Provider.

Asymmetric algorithm   A cryptographic algorithm that utilizes a different key for encrypting data from the one used to decrypt the data.

Asynchronous Transfer Mode over Asymmetric Digital Subscriber Line (ATM over ADSL)   ADSL offers a new technology aimed at small businesses and residential customers. It offers a higher throughput than Public Switched Telephone Network (PSTN) and Integrated Services Digital Network (ISDN) connections, but the bit rate is higher downstream than upstream—typically 384 Kbps when going out and 384 Kbps–1.544 Mbps when coming in (this usually suits Internet traffic usage where users download a much higher percentage of data than they upload). ADSL equipment can appear to a Windows 2000 server as one of two interfaces: Ethernet or dial-up. When seen as an Ethernet interface, the ASDL behaves in the same way as a standard network adapter connected to the Internet. When seen as a dial-up interface, ADSL provides the physical connection for ATM traffic.

Auditing   Windows 2000 gives the ability to audit security-related events, track access to objects and use of user rights, and detect attempted and successful access (authorized and unauthorized) to the network. Auditing is not enabled by default, but once enabled, a security log is generated that provides information in regard to specific activities performed on the computer.

Authenticated data exchange   The only problem with confidential data exchange is that there is no assurance that the person who used your public key to encrypt and send you a message is really whomever he or she claims to be. How can we ensure that? What if the sender encrypted the message using his or her private key, and then you decrypted it using his or her public key? What would this accomplish? We get the same confidentiality of the data as with the first method, but since presumably only the sender has the private key, we can be confident of his identity. Now we have an authenticated data exchange.

Authentication   Authentication is when a user is identified (usually by means of a username and password). If this is done in an encrypted form, an authentication protocol is used. A successful authentication proves that users are who they say they are, but has nothing to do with what resources they can access.

Authentication Header (AH)   The Authentication Header ensures data integrity and authentication. The AH does not encrypt data, and therefore provides no confidentiality, but does protect the data from modification. When the AH protocol is applied in transport mode, the Authentication Header is inserted between the original Internet Protocol (IP) header and the Transmission Control Protocol (TCP) or User Datagram Protocol (UDP) header.

Authorization   Authorization occurs when it is determined that users can have access to requested resources based on their identity. By definition, this can only happen after a successful authentication. In the context of Routing and Remote Access (RRAS), remote users' connection attempts can be authenticated (because they have proved who they are), but their connection can still be denied because their authorization failed if they did not have permission to dial in, for example.

Automatic Partner Discovery   You can configure your Windows Internet Name Server (WINS) servers to find other WINS servers on the network and create a replication partnership with them automatically. When you enable Automatic Partner Discovery, WINS servers use the multicast address 224.0.1.24 to discover or find other WINS servers.

Automatic Private Internet Protocol Addressing (APIPA)   APIPA, or Automatic Client Configuration, is a new feature initially available in Windows 98. The feature has been extended to Windows 2000 and allows Dynamic Host Control Protocol (DHCP) client computers to self-configure their IP addressing information in the event a DHCP server is not available when the computer issues a DHCPDISCOVER message. It also allows self-configuration when it senses that it has been moved from a previous network via Windows 2000 media sensing capabilities.

Backup Domain Controller (BDC)   A backup file or copy of the Primary Domain Controller (PDC). Periodically, the BDC is synchronized with the PDC.

Backup Logs   Windows Backup generates a backup log file for every backup job. These files are the best place to review the backup process in case some problem is encountered by the program. The backup log is a text file that records all the events during the backup process.

BACP   *See* Bandwidth Allocation Control Protocol.

Bandwidth Allocation Control Protocol (BACP)   BACP polices multiple peers using Multilink Point-to-Point Protocol (MP); for example, electing a favored peer when more than one PPP peer requests to add or remove a connection at the same time. The sole job of this protocol is to elect a favored peer when necessary. If both peers of an MP- and BAP-enabled connection send a BAP Call Request or BAP Link Drop Query Request message at the same time, only one request can succeed, and it is the responsibility of this protocol to elect which peer wins.

Bandwidth Allocation Protocol (BAP)   BAP is a Point-to-Point Protocol (PPP) that is used to dynamically add or remove additional links to an MP connection.

BAP   *See* Bandwidth Allocation Protocol.

Basic Input/Output System (BIOS)   A set of programs encoded in ROM on IBM PC-compatible computer programs handle startup operations such as Power On Self Test (POST) and low-level control for hardware such as disk drives, keyboards, etc.

BDC   *See* Backup Domain Controller.

BIOS   *See* Basic Input/Output System.

Black holes   Because the Routing Information Protocol (RIP) is a distance vector-based routing protocol that uses unacknowledged delivery, data can often be lost without trace. One router could realize that its neighboring router was unavailable and send out information to broadcast this, but if the information is never received, other routers can continue to send data to the downed router in the mistaken belief it is still available. This is a black hole because there is nowhere for the packets to go but the sending system hasn't realized this. Link state routing protocols that use directed and acknowledged announcements are not vulnerable to this problem.

B-Node   A b-node (broadcast node) client uses broadcasts instead of a WINS server. A Windows NetBIOS client computer without a configured WINS server is a b-node client.

Boot   The process of loading an operating system into the computer's memory (RAM) so those applications can be run on it.

Boot ROM   A boot ROM is a chip on the network adapter that helps the computer boot from the network. Such a computer need not have a previously installed operating system. The BIOS of the computer that has a PXE-based boot

ROM must be configured to boot from the network. Windows 2000 Server RIS supports PXE ROM versions 99 or later.

BOOTP   *See* Bootstrap Protocol.

Bootstrap Protocol (BOOTP)   Bootstrap Protocol (BOOTP) is the predecessor to DHCP. It was originally designed to provide IP address configuration to diskless workstations, which not only received IP addressing information from a BOOTP server, but also received information regarding where to download its operating system image. DHCP was developed to improve on the host configuration services offered by BOOTP, and address some of the problems encountered in using it.

Bottleneck   A bottleneck in computer terms is also a component of the system as a whole that restricts the system from operating at its peak. When a bottleneck occurs, the component that is a bottleneck will have a high rate of usage and other components will have a low rate of usage. A lack of memory is a common cause of bottleneck when your computer doesn't have enough memory for the applications and services that are running.

Burst mode   When the Windows Internet Name Server (WINS) server is in burst mode, any name registration requests received over a predefined number receive immediate acknowledgment. However, the WINS server does not check the NetBIOS against the WINS database; it does not issue a challenge against duplicate names, and it does not write an entry to the WINS database.

CA   *See* Certificate Authority.

Caching resolver   The caching resolver not only caches queries that have been answered positively, but also caches negative results as well. When a Domain Name System (DNS) query fails, this failed result is placed in cache for five minutes, by default. If the machines issues a DNS query for the same object within five minutes, no query will be sent, and a failure message will be retrieved from cache. This can significantly reduce the overall DNS query traffic on a large network.

Caching-only DNS server   The caching-only Domain Name System (DNS) server does not contain any zone information; it only stores (caches) the results of previous queries it has issued. You might want to place a caching-only server on the other side of a slow Wide Area Network (WAN) link, since they do not generate zone transfer traffic.

Caching-only server   All Domain Name System (DNS) servers cache results of queries they have resolved. The caching-only DNS server does not contain zone information or a zone file. The caching-only server builds its database of host name and domain mappings over time from successful DNS queries it has resolved for DNS clients.

CAL   *See* Client Access License.

Callback   Callback is when the remote user dials in and requests the server to call back, so the connection cost of the remote access session is charged to the server's line and not the user.

Canonical Name (CNAME)   This is an alias for a computer with an existing A Address record. For example, if you have a computer called "bigserver" that is going to be your Web server, you could create a CNAME for it, such as "www." It is important to note that you must have an A record for the host that you intend to create the alias for, since the CNAME record requests that you include the host name of the computer for which you wish to create the alias.

CAPI   *See* CryptoAPI.

Capture filter   A capture filter works somewhat like a database query; you can use it to specify the types of network information you want to monitor. For example, you can capture packets based on the protocol or based on the addresses of two computers whose interactions you wish to monitor. When a capture filter is applied, all packets are examined and compared to the filter's parameters; those that do not fulfill the filter requirements are dropped. This can be a processor-intensive activity during periods of moderate or high network utilization when the network card is placed in promiscuous mode.

Centralized model   This model consolidates administrative control of group policies. A single team of administrators is responsible for managing all Group Policy Objects (GPOs) no matter where they are. This is usually applied by giving all the top-level Organizational Unit (OU) administrators full control to all GPOs no matter where are located. They give each second-level OU administrator Read permission only to each GPO. You can also decentralize other resources or keep all resources centralized, depending on the environment.

Certificate   A message that contains the digital signature of a trusted third party, called a certificate authority, which ensures that a specific public key belongs to a specific user or device.

Certificate Authority (CA)   An authority/organization that produces digital certificates with its available public key. A Certificate Authority (CA) is a public key certificate issuer (for example, Verisign). To use a public key certificate, you must trust the issuer (CA). This means that you have faith in the CA's authentication policies. The CA is used for doing things such as authorizing certification authenticity, revoking expired certificates, and responding to certification requests. Windows 2000 offers an alternative to a third-party CA. You can become a CA within your own Intranet. Thus you can manage your own certificates rather than relying on a third-party Certification Authority.

Certificate service   Provides security and authentication support, including secure e-mail, Web-based authentication, and smart card authentication.

Challenge Handshake Authentication Protocol (CHAP)   A protocol (Point-to-Point Protocol or PPP) in which a password is required to begin a connection as well as during the connection. If the password fails any of these requirements, the system breaks the connection.

Change Permission   You can use this permission to allow users the ability to change permissions on files and folders without giving them the Full Control permission. You can use this permission to give a user or group access to modify permissions on file or folder objects without giving them the ability to have complete control over the object.

CHAP   *See* Challenge Handshake Authentication Protocol.

Cipher   The process that turns readable text data into ciphertext, which is encrypted data that must be deciphered before it is readable.

Cipher Block Chaining (CBC)   Because the blocks of data are encrypted in 64-bit chunks, there must be a way to "chain" these blocks together. The chaining algorithm will define how the combination of the unencrypted text, the secret key, and the encrypted text (also known as ciphertext) will be combined to send to the destination host. Data Encryption Standard (DES) can be combined with Cipher Block Chaining (CBC) to prevent identical messages from looking the same. This DES-CBC algorithm will make each ciphertext message appear different by using a different "initialization vector" (IV).

Cipher command   The cipher command is another way to encrypt and decrypt data. You can use it from the command line and it has many switches, so you can define exactly what you want to have done. The Cipher.exe command syntax is simply CIPHER, followed by the switches that you would like to use, followed by the path and directory/file name. The most common switches are the /E switch (encrypts the specified directories) and the /D switch (decrypts the specified directories). You can also use wildcards with the cipher command. For example, C:\>cipher /e /s *win* will encrypt all files and folders with "win" in the name and all files within them.

CIW   *See* Client Installation Wizard.

Class A Addresses   Class A addresses are for the "large size" networks, those that have a tremendous number of computers, and thus a need for many host addresses. Class A addresses always begin with a 0 in the first octet (also called the W octet). This will be the first bit on the left. This leaves seven bits for the individual network ID, and 24 bits to identify the host computers. When we convert to decimal, we see that this means a Class A address will have a decimal value in the first octet of 127 or less. Class A addresses, because they use only the first octet to identify the network, are limited in number. However, each Class A network can have a huge number of host computers, over 16 million. The Class A network numbers were all used up some time ago; they have been assigned to very large organizations such as IBM, MIT, and General Electric.

Class B Addresses   Class B networks are the "medium size" networks. Class B networks use the first two octets (the 16 leftmost bits) to identify the network, and the last two octets (or the 16 rightmost bits) to identify the host computers. This means there can be far more Class B networks than Class As (over 16,000), but each can have fewer hosts ("only" 65,535 each). Class B addresses always begin with a 10 for the two leftmost bits in the W octet, and the network is defined by the first two octets, which translates to decimal values of 128 through 191 for the first octet, 16 bits identify the Network ID, and the remaining 16 bits identify the Host ID. Microsoft's network is an example of a Class B network.

Class C Addresses   The smallest sized block of addresses designated by a class is the Class C network, each of which can have only 254 hosts. However, there can be over two million Class C networks. A Class C network always has 110 as its first three bits. This leaves 24 bits to identify the network, with only 8 bits to use for host IDs. A Class C network, in decimal notation, will have a first octet decimal value of 192 through 223.

Class D Addresses   Class D addresses, whose four high order (leftmost) bits in the W octet are 1110, are used for multicasting. This is a method of sending a message to multiple computers simultaneously.

Class E Addresses   Class E addresses, with four high order bits of 1111, are reserved for experimental and testing purposes.

Classless Addressing (CIDR)   The use of address classes is the traditional way of working with Internet Protocol (IP) addressing and subnetting. A more recent development is called Classless InterDomain Routing (CIDR). CIDR networks are referred to as "slash x" networks, with the "x" representing the number of bits assigned originally as the network ID (before subnetting). Think of this as the number of bits that don't "belong" to you. With CIDR, the subnet mask actually becomes part of the routing tables. CIDR allows us to break networks into subnets and combine networks into supernets.

Client Access License (CAL)   The CAL allows clients to access the Windows 2000's network services, shared folders, and printers. There are two types of CAL modes: Per Seat and Per Server. It important to understand the difference between the two modes: Per Seat and Per Server. When you use the Per Seat mode, each computer that accesses the server must have a CAL. The Per Server mode requires a CAL for each connection to the server. This is a subtle but significant difference. In addition, the CAL allows clients to access the Windows 2000 Server's network services, shared folders, and printers. The licensing modes are the same as under Windows NT 4.0.

Client impersonation   This is when somebody takes over an existing authenticated connection by obtaining connection parameters from a successfully authenticated client, disconnecting the client, and then taking control of the original connection.

Client Installation Wizard (CIW)   When a client computer boots using either the Remote Boot Disk or the PXE-based Boot ROM, it tries to establish a connection to the Remote Installation Service (RIS) server. If the RIS server is preconfigured to service the RIS clients, it helps the client get an Internet Protocol (IP) address from the Dynamic Host Control Protocol (DHCP) service. The CIW is then downloaded from the RIS server. This wizard has four installation options. The options that are presented to the user depend on the group policy set in the Active Directory. A user may get all four options, or may not get any of the options starting an automatic setup.

Client reservations   Client reservations allow you to manage virtually the entirety of your Internet Protocol (IP) addresses space centrally, with the exception being your Dynamic Host Control Protocol (DHCP) servers.

Cloning   *See* Disk imaging/cloning.

CNAME   *See* Canonical Name.

Comprehension   The process of distinguishing between situations, discussing, estimation, explaining, indicating, paraphrasing, and giving examples.

Computer account   A computer account is an account that is created by a domain administrator and uniquely identifies the computer on the domain. A newly created account is used so that a computer may be brought into a Windows 2000 Domain.

Confidential data exchange   Think of the method used to secure safety deposit boxes at banks. When you rent a box, you have a key to it—but your key alone won't unlock it. The bank officer also has a key, but again, that key by itself isn't of much value. When both keys are used, however, the authorized person can access the box. Likewise, with public key encryption technologies, it takes two keys to tango. One is the public key, which is made available to all those who want to send you an encrypted message. They can all use that public key to encrypt their messages, but they cannot use it to decrypt them—only your private key, which you keep secret, can do that. This is called a confidential data exchange.

Configuration   Configuration of an operating system involves specifying settings that will govern how the system behaves.

Container Object   Container objects can contain other objects. A special type of container object you can create in the Active Directory is the Organizational Unit (OU).

Containers   Containers are used to describe any group of related items, whether they are objects, containers, domains, or an entire network.

Control Panel Accessibility Options   These are options which include StickyKeys, FilterKeys, ToggleKeys, SoundSentry, ShowSounds, High Contrast, MouseKeys, and SerialKeys.

Convergence   When all the routers on the internetwork have the correct routing information in their routing tables, the internetwork is said to have converged. When convergence is achieved, the internetwork is in a stable state and all routing occurs along optimal paths. When a link or router fails, the internetwork must reconfigure itself to reflect the new topology and to achieve this, routing tables must be updated. Until the internetwork has converged once again, routing will be vulnerable to loops and black holes. The time it takes for the internetwork to reconverge is known as the convergence time and the optimal aim is for the shortest convergence time with minimum traffic.

Cooperative multitasking   An environment in which application relinquishes its use of the computer's Central Processing Unit (CPU) so that another application could use the CPU.

Copy backup   This type of backup simply copies the selected files. It neither looks for any markers set on the files nor does it clear them. The Copy backup does not affect the other Incremental or Differential backup jobs and can be performed along with the other types of backup jobs.

Counter logs   Counter logs are maintained similarly to the way they were in Windows NT 4.0, but the procedure for configuring the Counter logs is a bit different. Trace logs are much easier to configure in Windows 2000 because you now can set them up from the console, rather than having to edit the registry as you had to do in Windows NT 4.0.

CryptoAPI (CAPI)   CryptoAPI (CAPI) architecture is a collection of tasks that permit applications to digitally sign or encrypt data while providing security for the user's private key data.

Cryptography   The science of encrypting and decrypting data. The science (and art) of breaking cryptographic code is called cryptanalysis.

Daily backup   This type of backup does not use any markers to back up selected files and folders. The files that have changed during the day are backed up every day at a specified time. This backup will not affect other backup schedules.

Data backup   A backup and disaster protection plan is an essential part of a network administrator's duties. Windows 2000 provides a built-in Backup utility used to back up data to tape or file, or to create an Emergency Repair Disk (ERD). An ERD can be used to repair a computer with damaged system files.

Data compression   Windows 2000 offers the capability of compressing data on a file-level basis, so long as the files and folders are located on an NT File System (NTFS) formatted partition or volume. Compression saves disk space; however, NTFS compression cannot be used in conjunction with file encryption.

Data Encryption Standard (DES)   The most commonly used encryption algorithm used with Internet Protocol Security (IPSec) is the Data Encryption Standard (DES) algorithm. The widely used Data Encryption Standard (DES) uses secret key algorithms. Standard DES operates on 64-bit blocks of data, and uses a series of complex steps (even more complex than our Bible-assisted method) to transform the original input bits to encoded output bits. DES is the current U.S. government standard for encryption. The DES algorithm is an example of a symmetric encryption algorithm.

Data Link Control (DLC)   DLC is a nonroutable protocol used for connecting to IBM mainframes and some network-connected laser printers.

Debugging Mode   This is the most advanced startup option of all. To use this option you will need to connect another computer to the problematic computer through a serial cable. With proper configuration, the debug information is sent to the second computer.

Decentralized model   This model is appropriate for companies that rely on delegated levels of administration. They decentralize the management of Group Policy Objects (GPOs), which distributes the workload to a number of domains. To apply this model, simply give all Organizational Unit (OU) administrators full control of their respective GPOs.

Dedicated Server   A dedicated printer server is a Windows 2000 server whose only role is to provide printing services. The server does not provide directory space for users other than storage for spooled print jobs. It does not provide authentication services, does not host database services, does not act as a Domain Name System (DNS) server, and so on. A dedicated print server can host several hundred printers and print queues, however. Though it may not be obvious, the printing process does have an impact on the performance of the server providing the printing services. An environment with a large number of printers or print jobs should strongly consider using at least one dedicated print server.

Defragmentation   The task of finding fragmented files and moving them into contiguous space is called defragmentation.

Demand-dial routing   Dial-on demand connections are normally used when a permanent connection is not available, so demand-dial routing is used connect your router to the required host or router when there is no permanent connection to do this. They can be used as a backup to a permanent connection or if no permanent connection is possible. Because dial-up connections are usually charged on a time basis, a demand-dial connection is an efficient method of only paying for a connection when you have data to transfer. An idle timeout value allows the connection to automatically terminate when there is no more data to transfer.

Deny Permissions   Unlike the Allow permission, the Deny permission overrides all other permissions set for a file or folder. If a user is a member of one group with a Deny Write permission for a folder and a member of another group with a Allow Full Control permission, the user will be unable to perform any of the Write permission tasks allowed because permission has been denied. The Deny permission should be used with extreme caution, as it can actually lock out all users, even administrators, from a file or folder. The proper way to remove a permission from a user or group on a file or folder is to uncheck the Allow permission for that user or group, not to check the Deny permission.

DER Encoded Binary X.509   This is the format used for non-Windows 2000 certification authorities. Since the Internet is still dominated by non-Windows servers, it is supported for interoperability. DER certificate files use the .cer file extension.

DES   *See* Data Encryption Standard.

Dfs   *See* Distributed File System.

DHCP   *See* Dynamic Host Control Protocol.

Dictionary attack   Dictionary attack occurs when a malicious user attempts to gain access by "cracking" a password by automatically trying a list of words or commonly used phrases.

Differential backup   The Differential backup checks and performs a backup of only those files that are marked. It does not clear the markers after the backup, which means that any consecutive differential backups will backup the marked files again. When you need to restore from a differential backup, you will need the most current full backup and the differential backup performed after that.

Diffie-Hellman key exchange   Provides a method for two parties to construct a shared secret (key) that is known only to two of them, even though they are communicating via an insecure channel.

Digital signature   A string of bits that is added to a message (an encrypted hash), which provides for data integrity and authentication.

Digital Subscriber Line (DSL)   There are many variants of digital subscriber line (xDSL). All versions utilize the existing copper loop between a home and the local telco's Central Office (CO). Doing so allows them to be deployed rapidly and inexpensively. However, all DSL variants suffer from attenuation, and speeds drop as the loop length increases. Asymmetrical DSL (ADSL) and Symmetrical DSL (SDSL) may be deployed only within 17,500 feet of a CO, and Integrated Services Digital Network emulation over DSL (IDSL) will work only up to 30,500 feet. All DSL variants use Asynchronous Transfer Mode (ATM) as the data-link layer.

Direct Memory Access (DMA)   DMA is a microprocessor capable of transferring data between memory units without the aid of the Central Processing Unit (CPU). Occasionally, built-in circuitry can do this same function.

Directory   A directory is a database that contains information about objects and their attributes.

Directory service   The directory service is the component that organizes the objects into a logical and accessible structure, and provides for a means of searching and locating objects within the directory. The directory service includes the entire directory and the method of storing it on the network.

Directory Services Restore Mode This startup mode is available on Windows 2000 Server domain controller computers only. This mode can be used to restore the SYSVOL directory and Active Directory on the domain controller.

Discover A Dynamic Host Control Protocol (DHCP) client begins the lease process with a DHCPDISCOVER message. The client broadcasts this message after loading a minimal Transmission Control Protocol/Internet Protocol (TCP/IP) environment. The client does not know the address of the DHCP server, so it sends the message using a TCP/IP broadcast, with 0.0.0.0 as the source address and 255.255.255.255 as the destination address. The DHCPDISCOVER message contains the clients network hardware address, its computer name, a list of DHCP options the client supports, and a message ID that will be used in all messages between the client and server to identify the particular request.

Disk compression This compression allows you to compress folders, subfolders, and files to increase the amount of file storage, but slow down access to the files.

Disk Defragmenter Disk Defragmenter can analyze your volumes and make a recommendation as to whether or not you should defragment it. It will also give you a graphical display showing you the fragmented files, contiguous files, system files and free space. Disk Defragmenter does not always completely defragment free space; instead, it often moves it into just a few contiguous areas of the disk, which will still improve performance. Making the free space one contiguous space would have little added benefit.

Disk imaging/cloning The deployment of a new operating system is one of the most challenging and time-consuming tasks that a network administrator has to perform. The disk duplication methods are particularly useful when you need to deploy Windows 2000 Professional on a large number of computers. This is also known as disk imaging or cloning. These tools make the rollout fast and easy.

Disk quota Windows 2000 comes with a disk quota feature that allows you to control users' disk consumption on a per user/per partition basis. To begin setting disk quotas for your users, right-click any partition in either Windows Explorer or the My Computer object. Click Properties and then click the Quota tab. Also, a disk quota allows you to limit the amount of disk space used by each user.

Distance vector protocol   Routing Information Protocol (RIP) is known as a distance vector protocol. This means that it has a maximum path length of 15 hops. If a packet must pass through more than 15 routers (gateways) to reach its destination, RIP considers the destination "unreachable."

Distinguished Name (DN))   DN, in Active Directory parlance, is a Lightweight Directory Access Protocol (LDAP) way of uniquely identifying an object.

Distributed File System (Dfs)   The Windows 2000 Distributed File System provides you a method to centralize the organization of the shared resources on your network. In the past, shared resources were most often accessed via the Network Neighborhood applet, and users would have to wade through a number of domains and servers in order to access the shared folder or printer that they sought. Network users also had to remember where the obscure bit of information was stored, including both a cryptic server name and share name. The Distributed File System (Dfs) allows you to simplify the organization of your network resources by placing them in central shares accessed via a single server. Also, the Dfs allows you to create a central share point for shared resources located through the organization on a number of different servers.

Distribution Server   This is a server on which the Windows 2000 installation files reside. When you install the operating system over the network, the client machine does not need a CD-ROM drive. The first requirement for network installation is a distribution server that contains the installation files. The distribution server can be any computer on the network to which the clients have access.

DLC   *See* Data Link Control.

DMA   *See* Direct Memory Access.

DN   *See* Distinguished Name.

DNM   *See* Domain Naming Master.

DNS   *See* Domain Name System.

Domain   A collection of connected areas. Routing domains provide full connectivity to all end systems within them. Also, a domain is a collection of accounts and network resources that are grouped together using a single domain name and security boundary.

Domain controller   Domain controllers validate logons, participate in replication of logon scripts and policies, and synchronize the user account database. This means that domain controllers have an extra amount of work to perform. Since the Terminal Server already requires such heavy resources, it is not a good idea to burden a Terminal Server with the extra work of being a domain controller. Also, all user accounts, permissions, and other network details are all stored in a centralized database on the domain controllers.

Domain Local Groups   Domain Local Groups are used for granting access rights to resources such as file systems or printers that are located on any computer in the domain where common access permissions are required. The advantage of Domain Local Groups being used to protect resources is that a member of the Domain Local Group can come from both inside the same domain and from outside as well.

Domain Name System (DNS)   Because the actual unique Internet Protocol (IP) address of a web server is in the form of a number difficult for humans to work with, text labels separated by dots (domain names) are used instead. DNS is responsible for mapping these domain names to the actual Internet Protocol (IP) numbers in a process called resolution. Sometimes called a Domain Name Server.

Domain Naming Master (DNM)   A Domain Naming Master is one of the operations masters roles played by domain controllers in a Windows 2000 network.

Domain restructure   Domain restructure, or domain consolidation, is the method of changing the structure of your domains. Restructuring your domains can allow you to take advantage of the new features of Windows 2000, such as greater scalability. Windows 2000 does not have the same limitation as the Security Accounts Manager (SAM) account database in Windows NT. Without this limitation, you can merge domains into one larger domain. Using Windows 2000 Organizational Units (OUs), you have finer granularity in delegating administrative tasks.

Domain Tree   A domain tree is a hierarchical collection of the child and parent domains within a network. The domains in a domain tree have contiguous namespaces. Domain trees in a domain forest do not share common security rights, but can access one another through the global catalog.

Downlevel clients   Downlevel clients with static Internet Protocol (IP) addresses are not able to communicate directly with the Dynamic Domain Name System (DDNS) server. DDNS entries for these clients must be manually reconfigured at the DDNS server. Downlevel clients are not able to communicate directly with a DDNS server.

Driver signing   One of the most frustrating things about Windows operating systems is that any software vendors can overwrite critical system level files with their own versions. Sometimes the vendor's version of a system level file is buggy or flawed, and it prevents the operating system from functioning correctly, or in the worst case, prevents it from starting at all. Windows 2000 uses a procedure called Driver Signing that allows the operating system to recognize functional, high-quality files approved by Microsoft. With this seal of approval, you should be confident that installing applications containing signed files will not disable your computer. Windows 98 was the first Microsoft operating system to use digital signatures, but Windows 2000 marks the first Microsoft operating system based on NT technology to do this.

DSL   *See* Digital Subscriber Line.

Dynamic compulsory tunnels   Dynamic compulsory tunnels occur where a connection is dynamically assessed and the tunnel directed accordingly. For example, based on certain criteria, the same user may be directed to different Virtual Private Network (VPN) servers depending on what time of day the connection is made. Or, realms can be further divided into usernames, departments, the telephone number being used, and so forth. In this way, dynamic compulsory tunnels offer the highest degree of flexibility and granularity. An additional advantage for the owner of the Network Access Server is that it can simultaneously support both tunneling and nontunneling connections.

Dynamic disks   Dynamic disks introduce conceptual as well as technical changes from traditional basic disk structure. Partitions are now called volumes, and these can be created or changed without losing existing data on the disk. Recall that when using basic disks, you must first create primary partitions (up to a maximum of four), then extended partitions (a maximum of one) with logical drives. Dynamic disks allow you to create volume after volume, with no limit on the number or type that can exist on a single disk; you are limited only by the capacity of the disk itself.

Dynamic Host Configuration Protocol (DHCP)   A software utility that is designed to assign Internet Protocol (IP) addresses to clients and their stations logging onto a Transmission Control Protocol/Internet Protocol (TCP/IP) and eliminates manual IP address assignments.

Dynamic Host Control Protocol (DHCP) allocator   A Dynamic Host Control Protocol (DHCP) allocator is a simplified DHCP service without the database or configurable options. Invoking the DHCP allocator means that the computer will automatically assign Internet Protocol (IP) addresses to other workstations on the same subnet using a private address range, and it will assign the default gateway and the DNS server to be the same IP address as the computer running Internet Connection Sharing (ICS). Note there is no Windows Internet Name Server (WINS) server allocation.

Dynamic routing   Dynamic routing uses routing protocols such as the Routing Information Protocol (RIP) or Open Shortest Path First (OSPF) to allow routers to communicate with one another and automatically, dynamically update their routing tables without human intervention.

EAP   *See* Extensible Authentication Protocol.

EFS   *See* Encrypting File System.

Encapsulating Security Payload (ESP)   A header used by Internet Protocol Security (IPSec) when encrypting the contents of a packet.

Encrypting File System (EFS)   Unlike Windows NT 4.0, Windows 2000 provides the Encrypting File System (EFS) that allows you to encrypt and decrypt data on a file-by-file basis without the need for third-party software, as long as it is stored on an NTFS formatted partition or volume. EFS is based on public key cryptography.

Encryption   Scrambling of data so as to be unreadable; therefore, an unauthorized person cannot decipher the data.

ESP   *See* Encapsulating Security Payload.

Ethernet   A networking protocol and shared media (or switched) Local Area Network (LAN) access method linking up to 1K nodes in a bus topology.

Evaluation   Evaluation is the process of assessing, summarizing, weighing, deciding, and applying standards.

Event Viewer   The Windows 2000 Event Viewer has a dedicated log for DNS-specific information. The Event Viewer can provide information on when zone transfers have taken place, if there was a problem with a zone transfer, when changes have taken place within the zone, or even report that an excessive number of changes have occurred to the zone for a specific period of time.

Extended Partitions   Although extended partitions cannot be used to host operating systems, they can store other types of data and provide an excellent way to create more drives above the four-partition limit. Extended partitions do not represent one drive; rather, they can be subdivided into as many logical drives as there are letters in the alphabet. Therefore, one extended partition can contain several logical drives, each of which appears as a separate drive letter to the user.

Extensible Authentication Protocol (EAP)   The Extensible Authentication Protocol is an extension to Point-to-Point Protocol (PPP) that allows for arbitrary authentication mechanisms to be used to validate a PPP connection. Its design is such that it allows authentication plug-in modules at both the client and server. One example is using security token cards ("smart cards"), where the remote access server queries the client for a name, PIN, and card token value. Another example is using biometrics; for example, a retina scan or finger print match to uniquely identify an individual. Once the connection authentication phase is reached, the client negotiates which EAP authentication it wants to use, which is known as the EAP type. Once the EAP type is agreed upon, the server can issue multiple authentication requests to the client (as in the client name, then PIN, then card token value).

Fast Transfer   The Windows 2000 Domain Name System (DNS) Server supports a method of zone transfer that allows multiple records to be included in a single message. This compressed form of zone file transfer is referred to as a fast transfer. Not all DNS servers support the fast transfer mode, although most of the popular ones do. One popular DNS server that does not support fast transfers is Berkeley Internet Name Domain (BIND) versions before 4.9.4. Subsequent versions of BIND do support the fast transfer mode. If you do maintain BIND versions lower than 4.9.4, you can use the Advanced Options in the DNS server to indicate you have BIND Secondaries, and this disables the fast transfer mode.

FAT   *See* File Allocation Table.

Fault tolerance   Fault tolerance is high-system availability with enough resources to accommodate unexpected failure. Fault tolerance is also the design of a computer to maintain its system's performance when some internal hardware problems occur. This is done through the use of backup systems.

FEK   *See* File Encryption Key.

File Allocation Table (FAT)   A FAT is an area on a disk that indicates the arrangement of files in the sectors. Because of the multi-user nature of Terminal Server, it is strongly recommended that the NTFS file system be used rather than the FAT file system. FAT does not offer file and directory security, whereas with NTFS you can limit access to subdirectories and files to certain users or groups of users.

File Allocation Table 16 (FAT16)   The earlier version of the FAT file system implemented in MS-DOS is known as FAT16, to differentiate it from the improved FAT32.

File Allocation Table 32 (FAT32)   FAT32 is the default file system for Windows 95 OSR2 and Windows 98. The FAT32 file system was first implemented in Windows 95 OSR2 and was supported by Windows 98 and now Windows 2000. While FAT16 cannot support partitions larger than 4GB in Windows 2000, FAT32 can support partitions up to 2TB (Terabytes) in size. However, for performance reasons, the creation of FAT32 partitions is limited to 32GB in Windows 2000. The second major benefit of FAT32 in comparison to FAT16 is that it supports a significantly smaller cluster size—as low as 4K for partitions up to 8GB. This results in more efficient use of disk space, with a 15 to 30 percent utilization improvement in comparison to FAT16.

File Encryption Key (FEK)   A random key called a file encryption key (FEK) is used to encrypt each file and is then itself encrypted using the user's public key. At least two FEKs are created for every encrypted file. One FEK is created with the user's public key, and one is created with the public key of each recovery agent. There could be more than one recovery agent certificate used to encrypt each file, resulting in more than two FEKs. The user's public key can decrypt FEKs created with the public key.

File Transfer Protocol (FTP)   This transfers files to and from a computer running an FTP server service (sometimes called a *daemon*).

Filter Actions   Filter actions define the type of security and the methods in which security is established. The primary methods are: Permit, Block, and Negotiate security.

FireWire   Also known as IEEE 1394. An Apple/Texas Instruments high-speed serial bus allowing up to 63 devices to connect; this bus supports hot swapping and isochronous data transfer.

Forest   A forest is a grouping of one or more domain trees that do not share a common namespace but do share a common schema, configuration, and global catalog; in fact, it forms a noncontiguous (or discontiguous) namespace. The users in one tree do not have global access to resources in other trees, but trusts can be created that allow users to access resources in another tree.

Forward Lookup Query   A forward lookup query occurs when a computer needs to get the Internet Protocol (IP) address for a computer with an Internet name. The local computer sends a query to a local Domain Name System (DNS) name server, which resolves the name or passes the request on to another server for resolution.

Forward lookup zones   Forward lookup zones are used to provide a mechanism to resolve host names to IP addresses for DNS clients. A forward lookup zone will contain what are known as resource records. These resource records contain the actual information about the resources available in the zone.

Forwarder   A DNS forwarder accepts requests to resolve host names from another DNS server. A forwarder can be used to protect your internal DNS server from access by Internet users.

FQDN   *See* Fully Qualified Domain Name.

FTP   *See* File Transfer Protocol.

Fully Qualified Domain Name (FQDN)   A full site name of a system rather than just its host name. The FQDN of each child domain is made up of the combination of its own name and the FQDN of the parent domain. The FQDN includes the host name and the domain membership of that computer.

Gateway   In networking, gateway refers to a router or a computer functioning as one, the "way out" of the network or subnet, to get to another network. You also use gateways for software that connects a system using one protocol to a system using a different protocol, such as the Systems Network Architecture (SNA) software (allows a Local Area Network (LAN) to connect to an IBM mainframe). You can also use Gateway Services for NetWare used to provide a way for Microsoft clients to go through a Windows NT or Windows 2000 server to access files on a Novell file server.

Global Groups   Global Groups are used for combining users who share a common access profile based on job function or business role. Typically organizations use Global Groups for all groups in which membership is expected to change frequently. These groups can have as members only user accounts defined in the same domain as the Global Group.

Globally Unique IDentifier (GUID)   The Globally Unique IDentifier (GUID) is a unique numerical identification created at the time the object is created. An analogy would be a person's social security number, which is assigned once and never changes, even if the person changes his or her name, or moves.

Glue record   The Host (A) Address record is referred to as a glue record. It is called a glue record because it associates the host name in the Name Server (NS) record with an Internet Protocol (IP) address of the machine noted in the NS record. It glues together the name server's host name and IP address in this way.

GPC   *See* Group Policy Container.

GPO   *See* Group Policy Object.

GPT   *See* Group Policy Template.

Graphical User Interface (GUI)   An overall and consistent system for the interactive and visual program that interacts (or interfaces) with the user. GUI can involve pull-down menus, dialog boxes, on-screen graphics, and a variety of icons.

Group policy   Group Policy provides for change management and desktop control on the Windows 2000 platform. You are familiar with the control you had in Windows NT 4.0 using System Policies. Group Policy is similar to System Policies but allows you a much higher level of granular configuration management over your network. Some of the confusion comes from the change of names applied to different groups in Windows 2000. You can apply Group Policy to sites, domains, and organizational units. Each of these represents a group of objects, so Group Policy is applied to the group of objects contained in each of these entities. Group Policy cannot be directly applied to Security Groups that are similar to the groups you are used to working with in Windows NT 4.0. However, by using Group Policy Filtering, you can successfully apply Group Policy to individual Security Groups.

Group Policy Container (GPC)   The Active Directory object Group Policy Containers (GPCs) store the information for the Folder Redirection snap-in and the Software Deployment snap-in. GPCs do not apply to local group policies. They contain component lists and status information, which indicate whether Group Policy Objects (GPOs) are enabled or disabled. They also contain version information, which ensures that the information is synchronized with the Group Policy Template (GPT) information. GPCs also contain the class store in which GPO group policy extensions have settings.

Group Policy Object (GPO)   After you create a group policy, it is stored in a Group Policy Object (GPO) and applied to the site, domain, or Organizational Unit (OU). GPOs are used to keep the group policy information; essentially, it is a collection of policies. You can apply single or multiple GPOs to each site, domain or OU. Group policies are not inherited across domains, and users must have Read permission for the GPO that you want to have applied to them. This way, you can filter the scope of GPOs by adjusting who has read access to each GPO.

Group Policy Template (GPT)   The subset of folders created on each domain controller that store Group Policy Object (GPO) information for specific GPOs are called Group Policy Templates (GPTs). GPTs are stored in the SysVol (System Volume) folder on the domain controller. GPTs store data for Software Policies, Scripts, Desktop File and Folder Management, Software Deployment, and Security settings. GPTs can be defined in computer or user configurations. Consequently, they take effect either when the computer starts or when the user logs on.

GUI   *See* Graphical User Interface.

GUID   *See* Globally Unique IDentifier.

HAL   *See* Hardware Abstraction Layer.

Hardware Abstraction Layer (HAL)   Windows NT's translation layer existing between the hardware, kernel, and input/output (I/O) system.

Hardware Compatibility List (HCL)   The Hardware Compatibility List is published by Microsoft for each of its operating systems, and is updated on a monthly basis. There is a copy of the HCL on the Windows 2000 Professional CD, located in the Support folder and named Hcl.txt.

Hardware profile   A hardware profile is a set of instructions that tells your computer how to boot the system properly, based on the setup of your hardware. Hardware profiles are most commonly used with laptops. This is because laptops are frequently used in at least two different settings: stand-alone and in a docking station on a network. For example, when the laptop is being used at a docking station, it requires a network adapter. However, when the laptop is used away from the network, it does not. The hardware profile dialog manages these configuration changes. If a profile is created for each situation, the user will automatically be presented these choices on Windows startup.

Hash function   A mathematical calculation that produces a fixed-length string of bits, which cannot be reverse-engineered to produce the original.

HCL   *See* Hardware Compatibility List.

HINFO   *See* Host Information.

HKEY_CLASSES_ROOT   Contains information used for software configuration and object linking and embedding (OLE), as well as file association information.

HKEY_CURRENT_CONFIG   Holds data about the current hardware profile that is in use.

HKEY_CURRENT_USER Has information about the user who is currently logged on.

HKEY_LOCAL_MACHINE Stores information about the hardware, software, system devices, and security information for the local computer.

HKEY_USERS Holds information and settings for the environments of all users of the computer.

H-Node H-node (hybrid node) Windows Internet Name Server (WINS) clients are similar to M-node, but use WINS NetBIOS name resolution first, before initiating a NetBIOS broadcast message.

Host Information (HINFO) HINFO records provide information about the Domain Name System (DNS) server itself. Information about the CPU and operating system on the host can be included in the HINFO record. This information is used by application protocols such as File Transfer Protocol (FTP) that can use special procedures when communicating between computers of the same CPU and OS type (RFC 1035).

Host routing Host routing occurs when a computer forwards a packet to a router rather than sending the packet directly on its own network.

Host-to-host layer This layer is basically the same as the Transport layer in the OSI model. It is responsible for flow control, acknowledgments, sequencing (ordering) of packets, and establishment of end-to-end communications. Transmission Control Protocol (TCP) and the User Datagram Protocol (UDP) operate at this level.

HTML *See* HyperText Markup Language.

HTTP *See* HyperText Transfer Protocol.

HyperText Markup Language (HTML) The format used to create documents viewed on the World Wide Web (WWW) by the use of tags (codes) embedded within the text.

HyperText Transfer Protocol (HTTP)   HTTP is an Internet standard supporting World Wide Web (WWW) exchanges. By creating the definitions of Universal Resource Locators (URLs) and their retrieval usage throughout the Internet.

IAS   *See* Internet Authentication Services.

ICS   *See* Internet Connection Sharing.

IDE   *See* Integrated Drive Electronics.

IIS   *See* Internet Information Service.

IKE   *See* Internet Key Exchange.

in-addr.arpa domain   The in-addr.arpa domain indexes host names based on Network IDs and makes reverse lookups much more efficient and speedy.

Incremental backup   This backup process is similar to the Differential backup, but it clears the markers from the selected files after the process. Because it clears the markers, an incremental backup will not back up any files that have not changed since the last incremental backup. This type of backup is fast during the backup but is very slow while restoring the files. You will need the last full backup and all of the subsequent incremental backups to fully restore data. The positive side of this backup type is that it is fast and consumes very little media space.

Indexing service   Provides indexing functions for documents stored on disk, allowing users to search for specific document text or properties.

Industry Standard Architecture (ISA)   A PC's expansion bus used for peripherals plug-in boards.

Infrastructure   Infrastructure of a computer network consists of the basic components upon which it is built.

Initialization Vector (IV)   The IV is a random block of encrypted data that begins each chain. In this fashion, we are able to make each message's ciphertext appear different, even if we were to send the exact same message a hundred times.

Integrated Drive Electronics (IDE) drive   An IDE drive is a hard disk drive for processors containing most controller circuitry within the drive. IDE drives combine Enhanced System Device Interface (ESDI) speed with Small Computer System Interface (SCSI) hard drive interface intelligence.

Integrated Services Digital Network (ISDN)   Integrated Services indicates the provider offers voice and data services over the same medium. Digital Network is a reminder that ISDN was born out of the digital nature of the intercarrier and intracarrier networks. ISDN runs across the same copper wiring that carries regular telephone service. Before attenuation and noise cause the signal to be unintelligible, an ISDN circuit can run a maximum of 18,000 feet. A repeater doubles this distance to 36,000 feet.

Internal Router (IR)   An Internal Router as its name suggests, is a router that sits in its area, and only in its area and handles intra-area routing.

Internet Authentication Services (IAS)   IAS performs authentication, authorization, and accounting of dial-up and Virtual Private Networking (VPN) users. IAS supports the Remote Access Dial-In User Service (RADIUS) protocol.

Internet Connection Sharing (ICS)   ICS can be thought of as a less robust version of Network Address Translation (NAT lite). ICS uses the same address translation technology. ICS is a simpler version of NAT useful for connecting a few computers on a small Local Area Network (LAN) to the Internet or useful for a remote server through a single phone line and account.

Internet Control Message Protocol (ICMP)   The Internet Control Message Protocol (ICMP) is a Transmission Control Protocol/Internet Protocol (TCP/IP) standard that allows hosts and routers that use IP communication to report errors and exchange limited control and status information. The PING utility works by sending an ICMP echo request message and recording the response of echo replies.

Internet Group Management Protocol (IGMP)   The Internet Group Management Protocol is used for multicasting, which is a method of sending a message to multiple hosts but only addressing it to a single address. Members of a multicast group can be defined, and then when a message is sent to the group address, only those computers that belong to the group will receive it. IGMP is used to exchange membership status information between IP routers that support multicasting and members of multicast groups.

Internet Information Service (IIS)   Windows NT web browser software that supports Secure Sockets Layer (SSL) security protocol from Netscape. IIS provides support for Web site creation, configuration, and management, along with Network News Transfer Protocol (NNTP), File Transfer Protocol (FTP), and Simple Mail Transfer Protocol (SMTP).

Internet Key Exchange (IKE)   Automated Key Management uses a combination of the Internet Security Association Key Management Protocol and the Oakley Protocol (ISAKMP/Oakley). This combination of protocols is often referred to collectively as the Internet Key Exchange (IKE). The IKE is responsible for exchange of "key material" (groups of numbers that will form the basis of new key), session keys, SA negotiation, and authentication of peers participating in an Internet Protocol Security (IPSec) interaction. During this exchange, the Oakley protocol protects the identities of the negotiating parties.

Internet Packet eXchange (IPX)   Novell NetWare's built-in networking protocol for Local Area Network (LAN) communication derived from the Xerox Network System protocol. IPX moves data between a server and/or workstation programs from different network nodes. Sometimes called an Internetnetwork Packet eXchange.

Internet Protocol Security (IPSec)   IPSec is a new feature included in Windows 2000 and provides for encryption of data as it travels between two computers, protecting it from modification and interpretation if anyone were to see it on the network.

Internet Security Association and Key Management Protocol (ISAKMP)   An Internet Protocol Security (IPSec) protocol required as part of the IPSec implementation, which provides a framework for Internet key management.

Internet Service Provider (ISP)   The organization allowing users to connect to its computers and then to the Internet. ISPs provide the software to connect and sometimes a portal site and/or internal browsing capability.

Internetwork layer   This layer matches the Network layer in the OSI model. The Internet Protocol (IP) works here to route and deliver packets to the correct destination address. Other protocols that operate at this layer include the Address Resolution Protocol (ARP), Reverse Address Resolution Protocol (RARP), and the Internet Control Message Protocol (ICMP).

Interrupt ReQuest (IRQ)   An electronic signal that is sent to the computer's processor requiring the processor's attention. Also, a computer instruction designed to interrupt a program for an Input/Output (I/O).

IPCONFIG command-line utility   IPCONFIG is used to gather information about the Transmission Control Protocol/Internet Protocol (TCP/IP) configuration on the computer. Typing IPCONFIG at the command line will display the computer's Internet Protocol (IP) address, subnet mask, and default gateway. Adding the /all switch will display additional information such as the host name, Media Access Control (MAC) address, node type, and much more. IPCONFIG includes new switches that increase its usefulness beyond being a great tool for getting IP addressing information about your machines.

IPSec   *See* Internet Protocol Security.

IPX   *See* Internet Packet eXchange.

IR   *See* Internal Router.

IRQ   *See* Interrupt ReQuest.

ISA   *See* Industry Standard Architecture.

ISDN   *See* Integrated Services Digital Network.

ISP   *See* Internet Service Provider.

Iterative query   Iterative queries allow the Domain Name System (DNS) server responding to the request to make a best-effort attempt at resolving the DNS query. If the DNS server receiving an iterative query is not authoritative for the domain included in the query, it can return a Referral response.

JetBEUI   Microsoft had intended NetBEUI to become even more robust, and even routable. They were working on a networking protocol dubbed "JetBEUI" that would have been a routable implementation of NetBEUI.

Kerberos   Kerberos guards against this username and password safety vulnerability by using tickets (temporary electronic credentials) to authenticate. Tickets have a limited life span and can be used in place of usernames and passwords (if the software supports this). Kerberos encrypts the password into the ticket. It uses a trusted server called the Key Distribution Center (KDC) to handle authentication requests. Kerberos speeds up network processes by integrating security and rights across network domains and also eliminates workstations' need to authenticate themselves repeatedly at every domain they access. Kerberos security also makes maneuvering around networks using multiple platforms such as UNIX or NetWare easier.

Knowledge   Knowledge is the very lowest level of learning. It is, of course, important that a network administrator have this knowledge. Knowledge involves the processes of defining, locating, recalling, recognizing, stating, matching, labeling, and identifying.

L2TP   *See* Layer-Two Tunneling Protocol.

Last Known Good Configuration   This mode starts the system using the configuration that was saved in the registry during the last system shutdown. This startup option is useful when you have changed some configuration parameters and the system fails to boot. When you use this mode to start the system, all changes that were made after the last successful logon are lost. Use this option when you suspect that some incorrect configuration changes are causing the system startup failure. This mode does not help if any of the installed drivers have been corrupted or any driver files are deleted by mistake.

Layer Two Tunneling Protocol (L2TP)   L2TP offers better security through the use of IPSec and creates Virtual Private Networks (VPNs). Windows 2000 uses L2TP to provide tunneling services over Internet Protocol Security (IPSec)-based communications. L2TP tunnels can be set up to traverse data across intervening networks that are not part of the VPN being created. L2TP is used to send information across intervening and nonsecure networks.

LDAP   *See* Lightweight Directory Access Protocol.

Lease   A lease is an agreement to let someone use something for a defined length of time. The Dynamic Host Control Protocol (DHCP) client leases Internet Protocol (IP) addressing information from the DHCP server. The DHCP client does not own this information, and does not get to keep it forever.

Legend   The legend displays information about the counters that are being measured. It is the set of columns at the bottom of System Monitor.

Lifetime   This is the "shelf-life" of a route—how long it is considered valid. Static routes automatically have an infinite lifetime, but dynamic routes have a finite lifetime; the route must be refreshed before the lifetime expires in order to be retained in the routing table.

Lightweight Directory Access Protocol (LDAP)   A simplified Directory Access Protocol (DAP) accessing a computer's directory listing. LDAP is able to access to X.500 directories.

Line Printer Daemon (LPD)   LPD is the server process that advertises printer queues and accepts incoming print submissions, which are then routed to the print device.

Line Printer Remote (LPR)   LPR is a process that spools a print job to a remote print spool that is advertised by the Line Printer Daemon (LPD).

Link State Routing   Link state routing was designed specifically to overcome some of the shortcomings of the older distance vector routing protocol, which was never designed for today's wide-scale enterprise internetworks.

LMHOSTS   An LMHOSTS file is a plain-text file that contains NetBIOS names to IP address mappings. LMHOSTS can be useful as a backup method of resolving names of especially important computers when other methods fail.

Load balancing   The fine tuning process of a system (computer, network, etc.) to allow the data to be distributed more efficiently and evenly. Load balancing is an add-on feature of MetaFrame that must be purchased separately from the base product. Load balancing allows the administrator to group servers in a server farm which can act as a single point of access for clients accessing published applications.

Local policy   A group policy stored locally on a Windows 2000 member server or a Windows 2000 professional computer is called a local policy. The local policy is used to set up the configuration settings for each computer and for each user. Local policies are stored in the \%systemroot%\system32\grouppolicy folder on the local computer. Local policies include the auditing policy, user rights and privilege assignment, and various security options.

Local printer   A print device that is directly attached, via a parallel or serial cable, to the computer that is providing the printing services. For a Windows 2000 Professional workstation, a local printer is one that is connected to the workstation. For a Windows 2000 Server, a local printer is one that is connected to the server. Drivers for the print device must reside on the computer that connects to the printer.

Local user profiles (local profiles)   Local user profiles are kept on one local computer hard drive. When a user initially logs on to a computer, a local profile is created for them in the \%systemdrive%\Documents and Settings\<username> folder. When users log off the computer, the changes that they made while they were logged on will be saved to their local profile on that client computer. This way, subsequent logons to that computer will bring up their personal settings. When users log on to a different computer, they will not receive these settings, as they are local to the computer in which they made the changes. Therefore, each user that logs on to that computer receives individual desktop settings. Local profiles are ideal for users who only use one computer. For users that require access to multiple computers, the Roaming profile would be the better choice.

Logical infrastructure   Logical infrastructure is the networking protocols, the Domain Name System (DNS) namespace and services, the Internet Protocol (IP) addressing scheme and Dynamic Host Control Protocol (DHCP) strategy, the remote access services, and security protocols. Components of the logical infrastructure includes Network Protocols, IP Addressing Schemes, Name Resolution Services, Remote Access, Routing and Network Address Translation, and Security Infrastructure (Certificate Services).

LogicalDisk object   The LogicalDisk object measures the transfer of data for a logical drive (i.e., C: or D:) or storage volumes. You can use the PhysicalDisk object to determine which hard disk is causing the bottleneck. Then, to narrow the cause of the bottleneck, you can use the LogicalDisk object to determine which, if any, partition is the specific cause of the bottleneck. By default, the PhysicalDisk object is enabled and the LogicalDisk object is disabled on Windows 2000 Server.

LPD   *See* Line Printer Daemon.

LPR   *See* Line Printer Remote.

MAC   *See* Media Access Control; Message Authentication Code.

Mail eXchanger (MX)   Identifies the preferred mail servers on the network. If you have several mail servers, an order of precedence will be run. Note that the MX record has similar requirements to the Canonical Name (CNAME) record. You must have an existing A record for the machine that you wish to create a MX record for.

Mandatory Roaming profiles   Mandatory roaming profiles are mandatory user profiles the user cannot change. They are usually created to define desktop configuration settings for groups of users in order to simplify administration and support. Users can make changes to their desktop settings while they are logged on, but these changes will not be saved to the profile, as Mandatory profiles are read-only. The next time they log on, their desktop will be set back to the original Mandatory profile settings.

Many-to-One Certificate Mapping   This involves mapping many certificates to a single user account. This is particularly convenient when organizations need to share specific information with each other. An administrator must install the Root Certificate Authority (CA) certificates of all the desired CAs as trusted Root CAs in their enterprise. The administrator can then set a rule that maps all certificates installed by the trusted CAs to a single Windows 2000 account. Users using these mapped certificates possess access rights defined by the rights set on the mapped account.

Master File Table (MFT)   The MFT stores the information needed by the operating system to retrieve files from the volume. Part of the MFT is stored at the beginning of the volume and cannot be moved. Also, if the volume contains a large number of directories, it can prevent the free space from being defragmented.

Master image   After configuring one computer with the operating system and all the applications, Sysprep is run to create an image of the hard disk. This computer serves as the master or model computer that will have the complete setup of the operating system, application software, and any service packs. This hard disk image is the master image and is copied to a CD or put on a network share for distribution to many computers. Any third-party disk-imaging tool can then be used to replicate the image to other identical computers.

MCSE   *See* Microsoft Certified Systems Engineer.

Media Access Control (MAC)   A sublayer in the Open System Interconnection (OSI) data link layer that controls access, control, procedures, and format for a Local Area Network (LAN), for example, Institute of Electronic and Electrical Engineers (IEEE) 802.3, 802.5, and 802.5 standards.

Message Authentication Code (MAC)   A cryptographically generated fixed-length code associated with a message in order to ensure the authenticity of the message (a digital signature is a public key MAC).

Message queuing service   Provides a communication infrastructure and a development tool for creating distributed messaging applications. Such applications can communicate across heterogeneous networks and with computers that might be offline. Message queuing provides guaranteed message delivery, efficient routing, security, transactional support, and priority-based messaging.

Metric   A metric is the cost of using a particular route from one destination to another. Generally this will be the number of hops to the Internet Protocol (IP) destination. Anything on the local subnet is one hop, and every time a router is crossed, this adds 1 to the hop count. The value of this is that it lets Windows 2000 select the route with the lowest metric if there are multiple routes to the same destination.

MFT   *See* Master File Table.

Microsoft Certified Systems Engineer (MCSE)   An engineer who is a technical specialist in advanced Microsoft products, specifically NT Server and NT Workstation.

Microsoft Challenge Handshake Authentication Protocol (MS-CHAP) This is Microsoft's version of the Challenge Handshake Authentication Protocol, and offers the same features as CHAP with some additional advantages. It is supported on all versions of Windows, and as such, makes a suitable default authentication protocol. However, where you have the choice, you should instead use the later version, MS-CHAPv2, which is a more secure protocol that protects against server impersonation. If mutual authentication (where both sides can verify they are who they say they are) is important to your security policies, then you should ensure that Microsoft clients have the latest MS-CHAPv2 and disable MS-CHAP on the server.

Microsoft Management Console (MMC)   The MMC provides a standardized interface for using administrative tools and utilities. The management applications contained in an MMC are called Snap-ins, and custom MMCs hold the Snap-ins required to perform specific tasks. Custom consoles can be saved as files with the .msc file extension. The MMC was first introduced with NT Option Pack. Using the MMC leverages the familiarity you have with the other snap-ins available within MMC, such as SQL Server 7 and Internet Information Server 4. With the MMC, all your administrative tasks can be done in one place.

Mini-Setup Wizard   The purpose of this wizard is to add some user-specific parameters on the destination computer. These parameters include: End-user license agreement (EULA); Product key (serial number); Username, company name, and administrator password; Network configuration; Domain or workgroup name; and Date and time zone selection.

Mirror Set   In a mirror set, all data on a selected partition or drive are automatically duplicated onto another physical disk. The main purpose of a mirror set is to provide fault tolerance in the event of missing or corrupt data. If one disk fails or contains corrupt files, the data is simply retrieved and rebuilt from the other disk.

Mirrored Volume   Like basic disks, dynamic disks can also be mirrored, and are called mirrored volumes. A continuous and automatic backup of all data in a mirrored volume is saved to a separate disk to provide fault tolerance in the event of a disk failure or corrupt file. Note that you cannot mirror a spanned or striped volume.

Mirroring   Also called RAID 1. RAID 1 consists of two drives that are identical matches, or mirrors, of each other. If one drive fails, you have another drive to boot up and keep the server going.

Mixed Mode   When in Mixed Mode, the domain still uses master replication with a Windows 2000 DC. The Windows NT Backup Domain Controllers (BDCs) replicate from the Windows 2000 server, as did the Windows NT Primary Domain Controller (PDC). When you are operating in Mixed Mode, some Windows 2000 functionality will not be available. You will not be able to use group nesting or transitive trusts. Mixed Mode is the default mode.

MMC   *See* Microsoft Management Console.

M-Node   M-node (mixed node) Windows Internet Name Server (WINS) clients use both broadcasts and WINS servers to resolve NetBIOS names to Internet Protocol (IP) addresses. The mixed-node client preferentially uses broadcasts before querying a WINS server.

MP   *See* Multilink Point-to-Point Protocol.

MSCHAP   *See* Microsoft Challenge Handshake Authentication Protocol.

MX   *See* Mail eXchanger.

Multilink Point-to-Point Protocol (MP)   MP allows multiple physical links to appear as a single local link over which data can be sent and received at a higher throughput than if going over a single physical link.

Name collision   When a machine tries to update its name in the zone database, and finds that its name is already there with a different IP address, it has experienced a name collision. The default behavior of the DNS client is to overwrite the existing record with its own information.

Name Server (NS)   An NS record lists the Domain Name System (DNS) servers that can return authoritative answers for the domain. This includes the Primary DNS server for the zone, and any other DNS servers to which you delegate authority for the zone. The NS record is also used to direct DNS client requests to other DNS servers when the server is not authoritative for a zone. For example, when you issue a query for the microsoft.com domain, the .com domain DNS server is not authoritative for the microsoft.com domain. However, an NS record is contained on the .com DNS server that can return a referral answer to the requesting client, which will direct it to the microsoft.com DNS server.

NAT   *See* Network Address Translation.

Native Mode   Native Mode allows only Windows 2000 domain controllers to operate in the domain. When all domain controllers for the domain are upgraded to Windows 2000 Server, you can switch to Native Mode. This allows you to use transitive trusts and the group-nesting features of Windows 2000. When switching to Native Mode, ensure you no longer need to operate in Mixed Mode, because you cannot switch back to Mixed Mode once you are in Native Mode.

NBMA   *See* Non-Broadcast Multiple Access.

NBNS   *See* NETwork Basic Input/Output System Name Server.

NBTSTAT   NBTSTAT is used to display the local NetBIOS name table, a table of NetBIOS names registered by local applications, and the NetBIOS name cache, a local cache listing of NetBIOS computer names that have been resolved to IP addresses.

NDS   *See* NetWare Directory Service.

Net Shell (Netsh)   Net Shell (Netsh) is a command-line and scripting tool for both local and remote Windows 2000 servers running Routing and Remote Access. It can be used in conjunction with remote access settings, but is also for routing, Dynamic Host Control Protocol (DHCP) Relay, and Network Address Translation (NAT).

NetBEUI   *See* NETwork Basic Input/Output System Extended User Interface.

NetBIOS   *See* Network Basic Input/Output System.

NETDIAG   The Resource Kit for Windows 2000 Professional includes the NETDIAG utility. This is a command-line diagnostic tool that helps isolate networking and connectivity problems. It does this by performing a series of tests designed to determine the state of the network client software, and ascertain whether it is functional. This tool does not require that parameters or switches be specified, which means support personnel and network administrators can focus on analyzing the output, rather than training users on how to use the tool.

NETSTAT command-line utility   NETSTAT is used to display protocol statistics and current TCP/IP network connections.

NetWare Directory Service (NDS)   NDS (created by Novell) has a hierarchical information database allowing the user to log on to a network with NDS capable of calculating the user's access rights.

Network   Two or more computers connected together by cable or wireless media for the purpose of sharing data, hardware peripherals, and other resources.

Network Address Translation (NAT)   With NAT, you can allow internal users to have access to important external resources while still preventing unauthorized access from the outside world.

NETwork Basic Input/Output System (NetBIOS)   A program in Microsoft's operating system that links personal computers to a Local Area Network (LAN).

NETwork Basic Input/Output System Extended User Interface (NetBEUI)   The transport layer for the Disk Operating System (DOS) networking protocol called Network Basic Input/Output System (NetBIOS).

NETwork Basic Input/Output System Name Server   A NetBIOS Name Server (NBNS) is a machine that runs server software dedicated to resolving NetBIOS names to IP addresses. The NBNS contains a database file that can accept dynamic NetBIOS name registrations and answer queries for NetBIOS name resolution.

Network Interface Card (NIC)   A board with encoding and decoding circuitry and a receptacle for a network cable connection that, bypassing the serial ports and operating through the internal bus, allows computers to be connected at higher speeds to media for communications between stations.

Network interface layer   This bottom layer of the U.S. Department of Defense (DoD) model corresponds to both the Data Link and Physical layers of OSI. It provides the interface between the network architecture (Ethernet, Token Ring, AppleTalk, etc.) and the upper layers, as well as the physical (hardware) issues.

Network News Transfer Protocol (NNTP)   The Network News Transfer Protocol is used for managing messages posted to private and public newsgroups. NNTP servers provide for storage of newsgroup posts that can be downloaded by client software called a newsreader. Windows 2000 Server includes an NNTP server with IIS, and Outlook Explorer version 5, which is part of the Internet Explorer software included with Windows 2000, provides both an e-mail client and a newsreader

Network protocol   Network protocol usually refers to the network and transport layer protocols (often part of a protocol "stack" or "suite") used for communication over a Local Area Network (LAN).

Network printer   A print device that has a built-in network interface or connects directly to a dedicated network interface. Both workstations and servers can be configured to print directly to the network printer, and the network printer controls its own printer queue, determining which jobs from which clients will print in which order. Printing clients have no direct control over the printer queue and cannot see other print jobs being submitted to the printer. Administration of a network printer is difficult. Drivers for the print device must reside on the computer that connects to the printer.

NIC   *See* Network Interface Card.

NNTP   *See* Network News Transfer Protocol.

Non-Broadcast Multiple Access (NBMA)   This represents a network that can connect more than two routers, but which cannot support hardware broadcasts. In this particular case, because multicasts cannot be used, Open Shortest Path First (OSPF) must be configured to use unicast to the specific IP addresses of the routers on the NBMA network.

Nondedicated server   A nondedicated print server is a Windows 2000 server that hosts printing services in addition to other services. A domain controller, database server, or Domain Name System (DNS) server can provide printing services as well, but should be used only for a smaller number of printers or for printers that are not heavily used. Anyone setting up a nondedicated print server should monitor the performance of the printing process and the other tasks running on the server and be prepared to modify the server configuration if the performance drops below acceptable levels.

Nonmandatory Roaming profiles   Roaming user profiles are stored on the network file server and are the perfect solution for users who have access to multiple computers. This way their profile is accessible no matter where they log on in the domain. When users log on to a computer within their domain, their Roaming profile will be copied from the network server to the client computer and the settings will be applied to the computer while they are logged on. Subsequent logins will compare the Roaming profile files to the local profile files. The file server then copies only any files that have been altered since the user last logged on locally, significantly decreasing the time required to logon. When the user logs off, any changes that the user made on the local computer will be copied back to the profile on the network file server.

Normal backup   This is the most common type and is also known as a full backup. The Normal backup operation backs up all files and folders that are selected irrespective of the archive attributes of the files. This provides the easiest way to restore the files and folders but is expensive in terms of the time it takes to complete the backup job and the storage space it consumes. The restore process from a Normal backup is less complex because you do not have to use multiple tape sets to restore data completely.

NS   *See* Name Server.

NSLOOKUP command-line utility   NSLOOKUP is used to check records, domain host aliases, domain host services, and operating system information by querying Domain Name System (DNS) servers. NSLOOKUP works in two modes: interactive mode and command mode. Command mode is used when you only want to do a single query.

NT File System (NTFS)   The NT File System (with file names up to 255 characters) is a system created to aid the computer and its components recover from hard disk crashes.

NTFS   *See* NT File System.

NWLink IPX/SPX/NetBIOS Compatible Transport Protocol (NWLink)   Microsoft's implementation of Novell's Internet Packet eXchange/Sequenced Packet eXchange (IPX/SPX) protocol stack, required for connecting to NetWare servers prior to version 5. NWLink can also be used on small networks that use only Windows 2000 and other Microsoft client software. NWLink is a Network Driver Interface Specification (NDIS) compliant, native 32-bit protocol. The NWLink protocol supports Windows sockets and NetBIOS.

ODBC   *See* Open DataBase Connectivity.

Offer   After the Dynamic Host Control Protocol (DHCP) server receives the DHCPDISCOVER message, it looks at the request to see if the client configuration request is valid. If so, it sends back a DHCPOFFER message with the client's network hardware address, an IP address, a subnet mask, the length of time the lease is valid, and the IP address of the server that provided the DHCP information. This message is also a Transmission Control Protocol/Internet Protocol (TCP/IP) broadcast, as the client does not yet have an Internet Protocol (IP) address. The server then reserves the address it sent to the client so that it is not offered to another client making a request. If there are more than one DHCP servers on the network, all servers respond to the DHCPDISCOVER message with a DHCPOFFER message.

Off-Subnet Addressing   When the Dynamic Host Control Protocol (DHCP) server allocates an Internet Protocol (IP) address that is on a different subnet to the remote access server itself; this is called off-subnet addressing.

On-Subnet Addressing   When the allocated addresses are on the same subnet as the remote access server, this is called on-subnet addressing and is by far the more common setup.

One-to-One Certificate Mapping   This type of mapping simply involves mapping a single user certificate to a single Windows 2000 user account. Certificates may be issued from your own Enterprise CA or from a trusted CA. These certificates are then manually mapped to their respective user accounts.

One-way initiated demand-dial connections   A one-way initiated connection restricts one router to being the calling router and the other to being an answering router. In many ways, this is the easiest of configurations because there is less to configure. It also offers a more secure routing environment from the perspective of the calling router because it has complete control over when a connection is made.

Open DataBase Connectivity (ODBC)   A database programming interface that allows applications a way to access network databases.

Open Shortest Path First (OSPF)   Open Shortest Path First is a link-state routing protocol designed for use in large scale internetworks and seeks to redress some of the shortcomings associated with traditional distance vector-based routing protocols. OSPF is a new and unfamiliar routing protocol. It is outside the scope of this chapter to give a complete and detailed description on every aspect of OSPF but it does aim to provide the basic understanding and provide a framework of concepts and terminology to get you started. Without this, the OSPF configuration options themselves will make little sense, let alone understanding the consequences of setting their values.

Open Systems Interconnection (OSI) model   This is a model of breaking networking tasks into layers. Each layer is responsible for a specific set of functionality. There are performance objects available in System Monitor for analyzing network performance.

Organizational Units (OUs)   OUs in Windows 2000 are objects that are containers for other objects, such as users, groups, or other organizational units. Objects cannot be placed in another domain's OUs. The whole purpose of an OU is to have a hierarchical structure to organize your network objects. You can assign a group policy to an OU. Generally, the OU will follow a structure from your company. It may be a location, if you have multiple locations. It can even be a department-level organization. Also, OUs are units used to organize objects within a domain. These objects can include user accounts, groups, computers, printers, and even other OUs. The hierarchy of OUs is independent of other domains.

OSI   *See* Open Systems Interconnection.

OSPF   *See* Open Shortest Path First.

OU   *See* Organizational Unit.

Paging   When enough memory is not available for the running applications, pages of memory can be swapped from physical memory to the hard disk too much and slow the system down. This is also known as paging because pages of memory are swapped at a time. Windows 2000 separates memory into 4KB pages of memory to help prevent fragmentation of memory. Swapping can even get bad enough that you can hear your hard disk running constantly.

Paging file   A file on the hard disk (or spanning multiple disks) that stores some of the program code that is normally in the computer's RAM. This is called virtual memory, and allows the programs to function as if the computer had more memory than is physically installed.

PAP   *See* Password Authentication Protocol.

Password Authentication Protocol (PAP)   The Password Authentication Protocol is the least secure of the authentication protocols provided using a simple, plain-text authentication. It offers no protection against replay attacks, client impersonation, or server impersonation. However, it is offered in Windows 2000 Routing and Remote Access for downward compatibility for older clients and non-Microsoft clients that cannot support a stronger authentication protocol.

Password policy   A password policy regulates how your users must establish and manage their passwords. This includes password complexity requirements and how often passwords must change. There are several settings that can be used to implement a successful password policy. You can enforce password uniqueness so those users cannot simply switch back and forth between a few easy to remember passwords. This can be set to low, medium, or high security. With low security, the system remembers the user's last 1–8 passwords (it is your choice as administrator to decide how many); with medium, it remembers the last 9–16 passwords; with high, it remembers the last 17–24 passwords.

PathPing   This is new to Windows 2000 and combines features from both Ping and Tracert by sending packets to each router in the source to destination route, and then computing results based on the information returned from each discovered router. It helps to indicate the degree of packet loss at each link of the route, allowing you to identify which routers or links might be causing problems in the way of packet loss and delays.

PATHPING command-line utility   PATHPING is used to verify configurations and test IP connectivity by name or IP address. PATHPING combines features of PING and TRACERT with added functionality, and is used to trace the route a packet takes to a destination and display information on packet losses for each router in the path. PATHPING can also be used to troubleshoot Quality of Service (QoS) connectivity.

PCMCIA   *See* Personal Computer Memory Card Interface Adapter.

PDC   *See* Primary Domain Controller.

Peer-to-peer network   A workgroup is also referred to as a peer-to-peer network, because all the computers connected together and communicating with one another are created equal; that is, there is no central computer that manages security and controls access to the network.

Performance logging   Performance logging has many features. The data collected are stored in a comma-delimited or tab-delimited format, which allows for exportation to spreadsheet and database applications for a variety of tasks such as charting and reports. The data can also be viewed as collected. You can configure the logging by specifying start and stop times, the name of the log files and the maximum size of the log. You can start and stop the logging of data manually or create a schedule for logging. You can even specify a program to run automatically when logging stops. You can also create trace logs. Trace logs track events that occur rather than measuring performance counters.

Permissions Inheritance   By default, all permissions set for a folder are inherited by the files in the folder, the subfolders in the folder, and the contents of the subfolders. When the permissions on a folder are viewed in the Security tab of the file or folder Permissions window, inherited permissions are indicated with a gray check box.

Personal Computer Memory Card Interface Adapter (PCMCIA)
An interface standard for plug-in cards for portable computers; devices meeting the standard (for example, fax cards, modems) are theoretically interchangeable.

Personal Information Exchange   The Personal Information Exchange format is an industry format that facilitates backup and restoration of a certificate and its private key. This vendor-independent certificate format enables certificates and their corresponding private keys to be transferred from one computer to another or from a computer to removable media. Personal Information Exchange format is the only format used by Windows 2000 when exporting certificates and private keys because it avoids exposing the keys to unintended parties.

Physical infrastructure   Physical infrastructure is the machines themselves along with the cables and network interface cards, and hubs and routers.

Physical layer protocols   Physical layer protocols consist of specifications or standards governing the hardware components.

Physical memory   Physical memory is the actual Random Access Memory (RAM) on the computer. When the physical memory becomes full, the operating system can also use space on the hard disk as virtual memory. When memory becomes full, rather than locking up the computer, the operating system stores unused data on the hard disk in a page file (also called paging or swap file). Data are swapped back and forth between the hard disk and physical memory as needed for running applications. If memory is needed that is in virtual memory, it is swapped back into physical memory.

PhysicalDisk object   The PhysicalDisk object measures the transfer of data for the entire hard disk. You can use the PhysicalDisk object to determine which hard disk is causing the bottleneck. By default, the PhysicalDisk object is enabled and the LogicalDisk object is disabled on Windows 2000 Server.

PKI   *See* Public Key Infrastructure.

Plug and Play (PnP)   A standard requiring add-in hardware to carry the software to configure itself in a given way supported by Microsoft Windows 95. Plug and Play can make peripheral configuration software, jumper settings, and Dual In-line Package (DIP) switches unnecessary. PnP allows the operating system to load device drivers automatically and assign system resources dynamically to computer components and peripherals. Windows 2000 moves away from this older technology with its use of Kernel-mode and User-mode PnP architecture. PnP autodetects, configures, and installs the necessary drivers in order to minimize user interaction with hardware configuration. Users no longer have to tinker with IRQ and I/O settings.

P-Node   A p-node (peer node) Windows Internet Name Server (WINS) client uses a WINS server and does not issue broadcasts. When a WINS client is configured as a p-node WINS client, it will *not* broadcast to resolve a NetBIOS name to an IP address. The advantage of configuring WINS clients as p-nodes is that there is no possibility of NetBIOS broadcast traffic using up valuable network bandwidth. On the other hand, if the p-node client is not able to access a WINS server, it will have to use alternate methods to resolve the NetBIOS name to an IP address, even if the destination host is local. This can lead to strange things, like the p-node client accessing a remote Domain Name System (DNS) server to resolve the Internet Protocol (IP) address of a host on the local segment.

PnP   *See* Plug and Play.

Point-to-Point Protocol (PPP)   A serial communication protocol most commonly used to connect a personal computer to an Internet Service Provider (ISP). PPP is the successor to Serial Line Internet Protocol (SLIP) and may be used over both synchronous and asynchronous circuits. Also, PPP is a full-duplex, connectionless protocol that supports many different types of links. The advantages of PPP make it de facto standard for dial-up connections.

Point-to-Point Tunneling Protocol (PPTP)   One of two standards for dial-up telephone connection of computers to the Internet, with better data negotiation, compression, and error corrections than the other Serial Line Internet

Protocol (SLIP), but costing more to transmit data and unnecessary when both sending and receiving modems can handle some of the procedures.

Pointer record (PTR)   The Pointer record is created to allow for reverse lookups. Reverse lookups are valuable when doing security analysis and checking authenticity of source domains for e-mail.

Policy Inheritance   Group policies have an order of inheritance in which the policies are applied. Local policies are applied first, then group policies are applied to the site, then the domain, and finally the Organizational Unit (OU). Policies applied first are overwritten by policies applied later. Therefore, group policies applied to a site overwrite the local policies and so on. When there are multiple Group Policy Objects (GPOs) for a site, domain, or OU, the order in which they appear in the Properties list applies. This policy inheritance order works well for small companies, but a more complex inheritance strategy may be essential for larger corporations.

Ports   A channel of a device that can support single point-to-point connections is known as a port. Devices can be single port, as in a modem.

Power options   Power options are dependent on the particular hardware. Power options include Standby and Hibernation modes. Standby mode turns off the monitor and hard disks to save power. Hibernation mode turns off the monitor and disks, saves everything in memory to disk, turns off the computer, and then restores the desktop to the state in which you left it when the computer is turned on.

PPP   *See* Point-to-Point Protocol.

PPTP   *See* Point-to-Point Tunneling Protocol.

Preboot eXecution Environment (PXE)   The PXE is a new Dynamic Host Control Protocol (DHCP)-based technology used to help client computers boot from the network. The Windows 2000 Remote Installation Service (RIS) uses the PXE technology along with the existing Transmission Control Protocol/Internet Protocol (TCP/IP) network infrastructure to implement the RIS-based deployment of Windows 2000 Professional. The client computer that has the PXE-based ROM uses its Basic Input/Output System (BIOS) to contact an existing RIS server and get an Internet Protocol (IP) address from the DHCP server running on the network. The RIS server then initializes the installation process on the client computer.

Preemptive multitasking   An environment in which timesharing controls the programs in use by exploiting a scheduled time usage of the computer's Central Processing Unit (CPU).

Preshared keys   A preshared key is a secret key agreed upon previously by two users conducting the transaction. This method, like the public key certificate, has the advantage of working with computers that are not running Kerberos v5. The disadvantage is that Internet Protocol Security (IPSec) must be configured, on both sides, to use the specified preshared key. However, this simple method is also appropriate for non-Windows 2000 computers, and works well in cases where only authentication protection is required.

Primary Domain Controller (PDC)   An NT security management for its local domain. The PDC is periodically synchronized to its copy, the Backup Domain Controller (BDC). Only one PDC can exist in a domain. In an NT 4.0 single domain model, any user having a valid domain user account and password in the user accounts database of the PDC has the ability to log on to any computer that is a member of the domain, including MetaFrame servers.

Primary Domain Name System (DNS) Server   The Primary DNS server maintains the master copy of the DNS database for the zone. This copy of the database is the only one that can be modified, and any changes made to its database are distributed to secondary servers in the zone during a zone transfer process. The server can cache resolution requests locally so a lookup query does not have to be sent across the network for a duplicate request. The primary server contains the address mappings for the Internet root DNS servers. Primary servers can also act as secondary servers for other zones.

Primary Partitions   Primary partitions are typically used to create bootable drives. Each primary partition represents one drive letter, up to a maximum of four on a single hard disk. One primary partition must be marked as active in order to boot the system, and most operating systems must be loaded on a primary partition to work.

Print Device   The hardware that actually does the printing. A print device is one of two types as defined in Windows 2000: local or network-interface. A local print device connects directly to the print server with a serial or parallel interface. A network-interface print device connects to the printer across the network and must have its own network interface or be connected to an external network adapter.

Print Driver   A software program used by Windows 2000 and other computer programs to connect with printers and plotters. It translates information sent to it into commands that the print device can understand.

Print Server   A print server is a computer that manages printing on the network. A print server can be a dedicated computer hosting multiple printers, or it can run as one of many processes on a nondedicated computer.

Printer permissions   Printer permissions are established through the Security tab in the printer's Properties dialog. The security settings for printer objects are similar to the security settings for folder shares.

Private key   A digital code used to decrypt data, which is kept secret and works in conjunction with a published public key.

Protocol stack   A protocol stack consists of two or more protocols working together to accomplish a purpose (communication with another computer across a network). Transmission Control Protocol (TCP) and Internet Protocol (IP) make up the stack, which handles the most important tasks of communication such as handling addressing and routing issues, error checking, and flow control.

Protocol suite   A protocol suite is a more elaborate collection of communication protocols, utilities, tools, and applications. The suite includes a large number of additional protocols, used in various situations and for different purposes. Different vendors may include different tools and utilities in their implementations of the Transmission Control Protocol/Internet Protocol (TCP/IP) suite.

Protocols   Protocols are sets of rules that computers use to communicate with one another. Protocols usually work together in stacks, so called because in a layered networking model, they operate at different layers or levels. These protocols govern the logic, formatting, and timing of information exchange between layers.

Proxy autodiscovery   Proxy autodiscovery is used only by clients that have Internet Explorer 5.0. This option informs the client of the location of the Internet Explorer 5.0 automatic configuration file.

PSTN   *See* Public Switched Telephone Network.

PTR   *See* Pointer record.

Public key   A digital code used to encrypt or decrypt data, which is published and made available to the public, used in conjunction with a secret private key.

Public Key Certificate   A Public Key Certificate is a security token that is passed between a certificate server and a client that causes data exchanged between the two to be encrypted. Public encryption keys include the public key certificates are responsible for encoding the data. Certificates can be either single use (e.g., secure e-mail (S/MIME) only) or multi-use (e.g. secure e-mail (S/MIME, Encrypting File System, and client authentication). So, we can easily see the certificates can be applied in various scenarios.

Public Key Infrastructure (PKI)   A key and certificate management system that is trusted.

Public Switched Telephone Network (PSTN)   Also known as POTS (Plain Old Telephone Service), this is the analog telephone system originally designed to transfer human voice. The dial-up equipment consists of an analog modem at the client and at the server. The maximum bit rate is low.

Publishing resources   Resources, such as folders and printers, which are available to be shared on the network, can be published to the Active Directory. The resources are published to the directory and can be located by users, who can query the directory based on the resource's properties (for example, to locate all color printers).

Push replication   Push replication causes the push partner to send changes based on the number of changes made in the Windows Internet Name Server (WINS) database. After the minimum number of changes have been made, the push partner sends a pull notification to the WINS server to request the changes. Windows 2000 WINS Servers are able to maintain persistent connections, which allow push partners to push changes as soon as they take place.

PXE   *See* Preboot eXecution Environment.

QoS   *See* Quality of Service.

Quality of Service (QoS) Admission Control   Admission control allows you to control how applications are allotted network bandwidth. You can give important applications more bandwidth, less important applications less bandwidth.

RADIUS   *See* Remote Access Dial-In User Service.

RAID   *See* Redundant Array of Inexpensive Disks.

RARP   *See* Reverse Address Resolution Protocol.

RAS   *See* Remote Access Service.

RDP   *See* Remote Desktop Protocol.

Realm-based tunneling   Realm-based tunneling is where the access concentrator makes decisions on the tunnel's final destination (Virtual Private Network—VPN—server) based on additional group information about the user (referred to as the realm).

Rebinding Time Value   The Rebinding Time Value represents 87.5 percent of the lease period. If the lease period is eight days, then the rebinding interval is 168 hours. The client will attempt to rebind its IP address at this time only if it was not able to renew its lease at the Renewal Time (T1). The client broadcasts a DHCPREQUEST message. If the server that granted the Internet Protocol (IP) address does not respond, the client will enter the Rebinding State and begin the DHCPDISCOVER process, attempting to renew its IP address with any Dynamic Host Control Protocol (DHCP) server. If it cannot renew its IP address, it will try to receive a new one from any responding DHCP server. If unsuccessful, TCP/IP services are shut down on that computer.

Recovery agent   The recovery agent restores the encrypted file on a secure computer with its private recovery keys. The agent decrypts it using the cipher command line and then returns the plain text file to the user. The recovery agent goes to the computer with the encrypted file, loads the recovery certificate and private key, and performs the recovery. It is not as safe as the first option because the recovery agent's private key may remain on the user's computer.

Recovery Console   The Recovery Console is a new command-line interpreter program feature in Windows 2000 that helps in system maintenance activities and resolving system problems. This program is separate from the Windows 2000 command prompt.

Recursive query   The Domain Name System (DNS) client most often will send a recursive query. When a recursive query is sent to the client's Preferred DNS server, the server must respond to the query either positively or negatively. A positive response returns the Internet Protocol (IP) address; a negative response returns a "host not found" or similar error. A recursive query is one that requires a definitive response, either affirmative or negative.

Redundant Array of Inexpensive Disks (RAID)   Although mirroring and duplexing are forms of RAID, most people think of RAID as involving more than two drives. The most common form of RAID is RAID-5, which is the striping of data across three or more drives, providing fault tolerance if one drive fails. For the best disk performance, consider using a SCSI RAID (Redundant Array of Independent Disks) controller. RAID controllers automatically place data on multiple disk drives and can increase disk performance. Using the software implementation of RAID provided by NT would increase performance if designed properly, but the best performance is always realized through hardware RAID controllers.

Redundant Array of Inexpensive Disks 5 (RAID-5) Volume   A RAID-5 volume on a dynamic drive provides disk striping with parity, and is similar to a basic stripe set with parity. This disk configuration provides both increased storage capacity and fault tolerance. Data in a dynamic RAID-5 volume are interleaved across three or more disks (up to 32 disks), and parity information is included to rebuild lost data in the event of an individual disk failure. Like a spanned or striped volume, a RAID-5 volume cannot be mirrored.

Referral response   The Referral response contains the Internet Protocol (IP) address of another Domain Name System (DNS) server that may be able to service the query. The Referral is based on information contained in delegations (NS records) on the DNS server being queried.

Registry   The Registry is the hierarchical database that stores operating system and application configuration information. It was introduced in Windows 9x and NT and replaced much of the functionality of the old initialization, system, and command files used in the early versions of Windows (.ini, .sys, and .com extensions). The registry is also a Microsoft Windows program allowing the user to choose options for configuration and applications to set them; it replaces confusing text-based .INI files.

Remote   The word "remote" can take on a number of different meanings depending on the context. In the case of an individual computer, the computer you are sitting in front of is sometimes referred to as being "local" while any other computer is considered "remote." In this context any machine but your own is considered a remote computer. In discussions related to network configuration and design, "remote" may refer to segments and machines that are on the far side of a router. In this context, all machines on your physical segment are considered "local" and machines located on other physical segments are referred to as remote.

Remote access   Remote access is when a workstation connects to a remote network so that remote resources can be transparently accessed. All applications are still run on the workstation—the only processing done on the remote access server involves the connection process (e.g., routing, authentication, encryption) rather than running any applications for the remote client.

Remote Access Dial-In User Service (RADIUS)   RADIUS is an industry-standard protocol providing what's often referred to as the three "A"s—Authentication, Authorization, and Accounting services for distributed dial-up networking. RADIUS is actually a client/server protocol. In the context of Windows 2000 Routing and Remote Access, the RAS server is actually the RADIUS client because although it physically accepts the incoming connections, it passes all connection requests and information about the connections to the RADIUS server. That RADIUS server is usually devoted to running a large user account database against which it can identify remote users.

Remote Access Policy   Remote access policies allow you to create demand-dial connections to use specific authentication and encryption methods. In Windows NT versions 3.5x and Windows NT 4.0, authorization was much simpler. The administrator simply granted dial-in permission to the user. The callback options were configured on a per-user basis.

Remote Access Service (RAS)   Remote Access Service is a built-in feature of the Microsoft NT operating system. It allows users to establish a connection to an NT network over a standard phone line. Remote Access allows users to access files on a network or transfer files from a remote PC, over a Dial-Up Networking connection. The performance of transferring files over a dial-up connection is very similar to the performance you would get if you were downloading a file from the Internet.

Remote control   Remote control is when a workstation shares (controls) a remote machine's resources (screen, keyboard, mouse, processor) over a remote link. This means that the remote machine can run applications for the client workstation because the CPU is shared. In this case, the workstation effectively becomes a dumb terminal, because it is not running applications itself but using the CPU on the remote machine.

Remote Desktop Protocol (RDP)   Remote Desktop Protocol (RDP) is the application protocol between the client and the server. It informs the server of the keystrokes and mouse movement of the client and returns to the client the Windows 2000 graphical display from the server. RDP is a multi-channel, standard protocol that provides various levels of compression so that it can adapt to different connection speeds and encryption levels from 40 to 128 bit. Transmission Control Protocol/Internet Protocol (TCP/IP) carries the messages, and RDP is the language in which the messages are written. Both are needed to use Microsoft's implementation of Terminal Services.

Remote Installation Preparation (RIPrep)   RIPrep is a disk duplication tool included with Windows 2000 Server. It is an ideal tool for creating images of fully prepared client computers. These images are the customized images made from the base operating system, local installation of applications such as Microsoft Office, and customized configurations.

Remote Installation Preparation (RIPrep) Wizard   The RIPrep wizard enables the network administrator to distribute to a large number of client computers a standard desktop configuration that includes the operating system and the applications. This not only helps in maintaining a uniform standard across the enterprise; it also cuts the costs and time involved in a large-scale rollout of Windows 2000 Professional.

Remote Installation Service (RIS)   The RIS, part of Windows 2000 Server, allows client computers to install Windows 2000 Professional from a Windows 2000 Server with the service installed. The Remote Installation Services (RIS) facilitates installation of Windows 2000 Professional remotely on a large number of computers with similar or dissimilar hardware configurations. This not only reduces the installation time but also helps keep deployment costs low. Also, the Windows 2000 Remote Installation Services allow you a way to create an image of Windows 2000 Professional you can use to install Windows 2000 Professional on your network client systems. This image actually consists of the installation files from the Windows 2000 Professional CD-ROM.

Remote local printer   A print device connected directly to a print server but accessed by another print server or by workstations. The queue for the print device exists on the server, and the print server controls job priority, print order, and queue administration. Client computers submit print jobs to the server and can observe the queue to monitor the printing process on the server. Drivers for the print device are loaded onto the client computer from the print server.

Remote network printer   A network printer connected to a print server that is accessed by client workstations or other print servers. Like the remote local printer, the printer queue is controlled by the print server, meaning that the client computers submit their print jobs to the print server, rather than to the print device directly. This allows for server administration and monitoring of the printer queues. Drivers for the print device are loaded onto the client computers from the print server.

Renewal Time Value   The Renewal Time Value represents 50 percent of the lease period. If the lease period were eight days, then the Renewal Time Value (T1) would be four days. At T1, the DHCP client will attempt to renew its IP address by broadcasting a DHCPREQUEST message containing its current Internet Protocol

(IP) address. If the Dynamic Host Control Protocol (DHCP) server that granted the IP address is available, it will renew the IP address for the period specified in the renewed lease. If the DHCP server is not available, the client will continue to use its lease, since it still has 50 percent of the lease period remaining.

Replay attack   This is when somebody captures the packets of a successful connection attempt and then later replays the same packets in an attempt to obtain an authenticated connection.

Request   After the client receives the DHCPOFFER message and accepts the Internet Protocol (IP) address, it sends a DHCPREQUEST message out to all Dynamic Host Control Protocol (DHCP) servers indicating that it has accepted an offer. The message contains the IP address of the DHCP server that made the accepted offer, and all other DHCP servers release the addresses they had offered back into their available address pool.

Reserved client   A reserved client is a Dynamic Host Control Protocol (DHCP) client that you configure to always receive the same Internet Protocol (IP) address. Creating reserved clients allows you to assign functionally static IP addresses to computers that require these, such as Windows Internet Name Service (WINS) and DNS servers. DHCP servers also require a static IP address. However, the DHCP server itself cannot be a DHCP client, so creating a client reservation for them would be a waste of IP addresses.

Resolver software   Resolver software on the Domain Name System (DNS) client formulates and issues query statements sent to the DNS server. Resolver software can be included in the WinSock application, or in the case of Windows 2000, be a component of the operating system. The Windows 2000 operating system has a system-wide caching resolver. Examples of WinSock programs that make use of resolver software include: Web browsers (such as Microsoft Internet Explorer), File Transfer Protocol (FTP) clients (such as the command-line FTP program found in Windows 2000), Telnet clients, and DNS servers.

Resource record   The resource record contains data about the resources contained in the domain. The resource record that you will use most is the A, or Host Address, record. This record contains the host name to Internet Protocol (IP) address mappings that most Domain Name System (DNS) clients will ask for when seeking to resolve a host name to an IP address.

Retry Interval   The Retry Interval defines the period of time the Secondary should wait until sending another pull request message. The Secondary will continue to retry the zone transfer until it is successful in contacting the Primary for its zone.

Reverse Address Resolution Protocol (RARP)   RARP does the same thing as the Address Resolution Protocol (ARP) in reverse; that is, it takes a physical address and resolves it to an IP address. The **arp –a** command can be used to view the current entries in the ARP cache.

Reverse lookup   The process of resolving a known Internet Protocol (IP) address to a host name is called a reverse lookup, in contrast to the forward lookup where a host name is resolved to an IP address. Reverse lookups query reverse lookup zones.

Reverse Lookup Query   A reverse lookup query resolves an Internet Protocol (IP) address to a Domain Name System (DNS) name, and can be used for a variety of reasons. The process is different, though, because it makes use of a special domain called in-addr.arpa. This domain is also hierarchical, but is based on IP addresses and not names. The sub-domains are organized by the *reverse* order of the IP address. For instance, the domain 16.254.169.in-addr.arpa contains the addresses in the 169.254.16.* range; the 120.129.in-addr.arpa domain contains the addresses for the 129.120.*.* range.

Reverse lookup zones   While forward lookup zones allow Domain Name System (DNS) clients to resolve a host name to an IP address, a reverse lookup zone allows the DNS client to do the opposite: resolve an IP address to a host name. Reverse lookup zones are especially helpful if your organization is using inventory or security software that depends on reverse lookups to identify the host names of the Internet Protocol (IP) addresses they discover.

RIPrep   *See* Remote Installation Preparation.

Rogue DHCP server   A rogue Dynamic Host Control Protocol (DHCP) server (a DHCP server that has not been approved by the IT department) is likely to contain invalid scopes and DHCP options. Rogue DHCP servers can assign inaccurate IP addressing information to DHCP clients, which may disrupt network communications for these hapless clients.

Rollback Strategy   As with any upgrade, problems can sometimes require going back to the previous state. This possibility also applies to upgrading your domain to Windows 2000. You need to create a plan to roll back your network to its previous state if the upgrade to Windows 2000 fails. When upgrading the domain controllers, do not upgrade the Backup Domain Controller (BDC) that has the current directory database. Make sure the BDC is synchronized with the Primary Domain Controller (PDC), and then take it offline. Leave the BDC as is until the upgrade is successful. If you run into problems during the upgrade, you can bring the BDC back online, promote it to the PDC, and recover the Windows NT state. If this process is successful, you can upgrade the BDC to Windows 2000.

ROUTE command-line utility   ROUTE is used to display or make modifications to the local routing table.

Router   When the word "router" is used, typically people think of a physical box which is dedicated to just routing—Cisco, Bay Networks, Digital, and Cabletron Systems, for example, are just a few of the best known vendors offering this kind of technology.

Router routing   Router routing occurs when a router receives a packet that is not destined for another computer so it must send the packet to either the destination computer (if directly attached) or another router.

Routing and Remote Access (RRAS)   Within Windows NT, a software routing and remote access capability combining packet filtering, Open Shortest Path First (OSPF) support, etc.

Routing Tables   Each router uses a list of known routes (either static routes or dynamic routes or a mixture of the two) which it amalgamates into one or more routing tables. When it receives a packet to forward, it consults its routing table to see which interface should be used to forward the packet. There may be more than one possible route, in which case the better path will also be evaluated to see which one should be used.

RRAS   *See* Routing and Remote Access.

SA   *See* Security Association.

Safe Mode   Safe Mode starts Windows 2000 using only some basic files and device drivers. These devices include monitor, keyboard, mouse, basic VGA video, CD-ROM, and mass storage devices. The system starts only those system services that are necessary to load the operating system. Networking is not started in this mode. The Windows background screen is black in this mode, and the screen resolution is 640 by 480 pixels with 16 colors.

Safe Mode with Command Prompt   This option starts the operating system in a safe mode using some basic files only. The Windows 2000 command prompt is shown instead of the usual Windows desktop.

Safe Mode with Networking   This mode is similar to the Safe Mode, but networking devices, drivers, and protocols are loaded. You may choose this mode when you are sure that the problem in the system is not due to any networking component.

SAM   *See* Security Accounts Manager.

Scavenging   Scavenging is the process of removing stale entries from the zone. The default setting is not to allow scavenging from the Domain Name System (DNS) database. Scavenging can be set on a per-server or per-zone basis.

Scope   A scope is a collection or pool of Internet Protocol (IP) addresses. A single scope includes all the IP addresses that you wish to make available to Dynamic Host Control Protocol (DHCP) clients on a single subnet. Only one scope can be created for each subnet. A single DHCP server can manage several scopes.

Scope options   Scope options allow you to specify Dynamic Host Control Protocol (DHCP) options that apply to a single scope. A good example of when you want to set scope options is when you automatically want to configure the Internet Protocol (IP) address of the default gateway for the DHCP clients. Each subnet must have a different default gateway, since the default gateway must be local to each subnet. It wouldn't make much sense to assign the same default gateway to all the scopes. Therefore, you configure a scope option for the default gateway for each scope that has a different default gateway.

Scripted method   This method for Windows 2000 Professional installation uses an answer file to specify various configuration parameters. This is used to eliminate user interaction during installation, thereby automating the installation process. Answers to most of the questions asked by the setup process are specified in the answer file. Besides this, the scripted method can be used for clean installations and upgrades.

SCSI   *See* Small Computer System Interface.

Second-level domain name   The second-level domain name distinguishes your organization from all others on the Internet. Examples of second-level domains are microsoft.com, osborne.com, and syngress.com.

Secondary Domain Name System (DNS) Server   Secondary DNS servers provide fault tolerance and load balancing for DNS zones. Secondary servers contain a read-only copy of the zone database that it receives from the primary server during a zone transfer. A secondary server will respond to a DNS request if the primary server fails to respond because of an error or a heavy load. Since secondary servers can resolve DNS queries, they are also considered authoritative within a domain, and can help with load balancing on the network. Secondary servers can be placed in remote locations on the network and configured to respond to DNS queries from local computers, potentially reducing query traffic across longer network distances. While there can be only one primary server in a zone, multiple secondary servers can be set up for redundancy and load balancing.

Secondary server   The server receiving the zone files can be called either a Slave server or a Secondary server. It is preferred to refer to the machine receiving the zone file as a secondary, because the term Slave DNS server has another meaning that refers to an inability to perform recursion for DNS clients.

Secret key   Also called a shared secret, a digital code shared between two parties and used for both encrypting and decrypting data.

Secure callback   This is when the remote access server calls back the remote client after a successful authentication, and is used particularly when the connection charge should be the responsibility of the server rather than the client. Either the client can specify the number that should be called back (greatest flexibility so they can dial in from anywhere), or this feature can be restricted for security to only call back on a specific number (secure callback).

Security Accounts Manager (SAM)   The Security Accounts Manager (SAM) is the portion of the Windows NT Server registry that stores user account information and group membership. Attributes that are specific to Terminal Server can be added to user accounts. This adds a small amount of information to each user's entry in the domain's SAM.

Security Association (SA)   Security Associations (SAs) define Internet Protocol Security (IPSec) secured links. One of the tasks of IPSec is to establish a Security Association between the two computers desiring to communicate with one another securely. This could include: communications between remote nodes and the network; communications between two networks; and communications between two computers on a Local Area Network (LAN).

Security Groups   The Windows 2000 Security Groups allow you to assign the same security permissions to large numbers of users in one operation. This ensures consistent security permissions across all members of a group. Using Security Groups to assign permissions means the access control on resources remains fairly static and easy to control and audit. Users who need access are added or removed from the appropriate security groups as needed, and the access control lists change infrequently.

Security Negotiation   Security negotiation ensures that the authentication and encryption methods used by the sending and receiving computers are the same. If they are not, reliable communication cannot take place. To provide for compatibility between the security systems being used, there must be protocols in place to negotiate the security methods. Internet Protocol Security (IPSec) uses ISAKMP and IKE to define the way in which security associations are negotiated.

Security Parameters Index   A Security Parameters Index (SPI) tracks each Security Association (SA). The SPI uniquely identifies each SA as separate and distinct from any other Internet Protocol Security (IPSec) connections current on a particular machine. The index itself is derived from the destination host's IP address and a randomly assigned number. When a computer communicates with another computer via IPSec, it checks its database for an applicable SA. It then applies the appropriate algorithms, protocols, and keys, and inserts the SPI into the IPSec header.

Security Templates   Windows 2000 comes with several predefined Security Templates. These templates address several security scenarios. Security Templates come in two basic categories: Default and Incremental. The Default or Basic templates are applied by the operating system when a clean install has been performed. They are not applied if an upgrade installation has been done. The incremental templates should be applied after the Basic Security Templates have been applied. There are four types of incremental templates: Compatible, Secure, High Secure, and Dedicated Domain Controller.

Segment   In discussions of Transmission Control Protocol/Internet Protocol (TCP/IP), segment often refers to the group of computers located on one side of a router, or sometimes a group of computers within the same collision domain. In TCP/IP terminology, "segment" can also be used to describe the chunk of data sent by TCP over the network (roughly equivalent to the usage of "packet" or "frame"). In discussions of the physical networking infrastructure, "segment" usually refers to a length of cable, or the portion of the network connected to a length of backbone between repeaters.

Sequenced Packet eXchange (SPX)   The communications protocol (from NetWare) used to control network message transport.

Serial Line Interface Protocol (SLIP)   The SLIP is an older Wide Area Network (WAN) link protocol that does not support encryption or compression, and requires a manually configured static Internet Protocol (IP) address. It can be used only on the Windows 2000 RAS client, and is used now primarily to connect to remote servers running the UNIX operating system.

Server   The word "server" can take on a variety of different meanings. A server can be a physical computer, such as "Check out that Server over in the Accounting Department." A server can also represent a particular software package. For example, Microsoft Exchange 2000 is a mail and groupware Server application. Often server applications are just referred to as "servers," as in "Check out what the problem is with the mail server." The term "server" is also used to refer to any computer that is currently sharing its resources on the network. In this context, all computers, whether Windows 3x or Windows 2000, can be servers on a network.

Server impersonation   This is when a bogus server appears to be a valid server so that it can capture credentials of a remote user trying to connect so it can use these to the valid server.

Server options   Server options apply to all scopes configured on a single DHCP server. Server options were known as global options on the Windows NT 4.0 DHCP Server.

Service Identifiers   A computer running the TCP/IP NetBIOS interface actually has several NetBIOS names. Each name is used by a service to "advertise" that the service is running on that particular computer. It's like putting a sign on the door saying "these people live here." For example, if a Windows 2000 machine is running both the Server service and the Workstation (Microsoft Redirector) service, it will register two NetBIOS names, one for each of the services running. This is a way for the NetBIOS applications to let other machines know that they are running and available.

Service pack   A service pack typically contains bug fixes, security fixes, systems administration tools, drivers, and additional components. Microsoft recommends installing the latest service packs as they are released. In addition, as a new feature in Windows 2000, you do not have to reinstall components after installing a service pack, as you did with Windows NT. You can also see what service pack is currently installed on a computer by running the WINVER utility program. WINVER brings up the About Windows dialog box. It displays the version of Windows and the version of the service pack you are running.

Service record (SRV)   The SRV record provides information about available services on a particular host. This is similar to the "service identifier" (the hidden 16th character) in NetBIOS environments. If a particular host is looking for a server to authenticate against, it will check for a SRV record to find an authenticating host. SRV records are particularly important in Windows 2000 domains. Since the DNS server is now the primary domain locator for Windows 2000 clients, the appropriate SRV records must be contained on the DNS server to inform Windows 2000 clients of the location of a Windows 2000 domain controller that can authenticate a logon request.

Setup Manager   The Setup Manager is the best tool to use when you have no idea of the answer file syntax or when you do not want to get into the time-consuming task of creating or modifying the sample answer file. When you choose to use the Setup Manager for unattended installations, you need to do a lot of planning beforehand. It is understood that you will not be using Setup Manager for automating installations on one or two computers; that would be a waste of effort. Setup Manager is useful for mass deployments only.

SETUPACT.LOG   The Action log file contains details about the files that are copied during setup.

SETUPAPI.LOG   This log file contains details about the device driver files that were copied during setup. This log can be used to facilitate troubleshooting device installations. The file contains errors and warnings along with a time stamp for each issue.

SETUPCL.EXE   The function of the SETUPCL.EXE file is to run the Mini-Setup wizard and to regenerate the security IDs on the master and destination computers. The Mini-Setup wizard starts on the master computer when it is booted for the first time after running SysPrep.

SETUPERR.LOG   The Error log file contains details about errors that occurred during setup.

SETUPLOG.TXT   This log file contains additional information about the device driver files that were copied during setup.

Shared Folders   Sharing folders so that other users can access their contents across the network is easy in Windows 2000, as easy as right-clicking on the folder name in Windows Explorer, selecting the Sharing tab, and choosing Share This Folder. An entire drive and all the folders on that drive can be shared in the same way.

Shared Folders Permissions   As only folders, not files, can be shared, shared folder permissions are a small subset of standard NT File System (NTFS) permissions for a folder. However, securing access to a folder through share permissions can be more restrictive or more liberal than standard NTFS folder permissions. Shared folder permissions are applied in the same manner as NTFS permissions.

Shared Printers   The process for sharing a printer attached to your local computer is similar to that for sharing a folder or drive. If the users who will access your printer will do so from machines that don't run the Windows 2000 operating system, you will need to install drivers for the other operating system(s).

Shared resource   A shared resource is a device, data, or program that is made available to network users. This can include folders, files, printers, and even Internet connections.

Shiva Password Authentication Protocol (SPAP)   The Shiva Password Authentication Protocol is a reversible encryption mechanism used by Shiva remote access servers. Although a remote access client might use SPAP to authenticate on a Windows 2000 Routing and Remote Access server, this protocol is more likely to be used by clients who need to connect to a Shiva remote access client. This protocol is more secure than Password Authentication Protocol (PAP), but less secure than the other protocols, and offers no protection against server impersonation. It is unlikely you would need it on a server running Windows 2000 Routing and Remote Access Service.

Silent Routing Information Protocol for Internet Protocol (Silent RIP for IP)   Silent RIP for IP occurs when an IP router (using the RIP routing protocol) dynamically updates its own routing table with information obtained from other RIP routers without sending out its own routing information. In this case, the routing "exchange" between the Silent RIP router and other routers is not complete because the information is one-way only—listening for routing information but not reciprocating. You can use Silent RIP on a workstation too, but this requires modifying the registry. On Windows 2000 RRAS router, it is configured as one of the RIP interface properties.

Simple Mail Transfer Protocol (SMTP)   The Simple Mail Transfer Protocol is used for sending e-mail on the Internet. SMTP is a simple ASCII protocol and is non-vendor specific.

Simple Network Management Protocol (SNMP)   The Simple Network Management Protocol provides a way to gather statistical information. An SNMP management system makes requests of an SNMP agent, and the information is stored in a Management Information Base (MIB).

Simple volume   A simple volume is a volume created on a dynamic disk that is not fault tolerant, and includes space from only one physical disk. A simple volume is just that—it is a single volume that does not span more than one physical disk, and does not provide improved drive performance, extra capacity, or fault tolerance. One physical disk can contain a single, large simple volume, or several smaller ones. Each simple volume is assigned a separate drive letter. The number of simple volumes on a disk is limited only by the capacity of the disk and the number of available letters in the alphabet.

Single-Instance-Store (SIS) Volume   When you have more than one image on the Remote Installation Service (RIS) server, each holding Windows 2000 Professional files, there will be duplicate copies of hundreds of files. This may consume a significant hard drive space on the RIS server. To overcome this problem, Microsoft introduced a new feature called the Single-Instance-Store, which helps in deleting all the duplicate files, thus saving on hard drive space.

SIS   *See* Single-Instance-Store Volume.

Site Server Internet Locator Server (ILS) Service   This service supports Internet Protocol (IP) telephony applications. Publishes IP multicast conferences on a network, and can also publish user IP address mappings for H.323 IP telephony. Telephony applications, such as NetMeeting and Phone Dialer in Windows Accessories, use Site Server ILS Service to display user names and conferences with published addresses. Site Server ILS Service depends on Internet Information Services (IIS).

Slave server   Slave servers are a special type of forwarder, which is configured not to attempt to resolve the host name on its own. The server receiving the zone files can be called either a Slave server or a Secondary server. It is preferred to refer to the machine receiving the zone file as a secondary because the term Slave Domain Name System (DNS) server has another meaning that refers to an inability to perform recursion for DNS clients.

Slave server/caching-only forwarder   The slave server/caching-only forwarder combination is very helpful in protecting your intranet zone data from Internet intruders. We can use this combination to prevent users on the other side of a firewall from having access to information on our Internal Domain Name System (DNS) server.

SLIP   *See* Serial Line Interface Protocol.

Small Computer System Interface (SCSI)   A complete expansion bus interface that accepts such devices as a hard disk, CD-ROM, disk drivers, printers, or scanners.

Small Office/Home Office (SOHO)   A SOHO network typically has the following characteristics: a single segment network; peer-to-peer networking; a single protocol (e.g., TCP/IP); and a demand-dial or dedicated link connection to the Internet via an Internet Service Provider (ISP). A user on a SOHO network frequently needs to use more than one computer, and also needs to be able to share resources from one computer to another, such as files, applications, and printers.

SMP   *See* Symmetric Multiprocessing.

SMS   *See* Systems Management Server.

SMTP   *See* Simple Mail Transfer Protocol.

SNA   *See* Systems Network Architecture.

SNMP   *See* Simple Network Management Protocol.

SOA   *See* Start of Authority.

SOHO   *See* Small Office/Home Office.

Spanned volume   A spanned volume is similar to a volume set in NT 4.0. It contains space from multiple disks (up to 32), and provides a way to combine small "chunks" of disk space into one unit, seen by the operating system as a single volume. It is not fault tolerant. When a dynamic volume includes the space on more than one physical hard drive, it is called a spanned volume. Spanned volumes can be used to increase drive capacity, or to make use of the leftover space on up to 32 existing disks. Like those in a basic storage volume set, the portions of a spanned volume are all linked together and share a single drive letter.

SPAP   *See* Shiva Password Authentication Protocol.

SPI   *See* Security Parameters Index.

SPX   *See* Sequenced Packet eXchange.

SQL   *See* Structured Query Language.

SRV   *See* Service record.

Stack   A data structure in which the first items inserted are the last ones removed, unlike control structure programs that use the Last In First Out (LIFO) structure.

Start of Authority (SOA)   The SOA identifies which Domain Name System (DNS) server is authoritative for the data within a domain. The first record in any zone file is the SOA.

Static Internet Protocol (IP) address   A static IP address allows users to use a domain name that can be translated into an IP address. The static IP address allows the server to always have the same IP address, so the domain name always translates to the correct IP address. If the address was assigned dynamically and occasionally changed, users might not be able to access the server across the Internet using the domain name.

Stripe Set   The term "striping" refers to the interleaving of data across separate physical disks. Each file is broken into small blocks, and each block is evenly and alternately saved to the disks in the stripe set. In a two-disk stripe set, the first block of data is saved to the first disk, the second block is saved to the second disk, and the third block is saved to the first disk, and so on. The two disks are treated as a single drive, and are given a single drive letter.

Stripe Set with Parity   A stripe set with parity requires at least three hard disks, and provides both increased storage capacity and fault tolerance. In a stripe set with parity, data is interleaved across three or more disks, and includes parity (error checking) information about the data. As long as only one disk in the set fails, the parity information can be used to reconstruct the lost data. If the parity information itself is lost, it can be reconstructed from the original data.

Striped volume   Like a stripe set in NT 4.0, a striped volume is the dynamic storage equivalent of a basic stripe set and combines free space from up to 32 physical disks into one volume by writing data across the disks in stripes. This increases performance but does not provide fault tolerance. A striped volume improves drive performance and increases drive capacity. Because each data block is written only once, striped volumes do not provide fault tolerance.

Striping   Striping is when the data are striped across the drives and there is parity information along with the data. The parity information is based on a mathematical formula that comes up with the parity based on the data on the other drives.

Structured Query Language (SQL)   A concise IBM query language (only 30 commands) structured like English, widely used in database management applications for mainframes and minicomputers.

Stub Areas   You can import external routes into an Open Shortest Path First (OSPF) AS with an AS Border Router, but to stop external routes from flooding into an area you can use what is called a Stub Area. A stub area applies the default route 0.0.0.0 to keep the topology database size small. In OSPF, you can assume that any destination that you can't reach through a designated route is reachable through the default route. To implement a stub area, one or more of the stub area's Area Border Routers must advertise the default route 0.0.0.0 to the stub area and the route summary.

Subnetting   Using several data paths to reduce traffic on a network and avoid problems if a single path should fail; usually configured as a dedicated Ethernet subnetwork between two systems based on two Network Interface Cards (NICs).

Supernetting   Supernetting is a way of combining several small networks into a larger one. For example, a company may need a Class B network, but because those have all been assigned, it can't get one. However, Class C networks *are* available, so the company can be assigned multiple Class C networks with contiguous addresses. By "stealing" bits again, but in the opposite direction (sort of like taking from the poor and giving to the rich instead of vice versa), you can use some of the bits that originally represented the network ID to represent host IDs, reducing the number of networks but increasing the number of hosts available per network.

Superscope   A superscope is a Windows 2000 Dynamic Host Control Protocol (DHCP) feature that lets you use more than one scope for a subnet. The superscope contains multiple "child" scopes, grouped together under one name and manageable as one entity. The situations in which superscopes should be used include: when many DHCP clients are added to a network, so that it has more than were originally planned for; when the Internet Protocol (IP) addresses on a network must be renumbered; and when two (or more) DHCP servers are on the same subnet for fault tolerance purposes.

Symmetric algorithm   A cryptographic algorithm that uses the same key to both encrypt and decrypt, also called a secret key algorithm.

Symmetric Multiprocessing (SMP)   SMP is a system in which all processors are treated as equals, and any thread can be run on any available processor. Windows 2000 also supports processor affinity, in which a process or thread can specify which set of processors it should run on. Application Programming Interfaces (APIs) must be defined in the application.

Synthesis   The process of design, formulation, integration, prediction, proposal, generalization, and show relationships.

SYSPREP.INF   SYSPREP.INF is an answer file. When you want to automate the Mini-Setup wizard by providing predetermined answers to all setup questions, you must use this file. This file needs to be placed in the %Systemroot%\Sysprep folder or on a floppy disk. When the Mini-Setup wizard is run on the computer on which the image is being distributed, it takes answers from the SYSPREP.INF file without prompting the user for any input.

System Monitor   The System Monitor is part of the Administrative Tools utility that allows you to collect and view data about current memory usage, disk, processor utilization, network activity, and other system activity. The System Monitor replaces the Performance Monitor used in Windows NT. System Monitor allows you to collect information about your hardware's performance as well as network utilization. System Monitor can be used to measure different aspects of a computer's performance. It can be used on your own computer or other computers on the network.

System policy   Group policies have mostly replaced system policies since group policies extend the functionality of system policies. A few situations still exist in which system policies are valuable. The system policy editor is used to provide user and computer configuration settings in the Windows NT registry database. The system policy editor is still used for the management of Windows 9*x* and Windows NT server and workstations and stand-alone computers using Windows 2000.

System Preparation (Sysprep)   SysPrep provides an excellent means of saving installation time and reducing installation costs. Sysprep is the best tool to copy the image of a computer to other computers that have identical hardware configurations. It is also helpful in standardizing the desktop environment throughout the organization. Since one Sysprep image cannot be used on computers with identical hardware and software applications, you can create multiple images when you have more than one standard. It is still the best option where the number of computers is in the hundreds or thousands and you wish to implement uniform policies in the organization.

Systems Management Server (SMS) This Windows NT software analyzes and monitors network usage and various network functions.

Systems Network Architecture (SNA) Systems Network Architecture (SNA) was developed by IBM in the mainframe computer era (1974, to be precise) as a way of getting its various products to communicate with each other for distributed processing. SNA is a line of products designed to make other products cooperate. In your career of designing network solutions, you should expect to run into SNA from time to time because many of the bigger companies (i.e., banks, healthcare institutions, government offices) bought IBM equipment and will be reluctant to part with their investment. SNA is a proprietary protocol that runs over SDLC exclusively, although it may be transported within other protocols, such as X.25 and Token Ring. It is designed as a hierarchy and consists of a collection of machines called nodes.

Take Ownership Permission This permission can be given to allow a user to take ownership of a file or folder object. Every file and folder on an NT File System (NTFS) drive has an owner, usually the account that created the object. However, there are times when ownership of a file needs to be changed, perhaps because of a change in team membership or a set of new responsibilities for a user.

Task-based model This model is appropriate for companies in which administrative duties are functionally divided. This means that this model divides the management of Group Policy Objects (GPOs) by certain tasks. To apply this model, the administrators that handle security-related tasks will also be responsible for managing all policy objects that affect security. The second set of administrators that normally deploy the companies' business applications will be responsible for all the GPOs that affect installation and maintenance.

TCP/IP *See* Transmission Control Protocol/Internet Protocol.

Telnet   Telnet is a Transmission Control Protocol/Internet Protocol (TCP/IP-based) service that allows users to log on to, run character-mode applications, and view files on a remote computer. Windows 2000 Server includes both Telnet server and Telnet client software.

Terminal Services   In application server mode, Terminal Services provides the ability to run client applications on the server, while "thin client" software acts as a terminal emulator on the client. Each user sees an individual session, displayed as a Windows 2000 desktop. The server manages each session, independent of any other client session. If you install Terminal Services as an application server, you must also install Terminal Services Licensing (not necessarily on the same computer). However, temporary licenses can be issued for clients that allow you to use Terminal servers for up to 90 days. In remote administration mode, you can use Terminal Services to log on remotely and manage Windows 2000 systems from virtually anywhere on your network (instead of being limited to working locally on a server). Remote administration mode allows for two concurrent connections from a given server and minimizes impact on server performance. Remote administration mode does not require you to install Terminal Services Licensing.

TFTP   *See* Trivial File Transfer Protocol.

TKEY   The TKEY resource record is used to transfer security tokens between the DNS client and server. It allows for the establishment of the shared secret key that will be used with the TSIG resource record.

Token Ring   A Local Area Network (LAN) specification that was developed by IBM in the 1980s for PC-based networks and classified by the (Institute of Electrical and Electronics Engineers) IEEE as 802.5. It specifies a star topology physically and a ring topology logically. It runs at either four Mbps or 16 Mbps, but all nodes on the ring must run at the same speed.

Tombstoning   Windows 2000 allows you to manually mark a record to eventually be deleted. This is called tombstoning. The tombstone state of the record replicates to other Windows Internet Name Service (WINS) servers, and this prevents any replicated copies of the deleted records from reappearing at the same server where they were originally deleted.

Top-level domain names   Top-level domain names include .com, .net, .org, and .edu. Organizations that seek to have an Internet presence will obtain a domain name that is a member of one of the top-level domain names.

Trace log   The Windows 2000 DNS Server allows you to enable trace logging via the Graphical User Interface (GUI) interface if you require extremely detailed information about the Domain Name System (DNS) server's activities. The information gathered in the trace is saved to a text file on the local hard disk. A trace log can track all queries received and answered by the DNS server.

TRACERT command-line utility   TRACERT is used to trace the route a packet takes to a destination.

Transmission Control Protocol/Internet Protocol (TCP/IP)   A set of communications standards created by the U.S. Department of Defense (DoD) in the 1970s that has now become an accepted way to connect different types of computers in networks because the standards now support so many programs.

Transport Mode   When Internet Protocol Security (IPSec) is used to protect communications between two clients (for example, two computers on the same Local Area Network or LAN), the machines can utilize IPSec in what is known as transport mode. In this example, the endpoints of the secure communication are the source machine and the destination host.

Trees   Trees are groups of domains that share a contiguous namespace. It allows you to create a hierarchical grouping of domains that share a common contiguous namespace. This hierarchy allows global sharing of resources among domains in the tree. All the domains in a tree share information and resources with a single directory, and there is only one directory per tree. However, each domain manages its own subset of the directory that contains the user accounts for that domain. So, when a user logs in to a domain, the user has global access to all resources that are part of the tree, providing the user has the proper permissions.

Trivial File Transfer Protocol (TFTP)   A simplified version of the File Transfer Protocol (FTP), associated with the Transmission Control Protocol/Internet Protocol (TCP/IP) family, that does not provide password protection or a user directory.

Trust   The users in one tree do not have global access to resources in other trees, but trusts can be created that allow users to access resources in another tree. A trust allows all the trees to share resources and have common administrative functions. Such sharing capability allows the trees to operate independently of each other, with separate namespaces, yet still be able to communicate and share resources through trusts.

Trust relationship   A trust relationship is a connection between domains in which users who have accounts in and log on to one domain can then access resources in other domains, provided they have proper access permissions.

TSIG   The TSIG resource record is used to send and verify messages that have been signed with a hash algorithm.

Tunnel Mode   The second communication mode is a gateway-to-gateway solution. Internet Protocol Security (IPSec) protects information that travels through a transit network (such as the Internet). Packets are protected as they leave the exit gateway, and then decrypted or authenticated at the destination network's gateway. When gateways represent the endpoints of the secure communication, IPSec is operating in tunnel mode. A tunnel is created between the gateways, and client-to-client communications are encapsulated in the tunnel protocol headers.

Two-way initiated demand-dial connections   A two-way initiated demand-dial connection is where routers can both initiate a connection when needed, and also respond to the same router calling it over the same demand-dial interface. In other words, in a two-way initiated connection, both routers can be a calling router, or an answering router on the same interface. Use two-way initiated connections when traffic from either router can create the demand-dial connection. This offers the greatest flexibility but also requires the greatest configuration since not only do both routers need to be configured, but also they have to be configured similarly to ensure their configurations match.

UDF   *See* Unique Database File.

UDP   *See* User Datagram Protocol.

Unattended method   The unattended method for Windows 2000 Server installation uses the answer file to specify various configuration parameters. This method eliminates user interaction during installation, thereby automating the installation process and reducing the chances of input errors. Answers to most of the questions asked by the setup process are specified in the answer file. In addition, the scripted method can be used for clean installations and upgrades.

UNATTEND.TXT file   The creation of customized UNATTEND.TXT answer files is the simplest form of providing answers to setup queries and unattended installation of Windows 2000. This can either be done using the Setup Manager or by editing the sample UNATTEND.TXT file using Notepad or the MS-DOS text editor. The UNATTEND.TXT file does not provide any means of creating an image of the computer.

UNATTEND.UDF   This file is the Uniqueness Database File, which provides customized settings for each computer using the automated installation.

UNC   *See* Universal Naming Convention.

UNICODE   UNICODE is a 16-bit character encoding standard developed by the Unicode Consortium between 1988 and 1991 that uses two bytes to represent each character and enables almost all of the written languages of the world to be represented using a single character set.

Uninterruptible Power Supply (UPS)   A battery that can supply power to a computer system if the power fails. It charges while the computer is on and, if the power fails, provides power for a certain amount of time allowing the user to shut down the computer properly to preserve data.

Unique Database File (UDF)   When you use the WINNT32.EXE command with the /unattend option, you can also specify a Unique Database File (UDF), which has a .UDB extension. This file forces Setup to use certain values from the UDF file, thus overriding the values given in the answer file. This is particularly useful when you want to specify multiple users during the setup.

Universal Groups   Universal Groups are used in larger, multi-domain organizations in which there is a need to grant access to similar groups of accounts defined in multiple domains. It is better to use Global Groups as members of Universal Groups to reduce overall replication traffic from changes to Universal Group membership. Users can be added and removed from the corresponding Global Groups with their account domains, and a small number of Global Groups are the direct members of the Universal Group. Universal Groups are used only in multiple domain trees or forests. A Windows 2000 domain must be in native mode to use Universal Groups.

Universal Naming Convention (UNC)   A UNC is an identification standard of servers and other network resources.

Universal Serial Bus (USB)   A low-speed hardware interface (supports MPEG video) with a maximum bandwidth up to 1.5 MBytes per second.

UPS   *See* Uninterruptible Power Supply.

USB   *See* Universal Serial Bus.

User account   The information that defines a particular user on a network, which includes the username, password, group memberships, and rights and permissions assigned to the user.

User classes   User classes allow Dynamic Host Control Protocol (DHCP) clients to identify their class membership to a DHCP server. The server can return to the client a specific set of options relevant to the class. The process is the same as how vendor class options are requested by the client and sent by the DHCP server.

User Datagram Protocol (UDP)   A Transmission Control Protocol/Internet Protocol (TCP/IP) normally bundled with an Internet Protocol (IP) layer software that describes how messages received reached application programs within the destination computer.

User Principle Name Mapping This is a special kind of one-to-one mapping only available through the Active Directory. Enterprise CAs insert an entry called a User Principle Name (UPN) into each of its certificates. UPNs are unique to each users account within a Windows 2000 Domain and they are of the format *user@domain* . The UPN is used to locate the user account in Active Directory and that account is logged on.

Value Bar The value bar is positioned below the graph area. It displays data for the selected sample, the last sample value, the average of the counter samples, the maximum and minimum of the samples, and the duration of time the samples have been taken over.

Vendor class options RFCs 2131 and 2132 define Dynamic Host Control Protocol (DHCP) vendor class options, which allow hardware and software vendors to add their own options to the DHCP server. These options are additions to the list of standard DHCP options included with the Windows 2000 DHCP Server.

Virtual Private Networking (VPN) VPNs reduce service costs and long distance/usage fees, lighten infrastructure investments, and simplify Wide Area Network (WAN) operations over time. To determine just how cost-effective a VPN solution could be in connecting remote offices, use the VPN Calculator located on Cisco's Web site at www.cisco.com.

Volume Set The term "volume" indicates a single drive letter. One physical hard disk can contain several volumes, one for each primary partition or logical drive. However, the opposite is also true. You can create a single volume that spans more than one physical disk. This is a good option when you require a volume that exceeds the capacity of a single physical disk. You can also create a volume set when you want to make use of leftover space on several disks by piecing them together as one volume.

VPN *See* Virtual Private Networking.

WDM *See* Windows32 Drive Model.

Windows 3x Windows 3 changed everything. It was a 16-bit operating system with a user interface that resembled the look and feel of IBM's (at that time not yet released) OS/2, with 3D buttons and the ability to run multiple programs simultaneously, using a method called cooperative multitasking. Windows 3 also provided virtual memory, the ability to use hard disk space to "fool" the applications into behaving as if they had more RAM than was physically installed in the machine.

Windows 9x In August of 1995, Microsoft released its long-awaited upgrade of Windows, Windows 95. For the first time, Windows could be installed on a machine that didn't already have MS-DOS installed. Many improvements were made: the new 32-bit functionality (although still retaining some 16-bit code for backward compatibility); preemptive multitasking (a more efficient way to run multiple programs in which the operating system controls use of the processor and the crash of one application does not bring down the others that are currently running); and support for filenames longer than the DOS-based eight-character limit.

Windows32 Driver Model (WDM) The Win32 Driver Model (WDM) provides a standard for device drivers that will work across Windows platforms (specifically Windows 98 and 2000) so that you can use the same drivers with the consumer and business versions of the Windows operating system.

Windows 2000 Microsoft's latest incarnation of the corporate operating system was originally called NT 5, but the name was changed to Windows 2000 between the second and third beta versions—perhaps to underscore the fact that this is truly a *new* version of the operating system, not merely an upgrade to NT.

Windows 2000 Control Panel The Control Panel in Windows 2000 functions similarly to the Control Panel in Windows 9x and NT, except that "under the hood" there are now two locations that information is stored, which is modified by the Control Panel applets. The Control Panel in previous operating systems was a graphical interface for editing Registry information.

Windows Backup Windows Backup is a built-in Backup and Restore utility which has many more features than the backup tool provided in Windows NT 4.0. It supports all five types of backup: Normal, Copy, Differential, Incremental, and Daily. Windows Backup allows you to perform the backup operation manually or you may schedule it to run at a later time in unattended mode. Included with the operating system, it is a tool that is flexible and easy to use.

Windows Internet Name Service (WINS)   WINS provides name resolution for clients running Windows NT and earlier versions of Microsoft operating systems. With name resolution, users can access servers by name, instead of having to use Internet Protocol (IP) addresses that are difficult to recognize and remember. WINS is used to map NetBIOS computer names to IP addresses. This allows users to access other computers on the network by computer name. WINS servers should be assigned a static IP address, which allows clients to be able to find the WINS servers. Clients cannot find a WINS server by name because they need to know where the WINS server is in order to translate the name into an IP address.

Windows Internet Name Service (WINS) Name Registration   Each WINS client has one or more WINS server identified in the network configuration on the computer, either through static assignment or through DHCP configuration. When the client boots and connects to the network, it registers its name and IP address with the WINS server by sending a registration request directly to the server. This is not a broadcast message, since the client has the address of the server. If the server is available and the name is not already registered, the server responds with a successful registration message containing the amount of time the name will be registered to the client, the Time To Live (TTL). Then the server stores the name and address combination in its local database.

Windows Internet Name Service (WINS) Name Release   When a WINS client shuts down properly, it will send a name release request to the WINS server. This releases the name from the WINS server's database so that another client can use the name if necessary. The release request contains the WINS name and address of the client. If the server cannot find the name, it sends a negative release response to the client. If the server finds the matching name and address in its database, it releases the name and marks the record as inactive. If the name is found but the address does not match, the server ignores the request.

Windows Internet Name Service (WINS) Name Renewal   As with Dynamic Host Control Protocol (DHCP), WINS name registrations are temporary and must be renewed to continue to be valid. The client will attempt to renew its registration when half (50 percent) of the Time To Live (TTL) has elapsed. If the

WINS server does not respond, the client repeatedly attempts to renew its lease at ten-minute intervals for an hour. If the client still receives no response, it restarts the process with the secondary WINS server, if one is defined. The client will continue attempting to renew its lease in this manner until it receives a response from a server. At that time, the server sends a new TTL to the client and the process starts over.

Windows Internet Name Service (WINS) Proxy Agent   The WINS Proxy Agent has a single purpose: to resolve NetBIOS names for non-WINS clients. The non-WINS clients can be UNIX servers, or even Windows computers that are configured as b-node clients. Keep in mind that the WINS Proxy Agent resolves NetBIOS names, it does not register them. When a non-WINS client starts up, it may broadcast its name to the local segment, but the WINS Proxy Agent on that segment does not register the non-WINS client name in the WINS database. The WINS Proxy Agent solves the problem of NetBIOS name resolution for non-WINS clients. The other side of the coin is resolving the NetBIOS name of a non-WINS client. A non-WINS client does not register its name in the WINS database. If a WINS client tries to resolve the name of a non-WINS client, the attempt fails because there is no entry in the WINS database for the non-WINS client. The solution to this problem is to add a *static entry* into the WINS database for the non-WINS client.

Windows Internet Name Service (WINS) Referral Zone   A WINS Referral Zone is usually a forward lookup zone that has no resource records in it. After creating the WINS Referral Zone, you disable WINS Referral for all other zones. After you have done this, any queries that are resolved via WINS are returned with the Fully Qualified Domain Name (FQDN) that contains the NetBIOS name returned from the WINS server with the WINS Referral Zone's domain name appended to it. In this way, it is easy to identify what queries have been resolved via WINS lookups.

Windows Internet Name Service (WINS) Snap-in   With the snap-in, you can view the active WINS entries under the Active Registrations folder. In addition, you can supply static mappings for non-WINS clients on the network through the snap-in. To configure a static mapping, select the Active Registrations folder and then select New Static Mapping from the Action menu. Once a static mapping is entered into the WINS database, it cannot be edited. If you need to make changes to a static mapping, you must delete and recreate the entry.

Windows NT   The NT kernel (the core or nucleus of the operating system, which provides basic services for all other parts of the operating system) is built on a completely different architecture from consumer Windows. In fact, NT was based on the 32-bit preemptive multitasking operating system that originated as a joint project of Microsoft and IBM before their parting of the ways, OS/2. NT provided the stability and security features that the "other Windows" lacked, albeit at a price, and not only a monetary one; NT was much pickier in terms of hardware support, did not run all of the programs that ran on Windows 9*x* (especially DOS programs that accessed the hardware directly), and required more resources, especially memory, to run properly.

WINNT.EXE program   The WINNT.EXE program is used for network installations that use an MS-DOS network client. The WINNT32.EXE program is used to customize the process for upgrading existing installations. The WINNT32.EXE program is used for installing Windows 2000 from a computer that is currently running Windows 95/98 or Windows NT.

WINS   *See* Windows Internet Name Service.

Workgroup   A workgroup is a logical grouping of resources on a network. It is generally used in peer-to-peer networks. This means that each computer is responsible for access to its resources. Each computer has its own account database and is administered separately. Security is not shared between computers, and administration is more difficult than in a centralized domain.

X25   X25 uses an international standard for sending data across public packet-switching networks. The Windows 2000 Routing and Remote Access server will only support direct connections to X25 networks by using an X25 smart card.

Zone delegation   Zone delegation provides a way for you to distribute responsibility for zone database management, and provides a measure of load balancing for Domain Name System (DNS) servers. When you create a delegation for a zone, you are "passing the buck" to another DNS server to answer DNS queries for a particular zone. Zones can be delegated to Secondary DNS Servers or Primaries.

Zone transfer The zone transfer process can be considered a "pull" operation. This is because the Secondary Domain Name System (DNS) server initiates the zone transfer process. The Secondary DNS server will initiate a zone transfer when a Primary DNS server sends a "notify" message to the Secondary DNS server. Informing it that there has been a change to the zone database, the Secondary DNS server boots up, or the Secondary DNS server's *Refresh Interval* has expired.

Zones of Authority The Domain Name System (DNS) name space is divided into zones, and each zone must have one name server that is the authority for the name mapping for the zone. Depending on the size of the name space, a zone may be subdivided into multiple zones, each with its own authority, or there may be a single authority for the entire zone. For instance, a small company with only 200-300 computers could have one DNS server handle the entire namespace.

INDEX

D

E

S

Custom Corporate Network Training

Train on Cutting Edge Technology   We can bring the best in skill-based training to your facility to create a real-world hands-on training experience. Global Knowledge has invested millions of dollars in network hardware and software to train our students on the same equipment they will work with on the job. Our relationships with vendors allow us to incorporate the latest equipment and platforms into your on-site labs.

Maximize Your Training Budget   Global Knowledge provides experienced instructors, comprehensive course materials, and all the networking equipment needed to deliver high quality training. You provide the students; we provide the knowledge.

Avoid Travel Expenses   On-site courses allow you to schedule technical training at your convenience, saving time, expense, and the opportunity cost of travel away from the workplace.

Discuss Confidential Topics   Private on-site training permits the open discussion of sensitive issues such as security, access, and network design. We can work with your existing network's proprietary files while demonstrating the latest technologies.

Customize Course Content   Global Knowledge can tailor your courses to include the technologies and the topics which have the greatest impact on your business. We can complement your internal training efforts or provide a total solution to your training needs.

Corporate Pass   The Corporate Pass Discount Program rewards our best network training customers with preferred pricing on public courses, discounts on multimedia training packages, and an array of career planning services.

Global Knowledge Training Lifecycle   Supporting the Dynamic and Specialized Training Requirements of Information Technology Professionals

- Define Profile
- Assess Skills
- Design Training
- Deliver Training
- Test Knowledge
- Update Profile
- Use New Skills

College Credit Recommendation Program   The American Council on Education's CREDIT program recommends 53 Global Knowledge courses for college credit. Now our network training can help you earn your college degree while you learn the technical skills needed for your job. When you attend an ACE-certified Global Knowledge course and pass the associated exam, you earn college credit recommendations for that course. Global Knowledge can establish a transcript record for you with ACE, which you can use to gain credit at a college or as a written record of your professional training that you can attach to your resume.

Registration Information

COURSE FEE: The fee covers course tuition, refreshments, and all course materials. Any parking expenses that may be incurred are not included. Payment or government training form must be received six business days prior to the course date. We will also accept Visa/MasterCard and American Express. For non-U.S. credit card users, charges will be in U.S. funds and will be converted by your credit card company. Checks drawn on Canadian banks in Canadian funds are acceptable.

COURSE SCHEDULE: Registration is at 8:00 a.m. on the first day. The program begins at 8:30 a.m. and concludes at 4:30 p.m. each day.

CANCELLATION POLICY: Cancellation and full refund will be allowed if written cancellation is received in our office at least six business days prior to the course start date. Registrants who do not attend the course or do not cancel more than six business days in advance are responsible for the full registration fee; you may transfer to a later date provided the course fee has been paid in full. Substitutions may be made at any time. If Global Knowledge must cancel a course for any reason, liability is limited to the registration fee only.

GLOBAL KNOWLEDGE: Global Knowledge programs are developed and presented by industry professionals with "real-world" experience. Designed to help professionals meet today's interconnectivity and interoperability challenges, most of our programs feature hands-on labs that incorporate state-of-the-art communication components and equipment.

ON-SITE TEAM TRAINING: Bring Global Knowledge's powerful training programs to your company. At Global Knowledge, we will custom design courses to meet your specific network requirements. Call 1 (919) 461-8686 for more information.

YOUR GUARANTEE: Global Knowledge believes its courses offer the best possible training in this field. If during the first day you are not satisfied and wish to withdraw from the course, simply notify the instructor, return all course materials, and receive a 100% refund.

In the US:

CALL: 1 (888) 762-4442

FAX: 1 (919) 469-7070

VISIT OUR WEBSITE:

www.globalknowledge.com

MAIL CHECK AND THIS FORM TO:

Global Knowledge

Suite 200

114 Edinburgh South

P.O. Box 1187

Cary, NC 27512

In Canada:

CALL: 1 (800) 465-2226

FAX: 1 (613) 567-3899

VISIT OUR WEBSITE:

www.globalknowledge.com.ca

MAIL CHECK AND THIS FORM TO:

Global Knowledge

Suite 1601

393 University Ave.

Toronto, ON M5G 1E6

REGISTRATION INFORMATION:

Course title ——————————————————————————

Course location ———————————————————— Course date ————

Name/title ———————————————————— Company ————————

Name/title ———————————————————— Company ————————

Name/title ———————————————————— Company ————————

Address ————————————— Telephone ———————— Fax ——————

City —————————————— State/Province ———— Zip/Postal Code ————

Credit card ———————— Card # ———————————— Expiration date ————

Signature ——————————————————————————

MCSE Windows® 2000 Study Guide

A COMPLETE STUDY PROGRAM BUILT UPON PROVEN INSTRUCTIONAL METHODS

Self-study features include:

Expert advice on how to take and pass the test:

"Because Exam 70-221 focuses on skills needed to design a large TCP/IP network, it is imperative that you be intimately familiar with the more "advanced" aspects of TCP/IP, such as dynamic routing and how to integrate TCP/IP with existing WAN requirements."

Step-by-Step Certification Exercises focus on the specific skills most likely to be on the exam. The **CertCam** icon guides you to diagrams with descriptive audio that demonstrates this skill set on CD-ROM.

CertCam 1-1

Special warnings that prepare you for tricky exam topics:

exam
Watch

"Group policies are a new method for applying system configuration changes across all or some of the systems in your domain. Expect Microsoft to test your knowledge of group policies in designing an IPSec network as well as the simpler configuration done through the adapter property sheets."

MCSE Designing a Windows 2000 Network **On The Job Notes** present important lessons that help you work more efficiently:

on the
Job

"Try to avoid assigning a router address as a global variable. Rather, use a scope variable. Even if your network is small and you only have one subnet (and consequently one gateway), your network is sure to grow. Different segments cannot share the router address because they would need different gateway addresses."

Two-Minute Drills at the end of every chapter quickly reinforce your knowledge and ensure better retention of key concepts:

"When enabled, the DNS Server service will perform additional trace-level logging of events or messages to assist in troubleshooting and debugging the server."

Scenario & Solution sections lay out problems and solutions in a quick-read format. For example:

I have multiple ISDN lines and would like to have another line come up when one is being used at 75 Percent. Is there anything that can do this?

Yes. BAP can be configured to automatically bring up another multi-link PPP line if you exceed a pre-set threshold.

More than 200 realistic practice questions with answers help prepare you for the real test.

Your organization has decided to increase security on the network. The servers on the network are under-powered and processing power is at a premium. How could you best improve security by encrypting and authenticating the data at a minimum of processing power?

A. Configure IPSec to use the 3DES encryption and the SHA authentication

B. Configure IPSec to use the 40-bit DES encryption and the SHA authentication

C. Configure IPSec to use 56-bit encryption and the MD7 authentication

D. Configure IPSec to use 40-bit encryption and MD5 authentication

☑ **D.** Configuring IPSec to use the lowest authentication and encryption will reduce the overhead associated with processing the information.

☒ **A, B,** and **C** are incorrect. SHA will authenticate using 160-bit keys, while MD5 uses only 128-bit. 3DES uses 128-bit encryption, while the other forms of DES encrypt at 40 or 56-bit. MD7 is a red herring.